CONTEMPORARY
ISLAMIC FINANCE

The *Robert W. Kolb Series in Finance* provides a comprehensive view of the field of finance in all of its variety and complexity. It covers all major topics and specializations in finance, ranging from investments, to corporate finance, to financial institutions. Each volume is written or edited by a specialist (or specialists) in a particular area of finance and is intended for practicing finance professionals, graduate students, and advanced undergraduate students. The goal of each volume is to encapsulate the current state of knowledge in a particular area of finance so that the reader can quickly achieve a mastery of that discipline.

Please visit www.wiley.com/go/kolbseries to learn about recent and forthcoming titles in the Kolb Series.

CONTEMPORARY ISLAMIC FINANCE

Innovations, Applications, and Best Practices

Editor

Karen Hunt-Ahmed

The Robert W. Kolb Series in Finance

John Wiley & Sons, Inc.

Published by John Wiley & Sons, Inc., Hoboken, New Jersey.
Published simultaneously in Canada.

Cover image: © infrontphoto / iStockphoto
Cover design: Leiva–Sposato

For general information on our other products and services or for technical support, please
contact our Customer Care Department within the United States at (800) 762-2974, outside
the United States at (317) 572-3993 or fax (317) 572-4002.

Wiley publishes in a variety of print and electronic formats and by print-on-demand. Some
material included with standard print versions of this book may not be included in
e-books or in print-on-demand. If this book refers to media such as a CD or DVD that is
not included in the version you purchased, you may download this material at
http://booksupport.wiley.com. For more information about Wiley products, visit
www.wiley.com.

Library of Congress Cataloging-in-Publication Data:

Contemporary Islamic finance : innovations, applications, and best practices / Karen
Hunt-Ahmed, editor.
    p. cm. – (The Robert W. Kolb series in finance)
    Includes indexes.
    ISBN 978-1-118-18090-7 (cloth); ISBN 978-1-118-22739-8 (ebk); ISBN 978-1-118-24033-5
(ebk); ISBN 978-1-118-26497-3 (ebk)
1. Finance–Islamic countries.   2. Finance–Religious aspects–Islam.
I. Hunt-Ahmed, Karen.
    HG187.4.C66 2013
    332.088'297–dc23
                                                                        2012028585

10   9 8 7 6 5 4 3 2 1

To Ozakh and Hazar, my loving daughters

To Martha Hunt

In memory of Thomas Daniel Hunt

Contents

Acknowledgments

Many people worked together to make this book possible. I would like to begin by thanking Bob Kolb for presenting me with the idea for an "Islamic Finance" volume, and my colleague at DePaul University, Timur Gok, for introducing us in the first place. I am forever grateful to the contributors to this volume: they supported the vision and were rewarded for that support with pesky follow-up questions and edit requests, which they endured with good humor. Those who have known me for years have seen a new side of me; I hope my editorial persona has not scared them away or scared away those authors who are new to my professional network. Emilie Herman and Kevin Commins at John Wiley & Sons kept all of us on track. Emilie's patience apparently knows no bounds.

I would also like to thank colleagues and friends who have supported me in the writing process. Annette Iskra, Suzanne Gaskins, Richard Taub, John Lucy, Rick Shweder, Sheikh Nizam Yacouby, Imam Senad Agic, Aminah McCloud, Juliet Bromer, and Jack Mosevich have patiently helped me sort through priorities in the continuing struggle to balance professional and personal life. Ali Fatemi, the chair of DePaul's Finance Department, made life easier at work so I could dedicate time for the book. I owe a huge debt of gratitude to my research assistant, Sarah Lalji, who put in many hours of work to take care of book details, in addition to her full-time school schedule.

My daughters, Ozakh and Hazar, are the most wonderful people in my life. They make life rich and help me grow as a person, as I hope I am helping them grow. They are the best at supporting my work and also at letting me know when it is time to take a break. I would like to thank Omer Ahmed for introducing me to the life that led to a long association with Islamic finance and its professionals. He made it possible for me to do fieldwork in Dubai, with children, and to meet many of the contributors to this book. Finally, I would like to thank my parents, Tom and Martha Hunt, for telling me I could accomplish whatever I wanted to in life and then supporting me while I did.

CHAPTER 1

Introduction

Islamic Finance in the World Economy

KAREN HUNT-AHMED
President, Chicago Islamic Microfinance Project
Lecturer, DePaul University

The religion of Islam has existed for 1,400 years but Islamic economic theory and its financial institutions as an industry emerged only in the 1970s. Islamic banks are late twentieth-century institutions designed, against the backdrop of a global economy dominated by capitalist business practices, to help Muslims conduct business internationally while simultaneously upholding traditional Islamic values related to trade finance and currency movement. The basis for their existence is the Islamic moral prohibition on charging interest—interest is a central component of capitalist banking—yet Islamic banks conduct billions of dollars of business annually in the world economy and the *de facto* Islamic banking transaction is—in most cases—virtually identical to a capitalist banking transaction. The industry of Islamic Banking and Finance (IBF)[1] is the manifestation of attempts to apply Islamic law and Islamic economic theory to financial dealings.

An Islamic Financial Institution (IFI) refers to any financial institution that performs Islamic transactions derived from either Islamic law or Islamic economic theory. An Islamic Bank is an institution that performs conventional banking services[2] (or their Islamic equivalent) such as checking accounts, savings accounts, loans, and so forth. An IFI may or may not be a bank but an Islamic bank is always an IFI. Islamic financial institutions include venture capital firms and insurance companies, and may be distinguished from conventional banks by three primary elements (Bahrain Monetary Agency 2002):

1. Prohibition of prohibited financing arrangements and business practices. The most important prohibition in Islamic finance is the prohibition of *riba* (interest or usury). This means not only that financing transactions are structured differently than in conventional finance, but also that the asset structure of the institution is based entirely upon tangible assets and partnership arrangements instead of on interest-based financial assets. *Gharar* (speculation) and *maysir* (gambling) are prohibited, as well as trading in *haram* (forbidden) goods such as alcohol, pork, and owning equity in riba-based institutions (Lewis and Algaoud 2001).

1

2. Integration of religious practices into daily life by governing business under Islamic law.
3. Existence of a Shari'a Standards Board (SSB) composed of Islamic scholars. The SSB's purpose is to insure that Islamic law is being followed accurately in the business practices and financial arrangements of the IFI. A member of the SSB (called a Shari'a Scholar) has been trained formally in Islamic law, but has not necessarily been trained in finance. A separate financial standards board evaluates the efficacy of financial transactions, just as it does in a conventional institution, and the two boards often work together.

Ideally, an IFI should combine the elements of Islamic financial practices with some effort to uphold Islamic daily life practices (Lewis and Algaoud 2001).

The industry of Islamic banking and finance is growing daily. There are hundreds of Islamic financial institutions worldwide and the world's potential market for Islamic finance consists of more than one billion Muslims, in addition to non-Muslims, who are welcome and encouraged to participate in Islamic finance. When I began my fieldwork in 2002, Islamic assets were estimated to be around USD 200–300 billion. By 2011, estimated industry assets under management topped USD 1 trillion and is growing at a rate of at least 10 percent per year.[3] The *Financial Times* reports that at least one bank, Dubai-based Saadiq (the Islamic banking arm of Standard Chartered Bank), saw revenue growth of 65 percent in 2011 over 2010.[4]

This book speaks to an audience that is dynamically involved in—or thinking of being involved in—the Islamic finance industry. As the industry grows rapidly, finance professionals, investors, attorneys, educators, and students demand more detailed and sophisticated knowledge. Innovations abound as practitioners find ways to reconcile existing practices and regulations with Shari'a requirements. This volume will provide a useful and timely guide to Islamic finance for anyone interested in learning about basic concepts, current issues, and best practices predominant in the industry today.

GLOBALIZATION AND MUSLIM SUBJECTIVITY

World conditions due to globalization have contributed to the formation of the industry of Islamic finance. (Please see Chapter 4 of this volume.) Geographic mobility and technological advances made possible (and desirable) by globalization have profoundly changed definitions of personal, community, and religious identities of humankind. Islamic law does not allow for individuals or institutions that lend money to charge interest on that money. Muslims who orient themselves according to Islamic practices would be acting against their moral constitutions to participate in transactions that involve the charging of interest. Yet in the early twenty-first century global economy, trade finance and other crucial banking transactions are clearly dominated by capitalist financial institutions whose return on investment is based upon charging interest. Heretofore, a Muslim wishing to participate in the global economy has had to invest in capitalist institutions and act in opposition to his or her religious and moral belief system. As financial resources in the Islamic world have grown over the past three decades, Muslims have increasingly sought alternatives to capitalist investment that are more in keeping with Islamic practice. Islamic banks provide a framework for

Muslims to invest their money "morally," in accordance with Islamic law, while at the same time they do not miss out on profit opportunities provided by the global form of capitalist exchange. Islamic banking must locate itself as a Muslim institution in the world economy, yet it is also an industry that explicitly engages with the capitalist institution of banking and as such must be studied in the context of globalization and its relation to capitalism.

Throughout history, Jewish and Christian religious doctrines have objected to what they defined as unsavory business practices, including the practice of usurious loans. De Roover (1974) emphasizes that usury at that time in history referred to *any increase* over principle and that usury was prohibited; consequently, any increase was considered excessive. Christianity and Judaism resolved this moral problem in a way that advances capitalist enterprise—by declaring loans at interest as acceptable transactions as long as they are not usurious, whereas Islam seems to be engaging with capitalism in a way that critiques capitalism while at the same time advances it. The industry and its resultant institutional structure act as a culture broker (cf. Mazzarella 2004), providing a bridge between capitalist business practices and a competing Muslim sensitivity for its practitioners, who are comfortable in both cultural systems. Furthermore, IBF acts as a bridge between competing subjectivities—or practices of Islam—within Islam itself.

HISTORY OF ISLAMIC FINANCE

Islamic finance is a subcategory of the discipline of Islamic economics, which is in turn informed by Islamic legal thought. Chapters 2 and 3 of this volume (Farooq's "Contemporary Islamic Economic Thought" and Shawamreh's "The Legal Framework of Islamic Finance," respectively) introduce those two concepts. In this section, I take you through a brief history of the industry's evolution. This account is informed by Kuran (2004), Warde (2010), and Askari et al. (2010), and draws upon the history of economic thought as its basis. This chapter is meant to be a brief introduction to the formation of the industry from a psychological perspective; the specifics of Islamic economic thought, and a critique of that thought, are discussed elsewhere in this volume (Chapter 2 and Chapter 5).

Whereas textual and traditional sources of Islamic law date to the time of the Prophet Mohammed and the ensuing three hundred years or so, Islamic economic theory is a contemporary theory. It has its roots in postcolonial India and its tenets have been widely debated since the middle of the twentieth century. Islamic economics is always written about with reference to classical economic theories that form the basis of capitalism. Early writings about Islamic economics were often presented as critiques of one or more economic theories prevalent in the world, such as communism, socialism, or capitalism (cf. Chapra 1976; Zarqa 1981; Siddiqui 1981). Since the fall of the Soviet Union and the apparent victory of capitalist economics over other forms of economic structures, critiques of communism and socialism are no longer at issue, so most of the contemporary critiques are direct reactions to capitalist economic values. Timur Kuran, in his book *Islam and Mammon*, recognizes the emphasis of values in the theory of Islamic economics: "at least initially, the *economics* of 'Islamic economics' was merely incidental to its *Islamic* character" (italics in original; Kuran 2004, p. 82).

The framework of Islamic economic theory was developed in India in the early twentieth century by Islamic scholar Mawlana Mawdudi (1903–1979) and expounded upon by one of his students, economist Khurshid Ahmad. Indian Muslims as a group were relatively disadvantaged economically compared with the majority population of Hindus. The British Raj had provided some economic protections to Muslims, farmers in particular, but it was unclear how or if a Hindu-led government would provide the same protection (Kuran 2004). Mawdudi believed that economic activity and technology were crucial to the success in the modern world, and he was dedicated to providing Muslims in India with economic opportunities that allowed them both to function in the modern world and to retain their Muslim identity. Many Muslims did not participate in conventional banking activities because of the prohibition against riba. Mawdudi himself adhered to this belief, as we learn from reading the notes to his own translation of the *Qur'an*. In particular, Mawdudi stresses different ways in which loaning at interest can erode communal bonds between men (1988). Nonetheless, Mawdudi believed it was detrimental to the Muslim community in India to abstain from banking activities. He and Ahmad believed that it was possible and desirable for Indian Muslims to embrace systems and institutions of Western modernity while at the same time adhering to the teachings and practices of Islam (Mawdudi 1980). One goal of Mawdudi was to redefine Islamic practices to conform to economic changes. He felt that Muslims in India could use practices to retain their Muslim identity in the face of the postcolonial Indian modernization project. In one of his last books, a short history of the founding of Islam, Mawdudi wrote (1974, p. 11):

> The Islamic way of life can be revived and reconstructed again and again with the help of the *Qur'an* and the traditions if ever, God forbid, the freshness of its true spirit wanes. The world no longer requires any new Prophet to revive Islam to its pristine glory. It is enough to have among us the learned people who know the *Qur'an* and the traditions of the Prophet and who are able to apply their teachings to their own lives and stimulate others to adopt and apply them in their lives as well. This is how the stream of Islam will continue to flow, refreshing the eternal thirst of mankind.

Khurshid Ahmad argued that economic systems are value-based systems; even the capitalist economic system was founded on certain cultural values, which are reflected in that system. This belief is not unlike Max Weber's (1930) assertion that Calvinist religious practices served to advance capitalism. Therefore, if Muslims are to be economically empowered, a theory of Islamic economics is necessary. Other theorists took up that line of thought, such as Umer Chapra, who states: "Virtue lies . . . not in shunning the bounties of God, but in enjoying them within the framework of the values for 'righteous living' through which Islam seeks to promote human welfare" (Chapra 1976, p. 173). In Islam, all fields of life are interrelated. Goals and values of each segment of life should be aligned, so the economic system's values are aligned with those of society.

Kuran (2004) asserts that the emergence of the industry grew out of the debate on whether or not Muslims in India should have a separate homeland or remain part of a greater India after the Partition of 1947. Mawdudi favored the latter proposition—cultural reassertion—and contended that a separate homeland was unnecessary because if Muslims practiced their religious duties faithfully, the matter of a national homeland would be irrelevant. In this view, group solidarity depends more on shared beliefs and practices than on shared geographical territory. This principle foreshadows many of the basic principles of globalization, namely the belief that group solidarity or identity can be based on something other than geographical place.

Mawdudi favored thinking of Islam as a *way of life*, rather than as a system of faith. In a treatise of his interpretation of the *Qur'an* published immediately after his death (1980), Mawdudi asserts that the *kalimah*[5] affirms that there is one God, Allah, and Mohammed is his Prophet. Mawdudi considers this to be the primary doctrine of Islam: The real difference between believers and unbelievers "lies in the acceptance of this doctrine and complete adherence to it in practical life." (Mawdudi 1980, p. 62) An emphasis of the connection between belief and practice is the foundation for Mawdudi's entire project of strengthening Islam worldwide. A Muslim must not only believe in the doctrine of Islam, but internalize and incorporate its practices in everyday life. It is only in this way that Islam (and Muslims) will survive in a world that is increasingly influenced by modern inventions and systems. We can see this idea at work in the thinking of contemporary scholars of Islam. It had particular relevance in the anxious times of postcolonial India, and has gained relevance in a globalized and post-9/11 world in which Islam has frequently come under attack from the prevailing world order.

In contrast to politicians who wanted a territorial solution for Muslim independence (Pakistan), Mawdudi sought to keep Islam salient in the minds of its practitioners without necessitating a territorial division. He fully recognized the prudence of tying economic behavior to religious beliefs. According to Kuran (2004), a technologically advanced world requires complicated economic decisions. In the dominant world economic order, those decisions are thought of as secular decisions. If Muslim traders and customers were making daily economic choices based on religious thought instead of on secular economic principles, the average person could think of business activities as religious activities. Therefore, religion would always be prominent in their minds (Kuran 2004). In this way, Muslims would remain politically visible despite their minority status. In this sense, Mawdudi advocated the creation of an Islamic economic actor in order to allow citizens to pursue economic activities in a morally acceptable way.

According to a comprehensive survey of Islamic economic literature, Professor Muhammad Siddiqui has outlined some of the key philosophical underpinnings of Islamic economic theories. The practitioner is meant to use these philosophical points as a guideline for developing practices in an (theoretical) Islamic economic system. Of course, no purely Islamic economic system exists in the world today, but it is held up as a goal to which Muslims should strive. Some of the major Islamic economic values are (Siddiqui 1981):

- A person should be a "God-conscious" human being. He or she should practice *tawhid*, or unity, at all times. This means that all earthly actions must be pleasing to the will of Allah.
- Economic enterprise is encouraged, as long as moderation is practiced and special attention is paid to social justice.

- Ownership has both an individual and communal component. Private property ownership is encouraged but it is a human responsibility to make sure that all humans have their basic needs met.
- Humans are encouraged to cooperate with each other in production relations, rather than to compete (i.e., as in capitalism).
- Economic development is a necessary human condition and must be undertaken in the spirit of social justice.

Throughout this volume, we will see much evidence that Islamic finance practitioners pay particular attention to these principles of Islamic economics in discourse and in practice.

ISLAMIC BANKING: ORIGINS IN PRACTICE

Whereas the theory of Islamic economics was never actually enacted systematically in Mawdudi's India, it was put into practice in the Arabian Gulf. The first successful Islamic bank—Dubai Islamic Bank—opened in Dubai, United Arab Emirates, in 1975.[6] Until this time, Muslims had been carrying on their business activities in one of two ways: Either they used conventional banks or they just used other, private methods of financing outside of the capitalist banking system. Islamic financing was originally part of interpersonal business dealings and not meant to be an institutional function (Udovitch 1970). But by the late twentieth century, if Muslims wanted to participate in the world economy, they would have to engage in some way with the capitalist banking system. In particular, the Arabian Gulf of the 1970s was undergoing tremendous and rapid changes as significant cash poured into the region from recently discovered oil (Ali 2002). Businessmen sought to use their newly acquired oil wealth to put into practice an idea that was theoretically conceived to solidify Muslim identity. The formation of Islamic banking was introduced as a practical solution to this problem.

There were several political developments in the Arab world around the same time that contributed to heightened sense of urgency about asserting pan-Islamism. In an article written on September 9, 2001 in the online version of *Le Monde*, Ibrahim Warde, a researcher of Islamic finance and adjunct professor at Tufts' Fletcher School of Business, reminds us that in 1967 Arab losses in the Six Day War had given birth to Nasser's secular pan-Arabism as well as to Saudi Arabia's Islamist domination in the Arabian Gulf region.[7] These political developments in addition to the inflow of cash into the Gulf provided the impetus for the establishment of the Organization of Islamic States (OIS) in 1970. Banking reform quickly made its way onto the OIS agenda (Warde 2010).

Dubai Islamic Bank (DIB) was the first Islamic bank in the context of the contemporary Islamic banking industry formation (Henry and Wilson 2004). There has always been considerable trade between Dubai and the Indian subcontinent, especially in the late twentieth century, when large numbers of Indians/Pakistanis migrated to the Gulf as guest workers. It is highly likely that ideas such as the theory of Islamic economics accompanied the people and goods that have always been traded between these places. In addition, Gulf Arabs also go to India or Pakistan for an education and must have been exposed to theories such as Mawdudi's during their stay. I consider it a natural extension of the theoretical origins of Islamic banking that its practice was taken up in the Gulf: Material prosperity enabled the theory to be enacted. This origin story seems to be important to bankers in Dubai, at least, and at any rate DIB is one of the most active of the purely Islamic banks.

A CONTEMPORARY INDUSTRY

Trade and finance have always been part of Islam's history. The Prophet Mohammed, the founder of Islam, was a business owner in the seventh century of the Christian era, as was his wife Khadijah. Nonetheless, there was no such thing as an Islamic bank until the late twentieth century. Classical Islamic jurisprudence has always been concerned with regulating trade and financial transactions between individuals and has produced a large body of rules on the subject; however, those rules did not give rise to an Islamic financial system until the 1970s. Udovitch (1970) points out that trade finance was always prevalent in Muslim societies, but that merchants would provide financing instead of financial institutions. This arrangement is similar to the function of merchant lending in Europe at the same time (Udovitch 1970). For example, *bancherius*, or merchant institutions in Venice that accepted deposits and made loans, were not specialized and were usually part of larger business operations, like cloth merchants. In the mid-twentieth century, a few individual Islamic banks were started in Egypt and Turkey, but they either failed on financial terms or were folded into the national banking system and converted to conventional banks (Kuran 2004, 2001). A corporation founded in Malaysia in 1963 eventually evolved into the Bank Islam Malaysia, incorporated in 1983.

Contemporary Islamic banks were formed in the 1970s when considerable oil wealth became available in the Arabian Gulf States. Muslim populations in other parts of the world—notably Indonesia, Pakistan, and Malaysia—have since generated sufficient steady income growth to develop a network of Islamic financial institutions that strive to integrate themselves into the global financial system. Growing Muslim populations in the United States and Great Britain have very recently begun to contribute to the Islamic financial network both institutionally and intellectually.

MY HISTORY WITH ISLAMIC FINANCE

Many people wonder how I got involved with Islamic finance. The story of how and why I got involved with the industry is a large part of the story of how I study the industry, so I will tell the story briefly. While studying for an MBA at Washington University in St. Louis, I learned about microfinance. I began to pay attention to and explore how people who cannot or chose not to participate in the conventional financial system get their businesses financed. I recognized that there may often be something else driving business practices other than the profit motive, as we are traditionally taught in a capitalist economic system. Ideas about morality play a role in business decisions more often than I had thought possible and it was interesting to me to explore those ways of thinking, especially in the world of finance.

After working for a time in commercial banking in Chicago, my family and I moved to Dubai, United Arab Emirates, where I worked in a private equity firm that had some "Islamic" transactions on its books. I observed that the money flows in a Shari'a-compliant transaction looked the same, but that the philosophy behind the transactions expressed a concern with a holistic view of the business relationship rather than focusing on whether that particular transaction was going to be profitable. This was interesting, of course, but life and work took over and I filed away this observation while I got on with living.

As fate would have it, my family was transferred back to Chicago for my husband's job as an asset manager. In addition to raising children and in lieu of getting a "real" job I entered into the PhD program at the University of Chicago. I did not intend to study business *per se*, so I applied and was admitted to an interdisciplinary social science program called Psychology: Human Development, which was more closely aligned with my undergraduate degree in psychology than a PhD in business would have been. A discussion in one of my classes led me to recall the Islamic (Shari'a-compliant) transactions I had worked with in Dubai and prompted me to think about the implications of applying one's moral values in a business setting, especially when those moral values did not always correspond to prevailing practices. Thus, my research idea—and my career—was formed. I asked the question that began this chapter: The religion of Islam has existed for 1400 years. Why did Islamic finance emerge in the world financial system in the late twentieth century? To answer this question, I needed to talk to Islamic bankers in the place where it all began: Dubai, United Arab Emirates.

My family and I moved back to Dubai for a year so that I could do dissertation fieldwork. We had family and professional connections there and had lived and worked in Dubai, so the move was almost seamless for us. After almost a year of ethnographic observations and in-depth interviews, and almost 20 years of traveling to and/or living in the UAE while observing Islamic finance, I now conceive of IBF as a particularized industry highly relevant to the plight of Muslims in the context of contemporary globalization. The existence of this industry is a partial answer to the question: How can Muslims living in the diaspora integrate their identities as Muslims with identities as global citizens? In a sense, the existence of IBF is an answer to the question of what happens when Muslims—and Islam—travel and live around the globe.

CONVENTIONAL FINANCE VERSUS IBF

IBF claims to be different from conventional finance but most of the financial transactions look the same to most people who examine them. Islamic finance professionals often explain Islamic finance with reference to conventional finance, though there is a movement in the industry to progress beyond this practice. When asked to compare and contrast with conventional finance, most Islamic finance professionals I talk to concede that Islamic finance is just like conventional finance, but without the immorality. "Immorality" in this case is related to both business practices (specific and general) and to the details of financial transactions. When asked, most Islamic bankers will tell you that the most immoral financial practice is charging interest on loans.

Because a large part of a conventional bank's income "is in the form of interest on the claims it holds" (usually loans) (Moss 2004), Islamic finance seeks to retain the useful features of conventional finance while adjusting practices to adhere to

Islamic principles. IBF began as a response to the needs of investment bankers and corporate finance professionals, although more recent activities have focused on retail banking, or personal finance. Chapters in this volume address both institutional and personal or retail financial activities.

Credit and Risk

Just as Jews and Christians found trade to be impossible without some kind of financing situation, Muslims recognize the necessity of finance. As with conventional finance, Islamic finance falls under two types: equity financing and debt financing. Equity financing means, generally, that the financier and the manager of a business are partners. There are different ways to structure a partnership, but the implication of an equity partnership is that each partner will receive a return (or profit) proportionate to the amount of the investment. Debt financing simply means that one party (the financier) provides money for a business venture. The financier expects to make a profit on the investment whether or not the business is successful. Islamic law allows most types of equity financing, but debt is problematic. Lending can occur, technically, but it must be interest-free, a so-called benevolent loan. The industry of Islamic finance was formed to address the prohibition of interest-bearing debt finance. As we will see throughout this volume, there are various ways to finance trade using debt instruments, but we must begin with a discussion of credit and risk, and why interest is prohibited under Islamic law.

Some standard definitions of *credit* are as follows (quotes from dictionary.com):

- Trustworthiness; credibility.
- Confidence in a purchaser's ability and intention to pay, displayed by entrusting the buyer with goods or services without immediate payment.
- Reputation of solvency and probity, entitling a person to be trusted in buying or borrowing: *Your credit is good.*
- Influence or authority resulting from the confidence of others or from one's reputation.
- Time allowed for payment for goods or services obtained on trust: *90 days' credit.*
- Repute: reputation; esteem.
- A sum of money due to a person; anything valuable standing on the credit side of an account: *He has an outstanding credit of $50.*

The definitions of credit listed above are seven of the ten definitions found on dictionary.com. The extension of credit can potentially lead to something called usury. The Islamic finance industry is premised on one concept: avoidance of riba, which is often translated to English as usury. This translation is disputed, as we will learn throughout this study, but IBF practitioners generally agree that the prohibition of something called riba is the basis for the industry. Usury is defined in today's terminology as "an exorbitant amount or rate of interest" or at a rate higher than the legal rate (dictionary.com); however, usury at one time referred to any increase over the amount of money lent.

The definition of credit, as we can see, encompasses concepts such as trustworthiness, repute, or confidence. These are not merely descriptions of a transaction, but meanings embedded in the concept of credit that speak to how humans relate to one another. For this reason, participation in a credit transaction is a situation in which people make judgments about one another. Credit, and by extension usury, becomes a symbol or metaphor of certain aspects of the human existence. Credit speaks to the temporal aspects of economic life. Credit provides a way to deal with the future in the present.

Due to the symbolic nature of credit and risk, their definitions and views about them are subject to human variations and interpretations. As such, there will be cultural differences between interpretations of credit. For example, usury can be used as a way to work out uncertainty about definitions of the self versus the other, the sociocultural institution's obligations for the well-being of individuals, and the extent to which divine morality is encoded in secular law. Credit, in the sense of loaning money for a definite period of time and for a specific purpose, has been seen as both necessary and somehow sinister.

Another crucial difference between bank credit and financial markets is the concept of risk. Bank credit evolved as a way to mitigate risk. Future uncertainty is embodied in the calculation of interest and part of the function of interest is to reimburse the lender for potential future losses and for the lost opportunity to use that money in the present. Risk in this case is a negative concept, one that must be eliminated as much as possible from the equation. On the contrary, risk has a very different meaning in financial markets. Investment risk is a positive concept, one without which financial markets would not even exist (cf. Knorr-Cetina and Preda 2005). In this case, risk means the opportunity for gain. The Islamic finance industry was created to address matters of bank and investment credit for institutional and large investors, not the credit needs of small investors. Credit is the crucial way by which investments and trade are facilitated. The prohibition of usury creates a special circumstance for the Muslim investor that distances him or her from international financial markets. As a result, matters of risk management are salient topics in the discourse of Islamic finance professionals (see in particular Chapter 7 of this volume).

General Business Ethics

In addition to specific prohibitions and requirements of an Islamic bank and its financial transactions (see Chapter 3 of this volume), an Islamic financial institution encourages adherence to general Islamic behavioral ethics. Lewis and Algaoud (2001) consider this increased attention to business ethics to be an important part of the corporate culture of an Islamic financial institution. They state that, ideally:

> [T]he corporate culture of an Islamic bank should be one in which Islamic values are reflected in all facets of behaviour ranging from internal relations, dealings with customers and other banks, policies and procedures, business practices through to dress, décor, image, and so on, consistent with Islam as a complete way of life. The purpose is to create a collective morality and spirituality which, when combined with the production of goods and services, sustains the growth and advancement of the Islamic way of life. (Lewis and Algaoud 2001, p. 165)

IFIs do take seriously the commitment to providing an Islamic environment, and this commitment is illustrated both in the literature and in my observations. For example, in a chapter of the book entitled *The Politics of Islamic Finance* (Henry and Wilson 2004), Kristen Smith of Harvard's Kennedy School of Government illustrates how Kuwait Finance House (KFH) takes public steps to foster a religious environment by organizing communal prayer in the office, showing a hiring preference for men who have demonstrated their devotion to Islam and by conducting non-banking business in a recognizably "Islamic" manner (Smith 2004). Islamic practices include providing a prayer room and encouraging prayer breaks, striving to maintain ethical business practices, structuring financial transactions to conform to Islamic law, maintaining gender segregation, and any other activity that falls under the jurisdiction of Islamic law. In practice, IFIs primarily strive to adhere to financial regulations, though some organizations take into consideration other aspects of human resources practices (see Martin and Hunt-Ahmed 2011 and Chapter 13 of this volume).

AN OVERVIEW OF THE BOOK CONTENTS

The idea for this book was developed after I had been teaching Islamic finance for a few years to overflowing classes of students at DePaul University's Driehaus School of Business in Chicago, Illinois. There are few Islamic finance classes taught in business schools in the United States and I found that young business students were eager to learn about this growing industry because they had heard so much about it in the media. My students were Muslim and non-Muslim, and all held a deep interest in international business. Most realized that if they wanted to be a part of the global financial industry, they would need to understand the basic ideas of Islamic finance, as they were likely to encounter these concepts as a matter of course in international business.

Most of the books I used for teaching purposes provided excellent introductory, legal, or technical material on Islamic finance, but the idea for the present volume was conceived when I realized there was room in the literature for a book that advanced the industry beyond descriptive terms and onto a broader, more academic discussion of some of the innovations and applications of earlier research and practical developments based on daily practices. It is my hope that this book will appeal to those new to the industry and also to practitioners and researchers already familiar with the industry. For this reason, I have divided the book into two primary parts: Part I, "The Contemporary Islamic Finance Landscape," addresses the most current thinking about Islamic economic theory and Islamic legal thought, then moves on to a series of chapters that present a new level of thinking about a wide variety of topics in the industry. While the topics may be familiar to the reader, these chapters represent the latest thoughts on the subject. All chapters are written by innovative academics and innovative practitioners who are on the ground and see what works and what does not work in the industry environment today.

Most chapters in this volume presume that readers have a rudimentary understanding of the basic principles of Islamic finance, but will be accessible to readers new to the industry as well. For this reason, I have foregone the inclusion of chapters specifically dedicated to describing the technical aspects of basic structures.

Individual chapters include descriptions as necessary. For readers who want to learn more about Shari'a-compliant financial structures in detail, there are many excellent books containing this information. I particularly recommend Ayub's *Understanding Islamic Finance*, Kettell's *Islamic Finance in a Nutshell: A Guide for Non-Specialists*, or Iqbal and Mirakhor's *An Introduction to Islamic Finance Theory and Practice*.

Novice readers may want to pay particular attention to Chapters 2 and 3 of this volume and may use these chapters as an abbreviated introductory text. In Chapter 2, "Contemporary Islamic Economic Thought," Farooq traces the history of Islamic economic thought from pre-modern times though the present, highlighting themes and concerns of the discipline and its relationship to both conventional (i.e., neoclassical) economic thought and what we now know as Islamic finance. Farooq advances scholarship in this area by comparing current formulations of Islamic economic thought and urging us to move beyond reliance on the neoclassical economics paradigm by developing a more theoretically and empirically rich body of work on Islamic economics.

In Chapter 3, "The Legal Framework of Islamic Finance," Shawamreh provides the reader with a basic introduction to the principles of Islamic legal thought. This framework is based in a system originating in the seventh century and refined through a precise juristic process in the intervening centuries. Shawamreh's contribution to the literature is the recognition that Islamic finance operates within a legal framework that developed concurrently—sometimes parallel with, sometimes separately from—an Islamic legal system. An often difficult task for practitioners new to Islamic finance is making the connection between centuries-old legal opinions and contemporary international regulatory environments. In this chapter, Shawamreh discusses some particular challenges associated with constructing and enforcing Shari'a-compliant financial transactions within a dual legal framework. This chapter is a particularly timely primer of Islamic legal thought and its resulting financial structures, followed by a discussion that makes the evolution of legal thought relevant to today's applications.

The cultural origin of Islamic finance is often overlooked in more practical treatises on the subject. Yet those new to Islamic finance often ask, "The financial structures look the same as conventional finance. If that is the case, why do we need this industry anyway?" Chapter 4, "Globalization and Islamic Finance," provides a social scientific explanation for the question of why we need this industry. I reach beyond a discussion of whether the financial structures are the same or different to explore motivations of individual practitioners and how they think about their participation in the industry.

Waleed El-Ansary, in Chapter 5's "Islamic Science and the Critique of Neoclassical Economic Theory," moves scholarship beyond a neoclassical interpretation of Islamic economics, just as Farooq has suggested that scholars approach the subject. El-Ansary dives into this critique by connecting the analytical tools of economic theory and the sciences of nature. In this groundbreaking work, the author connects the spiritual roots of Islamic thought with its economic principles in a new way. He contends that the debate between Islamic and neoclassical economics ultimately depends on the all-important debate over the hierarchy of levels of reality and the secular philosophy of science. He critiques the overly scientific analytical tools currently used to evaluate the theoretical claims of Islamic and neoclassical economics and urges greater synthesis of the spiritual and scientific when addressing such questions.

No serious industry or academic discipline is without controversy. In Chapter 6, "Juristic Disagreement," Shoiab Ghias provides evidence for the seriousness of the Islamic finance industry in the form of a controversy over the permissibility of the existence of the industry itself. In virtually all of the prevailing industry literature, two chief principles motivate thinking on the subject: first, that riba (interest) is banned under Islamic law and second, that Islamic banking is the inevitable practical expression of this ban. Ghias finds that in 2008, a panel of Pakistani Shari'a scholars issued a *fatwa* (legal opinion) stating that Islamic banking is unacceptable under Islamic law. For this volume, Ghias has translated this *fatwa*, provides a discussion of its authority, presents arguments for its validity, and presents us with a resolution of the matter. Because this volume is meant to address contemporary issues in Islamic finance, the editor finds this chapter a particularly important tool to stimulate discussions within the industry.

Innovations

Chapter 7, "Managing Liquidity Risk in Islamic Finance," written by Muhammad Al-Bashir Muhammad Al-Amine, and Chapter 8, "Elements of Islamic Wealth Management," written by Paul Wouters, are exceptionally relevant and timely topics for inclusion in any finance volume during and after the 2007 worldwide economic crisis. For this reason, this volume devotes considerable attention to the theory and application of products in these categories. Chapters 7 and 8 present the reader with a general discussion of each topic, with special emphasis on products that connect the investor to international capital markets and allow individual and institutional investors to manage wealth and the risk inherent in wealth management. Chapters 9 through 12 discuss contemporary formulations of specific products used in these endeavors.

Michael McMillen, the author of Chapter 9, "*Sukūk* and the Islamic Capital Markets," is an internationally respected attorney and pioneer in the development of *sukūk* structures. Sukūk are relatively new products in international finance and are designed to bridge Islamic and conventional capital markets as a risk management tool. He explains the connection in Chapter 9:

> Islamic capital markets will emerge from the current financial downturn as a central feature of the Islamic finance and investment industry and will increasingly be integrated with the larger conventional capital markets. *Sukūk* will likely be the vehicle of choice in achieving that integration.

Chapters 10 and 11 focus on Shari'a-compliant mutual funds and the indices that measure their returns. Monem Salam (Chapter 10, "Shari'a-Compliant Mutual Funds") has managed one of the most successful mutual funds of all time; that this fund is Shari'a-compliant is a boon to the industry and a particular bonus for mutual fund investors looking to invest their money according to Islamic principles. This success appears to be a feature of Shari'a-compliant funds, as Tariq Al-Rifai discusses in Chapter 11, "The Evolution of Shari'ah-Compliant Indexes and Why They Outperform Conventional Indexes over the Long Term." Al-Rifai has been an industry leader in evaluating Shari'a-compliant financial products since the 1990s and has extensive knowledge of the field. He is optimistic in his outlook for the industry, an opinion based on solid evidence and its track record.

A relatively new product on the scene is *takaful*, or Shari'a-compliant insurance. Insurance is both a risk management tool and a wealth management product, as it can be structured as an investment. Insurance was originally a controversial topic in Islamic finance, as Farrukh Siddiqui explains in Chapter 12, "Takaful." Siddiqui traces the history and evolution of opinions on this issue and illuminates contemporary structures and *fatawa* supporting the creation and sustainability of *takaful* as a viable and necessary part of a functioning international financial industry.

Chapters 13 through 15 complete the section on innovations by discussing relatively unexplored topics. Because the industry is so new, it has taken time to develop scholarship on the arguably less glamorous (than international financial structures) but crucial inner workings of an industry. In Chapter 13, "Islamic Human Resources Practices," William Martin examines the relatively unexplored topic of human resource management. He reviews the purpose of attending to issues of human development in the workplace and reminds us that Islam puts great emphasis on this very issue. A truly Islamic financial institution must pay attention to the needs of its employees including, but not limited to, providing Shari'a-compliant methods of compensating employees for their work.

Chapters 14 and 15 address the uncomfortable yet vital topic of poverty alleviation. If Islamic finance intends to stay true to its stated principles of attending to social justice concerns, it must not ignore the parts of society that are not able to participate in big-money financial transactions. In fact, the competitive advantage of Islamic finance is that it is self-reflective about its role in the whole economy, not just international financial institutions. In Chapter 14 "An Integrated Islamic Poverty Alleviation Model," Kabir Hassan and his student Ali Ashraf present a model for poverty alleviation that utilizes the institutions of *Zakat* and *Awqaf*— also, not coincidentally, wealth management tools—to achieve its purposes. Sabur Mollah and Hamid Uddin, in Chapter 15, "How Does an Islamic Microfinance Model Play the Key Role in Poverty Alleviation?" further this discussion with a more focused look at how Islamic microfinance can work and is working toward this goal in Europe.

Applications and Best Practices

Part II, "Case Studies," the last part of this volume, moves away from theory to present the reader with examples of how products and structures are implemented in real life. Chapters 16 through 23 show us how international marketing and financial structures are implemented in a globalized world. Offshore banking structures are a major part of globalization and make the international focus of Islamic finance a reality. Mutual funds are active all over the world and we see how mutual funds in Saudi Arabia perform, as well as how the realities of ratings services function worldwide. Because this is such a global industry, it is easy to forget that the United States is a relatively new market for Islamic finance, and we explore its opportunities and challenges as a case study. We revisit the challenges of risk management by discussing individual situations in more detail. Finally, we conclude our section on best practices by comparing efforts to institute Islamic microfinance in various parts of the world.

A FINAL NOTE

The global nature of this industry necessitates a final word about translations and spellings. The editor chose authors based on their proven innovative thinking and practical experience; therefore, the authors come from many disciplinary backgrounds, industries, and writing styles. We have chosen to leave intact each author's spellings and translations of non-English terminologies. We believe these differences reflect the true nature of the industry, which is to provide a central institutional structure in which many different opinions can flourish and prosper. It is the editor's hope that readers will appreciate our efforts to provide a diversity of opinion and a format for ongoing discussions of advancements in the industry of Islamic finance.

NOTES

1. I will shorten the reference to 'IBF' throughout this Introduction.
2. A "conventional" bank is the industry term that refers to existing international, interest-based banks.
3. www.zawya.com/story/ZAWYA20110505062447/Global_Islamic_Finance_Report_2011_Released/; accessed 5/21/12.
4. www.ft.com/intl/cms/s/0/09a99422–7291–11e1–9be9–00144feab49a.html#axzz1yS3ndpCe; accessed 6/21/12.
5. *La ilaha illallah, Mohammed ur-Rasulallah* (there is only one God and Mohammed is his prophet). This is also called the *Shahadah.*
6. The Islamic Development Bank was begun in Saudi Arabia in 1975 as well.
7. http://mondediplo.com/2001/09/09islamicbanking; accessed 6/21/12.

REFERENCES

Ali, Ahmad Mohamed. 2002. "The Emerging Islamic Financial Architecture: The Way Ahead." Paper presented at the Fifth Harvard University Forum on Islamic Finance, April 6–7.

Askari, H., Z. Iqbal, and A. Mirakhor. 2010. *Globalization and Islamic Finance: Convergence, Prospects & Challenges.* Hoboken, NJ: John Wiley & Sons.

Bahrain Monetary Agency. 2002. *Islamic Banking & Finance in the Kingdom of Bahrain.* Bahrain: Arabian Printing Press.

Chapra, Muhammad Umar. 1976. "Objectives of the Islamic Economic Order." In Khurshid Ahmad, ed. *Islam: Its Meaning and Message.* London: Islamic Council of Europe.

De Roover, Raymond. 1974. "New Interpretations of the History of Banking." In Julius Kirshner, ed. *Business, Banking and Economic Thought in Late Medieval and Early Modern Europe: Selected Studies of Raymond de Roover*, 200–238. Chicago: The University of Chicago Press.

Henry, Clement M., and Rodney Wilson. 2004. "Introduction." In Clement M. Henry and Rodney Wilson, eds. *The Politics of Islamic Finance.* Edinburgh: Edinburgh University Press.

Knorr-Cetina, Karin, and Alex Preda, eds. 2005. *The Sociology of Financial Markets.* Oxford: Oxford University Press.

Kuran, Timur. 2004. *Islam & Mammon: The Economic Predicaments of Islamism*. Princeton: Princeton University Press.

Lewis, Mervyn K., and Latifa M. Algaoud. 2001. *Islamic Banking*. Cheltenham, UK: Edward Elgar.

Martin, W. M., and Karen Hunt-Ahmed. 2011. "Executive Compensation: The Role of Shari'a Compliance," *International Journal of Islamic and Middle Eastern Finance and Management*, 4:3, 196–210.

Mawdudi, Sayyid Abul A'la. 1988. *Towards Understanding the Qur'an, Vol. I*. Chichester, United Kingdom: The Islamic Foundation.

Mawdudi, Abu'l A'la. 1980. *Towards Understanding Islam*. United Kingdom: The Islamic Foundation.

Mawdudi, Abu'l A'la. 1974. *Islam: An Historical Perspective*. United Kingdom: The Islamic Foundation.

Mazzarella, William. 2004. *Shoveling Smoke: Advertising and Globalization in Contemporary India*. Durham, NC: Duke University Press.

Moss, Rita. 2004. *Strauss's Handbook of Business Information: A Guide for Librarians, Students, and Researchers*. 2nd edition. Westport, CT: Libraries Unlimited.

Siddiqui, Muhammad Nejatullah. 1981. "Muslim Economic Thinking: A Survey of Contemporary Literature," In Khurshid Ahmad, ed. *Studies in Islamic Economics*. Chichester, United Kingdom: International Centre for Research in Islamic Economics.

Smith, Kristin. 2004. "The Kuwait Finance House and the Islamization of Public Life in Kuwait." In Clement M. Henry and Rodney Wilson, eds. *The Politics of Islamic Finance*. Edinburgh: Edinburgh University Press.

Udovitch, Abraham L. 1970. *Partnership and Profit in Medieval Islam*. Princeton: Princeton University Press.

Warde, I. 2010. *Islamic Finance in the Global Economy*. 2nd edition. Edinburgh: Edinburgh University Press.

Weber, Max. 1930. *The Protestant Ethic and the Spirit of Capitalism*. London: Routledge.

Zarqa, Anas. 1981. "Islamic Economics: An Approach to Human Welfare." In *Studies in Islamic Economics*, ed. Khurshid Ahmad. Chichester, United Kingdom: International Centre for Research in Islamic Economics.

PART I

The Contemporary Islamic Finance Landscape

CHAPTER 2

Contemporary Islamic Economic Thought

MOHAMMAD OMAR FAROOQ[1]
Head of the Centre for Islamic Finance, Bahrain Institute of Banking and Finance

Economics as a specialized field of social science that systematically studies and explores the economic dimensions of life is a modern phenomenon. Thus, it can be safely argued that there was no Islamic economics until modern economics was developed.[2] Yet, Muslims had a vibrant and dynamic civilization, where the economic life did go on both at the individual and collective level. And, the Qur'an as the anchor of the Islamic way of life has some fundamental principles affecting the economic dimensions of life. Gradually the Muslim world faced decay and Western civilization emerged as dominant. In the civilizational encounter, the Muslim world, similar to many other parts of the world, became a victim of colonization and was dismembered and disfigured in many ways.

In the twentieth century the Muslim world experienced a new revivalism, which was also instrumental in challenging Western colonialism. This revivalism unfolded in both Islamic and nationalistic form. With few exceptions, Islamic revivalism was central to the aspiration for freedom and independence in the Muslim world. The pan-Islamic contributions of, among others, Jamal Al-din Afghani (d. 1897 AD), his disciple Muhammad Abduh (d. 1905) and Abduh's disciple Rashid Rida (d. 1935 AD) paved the way for Islamic movements, such as Jamaat-e-Islami in South Asia, Ikhwan al-Muslimoon in the Middle East and so on. This revivalism was rooted in the notion that Islam is a complete code/way of life and thus every aspect of life, including the economy, must be reshaped based on the foundation of Islam. Thus, as part of the revivalist Islamic ethos, there was call for the economies of the Muslim world to be transformed and built on the foundation of Islam. During the twentieth century one finds works on Islamic economics outlining and detailing the Islamic economic system, as distinguished from its conventional—both capitalist and socialist—counterparts. In this chapter we provide a brief survey of some of the major aspects of contemporary Islamic economic thought. Given the space limitation of such a chapter, this of course is not an exhaustive survey of the subject.

THE CONTINUUM OF THE PREMODERN ISLAMIC ECONOMIC THOUGHT

Since Islamic civilization from the time of the Prophet Muhammad had a vibrant and strong economy spanning over a millennium, it is also natural to expect that such an economy did not exist in a vacuum of economic thought.[3] The Qur'an and hadith (narrations quoting the Prophet or describing/reporting his actions or reactions) contain many verses/narrations of direct and indirect economic implications. Gradually, with the development of *fiqh* (Islamic law and jurisprudence) as the predominant field of Islamic knowledge, Islamic economic thought generally dealt with practical policy or moral aspects of the economy and evolved as text-oriented legalism or polemics.

Much of the early or premodern economic thought centered around religious rulings and economic policies. Contrary to the "Great Gap" perspective of Joseph Schumpeter (Ghazanfar 2003), economic thought has had an unbroken legacy in the Muslim world since the very first century after the Prophet Muhammad. Among notable contributions throughout the premodern period, for example, are: *Kitab al-Kharaj* (Treatise on Taxation) by Imam Abu Yusuf (d. 767 AD), *Kitab al-Amwal* (Treatise on Wealth) by Abu Ubayd Al-Qasim (d. 837 AD), *Al-Ahkam al-Sultaniyyah* (The Laws of Governance) by Abul Hasan Al-Mawardi (d. 974 AD), and *Al-Hisbah fil-Islam* (Public Duties in Islam) by Taqi Uddin Ibn Taymiyah (d. 1328 AD). Ibn Khaldun (d. 1404 AD) and his *Muqaddimah* (Prolegomena)[4] must be mentioned in this context, but separately, because while the other names and their works just mentioned represent the vitality of economic thought from the Islamic perspective, Ibn Khaldun's contribution was a fundamental break from the text-oriented, legalistic, or polemical legacy and served as a significant bridge to the modern period.

Until the period of Ibn Khaldun, no work can be identified and categorized as a systematic study of any social phenomena, such as the economy, that can be labeled as theorization—"the process of formulating general concepts by abstracting common properties of instances."[5] The pivotal contribution of Ibn Khaldun could have led Muslim scholars to shift away from legalistic or philosophical treatises, but the predominance of legalism was so entrenched that Ibn Khaldun had to be rediscovered by Western scholars, who fundamentally benefited from his works before the Muslims, which led to the development of modern sociology to study social phenomena.

CONTEMPORARY ISLAMIC ECONOMIC THOUGHT

Contemporary Islamic economic thought has its roots in the Islamic revivalism of the twentieth century (Zaman 2008). Among the pioneers who not only called for reshaping the economic system based on Islam, but also made pioneering contributions to the discourse about what such an economic system would be like, were Sayyid Abul A'la Mawdudi (d. 1979 AD)[6] and Muhammad Baqir Al-Sadr (d. 1980 AD).[7] The earliest titles on Islamic economics were authored not by economists or anyone with experience in dealing with economy (Al-Sadr 1994; Mawdudi 1969, 1975). Compared to later contributions, these early contributions were less pragmatic, rigorous, and nuanced, but nonetheless pivotal.

Several institutional developments need to be noted in this context. In 1969 the Organization of Islamic Conference (OIC) was established in Jeddah, Saudi Arabia—not proactively, but triggered by arson at al-Aqsa Mosque in Jerusalem. As part of a comprehensive agenda, the Islamic Development Bank (IDB) was established in 1975, also based in Jeddah. One of the important milestone undertakings of IDB was holding the First International Conference on Islamic Economics in Makkah in 1976. Organized by the King Abdul Aziz University in Jeddah, it was the first time such a major and robust gathering of economists and *Ulama* from across the globe was convened. In the presence of two hundred such participants, 30 papers were presented covering a broad range of topics in Islamic economics: concept and methodology, production and consumption, role of the state, insurance, riba-free banking (riba is generally equated with interest), zakat and fiscal policy, and so on (Ahmad 1980, p. xvii) The conference led to the establishment of the International Centre for Research in Islamic Economics at King Abdul Aziz University, Jeddah, in 1977.

At a different level, and not necessarily connected with the previously mentioned institutional developments, in 1979 the military junta of General Ziaul Huq (d. 1988 AD), who came to power in Pakistan through a military coup (an un-Islamic means), initiated an Islamization or Shariah implementation program, an integral part of which was to Islamize the entire economy and restructure it as an economy free of interest. Similar changes followed in Iran in the aftermath of the Islamic revolution there. While Iran has shown a better Islamic commitment, neither of these two countries can be taken as a proper example, with the experience of Pakistan since its independence in 1947 being simply terrible. Notably, each of these two countries pursued an agenda of Islamization of the economy as part of its public and explicit policy. In contrast, Malaysia became independent in 1957, and did not undertake an explicit Islamization program; yet, with a clear Islamic undertone and commitment, it not only transformed itself into a modern economy, but also did so with a clear Islamic vision and direction.

The Islamization or Shariah implementation agenda was part of the revivalist ethos,[8] but in none of the regions where Islamic movements have been prominent did the economy take an Islamic direction in a substantive manner. The development of the field of contemporary Islamic economic thought needs to be understood in this context, as the economic thought developed without a meaningful link to any real economy.

MAJOR THEMES AND CONCERNS

The aforesaid institutional development and conferences raised greater awareness, facilitated mobilization of resources, and encouraged networking among Islamic economics experts and enthusiasts. Soon it was recognized that there was a great deal of interest in this field and a good deal of work—polemical or not—was already there. One of the pioneering Islamic economists, Dr. Muhammad Nejat-ullah Siddiqi, who worked as a professor at the International Centre for Research in Islamic Economics, King Abdul Aziz University in Jeddah, presented at that 1976 conference a significant work, a survey of the literature on Islamic economics, "Muslim Economic Thinking: A Survey of Contemporary Literature" (Ahmad 1980, 191–315).[9] The survey included 700 works in English, Arabic, and Urdu covering virtually all areas pertaining to an economy. This further boosted the confidence of those interested in Islamic economics as a field and in Islamization of the economy[10] as a pursuit that made everyone aware that even before such major organized events as in 1976, considerable contributions already existed. The survey categorized the works in Islamic economics under five major headings:

1. Economic philosophy of Islam [1–90]
2. Economic system of Islam [91–498]
3. Islamic critique of contemporary economics [499–610]
4. Economic analysis in an Islamic framework [611–647]
5. History of economic thought in Islam and Misc. [648–698]

As can be noticed from the number of works under each category, the two largest categories are the economic system of Islam and the Islamic critique of contemporary economics. It should be noted that most of the works under the former category also were rather heavy with critique of contemporary economics. Thus, the two primary foci of the literature during this period were polemical in nature in their attempts to expose the weaknesses and shortcomings of the contemporary economics and the dominant economic systems and to delineate the economic system of Islam, also polemically.[11] This chapter does not, of course, as mentioned earlier, provide exhaustive coverage of the contemporary contributions.[12] In the remainder of this chapter, a few salient trends in light of the major contributors and contributions are discussed briefly.

THE SHADOW OF MAINSTREAM ECONOMICS

Two important realities, among others, that the field of Islamic economics had to contend with were: (1) the current world is dominated by two competing systems, the capitalist (market-oriented) system and the communist/socialist (command- or central-planning-oriented) system; and (2) over the second half of the twentieth century, the world has converged closer to the market-oriented, mixed economy, and mainstream economics, especially in academia, which primarily deals with and articulates this type of mixed economy.

In terms of praxis, until recently there have been quite a few economies based on socialism (the former Soviet Union, Eastern European countries, Cuba, and North Korea), while the rest were either essentially capitalist or closer to capitalism. Advocates of socialism could look to the socialist countries for their reference, and advocates of capitalism could refer to many more countries. However, the advocates of Islamic economics had no specific economy to refer to as a prototype. Thus, the discourse about Islamic economics is essentially conceptual or theoretical, yet to be linked to any actual economy.

As the world economies converged more to the market-oriented system, in the academic world the dominance was of the mainstream economics that is based on the market-oriented, mixed economy, where both private enterprise and property reign supreme, yet there is coexistence of a robust private as well as public sector. Call it mainstream or conventional economics, it is formally traced to Adam Smith as its father. From his time emerged the classical school, with essentially no distinction between macro- and microeconomics. Then came the marginalist, neoclassical revolution, with its more microeconomic focus. Neoclassical economics did not have much of an issue with its classical predecessors, and in line with the classical school, it dominated the field until the Great Depression of the early twentieth century.

Modern economics with its graphical and mathematical orientation is more indebted to neoclassical economics. From the Great Depression era came the Keynesian revolution, which challenged Classical economics and its postulates, while also placing Keynesianism at odds with the classical macroeconomic thoughts, and thus with the neoclassical economics as well because the latter accepted the macroeconomic postulates of the former. Despite the major differences between classical-neoclassical on the one hand and Keynesian on the other, modern economics as it is taught in the introductory undergraduate textbooks today is a fusion of both neoclassical and Keynesian ideas, facilitated by, for example, synthesizing works of the late Nobel laureate Paul Samuelson, and as encapsulated in the first modern economics text book authored by him.[13] This synthesis is based on both macroeconomic and microeconomic focus and both neoclassical and Keynesian contributions, while acknowledging and delineating the differences between the two. Notably, this modern, mainstream economics is based essentially on pedagogical tools contributed by the neoclassical school and expanded or refined further by others, especially as part of the legacy of the "formalist revolution."[14]

This background is very important to understand contemporary Islamic economic thought, because Islamic economists were generally also trained in modern universities or institutions within the legacy of the mainstream economics.[15]

SHIFT FROM ISLAMIC ECONOMICS TO ISLAMIC FINANCE

The revivalist ethos, especially pertaining to Islamizing the economy, was tempered by the mid-1980s, as the experience of Pakistan (the military junta's Shariah implementation program), Iran (in the grip of post-Revolution ideological zeal and fervor), and Afghanistan (the chokehold of Taliban-style Shariah) did not meet the positive expectations of the Muslim masses. Thus, not finding an economy, where ideas could be experimented with, and also due to the vast oil wealth after the crisis that sought Islamic (or, Shariah-compliant) investment opportunities, the focus shifted to Islamic finance. Instead of focusing on macro-level changes in the broader economy, micro-level changes in financial institutions proved much easier to pursue.

Thus emerged the subdiscipline of Islamic finance, basically to have institutions for financial intermediation that are legalistically interest-free, providing Islamic alternatives to the services and mechanisms available in the conventional financial system. While a vast number of earlier works were focused on various aspects of an Islamic economy, the later focus shifted to development, operation, and promotion of Islamic financial institutions. This shift was not just at the level of praxis, but also at the level of thought.

Earlier literature on Islamic economics was highly idealistic (Siddiqi 1972; Rahman 1974; Mawdudi 1975[16]), where profit-loss sharing (PLS) or participatory modes were glorified, almost in exclusion of other modes. Several major works of this period dealt with riba (and interest, as part of equating interest with riba in a blanket manner),[17] enunciating the deleterious role of interest, the wisdom of prohibition of *riba* (read: interest), how the economy needs to be free from interest, and how such an interest-free economy can be structured and implemented (Ahmad 1969; Mannan 1968; Siddiqi 1973; Uzair 1955).

GROWTH OF MORE SOPHISTICATED AND ROBUST LITERATURE

During the decade after the 1976 conference, as more and more Western-trained economists among the Muslims started taking an interest in Islamic economics and finance, gradually more sophisticated works that could appeal to those with modern economics backgrounds started appearing (Chapra 1979; Naqvi 1981; Choudhury 1983). This pool was further strengthened by a few high-profile economists at globally known institutions, such as the International Monetary Fund (IMF) and the World Bank. Abbas Mirakhor and Mohsin Khan, both at the IMF at that time, contributed a number of works that raised the profile of Islamic economics and/or finance significantly (Khan 1986; Iqbal and Mirakhor 1987).

While a good number of Muslim economists embraced the new field and continued to make contributions, an important wedge developed in terms of the methodology.[18] As mentioned earlier, modern economics in the academic context—including pedagogy and research—is shaped by the neoclassical-Keynesian conceptual and analytical toolkit. Thus, those economists with an Islamic persuasion—and for lack of a better term we will refer to them as Islamic economists—were generally trained in the tradition of mainstream economics. Generally speaking, from the viewpoint of comparative economic systems, there was hardly anyone who could advocate for Islamic economics while embracing either the capitalist or socialist system. But at the level of economic thought, there was no consensus regarding embracing the entire body of accumulated thoughts and contributions in modern economics. Thus, while most Islamic economists critiqued various conventional theories and at the same time embraced modern economics in general, there were others who were of the thought that Islamic economics must be completely free from conventional economics and be on its own unique foundation (Choudhury 2003).

However, while there could arguably be rejection of the body of mainstream economic thought, the toolkit of modern economics could not be ignored, let alone set aside, so easily. Therefore there were a number of reasons why new works in Islamic economics continued to resort to the toolkit of modern economics. Among these reasons are: (1) many of these Islamic economists were originally trained in conventional economics; (2) there was no separate toolkit from an Islamic perspective; and (3) there was an urge to penetrate the academic world of research and publication and raise the profile that required employing an accepted, standard tool kit with which the peer economists—conventional and otherwise—were familiar. Also, by this time the Islamic economists already were producing more specialized works focusing on or covering various subfields of economics: micro, macro, development, monetary, financial, and so on (Kahf 1978; Choudhury 1986a). Gradually, of course, as the focus shifted from Islamic economics to Islamic finance, many more contributors came forward covering broader areas, with increasing emphasis on empirical works, but most such works have been in the context of Islamic finance rather than Islamic economics. The following subsections discuss a few important and broad themes in Islamic economics.

Narrative and Polemical Discourse versus Theorization

As mentioned earlier in this chapter, in the premodern period, the contributions to economic thinking in the Muslim world were essentially conceptual, philosophical and/or polemical, dealing with policies, legal rulings, normative conducts, and so on. There was a fundamental break in this legacy through the contribution of Ibn Khaldun. His was the first attempt to identify patterns of change affecting society in a historical context and continuum. His contributions are considered as a precursor to various areas, such as modern historiography, sociology, and economics. Unfortunately, it was not the Muslims who took up, embraced, and built upon his legacy. Rather, as mentioned earlier, it had to wait for the Western scholars to discover Ibn Khaldun and benefit from his works with due acknowledgement before Muslims would rediscover and reclaim him.[19]

The relevance of Ibn Khaldun in this context is related to the role of theorization in the development of a field, particularly in social science. While during the twentieth century there were numerous works on Islamic economics, there was no comprehensive, coherent theoretical or conceptual approach to Islamic economics. Only one author stands out in this context: Masudul Alam Choudhury, probably the most prolific author and scholar in the field of Islamic economics and related areas. He has written numerous scholarly books and research papers that are distinguished from the contributions of others due to the fact that his works, at least from his viewpoint, represent a comprehensive, holistic paradigm based on a "phenomenological model of unity of knowledge in economics, ethics, science and society" (Choudhury 2007).[20]

While there are many major contributors to the field of Islamic economics, there is nothing comparable in its comprehensiveness and robustness as a unifying model that Choudhury presents as the Tawhidi paradigm, where Tawhid, being oneness of God and a unifying principle, enables ideas and concepts, theories and models, methods and solutions to come together to bear upon human life as guidance from the Islamic perspective. Thus, he presents his contributions as the "universal paradigm" that deals with not just the micro and macro dimensions of the economy, but also as "a methodology that explains *macrocosmic* phenomena by a process of complex aggregation of micro-phenomena" (Choudhury 2007, p. 1, emphasis added).

However, pushing it all the way from macroeconomic to "macrocosmic," as ambitious as it sounds and appears, as indicated, this is from the author's viewpoint. Hardly any known Islamic economist has embraced or validated this paradigm, let alone adopted it as a basis for further development of their own theories, models, or studies. Thus, Choudhury's paradigm is not in the Kuhnian sense of "universally recognized scientific achievements that for a time provide model problems and solutions to a community of practitioners" (Kuhn 1970, p. 158).

Rather, it is simply a body of knowledge and someone's contribution to understanding. While in its holistic scope and robustness the contribution of

Choudhury remains distinctive, there might be an important reason why it has not been received well or seriously by peers, which is discussed in the following pages.

Theories/Models versus Reality

To appreciate this particular aspect, some reflections once again on the status of the mainstream economics are warranted. To put this in perspective, let's note that recently there have been calls to abolish the Nobel Prize in economics (Bergmann 1999). Many scientists as well as social scientists are among those who are not at all happy with this award (Henderson 2004). The highly acclaimed and provocative author of *The Black Swan* has proposed that investors should sue the authorities who awarded the Nobel Prize in economics (Baker 2010). What is this hullabaloo about?

Strictly speaking, the Nobel Memorial Prize in economics is the ultimate recognition for economists. This field in modern times has become sophisticated through rigorous application of advanced mathematical and statistical modeling and studies, overburdened by most unrealistic assumptions, yet claiming to be akin to a positive, scientific endeavor. The original purpose and intent of everything in this field were to understand how the economy works, in a way similar to natural scientists' attempting to discover the ways of nature.[21] However, not alone but most overwhelmingly in economics, the enterprise of understanding the economy has become a highly sophisticated, mathematics-and-statistics-laden exercise that tries to achieve internal consistency and rigor that is undoubtedly elegant, robust, advanced, and complex, but far removed from the reality. In historical perspective, it was this kind of tendency to develop an internally coherent, elegant, and robust model in the neoclassical tradition, but delinked from the real economy, that confounded them, so it was no surprise that when the Great Depression occurred, neoclassical economics (the dominant paradigm) could not predict, explain, or solve the problem of the Great Depression. Arguably, capitalism was saved by the Keynesian revolution. For nearly half a century, the Keynesian paradigm in economics dominated the economics discourse as well as policy making to the extent that the Keynesian policy regime became deeply integrated into the monetary and financial systems of modern economies. However, as realistic as Keynesian economics appeared to be in the aftermath of the Great Depression, gradually Keynesian economists also developed the tendency to create their own fantasy world that was internally coherent, elegant, and robust, but gradually lost touch with the reality to the extent that when stagflation—high unemployment accompanied by high inflation—reared its ugly head in the 1970s, they were caught completely unprepared and could not predict, explain, or solve the problem of stagflation either.

The result was the gradual reemergence of the new generation of economists in the footsteps of the classical-neoclassical economics and taking up the mantle. The rational expectation school, real business cycle theory, and new classical macroeconomics are some of the variants of this new generation. While all of these paradigmatic mazes were being fought out within economics, the first global economic/financial crisis of the twenty-first century caught economists of all mainstream persuasions off-guard. They are still scratching their heads, and only a few brave souls, even among the large pool of Nobel laureates in economics, are going public and sticking their necks out that they understand what is going on and thus can solve the problem. What is the relevance of all this to the niche field of Islamic economics? Well, this has to do at least partly with the normative versus positive discourse in economics, and its implication for Islamic economics.

Positive, Normative, and Transformative

Modern economics had its origin more in political economy. However, since the emergence of neoclassical economics, the field has been pushed in the positive direction with exaggerated claims and aspirations as if economics is like the natural sciences. Gradually, not only did the endeavor to develop positive economics largely delink economics from its normative dimensions, but also the mainstream economics in academia and research institutions increasingly became dominated by those with sophisticated modeling (abstracting from reality) using advanced mathematics and statistics. While modeling and theorization are essential for understanding how things work, and in this context, how the economy and the participating agents behave at the micro and macro levels, the relentless pursuit of mathematical and quantitative rigor, sophistication, and robustness of the economic models made the whole discipline internally more coherent, but delinked from the normative considerations on the one hand and from the real economy on the other.

In light of this experience of mainstream economics, Islamic economics literature and discourse are primarily focused on the normative dimensions of a "moral economy"[22]—that is, instead of how an economy functions in general or in an Islamic framework, what the economy's function and behavior should be; how the participating agents (consumers, producers, traders, markets) should behave; and so on. While the mainstream economics is overwhelmingly biased toward the positive, the normative side is largely ignored. Islamic economists' focus has been just the opposite. From the Islamic viewpoint, there is also a transformative dimension (Zaman 2008), because Islam does not merely focus on the normative; it also shows ways in which the normative dimensions can be achieved. However, between the normative and transformative dimensions, there is a legitimate and valuable role of the positive (dealing with *What is*, instead of *What should be*?) as well. Thus, for example, the Qur'an does offer precious insight about human behavior and propensities, which needs to be identified and studied as a baseline to seek transformation toward the normative. In this context, there are differences in *Homo economicus* and *Homo islamicus*, but the differences might be highly exaggerated by Islamic economists, which might explain why the experience of the participants in the Islamic finance industry is that they behave more like *Homo economicus* than the presumed or idealized *Homo islamicus* (Farooq 2011; Kuran 1996; Warde 2000).

For most of the contributions in the Islamic economics literature, either the neoclassical assumptions about the positive dimensions are adopted or *Homo islamicus*[23] is assumed, but the study of *Homo islamicus* in a systematic and coherent framework is absent. The works based on the *Tawhidi* paradigm of Choudhury could have been an important difference in this regard, as the paradigm approaches the pertinent issues and problems from a holistic perspective. However, this paradigm has not been embraced or taken seriously even by the peer

Islamic economists. One might argue that Islamic economists are generally not only trained by mainstream economics, but also brainwashed or enamored with it, and therefore cannot step outside the shadow of mainstream economics (Zaman 2008). Indeed, Choudhury claims that "The predictions and scope of economics in its mainstream outlook, therefore, are almost always incorrect, evasive, unjust and inequitable" (2007, p. 2), and thus it is not surprising that the current Islamic economics in the shadow of mainstream economics is also without adequate coherence or relevance.

However, at least two reasons might be behind the lack of interest in the Tawhidi paradigm. First, this paradigm is based on rather advanced philosophical garb of epistemology on the one hand and highly advanced, mathematical theories and models on the other (Farooq 2009c). Very few among the peer Islamic economists, let alone the peers beyond economics or especially the religious scholars, probably fathom what the paradigm amounts to or has to offer. Second, the product of this Tawhidi paradigm seems to be a robust theoretical edifice that reflects more a romance with theorization than the world of reality, the same kind of problem that continues to plague mainstream economics. Thus, the contributions to Islamic economics to date include mostly works that lack any distinctive paradigm or holistic approach of their own and focus largely on the normative dimensions. For the sole remainder, Choudhury, who has attempted a new paradigm with some positive bent—actually presenting it as "positive science"—the contributions in fact are confined to the realm of high theorization, also without any meaningful empirical bent.

Quite ironically, while repudiating neoclassical economics, which claimed to be positive science dealing with "rational" human beings and in the process delinked from the normative aspects and ultimately from the reality, Choudhury himself ends up viewing his contributions as "positive science" while assuming that human beings are essentially "rational." From this viewpoint: ". . . economics is a positive science, rather than a normative rhetoric, about the socio-scientific order where the use of ethics and values when agents are optimizing [is] completely rational" (2007, p. xiv). Thus, whether the Islamic economists have focused on addressing various micro or macro issues in a fragmented manner without a coherent and robust underlying theoretical edifice, or have focused on the coherent and robust underlying theory based on advanced mathematical tools and concepts, in either case the real-world problems remain as elusive as ever.

Lack of Problem-Solving Orientation

Islamic economics discourse is primarily an enterprise that has attempted Islamization of economics, where in terms of concepts, tools, and priorities it is basically to come up with Islamic alternatives to everything that mainstream economics has. Thus, if mainstream economics has utility function as part of its theoretical structure, we must have "Islamic" utility function (Choudhury 1986a). If it has supply curve, then it must be Islamized and Muslims must have Islamic supply curve (Aziz 2011).

The reality is that the whole legacy of Islamic economics does not have anything equivalent to Adam Smith's *An Inquiry into the Nature and Causes of the Wealth of Nations* (1937) that laid the foundation of a systematic way to better understand the economic behavior at the micro and macro levels. Nor does it have anything equivalent to the late Nobel laureate Gunnar Myrdal's *Asian Drama* (1968), a systematic inquiry to better understand the problems of development and underdevelopment, for example, in South Asia. Smith was a moral philosopher and did not see his inquiry delinked from its moral and normative anchor, and Myrdal was an institutionalist who did not believe that positive economics was without any underlying normative biases, and his positive inquiry was on the basis of his own normative biases explicitly stated or identified.

In the history of Muslim civilization, there have been continuous endeavors to deal with the issues of poverty and prosperity. However, except in some very brief periods of early experience after the Prophet Muhammad there is no identified or established record that alleviation, let alone elimination, of poverty has ever been the focus of any systematic effort. Moreover, except in the contribution of Ibn Khaldun, there has never been any systematic effort to inquire, investigate, and understand the socioeconomic reality in general, let alone the problem of poverty and why it persists. (Farooq 2008, 2009a).

It is no wonder that Siddiqi's 1976 survey and the resulting bibliography on Islamic economics literature to that date included 700 entries under 51 subcategories over 115 pages, and poverty is not one of those categories. The same is true about Khan's 1983 survey (221 pages). While there seems to be extensive literature in Islamic economics, and policy recommendations and ready-made solutions are confidently offered, no systematic inquiry into the real-world problems is undertaken. The Islamic Research and Training Institute (IRTI), the research and training wing of the Islamic Development Bank, has made a valuable contribution and produced hundreds of treatises, including some touching on poverty, but not a single one that has focused on investigating and understanding the nature and the challenges of poverty. Attempting to provide solutions, especially with the presumption that solutions are readily available in the scriptural sources, without studying and understanding the problem in the *inquiring* legacy of Ibn Khaldun or Adam Smith is a fundamental shortcoming of the current body of Islamic economics. Thus, if one takes the subject of poverty, there does not seem to be any study of the problem, but there are plenty of studies providing solutions (Islamic Council of Europe 1979; Khan 1994).

Without proper study of the problem (Bonner 2005), it is only predictable that there is hardly any mapped-out solution to the problem of poverty and underdevelopment. Thus, if one reviews a book on Islamic economics, the typical content would be as in Khan (1994): Islamic economics—an overview: Islamic worldview, basic assumptions, economic organization, role of money (usually constituting a longer topic in the context of prohibition of riba), consumer behavior, poverty, fiscal management, the nature of Islamic economics, the methodology of Islamic economics, Islamic economics in practice, and so on.

In the segment under poverty, the opening sentences are revealing. "Poverty is a complex phenomenon. Islamic scholars are developing a body of doctrines to analyze and solve this problem" (Khan 1994, p. 20). With this recognition of the complexity and the assurance that the scholars are developing the relevant "doctrines," the book right away jumps to ideas for solutions. In the list of ideas, one comes across comments like the following: "The Islamic concept of economic justice revolts against the prevalent strategy of unbalanced development between rural and urban areas" (p. 21). Unfortunately, there is no explanation or analysis as to why the rural-urban dichotomy develops and persists, what the pattern is, or contextual differences among contributing underlying factors. This might be the "poverty of Islamic economics" (Farooq 2008) that needs to be addressed before major challenges such as poverty can be approached in a problem-solving manner. The problem is accentuated as Islamic finance, an offshoot of the Islamic revivalist movement, though it was supposed to be a part of the Islamic economic system, as mentioned earlier, eclipsed Islamic economics, obscuring as well as reducing the latter in importance.

Islamic Finance without an Islamic Economy and Delinked from Islamic Economics

The literature on Islamic economics during the 1970s and 1980s was dominated by themes pertaining to various aspects of an Islamic economic system. Thus, from theorization to polemics to research works, one can find numerous works trying to articulate concepts, models or policy propositions in the context of an Islamic economic system (Islahi 2007). However, as explained earlier, the Islamic revivalist movements failed to find any serious opportunity to Islamize an economy, while a variety of factors converged favorably for developing and establishing Islamic finance. Many joined in the fray, and even the leadership of it was seized by the conventional financial powerhouses, such as Citibank, HSBC, and BNP Paribas.

Several high-profile institutional involvements brought a new level of global exposure to Islamic finance. Islamic finance reached and was embraced by Main Street and Wall Street, through the Dow Jones Islamic Index. In academia, Harvard Law School initiated the biennial Harvard University Forum on Islamic Finance. Several notable universities, such as the University of Durham in the United Kingdom, introduced a full range of degree and professional programs. Major professional bodies initiated programs; for example, the Chartered Institute of Management Accountants (CIMA) introduced CIMA Islamic. But the most important catalyst for Islamic finance gaining global attention was the access to the capital market using Islamic financial modes. This profile was further reinforced during the aftermath of the recent global financial crisis, where a number of studies indicated that Islamic finance seems to be more resilient during economic downturns,[24] and several notable global luminaries, such as the Vatican, drew attention to Islamic finance.[25]

The 1990s and early 2000s saw an explosion of literature on Islamic finance. The number of books, research papers, monographs, and policy papers that became available essentially eclipsed Islamic economics. With the rise of the so-called Shariah scholars (should rather be called Shariah experts or Shariah finance experts)[26] bringing the Islamic finance industry to prominence, even Islamic economists have felt marginalized (Siddiqi 2006). Indeed, the number of works dealing with Islamic economics dwindled significantly, while Islamic finance literature became dominant.

It can be argued that Islamic finance should have enhanced the Islamic economics literature as well. However, the reality is that Islamic finance seems to have emerged as a cart before the horse. There seems to be little acknowledgment that the financial system is part of an economic system, and a normative financial system, which Islamic finance claims to be, cannot be merely a technical infrastructure that can function and achieve its normative goals without a broader, underlying economy supporting it. Regardless of the relationship between Islamic finance and Islamic economics, the interest in and appetite for Islamic economics do not seem to be as strong as for Islamic finance.[27] That takes us to the last aspect of this survey.

What Is and Whither Islamic Economics?

Even though there are differences in the definition of economics in the conventional sense, modern texts have converged to definitions that capture the essence of economics. This has happened over the past two to three centuries. In comparison, Islamic economics is a newer field and significant divergence exists in defining it (Chapra 1996). This is partly due to the fact that, unlike economists as a profession and economics as a recognized and established field of study, Islamic economics still does not have a professional foundation and there is hardly any global standard or broad agreement regarding most aspects of Islamic economics. Thus, one can find remarkable differences among the works of the past few decades—for example, Mannan (1980), Naqvi (1981) and Khan (1994). While the works of Mannan and Khan are descriptive, polemical, and prescriptive, Naqvi's are analytically and theoretically robust.

Yet, there is considerable agreement or common ground between conventional and Islamic economics. A review of major Islamic economists, such as Chapra, Siddiqi, and others, demonstrates that except the religious prohibitions, such as riba (interest), *gharar* (excessive uncertainty), *maisir* (gambling), and the emphasis on ethical foundations and the *maqasid* (broader objectives), Islamic economics shares the primary macroeconomic goals at the operational level, and those are achievement of full employment, economic growth, price level stability, and so on (Chapra 1996).

Major aspects of an Islamic economic system do not necessarily have many unique features, but its uniqueness lies in the comprehensive way it tries to balance the extremes of competing economic systems while pursuing broader socioeconomic goals. Thus, on private property, while socialism denies private property and capitalism embraces it at its core, Islamic economics affirms private property, but allows the government to set limits on private property and related property rights. On the roles of the market and government, the Islamic economic system upholds the market as a core institution and mechanism, but also allows the government to intervene whenever there are greater collective interests to call for such interventions. Thus, the Islamic economy cannot necessarily be understood or defined in black-and-white terms with unique characteristics of systems such as socialism and capitalism, and, on the basis of which, strong polemical cases can be made. However, its uniqueness lies in the balance that the Islamic economy seeks in the pursuit of individual and collective goals in the context of broader objectives, such as *maqasid al-Islam* (alternatively known as *maqasid ash-Shariah*) (Siddiqi 2008). Because balance is an elusive and dynamic goal, only through human experience of trial and error can a practical and functioning model of an Islamic economy be presented, which will be its true validation.

CONCLUSION

Islamic economics is a rather young field that attempts to study and shape economic aspects of life from the Islamic perspective. The field is dominated by those who were trained in the Western, conventional tradition. It is not surprising that many among the advocates of Islamic economics are quite comfortable, if not enamored, with the conventional economics. Even those who vehemently oppose the conventional legacy seem to be unable to come out of the shadow of the conventional economics in terms of its models, theories, tools and methodologies.

Islamic economics has been basically eclipsed by Islamic finance, but the success of Islamic finance at least in form indicates that there needs to be greater attention to Islamic economics and shaping the economy from the Islamic viewpoint is integrally related to achieving the broader goals of an Islamic economy or of *maqasid al-Islam*.

The Qur'an does lay out a number of essential economic principles, some of which are injunctions and some prohibitions. The legacy of the Prophet Muhammad is also focused primarily on mobilizing the resources as the bounties of God toward ensuring that people enjoy a healthy and prosperous life, that such prosperity—without worldly indulgence—is widely or universally shared and that all such aspects are addressed as part of *akhirah* (hereafter)-bound, just way of life. After the first global economic/financial crisis of this century, the hollowness or even danger of conventional economic thought stands bare. Humanity is looking for fresh guidance, and the ever-fresh principles in the Qur'an and exemplified in the Prophetic legacy are as compellingly needed as ever. From that perspective, there is a genuine need to transform the economies embracing the economic principles of Islam that are almost universal. And, toward the realization of such an economy, much more focused and coherent works in Islamic economics that are both theoretically and empirically rich are greatly needed.

NOTES

1. The author is the Head of the Centre for Islamic Finance at the Bahrain Institute of Banking and Finance and he gratefully acknowledges the feedback on the draft from the following individuals: Dr. Muhammed Nejatullah Siddiqi (former Professor, King Abdul Aziz University, Jeddah), Dr. Munir Quddus (Dean of College of Business, Prairie View A&M University, Texas), Dr. Salim Rashid (Professor Emeritus of Economics, University of Illinois, Urbana-Champaign), Dr. Syed Nawab Haider Naqvi (Professor of Economics at Federal Urdu University of Arts, Science and Technology, Pakistan), Shah Abdul Hannan (former Chairman, Islami Bank Bangladesh Limited), Dr. Ahmad Asad (Senior Lecturer, BIBF), Nedal El Ghattis (Senior Lecturer, BIBF), Alfatih Gessan P. Aryasantana (Senior Lecturer, BIBF), and Hussam Sultan (Fajr Capital, Brunei). The opinions expressed in this paper do not necessarily reflect the views of BIBF or any individual or institution other than the author.

2. About the pursuit of the "discovery" of Islamic economics, Charles Tripp correctly observes in *Islam and the Moral Economy*: "In doing so, however, many of them were clearly influenced by the very act of imagining a separate domain of the economy. Thinking about the economy as a distinct sphere of knowledge, of understanding and of explanation of human behaviour seemed to bring its own rules, reasoning and criteria. By entering into arguments about the economy as a particular realm of human activity,

many of the Muslim intellectuals seemed to accept—with various degrees of unease, some acknowledged, others not—that they were engaging with a discourse not of their own making" (2006, pp. 104–105).

3. Here this author differs with El-Ashker and Wilson in *Islamic Economics: A Short History*, where they present their narrative about "Islamic economics" as if it existed from the time of the Qur'an and the Prophet Muhammad. This author differs with their viewpoint on this on the basis that until during the modern period, economy was not considered and treated as a separate and distinct domain. Thus, while a convincing case can be made that there was a continuous legacy of economic thought from Islamic perspective, economics or Islamic economics as a separate discipline did not exist during the premodern period. Also see Mirakhor (2007, pp. 7, 9) to appreciate why he views Islamic economics as a discipline in its infancy, or why Hasan states: "Islamic economics started as a formal academic discipline only after 1975. . . ." (Hasan 2005, pp. 29–46).

4. Ibn Khaldun, *The Muqaddimah: An Introduction to History*, trans. Franz Rosenthal (Princeton, NJ: Princeton University Press, 1969).

5. www.thefreedictionary.com/generalisation.

6. Chapra 2004, pp. 163–180; Kuran 1997, pp. 301–304.

7. El-Ashker and Wilson (2006), pp. 392–399.

8. The term *Islamization* in the context of Shariah implementation is much broader than the Islamization in the context of knowledge and science. The latter became popularized with the highly respected works of the late Professor Ismail al-Faruqi, who is generally credited to have introduced the paradigm of Islamization of knowledge, especially in the areas of the social sciences. He offered a 12-step work plan. Islamic movements in particular seized upon this agenda and a major institutional network for research, such as the International Institute of Islamic Thought (Herndon, Virginia), and academic institutions, such as the International Islamic University Malaysia, emerged. For a general review of Islamization of knowledge, see Sulaiman (2000). For a critical perspective, see Siddiqi (2011), pp. 15–34; Nasr (1992); Hasan 1998, pp. 1–40; and Haneef (2005).

9. As the author, Siddiqi, notes, the work was developed in 1974 and presented in 1976, and by the time it was published as part of an edited volume—*Studies in Islamic Economics* (Ahmad 1980)—comprising a number of papers from 1976 conference, the survey had been further expanded to include the contributions since 1976. In the same volume, there was also a separate chapter on contributions in Turkish language, which included 219+ entries: Sabahuddin Zaim, "Contemporary Turkish Literature on Islamic Economics," in Ahmad (1980, pp. 317–350).

10. Al-Zarqa (2003), p. 4.

11. Another relevant survey, further updated and annotated, is Muhammad Akram Khan, *Islamic Economics: Annotated Sources in English and Urdu* (Leicester, UK: Islamic Foundation, 1983).

12. Due to space limitation, not all the relevant works and ideas could be mentioned or cited, let alone be elaborated upon, in this chapter.

13. Samuelson (1948), p. 861.

14. Carsten Köllmann (2008), pp. 575–599.

15. For example, Muhammad Umer Chapra received a PhD in economics from the University of Minnesota, Masudul Alam Choudhury from the University of Toronto, Monzer Kahf from the University of Utah, Mohsin Khan from the London School of Economics, Abbas Mirakhor from Kansas State University, Syed Nawab Haider Naqvi from Princeton University, and so on.

16. Originally, this was a speech in Urdu, delivered by Mawdudi in 1941 at Aligarh Muslim University.

17. A constant theme of the Islamic economics literature is about riba, which is categorically prohibited in the Qur'an. The orthodox position revolves around the riba-interest

equation in a blanket manner. This is one of the most discussed themes in the literature on Islamic economics and finance. For a comprehensive survey, see Siddiqi (2004). For a minority view that does not accept the *riba*-interest equation in a blanket manner, see El-Gamal (2000); Farooq (2009b); and Rahman (1964). Such equation or reductionism might have resulted into delinking the issue of interest from injustice and exploitation. See Farooq (2012, forthcoming).

18. A typology of methodology in Islamic economics is presented in Furqani and Haneef (2011).

19. Renowned historian Arnold J. Toynbee hailed the *Muqaddimah* as "a philosophy of history which is undoubtedly the greatest work of its kind that has ever yet been created by any mind in any time or place" (Toynbee 1961, p. 322). Robert Flint, the British philosopher, viewed Ibn Khaldun as follows: "[A]s a theorist of history he had no equal in any age or country until Vico appeared, more than three hundred years later. Plato, Aristotle, and Augustine were not his peers, and all others were unworthy of being even mentioned along with him" (Flint 1894, 87).

20. The theme of phenomenology itself is complicated enough to preclude any meaningful exposition of it here. Interestingly, while making such a bold claim about uniting almost everything relevant, Choudhury does not bother to initiate his readers into phenomenology (see, for example, Choudhury 2007). For a relevant work pertaining to phenomenological perspective as applied to economics, see Till Düppe, *The Phenomenology of Economics: Life-World, Formalism, and the Invisible Hand* doctoral dissertation, 2009), available at http://repub.eur.nl/res/pub/16075/Proefschrift%20Till%20Duppe%5Blr%5D.pdf.

21. The late Paul Samuelson, the first American recipient of the Nobel Prize in economics, approached modern economics from the viewpoint of thermodynamics (Mirowski 1991, p. 384).

22. Tripp (2006).

23. Ibid., 121–122.

24. Hasan and Dridi (2010). For an empirical work disputing the idea that Islamic finance is more resilient, see Charles, Darné, and Adrian Pop (2011).

25. Totaro (2009).

26. The scholarly output of most of the top "Shariah scholars" is rather scanty.

27. This does not mean that we should not have Islamic finance if we do not have an Islamic economy. The observation here is to underscore the importance of having an Islamic economy underlying Islamic finance and the potential limitation of Islamic finance without being appropriately interfaced with an Islamic economy and grounded in Islamic economics.

REFERENCES

Ahmad, Khurshid, ed. 1980. *Studies in Islamic Economics*. Leicester, UK: Islamic Foundation, 271–272.

Ahmad, Sheikh Mahmud. 1969. "Banking in Islam." *Muslim New International* 8:1, June, 5–11.

Al-Sadr, Muhammad Baqir. 1994. *Our Economics: Discovery Attempt on Economic Doctrine in Islam* (English translation of *Iqtisaduna*) (2 vols.). Tehran, Iran: World Organization for Islamic Services.

Al-Zarqa, Muhammad Anas. 2003. "Islamization of Economics: The Concept and Methodology," *Journal of KAU: Islamic Economics* 16:1, 3–42.

Aziz, M. Abdul. 2011. *Reference Book on Course Outlines: Conventional as Well as Islamic Approaches in Selected Disciplines of Public & Private Universities of Bangladesh*. Dhaka: Bangladesh Institute of Islamic Thought.

Baker, Stephanie. 2010. "'Black Swan' Author Says Investors Should Sue Nobel for Crisis." *Bloomberg*, October 8. Available at www.bloomberg.com/news/2010-10-08/taleb-says-crisis-makes-nobel-panel-liable-for-legitimizing-economists.html (accessed November 2, 2011).

Bergmann, Barbara. 1999. "Abolish the Nobel Prize for Economics." *Challenge* 42:2, March–April, 52–67.

Bonner, M. 2005. "Poverty and Economics in the Qur'an." *Journal of Interdisciplinary History* 35:3, 391–406.

Chapra, Muhammad Umer. 1979. *Objectives of the Islamic Economic Order*. Leicester, UK: Islamic Foundation.

Chapra, M. Umer. 1983. *Monetary Policy in an Islamic Economy*. Islamabad, Pakistan: Institute of Policy Studies, 27–68.

Chapra, M. Umer. 1996. "What Is Islamic Economics?" IDB Award Lecture Series 9.

Chapra, M. Umer. 2004. "Mawlana Mawdudi's Contribution to Islamic Economics." *The Muslim World* 94 (April): 163–180.

Chapra, M. Umer. 2008. "Ibn Khaldun's Theory of Development: Does It Help Explain the Low Performance of the Present-Day Muslim World?" *Journal of Socio-Economics* 37:2, 836–863.

Chapra, M. Umer. 2010. "Islamic Economics: What It Is and How It Developed." Paper written for EH.net's Online Encyclopedia of Economic and Business History. Available at http://eh.net/encyclopedia/article/chapra.islamic (accessed September 29, 2011).

Charles, Amélie, Olivier Darné, and Adrian Pop. 2011. "Is the Islamic Finance Model More Resilient than the Conventional Finance Model? Evidence from Sudden Changes in the Volatility of Dow Jones Indexes." Paper presented at Asian Finance Association 2011 International Conference, July 10–13, available at http://affi2011.etud.univ-montp1.fr/wp-content/themes/blog_um1_ouvert_affi2011/Papers/118C.pdf (accessed January 7, 2012).

Choudhury, Masudul Alam. 1983. "Principles of Islamic Economics." *Middle Eastern Studies* 19:1, 93–103.

Choudhury, Masudul Alam. 1986a. *Contributions to Islamic Economic Theory: A Study in Social Economics*. Macmillan.

Choudhury, Masudul Alam. 1986b. "The Micro-Economics Foundations of Islamic Economics: A Study in Social Economics." *American Journal of Islamic Social Sciences* 3:2, 231–245.

Choudhury, Masudul Alam. 2003. *The Islamic World-System: A Study in Polity-Market Interaction*. London and New York: Routledge.

Choudhury, Masudul Alam. 2007. *The Universal Paradigm and the Islamic World-System: Economy, Society, Ethics and Science*. London: World Scientific.

El-Ashker, Ahmed, and Rodney Wilson. 2006. *Islamic Economics: A Short History*. Leiden and Boston: Brill.

El-Gamal, Mahmoud. 2000. "An Economic Explication of the Prohibition of Riba in Classical Islamic Jurisprudence." *Proceedings of the Third Harvard University Forum on Islamic Finance*, Cambridge, Massachusetts, 31–44.

Farooq, Mohammad Omar. 2008. "The Challenge of Poverty and the Poverty of Islamic Economics." *Journal of Islamic Economics, Banking and Finance* 4:2, May–August, 35–58.

Farooq, Mohammad Omar. 2009a. "The Challenge of Poverty and Mapping Out Solutions: Requisite Paradigm Shift from a Problem-Solving and Islamic Perspective." *Journal of Islamic Economics, Banking and Finance* 5:2, May–August, 45–76.

Farooq, Mohammad Omar. 2009b. "Islam and the Riba-Interest Equation: Reexamination of the Traditional Arguments." *Global Journal of Finance and Economics* 6:2, September, 99–111.

Farooq, Mohammad Omar. 2009c. "On Overstretched Critique and Mathematization of Islamic Economics." *Journal of King Abdul Aziz University in Islamic Economics* 22:2, 83–89.

Farooq, Mohammad Omar. 2011. "Self-Interest, Homo Islamicus and Some Behavioral Assumptions in Islamic Economics and Finance," *International Journal of Excellence in Islamic Banking and Finance* 1:1, January, 52–79.

Farooq, Mohammad Omar. 2012, forthcoming. "Exploitation, Profit and Riba-Interest Reductionism." *International Journal of Islamic and Middle Eastern Finance and Management.*

Flint, Robert. 1894. *Historical Philosophy in France and French Belgium and Switzerland.* New York: Scribners.

Furqani, Hafas, and Mohamed Aslam Haneef. 2011. "Methodology of Islamic Economics: Typology of Current Practices, Evaluation and Way Forward." Paper presented at the 8th conference on Islamic Economics, Doha, Qatar, December 25–27.

Ghazanfar, S. M. 2003. *Medieval Islamic Economic Thought: Filling the "Great Gap" in European Countries.* New York: Rutledge-Curzon.

Haneef, Mohamed Aslam. 2005. *A Critical Survey of Islamization of Knowledge.* Kuala Lumpur: International Islamic University of Malaysia.

Hasan, Zubair. 1998. "Islamization of Knowledge in Economics: Issues and Agenda," *IIUM Journal of Economics and Management* 1:6, 1–40.

Hasan, Zubair. 2005. "Treatment of Consumption in Islamic Economics: An Appraisal," *Journal of King Abdul Aziz University in Islamic Economics* 18:2, 29–46.

Hasan, Zubair, and Jemma Dridi. 2010. "The Effects of the Global Crisis on Islamic and Conventional Banks: A Comparative Study." IMF Working Paper, available at www.imf.org/external/pubs/cat/longres.cfm?sk=24183.0 (accessed January 7, 2012).

Henderson, Hazel. 2004. "Abolish the 'Nobel' in Economics: Many Scientists Agree." December. Available at www.alia2.net/article3237.html (accessed November 2, 2011).

Iqbal, Zubair, and Abbas Mirakhor. 1987. "Islamic Banking." IMF Occasional Paper 49.

Islahi, Abdul Azim. 2007. "Thirty Years of Research in the History of Islamic Economic Thought: Assessment and Future Directions." Paper for the Seventh International Conference on Islamic Economics, Islamic Economics Research Center, King Abdulaziz University, Jeddah, Kingdom of Saudi Arabia, April 1–3, 2008.

Islamic Council of Europe. 1979. *The Muslim World and the Future Economic Order*, London.

Kahf, Monzer. 1978. *Islamic Economy: Analytical Study of the Functioning of the Islamic Economic System.* Plainfield, Indiana, American Trust Publications.

Khan, Mohsin. 1986. *Islamic Interest-Free Banking: A Theoretical Analysis.* IMF Staff Papers 4.

Khan, Muhammad Akram. 1994. *An Introduction to Islamic Economics.* Herndon, VA: International Institute of Islamic Thought.

Khan, Muhammad Akram. 1983. Islamic Economics: Annotated Sources in English and Urdu. Leicester, UK: Islamic Foundation. See Classification System, pp. 17–23.

Köllmann, Carsten. 2008. "General Equilibrium Theory and the Rationality in Economics," *Analyse & Kritik* 30:575–599.

Kuhn, Thomas. 1970. *The Structure of Scientific Revolutions.* Chicago, IL: University of Chicago Press.

Kuran, T. 1996. "The Discontents of Islamic Economic Morality." *American Economic Review* 86:2, 438–442.

Kuran, Timur. 1997. "The Genesis of Islamic Economics: A Chapter in the Politics of Muslim Identity," *Social Research* 64:2, Summer, 301–304.

Mannan, M. A. 1968. "Islam and Trends in Modern Banking: Theory and Practice of Interest-Free Banking." *Islamic Review* (London) 56:11, 12, November–December, 5–10.

Mannan, M. A. 1980. *Islamic Economics: Theory and Practice.* Lahore, Pakistan: Sh. Muhammad Ashraf.

Mawdudi, Sayyid Abul A'la. 1969. "Principles and Objectives of Islam's Economic System." *Criterion* (Karachi) 4:2, March–April, 44–58.

Mawdudi, Sayyid Abul A'la. 1975. *The Economic Program of Man and Its Islamic Solutions.* Lahore, Pakistan: Islamic Publications.

Mirakhor, Abbas. 2007. *A Note on Islamic Economics: IDB Prize Lecture.* Jeddah, Saudi Arabia: IRTI/IDB.

Mirowski, Philip. 1991. *More Heat than Light: Economics as Social Physics, Physics as Nature's Economics.* Cambridge, United Kingdom: Cambridge University Press.

Myrdal, Gunnar. 1968. *Asian Drama: An Inquiry into the Poverty of Nations.* New York: Twentieth Century Fund/Pantheon.

Naqvi, Syed Nawab Haider. 1981. *Ethics and Economics: An Islamic Synthesis.* Leicester, UK: Islamic Foundation.

Nasr, Syed Vali Reza. 1992. "Islamization of Knowledge: A Critical Overview." IIIT Occasional Paper.

Rahman, Afzal-ur. 1974. *Economic Doctrines of Islam* (3 vols.). Lahore, Pakistan: Islamic Publications.

Rahman, Fazlur. 1964. "Riba and Interest." *Islamic Studies* 3:1, March, 1–43.

Samuelson, Paul. 1948. *Economics.* New York: McGraw-Hill, 861.

Siddiqi, Mohammad Nejatullah. 1972. *Economic Enterprise in Islam.* Lahore, Pakistan: Islamic Publications.

Siddiqi, Mohammad Nejatullah. 1973. *Banking without Interest.* Lahore, Pakistan: Islamic Publications.

Siddiqi, Mohammad Nejatullah. 2004. *Riba, Bank Interest, and the Rationale of Its Prohibition.* Visiting Scholars Research Series. Jeddah, Saudi Arabia: Islamic Development Bank.

Siddiqi, Mohammad Nejatullah. 2006. "Shariah, Economics and the Progress of Islamic Finance: The Role of Shariah Experts." Paper presented at Seventh Harvard Forum on Islamic Finance, April 21, 2006, Cambridge, Massachusetts. Retrieved on July 24, 2008, from www.siddiqi.com/mns/Role_of_Shariah_Experts.htm.

Siddiqi, Mohammad Nejatullah. 2008. "Obstacles to Islamic Economics Research." Paper presented at the Seventh International Conference on Islamic Economics, Islamic Economics Research Center, KAAU, Jeddah, April 1–3. Retrieved July 30, 2008, from www.siddiqi.com/mns/OBSTACLES_TO_ISLAMIC_ECONOMICS_RESEARCH.htm.

Siddiqi, Mohammad Nejatullah. 2011. "Islamization of Knowledge: Reflection on Priorities," *American Journal of Islamic Social Sciences* 28:3, 15–34.

Smith, Adam. 1937. *An Inquiry into the Nature and Causes of the Wealth of Nations.* New York: Modern Library.

Sulaiman, Sa'idu. 2000. *Islamization of Knowledge: Background, Models and the Way Forward.* Herndon, VA: International Institute of Islamic Thought.

Totaro, Lorenzo. 2009. "Vatican Says Islamic Finance May Help Western Banks in Crisis." *Bloomberg*, March 4. Available at www.bloomberg.com/apps/news?pid=newsarchive&sid=aOsOLE8uiNOg (accessed October 15, 2011).

Toynbee, Arnold. 1961. *A Study of History* (vol. 3). Oxford: Oxford University Press.

Tripp, Charles. 2006. *Islam and the Moral Economy: The Challenge of Capitalism.* Cambridge, UK: Cambridge University Press.

Uzair, Muhammad. 1955. *An Outline of Interestless Banking.* Karachi, Pakistan: Raihan Publications.

Warde, I. 2000. *Islamic Finance in the Global Economy.* Edinburgh, UK: Edinburgh University Press.

Zaman, Asad. 2008. "Islamic Economics: A Survey of the Literature." MPRA Paper 11024, June. Available at http://mpra.ub.uni-muenchen.de/11024 (accessed October 15, 2011).

CHAPTER 3

The Legal Framework of Islamic Finance

CYNTHIA SHAWAMREH
Lecturer in Law at the University of Chicago Law School; Senior Counsel,
City of Chicago Department of Law, Finance and Economic Development Division

The Islamic finance industry has developed into a significant sector integrated into the global economy. The legal framework for contemporary Islamic finance is dual in nature. Contemporary Islamic finance is practiced all over the world, subject to the secular legal systems that govern the places of the industry's operations. Islamic finance is also subject, in its very reason for being, to the theories, principles, and holdings of Islamic law. This chapter provides an overview of the legal framework for contemporary Islamic finance. Islamic legal theory and jurisprudential reasoning are outlined. The basic rules of Islamic finance, including the prohibition of riba, gharar, and haram activities, and the objective to promote social welfare are covered. The fundamentals of Islamic contract formation are discussed, including sales contracts, profit and loss sharing partnerships, leasing, and Sukuk. The essential question of who interprets Islamic law is considered, exploring the role and function of Shari'a scholars in contemporary Islamic finance and efforts toward industry standardization. The chapter raises questions presented by the operation of Islamic finance in dual regulatory systems, driven by the need to comply with both Islamic law and the multiple secular governmental frameworks within which the industry operates around the world. The challenges these questions present are considered in the context of both closing transactions and the enforceability of contracts.

ISLAMIC LEGAL THEORY

Islamic legal theory posits that law is divine in nature and in substance, and that there is a "right" answer for every imaginable question contained in the Shari'a. The Shari'a, however, as divine law, is transcendent and essentially unknowable. The human effort to determine the content of the Shari'a is known in Islamic legal theory as "fiqh." Classical Sunni legal theory crystallized around the tenth century C.E. with the emergence of four distinct schools of orthodox Sunni jurisprudence.[1] Named after the founding scholar of each school, the Hanafi, Shafi'i, Maliki, and Hanbali schools today generally tend to be spread geographically across the Muslim world. At certain historical periods and in certain places, however, a Qadi, or religious judge, would be selected to represent each school within a single city, coexisting in pluralistic mutual tolerance. Shi'i legal theory developed distinctly from Sunni theory, although it followed generally similar patterns and methodologies. While the schools differ from one another in both legal methodology and in content, certain broad parameters of thought are held in common. The general parameters of Sunni legal thought are known as "usul-i-fiqh," translated roughly as the fundamental principles of jurisprudence.

SOURCES OF ISLAMIC LAW

Usul-i-fiqh posits that there are four basic sources of Islamic law. These sources are the Qur'an, Hadith, consensus (ijma'), and ijtihad.[2] The text of the Qur'an is the first of these four sources. Qur'anic text, revealed by God to the Prophet Muhammad, contains around 6,200 verses, of which approximately 500 verses include specifically legal content.[3] There is widespread consensus among Muslims about the text of the Qur'an, which was standardized and codified during the reign of the third Sunni caliph, Uthman (r. 644–656 C.E.).[4] During the formative period of Islamic history, a distinct class of scholars emerged, who meticulously studied religious text and grappled with the meaning of the text for governing human society. If a legal situation was covered by explicit Qur'anic text, the result was relatively straightforward. However, even in these relatively clear cases, these early scholars wrestled with questions of interpretation.[5]

Complex study of the rules of Arabic grammar developed to better analyze text. The choices individual scholars made regarding linguistic analysis were applied consistently to different portions of Qur'anic text, making selection of those choices extremely important. Different scholars came to different conclusions about the meaning of the same text through different linguistic assumptions. For example, if a scholar determined that use of the imperative verb form in a text implied a binding command from God rather than an exhortation, that determination would have implications in other textual examples. Grammatical analysis helped in the evaluation of several types of linguistic ambiguity in text. Certain verses were considered to be "clear" in meaning while others contained meaning that was "hidden." Certain verses were considered to be "general" ('amm) while others were considered "specific" (khass). Specific Arabic words in the text had fallen out of common usage, or had multiple possible meanings, like the word *eye* or *bank* in English.[6]

In addition to the development of grammatical analysis, scholars gathered as much historical material as possible in order to pair the text with the "circumstances of revelation," a field known as asbab al-nazul. The historical sources were checked and cross-checked in order to place the verses in their precise context, shedding light on the nuances and possible meanings of the text. Finally, scholars developed a theory of abrogation (naskh) to reconcile portions of Qur'anic text that were in seeming conflict with other portions of Qur'anic text. In these cases, one of the texts was determined to have repealed the other. Several factors were considered in determining which text would repeal another, including chronological sequence of revelation.[7] Common examples of abrogation include the progressive nature of revelation regarding the prohibition of wine-drinking, and the command to face toward Mecca in prayer, repealing the practice of facing toward Jerusalem.

The next source of Islamic law is the text of the Hadith, which are generally collections of sayings and actions of the Prophet Muhammad reported by his companions. The Hadith were meticulously sifted by scholars in the ninth century C.E., with many thousands of Hadith discarded as unreliable. Hadith are generally presented with two parts. The content of the report of the saying or action of the Prophet Muhammad is preceded by a "chain of transmission" known as the isnad. These chains of transmission identify which individual heard from which individual and so on back to a companion of the Prophet himself, who states what he or she witnessed firsthand. Scholars vigorously examined these chains of transmission of the Hadith, and developed a system of evaluating their trustworthiness. The biographical history of each individual in the chain of transmission was explored ('ilm al-rijal). The individual's reliability and personal trustworthiness of character were evaluated. Any gaps in the chain of transmission were identified. Similarly, any spots in the chain that were improbable due to the individuals not living at the same time or in the same place were identified. The number of times the content of a particular Hadith was repeated from different sources (tawatur) was noted. The remaining Hadith are contained in several well-known collections and are considered reliable or sound. Hadith are divided into categories indicating their strength, as "trustworthy," "well-known," "good," "weak," and "disliked."[8] The relative strength or weakness of a Hadith is taken into account in legal rulings. The evaluation and content of the Hadith is a significant point of difference between Shi'i and Sunni legal thought.[9]

The third source of Islamic law is consensus (ijma'). Early scholars debated the meaning of consensus in the context of determining binding law. The concept of consensus relates to agreement on the meaning of text contained in the first two sources of law, Qur'anic text and Hadith. The question of whose agreement was necessary for a consensus was critical. Most felt that it was the agreement of qualified scholars that was necessary, rather than the entire Muslim community. Even with that narrower definition, however, pressing questions remained unanswered. What level of scholarship was necessary to be counted among the qualified scholars? Was the agreement of local scholars sufficient? Did all scholars everywhere have to participate for consensus to be reached? Was silence, or lack of objection, the same as assent to a legal position, or did an affirmative declaration of agreement have to be obtained? Was it sufficient to consider only living scholars at a given time to declare a consensus, or were earlier scholars to be included? What about scholars not yet alive? With these difficult logical concerns, only a relatively few matters are considered to be contained within this legal category.[10]

The fourth and final basic source of Islamic law is ijtihad. The concept of ijtihad developed very early in the formative period of Islamic law. Ijtihad means to strive, to make an effort in the sense of using one's utmost rational intellect. Qiyas, or reasoning by analogy, is the most common form of ijtihad in Islamic jurisprudence. The scholar Shafi'i (founder of one of the four Sunni legal schools) articulated this concept in his landmark work Al-Risala around 815 C.E. To illustrate the concept of ijtihad, Shafi'i used the example of the Qur'anic injunction for Muslims to pray in the direction of the Ka'ba in Mecca.[11] What is one to do when the Ka'ba is beyond the range of vision? What if one is in a desert far away from Mecca? Shafi'i wrote that God has given humans signs in the natural world such as the stars, the mountains, the rivers, the moon, light, darkness, and the movement of the sun. From these signs, humans can strive to use their rational intellect (ijtihad) to determine, according to the best of their ability, the direction of Mecca. Even if one errs in this determination, having striven to the best of one's ability to deduce the proper direction for prayer is praiseworthy in the sight of God. Similarly to the signs of the natural world, Shafi'i argued, God has given humanity signs in the verses of the Qur'an. The Arabic word for Qur'anic verses, ayat, literally means signs. We must use these signs to guide us in the determination of legal results through reasoning by analogy when the text is not explicit. Although these legal results can never be absolutely certain, the use of intellect to strive to reach the right result with as much probability as possible is pleasing to God. The context of Shafi'i's work was the struggle between people who advocated freely using their opinions (ra'ay) for legal decisions and people who argued for strict use of Hadith. Shafi'i's theory managed to reconcile these positions, allowing for legal jurisdiction in a wider context of situations not explicitly covered by text without abandoning text entirely. By tying legal decision-making to strict analogical reasoning from text, Shafi'i set the groundwork for the most essential parameter in the development of Sunni legal theory during the following centuries.

Reasoning by analogy is common in some form in most legal systems. In Islamic law qiyas takes several forms. Two simple examples of classical qiyas will illustrate this point. One form of qiyas, reasoning by analogy, is the following: Case A is like Case B. Case A results in ruling X; therefore Case B also results in ruling X. As an example, Qur'anic text prohibits the consumption of "khamr," usually translated as grape wine. The question arose in the early period whether date wine was also prohibited. The text does not explicitly prohibit the consumption of date wine, so how did scholars determine that it, too, was prohibited? Case A (grape wine is prohibited) had a ruling with explicit text. Case B (consumption of date wine) was determined by analogy to be like Case A, and therefore the text-based ruling of Case A was transferred to Case B (consumption of date wine is prohibited because it is like drinking grape wine). The difficult part of this process is determining the meaning of the word *like* in the example. How is drinking date wine like drinking grape wine? Is it because both are liquids? How do we know the reason drinking grape wine is prohibited is not just because it is red in color, so the ruling is not transferable? Scholars of course determined that the most probable reason for the prohibition of grape wine was that it is an intoxicant. Since date wine is also an intoxicant, the consumption of date wine was also forbidden. It is the determination of the reason for the text-based ruling, known as the effective cause ('illa), that is the key to reasoning by analogy in Islamic law. In this simple example, the effective cause is easily determined to be the property of intoxication. In countless other examples over the centuries, and in modern Islamic finance, determining the effective cause of a text-based ruling is not so simple.

The second example of how reasoning by analogy might be structured in classical qiyas is as follows: Case A has ruling X. Case B is contained within Case A and it therefore also has ruling X. The simple illustration of this point is the text-based prohibition on cursing one's parents. The question arises: is one allowed to hit one's parents? The text does not explicitly prohibit hitting one's parents. It is, however, obvious that if one must not curse one's parents, one must not hit one's parents. The logical reasoning here is that hitting one's parents exceeds the prohibition of cursing one's parents and is therefore contained within it. Once again, this simple example illustrates an easily determined ruling, but it is not so easy to determine and transfer all rulings, which are arguably "contained within" a text-based ruling.[12]

SECONDARY PRINCIPLES OF ISLAMIC JURISPRUDENCE

These four basic sources of Islamic law (Qur'an, Hadith, consensus, and ijtihad) provide the main outline of classical Sunni jurisprudence. Certain secondary principles are also used when these sources alone are not sufficient. Necessity (darura) is sometimes invoked to override a text-based result. The most common example of necessity is the permissibility of eating pork (which is textually forbidden) if one would otherwise starve. Other secondary principles include "maqasid," looking to the purposes of the law, "istihsan," or juristic preference, and "maslaha," or rulings in the best interests of the community. Different schools vary in how much flexibility they permit scholars to use in the application of these secondary principles to go beyond the text.

Maqasid, or looking to the general purposes of the law, can be used to assist in the determination of the effective cause ('illa) in classical reasoning by analogy (how Case B is like Case A). By the fourteenth century C.E., scholars had developed a theory of maqasid that identified five general purposes or higher objectives in the content of the law. These purposes are the protection of: (1) life; (2) religion, or the ability to practice Islam; (3) property; (4) children; and (5) human rationality.[13] By using this theory of the general purposes of the law, scholars would analyze the proposed 'illa to ensure that it promoted one of these general purposes. If the proposed 'illa could be tied to one of these general purposes, the probability that it was the correct effective cause in a rule was increased, thus making application to another ruling more credible. The principle of istihsan was invoked when a number of credible rulings were available to choose from, with no clear compelling outcome. Jurists could reasonably select from among the possible rulings by invoking this principle of juristic preference. Maslaha, or rulings in the best interest of the community, evolved over time to have broad applicability. Some jurists would even override the dictates of specific text by using the principal of maslaha, arguing that compelling circumstances justify the setting aside of specific text for the good of the community.

Scholars also developed five legal categories into which all human behavior can be divided in order to more clearly analyze Islamic law. These categories are: (1) prohibited, (2) discouraged, (3) neutral, (4) recommended, and (5) obligatory. For example, prayer and fasting are obligatory (category 5). Consumption of pork and alcohol are prohibited (category 1). Smoking, on the other hand, is discouraged but not specifically prohibited (category 2). Another set of categories developed by scholars to help sort through the complexity of Islamic law is the division of rules into two categories: (1) 'ibadat and (2) mu'amalat. 'Ibadat concerns the rules that govern the relationship between humans and God. For example, prayer and fasting fall into this category. Mu'amalat concerns the rules that govern the relationships among and between humans. Laws of contract and Islamic finance generally fall into this category.

THEORETICAL LEGAL SYSTEMS

Islamic legal theory over the centuries developed into a complex and sophisticated legal system. Western legal systems are generally considered to be based in common law (cases decided by judges govern as a body of binding precedent) or based in codified law (cases are decided based on predetermined statutory legal codes). Some legal systems, like that of the United States, present a combination of these two approaches. Islamic legal theory offers a third model, which is sometimes called juristic law.[14] In this system, individual judges must determine the right result in each case. While previous decisions in similar cases may be informative, they are not binding, as capable scholars are expected to engage with the text and perform their own legal analysis through ijtihad.

Theoretical Islamic law has been described as a microcosmic system.[15] The ideal in the microcosmic system is the determination, through the use of the utmost capacity of human rational intellect, of the most probable result in each individual case. The Shari'a, or God's unknowable, divine, and transcendent law, contains a just result for every imaginable situation. The human effort to determine what that result might be (fiqh) will only ever be probable at best and can never be known with absolute certainty. This theoretical approach conceptually permits, and even favors, tolerance and pluralism. The microcosmic system can be juxtaposed to rule-based systems such as common law or codified law, which can be identified as macrocosmic systems. In the theory of a macrocosmic system, the law is external and the rules are predetermined and broadly applied. This theoretical approach, however, in actual implementation is modified by the legal principle of equity.

The limitation of macrocosmic theory is the problem of extenuating circumstances. In some instances, straightforward application of a predetermined set of rules dictates an obviously unjust result. The legal principle of equity is then brought in to modify the unjust result by taking into account the extenuating circumstances. This modification is essential to a sense of fairness in a macrocosmic system. Conversely, the limitation of the theory of a microcosmic system is the risk of unpredictability associated with not knowing the rules in advance. In actual implementation, Islamic legal systems have modified this risk through the extreme deference scholars give to the work of earlier scholars, increasing the stability and predictability of the systems. In practice, most scholars have usually followed the legal determinations contained within their respective various schools, or at most patched rulings across the schools (a controversial practice known as talfiq) even when in theory they are charged with the task of individual ijtihad. This practical modification of theory created the stability and predictability necessary for functioning legal systems while still allowing for flexibility, mutual tolerance, and the possibility of adaptation over time and location.

BASIC RULES OF ISLAMIC FINANCE

Islamic scholars have classified and analyzed the rules of Islamic law relating to property, contracts, and finance over many centuries. The modern Islamic finance industry, which has arisen since the 1970s and grown into a contemporary sector of the global economy valued in the many billions of U.S. dollars, draws on these classical rules and on the legal determinations of modern Islamic scholars for its operations. The defining difference between Islamic finance and conventional finance has been articulated as: "while 'conventional' finance usually seeks profit-maximization within a given regulatory framework, Islamic finance is also guided by other, religiously-inspired goals."[16] These goals include the quest for social justice and other ethical and religious concerns about how to create a society pleasing to God.

Theorists of modern Islamic finance were concerned about developing an economic system that did not succumb to the injustices of either capitalism or socialism.[17] A principal element of this theory is the philosophy of risk sharing.[18] The system of interest rates utilized in conventional finance guarantees a return to the lender without regard to the condition of the borrower. This is considered exploitative. The alternative form of financing that avoids this injustice is profit and loss sharing (PLS). This takes into account the need of one party to access capital, which another party may be willing and able to provide. By sharing in the profits and losses of a given business venture, exploitation of a weaker party (one who needs capital) by a stronger party (one who has a surplus of capital) is minimized by spreading the risk.

The promotion of social and economic development through business activity, which has an actual, productive basis in the real economy, is an important component in the theory of Islamic finance. Zakat (charitable giving) is one of the five essential pillars of Islam, and can also be used to further the social goal of creating a just and ethical economic system. Any system of Islamic finance must also take into account the rules of Islamic law regarding permissible (halal) and forbidden (haram) activities. Islamic finance institutions will not generally finance the trade in forbidden products, such as pork, alcohol, drugs, or pornography. Some Islamic finance institutions will tolerate trade in forbidden products by a business they have financed, provided the trade is not the primary activity of the business and constitutes a de minimis percentage of the activity. Examples of these types of business include hotels or airlines, which may make alcohol available to patrons.[19] Islamic law also forbids both riba (unjustified increase) and gharar (excessive risk), the precise content of which is subject to interpretation. Modern Islamic scholars are regularly called upon to make determinations around the parameters of these legal questions for the Islamic finance industry.

PROPERTY, TRADE, AND FINANCIAL ETHICS

Reviewing text[20] is useful in constructing an outline of the basic orientation of Islamic law toward property, trade, and finance. Conceptually, property belongs to God, who has entrusted it to humans while on earth. Islamic law protects the idea of private ownership of property and the free trade in that property, but only within certain parameters. Humans are encouraged and expected to engage in economic activity, but to observe ethical principles in that activity.

Some Qur'anic examples are as follows:

> "The earth belongs to God." "He gives it as a heritage to those whom He wills of His servants." 7:128
> "When the prayer is ended, disperse through the earth and seek something of God's bounty." 62:10

"O Children of Adam. Adorn yourselves beautifully for every time and place of prayer; eat and drink; but do not waste. . . Who is there to forbid the beautiful things which God has brought forth for His servants, and the good things from among the means of sustenance?" 7:31–32

"Do not covet the bounties which God has bestowed more abundantly on some of you than on others. Men are allotted what they earn and women are allotted what they earn. Ask God for something of His bounty." 4:32

"Behold, the pious [who] in their property acknowledge a due share [right, haqq] to those who ask and to those who are deprived." 51:15–19; see 70:24–25

"Do not devour one another's property wrongfully, nor throw it before the judges [i.e., to influence them corruptly] in order to devour a portion of others' property sinfully and knowingly." 2:188

"Behold, those who unjustly devour the property of orphans but fill their bellies with fire; they will soon endure a blazing flame!" 4:10; see 4:2

"Do not devour one another's property wrongfully—unless it be by trade based on mutual consent [taradin]—and do not kill [or destroy] yourselves [or one another]. . . One who does this with rancor and wickedness—him shall We make to endure fire." 4:29–30

Some examples from the Hadith include the following:

"Asked 'What form of gain is best?' [the Prophet] said, 'A man's work with his hands, and every legitimate sale.'"

"[The Prophet gave one of his Companions] a dinar to buy for him sacrifice animals or a ewe. He bought with it two ewes, then sold one of them for a dinar. He brought with him a ewe and a dinar, and [the Prophet] invoked God's blessing for him in his trade. 'For were he to buy dirt he would make a profit in it.'"

"For the property of a man is not permissible except by a willing consent from him."

Many Qur'anic verses contain exhortations to trustworthy, charitable, and ethical behavior, including:

"Give full measure whenever you measure, and weigh with the true balance; this will be [for your own] good, and best in the end." 17:35

"Fulfill every pledge ['ahd]—for verily [on Judgment Day] the pledge will be inquired into!" 17:34

"Fulfill your covenant ['ahd] with God whenever you bind yourselves by a pledge ['ahadtum], and do not break oaths [ayman] after you have confirmed them; indeed, you have made God your surety; behold, God knows all that you do." 16:91

"God commands you to deliver your trusts [amanat] to those entitled to them." 4:58

"If [the debtor] is in difficulty, [then grant] a delay until a time of ease; if you were to remit [the debt] by way of charity it would be good for you—if you but knew." 2:280

Intention (niyyah) is an essential element of Islamic law in contracts, as well as in other legal categories. From the Qur'an:

"Man has [i.e., is held accountable for] only what he strives for." 53:39

A Hadith reads:

"Actions are only according to their intentions."

As a general summary, in Islamic law property belongs to God and humans are the caretakers of God's earth and of the wealth abundantly contained within it. Trade is favored, but only in the context of mutual consent. Islamic text contains numerous exhortations for ethical conduct and trustworthiness in trade and exhortations to fulfill pledges and covenants, and clearly forbids wrongful takings and exploitation. While debt is permissible, exploitation in lending is not. Text counseling leniency toward the debtor, however, must be read in conjunction with the command to fulfill one's covenants and pledges. Intention is an essential element of contract formation and of legally binding obligations. The promotion of fairness and ethical principles underlies all rules of contract and trade.

PROHIBITION OF RIBA

One of the most complex areas that Islamic scholars struggle with in contemporary Islamic finance revolves around the prohibition of riba. Riba is sometimes misleadingly defined as "interest," but may be more accurately described as "unjustified increase." The exact rules of which precise activities constitute riba are the source of much scholarly attention.

Textual Qur'anic references to riba include the following:

"Devour not usury [riba] doubled and re-doubled." 3:130

"Those who devour usury [riba] do not stand except as one stands whom Satan has confounded with his touch: for they say 'Buying and selling [bay'] is like usury'—the while God has made buying and selling lawful and usury unlawful. One who becomes aware of his Lord's admonition and desists, may keep his past gains, and his affair is for God [to judge]; but as for those who return to it, they are Companions of the Fire; they will abide in it! God effaces [the gains of] usury, while He makes acts of charity increase. . . Give up what remains of usury, if you are believers, for if you do it, take notice of war from God and His Apostle. But if you repent, then you shall be entitled to your principal: you will do no wrong, and neither will you be wronged." 2:275–279; see also 4:161

The rules around riba have been a complicated area of jurisprudence from the earliest times as well as for modern scholars. One type of riba that scholars consider clearly prohibited was known as "riba al-jahiliyya" (riba of the "Age of Ignorance"). This refers to the pre-Islamic Arabian practice identified in the preceding text in which a person's debt was doubled if not paid at a certain predetermined time. Scholars have also subdivided riba into two additional types: (1) riba al-fadl (riba of excess) and (2) riba al-nasi'a (riba of delay). The text of an important Hadith reads as follows:

> Gold for gold, silver for silver, wheat for wheat, barley for barley, dates for dates, salt for salt, like for like, equal for equal, hand to hand. If these types differ, then sell them as you wish, if it is hand to hand.

This Hadith specifies that trade in one of these six commodities (gold, silver, wheat, barley, dates, salt) must be "like for like, equal for equal," or in the same quality and in an equal amount. It is prohibited to trade within a single type with inequality of quality or amount, with or without a time delay. This is riba al-fadl (riba of excess). The Hadith also specifies that trade in the six commodities must be "hand to hand," or a simultaneous transaction. It is prohibited to trade with a time delay among the listed commodities.[21] This is riba al-nasi'a (riba of delay). What are the implications of this text?

The "gold for gold" Hadith is extremely thought provoking. It is hard to imagine why anyone would trade an equal amount of equal quality ("like for like, equal for equal") of any of the six listed commodities (gold, silver, wheat, barley, dates, salt) at the same time ("hand to hand"). Are only these six commodities to be treated in this fashion, or should scholars extend the ruling to other commodities by analogy? Why would the parties ever trade any of these six commodities at exactly the same time in exactly the same amount and quality instead of simply keeping what they had instead? What would be the purpose of such a transaction? What then is the purpose behind the text? What is the effective cause ('illa) that would allow transfer of the ruling to other situations?

It is of course impossible to answer these questions with certainty. Scholars have proposed various possible answers over time, and the four Sunni schools have different interpretations of the implications of this Hadith.[22] All four schools allow the extension of the ruling by analogy to specific other commodities, called "ribawi." Shafi'is hold the effective cause for the list of six (allowing the transfer of the ruling) to be commodities with the properties of currency and food. Malikis consider the effective cause to be the properties of currency and basic preservable foodstuffs. Hanafis and Hanbalis consider the effective cause to be that the goods are sold by weight or volume, and in highly precise measure. Crude oil is therefore a ribawi good (meaning the ruling extends by analogy from the six listed commodities to this good) for Hanafis and Hanbalis, but not for Malikis and Shafi'is.

Islamic law allows trade with excess and time delay among goods not ruled to be of the same genus or type, as prohibited by the "gold for gold" Hadith. Why the distinction? Some of the possible purposes for the Hadith articulated by Islamic scholars over the centuries include (1) mathematical equivalency (Ibn Rushd, d. 1198), (2) avoiding commercial exploitation (Ibn Qayyim, d. 1350), and minimizing commerce in currency and foodstuffs (Ibn Qayyim).[23] The last clause of the "gold for gold" Hadith seems to encourage trade between different types of commodities. The results of the rule seem to promote the use of currency as a financial intermediary, moving from a barter-based economy to a money-based economy. Encouraging the use of money and markets to allocate and moderate risks is one possible reason for the rule.[24] This is certainly how Islamic civilization developed over time, with standardized currency facilitating trade across a vast geographic empire.

Whatever the purpose of the "gold for gold" Hadith, the precise rules of the prohibition of riba remain complex and an area where not all scholars are in full agreement. Certain financial structures and products in the modern Islamic finance industry are considered by some scholars to be acceptable even while bordering on riba, while other scholars consider them to have crossed the line into forbidden activity. Uncertainty around the exact parameters of riba goes all the way back to the Companions of the Prophet. It is recounted that:

> [Umar said,] "The last verse revealed was the verse of riba, and [then] the Messenger of God was taken [in death]. He had not explained it to us. So leave riba and doubt [riba.]"[25]

PROHIBITION OF GHARAR

Another complex area that Islamic scholars struggle with in contemporary Islamic finance revolves around the prohibition of gharar. Gharar can be defined as "excessive risk." Since risk sharing is a key element of Islamic finance theory, it is essential to determine what level of risk is excessive or falls into the category of speculation more akin to gambling than to an appropriate risk associated with ordinary business ventures. The rules of gharar are complicated, without full agreement among scholars on what constitutes excessive risk taking and speculation.

Gharar is not specifically discussed in Qur'anic text. Qur'anic text prohibits gambling (maysir) in the following verse:

> "Intoxicants, games of chance [maysir], [worship of] idols, and [divination by] arrows are but an abomination, Satan's handiwork; avoid it then, so that you might prosper! By means of intoxicants and games of chance Satan wants only to sow enmity and hatred among you, and hinder you from the remembrance of God and from prayer. Will you not, then, desist?" 5:90–91

It is the Hadith that first introduce the term *gharar*. The following texts are examples:

> "The Messenger of God forbade the 'sale of the pebble' [hasah, sale of an object chosen or determined by the throwing of a pebble], and the sale of gharar."
> "Do not buy fish in the sea, for it is gharar."
> "The Prophet forbade sale of what is in the wombs, sale of the contents of the udders . . . and [sale of the] 'stroke of the diver' [darbat al-gha'is, sale in advance of the yield of a diver's dive, whatever it was]."
> "Whoever buys foodstuffs, let him not sell them until he has possession of them."
> "He who purchases food shall not sell it until he weighs it [yaktalahu]."
> "[T]he Prophet forbade the sale of grapes until they become black, and the sale of grain until it is strong."

These examples make it clear that gharar comes into play when uncertainty surrounds a transaction and the value of what is being sold or exchanged cannot be determined. A fish in the sea may or may not be caught, and may or may not be of consumable quality. A fish that has been netted and examined, on the other hand, can have a determinable value. Grapes (or grain) that have not ripened cannot be sold, because they may or may not come to fruition. So what would farmers do to ensure the sale of agricultural yields, when they needed capital in advance in order to grow their crops? While the gharar rules forbid the sale of specific crops (grapes or grain in this example) in advance of their yield, classical scholars did not interpret the text to prohibit the advance sale of crops in general. For example, a farmer could contract to provide a certain quantity and quality of wheat for delivery at a future date in exchange for advance payment of a determined amount of money. The prohibition was interpreted to prevent tying the determination of value to the uncertain yield of a specific field or grove, an inherently risky transaction.

Complex modern Islamic finance transactions carefully navigate the rules of gharar, with some scholars more liberal than others in interpretation. An example of a financial instrument carefully navigating the rules of gharar is the Islamic alternative to insurance. Conventional insurance is considered excessively speculative, since one will never know if the money paid in will ever be needed in the event of illness, death, or other calamity, and these types of events are destined by God. Takaful, the Islamic alternative financial product, allows for a pooling of funds for mutual self-help from which members can draw in the event of need. Careful design of this product in consultation with Islamic scholars resulted in a financial equivalent generally considered legally acceptable.

LIMITATIONS ON FREEDOM OF CONTRACT

Islamic law encourages trade and favors freedom of contract in general. Some text-based rules, however, specify certain limitations on freedom of contract in addition to the ethical exhortations already noted. Relevant Hadith include:

> "[The Prophet] forbade a sale and a stipulation [bay' wa-shart]."[26]
> "The Messenger of God forbade two bargains [safqah] in one."
> "The Messenger of God forbade two sales in one [bay'atayn fi bay'a]."
> "The Prophet forbade sale of the delayed obligation [al-kali'] for a delayed obligation."
> "Illicit are a loan and a sale [salaf wa-bay'], or two stipulations in a sale, or sale of what you do not have."

Modern scholars must grapple with tremendously complex financial transactions in contemporary Islamic finance while keeping these rules in mind. Clearly trade of one concrete specific existent asset of actual value ('ayn) (for example, "this specific house," "this specific airplane," "this specific car") for another concrete specific existent asset of actual value ('ayn) at the same time is permissible. Trade of one concrete specific existent asset of actual value ('ayn) for an abstract obligation (dayn) (for example, to pay $300,000 or to deliver 1,000 bushels of a particular quality of wheat) is also generally permissible. The obligation to pay the

$300,000 is an abstract obligation (dayn) because it is measured in value, rather than as an obligation to deliver these particular specific bills or coins. Trade in abstract obligations (dayn for dayn) is permissible only under certain very restrictive rules. Trade in dayn for dayn is prohibited when the exchange in both of the countervalues is delayed.[27] This is like the sale of the delayed obligation (al-kali') for a delayed obligation, clearly prohibited by the Hadith text cited earlier. Classical Islamic contracts also contained the concept of binding or nonbinding contracts, and promises that could be binding or nonbinding depending on the particular details. Application of these complicated rules requires modern scholars not only to understand the reasoning and holdings of the classical scholars, but also to adapt these holdings to modern financial transactions that contain both content (oil, other energy sources or products, airplane fleets, cars, factories, modern infrastructure like water or sewer systems) and structures that were unknown in the classical period.

STRUCTURES OF ISLAMIC FINANCE PRODUCTS

The Islamic finance industry offers numerous financial products and structures. It includes self-identified Islamic financial institutions, and also includes Islamic windows at many conventional financial institutions with a significant global presence. Islamic finance can also encompass nonfinancial institution–based transactions. How do these products and transactions operate without interest rates? According to Warde, "The answer is that [they] can through the development of profit-and-loss sharing mechanisms, or through alternatives such as imposing fixed service charges or acting as buying agents for clients."[28] Islamic financial institutions create these charges and structures to cover the cost of running the bank that a conventional bank covers through the interest rates it charges when lending money. More controversially, Islamic transactions can mimic the financial result of an interest rate in a variety of economic structures.

One of the most prevalent structures of Islamic financial products is a form of contract known as murabaha. Murabaha is a contract in which one party, often (but not exclusively) an Islamic bank, sells an asset to another party at cost plus a markup for profit. This can take the form of exchange of an asset for an agreed price, when both the purchase price and the asset are delivered at the same time. The basic idea of murabaha has several variations.[29] "Bay muajjal" is a credit sale in which payment of an agreed-upon price is deferred or made in installments over time, but the goods are delivered immediately. A simple example would be a transaction involving equipment financing. A business owner would notify an Islamic bank of an interest in purchasing particular equipment for the business. The bank would then acquire title to the equipment and sell it to the business owner for the bank's cost plus a markup. The business owner pays the bank the purchase price in installments over time. Another simple example is a common form of home financing. Instead of paying interest on a conventional home loan, a potential homeowner identifies the home he or she would like to purchase. An Islamic bank agrees to acquire title to the property and then sell it to the home buyer for cost plus a markup. The home buyer pays the bank the purchase price in installments over time. Scholars have ruled that the acquisition of title by the bank is essential to the legality of these transactions from an Islamic law perspective, and that the bank must take at least constructive possession of the asset sold at cost plus a markup.

Another variation on the basic idea of murabaha is "bay salam," which allows for advance payment or a forward sale. This is the sale of goods that are delivered to the purchaser at a future date in exchange for a payment of cash up front. This structure has particular value in the context of agricultural financing. Another example of cash payment in advance with future delivery is known as "istisna" or commissioned manufacture. A purchaser determines that exactly what is wanted does not yet exist, and so hires another party to manufacture that asset according to precise specifications. This can be accomplished directly between the producer and the consumer, or through an Islamic financial institution as an intermediary. Istisna can also be structured to allow the seller to defer delivery and the buyer to delay payment until that delivery, all for a preset purchase price. Many variations on the basic idea of sales for cost plus markup exist, sometimes as service or management fees.

Scholars generally consider murabaha structures permissible, but they are not the preferred form of Islamic finance. Murabaha structures technically fit into the Islamic legal rules of contract, but they often economically mimic conventional finance. The prevalence of murabaha in Islamic finance transactions has given rise to some critics accusing the Islamic finance industry of engaging in "hiyal," legally permissible ruses intended to comply in form but not in substance with the rules of Islamic law.[30] *Hiyal* was a word used in centuries past to identify schemes that were intentionally designed to avoid the rules of Islamic law while outwardly complying with them in form. Synthetic murabaha, where banks don't actually take possession of the asset in question, are particularly disfavored by scholars.

Islamic scholars, along with critics from outside the Islamic finance industry, have emphasized the need for less reliance on murabaha structures and the need for engaging in more transactions that follow a clear profit-and-loss-sharing model in order for Islamic finance to reach its potential to promote its social justice and ethical goals for economic development. The classic model of profit-and-loss sharing is the partnership. Two types of partnership structures are most common. A "musharaka" is like a joint venture agreement, or a general partnership. In this structure, both parties may come to the venture with funds (even if the amounts are not equal) and both may actively participate in the business venture. The partners agree in advance the ratio in which profits and losses will be shared and the risk distributed. The second type of partnership is called "mudaraba," and is similar to a limited partnership arrangement. In a mudaraba partnership, one party will typically provide the capital without participating in the day-to-day business activities of the venture. The second party does not usually provide capital to the partnership, but instead spends time and energy running the business. Again, the partners agree in advance on the ratio in which profits and losses will be shared and risk distributed.

Partnerships in Islamic finance can take place in the context of private individuals contracting with each other exclusive of a financial institution. They can also take place in the context of Islamic banks, which may act as either the mudaraba party contributing the capital to a business venture (like a lender, but with an equity stake) or the mudaraba party running the business (like a bank accepting the deposit of the customer, whose funds are then used to invest in other productive business ventures). In both of these structures, the Islamic bank may agree to fixed fees, service charges, and predetermined ratios for sharing risk with its customers.

Another important legal structure used in the Islamic finance industry is known as "ijara." Ijara is the sale of usufruct (manfaa), which is the right to use something that belongs to someone else. This is nearly identical to conventional leasing.[31] A party or an Islamic bank leases an asset (a home, a car, equipment, a building, agricultural land) to another party in exchange for payment of a specified rent over time. The asset and the risks of ownership (including loss or damage) remain with the lessor or the Islamic bank. Some contracts include a rent-to-own concept, where the property may be purchased at the end of the lease by the lessee. The sale price, however, may not be predetermined. Since usufruct (the right to use something) extends as a stream into the future and is not existing and tangible, it is inherently risky and unstable in value. Islamic law therefore favors the rights of the lessees, allowing them to cancel the lease if it proves to be less valuable than expected.[32]

Other products and instruments are offered by the Islamic finance industry. They include stocks, bonds, commodities, foreign currencies, derivatives, Islamic mutual funds, and variations on insurance. "Sukuk," which are comparable in economic substance to bonds, have grown tremendously important in recent years. Very large financings in certain industries and geographic locations have relied on the Sukuk structure for projects worth billions of dollars. The basic concept of Sukuk is that the investors have purchased ownership shares in a company through an up-front payment of capital. Sukuk certificates are issued to these investors. The investors own a piece of an underlying asset that is the subject of the business activity, which can be structured on a lease or sale basis. Investors then receive either rent payments or installment sale payments over time, allowing them to recoup their principal investment plus a profit. The underlying asset can be development land, as in the $700 million Qatar global Sukuk of 2003, or equipment, as in the $100 million Sukuk issued by Tabreed Financing Corporation in 2004 for certain specified central cooling plants in the United Arab Emirates. Both of these examples were lease-based Sukuk, with Tabreed using a sale-back at the end of the lease, and Qatar using a gift-back at the end of the lease to recover the property financed.[33]

SOCIAL AND ECONOMIC DEVELOPMENT

At the other end of the economic continuum, Islamic finance can be used to invest in microfinance to stimulate economic development of small businesses. In fact, it is argued that Islam encourages entrepreneurship and business development.[34] An important tool in financing economic development using conventional finance is microfinance, usually through interest-bearing micro-loans. Islamic microfinance, its Shari'a-compliant counterpart, is growing, although it is not yet widespread.[35] Microfinance options offer a way for Islamic finance to directly address the social justice and ethical goals that underlie its reason for being. Mudaraba (limited partnership) structures seem particularly well suited for this effort, although several Islamic finance products currently in use can be adapted for microfinance. With the rise of interest-based micro-lending, particularly in predominantly Muslim countries, Shari'a-compliant alternatives seem a logical development tool that can avoid some of the criticisms of conventional micro-lending, such as overly high interest rates and the burden of repayment regardless of success of the business venture. By using profit-and-loss-sharing structures, those with access to capital can help stimulate economic growth and development without overly burdening small businesses. Other development finance options also exist in the Islamic finance industry. Most common is development bank financing of infrastructure for basic services of benefit to the public.

INTERPRETATION OF ISLAMIC LAW

Who interprets Islamic law as it relates to Islamic finance? The development of Islamic legal theory allowed for plurality and mutual respect between scholars with different opinions on points of law. While this flexibility has served Islamic civilization well through time and place, this plurality creates uncertainty in the market with respect to the global practice of Islamic finance. The Islamicity of products can be called into question when not all scholars agree on the more borderline structures offered in the market. As an example, scholars in Malaysia have tended to be more liberal in their interpretations than scholars in the Arabian Gulf region.[36] The challenge this creates has led to numerous efforts to standardize and better harmonize legal rulings on Islamic finance products.

The Islamic finance industry since its modern development in the 1970s has relied heavily on Shari'a scholars for fatwas (legal opinions) on products presented. Essentially every Islamic financial institution retains at least one and usually several Shari'a scholars for consultation. These Shari'a scholars serve as advisers to Islamic financial institutions in the form of Shari'a boards. They are paid to advise on the Islamicity of new products or financial structures proposed to be presented to the market, and to audit the operations of financial institutions claiming to be Islamic. This is a vital role for the Islamic finance industry, and it is a perennial problem that not enough individual scholars are qualified to advise the growing number of Islamic financial institutions. Individual scholars often serve on multiple Shari'a boards and are stretched very thin in their ability to devote their time to the many pressing questions that arise. The training of increasing numbers of qualified scholars is an important area of development in Islamic finance.[37]

Another important area of development is increasing coordination among scholars. The recent trend is toward more unity in the approach of various scholars. This is being achieved in several ways, including conferences that gather scholars from different backgrounds and locations, and the establishment or strengthening of institutions that are aimed at standardizing and monitoring Islamic finance products. One of the most significant trends with implications for Islamic law beyond the Islamic finance industry is the development of Fiqh Academies. These conferences, research institutes, and Fiqh Academies gather scholars who together debate the merits of particular legal positions in a form of collective or "group ijtihad."[38] The consensus developed in these debates is then summarized and published as fatwas (legal opinions).[39] This development is an adaptation of the classical role of Islamic legal theory and scholarship well suited for the modern age with its revolutionary communications and transportation technologies. In the classical period, scholars were often geographically isolated from one another, guiding only the Muslims in their immediate location and those able to read precious copies of their written treatises. This was the norm, except for those vibrant urban centers of scholarship and learning that arose in various times and places. In today's world, however, scholars can much more easily come together regularly and much more easily distribute their knowledge to the global community. The trend toward group ijtihad does not carry any binding effect, in the tradition of Islamic legal theory, but it contains enormous potential to spread knowledge and bring credibility to these collective efforts and rulings. A significant percentage of the rulings issued by the Fiqh Academies have specifically addressed questions of Islamic finance.

Ultimately the Islamicity of Islamic finance products is determined by the consumer. The structure of Islamic legal theory relies on the credibility and the reputation of the individual scholar. In addition to the pluralism Islamic legal theory fosters among scholars, it is expected that individual members of the Muslim community will decide for themselves which scholar is most qualified and credible in the interpretation of Islamic law. Consumers of Islamic finance products rely on the Shari'a boards and individual scholars to issue fatwas on the Islamicity of the various products offered. These consumers have the ability to determine which scholar or scholars they consider most reliable and credible. The role of reputation also serves as a check on the Islamic scholar, whose credibility is at stake when he issues a fatwa on the permissibility of a particular product. Some statistical research, however, indicates that consumers of Islamic finance products do not actually exercise considered discretion in choosing which scholars to follow.[40] This is a significant risk. Consumers should never simply assume that any product calling itself "Islamic" actually complies with Islamic law. Some level of consumer diligence is obviously appropriate, especially in the absence of strong institutional regulatory systems to enforce truth in marketing Islamic products.

DUAL REGULATORY SYSTEMS

The fact that the Islamic finance industry operates all over the world presents numerous challenges. A major challenge for the Islamic finance industry is the absence of a single regulatory system that could monitor the Islamicity of products in the market. Much work has gone into efforts to coordinate consistent global standards for the Islamic finance industry. A leading organization in the development of available standards is the Accounting and Auditing Organization for Islamic Financial Institutions (AAOIFI). AAOFI prepares accounting, auditing, governance, ethics, and Shari'a standards for the Islamic finance industry and offers professional training and qualification programs for industry participants.[41] Other organizations work toward standardizing global conventions in the Islamic finance industry, such as the International Association of Islamic Banks, the Islamic Financial Services Board,[42] and the Dow Jones Islamic Market Index.[43] The current trend within the industry seems to be an increasing convergence of standards and voluntary practices, although diversity remains.

Each country in which Islamic finance operates has its own, usually secular, regulatory and legal systems with which the Islamic finance industry must comply.[44] These regulators are concerned only with the regulation of Islamic finance from a legal and economic perspective, not from the perspective of Islamic law.[45] The

development and strengthening of international standards for economic regulation, like Basel III, could be helpful to the Islamic finance industry. Basel III was
developed in response to the global financial crisis of 2008. It proposes bank capital adequacy, liquidity, and leverage requirements.[46] Participants in the Islamic
finance industry should be engaged in these deliberations to ensure that the proposals are workable from an Islamic finance perspective. The more internationally
standardized the economic rules, monitoring, and reporting requirements are, the
easier it will be for Islamic finance to function in the global economy in a more predictable and stable context. Similarly, the content and capacities of legal regulatory
systems within which Islamic finance must operate currently vary tremendously
depending on location and jurisdiction.

In recent years, the United States government has tried to create a friendlier
regulatory environment for Islamic finance.[47] While this has caused some political
backlash, the United States Department of the Treasury sponsored "Islamic Finance
101" trainings to educate various government officials about the Islamic finance
industry.[48] Before the implosion of the home mortgage market in the United States,
the U.S. government was actively cooperating with the Islamic finance industry to
try to reconcile U.S. regulations with Islamic finance practice so as not to disadvantage consumers of Shari'a-compliant mortgage financing. For example, banks
in the United States are generally restricted from owning real property. As discussed earlier, the Islamic finance products typically utilized to finance home purchases require the Islamic bank to acquire title to the asset being financed, in this
case the home, which is then sold or leased to the home buyer. The Office of the
Comptroller of the Currency (OCC) issued two directives that looked to the "economic substance" of ijara (lease-based) and murabaha (cost plus markup) transactions used in Islamic home mortgage finance and approved these products as permissible in the U.S. regulatory environment.[49] Another illustration of the challenge
of the dual regulatory system in Islamic home financing is the question of whether
consumers may treat the markup as interest payments for purposes of United States
tax law while not considering the markup as interest for purposes of Islamic law.[50]

Several additional challenges are presented under U.S. law for Islamic finance
transactions triggered by the need to comply with both secular regulation and the
requirements of Islamic law.[51] The Islamic law requirement of property ownership
in a financing transaction causes several burdens not faced by conventional banks.
For example, the various systems of state and local property transfer taxes can add
transaction costs. Entering the chain of title to property triggers potential environmental liability as well as risk of tort liability for injuries for an Islamic financial
institution. When financing equipment purchases, stepping into the chain of title
interrupts the flow of express and implied warranties from the supplier directly to
the ultimate consumer, and disclaimers of warranty by the Islamic financial institution may be unenforceable if not drafted correctly. In an Islamic financing transaction, prepayment of the obligation wouldn't reduce the amount owed, unlike
an interest-bearing loan, which can then bump up against consumer finance protection rules. Federal Deposit Insurance Corporation (FDIC) rules, which remove
the risk of loss from a depositor in a conventional bank, can be problematic from
the perspective of the Islamic law profit-and-loss-sharing requirement. These U.S.
examples illustrate some of the challenges of the dual regulatory system for Islamic
finance. Solutions have been possible when secular regulators show flexibility.

CHALLENGES IN CLOSING TRANSACTIONS

Among the many challenges faced by the Islamic finance industry, the specific challenges that are presented in closing business transactions must be mentioned. Closing financial transactions is a complex process whether the parties use conventional or Islamic financing. Documents outlining the transaction are drafted and negotiated, with their content determined according to the level of complexity of the underlying transaction. Due diligence documentation is received and meticulously reviewed by any party investing financing. Sophisticated financial transactions require opinion letters from lawyers, who opine on the enforceability of the underlying transaction and the corporate legal capacity of the represented party to enter into the transaction. Local and national filings are often required. Depending on the type of transaction, rating agencies may be utilized to rate the creditworthiness of the transaction. Each of these conventional procedures must be adapted to take Islamic law into account for Islamic finance transactions. For example, the nature and activities of the business financed must be reviewed. Ownership and liquidation preferences may have to be adjusted to ensure proper risk sharing from an Islamic perspective.[52] Bankruptcy and insolvency concerns must be considered.[53] Treatment of casualty and risk of loss have to be considered. Tax treatment of corporate ownership and property may be impacted. Choice of governing law provisions in transaction documents has proven important with respect to enforceability of contracts.

ENFORCEABILITY OF CONTRACTS

Perhaps the most pressing developing area of legal concern for Islamic finance transactions is the question of enforceability of contracts. Enforcement mechanisms, jurisdiction of courts, and choice of law issues riddle current Islamic finance transactions. For example, a dispute between two parties to an Islamic financing transaction ended up in a British court in the case of *Shamil Bank of Bahrain EC v. Beximco Pharmaceuticals Ltd.*[54] This case involved a dispute over murabaha and ijara financings that were restructured when Beximco did not pay its obligations when due. The transaction documents contained the clause "Subject to the Glorious Shari'a, this Agreement shall be governed by and construed in accordance with the laws of England." Beximco argued that the underlying murabaha and ijara structures were not really in accordance with the Shari'a. The British court awarded a $49.7 million judgment in favor of Shamil Bank, and held that it could not rule on the Islamicity of Islamic financial products. While this seems to be the right result, it leaves open the question of enforceability of contracts. Lawyers are now very careful to draft extremely specific clauses in contracts for Islamic financial transactions, so that secular courts rule only on enforcing contractual agreements between the parties, rather than on general compliance with Islamic law. This forces the determination of the applicable provisions of Islamic law to be clearly articulated in advance of any disputes.

Even in cases where the transaction's compliance with Islamic law is not at issue, enforcement of contracts can be an issue in Islamic finance. In 2009, Dubai World, a large property developer in Dubai, delayed repaying its debts, some of which were structured as Islamic finance transactions. The debt has been estimated at approximately $59 billion. Dubai World had to restructure approximately $26 billion, shaking global financial markets. Dubai World's property company, Nakheel, had an outstanding Sukuk (Islamic bond transaction) worth $3.5 billion that it was unable to repay. Three weeks after the announcement of the inability to repay the Nakheel Sukuk, Abu Dhabi bailed out the company with an estimated $10 billion.[55] Lawyers immediately went to work restructuring the debt. The enormous relief over the aversion of the crisis left open the question of how to enforce contracts in these circumstances. The Ruler of Dubai established the Dubai World Tribunal, a special court set up "to handle various matters pertaining to the settlement of the financial position of Dubai World and its subsidiaries."[56] An estimated $110 billion in debt is now held in Dubai, some percentage of which is conventional and some percentage of which is structured as Islamic finance. The Jebel Ali Free Zone FZE (Jafza) holds a $2 billion Sukuk scheduled to mature in November 2012. The Dubai International Financial Centre (DIFC Investments LLC) has a $1.25 billion Sukuk scheduled to mature in June 2012. It remains to be seen if refinancing or further restructuring will be necessary.[57] In the meantime, authorities in the United Arab Emirates are working on revised bankruptcy legislation.[58]

CONCLUSION

The legal framework for contemporary Islamic finance is complex and dual in nature. Classical Islamic legal theory and jurisprudence are essential to the operation of Islamic finance. Shari'a scholars interpret Islamic law in the modern context to determine the limits and parameters of Islamic financial practices and industry products. Contemporary Islamic finance is practiced all over the world, also subject to the secular legal systems that govern the places of the industry's operations. Islamic finance as an industry therefore must comply with both Islamic law and the secular legal systems that govern operations, presenting numerous challenges. While substantial effort has been invested in standardizing and harmonizing the diversity of Islamic law rulings for Islamic finance, progress needs to be made in standardizing the economic and legal rules of the global economy. International economic and legal institutions remain weak and underfunded, and rules are inconsistently applied across jurisdictions. Development of stronger standardized rules of international economic law could provide a more stable system within which both conventional and Islamic finance could flourish. In the increasingly interconnected international economy, movement toward more predictable and uniform rules and enforcement procedures across jurisdictions would benefit not only the Islamic finance industry, but also the global economy as a whole.

NOTES

1. Wael B. Hallaq, *The Origins and Evolution of Islamic Law* (Cambridge University Press, 2005).
2. See Bernard G. Lewis, *The Spirit of Islamic Law* (University of Georgia Press, 1998); Wael B. Hallaq, *Islamic Legal Theories: An Introduction to Sunni Usul Al-Fiqh* (Cambridge University Press, 1997); Knut S. Vikor, *Between God and the Sultan: A History of Islamic Law* (Oxford University Press, 2005).
3. See Vikor, page 33; Hallaq, *Islamic Legal Theories*, page 3.

4. Hugh Kennedy, *The Prophet and the Age of the Caliphates: The Islamic Near East from the Sixth to the Eleventh Century* (Pearson Education Limited, 2004); see also *The Cambridge Companion to the Qur'an*, edited by Jane Dammen McAuliffe (Cambridge University Press, 2006), for discussions of the compilation of the Uthmanic codex.

5. Some examples of the relevance and implications of grammar include analysis of the command form, exhortation versus permission, questions of gender, the plural versus the singular, and the use of the definitive article as it implies a general or a particular command. See Vikor, page 285.

6. See Lewis. The "eye" of a storm obviously has a different meaning than the "eye" on my face. The words "I went to the bank today," would have a completely different meaning when stated by an urban dweller in a monetary economy than if stated by a rural individual residing near the bank of a river.

7. See Jane Dammen McAuliffe, "The Tasks and Traditions of Interpretation" in *The Cambridge Companion to the Qur'an*, edited by Jane Dammen McAuliffe (Cambridge University Press, 2006). See also Hallaq, *Islamic Legal Theories*, pages 68–74, for a discussion of the nuances of the theory of abrogation (naskh). Scholars debated God's motives for abrogation, whether Qur'anic text could abrogate Hadith, whether Hadith could abrogate later Hadith, whether Hadith could abrogate Qur'anic text, the necessity of consensus in determining abrogation, and whether only certain epistemological types of text could abrogate other text.

8. Vikor, page 42. See also Lewis.

9. Shi'i scholars, for example, would not consider the transmission of Hadith witnessed by the Prophet's wife Aisha as trustworthy because of her rebellion after the Prophet's death against the first Shi'i Imam (and fourth Sunni Caliph) 'Ali ibn 'Abi Talib. Sayings and actions of the 12 Shi'i Imams have legal import in Twelver Shi'i legal theory, which they do not have in Sunni theory. See Moojan Momen, *An Introduction to Shi'i Islam: The History and Doctrines of Twelver Shi'ism* (Oxford: George Ronald, 1985) for a summary of Twelver Shi'i jurisprudential theory.

10. See Vikor, pages 74–86. See also Hallaq, *Islamic Legal Theories*, pages 75–81.

11. See Hallaq, *Islamic Legal Theories*, page 23.

12. See Hallaq, *Islamic Legal Theories*, for a fuller discussion of ijtihad, including these examples of these two forms of classical reasoning by analogy.

13. See Ahmad Al-Raysuni, *Imam Al-Shatibi's Theory of the Higher Objectives and Intents of Islamic Law* (International Institute of Islamic Thought, 2005).

14. See Vikor, pages 5–8.

15. See Frank Vogel, *Islamic Law and Legal System: Studies of Saudi Arabia* (Leiden: Brill, 2000), pages 23–32.

16. See Ibrahim Warde, *Islamic Finance in the Global Economy* (Edinburgh University Press, 2009), page 5.

17. See Chibli Mallat, *The Renewal of Islamic Law: Muhammad Baqer as-Sadr, Najaf and the Shi'i International* (Cambridge University Press, 1993); Charles Tripp, *Islam and the Moral Economy* (Cambridge University Press, 2006).

18. The classical Islamic legal maxim "al-kharaj bi al-daman" expresses the link between profit and risk in Islamic law. It means that yield must be associated with the possibility of loss.

19. Some Islamic finance institutions will tolerate up to 33 percent of business activity in a forbidden trade.

20. See Frank E. Vogel and Samuel L. Hayes, III, *Islamic Law and Finance: Religion, Risk and Return* (Leiden: Brill, 1998) for all Qur'anic and Hadith text included in this section. Translations are by Frank Vogel.

21. Additional Hadith text clarifies that time delay in sales (purchasing on credit) is permitted when currency is only one of the two considerations. See Vogel and Hayes, page 74. The time value of money may also be accounted for in price.

22. See Vogel and Hayes, pages 74–87, for discussion of the various interpretations of this Hadith.
23. See Vogel and Hayes, pages 78–83.
24. See Vogel and Hayes, page 85. See also Vogel and Hayes, page 74, which cites a Hadith specifically encouraging the use of money as a medium in a transaction involving dates of differing quality.
25. See Vogel and Hayes, page 63.
26. Ibn Hanbali rejects this Hadith, while other scholars accept it. See Vogel and Hayes, page 68.
27. See Vogel and Hayes, pages 114–125.
28. See Warde, page 6.
29. See Warde, pages 133–134.
30. See Mahmoud A. El-Gamal, *Islamic Finance: Law, Economics and Practice* (Cambridge University Press, 2006).
31. See Warde, page 135.
32. See Warde, page 135.
33. See El-Gamal, pages 4–7 and 107–108. One of El-Gamal's criticisms of some Sukuk are the methods used to determine the value of the payments to the Sukuk holders, which are sometimes benchmarked against the London Interbank Offered Rate (LIBOR), a conventional interest rate marker. Sukuk are discussed in detail later in this volume.
34. See Chapter 14, this volume.
35. See, for example, the Islamic Microfinance Challenge to promote the development of Islamic microfinance, www.cgap.org; the opening of an Islamic microfinance product at Bahrain's Family Bank, www.familybankbh.com; and the Islamic Microfinance Summit, www.islamicmicrofinance-summit.com.
36. This gap seems to be increasingly narrowing. See Warde.
37. See the discussion of Shari'a scholars contained later in this volume.
38. See Warde, pages 40–41.
39. See for example, the *Fiqh Academy Journal* of the Islamic Fiqh Academy in Jeddah under the auspices of the Organization of the Islamic Conference. See Vogel and Hayes, page 48. See also the website for the International Shari'a Research Academy for Islamic Finance (ISRA) in Malaysia, www.isra.my/.
40. See Warde.
41. See www.aaoifi.com/aaoifi.
42. See www.ifsb.org.
43. See http://djiindexes.com/islamicmarket.
44. A full discussion of the history and methodology of Islamic law courts, and the predominant use of secular court systems generally in modern Islamic finance transactions, is beyond the scope of this chapter.
45. See generally *Islamic Finance: The Regulatory Challenge*, edited by Simon Archer and Rifaat Ahmed Abdel Karim (John Wiley & Sons, 2007).
46. See www.bis.org/bcbs/basel3htm.
47. Interviews with various U.S. government officials confirm the willingness of such officials to try to accommodate the Islamic finance industry. See "Islamic Finance in the US: What Are the Challenges to Overcome in Order for the Industry to Subsist Viably under Secular Regulation?" by Fatimah S. Baeshen, unpublished MA thesis, Center for Middle Eastern Studies, University of Chicago (2009).
48. See United States Department of the Treasury website, www.treasury.gov/press-center/press-releases/Pages/po3068.aspx. See also the appointment in 2004 of Dr. Mahmoud El-Gamal as the Islamic Finance Scholar-in-Residence for the United States Department of the Treasury, www.treasury.gov/press-center/press-releases/Pages/js1706.aspx. The United States Department of the Treasury has worked with

Harvard University's Islamic Finance Project in educating U.S. government officials about the Islamic finance industry.

49. See the Office of the Comptroller of the Currency Interpretive Letter No. 806, www.occ.gov/interp/dec97/intdec97.htm, and Interpretive Letter No. 867, www.occ. gov/interp/nov99/intnov99.htm.

50. See "Is Sharif's Castle Deductible? Islam and the Tax Treatment of Mortgage Debt," by Roberta Mann in *William & Mary Bill of Rights Journal* 17 (2009): 1139, http://scholarship.law.wm.edu/wmborj/vol17/iss4/5.

51. See "Legal Issues Arising in Islamic Finance Transactions in the United States," by Isam Salah (2009), available at www.kslaw.com.

52. See "No Pain, No Gain: The State of the Industry in Light of an American Islamic Private Equity Transaction," by Umar F. Moghul in *Chicago Journal of International Law* 7:2 (Winter 2007).

53. See "An Introduction to Shari'a Considerations in Bankruptcy and Insolvency Contexts and Islamic Finance's First Bankruptcy (East Cameron)," by Michael J. T. McMillen (2011), http://ssrn.com/abstract=1826246, for discussion of the bankruptcy proceedings in connection with the East Cameron oil and gas Sukuk in the United States. In 2006, East Cameron Gas Company issued a $175 million Sukuk due in 2016 with quarterly redemptions. In 2008, East Cameron Partners, LP, filed a voluntary petition for Chapter 11 bankruptcy in a Louisiana court.

54. *Shamil Bank of Bahrain EC v. Beximco Pharmaceuticals Ltd.*, 1 WLR 1784 (CA 2004) (UK). See "Contractual Enforceability Issues: Sukuk and Capital Markets Development," by Michael J. T. McMillen in *Chicago Journal of International Law* 7:2 (Winter 2007) for discussion of the implications of the Shamil Bank case.

55. "Dubai's Debt Crisis: One Year On" by Katy Watson, November 25, 2010, BBC website at www.bbc.co.uk/news/business-11837714. Other estimates of the amount of the bailout are as high as $20 billion.

56. Decree No. 57 of 2009 established the Dubai World Tribunal, as amended by Decree No. 11 of 2010. See www.dubaiworldtribunal.org. The tribunal is modeled on the court system of the Dubai International Financial Centre and British law.

57. "Cautious Optimism over Dubai's Debt," by Simeon Kerr, *Financial Times*, February 8, 2012, www.ft.com/cms/s/0/82f8496c-5262–11e1-a155–00144feabdc0.html#axzz1nVUV1CBM.

58. "Mideast Money—Legal Limbo Stymies Banks' Recovery of Dubai Govt Debt," by David French, *Reuters*, February 22, 2012, www.reuters.com/article/2012/02/22/emirates-insolvency-idUSL5E8DK63020120222.

CHAPTER 4

Globalization and Islamic Finance

Flows and Consciousness

KAREN HUNT-AHMED

President, Chicago Islamic Microfinance Project and Lecturer, DePaul University

Islamic finance was made possible by the conditions of globalization. Globalization is an expansive topic and one that has different meanings in different contexts. It has been explored occasionally on a macro level in the context of Islamic finance (*cf.* Warde 2010 and Askari, Iqbal, and Mirakhor 2010) but rarely in the context of the individuals who work in the industry (see, for example, Hunt-Ahmed 2012, forthcoming). This chapter discusses the concepts of global flows and global consciousness to provide an overview of what the term *globalization* means vis-à-vis the industry of Islamic finance. It then discusses ways in which practitioners who interact with global conditions render Islamic finance a place that is at once created by individuals in search of a mediating environment and a tool through which its practitioners can negotiate relationships in a globalized world.

I use the term *globalization* as a heuristic model for thinking about industry and how the people I have interviewed experience their world through contact with Islamic finance. Both the industry's rhetoric and its participants place themselves at the crossroads between capitalist business practices and a transnational Muslim identity. I have found two sets of ideas to be particularly helpful in thinking about what aspects of globalization are most relevant to my project. Each set of literature contributes an idea about the world that was reinforced by the observations I made during fieldwork experience in Dubai, United Arab Emirates, and responses to interview questions by Islamic finance professionals. I designate these two categories of globalization literature *global flows* and *global consciousness*. This chapter examines some of the existential problems presented to the human experience by globalization and suggests how looking at the industry of Islamic banking and finance can help us understand some solutions to those problems.

GLOBALIZATION THEORIES

Globalization theories grew to prominence in the 1990s (see especially Appadurai 1996, 2000; Sassen 1998; Jameson and Miyoshi 1998; Hannerz 1996; Scholte 2000) and are still flourishing, both in social science theories and in the public's imagination. In the public imagination and on the nightly news, the term *globalization* is particularly linked to the effects of population growth and capital migration across borders in search of cheap labor. Events such as the World Trade Organization (WTO) annual meetings and the protests associated with them feed the anxiety that there will not be enough food to feed the world or enough jobs left, especially in the United States and other developed countries, as a result of the destructive force of globalization. Health, the environment, human rights (especially women's rights), and the outsourcing of jobs from wealthy to developing countries all fall under this category. As we may surmise from a vivid imagery of machines and factory workers, this form of globalization theory is mostly concerned with industrial production and particularly how workers are treated during the production process. This industrial approach is often more amenable to media images and easily translatable to the general public because it speaks directly to employment matters and draws upon Marxist imagery and terminology familiar to critics of capitalism.

Social science theories of globalization are also concerned with movements and images. Such theories of globalization can have several different meanings, depending on the context of specific subject matter. Jan Aart Scholte connects globalization with five broad definitions (Scholte 2000): internationalization, liberalization, universalization, modernization, and deterritorialization. Reading about these categories is helpful in organizing thoughts about globalization theories, but they do not exactly capture what I discovered from talking to Islamic finance practitioners in Dubai. Although I draw upon Scholte's categories, I will introduce my own categories of globalization theories in order to highlight those I consider most important to my own understanding of Islamic finance and its practitioners' experiences.

GLOBAL FLOWS

One basic idea related to the evolution of global culture is particularly important to the understanding of globalization. This idea is one I call *global flow* theories of globalization. Due to technological advances of the twenty-first century, people, things, and ideas move around the world more quickly and easily than they have at any time throughout history. Technologies such as the Internet, cell phone access (even in remote parts of the world), and the relative ease and safety of global travel make the world we live in today something unique and immensely unlike times past. Some people argue that there is nothing unique about the concept of globalization that appeared in the 1990s. For example, Anderson (1991) argues that the invention of the printing press altered the public imagination in a way that set up globalization; Thomas Friedman (2005) argues that the arrival of Columbus in the New World launched the age of globalization. Globalization is a process that has roots in these sorts of technological and migratory advances; however, my argument is that the specific time and space compressions due to the rapidity with which people, things, and ideas can move is something different and unique to the present period in history, which began in the middle of the twentieth century and rapidly picked up momentum.

Anthropologist Arjun Appadurai (1996) provides one of the earliest and most organized ways of looking at globalization in its sense of global flows. He begins his inquiry by asking: Why is globalization something new and different from historical interactive world systems? His answer is that technology and innovation led to colonialism, whose systems and subsequent collapse paved the way for individuals to begin to look at themselves in ways they had never before envisioned their lives, in great part because of media images made possible by technology and innovation. He contends that the old model of nation-states is not adequate for analyzing the present-day global situation because the global economy is so complex now that we need a new way of looking at the relationships among economy, culture, and politics. Things—objects, persons, images, and discourses—are in constant motion, which he illustrates using an imagery of flows. He suggests a framework that we can use to organize our thoughts about this idea of movement. He divides areas of life into five categories that are particularly affected by the new forms of technology and innovation typical of globalization, and calls these categories "-scapes" (Appadurai 1996, p. 33). Each category refers to a specific category of flows:

- *Ethnoscape:* movement of people (migration).
- *Mediascape:* movement of media images.
- *Financescape:* movement of capital across borders.
- *Technoscapes:* movement of technology, but technology makes all flows possible.
- *Ideoscape:* movement of ideas and knowledge.

This metaphor of "flows" resonates with people, myself included, who live significant portions of their lives straddling two or more cultures. I think of flows as a body of water whose current flows in many directions: the current is connected but is rarely evident to those who are unfamiliar with the context. The idea of scapes may be used as a guide to visualizing how people, ideas, and things move around the world. Two of these categories are particularly important to the present study and will be discussed in the following pages.

Financescapes: Capital Flows

Because this project is part of a more comprehensive ethnography of financial institutions, it is pertinent to point out some of the more important ways in which capital flows have been liberalized in the late twentieth century. Two important pieces of legislation have been important both to international financial systems in general and to Islamic finance in particular. The first is the Bretton Woods Act, an international agreement made at the end of World War II. The Act set forth guidelines for how to manage international commercial and financial relations and also provided for the creation of the World Bank and the International Monetary Fund. The result of this Act was that financial dealings became more interdependent worldwide while being controlled through fixed currency exchange rates. The system's collapse in the early 1970s opened up space for variable exchange rates that reduced barriers to commerce and capital movement. One result of this liberalization movement was the tremendous amount of cash that flowed into the Arabian Gulf's oil states, which in turn were the driving force behind the creation of Islamic finance. A more recent piece of legislation that has had a significant impact on Islamic finance was the repeal of the Glass-Steagall Act (Maurer 2006). This Act had separated investment banking from consumer banking activities in the United States. Under pressure from the world financial system's more liberal regulations, the Act was repealed in 1999, providing an opportunity for Islamic financial services to expand in the United States, which has become an important source of innovation in the industry.

Ethnoscapes: Deterritorialization

Viewing the world through metaphors of movement and flow opens up a space for us to think about how individuals and communities of people envision their relationships to one another. As citizens of the world become more interdependent, networks take on a supranational quality, which Scholte and others (*cf.* Gupta and Ferguson 1997) call *deterritorialization*. It is easier for people to travel and to communicate with family and friends around the globe than ever before, so it is not necessary or even desirable to identify so closely with other people from a particular geographic area. Aihwa Ong takes this situation a step further when she questions the relationship between the nation-state and globalization in her book *Flexible Citizenship: The Cultural Logics of Transnationality* (1999). In her study, she uses an imagery of flows to show how individual Asian investors blend strategies of migration and capital accumulation as they form ambivalent relationships with the nation-state in a globalized world. Hence, state affiliation—in this case to China—takes a secondary position to individual agency in a tension between national and personal identities, and citizenship or cultural affiliation has little to do with the passport one carries. I found that in my study as well, both individual agency and identification with a Muslim *umma* were more important to respondents than state affiliations. Olivier Roy (2004) also found this to be true in his study, *Globalized Islam*. This is an important concept, and one that I think is crucial to understand when thinking about Islamic finance.

Group identity is formed by an individual's relationship to a cultural community. Historically, geographic territory defined cultural groups, but that is no longer the criterion on which many people build their communities (Gupta and Ferguson 1997; Ong 1999). Instead, people more often turn to the media and technology to define their communities in the world. For example, Benedict Anderson (1991) described the relationship of the Indonesian diaspora in Holland with their compatriots back home in Indonesia. The involvement of diasporic Indonesians with politics in their homeland is made possible in large part by media technologies. Anderson formulated a model of "imagined communities," wherein the community a migrant remembers is no longer the community that exists, as a result of both the community and the migrant's changes over time and space.

Like Gupta and Ferguson, Appadurai asserts that as a result of migration and media images, people no longer live in stable, geographically bounded communities throughout the world. Instead, he believes that "an important fact of the world we live in today is that many persons on the globe live in . . . imagined worlds" (Appadurai 1996, 33). In the same way that Anderson's communities "imagined" their relationship to others in a close community, Appadurai's global subjects build a cultural world based on how they perceive like-minded people to be living. The crucial difference between Anderson and Appadurai is that Anderson's Indonesian diaspora envisioned its imaginary community through the lens of nation-state politics, whereas Appadurai's conception of imagined communities leaves open the possibility for communities to be based on mutual ideological membership without specific reference to geographic territory. Of course, every person lives his or her life embodied in some kind of territorial relationship. However, media and technology make it possible and easy for a person to live in one place and imagine himself or herself to be associated with people all over the world, without the constraints of space and time.

GLOBAL CONSCIOUSNESS

A particular kind of spatial orientation is a result of flows of globalization, but also has a direct bearing on another category of thought about globalization related to *global consciousness*. This category of globalization refers less to systems and movement and more to the mental state accompanying these structural features. Sociologist and globalization theorist Roland Robertson (1992) defines globalization in terms of a global consciousness as follows:

> Globalization as a concept refers both to the compression of the world and the intensification of consciousness of the world as a whole. The processes and actions to which the concept of globalization now refers have been proceeding, with some interruptions, for many centuries, but the main focus of the discussion of globalization is on relatively recent times. (p. 8)

Robertson believes the historical aspects of societal relations are important to our understanding of (1) the ways in which the world has always been interconnected and (2) the newness of the concept of globalization. Robertson believes that the historical roots of globalization have been ignored in favor of peripheral concerns, such as the ways in which economic matters have been privileged in an analysis of relations between societies. Whereas economic matters are tremendously important, Robertson considers them to be subject to cultural coding and therefore declares that we must pay attention to the cultural aspects of societies as well as to their material structures (Robertson 1992). Islamic finance professionals are embedded in both the economic and cultural/religious implications of globalization; therefore, it is helpful for us to look at both material flows *and* consciousness and, more importantly, how they interact.

Although Robertson concedes that the definition of globalization can be a contested field, he recognizes that certain relationships are to be privileged in a globalized world. In particular, he sees the individual as having various relationships with different aspects of the world: society, the state, the international system of states, and humankind in general. These relationships must be mediated, and that causes the main problem of the age of globalization. Individuals who must negotiate the set of circumstances related to globalization develop a consciousness that sees the world in terms of a myriad of relationships, many of them based on shared cultural or religious symbols instead of on a relationship with a state or an ethnic group. In other words, we must think of the world as a "global *whole*" (1992, p. 5; emphasis added). This focus on consciousness is well suited to the current project because I contend that Islamic finance exists in order to help mediate these types of relationships. Therefore, I believe that globalization gives rise to a certain kind of global consciousness that we can find in places like the industry of Islamic finance.

How individuals think about their relationship to a culture of globalization affects the way they think about their relationship to society and culture. Because of the movements involved in globalization, individuals regularly come into contact with, and live in geographical proximity to, people who may adhere to vastly different worldviews from their own. It becomes necessary to negotiate relations among people vis-à-vis the differences (Shweder, Minow, and Markus 2002).

Traditionally, there have been only two ways to think about culture and globalization: culture either becomes universal or irreparably splits apart. The former view suggests that the effects of worldwide interdependence will eradicate differences between cultures and make a stale, universal culture. Popular books entitled *The End of History and the Last Man* (Fukuyama 1992), *The World Is Flat* (Friedman 2005), and *The Corporation: The Pathological Pursuit of Profit and Power* (Bakan 2004) feed the imagination with images of globalization as a faceless machine that takes the form of corporations and is poised to flatten the world and remold it into its own form. The opposing image of a world being torn apart is contained in books like *Jihad vs. McWorld* (Barber 1995) and Huntington's *Clash of Civilizations* (1998). Either view—a flattened world or a world ripped apart—follows closely the vision Marx had of capitalism wreaking destruction upon humanity. Each critique makes a valid point, but I have found in my research that people who experience the effects of globalization in their daily lives do not usually see its relationship to culture as being so extreme. Indeed, most people find a way to incorporate the many elements of culture they encounter into a notion of culture that is more reflective of their own lives and identities.

For example, people have found ways to mediate cultural differences and pressures to conform under conditions of globalization. Ulf Hannerz uses the term *cosmopolitan* to describe a person with this "state of mind" or "mode of managing meaning" (Hannerz 1990). Cosmopolitanism describes one way to mediate diverse cultural experiences and incorporate them into one's own personal perspective (Hannerz 1990, 1996). In a more recent book, Kwame Anthony Appiah frames his view of cosmopolitanism specifically in terms of moral focus (2006). Islamic finance provides a particularly good example of how this framing of consciousness works: the identities of Islamic finance professionals are inseparable from their participation in that industry. Business practices within the industry reflect its practitioners' cosmopolitan perspectives even as their embodied experiences remain chiefly local. For the purposes of this chapter, I assume that under conditions of globalization, the "global" is the culture to which I am arguing that the cosmopolitan self anchors, particularly because there is already a discourse available in Islam for a transnational, deterritorialized community.

PROBLEMS CAUSED BY GLOBALIZATION

A key problematic of globalization is that an individual must develop a consciousness that sees itself as part of a myriad of relationships. For the purposes of this project, I have chosen to look at three types of relationships and the symbol systems, discourses, and practices that Islamic finance practitioners use to mediate those relationships. I draw upon Shweder's (1997) concept of the Big Three moral discourses, which are ways of describing the human experience, to look at the ways in which individuals conceptualize their relationships to self or identity (Autonomy or Self), members of a reference society (Community), and divine religious beliefs (Divinity). I argue that the industry of Islamic banking and finance solves certain problems of mediation in these three categories. For the remainder of this chapter, I outline the tensions faced by individuals in mediating three kinds of relationships in a globalized world and explain how Islamic finance as an industry alleviates those tensions.

Problem 1: Self and Identity

The first of these existential problems addressed by Islamic finance is the question of identity, or "Who am I?" in relation to the environment around me. Philosopher Charles Taylor (1989) explores the development of the modern self in terms of morality and associated lifestyle choices. According to Taylor, moral values are fundamental elements of worldview. He thinks about the modern self as a moral agent that locates itself in terms of "the good," which is a notion about morality and the proper way to live one's life. The world into which the self is born provides a metanarrative about "the good," and we locate our selves within this narrative. This relationship or dialogue between the preexisting metanarrative and the individual self is *constitutive*; that is, they "make each other up" (Shweder 1991). Taylor considers lifestyle—or the choices about how we live life every day—to be central to the construction of modern identity. Economic activity is one of the most important areas of human activity: therefore, making moral choices in a business setting contributes significantly to a person's self-representation.

Anthony Giddens, like Taylor, considers lifestyle choices to be very important in the construction of the modern self-identity. Under conditions of modernity, construction of self-identity is an ongoing process, which sociologist Giddens calls the "reflexive project of the self" (1991, 5). This reflexive project involves continuously revising personal biographical narratives as new lifestyle choices become known. Exposure to alternative lifestyles often poses moral or existential dilemmas for the modern self. In the past, close-knit communities may have provided guidance in solving these dilemmas, for example, through initiation rituals or familial involvement in marriage choices; however, the erosion of the modern community has left the individual alone to contemplate moral issues without the support of community traditions. Because there are so many different lifestyles from which to choose, the individual often turns to expert knowledge to filter information about daily life. The institution becomes like a community, in that it acts as a central organizing mechanism for lifestyle choices. I argue that Islamic bankers have made career choices in response to their understandings of morality. Career choice, by virtue of the community function of the institution, becomes a way in which the Islamic banker can address questions of self, community, and religious belief vis-à-vis a cultural and religious metanarrative.

Islamic Finance and Identity

According to Monger and Rawashdeh (2008), there are more than 300 Islamic financial institutions (IFIs) serving 1.2 billion Muslims or one-fifth of the global population. The growing industry is the manifestation of attempts to apply Islamic law (*Shari'a*) and Islamic economic theory to financial dealings. *Shari'a* law governs financial and other business transactions (Walsh 2008). Islamic law does not allow for individuals or institutions who lend or borrow money to charge or pay interest on that money, or to participate in gambling or unnecessary risk taking without the corresponding sharing of responsibility for potential losses, among other prohibitions, including those against illegal consumer goods: pork, alcohol, weapons, or illicit drugs. The size and the importance of IFIs (Smolarski, Schapek, and Tahir 2006), as well as the size and importance of Islamic capital market products and services (Sadeghi 2008) are growing. Islamic financial institutions include Islamic banks and Islamic windows at conventional banks, as well as companies providing other financial services such as venture capital, private equity, mutual funds, real estate financing, and *Shari'a*-compliant insurance (*Takaful*) companies.

Islamic banks as institutions came into existence in the world market in the early 1970s. In the mid-twentieth century, a few individual Islamic banks were started in Egypt and Turkey, but they either failed on financial terms or were folded into the national banking system and converted to conventional banks (Ayub 2008; Kettell 2008; Warde 2010; Kuran 2001, 2004). Contemporary Islamic banks were formed in the 1970s when considerable oil wealth became available in the Arabian Gulf states (Ali 2002). Muslim populations in other parts of the world—notably Indonesia, Pakistan, and Malaysia—have since generated sufficient steady income growth to develop a network of Islamic financial institutions that strive to integrate themselves into the global financial system. Growing Muslim populations in the United States and Great Britain have very recently begun to contribute to the Islamic financial network both institutionally and intellectually.

Problem 2: Self and Community

The second existential problem for Islamic financiers is the question of community: how does a person transcend definitions of community based on geographical references to form a community based on the universal facets of a transnational Muslim belief system? Because of global flows, people moving around the world with relative ease have presented individuals with the problem of how to identify with a community of people who may use different symbol systems to understand the world or whose worldview is vastly different from their own. Muslims have been particularly affected by negative portrayals of their culture and belief system in the media and are struggling to maintain their beliefs while attempting to interact with sometimes opposing belief systems. Muslims who wish to participate in the world economy while trying to adhere to standards prescribed by Islamic law regarding business and financial practices have a particular problem (Tripp 2006; Kuran 2004; Mirza and Halabi 2003). The problem occurs whether the individual

Muslim is a member of a minority Muslim community in the West or a citizen in a Muslim country receiving media images of a negative nature (*cf.* Said 1994, 1997).

During the 1980s and 1990s Muslim populations around the world—in Muslim countries like Indonesia, Pakistan, and Malaysia and in countries where Muslims live in the diaspora—generated enough steady income growth to develop a network of Islamic financial institutions. Innovations in institutional structures and products have encouraged growing Muslim populations to contribute to the Islamic financial network both institutionally and intellectually, especially in the United States and Great Britain. Many authors contend that in this manner, attempts to create an Islamic environment are an effect of globalization rather than a reaction against it (Roy 2004; Mamdani 2004; Gray 2003). To support this argument, I note that the language of business as well as of theoretical writings is English, tying the industry to its roots in the Anglo-American business model and mode of knowledge dissemination.

Islamic Finance and Community

In contrast to a close association with the conventional banking institutional structure, many authors assert that Islamic finance is a system that places more emphasis on the community and social justice concerns than conventional finance places on those same concerns. This idea has its roots in the spiritual concept of *adalah*, or social justice (Chapra 1992). For example, Mirza and Halabi (2003) contend that the Islamic banking in Australia's minority Muslim community has responded exceptionally well to the community focus and participates in Islamic banking partly to strengthen community ties. Kuran (2004) also asserts that Islamic finance is primarily a vehicle through which to call attention to a unique Muslim identity. I witnessed some of this kind of thinking among respondents I interviewed in Dubai, most of whom appeared to identify strongly with the idea that Islamic finance offers more equitable means of distributing wealth than conventional finance. Rather than seeing this difference as an irreconcilable problem, however, many practitioners agree with the contention of one author that the goal of those engaged in Islamic finance is to "increase competition within the world economic system rather than creating competition to it" (Al Saud 2000, xiii). This is not to suggest that Islamic bankers do not critique capitalism but merely to point out that the relationship is more complicated than a straightforward rejection of capitalist ideology or institutions. Islamic banking is not an *alternative* to capitalism, but an *improvement* upon it.

Problem 3: Self and Divinity

Finally, the industry of Islamic banking and finance addresses a third question for its practitioners: "To what extent can divine beliefs be encoded in daily life?" Islam as a religious belief system is particularly amenable to the examination of daily practices as they relate to spiritual beliefs. It is extremely important to note that *in Islam there is no single human who has been granted the authority to make decisions about religious matters.* Individual jurists or other learned people can offer opinions on a given situation, but it is always preferable to have a consensus of scholars. Some individuals appear to have more authority than others; however, that is due to the reality of human society and power structures, and is not built into the religion itself. When a moral decision arises, it is incumbent on each individual Muslim to think through the situation in his or her own personal process of *ijtihad* and to come to a conclusion that is consistent with his or her understanding of the religion. Many of the debates about financial matters happen because of different interpretations of central ideas and the meaning of specific practices.

Islamic Finance and Morality

In the present study, I included questions designed to elicit answers about how Islamic financiers explain their industry and financial activities to conventional bankers and to prospective participants in the industry. In these explanations, I found that participants in the industry of Islamic banking and finance make certain claims about the ideological and moral aims of their industry. Practitioners use terms familiar to conventional bankers to describe their activities. Moreover, certain words and phrases (in Arabic, no matter what is the speaker's native language) impart a selection of information to the public and to each other about the ideological aims of the industry. Taken together, the discourse and specialized business terminology are powerful ways to impart knowledge about the industry to members and nonmembers alike. Practitioners speak about their industry in terms of morality, but also in terms of flow and a global consciousness, while simultaneously upholding the practices they associate with an immoral industry—conventional finance.

CONCLUSION

In this chapter, I have reviewed some of the social science literature on globalization. I found that the understandings most related to my conception and to the conceptions of globalization as understood by my respondents fall into two general, but related, categories: *global flows* and *global consciousness.* Both categories build upon an imagery of flows of people, images, capital, and technology to create a consciousness about the world and relationships within it. Next, I looked at some of those relationships to ask what existential problems might be presented to a person in a globalized environment. I divided those questions into categories of self, community, and divinity so that in subsequent studies I will be able to examine more closely the discourse and practices within Islamic finance that render it a place that is created by individuals in search of a mediating environment and a tool through which its practitioners can negotiate relationships in a globalized world.

REFERENCES

Ali, Ahmad Mohamed. 2002. "The Emerging Islamic Financial Architecture: The Way Ahead." Paper presented at the Fifth Harvard University Forum on Islamic Finance, April 6–7.

Al Saud, M.A.F. 2000. "Forum opening address: A review of Islamic finance." In *Proceedings of the Third Harvard University Forum on Islamic Finance, October 1999,* xiii. Boston: Harvard University Center for Middle Eastern Studies.

Anderson, Benedict. 1991. *Imagined Communities: Reflections on the Origin and Spread of Nationalism.* London: Verso.

Appadurai, Arjun. 1996. *Modernity at Large: Cultural Dimensions of Globalization*. Minneapolis: University of Minnesota Press.

Appadurai, Arjun, ed. 2000. *Globalization*. Durham, NC: Duke University Press.

Appiah, K. A. 2006. *Cosmopolitanism: Ethics in a World of Strangers*. New York: W. W. Norton & Company, Inc.

Askari, H., Z. Iqbal, and A. Mirakhor. 2010. *Globalization and Islamic Finance: Convergence, Prospects and Challenges*. Hoboken, NJ: John Wiley & Sons.

Ayub, M. 2008. *Understanding Islamic Finance*. Chichester, UK: John Wiley & Sons.

Bakan, Joel. 2004. *The Corporation: The Pathological Pursuit of Profit and Power*. New York: Free Press.

Barber, B. R. 1995. *Jihad vs. McWorld*. New York: Times Books.

Chapra, M. U. 1992. *Islam and the Economic Challenge*. Herndon, VA: Islamic Foundation and International Institute of Islamic Thought.

Friedman, Thomas L. 2005. *The World Is Flat: A Brief History of the Twenty-First Century*. New York: Farrar, Straus & Giroux.

Fukuyama, Francis. 1992. *The End of History and the Last Man*. New York: Free Press.

Giddens, Anthony. 1991. *Modernity and Self-Identity: Self and Society in the Late Modern Age*. Cambridge: Polity Press.

Gray, John. 2003. *Al Qaeda and What It Means to Be Modern*. London: Faber & Faber.

Gupta, Akhil, and James Ferguson, eds. 1997. *Culture, Power, Place: Explorations in Critical Anthropology*. Durham, NC: Duke University Press.

Hannerz, Ulf. 1990. "Cosmopolitans and Locals in World Culture." *Theory, Culture & Society* Vol. 7, No. 2:237–251.

Hannerz, Ulf. 1996. *Transnational Connections*. London: Routledge.

Hunt-Ahmed, Karen. 2012 (forthcoming). "Finding a Jewel: Identity and Gendered Space in Islamic Finance." *Culture & Psychology*. Vol. 18, No. 4.

Huntington, Samuel. 1998. *The Clash of Civilizations and the Remaking of World Order*. New York: Simon & Schuster.

Jameson, Frederic, and Masao Miyoshi, eds. 1998. *The Cultures of Globalization*. Durham, NC: Duke University Press.

Kettell, B. 2008. "Definition of Islamic banking." In *Introduction to Islamic Banking and Finance*, 37–53. London: Brian Kettell Islamic Banking Training.

Kuran, Timur. 2001. "Comment: Speculations on Islamic Financial Alternatives." *Anthropology Today* 17:3, 28–29.

Kuran, Timur. 2004. *Islam & Mammon: The Economic Predicaments of Islamism*. Princeton, NJ: Princeton University Press.

Mamdani, Mahmood. 2004. *Good Muslim, Bad Muslim: America, the Cold War and the Roots of Terror*. New York: Pantheon Books.

Maurer, Bill. 2006. *Pious Property: Islamic Mortgages in the United States*. New York: Russell Sage Foundation.

Mirza, Abdul Malik, and Abdel Halabi. 2003. "Islamic Banking in Australia: Challenges and Opportunities." *Journal of Muslim Minority Affairs* 23:2, 347–359.

Monger, R., and M. Rawashdeh. 2008. "Islamic Finance Enters the Mainstream." *Management Accounting Quarterly* 9:3, 1–6.

Ong, Aihwa. 1999. *Flexible Citizenship: The Cultural Logics of Transnationality*. Durham, NC: Duke University Press.

Robertson, Roland. 1992. *Globalization: Social Theory and Global Culture*. London: Sage Publications.

Roy, Olivier. 2004. *Globalized Islam: The Search for a New Ummah*. New York: Columbia University Press.

Sadeghi, M. 2008. "Financial Performance of Shari'a-Compliant Investment: Evidence from Malaysia Stock Market." *International Research Journal of Finance and Economics* Issue 20:15–26.

Said, Edward W. 1994. *Orientalism.* New York: Vintage Books.

Said, Edward W. 1997. *Covering Islam: How the Media and the Experts Determine How We See the Rest of the World.* New York: Vintage Books.

Sassen, Saskia. 1998. *Globalization and Its Discontents.* New York: New Press.

Scholte, J. A. 2000. *Globalization: A Critical Introduction.* Houndmills, UK: Macmillan.

Shweder, Richard A. 1991. *Thinking through Cultures: Expeditions in Cultural Psychology.* Cambridge, MA: Harvard University Press.

Shweder, Richard A. 1997. "The 'big three' of morality (autonomy, community, divinity) and the 'big three' explanations of suffering." In Allan Brandt and Paul Rozin, eds. *Morality and Health.* New York: Routledge.

Shweder, Richard A., Martha Minow, and Hazel Rose Markus, eds. 2002. *Engaging Cultural Differences: The Multicultural Challenge in Liberal Democracies.* New York: Russell Sage Foundation.

Smolarski, J., M. Schapek, and M. I. Tahir. 2006. "Permissibility and Use of Options for Hedging Purposes in Islamic Finance." *Thunderbird International Business Review* 48:3, 425–443.

Taylor, Charles. 1989. *Sources of the Self: The Making of the Modern Identity.* Cambridge, MA: Harvard University Press.

Tripp, C. 2006. *Islam and the Moral Economy: The Challenge of Capitalism.* Cambridge: Cambridge University Press.

Walsh, C. 2008. "Ethics: Inherent in Islamic Finance through Shari'a Law: Resisted in American Business despite Sarbanes-Oxley." *Fordham Journal of Corporate & Financial Law* 12:753–777.

Warde, I. 2010. *Islamic Finance in the Global Economy.* 2nd ed. Edinburgh, UK: Edinburgh University Press.

CHAPTER 5

Islamic Science and the Critique of Neoclassical Economic Theory

WALEED EL-ANSARY
University Chair of Islamic Studies, Xavier University

Neoclassical economists often make two claims that preclude the possibility of "Islamic" economic theory. The first is that neoclassical economics accommodates any instrumentally rational, or internally consistent, set of values or tastes, making the theory of choice spiritually neutral (Robbins 1962; Heap et al. 1994). The second is that market exchange is compatible with a variety of ultimate ends, whether egoist or altruist, making industrial capitalism and the neoclassical theory of exchange spiritually neutral (Heyne 2000). According to such arguments, Islamic (or "Christian" or "Buddhist" or any other) economics is a "special case" of neoclassical economics *at best* (assuming that Islamic and other religious values are internally consistent).

Of course, economists admit that certain eighteenth- and nineteenth-century *classical* economic figures espoused "commerce without virtue" based on narrow self-interest.[1] But other economists during this period opposed that view, arguing that even enlightened self-interest was insufficient to provide the moral and legal constraints necessary for markets to exist in the first place.[2] Although this did not exclude greed as a potential motivation within industrial capitalism, it did not presuppose greed, either. Many neoclassical economists now insist that egoistic assumptions are neither necessary to the economic theory of exchange nor implied by the analytical tools of contemporary neoclassical thought (Novak 1982; Boulding et al. 1985).[3] Accordingly, the fact that some classical economists espoused materialism and greed is not sufficient to prove that industrial capitalism presupposes such criteria and motivations. Critics of economic thought either do not recognize the difference between classical and neoclassical economics or deliberately employ misleading arguments according to this view.[4] In short, religious economic *laws* obviously exist, but a religious economic *theory* does not, because religious values alter neither economizing nor exchange processes as such, nor the analytical tools for studying them.

In our opinion, the mainstream religious response to such arguments has not, by and large, been satisfactory.[5] In fact, economists of different religious affiliations generally appear to accept such neoclassical assertions, because they believe that industrial production processes are spiritually neutral, with all this implies for motivational assumptions and exchange processes, and that the standard analytical tools of neoclassical theory, which were imported from Newtonian mechanics and nineteenth-century physics, can be combined with moral constraints to accommodate spiritual values. As we shall see, both beliefs are erroneous.

Fortunately, leading philosophers such as Seyyed Hossein Nasr (1996, 1999, 2000) and scientists such as Wolfgang Smith (1984, 1995, 2003) provide an explicit refutation of the former and an implicit denial of the latter, even challenging the applicability of neoclassical theory's analytical tools to the "corporeal" world of perceptible qualities as opposed to the "physical" world of measured or measurable quantities that concerns physicists.[6] In fact, such a critique of the secular sciences of nature provides a profound, if not explicit, critique of neoclassical economics. Indeed, the "unity of method" within the secular philosophy of science is connected to industrial production processes on one hand, and to the unity of analytical tools between neoclassical theory and physics on the other. In this sense, the refutation of unity of method ultimately provides a profound critique of both industrial capitalism and the analytical tools of neoclassical economics; without Islamic metaphysics and sciences of nature, there is no such thing as Islamic economics in our opinion. But because the aforementioned authors articulate elements of these profound arguments in philosophical terms that many economists are not familiar with, and because different parts of these arguments are found in various writings that do not always explicitly draw their implications for economics, few economists either are aware of or understand the implications of such an approach.

Fortunately, E. F. Schumacher, the most important economist of the twentieth century from this perspective, is an exception (El-Ansary, forthcoming 2013). His personal library reveals the immense influence of contemporary Muslim philosophers, showing that he took far more extensive notes *within* the books of Rene Guenon (Shaykh Abdul Wahid Yahya), Frithjof Schuon (Shaykh 'Isa Nur al-Din), and Titus Burckhardt (Shaykh Ibrahim) than most other authors, including leading Catholic thinkers such as Jacques Maritain. Moreover, this Islamic influence appears in Schumacher's notes for a 24-lecture course he taught at London University in 1959 and 1960 entitled "Crucial Problems for Modern Living." His lecture notes are highly detailed with extensive commentary and references, including notes on the perennial philosophy and Burckhardt's *Alchemy: Science of the Cosmos, Science of the Soul* in German.[7] Tragically, Schumacher died a few weeks before a scheduled meeting with Nasr, a leading representative of another generation of Islamic philosophers, on Islamic economics in Tehran. Despite such profound influences, this foundation of Schumacher's work is not widely known. And because he left certain points implicit without rebutting elements of the aforementioned neoclassical arguments, even his admirers have misunderstood or misinterpreted his thought.[8]

It is therefore necessary to make such arguments explicit, integrating the writings of Schumacher and the aforementioned philosophers and scientists as well as other religious thinkers to respond to neoclassical claims that economic theory is neutral. It is also important to clarify certain details of neoclassical economics for other scholars who understandably may not be familiar with them. In our opinion, an intellectual division of labor is necessary in which economists of different religious affiliations build upon the foundation that has already been beautifully laid by the heavy lifting of these authors.[9]

The purpose of this chapter is to reveal the interconnections of these profound arguments with respect to contemporary economic theory, focusing on the first neoclassical claim to accommodate any internally consistent values or tastes, although the analysis begins with the second issue regarding the neutrality (or lack thereof) of industrial production processes (for a more detailed critique, see El-Ansary 2011). The article is divided into three sections. The first examines the three objectives of human work in relation to the division of labor from a religious perspective, as well as a spectrum of classical and neoclassical views. The second section challenges the claim that the analytical approach of neoclassical theory can accommodate the three objectives because it implies psychological hedonism, clarifying the need for an Islamic alternative. The third section considers the link between economics and physics, drawing the devastating implications of the Islamic sciences of nature for neoclassical theories of choice and welfare as well as policy issues such as "freedom of contract" in the context of Wolfgang Smith's distinction between the physical, corporeal, and higher levels of reality.[10]

TRADITIONAL OBJECTIVES OF HUMAN WORK

What are the objectives of work by which to evaluate production processes if man is created for a higher purpose? Brian Keeble points out that it would be inconceivable that work would *necessarily* entail conflict between spiritual and other needs (1998, p. 75).

> [Otherwise] we would have to face an awkward question: how it ever came about that, in order to sustain his earthly existence, man should be obliged to follow a course of physical action that seems a direct denial of his deepest nature, as if by some ghastly mistake of his Creator it is man's destiny to follow a direction that leads him away from the very thing it is his nature to be? If we are to avoid such a dilemma, we must conclude that in some way work is, or should be, profoundly natural and not something that must be avoided or banished as being beneath our dignity.

If work is not only supposed to help keep us alive, but is also supposed to help us strive toward perfection, then we can derive three purposes of human work, as Schumacher points out (1979, pp. 3–4):

> First, to provide necessary and useful goods and services.
> Second, to enable every one of us to use and thereby perfect our gifts like good stewards.
> Third, to do so in service to, and in cooperation with, others, so as to liberate ourselves from our inborn egocentricity.[11]

Of course, economists recognize the first objective of work. But some recognize the others to various degrees, acknowledging that different types of work have different effects. For example, Adam Smith acknowledged the second objective to some extent, arguing that an extremely high division of labor employing few of man's faculties could have serious social costs by reducing certain human capabilities. He states (see Schumacher 1997, pp. 99–100):

> The understandings of the greater part of men are necessarily formed by their ordinary employments. The man whose life is spent in performing a few simple operations . . . has no occasion to exert his understanding. . . . He naturally loses, therefore, the habit of such exertion and generally becomes as stupid and ignorant as it is possible for a human creature to become . . . but in every improved and civilised society this is the state into which the labouring poor, that is, the great body of the people, must necessarily fall, unless government takes some pains to prevent it.

Other figures such as James Mill, the father of John Stuart Mill, opposed this view, denying the existence of such harmful effects and arguing that all types of work were homogeneous in terms of the second objective (Pagano 1985). He also denied that the third objective was possible based on psychological hedonism, leaving only the first objective applicable to economics. More recently, some neoclassical economists have adopted a curious, syncretic position, assuming that all types of work are homogeneous on one hand (Pagano 1985) while asserting the legitimacy of all three objectives on the other.[12] These various positions clearly have important implications for one's assessments of industrial capitalism and socialism (El-Ansary 2006). Suffice it to say here that qualitatively different production processes affect all three objectives, and that any trade-offs between them can exist only in the short or medium term, not the long term, from the Islamic point of view. As Nasr states (1982, p. 89), "Equilibrium on the socio-economic plane is impossible to realize without reaching that inner equilibrium which cannot be attained save through surrender to the One and living a life according to the dictum of Heaven." From this point of view, what man makes, or man's art, should communicate a spiritual truth and presence analogous to nature, or God's art (Nasr 1987).

NEOCLASSICAL THEORY, PSYCHOLOGICAL HEDONISM, AND THE ISLAMIC ALTERNATIVE

We now consider whether neoclassical theory offers the analytical tools to accommodate the three objectives. Most economists take the following view (Heap et al. 1994, p. 5):

> The desires (of *Homo economicus*) can be "good," "bad," "selfish," "altruistic"— anything you like. The only proviso is that those desires generate a preference ordering; that is, the person can always say whether he or she prefers one bundle to another or is indifferent between them, and that the ordering satisfies the following conditions (reflexivity, completeness, consistency, and continuity).

This obviously implies that neoclassical theory can accommodate the spiritual objectives of work. However, most of the earliest neoclassical economists did not make this claim, for they explicitly defined the role of psychological hedonism in economic theory. As Georgescu-Roegen points out (1973, p. 456), Benthamism "was so much in the air" in England and the Continent during the rise of neoclassical theory that Edgeworth, with whom hedonism reached its apogee in economics, contended that actual pleasure "is measurable in terms of its 'atoms,' i.e. in terms of 'just perceptible increments'" (*Mathematical Psychics*, 1881).[13] Edgeworth therefore expressed his belief that a "hedonimeter" would be built for measuring actual pleasures, somewhat analogous to Bentham's wish for a "political thermometer." Because later economists were less enthusiastic about such prospects, they attempted to make economic theory independent of such speculations, shifting from "cardinal," or measurable, utility to "ordinal" utility, which requires a simple ranking of alternatives.[14]

But any such attempts to divorce economic theory from psychological hedonism fail so long as economists presuppose a "*mono*-utility function," an aggregate in which there are no qualitatively different needs or wants. This is the opposite of the Islamic approach to welfare based on a hierarchy of spiritual and other needs. The fundamental difference comes down to the distinction between a qualitative whole and a quantitative aggregate, which we shall return to in the context of Wolfgang Smith's distinction between the corporeal and physical realms. Suffice it to say here that a mono-utility function is not a "heuristic device" that can be successively adjusted for all rational values involving a single end, because it applies only to a particular domain of them (i.e., unethical preferences based on psychological hedonism).[15]

Such a "mental state" account of welfare does not even distinguish between "the mental states involved in believing something that really is true and a successful deception" (Griffin 1986, p. 13), with all this implies for the three objectives of work. Actually realizing the meaning of existence and being fully deluded that one has done so are the same in this view.[16] Griffin uses the example (p. 13) that "if a father wants his children to be happy, what he wants, what is valuable to him, is a state of the world, not a state of his mind; merely to delude him into thinking that his children flourish, therefore, does not give him what he values." The mental state account therefore subordinates truth to utility, admitting happiness that is false because the object of happiness does not exist, making this position an inversion of the Islamic (and other religions') doctrine that "there is no right superior to that of truth" (see Schuon 1981a, p. 112). This inversion is based on a confusion regarding the nature of the operation of the intelligence (Schuon 1987, p. 212):

> The good is a possibility of action; the true is not a possibility of knowledge, it is knowledge itself. Evil is a "willing," but error is not a "knowing," it is an ignorance. In other words, evil is an act of the will, but error is not an act of the intelligence. Intelligence is not, like will, free through its possible action; it is free through its very substance and so through the necessity of its perfection.[17]

In the next section, we will see that this debate over the analytical tools of economics has profound implications for the debate over freedom of contract in Islamic and secular approaches to economic law.

But first we must clarify how the conventional neoclassical approach excludes *spiritual* values in the three objectives of work and the source of confusion over this issue. Let us begin by considering the following example related to the third objective, to work "in service to, and in cooperation with, others, so as to liberate ourselves from our inborn egocentricity." Imagine that we have the authority to prevent an evil act, and someone is trying to bribe us to permit it. Although we may be unwilling to accept any amount of money to permit the evil act, we may also have a limit on how much we would be willing to pay to stop the same event that others have the authority to prevent. The two situations are different in the sense that the former is an "act" in which we participate to accomplish an evil, whereas the latter is an "event" others perform that perhaps we cannot afford to stop. The mono-utility approach, however, requires that willingness to accept (WTA) be equal to willingness to pay (WTP). This excludes the ethical values of one who "cannot be bought at any price," although it can accommodate the unethical preferences of a miser or a hedonist. In fact, if we constrain choice to alternatives that equate WTA and WTP, no alternative is more "right" or "wrong" than any other (in the absence of special assumptions that the cost of eliminating the damage equals WTA, the only basis on which it might be morally justifiable to accept a particular sum of money to compensate for the damage in permitting an otherwise evil act). Unconditionally equating WTA and WTP therefore implies an arbitrary choice from a normative point of view and denies a rational basis for ethics. Analogous arguments apply to choices of risk, in which an "expected" mono-utility function implies that one would be willing to accept one dollar for the additional risk of death if one would be willing to pay only a dollar to eliminate such a risk (Heap et al. 1994, p. 10). Moreover, Finnis points out (1990c, p. 12) that in this approach, "there is no difference in principle between buying the right to inflict injury intentionally and buying the right not to take precautions which would eliminate an equivalent number and type of injuries accidentally."

The moral requirement that WTA *not* equal WTP implies that there are *two* possible rankings for the desirability of a particular alternative rather than one depending on the "context" or the "direction of trade" (i.e., whether one is paying or accepting). In this case, there is a mathematical *relation* rather than a *function* between a given income and its moral desirability, depending on how the money was earned. (In terms of a two-dimensional graph, a mathematical relation has more than one value of y for each value of x, illustrating how "context matters," whereas a function has only one value of y for each value of x, illustrating that context may be irrelevant, at least to an egoist in our example.) The same divergence between WTA and WTP applies to production processes if they conflict with the second objective of work, "to enable every one of us to use and thereby perfect our gifts like good stewards."

Despite these crucial distinctions, leading Muslim economists such as Naqvi (1981, p. 63) appear to believe it is possible to add moral "constraints" to a mono-utility function.[18] This is internally inconsistent, because a moral constraint requires that WTA and WTP *diverge*, whereas the mono-utility approach equates them. Although Naqvi eloquently critiques greed and consumerism to distinguish between Islamic values and egoistic preferences, this does not by itself address the distinction between Islamic and neoclassical economic theories. The latter requires a response to the neoclassical claim to accommodate different motivational assumptions in its theory of choice, as well as the assertion that alternative motivational assumptions have limited relevance for production and exchange processes.

Some economists (Lutz and Lux 1988) therefore suggest a "lexicographic" or sequential function involving multiple ends rather than a mono-utility function to accommodate moral choices, allowing higher-priority ends such as honor to be fulfilled before lower-priority ends such as wealth.[19] Although this "sequential" structure successfully denies unethical trade-offs between alternatives to accommodate values better than the mono-utility approach, a lexicographic function cannot accommodate *spiritual* needs. This is because it substitutes a single spiritual end with a sequence of multiple independent ends, breaking the intimate linkage within a hierarchy of spiritual and other needs.[20] Moreover, a lexicographic function does not necessarily exclude egoism, as the case of a lexicographic hedonist who pursues various pleasures while equating WTA and WTP on moral choices suggests. Because diverse ends can also pose problems for the consistency of preferences (as ends "competing for position" within the sequence suggests) (May 1954), neoclassical economists generally object to this lexicographic approach in favor of a mono-utility function involving a single end.[21] We will return to the Islamic perspective on preference integration shortly.

Turning now to the first objective of work, "to provide necessary and useful goods and services," the mono-utility approach is also problematic, because it equates WTA and WTP across qualitatively different goods, thereby excluding any distinction within or between needs and wants. As Allen points out (see Lutz and Lux 1988, p. 21), "'need' is a non-word" in neoclassical economics, which excludes the possibility that one may not be able to abstain from or substitute for a particular good. Indeed, "The modern utility theory reduces all wants to one general abstract want called 'utility.' In line with this reduction, one need not say 'these people need more shoes': instead, 'these people need more utility' should suffice" (Georgescu-Roegen 1973, p. 458).[22] But common sense suggests that "He who does not have enough to eat cannot satisfy his hunger by wearing more shirts." A mono-utility approach therefore implicitly attributes "to man 'faculties which he actually does not possess,' unless we could drink paper, eat leisure, and wear steam engines" (Lutz and Lux 1988, p. 324).[23] Georgescu-Roegen (1966) points out that qualitatively different use values also apply to different uses of the *same* good, such as water, which we use to fully satisfy needs like thirst without driving the incremental value in other uses (such as sprinkling the lawn) to zero.[24] In short, "a mattress, knife, so much bread . . . are things that have by design particular qualities in virtue of which they are useful for particular purposes and meet particular needs, and they are inherently different" (Meikle 1995, p. 16). Thus, the economist's common inference from a downward-sloping demand curve (like the demand for water) to a single use value for *all* goods is a non sequitur.[25]

From an Islamic perspective, the mono-utility explanation of the economizing process involves the *post hoc, ergo propter hoc*, or "after this, therefore because of this," fallacy.[26] Erroneously equating WTA and WTP across different goods that fulfill different needs or wants (or combinations of the two in the case of goods with multiple use values or attributes) fundamentally misunderstands agents' choices, for changes in allocation involve changes in "each of the items in relation to the *whole*, rather than in relation to each other . . . changes happen at the *center* rather than at the margin" (Hobson as cited in Lutz and Lux 1988, p. 335).[27] In short, values transform the economizing process with all this implies for the analytical tools necessary to model it.

Consequently, some Muslim economists such as Khan (1995, ch. 2) have used a variation of the lexicographic approach in a commendable attempt to distinguish between needs and wants in consumer choices.[28] We certainly applaud these and other efforts to challenge the stranglehold of mono-utility functions in economics. However, as noted earlier, even a lexicographic function cannot accommodate a hierarchy of spiritual and other needs, which require a mathematical relation.

Despite the problems with the notion of a single use value, the conventional economic literature never (to our knowledge) discusses the analytical tool necessary for cases involving multiple use values on one hand and a single end on the other, which Islamic and other religious values require.[29] Perhaps most economists assume that this combination is impossible, thinking that a single end is incompatible with multiple use values, a correct conclusion if they are on the *same* level of reality. But this combination is possible and even necessary within a *hierarchy* of levels of reality. Classical Islamic treatises on philosophical ethics such as Naṣīr al-Dīn Ṭūsī's *The Nasirean Ethics* (1964) make such a distinction clear, explicitly establishing the ontological basis of multiple use values in the context of spiritual needs. We therefore suggest the term *multi-utility relation* for the analytical tool in the Islamic approach, since it entails multiple use values in a mathematical relation. Indeed, we believe that this approach resolves various paradoxes in economics, the most notable of which involve risk and uncertainty, which is crucial in understanding the religious prohibition of certain forms of risk trading and other aspects of religious economic law. (Although Mahmoud El-Gamal (2006) has attempted to draw the consequences of *inconsistent* preferences for the economic analysis of Islamic law, he makes no mention of the possibility of a multi-utility relation.[30]) In any case, the fundamental opposition between a multi-utility relation and a mono-utility function is based on the polarity between "unity" and "uniformity" according to contemporary Islamic philosophy (Guenon 2001).

The economic literature's pervasive neglect of a multi-utility relation in comparison to utility functions is indicated by the fact that a leading graduate textbook on microeconomic theory (Mas-Colell, Whinston, and Green 1995) simply makes no mention of any other possibility except irrational preferences. But this is a crucial error, because spiritual values can fulfill the economist's criteria for rational preferences; that is, they are complete (one can rank bundles A, B, and C, for example) and consistent (one prefers A to C if one prefers A to B and B to C).[31]

With only mono-utility and lexicographic utility functions left to choose between, economists select the former because a single end seems more plausible and appears to fulfill the consistency axiom more easily than multiple ends (a mono-utility approach also employs the analytical tools of Newtonian mechanics and nineteenth-century physics, as we shall see). Accordingly, neoclassical economists add another axiom, that of "continuity." Economics textbooks routinely present this as a technical mathematical condition that has no serious implications, since it simply excludes lexicographic utility functions. Even leading thinkers in the philosophy of economics such as Hausman neglect to critically assess this axiom, stating in his important book on ethics and economics that "Continuity is a technical condition, which we shall not discuss" (Hausman and McPherson 1996, p. 29). But the continuity axiom is *not* only a "technical" mathematical condition, since it rules out a multi-utility relation as well as a lexicographic utility function. Unlike the other axioms, the continuity axiom is not spiritually neutral, for it reintroduces the hedonistic assumptions of Jeremy Bentham, the founding father of modern utilitarianism, into neoclassical theory (Georgescu-Roegen 1966, 1973). As noted earlier, such a mental state theory of welfare subordinates truth to utility, treating the operation of the intelligence as an operation of the will, as if error was a type of knowing in the same way that evil is a type of willing.[32] The mental state account of welfare is therefore internally inconsistent (one can never offer a reason to subordinate truth to utility in any case).

It is important to note that economists often espouse an alternative "satisfaction of desire" view of welfare that partially corrects the mental state account by requiring that the object of desire actually exist to count toward utility (Hausman and McPherson 1996).[33] But this is not what the continuity axiom implies, which economists who believe that it is neutral do not recognize. In any case, Hausman asserts that economists do not take the satisfaction of desire account literally and often have in mind a substantive, mental state account of utility.[34]

Since this is what the continuity axiom entails, it is sobering to note that Bentham dreamed he was inspired by an "angel" shortly before the publication of his *Introduction to the Principles of Morals and Legislation* (see Crimmins 1990), which established the utilitarian principles on which the state should discard religious laws governing society and replace them with a secular science of legislation based on utilitarianism, attacking Church teachings while arguing that bans against such practices such as sexual indulgence and homosexuality decreased utility.[35] In the dream (pp. 314–315), the angel put into Bentham's hands a book that he "said he had just been writing with the quill of a phoenix . . . it was lettered on the back Principles and Legislation." Bentham viewed himself in the dream as "a founder of a sect, of course a person of great sanctity and importance," the savior of England and quite possibly the world. When he was asked by "a great man" what he should do "to save the nation," Bentham replied, "take up my book, & follow me." He clearly implied that the book the angel had delivered to him should replace Scripture as the best plan for the salvation of the world. According to the angel, it was a book with "the true flavour of the fruit of the tree of knowledge," and Bentham "had no occasion to eat it . . . as St. John did his: all I had to do was cram it as well as I could down the throats of other people." Bentham's subsequent sense of self-importance led to his will request made shortly before his death in 1832 that his skeleton be preserved, dressed in his own clothes, and placed in his chair (as an "Auto Icon") so that "personal friends and disciples . . . [could commemorate] the founder of the greatest happiness system of morals and legislation."[36]

Such details are obviously an embarrassment in the history of economic thought. Although few economists today explicitly subscribe to Bentham's view of welfare, it is intrinsic to the mono-utility approach. Contrary to this mental state account, a multi-utility relation requires that "our willing is not inspired by our desires alone, fundamentally it is inspired by the truth, and this is independent of our immediate interests" (Schuon 1987, p. 93). In the Islamic theory of welfare, happiness can be an *effect* rather than a motivating cause, because beauty and the love of beauty give the soul happiness; and virtue, or beauty of soul, is the highest form of beauty in this world. As Schuon explains (1981a, p. 94), "sensible beauties are situated outside the soul, and their meeting with it is more or less accidental; if the soul wishes to be happy in an unconditional and permanent fashion, it must carry the beautiful within itself." Virtue is a necessary part of man's total attachment to the Truth, or God, because man has a will to act in addition to an intelligence that knows.[37] The totality of this contemplation with the whole of one's being—intelligence, will, and sentiment—results in the virtues.[38] Happiness is, therefore, an effect that constantly accompanies virtue, and is not a motivating cause alone like truth. Consequently, there is an intrinsic connection between the "right" and the "good," between spiritual "needs" and corresponding "duties" as two sides of the same coin.[39] Thus, the Islamic view of welfare requires that the satisfaction of desires be based on true beliefs and that happiness be based on reality to count toward well-being. From this perspective, psychological hedonism rationalizes the sacrifice of spiritual and other needs for false happiness based on inferior intentions, providing a theory of choice and welfare of the "lower soul" (the *nafs al-ammārah* in Quranic terms).

We do *not* assert that economists must therefore completely banish the continuity axiom from the theory of choice. The axiom is not only necessary to model certain preferences of misers and hedonists; it is also appropriate for many *neutral* choices if applied locally rather than globally, such as those involving tastes. For example, if one is willing to pay a maximum of two apples for one pear in moving from bundle A to B, one should be willing to accept a minimum of two apples for one pear in moving back from bundle B to A. In this case, there is no qualitative difference between WTA and WTP, because they are simply movements between two bundles on the same indifference curve, a locus of points between which one is indifferent. But for values, the continuity axiom applies only within a given objective that can be fulfilled in a variety of morally equivalent ways. Thus, one can apply the continuity axiom locally *within* a given use value, but one cannot apply continuity globally *between* use values without implying unethical preferences (as the equation of WTA and WTP illustrates). In short, the misapplication of the continuity axiom to choices involving ethical values implies that "nothing is 'good' or 'evil' in itself, there is only 'more' or 'less'" (Schuon 1992, p. 61).

But if economists apply continuity globally because they believe that a single end is incompatible with a multi-utility framework, then neoclassical theory appears to offer the only possible theory of choice for a single end. In this case, neoclassical thought appears to offer a valuable "heuristic device" that can be successively adjusted for all such complete and consistent values rather than applying only to a particular domain of them.[40] The result is a vacuum in the literature on a multi-utility relation that is the central analytical tool of the Islamic approach, with all this implies for economic policy.

THE QUANTUM ENIGMA AND THE ISLAMIC CRITIQUE OF ECONOMICS

The preceding discussion clarifies important elements of the Islamic critique of neoclassical theory. However, this only sets the stage for far more devastating implications based on the intimate connection between the analytical tools of economic theory and the sciences of nature, a link that obviously could not exist if a mono-utility function accommodated all rational values or tastes for a single end. In fact, arguments regarding the Islamic natural sciences and "quantum paradox" not only demonstrate that the reduction of quality to quantity in a mono-utility function is a subjective construct that does not correspond to the nature of reality, but they also imply that the concept of a mono-utility aggregate is internally inconsistent, and that hedonists have inconsistent preferences. Accordingly, no one has ever had a mono-utility function and no one ever will, with all this implies for economic policy. In short, if the reduction of quality to quantity cannot apply to the world of nature, it does not apply to the human realm *a fortiori*.

Indeed, the neoclassical claim to accommodate any set of values and tastes has its roots in John Stuart Mill's analogy (1984) between classical economic theory and Newtonian mechanics.[41] Mill believed that just as Newton added constant forces such as gravity to "disturbance terms" such as friction to predict their aggregate effect, one could add constant causes such as greed to disturbance terms such as generosity to predict the aggregate result of economic phenomena. The "conflicting forces" of different motivating causes were analogous to the "conflicting forces" of mechanics, both of which a mathematical function could incorporate, thereby justifying the unity of analytical tools.[42]

But Ruskin (1938) rightly objected that disturbance terms such as generosity were not of the same quality as the supposedly constant force of greed, and the two could not be aggregated.[43] He even asserted that (see Clark and Wedderburn 1903–1912, vol. 27, p. 180):

> The modern Liberal politico-economist of the Stuart Mill school is essentially of the type of a flat-fish—one eyeless side of him always in the mud, and one eye, on the side that *has* eyes, down in the corner of his mouth,—not a desirable guide for man or beast.[44]

In short, Ruskin asserted that ethical values require a different analytical framework than composite causes to accommodate qualitative differences, thereby denying the validity of the unity of analytical tools.[45]

Analogous arguments apply to the subsequent founders of neoclassical theory who imported the mono-utility approach from nineteenth-century physics in an attempt to impose a "unity of analytical tools," not only unity of method, between the disciplines according to some historians of economic thought. Mirowski (1984), for example, maintains that:

> Neoclassical economic theory is bowdlerized nineteenth century physics. . . . [P]resent research techniques may be favoured *because* they were appropriated from physics. . . . [N]eoclassicism was not "simultaneously discovered" because it was "true," as Jevons and others would have it; instead, the timing of its genesis is explained by the timing of the energetics revolution in physics, and by the fact that scientifically trained individuals in different Western European countries at that time had access to the same body of knowledge and techniques. . . . One cannot predict where new theories will come from, but one can venture a broad inductive generalization from past patterns: that a substantial non-neoclassical economic theory will distinguish itself by consciously repudiating the energetics metaphor. (p. 377)

In a word, Mirowski and other critics claim that the neoclassical attempt to replace energy in physics equations with a mono-utility function in economics equations is arbitrary, is erroneous, and compromises economic analysis. He provides an enormous amount of supporting historical information to demonstrate the "sociology of knowledge" at work in economic theory. Leon Walras, one of the founders of neoclassical theory, even boasted that "the pure theory of economics is a science which resembles the physico-mathematical sciences in every respect" (Mirowski 1984, p. 363). This is not simply rhetorical flourish, since it is very nearly correct for his *rareté* equations (p. 368). Analogous comments apply to the work of Jevons, Edgeworth, Pareto, and other neoclassical economists, all of whom explicitly invoked the analogy between physics and economics (pp. 363–370). Accordingly, the timing (if not the possibility) of the mono-utility approach may be explicable primarily in terms of the sociology of knowledge.

Although arguments espousing the unity of tools are logically separable from arguments espousing the unity of method, the writings of the aforementioned economists clearly suggest that the latter is a necessary intellectual condition (in terms of the "sociology of knowledge") for the former. It is no accident that Ruskin challenged both. He even attacked the secular *natural* sciences, implicitly relying on a hierarchy of complementary human faculties and methods in premodern philosophy to study nature as "God's second book" (Rosenberg 1961, p. 6).[46] In this sense, Ruskin and Mill represent polar opposites on a spectrum of methodological positions, the former implicitly invoking the unity, plurality, *and* hierarchy of methods in the human *and* natural sciences, and the latter denying the plurality and hierarchy of methods in favor of unity of method *and* analytical tools.[47] According to Schuon (1984) and Nasr (1996, 2000), the danger of the latter increases the higher the level of being that is the subject matter of study, making it most hazardous in economics and other human sciences.[48]

Fortunately, "good physics is now refuting bad philosophy," as the philosopher and scientist Wolfgang Smith (1984, 1995, 2003) points out. In the context of the mind-boggling findings of quantum mechanics, he demonstrates (1995, 2003) that the reduction of quality to quantity does not even apply to the natural world, let alone to the human realm. Obviously, this has tremendous implications for the debate over the proper analytical tools in economics. Smith clarifies his solution to the paradoxes that the new physics poses for the understanding of the natural world in his seminal book *The Quantum Enigma: Finding the Hidden Key*, which Nasr (1997, p. 158) hails "as one of the most important books written in recent decades on the metaphysical interpretation of modern physics." One of the central distinctions that Smith makes is between the corporeal world of perceived qualities that we regularly experience and the physical world of measured or measurable quantities that occupies physicists. The world is not without qualitative differences as the "naïve realism" of billiard ball atomism (the notion that atoms alone "really exist") suggests. Although quantum mechanics has refuted atomism, the view that quality is reducible to quantity persists because of the desire for physics "without residue" (Smith 1995, p. 12).[49] "Quantum paradox" is the result, and Smith brilliantly demonstrates that the solution is to drop such a reductionist tenet (i.e., "bifurcation").[50] He states (2000, p. 475):

> The non-bifurcationist interpretation has the immediate advantage of eliminating at one stroke what is generally called "quantum paradox." There is no need any longer for this or that *ad hoc* hypothesis to make things fit; no need for "parallel universes" or new laws of logic! The one thing needful to avoid the semblance of paradox is to jettison bifurcation once and for all.[51]

Smith also demonstrates that this is the key to integrating the findings of physics into "higher orders of knowledge," showing that the findings of quantum mechanics reveal "reality is nonlocal." The "most striking" example according to him (1995, 2003, ch. 4) is the fact that the observation of photon A can have an *instantaneous* effect on photon B despite the fact that they are hundreds of meters apart traveling in opposite directions. Accordingly, Smith turns to the theory of hylomorphism in classical philosophy to explain the corporeal as the combination of "form," or what renders a thing intelligible, and "matter," the pre-existential recipient of form ("matter" here obviously differs from the conventional usage of this term today). This locates the physical as an intermediate realm of "potentiality" above the *materia prima* but below the "actual" corporeal, accounting for the lack of true self-identity for atoms (or other fundamental particles) on one hand, and explaining the "state-vector collapse," the actualization of potentiality on the physical level, by action from the corporeal level on the other.[52] Nasr (2006) also demonstrates that certain premodern Islamic philosophers and scientists such as Khayyam make an equivalent distinction between the physical and corporeal by distinguishing between *al-jism al-ta'līmī* (mathematical body) and *al-jism al-tabī'ī* (natural body). (Even if some other premodern scientists did not make this distinction, it is easily located as an intermediate level on their ontological map, for they certainly did not reduce the corporeal and higher levels of reality to the physical, which is scientism, not science.) This has extremely important implications for the understanding of premodern sciences, and is crucial for the ontological basis of the multi-utility relation in Islamic economic theory. Nasr makes the crucial point regarding traditional sciences as follows in his review of *The Quantum Enigma* (1997, pp. 151–152):

> [T]he qualities of the corporeal world are not accidents but come from the essence of corporeal objects which is not mathematical. Herein lies the key to the understanding of the significance of the traditional sciences which are precisely the sciences of the essence and attributes of corporeal objects. . . . In contrast quantitative and mathematical sciences in the modern sense refer not to the essence but to the material or material substratum of things. In this bold manner Smith destroys the stranglehold that modern scientism has exercised upon the traditional sciences since the 17th century when these sciences became interpreted as crude antecedents of modern science. . . Henceforth those interested in the traditional sciences of nature can pursue them as the sciences they are in reality, namely sciences dealing with the qualitative aspects of corporeal objects related to the very essence and attributes of these objects and providing knowledge of the corporeal world. This knowledge is, therefore, not in any way abrogated by the findings of modern physics which deals with another level of reality, ontologically speaking, namely the physical world in the sense that Smith uses this term and which he distinguishes from the corporeal world.

In short, integration (as well as every other positive quality) comes from above. As the astronomer Robert Jastrow has put it (see Smith 1995, p. 103): "For the scientist who has lived by his faith in the power of reason, the story ends like a bad dream. He has scaled the mountains of ignorance; he is about to conquer the highest peak; and as he pulls himself over the final rock, he is greeted by a band of theologians who have been sitting there for centuries."

The distinction between the physical and corporeal levels has catastrophic implications for the analytical tools of neoclassical economics as well as the theory of welfare. A mono-utility approach simply cannot accommodate qualitative differences in the corporeal realm, whereas both a lexicographic function based on a sequence of qualitatively different ends and a multi-utility relation based on a hierarchy of spiritual and other needs can. Even inconsistent preferences, the subject of behavioral economics, allow for qualitative distinctions, because the difficulty of choosing between qualitatively different goods and attributes can explain behavioral inconsistencies in the first place. But a mono-utility function requires an aggregate devoid of any qualitative differences whatsoever, which can apply only on the physical level. Choice (and existence itself) does not occur on this level, for it occurs in the corporeal realm. The mono-utility approach is thus eliminated from rational choice theory altogether, for egoistic preferences cannot be *globally* consistent over *corporeal* choices, although such preferences may be consistent within a *limited* range of choices.[53] Indeed, there is no "unitary self" insofar as the psyche is not integrated by the spirit (Coomaraswamy 1999). As Nasr explains (2004), we often try "in the modern world to achieve integration by bringing forces together on a single plane of reality," although this is metaphysically impossible given a hierarchy of levels of reality. "It is only a transcendent Principle that can integrate the various elements on a lower level of reality. And this repeats itself through all of the hierarchies of the universe."[54] Economists cannot therefore simultaneously combine the consistency and continuity axioms using a mono-utility approach, and the egoistic preferences of misers and hedonists are the subject of behavioral economics.[55] It is no accident that economic theory confuses this issue based on the confusion between the physical and corporeal levels, for neoclassical economists imported the mono-utility approach from a secular approach to physics.

Since a lexicographic function also excludes spiritual needs, it too implies behavioral inconsistencies (e.g., rivalry between ends for position in the function's sequence). In a word, bifurcation is a necessary, but not sufficient condition for the neoclassical theory of choice (and welfare) to be coherent. Such arguments regarding Islamic metaphysics and sciences of nature therefore imply that no one has ever had a mono-utility function (or a lexicographic function for that matter), and no one ever will, just as "No one has ever perceived a physical object, and no one ever will" (Smith 1995, p. 24).

Consequently, economic policy based on the neoclassical approach to welfare that assumes WTA *should* equal WTP breaks the links between preferences, choice, and welfare. Without true beliefs linking preferences to welfare, efficiency is misdirected and no longer normatively relevant. And without self-consistent preferences linking preferences to choice, "maximizing efficiency" is meaningless, because there is no stable goal as the object of efficiency (Hausman and McPherson 1996, p. 76). Since hedonistic preferences violate *both* of these conditions, as the distinction between the physical, corporeal, and higher levels of reality implies, neoclassical theory draws the wrong welfare and efficiency implications for ethical constraints.

According to this neoclassical view, laws should not reduce the choices available to consumers or producers because restrictions on voluntary transactions will decrease welfare and allocative efficiency; that is, voluntary transactions are in the welfare of both the buyer and seller, since they otherwise would not be willing to exchange (assuming the absence of certain "market imperfections"[56]). But this argument for the efficiency of "freedom of contract" and "complete markets" applies only when preferences are linked to both welfare and choice. This may be true for choices involving tastes, in which WTA equals WTP, but it is not necessarily true for choices involving values. Indeed, policies that institutionalize unethical preferences in the name of utility maximization lead individuals to internal disintegration and the community into social chaos. Hausman concludes, "It seems that those who are benevolent need to consider not just preferences, but the origins of preferences or the justifiability of preferences" (Hausman and McPherson 1996, p. 76).

This is particularly important when policies and institutions affect preferences systematically, as occurs in development and environmental programs. "Assessments of policy must then depend in part on one's views concerning which preferences to promote or concerning which institutions provide a suitable framework within which desirable preferences will develop" (p. 79). If freedom of contract and complete markets change values, not just tastes, then such policies can establish, maintain, or break the link between preferences and welfare.[57] But since mono-utility functions cannot support the distinction between values and tastes or intrinsic "good" and "evil," the neoclassical theory of choice favors libertarian policies while claiming to be neutral, thereby smuggling psychological hedonism into economic policy while suppressing the need for substantive philosophical debate over these policies.

Indeed, the Coase theorem, the central insight of the most cited paper in economics (by far) since World War II (Coase 1960), implies technical economic solutions to pollution based on the equation of WTA and WTP without the need for philosophical judgment.[58] The same applies to cost-benefit analysis. Analogous arguments apply to industrial production processes, which many economists assume are spiritually neutral like tastes, once again equating WTA and WTP with all this implies for the assessment of industrial capitalism. But if the paradigm behind such processes reduces the corporeal to the physical, then such an assumption is false (ultimately accounting for their disastrous unintended consequences on one hand and the impossibility of merely technical solutions to such problems on the other).

The Islamic critique of the unity of method is therefore critical for determining the areas within which WTA should *not* equal WTP, not just fully exposing the hedonistic presuppositions behind the neoclassical unity of analytical tools. In short, while market-based solutions may work well if WTA *should* equal WTP, they can fail miserably if they diverge. And to the extent that religious values are ultimately necessary to uphold the principle of justice (or that property rights are respected), the principle of contract (or that contracts [promises] are kept), and the principle of allegiance (or "that one loyally support a government that enforces the principles of justice and contract" [Wilson 1990, p. 4]), neoclassical theory espouses the very policies that in due course undermine the values necessary for markets to exist in the first place.[59]

The hierarchy of levels of reality thus implies the need for spiritual principles in public policy. As Islamic medicine asserts, vertical equilibrium in which the body is subordinate to the soul, and the soul is subordinate to the spirit, is necessary for welfare (Nasr 1996). In this way, man "avoids many unseen catastrophes and assures himself a life of wholeness and meaning" (Nasr 1994, p. 98). While some may object that accepting religious laws completely destroys human initiative, this criticism "fails to understand the inner workings of the Divine Law." Indeed, the Law places many paths before man, from which he chooses according to his nature and needs. "Initiative does not come only in rebelling against the Truth which is an easy task since stones fall by nature; initiative and creativity come most of all in seeking to live in conformity with the Truth and in applying its principles to the conditions which destiny has placed before man." By eliminating certain negative possibilities, Divine Law helps people in their internal struggle to have the will they want and to make the right choices in the face of path-dependent preferences. Consequently, Divine Law gives them the ultimate freedom of will by making it possible for them to integrate all of life around a Sacred Center that links preferences, welfare, and choice.

CONCLUSION

Muslim economists eloquently critique greed and consumerism to distinguish between spiritual values and egoistic preferences, but this does not by itself address the distinction between Islamic and neoclassical economic *theories*. The latter requires a response to the neoclassical claim to accommodate different motivational assumptions in its theory of choice, with all this implies for freedom of contract, production, and exchange processes.

Indeed, the debate between Islamic and neoclassical economics ultimately depends on the all-important debate over the hierarchy of levels of reality and the secular philosophy of science. If the distinction between the physical or corporeal and the higher levels of existence corresponds to the nature of reality, then no one has ever had a mono-utility function, and no one ever will, because quality is not reducible to quantity. Egoistic preferences are the province of behavioral economics, since spiritual principles are necessary for integration. Values fundamentally transform the economizing process, and a multi-utility relation is necessary for a theory of rational choice.[60]

Accordingly, the ongoing attempts of classical and neoclassical economists to apply the actual analytical tools of pre-quantum physics to prove equilibrium without spiritual principles, or economic laws without spiritual ones, is the height of scientism that has led to misunderstanding rather than understanding of both economizing and exchange processes. From the Islamic point of view, such attempts are parodies of doctrines on the correspondence between man and nature in theistic theoretical and practical sciences. Unfortunately, such scientism also leads to devastating consequences for both man and nature. At best, the reliance on a mono-utility approach in economics forces a trade-off between spiritual neutrality and logical completeness. One can either (1) apply mono-utility locally in a spiritually neutral way, leaving essential economic questions unanswered and the theory fatally incomplete, or (2) attempt to provide answers to essential questions by reducing values to tastes. Perhaps this is why E. F. Schumacher asserted that economics is either trivial or evil (see El-Ansary, forthcoming 2013).

At the very least, neoclassical economists must recognize that spiritual values are not reducible to a special case of neoclassical theory. The debate over which values are the necessary starting point of analysis is one that the economist qua economist cannot resolve. We can only hope that more economists will read the remarkable works of authors such as Schuon, Nasr, and Smith to set the stage for a serious debate within the field.

NOTES

1. For example, David Hume, who wrote about economics as well as philosophy, denied traditional conceptions of virtue in espousing his view of commercial society based primarily on egoism. For an important comparison and contrast with Adam Smith, see Fitzgibbons (1995).
2. Adam Smith opposed Hume's conception of "commerce without virtue," although Smith is routinely accused of espousing it. He attempted to integrate economic activity and moral virtue based on a diluted version of Stoicism, rejecting Aristotelian thought (Fitzgibbons 1995).
3. For example, Milton and Rose Friedman state (see Novak 1982, p. 94):
   Economics has been berated for allegedly drawing far-reaching conclusions from a wholly unrealistic "economic man" who is little more than a calculating machine, responding only to monetary stimuli. That is a great mistake. Self-interest is not myopic selfishness. It is whatever it is that interests the participants, whatever they value, whatever goals they pursue. The scientist seeking to advance the frontiers of his discipline, the missionary seeking to convert infidels to the true faith, the philanthropist seeking to bring comfort to the needy—all are pursuing their interests, as they see them, as they judge them by their own values.
   Friedman therefore declared in his Nobel acceptance address (see Machan 1995, p. 21), "The great Saints of history have served their 'private interest' just as the most money grubbing miser has served his interest."
4. It is particularly important for scholars in the humanities to note that many economists dismiss critiques of economics that do not recognize the distinction between classical and neoclassical theories.
5. For a variety of views, see, for instance, Boulding et al. (1985).
6. As we shall see, this crucial distinction reveals the proper domain assumptions for the analytical tools of physics, which do not apply to economic choices in the corporeal realm.
7. We would like to acknowledge the help of Joseph Lumbard in identifying the German passages in Schumacher's notes.
8. See for instance the preface to the 1989 edition of Schumacher's classic *Small Is Beautiful* by John McClaughry, who states:
   [Schumacher's] recurring diatribes about "greed and envy" showed a failure to appreciate the normal human urge to work to provide the good things for one's family. His attack on nuclear-generated electricity (Chapter 4, Part II) lacked any persuasive analysis of the costs, benefits, and risks of alternative energy sources; he chose instead to reject nuclear power on dubious environmental grounds, and also because its generation requires engineering complexity and large corporate and governmental organization. (p. xv)
   From a theistic perspective, McClaughry has essentially misunderstood Schumacher's critique of secular production processes.
9. For an application to Islamic economics, see El-Ansary (2006). For the specific contributions of Nasr to Islamic economics, see El-Ansary (2003).
10. We also apply these distinctions between the various levels of reality to production processes, drawing out their implications for the debate on whether industrial capitalism is compatible with diverse welfare criteria and for the debate on the definition of economics (El-Ansary 2006).
11. Regarding striving for perfection, Schumacher cites the Biblical injunction: "Be ye therefore perfect, even as your Father which is in heaven is perfect." He also cites: "Whichever

gift each of you have received, use it in service to one another, like good stewards dispensing the grace of God in its varied forms."

12. Some economists adopt this position implicitly by acknowledging the validity of religious beliefs while employing the neoclassical approach to work as "forgone leisure" (Pagano 1985, pp. 111–115). Pagano provides an excellent historical survey of classical and neoclassical approaches to work.

13. Although Georgescu-Roegen provides an excellent history of modern approaches to utility in this article, his interpretation of premodern views is highly debatable.

14. Lionel Robbins forcefully states the contemporary neoclassical position, which began developing with Irving Fisher in his doctoral dissertation in 1892, as follows (Robbins 1962, pp. 83–85):

It is sometimes thought, even at the present day, that [the economic theory of value] . . . depends upon the validity of particular psychological doctrines. The borderlands of Economics are the happy hunting grounds of minds averse to the effort of exact thought, and, in these ambiguous regions, in recent years, endless time has been devoted to attacks on the alleged psychological assumptions of Economic Science. . . .

Unfortunately, in the past, incautious utterances on the part of economists themselves have sometimes afforded a pretext [for such criticism]. . . . It is well known that certain of the founders of the modern subjective theory of value did in fact claim the authority of the doctrines of psychological hedonism as sanctions for their propositions. . . . The names of Gossen and Jevons and Edgeworth, to say nothing of their English followers, are a sufficient reminder of a line of really competent economists who did make pretensions of this sort. . . .

But it is fundamentally important to distinguish between the actual practice of economists, and the logic which it implies, and their occasional ex post facto apologia. It is just this distinction which the critics of Economic Science fail to make. They inspect with supererogatory zeal the external façade, but they shrink from the intellectual labour of examining the inner structure. Nor do they trouble to acquaint themselves with the more recent formulations of the theory they are attacking. . . . No one who was acquainted with recent value theory could honestly continue to argue that it has any essential connection with psychological hedonism, or for that matter with any other brand of Fach-Psychologie.

15. A "heuristic" analytical device makes simplifying assumptions that neither are negligible nor specify a domain of reality, but serves to discover truth (a classic example cited in the philosophy of science literature is Newton's assumption of a single planet in a solar system). For a classic discussion of negligibility, domain, and heuristic assumptions in economic theory see Musgrave (1981).

16. "Bentham, Mill, and Sidgewick all saw utility as having to enter our experience. But we desire things other than states of mind; I might sometimes prefer, say, bitter truth to comforting delusion" (Griffin 1986, p. 13). If one does not prefer "bitter truth to comforting delusion," such egoistic states of mind are not integrated according to the Islamic theory of choice, as we shall see.

17. Although the intelligence can be wrong by the falseness of its content, "then it is wrong as thought and not as knowledge; to speak of a false knowledge would be as absurd as to speak of a blind vision or a dark light" (Schuon 1981a, p. 102).

18. See particularly Naqvi's comments regarding the "allowability constraint." His opening paragraphs on the sacred dimension of all aspects of life are eloquent. But he does not write one word against the neoclassical claim to provide a formal theory of choice, although so much hinges on this claim. The majority of Muslim economists also appear to believe that the standard mono-utility approach can accommodate Islamic values with such constraints. With respect to the mainstream literature, Griffith and Goldfarb (1991) provide an overview of this debate, examining neoclassical attempts to amend the rational egoist model to include norms. The authors suggest that the results

are unsatisfactory, although for reasons that are not based on a hierarchy of spiritual and other needs or the difference between a relation and a function as discussed in this section.

19. At one point, we also espoused the lexicographic approach (Alwani and El-Ansary 1999), which we believe is still preferable to a mono-utility approach.

20. Although the lexicographic approach accommodates divergences between WTA and WTP in its "step-wise" approach to multiple ends, it is for reasons that are completely different from a single end involving multiple use values, since the latter presupposes a hierarchy of levels of reality, as we will discuss shortly. In any case, a mathematical relation may still apply *within* a lexicographic function in the sense that context may still be important for a particular term.

21. Economists generally view lexicographic functions as a mathematical curiosity applicable to peripheral cases such as the preferences of drug addicts.

22. Georgescu-Roegen therefore espouses a lexicographic approach to model the economizing process.

23. Lutz and Lux provide an important critique that is consistent with many elements of religious thought, even dedicating their first book to Schumacher, whom they refer to as "the gentle giant of humanistic economics." They also refer once to Rene Guenon's *The Reign of Quantity and the Signs of the Times* (2001) in light of the reduction of quality to quantity in economics, recommending his book in "A Reader's Guide to the Literature" (Lutz and Lux 1979). However, they appear to be unaware of Guenon's influence on Schumacher, and even place Ruskin and Schumacher, who espouse a theistic approach to economics, in the same group as Sismondi and Hobson, who adopt a nontheistic one. The solutions that Lutz and Lux propose are consequently somewhat syncretic.

24. Georgescu-Roegen argues (1966, pp. 196–197):
    If all wants were reducible [to a composite use value] we could not explain why in any American household water is consumed to the satiety of thirst—and therefore should have a zero "intensity" of utility at that point—while, since water is not used to satiety in sprinkling the lawn, it must have a positive "final degree of utility." Yet, no household would go thirsty—no matter how little—in order to water a flower pot. In other words, if a commodity satisfies several wants, it may very well happen that its "marginal utility" with respect to some wants may be zero (because these wants are completely satisfied) and yet the "utility" of the last unit be not null.

25. Economists like Heyne (1999) argue that needs are nonexistent, because higher prices always lead to lower consumption; that is, abstention or substitution is always possible unless a "demand curve" is vertical, which he calls a "fictional beast." However, substitution between alternatives *within* a need does not imply substitution *between* needs. For example, the ability to substitute rice for potatoes to satisfy one's need for starch when the (relative) price of potatoes increases does not imply that one does not need starch and that one can "wear more shirts" instead.

26. Georgescu-Roegen (1973) even points out that it is not possible to construct a mono-utility function based on the observation of consumer behavior alone, for this requires structuring the data according to *a priori* assumptions.

27. Hobson (see Lutz and Lux 1988, Appendix II) provides vivid examples of the "fallacy of allocation by marginal comparison" in neoclassical theory, ranging from a mother's response to a price increase for medicine required by a sick baby, to an artist's response to a price increase for a pigment for a painting, to charitable contributions. In all such cases, the comparison of marginal utilities is unconvincing and represents a fragmented rather than holistic view. It is important to note that Hobson, a disciple of John Ruskin, did not embrace a theistic approach to economics. Therefore, this critique based on qualitative differences within and between needs and wants is consistent with a broad range of views. Whether or not such views are internally consistent is a separate philosophical issue.

28. Khan combines the lexicographic and mono-utility approaches in the following sequence of choices: (1) "spending for worldly needs" versus "spending for the cause of Allah" using a mono-utility approach; (2) "future consumption" versus "present consumption" using a mono-utility approach; (3) consumption of "essentials" (*daruriyyat*), "complements" (*hajiyyat*), and "improvements to essentials" (*tahsiniyyat*) using a lexicographic approach; and (4) various substitutes within a particular end in a lexicographic function.

29. On the rare occasions the literature employs a multi-utility framework, it is always a lexicographic approach. Although some critics of neoclassical theory recognize the problems of conflating needs and wants, equating WTA and WTP, and so on, none has proposed an analytical solution corresponding to the Islamic point of view. In addition to the previous references, see, for instance, Etzioni (1986). Perhaps the most advanced critique that falls short of properly specifying a multi-utility relation is the work on law and economics by Finnis (1990a, 1990b, 1990c) (although his approach also introduces some questionable philosophical presuppositions, according to some theistic philosophers).

30. A multi-utility relation is obviously important when risk and uncertainty are unevenly distributed (e.g., when the *material* costs and benefits of actions are more uncertain than the corresponding *moral* costs and benefits). Ruskin maintains this is always the case (1968, pp. 117–118):

   [T]*he variety of circumstance which influence . . . reciprocal interests are so endless, that all endeavour to deduce rules of action from balance of expediency is in vain. And it is meant to be in vain. For no human actions ever were intended by the Maker of men to be guided by balances of expediency, but by balances of justice. He has therefore rendered all endeavours to determine expediency futile for evermore. No man ever knew, or can know, what will be the ultimate result to himself, or to others, of any given line of conduct. But every man may know, and most of us do know, what is a just and unjust act.*

   But the first step to any modification of economic theory is an alternative analytical tool for choices under certainty.

31. Although many Muslims, Christians, or other theists may not have internally consistent preferences, this does not imply that preferences are inconsistent *because* of spiritual values. We will return to this issue shortly.

32. The relativist assertion that the intelligence is incapable of objective knowledge is also self-contradictory (Schuon 1984).

33. The satisfaction of desire criterion is still subjective, however, because desirability defines goodness rather than goodness defining desirability (which may be appropriate for tastes, not for values, since the former are not subject to criticism and are unmodified by understanding). Even if people's preferences are based on false beliefs, the satisfaction of desire account of welfare requires that they be fulfilled. Hausman argues (Hausman and McPherson 1996, p. 76), "The only consistent ways out of this impasse are either to follow people's preferences, even if they depend upon beliefs that are false and unreasonable, or to employ some substantive theory of welfare." Thus, although the satisfaction of desire account "severs the link between 'fulfillment of desire' and the requirement that the person in some way experience its fulfillment," it does not rule out egoistic or illusory desires, just like the mental state account. Truth is still subordinate to utility. The satisfaction of desire is therefore not neutral as *the* criterion of *welfare* (although it can be neutral in a theory of *choice* if one drops the continuity axiom). Indeed, the criterion is self-defeating, denying preferences their authority by subordinating truth to utility while feeding off of them.

34. As Hausman points out (Hausman and McPherson 1996, p. 74), "Economists often slide from talking about utility to talking about happiness. Economists often talk about individuals 'seeking' utility, which makes no sense if utility is just a measure of the extent

to which preferences are satisfied." Moreover, talk of "moving to the highest indifference curve" makes "the temptation to equate utility and welfare . . . seemingly irresistible" (p. 117). Although some philosophers have attempted to modify state of mind accounts with "qualitative hedonism" and state of world accounts with "informed desires," a mono-utility function cannot support such qualitative distinctions. In any case, the debate over whether such nontheistic attempts avoid subordinating truth to utility is irrelevant if the difference between the physical and corporeal corresponds to the nature of reality, as we shall see.

35. John Colls, a former disciple of Bentham who turned against him, described Bentham's volumes on religion as "volumes of blasphemy and slander . . . against the Author of Christianity and His people" (Crimmins 1990, p. 148).

36. This aspect of Bentham's will is available online at www.ucl.ac.uk/Bentham-Project/info/will.htm.

37. Schuon explains the necessary connection between metaphysical truth and virtue as follows (1987, p. 183):
A spiritual virtue is nothing other than consciousness of a reality. It is natural—but immaterial—if it is accompanied by feeling. . . The key to understanding the spiritual necessity of the virtues is that metaphysical truths are also reflected in the will and not only in the intellect and reason. To a given principal truth there corresponds a volitional attitude. This is a necessary aspect—or a consequence—of the principle that "to know is to be."

In an Islamic context, Nasr (2004) explains the relationship between Truth (*al-Haqq*) and truth (*al-haqīqah*): "*Haqīqah* means truth as it is grasped, [and] *al-Haqq* is the Name of God which is associated with that truth."

38. See Part II of Schuon (1981a) for an incomparable exposition of this issue.

39. From this point of view, the alleged conflict between the "right" and the "good" in contemporary moral philosophy is a "false problem" resulting from an antimetaphysical approach in "desire-ethics" such as utilitarianism and "duty-ethics" such as deontological ethics. For an excellent refutation of both, see, for instance, Veatch (1971, 1985).

40. Michael Novak, a leading Catholic thinker who espouses much neoclassical dogma, even criticizes theologians for their supposedly ill-founded suspicions about economic theory (Novak 1985). He states (pp. 567–568):
Two words which cause theologians particular trouble in discussing the liberal tradition in economics are "self-interest" and "acquisitiveness." . . . When an economist uses these words, he means "autonomous choice." He says nothing at all about the moral content of that choice; in the eyes of the economist, that frame is deliberately kept empty. Self-interest means whatever a person has chosen, whether it is sanctity or truth, pleasure or material benefit. The concept is as general and empty as possible, in order to be universalizable.
But the global application of the continuity axiom proves Novak wrong and the supposedly ill-founded reservations of others right.

41. Mill espoused the unity of method between the sciences, because he believed that the natural and moral sciences are on a continuum in which there is no fundamental shift in outlook, only increasingly complex data. Mill (1984) cites Newtonian mechanics as the model for economics and the premier example of a science based on "composite" causes, or causes in which the order does not matter to predict the effect (e.g., the effect is the same whether the causes occur simultaneously or sequentially). Unlike "combination" causes, in which the effect is sensitive to causal order, composite causes may be examined separately, "one at a time" (p. 53). The resulting aggregate is quantitative and reducible to a sum of parts, an object for "analysis" in which no *a priori* vision of the whole is necessary, for there are no qualitative differences to integrate.

42. According to Mill (pp. 53–54), economic analysis dealt with the main cause of greed, and other sciences dealt with the "disturbing causes," because he defined each science according to a specific cause and each art according to desired effects. The *art of*

economic policy therefore drew on many sciences in addition to economics to incorpo-rate different disturbance terms. *Classical* economics was thus a "separate but inexact" science. Neoclassical economists would later import the approach of the *art* of economic policy making into the *science* of economics itself, apparently introducing the ability to incorporate the disturbance terms directly with mono-utility functions for *any* choice. For an excellent analysis of Mill's economic thought, see, for instance, Hausman (1992). In this regard, we believe that Mirowski goes too far when he claims that (1984, p. 365) "recourse to the history of mathematics and physics shows that the characterization of neoclassical economics as 'Newtonian' is both inept and misleading." Mono-utility functions clearly have a basis in Newtonian mechanics based on Mill's analogy, not just nineteenth-century physics. Although the difference between these two phases of pre-quantum physics helps to explain the expanded role of mono-utility functions in neoclassical theory, Newton's bifurcationist metaphysics is the necessary condition for both, and Mirowski underestimates this aspect of continuity between these phases of pre-quantum mechanics from an Islamic perspective. Indeed, the reduction of quality to quantity in the secular natural sciences implies production and exchange processes common to both classical and neoclassical thought. Thus, we believe that Mirowski also underestimates the continuity and overestimates the discontinuity between these phases of economic thought despite his admirable scholarship.

43. Ruskin states this objection in the opening paragraph of his renowned *Unto This Last* (1938, p. 115): "The social affections," says the economist, "are accidental and disturbing elements in human nature; but avarice and the desire of progress are constant elements. Let us eliminate the inconstants, and, considering the human being merely as a covetous machine, examine by what laws of labour, purchase, and sale, the greatest accumulative result in wealth is attainable. Those laws once determined, it will be for each indi-vidual afterwards to introduce as much of the disturbing affectionate element as he chooses. . . ."

    This would be a perfectly logical and successful method of analysis, if the accidentals afterwards to be introduced were of the same nature as the powers first examined. . . . But the disturbing elements in the social problem are not of the same nature as the constant ones; they alter the essence of the creature under examination the moment they are added; they operate, not mathematically, but chemically, introducing conditions which render all our previous knowledge unavailable.

44. Ruskin gives the following more diplomatic assessment of Mill in another passage (see Clark and Wedderburn 1903–1912, vol. 17, p. 478): "Mr. J. S. Mill is assuredly strong in some directions of thought, and entirely, by his nature, shut out from following others."

45. For an introduction to Ruskin's economic thought, see, for instance, Fain (1956).

46. However, Ruskin did not explicitly clarify the hierarchic methodology for this in which the senses occupy the lowest realm, reason and other faculties of the soul the interme-diate realm, and the intellect (as used in its original sense), or "eye of the heart," the highest level. As Nasr explains (1999, pp. 200–201):
    [T]he faculty of intellection symbolized by "the eye of the heart" . . . "sees" the spiritual world in a direct manner much like the physical eye which possesses the same power in the sensible world and in opposition to the faculty of reason which functions discursively and "knows" indirectly.

    It is important to emphasize that knowledge based on the intellect does not imply "non-verifiable . . . truth claims," as some (Aminrazavi 2000, p. 555) allege. Nasr (2000) responds to this charge in the same volume. For a synthesis of the traditional doctrine of the intellect pertaining to epistemology, see, for instance, Schuon (1981b, pp. 5–35). For a detailed examination of this in the context of the traditional sciences of nature, see, for instance, Nasr (1996).

47. Other thinkers such as Dilthey can be understood as taking an intermediate position on this spectrum, asserting unity of method *within* the natural sciences but not *between*

them and the human sciences. "Methodological anarchists" deny the unity of method as such, asserting plurality without hierarchy.

48. For a profound critique of secular methodological positions, see, for instance, Schuon (1984). For a remarkable discussion of the Islamic response to secular approaches to science, see Nasr (1996, 2000). For a discussion of secular approaches to the philosophy of science in relation to economics, see, for instance, Redman (1991).

49. Smith points out (1984, p. 15) that Newton was wrong in claiming in the *Principia* that we "justly infer the hardness of the undivided particles," because "the hardness of the whole arises from the hardness of the parts." Smith cites Schroedinger that "we have been compelled to dismiss the idea that such a particle is an individual entity which in principle retains its 'sameness' forever. Quite the contrary, we are now obliged to assert that the ultimate constituents of matter have no 'sameness' at all" (pp. 50–51). Because the idea that neither the atom nor the fundamental particles into which it can be decomposed have a true self-identity may be difficult to conceive, Schroedinger puts it in even more emphatic terms as follows:

And I beg to emphasize this, and I beg you to believe it: It is not a question of our being able to ascertain the identity in some instances and not being able to do so in others. It is beyond doubt that the question of "sameness," of identity, really and truly has no meaning.

However, a "totalist" physics that claims to be the complete explanation of the totality of the physical world "without residue" is obliged to accept bifurcation, almost as a "necessary evil" one might say (Smith 1995, p. 12).

50. Smith defines bifurcation (1995, p. 137) as the "Cartesian tenet which affirms that the perceptual object is private or merely subjective. The idea of bifurcation goes hand-in-hand with the assumption that the external world is characterized exclusively by quantities and mathematical structure. According to this view, all qualities (such as color) exist only in the mind of the percipient."

51. Bifurcation also poses major problems for philosophy, which Smith illustrates as follows (2000, p. 473):

The red apple which we do perceive . . . has become relegated to a private phantasm, a mental as distinguished from a real entity. This postulate, moreover, demands another: one is now forced— on pain of radical subjectivism—to assume that the red apple, which is unreal, is causally related to a real apple, which, however, is not perceptible. . . . [What] was one object has now become two; as Whitehead puts it: "One is the conjecture, and the other is the dream."

Smith argues (1995, pp. 10–12) that there are no possible grounds for proving bifurcation, for "if the dogma of bifurcation were true, then the corresponding 'two object' theory of perception would *ipso facto* be unverifiable, for the obvious reason that there would be no way of ever finding out whether the external object exists, let alone whether it is geometrically similar to the perceptual." Accordingly, "The 'two object' theory of perception, no less than the bifurcationist tenet on which it rests, constitutes . . . a metaphysical premise which can neither be verified nor falsified by any empirical or scientific means." In short, "No real philosophic advantage . . . results from the postulate of bifurcation, which is to say that the totalist claims of physics need in any case to be relinquished: In a word, not everything without exception can be understood or explained exclusively in quantitative terms."

52. As Smith explains (1995, p. 139), physicists define such potentiality in terms of the "state-vector," or "the mathematical entity which represents the state of a physical system in the formalism of quantum theory." The act of measurement itself causes the state-vector to "collapse" to an actual value from this range of potential values.

53. Economists often argue that individuals must have consistent preferences in the long run because of "survival of the fittest"—those with rational preferences will exploit those with irrational preferences until only rational actors remain. Yet, Hodgson shows that "survival of the fittest" applies only to firms, arguing that (1993, p. 41):

it is more difficult to attach such a notion to the supposedly "rational" consumer, as "non-rational" consumers do not go extinct in the same way. If "non-rationality" simply means inconsistent preferences, there is no obvious reason to assume a "rational" consumer will have a superior survival value in socio-economic evolution.

    This neoclassical argument on "survival of the fittest" clearly cannot account for empirical evidence suggesting the pervasiveness of intransitive preferences. As May (1954) points out, the evidence from several sources demonstrates that "intransitivity is a natural result of the necessity of choosing among alternatives according to conflicting criteria . . . the question is no longer 'Are preferences transitive?', but rather 'Under what conditions does transitivity fail?'" We examine this issue further in El-Ansary (2006). According to the Islamic view, if the only people to survive were those with integrated preferences, the world would contain only saints.

54. Nasr (2004) elucidates this point with the following example:
    Take the human being. It is composed of body, soul and spirit. There is no way you can integrate the body without the presence of the soul. That is why, when the soul departs, the body falls apart into dust. And this remarkable, integrated functioning of various parts of our body is one of the greatest miracles to which we pay very little attention. . . . The same is true for the soul. Our souls are scattered, like particles flowing out of the centre, and we live in a scattered world. The common everyday English usage of the words "scatter brain" reflects the fact that in a sense the mind is "scattered." There is absolutely no way to integrate it without the presence of the spirit. It is only the spirit that is able to integrate the psyche. The vital principle that is integration not only relates to God as the Supreme Reality, but to every level of reality down to the . . . world in which we live. Therefore, to really talk about integration, you must accept the vertical dimension of reality. The reason that we cannot integrate anything in our world is because of the eclipse of a knowledge of that vertical dimension.

55. As noted earlier, in philosophical terms, the "unity" required for consistency and the "uniformity" required for continuity are polar opposites. The former is associated with infinite quality whereas the latter is pure quantity.

56. Market imperfections include, for example, "asymmetric information" in which differences in the amount of information each party has can lead to exploitation, and "negative externalities" in which noncontracting third parties are harmed, such as pollution.

57. As noted earlier, the behavioral economic analysis of religious law is interesting, but not fully consistent with these arguments if the analysis neglects a multi-utility relation while assuming that a mono-utility function is rational.

58. We critique the Coase theorem and cost-benefit analysis from an Islamic perspective in Part II of El-Ansary (2006).

59. This is most obvious in the case of non-self-enforcing markets as opposed to on-the-spot exchange. For an interesting survey and taxonomy of views on the effects of markets on society, see, for instance, Hirschman (1986, ch. 5). For a theistic view of this issue, see, for instance, Lindbom (1982).

60. Analogous arguments apply to industrial production processes with all this implies for the theory of exchange. The Islamic critique of the secular philosophy of science therefore integrates the critique of the analytical tools of neoclassical theory, freedom of contract, and industrial capitalism.

REFERENCES

Alwani, Taha Jabir, and Waleed El-Ansary. 1999. *Linking Ethics and Economics: The Role of Ijtihād in the Regulation and Correction of Capital Markets.* Washington, DC: Georgetown University, Center for Muslim-Christian Understanding.

Aminrazavi, Mehdi. 2000. "*Philosophia perennis* and *Scientia sacra* in a postmodern world." In Randall Auxier, Lucian W. Stone, and Lewis Edwin Hahn, eds. *The Philosophy of Seyyed Hossein Nasr (Library of Living Philosophers)*, 551–562. Chicago: Open Court Publishing.

Boulding, Kenneth, Walter Block, Geoffrey Brennan, and Kenneth Elzinga, eds. 1985. *Morality of the Market: Religious and Economic Perspectives*. Vancouver, B.C.: Fraser Institute.

Clark, Edward T., and Alexander Wedderburn, eds. 1903–1912. *The Works of John Ruskin*. London: George Allen.

Coase, Ronald H. 1960. "The Problem of Social Cost." *Journal of Law and Economics* 3, October, 1–44.

Coomaraswamy, Rama. 1999. "Psychological Integration and the Religious Outlook." *Sacred Web* 3, June. Also available online at www.coomaraswamy-catholic-writings.com/articles.htm.

Crimmins, James. 1990. *Secular Utilitarianism: Social Science and the Critique of Religion in the Thought of Jeremy Bentham*. Oxford: Clarendon Press.

Edgeworth, Francis Y. 1881. *Mathematical Psychics: An Essay on the Application of Mathematics to the Moral Sciences*. London: C.K. Paul.

El-Ansary, Waleed. 2003. "Islamic economics and the sciences of nature: The contribution of Seyyed Hossein Nasr." In Mohammad Faghfoory, ed. *Beacon of Knowledge: Essays in Honor of Seyyed Hossein Nasr*, 491–520. Louisville, KY: Fons Vitae.

———. 2006. *The Spiritual Significance of Jihād in the Islamic Approach to Markets and the Environment*. Washington, DC: George Washington University.

———. 2011. "Linking ethics and economics: Integral development and the three dimensions of Islam." In Catherine Cornille and Glenn Willis, eds. *The World Market and Interreligious Dialogue*. Eugene, OR: Cascade Books.

———. 2013. *Not by Bread Alone: Lectures by E. F. Schumacher*. Bloomington, IN: World Wisdom Books (forthcoming).

El-Gamal, Mahmoud. 2006. *Islamic Finance: Law, Economics and Practice*. New York: Cambridge University Press.

Etzioni, Amatai. 1986. "The Case for a Multiple Utility Conception." *Economics and Philosophy*, 2, Fall, 159–183.

Fain, John T. 1956. *Ruskin and the Economists*. Nashville, TN: Vanderbilt University Press.

Finnis, John. 1990a. "Allocating Risks and Suffering Some Hidden Traps." *Cleveland State Law Review* 38:1, 193–207.

———. 1990b. "Concluding Reflections." *Cleveland State Law Review* 38:1, 231–250.

———. 1990c. "Natural Law and Legal Reasoning." *Cleveland State Law Review* 38:1, 1–15.

Fitzgibbons, Athol. 1995. *Adam Smith's System of Liberty, Wealth, and Virtue: The Moral Foundations of The Wealth of Nations*. Oxford: Clarendon Press.

Georgescu-Roegen, Nicholas. 1966. *Analytical Economics*. Cambridge, MA: Harvard University Press.

———. 1973. "Utility and value in economic thought." In Philip P. Weiner, ed. *Dictionary of the History of Ideas* (vol. 4), 450–458. New York: Scribners.

Griffin, James. 1986. *Well-Being*. Oxford: Oxford University Press.

Griffith, William, and Robert Goldfarb. 1991. "Can the rational egoist model be expanded to include norms?" In Kenneth Koford and Jeffrey Miller, eds. *Social Norms and Economic Institutions*, 39–84. Ann Arbor: University of Michigan Press.

Guenon, Rene. 2001. *The Reign of Quantity and the Signs of the Times*. Ghent, NY: Sophia Perennis.

Hausman, Daniel. 1992. *The Inexact and Separate Science of Economics*. Cambridge: Cambridge University Press.

Hausman, Daniel, and Michael McPherson. 1996. *Economic Analysis and Moral Philosophy*. Cambridge: Cambridge University Press.

Heap, Shaun Hargreaves, Martin Hollis, Bruce Lyons, Robert Sugden, and Albert Weale. 1994. *The Theory of Choice: A Critical Guide*. Oxford: Blackwell Publishers.

Heyne, Paul. 1999. *The Economic Way of Thinking*. Upper Saddle River, NJ: Prentice Hall.

———. 2000. *A Student's Guide to Economics*. Wilmington, DE: ISI Books. Online at www.isi.org/college_guide/student_guides/econ.pdf.

Hirschman, Albert. 1986. *Rival Views of Market Society and Other Recent Essays*. New York: Viking Penguin.

Hodgson, Geoffrey. 1993. "Calculation, habits and action." In Bill Gerrard, ed. *The Economics of Rationality*, 36–51. London: Routledge.

Keeble, Brian. 1998. *Art: For Whom and For What?* Ipswich, UK: Golgonooza Press.

Khan, M. Fahim. 1995. *Essays in Islamic Economics*. Leicester, UK: Islamic Foundation.

Lindbom, Tage. 1982. *The Tares and the Good Grain*. Macon, GA: Mercer University Press.

Lutz, Mark, and Kenneth Lux. 1979. *The Challenge of Humanistic Economics*. Menlo Park, CA: Benjamin/Cummings Publishing Company.

———. 1988. *Humanistic Economics: The New Challenge*. New York: Bootstrap Press.

Machan, Tibor. 1995. "Reason in Economics versus Ethics." *International Journal of Social Economics*, 22:7, 19–37.

Mas-Colell, Andreu, Michael Whinston, and Jerry Green. 1995. *Microeconomic Theory*. New York: Oxford University Press.

May, Kenneth. 1954. "Intransitivity, Utility, and the Aggregation of Preference Patterns." *Econometrica*, 22:1, January, 1–41.

Meikle, Scott. 1995. *Aristotle's Economic Thought*. Oxford: Oxford University Press.

Mill, John Stuart. 1984. "On the definition and method of political economy." In Daniel Hausman, ed. *The Philosophy of Economics: An Anthology*, 52–69. Cambridge: Cambridge University Press.

Mirowski, Philip. 1984. "Physics and the Marginal Revolution." *Cambridge Journal of Economics*, 361–379.

Musgrave, Alan. 1981. "'Unrealistic Assumptions' in Economic Theory: The F-Twist Untwisted." *Kyklos* 34:377–387.

Naqvi, Syed Haider. 1981. *Ethics and Economics: An Islamic Synthesis*. Leicester, UK: Islamic Foundation.

Nasr, Seyyed Hossein. 1982. "Review of *Ethics and Economics—An Islamic Synthesis*." *Hamdard Islamicus*, 109, Summer, 89–92.

———. 1987. *Islamic Art and Spirituality*. Albany: State University of New York Press.

———. 1994. *Ideals and Realities of Islam*. London: Allen & Unwin.

———. 1996. *Religion and the Order of Nature*. Oxford: Oxford University Press.

———. 1997. "Perennial Ontology and Quantum Mechanics: A Review Essay of Wolfgang Smith's *The Quantum Enigma: Finding the Hidden Key*." *Sophia: A Journal of Traditional Studies*, 3:1, Summer, 137–159.

———. 1999. *Islamic Life and Thought*. Lahore, Pakistan: Suhail Academy.

———. 2000. "Reply to Mehdi Aminrazavi." In Randall Auxier, Lucian W. Stone, and Lewis Edwin Hahn, eds. *The Philosophy of Seyyed Hossein Nasr (Library of Living Philosophers)*, 563–570. Chicago: Open Court Publishing.

———. 2004. "Sufism and the Integration of the Inner and Outer Life of Man." Singhvi Lecture. London: Temenos Academy.

———. 2006. *Islamic Philosophy: An Introductory Survey, Philosophy in the Land of Prophecy*. New York: State University of New York Press.

Novak, Michael. 1982. *The Spirit of Democratic Capitalism*. New York: Simon & Schuster.

———. 1985. "Overview." In Kenneth Boulding, Walter Block, Geoffrey Brennan, and Kenneth Elzinga, eds. *Morality of the Market: Religious and Economic Perspectives*. Vancouver, B.C.: Fraser Institute.

Pagano, Ugo. 1985. *Work and Welfare in Economic Theory*. Oxford: Basil Blackwell.

Redman, Deborah. 1991. *Economics and the Philosophy of Science*. New York: Oxford University Press.

Robbins, Lionel. 1962. *An Essay on the Nature and Significance of Economic Science.* New York: St. Martin's Press.

Rosenberg, John. 1961. *Darkening Glass: A Portrait of Ruskin's Genius.* New York: Columbia University Press.

Ruskin, John. 1938. *Unto This Last and Other Essays.* New York: E.P. Dutton.

———. 1968. *Unto This Last, The Political Economy of Art, and Essays on Political Economy.* New York: Everyman's Library.

Schumacher, E. F. 1979. *Good Work.* New York: Harper & Row.

———. 1989. *Small Is Beautiful.* New York: Harper & Row.

———. 1997. *This I Believe.* Foxhole, Dartington: Green Books, Ltd.

Schuon, Frithjof. 1981a. *Esoterism as Principle and as Way.* Middlesex: Perennial Books.

———. 1981b. *From the Divine to the Human.* Bloomington, IN: World Wisdom Books.

———. 1984. *Logic and Transcendence.* Middlesex: Perennial Books.

———. 1987. *Spiritual Perspectives and Human Facts.* Middlesex: Perennial Books.

———. 1992. *The Play of Masks.* Bloomington, IN: World Wisdom Books.

Smith, Wolfgang. 1984. *Cosmos and Transcendence: Breaking Through the Barrier of Scientistic Belief.* Peru, IL: Sherwood Sugden & Co.

———. 1995. *The Quantum Enigma: Finding the Hidden Key.* Peru, IL: Sherwood Sugden & Co.

———. 2000. "*Sophia perennis* and modern science." In Randall Auxier, Lucian W. Stone, and Lewis Edwin Hahn, eds. *The Philosophy of Seyyed Hossein Nasr (Library of Living Philosophers)*, 469–492. Chicago: Open Court Publishing.

———. 2003. *The Wisdom of Ancient Cosmology: Contemporary Science in Light of Tradition.* Herndon: Foundation for Traditional Studies.

Tūsī, Nasīr al-Dīn. 1964. *The Nasirean Ethics.* G. M. Wickens, tr. London: G. Allen & Unwin.

Veatch, Henry. 1971. *For an Ontology of Morals: A Critique of Contemporary Ethical Theory.* Evanston, IL: Northwestern University Press.

———. 1985. *Human Rights: Fact or Fancy?* Baton Rouge: Louisiana State University Press.

Wilson, Fred. 1990. *Psychological Analysis and the Philosophy of John Stuart Mill.* Toronto: University of Toronto Press.

CHAPTER 6

Juristic Disagreement

The Collective Fatwā Against Islamic Banking in Pakistan

SHOAIB A. GHIAS
J.D., Ph.D. candidate
University of California, Berkeley, School of Law

INTRODUCTION

Over the past two decades, several Islamic financial institutions have been established across the world. Many of these institutions are under the shar'ī supervision of Muftī Muḥammad Taqī 'Uthmānī (b. 1943), who is considered the architect of modern Islamic banking and finance.[1] 'Uthmānī is a Ḥanafī jurist (muftī), former scholar-judge of the Supreme Court of Pakistan, and the vice president of Dār al-'Ulūm, Karachi (est. 1951)—the most prominent Deobandi seminary in Pakistan.[2] He is often called the muftī-i a'ẓam (the grand jurist) by the Deobandi scholars in Pakistan.

In 2008, a group of Deobandi scholars issued a collective fatwā against 'Uthmānī's model of Islamic banks. The intellectual force behind the fatwā comes from the jurists at Jāmi'a 'Ulūm-i Islāmiyya, Banūrī Town (est. 1954)—another very prominent Deobandi seminary. But as the jurists at Banūrī Town are considered junior to 'Uthmānī, the fatwā's leadership comes from Jāmi'a Fārūqiyya's (est. 1967) founder, Mawlānā Salīmullah Khān (b. 1926),[3] who is among 'Uthmānī's few living teachers.[4] In the traditional system of religious knowledge and authority, where a teacher commands great respect and deference, Khān's role has particular symbolic importance in the fatwā against his former student's Islamic banking model. Moreover, Khān is the president of Wifāq al-Madāris al-'Arabiyya, the Deobandi board of education.[5] In the absence of formal hierarchical institutions among Deobandis, his position in the board of education is another symbolic aspect in the fatwā's authority.

Objections to 'Uthmānī's work on Islamic banking in Pakistan can be traced to the provocatively titled *al-Radd al-Fiqhī 'alā Justice Muḥammad Taqī* (*The Juridical Rebuttal against Justice Muhammad Taqi*) by Muftī Ḥabībullah Shaykh, the chair of ḥadīth studies at Jāmi'a Islāmiyya, Karachi.[6] The book was a response to 'Uthmānī's 1994 book, *Islām awr Jadīd Ma'īshat wa Tijārat* (*Islam and the Modern Economy and Commerce*), where he laid the groundwork for modern Islamic banking.[7] As Islamic banks expanded in Pakistan during early 2000s, Mawlānā Salīmullah Khān issued a circular to some Deobandi scholars to evaluate the contemporary Islamic banking practices.[8] Finally, on August 28, 2008, a conference was convened to issue the collective fatwā against Islamic banking.

In response to the collective fatwā, ʿUthmānī gave a fatwā that his former fatwās on Islamic banking stand in the absence of concrete arguments from the opposing side.[9] Shortly afterward, Banūrī Town published an article outlining the arguments for the fatwā against Islamic banking in its magazine *Bayyināt* (translated here),[10] and later wrote the book *Murawwaja Islāmī Baynkārī* (*Existing Islamic Banking*) to substantiate these arguments from Ḥanafī fiqh.[11] Since then, ʿUthmānī has authored *Ghayr Sūdī Baynkārī* (*Interest-Free Banking*) in response to Banūrī Town's objections.[12] Some of his supporters have also produced books to defend ʿUthmānī's fiqhī positions[13] and scholarly rank.[14] Whether ʿUthmānī's defense has satisfied the Deobandi critics of Islamic banking in Pakistan remains to be seen.

The Banūrī Town scholars have termed the collective fatwā against Islamic banking muttafiqa (collectively agreed upon) and jamhūrī (majority opinion), whereas ʿUthmānī's supporters have called the fatwā ikhtilāfī (dissenting opinion).[15] But such claims are difficult to assess in the absence of an objective method to measure the prestige and number of scholars on each side. Since the controversy, the mother seminary of the Deoband movement, Dār al-ʿUlūm, Deoband in India,[16] has issued a fatwā placing faith in ʿUthmānī's ability to address matters of Islamic fiqh and finance but not responding to the collective fatwā's substance. However, the Deobandi group Majlis al-ʿUlamā of South Africa has taken a strong position against ʿUthmānī's work on Islamic finance.[17]

While the collective fatwā deals with Islamic banking in Pakistan, the debate has implications for the Islamic finance industry beyond Pakistan. ʿUthmānī (chairman of the sharīʿa board, Guidance Residential; former chairman, Dow Jones Islamic Markets Index); his son Muftī ʿImrān Ashraf ʿUthmānī (member of the sharīʿa board, Guidance Residential); and the (American) Deobandi scholar Shaykh Yūsuf Ṭalāl DeLorenzo (member of the sharīʿa board, Dow Jones Islamic Markets Index) have played an important role in developing Islamic finance in the West. Interestingly, Shaykh DeLorenzo was educated at Banūrī Town and was among the students of Muḥaddith al-ʿAṣr Mawlānā Muḥammad Yūsuf Banūrī (d. 1977), the founder and eponym of Banūrī Town. In fact, both Dārul ʿUlūm and Banūrī Town claim the legacy of the late Mawlānā Banūrī in the present debate.[18]

Arguments, Style, and Scope

The critics of Islamic banking have often argued that Islamic banking holds on to Islamic contractual forms at the expense of ignoring Islamic economic substance.[19] But the collective fatwā against Islamic banking is premised on the inherent interdependence between form and substance in fiqh. The fatwā's basic argument is that Islamic banking does not have Islamic substance because it has deviated from Islamic legal forms. The fatwā may not be conclusive but it represents the liveliness and diversity of the intellectual debate on Islamic finance among scholars.

The fatwā's arguments are divided into two "reasons" or parts: The first part argues that even Islamic bankers, ʿUthmānī, and other intellectuals agree that existing Islamic banks are not following the theoretical foundations of modern Islamic finance. The second part argues that even the theoretical foundations of

Exhibit 6.1 Subject Matter of the Collective Fatwa's Objections

First Reason	Second Reason
Testimonials of 1. Bankers 2. Uthmānī 3. Intellectuals	1. Principles of Jurisprudence 2. Existing Murābaha and Ijāra as Stratagems 3. Existing Murābaha versus Fiqhī Murābaha 4. Agency in Murābaha 5. Ijāra for Purchase Finance 6. Benchmarking Rent to Market Interest Rate 7. Forced Charity as Penalty 8. Security Deposits 9. The Scope of Equity-Based Financing 10. Unilateral Amendments in Contracts 11. Dealing with the State Bank's Regulations 12. Service Fees in Muḍāraba Accounts 13. Allocation of Profit in Shirka and Muḍāraba 14. Diminishing Partnership 15. Corporate Personality of Banks 16. Interest-Based Elements in Banks

modern Islamic finance—devised by 'Uthmānī—violate the rules and principles of Ḥanafī fiqh. The objections cover 'Uthmānī's principles of jurisprudence as applied to aspects of modern Islamic banking (see Exhibit 6.1). According to the fatwā, 'Uthmānī has disfigured technical concepts, used weak (ḍaʿīf) and inaccurate (marjūḥ) opinions, engaged in talfīq muḥarram (unacceptable patchwork of doctrines from different schools),[20] and deliberately ignored correct (ṣaḥīḥ), explicit (ṣarīḥ), and clear (wāḍiḥ) rules. These arguments are elaborated at length in Banūrī Town's book *Murawwaja Islāmī Baynkārī* (*Existing Islamic Banking*).[21]

In a demonstration of the rhetorical style of the 'ulamā's internal discourse, the Banūrī Town jurists address 'Uthmānī with honorific terms such as ḥaḍrat (great presence), mawlānā (our lord), makhdūm al-'ulamā (master of scholars), and muftī-i aʿẓam (the grand jurist), and with prayers for long life such as dāmat barakātahu (may his blessings endure) and madda ẓillahu (my his shadow extend) while arguing in the same sentence that his jurisprudence is fundamentally flawed. Noticing the sarcasm embedded in the respectful terms, 'Uthmānī responds in *Ghayr Sūdī Baynkārī* with equally effective style, saying that "when, for some reason, the minds of these *young scholars* become certain about an *aged student* that after studying fiqh for half a century he is unaware of even the basic principles, and he will have to be taught those things about fiqh and uṣūl-i fiqh that even a fourth or fifth level student knows, then it is not surprising [for them] to get angry. And it is their grace if, as a concession for the addressed's age, they cover the anger with the curtain of honorifics and respect, and only rely on using metaphors, saying things between the lines, and employing satire."[22] (Emphasis mine.)

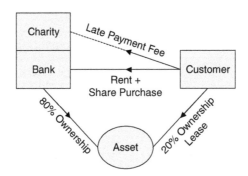

Exhibit 6.2 Diminishing Partnership for Home Financing

To understand some of the fatwā's substantive concerns, consider a diminishing partnership structure (shirka mutanāqiṣa) used in Islamic banks for home finance.[23] In the diminishing partnership structure, the customer and the bank jointly purchase the property. Instead of agreeing to pay interest on principal as in conventional finance, the customer makes an enforceable promise to lease the property and pay rent to the bank proportional to the bank's share of ownership. However, the rent is calculated based on the interest rate benchmark, for example the Karachi Interbank Offered Rate (KIBOR), plus some margin. Furthermore, instead of agreeing to pay back the principal to the bank, the customer makes an enforceable promise to purchase the bank's share over time. Last, instead of agreeing to pay late payment fees to the bank, the customer makes an enforceable promise to undertake charity in case of late payments. Exhibit 6.2 illustrates this transaction.

According to the collective fatwā's arguments, there are several problems with this transaction. First, the joint ownership is conditional upon the lease, the periodic purchase of the bank's share, and the charity undertaking, all of which violates the fiqhī rules for conditional sale (second reason, part 14). Second, the rent is benchmarked to the conventional interest rate, which is similar to ribā and therefore comes under the fiqhī rule for ribā (second reason, part 6). Third, the enforceable promise to undertake charity is not charity but forced payments for the bank's purpose and is therefore analogous to ribā (second reason, part 7).[24]

Note on Translation

I have translated Banūrī Town's article in *Bayyināt* consisting of the fatwā and its arguments against Islamic banking. I have also translated Dār al-ʿUlūm, Deoband's fatwā from India and a collective statement from Pakistan both endorsing ʿUthmānī's work. Rendering the fatwās and the article's rhetorical Urdu prose with Persian and Arabic legal terms and phrases into English can be challenging. I have mostly retained the prose's rhetorical flavor to convey the colorful descriptions despite some awkward English sentence structures. But occasionally I have also used simpler English to render the meaning more clearly. I have included a glossary of translated and untranslated terms at the end. Since there is often objections to translating ribā or sūd into "interest," I have generally included the original term in parentheses. I have also inserted subject headings in some places, and added explanatory terms within square brackets.

TRANSLATION: EXISTING ISLAMIC BANKING AND THE OUTLINE OF THE POSITION OF THE MAJORITY OF 'ULAMĀ[25]

The majority of jurists in the country declare existing banking associated with Islam to be against sharī'a. To collectively express this opinion, a conference of famous and well-known jurists from the country's four provinces was conducted on 25 Sha'bān al-Mu'aẓẓam in Jāmi'a Fārūqiyya, Shah Faisal Colony, Karachi, under the chairmanship of Shaykh al-Mashā'ikh (elder of learned elders), Ustādh al-'Ulamā wa al-Muftīyyīn (teacher of scholars and jurists), Ḥaḍrat Shaykh al-Ḥadīth Mawlānā Salīmullah Khān – may his blessings endure. A brief summary of the position on existing Islamic banking expressed by the participating jurists, after evaluation in the light of Qur'an and sunna, fiqh and fatwā, and facts and circumstances, is presented:

Dār al-Iftā: Jāmi'a 'Ulūm-i Islāmiyya, 'Allama Banūri Town, Karachi 29 Sha'bān 1429

We consider the banking system associated with Islam purely un-Islamic. In some regards, we consider this system even more dangerous than the conventional banking system. There are two reasons to call this system un-Islamic:

1. Existing Islamic banking does not follow the proposed Islamic way.
2. Even the proposed Islamic way of financing consists of several shortcomings from a shar'ī perspective. Observe the details:

First Reason

In practice, the banking system is not using the fiqhī foundations and conditions that the existing Islamic banking's architects (mujawwizīn) provided to Muslim bankers—even on the terms [of the foundations]. As a result, existing Islamic banking has remained unsuccessful in establishing its Islamic identity distinct from conventional banking, and is marching on such a shaky path that it can certainly not distinguish itself from conventional banking. Consequently, the end result is materially indistinct from ribā-based transactions. Note three incontrovertible testimonials of this point:

First Testimonial [Islamic Bankers]

The scholarly architects of existing Islamic banking and the people associated with existing Islamic banking accept the fact that the foundations of Islamic banking are shirka and muḍāraba, whereas existing murābaha and ijāra are merely stratagems that were conditionally declared permissible and feasible (qābil-i 'amal) for a limited time and interim period. Existing murābaha and ijāra are not the permanent foundations of Islamic banking in general. In fact, on the basis of being interest-based stratagems (sūdī ḥīla), making them permanent foundations is impermissible and against sharī'a. Nevertheless, our bankers are focused on ijāra and murābaha, instead of shirka and muḍāraba. They are not ready to abandon these stratagems, even though these are interest-based stratagems used in the framework of conventional standards and materially interest-bearing (sūdī) transactions. The reason is that using existing ijāra and murābaha in the framework of conventional standards produces the shape and form, and qualities and benefits, of precisely conventional banking, which is acceptable to every banker. In comparison, the elements of shirka and muḍāraba are almost absent (qalīl kal maʿdūm). Shirka and muḍāraba do not appeal to banks because of the Islamic principle of sharing profit and loss. Therefore, it can be rightly stated that existing Islamic banking has deviated from its original foundations such that return to its original foundations appears clearly impossible (maḥāl), because true foundations of Islamic banking are on one side, whereas the direction of existing Islamic banking is on the other side.

Second Testimonial [Muftī Muḥammad Taqī ʿUthmānī]

For this reason, the lead supporter of Islamic banking whose fatwā and personality are relied upon on this issue, Ḥaḍrat Mawlānā Muftī Muḥammad Taqī ʿUthmānī, may his blessings endure, is deeply sad and disappointed with this banking system. He has expressed this [sentiment] in various writings and lectures. As a result of these disappointments, he is showing signs of slowly distancing himself from this system, even frankly stating that "the wheel of existing Islamic banking is now going backwards." (We have the cassette and CD of the statement of Mawlānā, may his shadow extend, on file.)[26]

This can only mean that the fears and suspicions of the people who considered existing Islamic banking un-Islamic from the beginning are completely right. Moreover, even the people who were expecting improvements and Islamic compliance in these banks with great hopes are forced to consider the idea of improvements and Islamic compliance an unfulfilled dream. If the existing Islamic banks were using the standards proposed for them, then neither would these elders [i.e., ʿUthmānī] have faced disappointments, nor would our bankers have heard their suspicions.

Third Testimonial [Intellectuals]

[The third testimonial] is from those countless common people and intellectuals who interacted with both conventional and existing Islamic banks, but who could not find the least difference between the two despite search and effort. This category includes those ranging from common account holders to the greatest economists and famous bankers, for whom it can be said without hesitation (bilā khawf-i tardīd) that they know the finer aspects of the banking system with such depth and detail that their knowledge in this field begins where the knowledge of our modern Islamic bankers ends. These experts have learned the banking system not just from books and lectures, but after spending an important part of their lives in banks. Nevertheless, they could not feel any difference between conventional and Islamic banks apart from a few Islamic technical terms, which is a testament to the fact that the operation of existing Islamic banking is working on the financing structure of conventional banks instead of the proposed Islamic foundations. Therefore, conventional and Islamic banks differ only in a few terms. In operations and goals, the two are the same.

Second Reason

The second reason to consider existing Islamic banks to be against Islam is that even the foundations provided for existing Islamic banking are not, in any manner, free from gaps. The architects of existing Islamic banking have dangerously stumbled in sharʿī terms in the implementation (taṭbīq), elaboration (tashrīḥ), realization (taʿbīr), argumentation (istidlāl), and mode of argumentation (ṭarz-i istidlāl) of these foundations.

1. Principles of Jurisprudence

The fundamental mistake in the argumentation and the style of argumentation of these people is that in order to Islamize banking instruments, they disfigured (qaṭʿ wa barīd) several technical fiqhī terms; depended on weak (ḍaʿīf) and inaccurate (marjūḥ) opinions; authorized the practice of using [rules from] another school (madhhab ghayr) in a single transaction without completing sharʿī conditions, which is talfīq muḥarram (the impermissibility of combining different opinions) for all schools and thereby overall invalid.[27] Similarly, in order to prove the Islamic face of an instrument and to clad it in Islamic garb, remote and endless interpretations (dūr az kār taʾwīl dar taʾwīl) have been used, deliberately ignoring correct (ṣaḥīḥ), explicit (ṣarīḥ), and clear (wāḍiḥ) rules—something the [canonical] scholars have considered an insult, obstruction, and joke to sharīʿa, since this method falls in the category of invalid interpretation (taʾwīl fāsid).

2. Existing Murābaḥa and Ijāra as Stratagems

The murābaḥa and ijāra used in banks are merely stratagems (ḥīla). They are not agreed-upon Islamic financing instruments. Making them a permanent system is impermissible. The transaction completed through such stratagems is also considered impermissible. Just as the stratagem of sale-repurchase (bayʿ ʿayna) is impermissible before Imām Muḥammad,[28] the stratagems of murābaḥa and ijāra, and making them financial instruments, are impermissible. On the one hand, the architects of Islamic banking have ignored clear rules of this sort through endless interpretations (taʾwīl dar taʾwīl). On the other hand, to justify the penalties imposed by Islamic banks, [they have used] the Mālikī jurist Ibn Dinār's inaccurate (marjūḥ) and rejected as if non-existent (matrūk kal maʿdūm) opinion, when following this opinion was impermissible in sharīʿa and in principle. But the architects of Islamic banking have deliberately disregarded these jurisprudential (uṣūlī) subtleties, when these clear rules were not concealed to them.

3. Existing Murābaḥa versus Fiqhī Murābaḥa

There is no correspondence between fiqhī murābaḥa and the murābaḥa used in Islamic banks. In fiqhī murābaḥa, the determination and assignment of price [are done] up front, and the clear knowledge and existence of cost are necessary. However, in the murābaḥa used in banks, the bank does not pay the price first, and the cost does not even exist. Therefore, banking murābaḥa does not even fall under any sale, let alone technical fiqhī murābaḥa. In fact, naming this transaction murābaḥa is called deception in sharīʿa and considered impermissible. But this deception is named murābaḥa in existing Islamic banking.

4. Agency in Murābaḥa

In the murābaḥa used in existing Islamic banks, the bank's [master] contract on paper, signed beforehand, is the real contract (aṣal). Afterwards, the various steps of agency could not be agency in terms of sharīʿa. Rather, on account of the responsibility of buying and selling revolving around one person, they are clearly invalid agency (wakāla fāsida). Therefore, this method of agency is merely a manipulation of words in terms of sharīʿa. In reality, the same person is becoming the seller and the buyer, which is clearly against sharīʿa. This murābaḥa has no relation to the fiqhī murābaḥa. Thus the banking murābaḥa is purely a stratagem for interest (sūdī ḥila). And the earnings of these banks are interest (ribā), not profit (ribḥ).

5. Ijāra for Purchase Finance
The basic purpose of the contracting parties in existing ijāra is not a lease (ijāra) transaction, but rather a sale (bayʿ) transaction. Based on jurisprudential principles, the rule would apply to the basic purpose of sale, not the words of ijāra. So if this transaction is a sale, then it is a sale conditioned on lease (bayʿ mashrūṭ bil ijāra), which is against sharīʿa.

6. Benchmarking Rent to Market Interest Rate
It is basically wrong to use the conventional interest rate as a standard to determine the rent, because this is, first, similar (mushābiha) to interest (sūdī muʿāmalāt) and, second, suspicious (ishtibāh) as well. Furthermore, the conventional interest rate changes with time and inflation. An ijāra where the rent is not determined up front is impermissible. But our Islamic bankers are trying to give sharʿī grounds to non-sharʿī methods, ignoring basic rules as usual.

7. Forced Charity as Penalty
Similarly, making and taking forcible charity in case of prepayment or late payment from the customer in existing ijāra or any other contract is not charity, but penalty in terms of sharīʿa, custom, logic, and law, which is undoubtedly impermissible and purely interest (khāliṣ sūdī). In fact, [as for] the fiqhī text used by some scholars to justify this penalty, the same text [actually] proves that the penalty is clearly interest. This charity is paid for the bank's purpose, with the bank's conditions and preferences, and under the bank's compulsions. On this issue, the architects of existing Islamic banking have deliberately or inadvertently made a big fallacy—to prove a non-sharʿī business need of the bank based on sharīʿa, they have used a remote, impermissible logic. However, it is clear that when there is compulsion, there can be no charity; and when there is charity, there can be no compulsion.

8. Security Deposits
Similarly, there is no allowance in sharīʿa law for security deposits in ijāra or other contracts of existing banks. The technical concepts of shirka, mumilarl, ijāra, murābaḥa, and so forth are from the genus of trust (amānāt) instead of guaranty (ḍamānāt), whereas security (rahn) can be taken upon guaranty and only under the rules of security. So the security used in our Islamic banks is neither security nor loan, nor even trust. Rather, it is a non-sharʿī stratagem, pretext, and fabrication (talfīq) to benefit from someone else's money, which is impermissible and ḥarām.

9. The Scope of Equity-Based Financing
Even after accepting shirka and muen aft as real foundations, existing Islamic banks are not financing based on them. That is why the proportion of shirka and mu real in comparison with ijāra and murābapa, based on a survey and cautious

estimate, is at most 15 to 20 percent. Even if it is assumed 50 percent, applying the principle that "when ḥalāl and ḥarām gather, ḥarām dominates ḥalāl," and based on the present facts where ḥalāl modes of financing are almost absent (qalīl kal maʿdūm) and the element of non-sharʿī modes is greater, such a dominated mode of financing can only be called non-sharʿī. That is why there is no principled reason for considering existing Islamic banking's mode of financing to be based on sharīʿa. But still it is called permissible and its justification is emphasized.

10. Unilateral Amendments in Contracts

Existing mushāraka and muḍāraba use contracts against sharīʿa. For example, the application form to open an account in an Islamic bank includes the acceptance, without specifics (bilā tafṣīl), of the bank's conditions and policies as well as banking laws and notices. Furthermore, [the application form] includes the promise to abide by the regulations and notices of the State Bank of Pakistan. However, the Islamic bank's notices and policies keep changing, instead of staying the same. To make the customer bound by such indefinite (majhūl) and unknown (ghayr maʿlūm) notices is impermissible in sharīʿa. And a contract with indefinite and unknown conditions and responsibilities is considered invalid in sharīʿa, rather than correct and permissible.

11. Dealing with the State Bank's Regulations

Similarly, binding a Muslim customer to the notices and policies of the State Bank of Pakistan is completely impermissible because the un-Islamic nature of the State Bank and its violation of sharʿī rules are as clear as the sun. Importantly, some people argue that the State Bank of Pakistan has openly, legally, and in writing allowed the Islamic banks to make their policies according to Islam. If we accept this notion, disregarding the State Bank's un-Islamic nature, then it would mean that our existing Islamic banks, despite being practically and legally free to invest on their true [Islamic] foundations, are deliberately not expanding the concept of investing on the true foundations of Islamic banks (i.e., mushāraka and muḍāraba). If the excuse of the State Bank as an obstacle existed, then to some extent there would have been space for considering Islamic bankers under compulsion, just as some scholars have remained silent [about questionbale financing practices] because of this compulsion.

12. Service Fees in Muḍāraba Accounts

In muḍāraba, the account holder is rabb al-māl (investor) and the bank is muḍārib (working partner). The bank's portion in the māl muḍārib (generated wealth) is the agreed percentage of the obtained profit. Taking further money for personal and institutional expenses or taking various fees or any form of compensation or allowance from the māl muḍārib is impermissible for the bank. But Islamic banks take a muḍāraba fee and they are still called Islamic, which is synonymous with calling un-Islamic Islamic.

13. Allocation of Profit in Shirka and Muḍāraba

The proposed method of allocating profits in shirka and muḍāraba does not fulfill Islamic requirements. Rather, instead of the real rate of return, a fictional and estimated rate of return is used on the basis of "daily return" or in the name of "weighed return," which is completely against the fundamental principles of shirka and muḍāraba.

14. Diminishing Partnership

From the standpoint of sharī'a, shirka mutanāqiṣa (diminishing partnership) falls under forbidden gains (mamnū' mukāsib) and impermissible sales (nā jā'iz buyū'). This contract includes several problems such as transaction upon transaction (ṣafqa fī ṣafqa), sale and condition (bay' wa sharṭ), and sale subject to repurchase (bay' al-thanayā) and is therefore impermissible. But despite these textual principles (nuṣūṣ shar'iyya), the justification for shirka mutanāqiṣa has been given, and Islamic banks have made this a foundational mode of financing. Instead of calling shirka mutanāqiṣa an established (istiqrā'ī) Islamic mode of financing, calling it an un-Islamic mode was the responsibility of scholars. But some people have deliberately ignored this responsibility.

It should remain clear that the trustworthiness (amānat wa diyānat), religious-ness (tadyīn), and God-consciousness (taqwā) of the experts of Islamic sharī'a and fiqh are witness to the fact that the clear rules of Islamic fiqh are such that attempting to deny them or [re]interpreting them in any way falls under invalid interpretation (ta'wīl fāsid). Rather, [the practice] amounts to playing with, and making a joke of, shar'ī texts.

15. Corporate Personality of Banks

The oppressive, unjust, and exploitative notion of juristic person and its limited liability is not simply present in existing Islamic banking, but holds the status of the backbone.[29] The juristic person and the concept of its limited liability is non-shar'ī and prejudiced (nā rawā) to provide unlimited profits to the bank and its branches and holdings, and to protect them from the heavy burdens of loss. This concept embeds the best outcome for the juristic person's branches and holdings and the worst exploitation of the debtors. When the profits are high, the inanimate "juristic person" is more powerful than a real person, and when it is time to bear losses, the juristic person dons the shroud (kafan) of limited liability and descends into death's well. In addition to being against Islam, this concept insults the humanity as well, because making a real person a servant of the fictional person becomes necessary. Nevertheless, countless intellectual moves have been employed to prove this un-Islamic concept Islamic, and such arguments are made on this position that are not acceptable in principle.

16. Interest-Based Elements in Banks

The architects and associates of existing Islamic banking themselves admit that the transactions of existing Islamic banks are not purely without interest (ghayr sūdī), halāl, and permissible. Rather, some transactions are permissible and some are impermissible. Such [mixed] transactions are at least suspicious (mushtaba). Instead of general permissibility and lawfulness, according to principles of sharī'a, the rule of impermissibility and unlawfulness is applied on such transactions. For instance, if some transactions of existing Islamic banks are assumed permissible, even then there is no basis for presenting an absolute justification (muṭlaq jawāz). On such transactions, observe a fatwā of Makhdūm al-'Ulamā Ḥaḍrat Mawlānā

Muftī Muḥammad Taqī ʿUthmānī, may his blessings endure, that he gave on the rule for [bank] "counters without interest" (ghayr sūdī counters)[30] as an example:

> This analysis demonstrates that for now the business of these "counters without interest" is mixed with permissible and impermissible transactions, and some of it is suspicious. Therefore, until these shortcomings are addressed, the profit derived from them cannot be considered completely ḥalāl, and it is incorrect for Muslims to participate in such business. (*Fiqhī Maqālāt*, vol. 2, 264, Memon Publishers)[31]

This fatwā shows that there is no room in sharīʿa to permit and regularize such transactions, even if they include limited elements of permissibility. And it is impermissible for Muslims to participate in such transactions. But the transactions of existing Islamic banks are still considered and emphasized as permissible.

The point is that even the theoretical frameworks of existing Islamic banking devised by the architects of Islamic banking are against sharīʿa. Instead of Islamic banking, the color of conventional banking is obvious in them. And these frameworks have several sharʿī shortcomings. Even worse, the practical workings of such banks do not even accord with these theoretical frameworks. Therefore, even calling these existing Islamic banks "Islamic banks" is not permissible, because at most they can be called "stratagem banks" based on stratagems of ijāra and murābaḥa. But stratagem is one thing, and Islam's essence is another.

Fatwā

Therefore, on the basis of these reasons, the fatwā of the country's majority of scholars and jurists is as follows:

> In the past few years, the framework of banking in the name of some Islamic sharʿī technical terms was evaluated in the framework of Qur'ān and sunna; and along with the focus on the documents, forms, and principles of these banks, the works of great jurists were consulted. Finally, for a conclusive decision on this matter, a conference of respected scholars from the four provinces was conducted in Karachi on 28 August 2008, corresponding to 25 Shaʿbān al-Muʿaẓẓam 1429 on Thursday, under the chairmanship of Shaykh al-Ḥadīth Ḥaḍrat Mawlānā Salīmullah Khān— may his blessing endure. The leading jurists present in the conference collectively issued the fatwā that the banking (murawwaja baynkārī) associated with Islam is categorically (qaṭʿī) non-sharʿī and un-Islamic. Therefore, the contracts with these banks considered Islamic or sharʿī are impermissible and ḥarām; and the [sharʿī] rule about them is the same as the ribā-based banks.

From this detailed explanation, it has become clear that existing Islamic banking is in fact un-Islamic banking. But people are transacting with it thinking that it is Islamic banking. Therefore, the scholars of Muslim community consider existing Islamic banking more dangerous for Muslims in comparison with conventional banking. The reason is that engaging in an impermissible and against-sharīʿa transaction while considering it impermissible is a lesser wrong (kam darjay ka jurm), whereas considering it permissible is a greater wrong. Conventional bankers engage in interest-based (sūdī) transactions while considering them interest-based transactions. However, existing Islamic bankers engage in the same interest-based and against-sharīʿa transactions while considering them sharʿī, which is more dangerous than the former in relation to faith and afterlife (ākhira). A conventional Muslim banker, considering himself sharʿī wrongdoer and sinner, can reach the doors of repentance for the forgiveness of his impermissible and interest-based transactions. He can be given an opportunity (tawfīq) for repentance, whereas an existing Islamic banker would neither be drawn toward repentance nor get an opportunity for repentance because he does not even feel its need. God bestows repentance and forgiveness upon the one who turns toward God as a needy (muḥtāj) person.

Therefore, it is necessary and incumbent upon Muslims to make a complete effort to stay away from banking associated with Islam just as other ḥarām and against-sharīʿa matters, and engage in repentance and retraction from their past transactions. Undoubtedly, God forgives the one who returns to Him.

> Wallahu taʿālā aʿlam bi al-ṣawāb wa ilayhi al-marjaʿ wa al-maāb.

> Wa ṣalla allahu wa sallam ʿalā sayyidinā Muḥammad wa ʿalā ālihi wa ṣaḥbihi wa atbāʿihi ajmaʿīn.

Signatories to the Collective Fatwā[32]

Shaykh al-Ḥadīth Mawlānā Salīmullah Khān	Jāmiʿa Fārūqiyya, Karachi Jāmiʿa Ashrafiyya, Lahore, Punjab
Muftī Ḥamīdullah Jān	Majlis-i Taḥaffuz-i Khatm-i Nabuwwat, Karachi
Mawlānā Saīd Aḥmad Jalālpūrī	Jāmiʿa ʿUlūm Islāmiyya, Banūrī Town, Karachi
Muftī Muḥammad Inʿām al-Ḥaq	Jāmiʿa ʿUlūm Islāmiyya, Banūrī Town, Karachi
Muftī ʿAbdul Majīd Dīnpūrī	Dār al-ʿUlūm, Ḥaqqāniyya, Akora Khatak
Muftī Ghulām Qādir	Maʿhad al-Khalīl al-Islāmī, Bahādur Ābād, Karachi
Muftī Muḥammad Madanī	Jāmiʿa Fārūqiyya, Karachi
Mawlānā Manẓūr Aḥmad Mayngal	Jāmiʿa ʿUlūm Islāmiyya, Banūrī Town, Karachi
Muftī Rafīq Aḥmad Bālākūti	Jāmiʿa ʿUlūm Islāmiyya, Banūrī Town, Karachi
Muftī Shuʿayb ʿĀlim	Majlis-i Taḥaffuz-i Khatm-i Nabuwwat, Karachi
Muftī ʿAbdul Qayyūm Dīnpūrī	Jāmiʿa ʿUmar Kot, Sindh
Muftī Aḥmad Khān	Dār al-Hudā, Tayrī Khayrpūr, Sindh
Muftī Qaḍī Salīmullah	Jāmiʿa Rashīdiyya, Turbat Makrān, Balochistan
Muftī Ihtishāmul Ḥaq Āsiya Ābādī	Jāmiʿa Dhoronaro, Sindh
Muftī Imdādullah	Dār al-Iftā Rabbāniyya, Quetta, Balochistan
Muftī Rozī Khān	Jāmiʿa Ḥammādiyya, Karachi
Muftī ʿĀṣim ʿAbdullah	Jāmiʿa Fārūqiyya, Karachi
Muftī Samīullah	Jāmiʿa Dhoronaro, Sindh
Mawlānā Kalīmullah	Jāmiʿa Khulafā-i Rāshidīn, Karachi
Muftī Amānullah	Jāmiʿa Ashrafiyya, Sakkhar, Sindh
Muftī ʿAbdul Ghaffār	Dār al-ʿUlūm Kabīrwālā, Punjab
Muftī Ḥāmid Ḥasan	Jāmiʿa Khayrul Madāris, Multān, Punjab
Muftī ʿAbdullah	Jāmiʿa Islāmiyya, Clifton, Karachi
Muftī Ḥabībullah Shaykh	Jāmiʿa Fārūqiyya, Karachi
Muftī Aḥmad Khān	Jāmiʿa Fārūq-i ʿAẓam, Faisalabad, Punjab
Muftī Nazīr Aḥmad Shāh	Jāmiʿa ʿArabiyya Taʿlīmul Islām, Quetta, Balochistan
Muftī Saʿīdullah	Jāmiʿa Khulafā-i Rāshidīn, Karachi
Muftī Aḥmad Mumtāz,	Jāmiʿa Rahīmiyya, Sarkī Road, Quetta, Balochistan
Muftī Gul Ḥasan Bolānī	Jāmiʿa ʿArabiyya Ahsan al-ʿUlūm, Gulshan-i Iqbāl

Muftī Zar Walī Khān	Jāmiʿa Ḥalīmiyya, Darwahpīzo, Sarḥad
Muftī Saʿduddin	Jāmiʿa Muʿīnul Islām, Hāthazārī, Bangladesh
Muftī ʿAbdussalām Chatgāmī	

Unsigned Endorsements[33]

Ḥaḍrat Mawlānā Sarfarāz Khān Ṣafdar
Muftī ʿĪsā
Mawlānā ʿAbdul Ghanī

TRANSLATION: FATWĀ FROM DĀR AL-ʿULŪM, DEOBAND, INDIA[34]

I live in Pakistan. Here Islamic banking has progressed rapidly under the guidance of Muftī Muḥammad Taqī ʿUthmānī, may his blessings endure. Many scholars in Pakistan agree with it while many others strongly disagree with it. I want to find out: what is the position of the scholars of Dār al-ʿUlūm, Deoband on the Islamic banking model of Muftī Muḥammad Taqī ʿUthmānī? Are they in agreement with Muftī Ṣāḥib's Islamic banking method?

Dānish Aḥmad, Pakistan

Fatwā

The principles and policies and practical framework, et cetera, of the Islamic banking model established and issued by Ḥaḍrat Mawlānā Muftī Muḥammad Taqī ʿUthmānī, may his great shadow extend, are not before us. Therefore, it is difficult to write a conclusive opinion. Nevertheless, Ḥaḍrat Muftī Ṣāḥib, may his shadow extend, has a deep knowledge of fiqh and fatwās, the ability to run banking in the Islamic way, and the capacity to protect the system from interest (sūd) and other non-sharʿī matters. So under such circumstances the questioned model is presumed to be correct (rājiḥ). If the local (Pakistani) scholars and jurists have disagreement over any details, then there is nothing problematic with the scholars taking reformative steps (iṣlāḥī qadam) in private without publicity in the general public.

The answer is correct (al-jawāb ṣaḥīḥ).
28 Muharram 1430/25 January 2009

Ḥabībur Raḥmān, Zaynul Islām, Waqār ʿAli
Muftiyān-i Dār al-Iftā, Dār al-ʿUlūm, Deoband [India]

TRANSLATION: RESPONSE FROM PAKISTAN[35]

Recently when the fatwā of some scholars on Islamic banking was published, it was given the title of "collective fatwā" (muttafiqa fatwā). Then the book published in its support, *Murawwaja Islāmī Baynkārī*, declared [the fatwā] the majority's position over and over again and claimed that the support for the struggle for Islamic banking comes from just one person (Shaykh al-Islām Muftī Muḥammad Taqī ʿUthmānī) and his students whose [financial] interests are associated with Islamic banking.

The country's other serious scholars were not in agreement with this fatwā, and its manners and claims. So they took notice of these circumstances, and the country's famous jurist and spiritual leader (shaykh-i ṭarīqa) Ḥaḍrat Mawlānā Muftī Mukhtār al-Dīn, successor to [the late] Ḥaḍrat Shaykh al-Ḥadīth Mawlānā Muḥammad Zakariyya Sahāranpūrī, God's mercy be upon him, wrote a statement and sent it to the jurists and scholars of Sindh and Punjab provinces:

> Recently a fatwā was published against banking without interest (bilā sūd baynkārī) and it was claimed that it represents the majority of scholars. In reality, this is not the case. Rather, a great number of respected scholars and authentic jurists do not agree with this fatwā for strong reasons. Therefore, these scholars find it necessary to clarify that the fatwā issued against banking without interest is neither agreed upon (muttafiqa) nor the position of the majority. Years of research and effort of our elders and authentic personalities of the Islamic world exist behind Islamic banking. We find the efforts of the great scholars, engaged in improving this system even today, commendable.

[The statement was signed by 140 scholars.]

GLOSSARY

Untranslated Terms

sharīʿa, adj. sharʿī	the system of Islamic ethics, law, and normativity
fiqh, adj. fiqhī	the genre of sharīʿa literature or authoritative legal manuals
fatwā	juristic opinion or response
ḥalāl	allowed
ḥarām	forbidden
ijāra	lease
murābaḥa	cost-plus sale
muḍāraba	silent partnership
mushāraka, shirka	partnership
ribā	forbidden forms of interest
sūd, adj. sūdī	forbidden forms of interest (Urdu)

Common Translated Terms

jurist	muftī or ahl-i fatwā or arbāb-i fiqh wa fatwā
scholar	ʿālim, pl. ʿulamā or ahl-i ʿilm
stratagem	ḥīla, pl. ḥiyāl (Arabic) or ḥīlay (Urdu)
architects	mujawwizīn
existing [Islamic banks]	murawwaja
invalid	fāsid
impermissible	nā jāʾiz
permissible	jāʾiz
un-Islamic	ghayr islāmī
non-sharʿī	ghayr sharʿī
against-sharīʿa	khilāf-i sharʿ
transaction	muʿāmala, pl. muʿāmalāt (Arabic) or muʿāmalay (Urdu)

NOTES

1. For 'Uthmānī's intellectual biography, see Kelly Pemberton, "An Islamic Discursive Tradition on Reform as Seen in the Writing of Deoband's Mufti Muhammad Taqi Usmani," *The Muslim World* 99, no. 3 (2009).

2. Sunni Muslim scholars in South Asia are divided into three major groups—Deobandis, Barelwis, and Ahl-i Ḥadīth—among whom the Deobandis are by far the most organized. See Muhammad Qasim Zaman, *The Ulama in Contemporary Islam: Custodians of Change* (Princeton, NJ: Princeton University Press, 2002), page 11.

3. Asadulla Shah, "Ḥaḍrat Shaykh Al-Ḥadīth Mawlānā Salīmullah Khān," www.algazali.org/gazali/showthread.php?tid=3041, accessed April 14, 2012.

4. See Muftī Taqī 'Uthmānī's letter to Mawlānā Salīmullah Khān in Thāqib al-Dīn, *Islāmī Baynkārī awr Muttafiqa Fatway kā Tajziya* (Karachi, Pakistan: Memom Islamic Publishers, 2009), pages 52–63.

5. Khalid Rahman and Syed Rashad Bukhari, "Pakistan: Religious Education and Institutions," *The Muslim World* 96, no. 2 (2006): 326.

6. I have been unable to find the original book, but an English translation is available as Ḥabībullah Shaykh, "A Juridical Rebuttal against Justice Mufti Muhammad Taqi Uthmaani," http://books.themajlis.net/book/print/603, accessed April 14, 2012. Furthermore, the book is referenced at Thāqib al-Dīn, *Islāmī Baynkārī awr Muttafiqa Fatway kā Tajziya*, page 32.

7. Muḥammad Taqī 'Uthmānī, *Islām awr Jadīd Ma'īshat wa Tijārat* (Karachi, Pakistan: Quranic Studies Publishers, 1994; reprint 2009).

8. 'Abdul Wāḥid, *Ghayr Sūdī Baynkārī: Mawlānā Taqī 'Uthmānī Madda Zillahu kī Khidmat Mayn Hadya-i Jawāb* (Karachi, Pakistan: Majlis-i Nasharyāt-i Islām, 2009).

9. Muḥammad Taqī 'Uthmānī et al., "Islāmī Baynkārī kay Bāray Mayn Ayk Sawāl kā Jawāb," *al-Balāgh* 43, no. 10 (2008): 56.

10. Jāmi'a 'Ulūm Islāmiyya Banūrī Town, "Murawwaja Islāmī Baynkārī awr Jamhūr 'Ulamā kay Mawqaf kā Khulāṣa," *Bayyināt* 71, no. 9 (2008).

11. Jāmi'a 'Ulūm Islāmiyya Banūrī Town, *Murawwaja Islāmī Baynkārī: Tajziyātī Muṭāla'a, Shar'ī Jā'iza, Fiqhī Naqd wa Tabṣara* (Karachi, Pakistan: Maktaba-i Bayyināt, 2008).

12. Muḥammad Taqī 'Uthmānī, *Ghayr Sūdī Baynkārī: Muta'allaqa Fiqhī Masa'il kī Taḥqīq awr Ishkalāt kā Jā'iza* (Karachi, Pakistan: Quranic Studies Publishers, 2009).

13. Thāqib al-Dīn, *Islāmī Baynkārī awr Muttafiqa Fatway kā Tajziya*.

14. 'Abdur Ra'ūf, *Islāmī Baynkārī par Akābir 'Ulamā Mayn Ikhtilāf: Chand Uṣūlī Bātayn awr Uṣūlī Ḥal* (Multān, Pakistan: Idāra-i Tālīfāt-i Ashrafiyya, 2009).

15. *Islāmī Baynkārī awr 'Ulamā: Ikhtilāfī Fatway par Ahl-i 'ilm wa Fikr kay Tabṣaron kā Majmū'a*, (Karachi, Pakistan: al-Afnān Publisher, 2009).

16. For a history of the Deoband seminary, see Barbara Daly Metcalf, *Islamic Revival in British India: Deoband, 1860–1900* (New York, NY: Oxford University Press, 2004).

17. Majlisul Ulama of South Africa. "The Concept of Limited Liability: Untenable in the Shariah," http://books.themajlis.net/book/print/251, accessed April 14, 2012; Majlisul Ulama of South Africa, "Penalty of Default: Can Riba Be Legalized to Punish a Man for Late Payment of Instalments?" http://books.themajlis.net/book/print/67, accessed April 14, 2012; Majlisul Ulama of South Africa, "Shares, Unit Trusts and the Shariah," http://books.themajlis.net/book/print/297, accessed April 14, 2012.

18. For Banūrī Town's invocation of the late Banūrī in the debate, see Banūrī Town, *Murawwaja Islāmī Baynkārī: Tajziyātī Muṭāla'a, Shar'ī Jā'iza, Fiqhī Naqd wa Tabṣara*. For 'Uthmānī's invocation of Banūrī, see the preface to 'Uthmānī, *Ghayr Sūdī Baynkārī: Muta'allaqa Fiqhī Masa'il kī Taḥqīq awr Ishkalāt kā Jā'iza*.

19. See, for example, Mahmoud A. El-Gamal, *Islamic Finance: Law, Economics, and Practice* (New York: Cambridge University Press, 2008).

20. See Wael B. Hallaq and A. Layish, "Talfīk," in P. Bearman et al., eds., *Encyclopaedia of Islam*, 2nd edition, vol. 10, page 161 (Leiden, The Netherlands: Brill Publishers, 1998).
21. Banūrī Town, *Murawwaja Islāmī Baynkārī: Tajziyātī Muṭālaʿa, Sharʿī Jāʾiza, Fiqhī Naqd wa Tabṣara*.
22. ʿUthmānī, *Ghayr Sūdī Baynkārī: Mutaʿallaqa Fiqhī Masāʾil kī Taḥqīq awr Ishkalāt kā Jāʾiza*, pages 12–13.
23. See Muhammad Imran Ashraf Usmani and Zeenat Zubairi, eds., *Meezanbank's Guide to Islamic Banking* (Karachi, Pakistan: Darul Ishaat, 2002), page 108.
24. Instead of late payment fees given to charity, some banks use collection fees given to collection agencies. Since the collection fees are also forced payments for the bank's purpose, they appear to fall under the fatwā's reasoning.
25. Translated from Banūrī Town, "Murawwaja Islāmī Baynkārī awr Jamhūr ʿUlamā kay Mawqaf kā Khulāṣa."
26. The authors are anticipating the charge of mischaracterizing ʿUthmānī's position, which explains why they are pointing toward evidence.
27. In contrast to many Arab scholars, this point reflects the enduring centrality of the madhhab among the South Asian Ḥanafīs. For the conditions before engaging in talfīq and iftā bi madhhab ghayr, see Muḥammad Yūsuf Banūrī, "Qadīm Fiqh-i Islāmī kī Rawshanī Mayn Jadīd Masāʾil kā Ḥal," *Bayyināt* 2, no. 3 (1963); Muḥammad Yūsuf Banūrī, "Jadīd Fiqhī Masāʾil awr Chand Rahnumā Uṣūl," *Bayyināt* 2, no. 4 (1963).
28. Imām Muḥammad ibn al-Ḥasan al-Shaybānī (d. 805) was among the three leading students of Imām Abū Ḥanīfa (d. 767).
29. On ʿUthmānī's fiqhī perspective on corporate personality, see Muhammad Taqi Usmani, "The Principle of Limited Liability," in Muhammad Imran Ashraf Usmani and Zeenat Zubairi, eds., *Meezanbank's Guide to Islamic Banking* (Karachi, Pakistan: Darul Ishaat, 2002); ʿUthmānī, *Islām awr Jadīd Maʿīshat wa Tijārat*, pages 95–102.
30. The "counters without interest" were introduced by conventional banks in the 1980s consisting of separate counters in branches to deal with profit-and-loss-sharing accounts.
31. In response to the characterization of his position, ʿUthmānī has distinguished these ghayr sūdī counters from existing Islamic banking. See ʿUthmānī, *Ghayr Sūdī Baynkārī: Mutaʿallaqa Fiqhī Masāʾil kī Taḥqīq awr Ishkalāt kā Jāʾiza*, pages 36–40.
32. Banūrī Town, *Murawwaja Islāmī Baynkārī: Tajziyātī Muṭālaʿa, Sharʿī Jāʾiza, Fiqhī Naqd wa Tabṣara*, page 346.
33. Muftī Doctor ʿAbdul Wāḥid was mistakenly included among the endorsers. See ʿAbdul Wāḥid, *Ghayr Sūdī Baynkārī: Mawlānā Taqī ʿUthmānī Madda Zillahu kī Khidmat Mayn Hadya-i Jawāb*, page 4.
34. Translated from *Islāmī Baynkārī awr ʿUlamā: Ikhtilāfī Fatway par Ahl-i ʿilm wa Fikr kay Tabṣaron kā Majmūʿa*, pages 13–14.
35. Ibid., pages 228–247.

REFERENCES

ʿAbdul Wāḥid. 2009. *Ghayr Sūdī Baynkārī: Mawlānā Taqī ʿUthmānī Madda Zillahu kī Khidmat Mayn Hadya-i Jawāb*. Karachi, Pakistan: Majlis-i Nasharyāt-i Islām.

ʿAbdurRaʾūf. 2009. *Islāmī Baynkārī par Akābir ʿUlamā Mayn Ikhtilāf: Chand Uṣūlī Bātayn awr Uṣūlī Ḥal*. Multān, Pakistan: Idāra-i Tāʾlīfāt-i Ashrafiyya.

Banūrī, Muḥammad Yūsuf. 1963. "Jadīd Fiqhī Masāʾil awr Chand Rahnumā Uṣūl." *Bayyināt* 2:4, 194–198.

———. 1963. "Qadīm Fiqh-i Islāmī kī Rawshanī Mayn Jadīd Masāʾil kā Ḥal." *Bayyināt* 2:3, 130–133.

Banūrī Town, Jāmiʿa ʿUlūm Islāmiyya. 2008. "Murawwaja Islāmī Baynkārī awr Jamhūr ʿUlamā kay Mawqaf kā Khulāṣa." *Bayyināt* 71:9.

———. 2008. *Murawwaja Islāmī Baynkārī: Tajziyātī Muṭālaʿa, Sharʿī Jāʾiza, Fiqhī Naqd wa Tabṣara*. Karachi, Pakistan: Maktaba-i Bayyināt.

El-Gamal, Mahmoud A. 2008. *Islamic Finance: Law, Economics, and Practice*. New York, NY: Cambridge University Press.

Hallaq, Wael B., and A. Layish. 1998. "Talfīḳ." In P. Bearman, Th. Bianquis, C. E. Bosworth, E. van Donzel and W. P. Heinrichs, eds. *Encyclopaedia of Islam*, 2nd ed., vol. 10. Leiden, The Netherlands: Brill Publishers.

Islāmī Baynkārī awr ʿUlamā: Ikhtilāfī Fatway par Ahl-i ʿilm wa Fikr kay Tabṣaron kā Majmūʿa. 2009. Karachi, Pakistan: al-Afnān Publisher.

Majlisul Ulama of South Africa. n.d. "The Concept of Limited Liability: Untenable in the Shariah." http://books.themajlis.net/book/print/251

———. n.d. "Penalty of Default: Can Riba Be Legalized to Punish a Man for Late Payment of Instalments?" http://books.themajlis.net/book/print/67

———. n.d. "Shares, Unit Trusts and the Shariah." http://books.themajlis.net/book/print/297

Metcalf, Barbara Daly. 2004. *Islamic Revival in British India: Deoband, 1860–1900*. New York, NY: Oxford University Press.

Pemberton, Kelly. 2009. "An Islamic Discursive Tradition on Reform as Seen in the Writing of Deoband's Mufti Muhammad Taqi Usmani." *The Muslim World* 99:3, 452–477.

Rahman, Khalid, and Syed Rashad Bukhari. 2006. "Pakistan: Religious Education and Institutions." *The Muslim World*. 96:2, 323–339.

Shah, Asadulla. n.d. "Ḥaḍrat Shaykh Al-Ḥadīth Mawlānā Salīmullah Khān." http://www.algazali.org/gazali/showthread.php?tid=3041

Shaykh, Ḥabībullah. n.d. "A Juridical Rebuttal against Justice Mufti Muhammad Taqi Uthmaani." http://books.themajlis.net/book/print/603

Thāqib al-Dīn. 2009. *Islāmī Baynkārī awr Muttafiqa Fatway kā Tajziya*. Karachi, Pakistan: Memom Islamic Publishers.

Usmani, Muhammad Imran Ashraf. 2002. *Meezanbank's Guide to Islamic Banking*. Karachi, Pakistan: Darul Ishaat.

Usmani, Muhammad Taqi. 2002. "The principle of limited liability." In Muhammad Imran Ashraf Usmani and Zeenat Zubairi, eds. *Meezanbank's Guide to Islamic Banking*. 223–232. Karachi, Pakistan: Darul Ishaat.

ʿUthmānī, Muḥammad Taqī. 2009. *Ghayr Sūdī Baynkārī: Mutaʿallaqa Fiqhī Masaʾil kī Taḥqīq awr Ishkalāt kā Jāʾiza*. Karachi, Pakistan: Quranic Studies Publishers.

———. 2009. *Islām awr Jadīd Maʿīshat wa Tijārat*. Karachi, Pakistan: Quranic Studies Publishers.

ʿUthmānī, Muḥammad Taqī, Afḍal ʿAli Rabbānī, ʿAbdur Raʾūf Sakkharwī, Maḥmūd Ashraf ʿUthmānī, and Muḥammad ʿAbdul Mannān. 2008. "Islāmī Baynkārī kay Bāray Mayn Ayk Sawāl kā Jawāb." *al-Balāgh* 43:10, 51–56.

Zaman, Muhammad Qasim. 2002. *The Ulama in Contemporary Islam: Custodians of Change*. Princeton, NJ: Princeton University Press.

ACKNOWLEDGMENTS

This work was presented in the Islamic Finance course at the University of California, Hastings College of the Law, in Fall 2011, and the Jurisprudence and Social Policy Forum at the University of California, Berkeley, School of Law, in Fall 2010. The author/translator would like to thank Karen Hunt-Ahmed, Abrar Hussain, Arshad Ahmed, Muftī Miṣbāḥullah, and Mawlānā Samiʿullāh for their comments and feedback.

CHAPTER 7

Managing Liquidity Risk in Islamic Finance

DR. MUHAMMAD AL-BASHIR MUHAMMAD AL-AMINE
Group Head, Shari'ah Assurance Department, Bank Al Khair

INTRODUCTION

Liquidity refers to the promptness with which an asset can be converted into cash. Liquid assets are money and other financial assets that can be turned into money.[1] In banking, *liquidity* is defined as "proportion of the assets which is held in cash or near cash."[2] The liquidity of a bank represents a bank's ability to meet anticipated demand for its funds from depositors and borrowers.[3]

Liquidity problems arise when there is an unexpected decline in the bank's net cash flow and the bank is unable to raise resources at a reasonable cost in a Shari'ah-compatible manner. This would make it difficult for an Islamic bank to meet its obligations when new opportunities for profitable business arise. The mismatch between deposits and loans and investments exposes any bank, whether it is an Islamic bank or a conventional commercial bank, to liquidity problems. The bank may maintain too much liquidity to avoid getting into this difficulty. But this, in turn, may hurt its profitability. Creating a right balance between the two objectives of safety and profitability is thus the crux of the liquidity management problem.[4]

Monitoring and controlling liquidity is one of the most critical responsibilities of a bank's management. It has been a very important concern in the minds of Islamic banking practitioners since the early days of the inception of Islamic banks. This concern has become more pressing after the growth of the industry and the large liquidity in Islamic banks. Moreover, as the market gets competitive, the industry is forced to go toward project finance, which is mainly medium- and long-term in nature, and by consequence requires new means of fund-raising and liquidity management.

LIQUIDITY MANAGEMENT AND THE CRISIS

The recent crisis has clearly made it evident that the industry is facing a number of vulnerabilities, both in the liquidity risk management in individual banks and on a systemic basis. Although comparatively better, the situation in the Islamic banking industry is not so different from its conventional counterpart. Thus, uncertainty and lack of transparency over the holdings of toxic assets, in the conventional financial system in particular, led to general reluctance to provide funding to each other, which resulted in the freezing of the wholesale money market in several developed economies. Short-term liquidity evaporated, affecting participants that were too dependent on the market for funding. This largely stemmed from poor liquidity risk management practices and has now prompted the Basel Committee to develop new proposals for global liquidity management standards.[5]

Although the Islamic financial industry was relatively insulated from the first-round effects of the crisis because it did not invest in so-called toxic structured financial products, it has not been able to avoid the second-round effects. These have been manifested in a sharp reduction of liquidity in all markets and the effect of the global economic downturn on the creditworthiness of all borrowers, including those who are customers of Islamic financial institutions.[6] The issue has been top on the agenda of regulators and practitioners and frequently highlighted by rating agencies.

Addressing the challenges facing the Islamic finance industry, the governor of the Central Bank of Bahrain (CBB) notes:

> The second set of issues relates to risk management. This has a number of different dimensions, but two in particular are worth highlighting. The first relates to liquidity risk. The conventional financial industry received a wake-up call during the crisis concerning the importance of understanding, monitoring and controlling liquidity risks. The Islamic financial industry must recognise that it too needs good liquidity risk management. How Islamic financial institutions can manage their liquidity risk given the relative absence of short-term money market instruments has been a problem for the industry for some time. However, the events of recent years should give a greater sense of urgency to resolving these problems and we need to redouble our efforts to find a solution.[7]

Another regulator who pointed to the issue is governor of the Central Bank of the Republic of Turkey, who notes:

> As liquidity concerns played a major role in the deepening of the crisis, intense discussions on a new structure in global liquidity management have dominated the global arena. In this context, liquidity management issues in the Islamic financial services deserve a special attention. Successful implementation of a solid liquidity management system can be the key for sustaining the rapid growth of the industry.[8]

The issue has also been stressed by rating agencies. Thus, Standard & Poor's, for instance, notes:

> Liquidity is one of the most critical issues for IFIs, as only a small secondary market exists to enable them to manage their liquidity. Their assets are generally not sellable on a secondary market and they cannot invest in fixed-income instruments for treasury management purposes.[9]

The sound management of liquidity risk is critical to avert both a threat to the solvency of a banking institution and a loss of confidence in the broader financial system. The situation is not peculiar to Islamic banks in any one jurisdiction.[10]

Similarly, it has been stressed by a recent working paper by the International Monetary Fund (IMF) that while Islamic banks rely more on retail deposits and, hence, have more stable sources of funds, they face fundamental challenges when it comes to liquidity management.[11] Yet, the growing internationalization and cross-border activities in Islamic finance in recent years further accentuates the need to enhance the ability of Islamic financial institutions to withstand shocks. Thus, it is maintained that access to a robust liquidity management infrastructure will help to reduce the cost of intermediation, which is an important factor for a more efficient and competitive Islamic financial system.[12]

In fact, Islamic financial institutions have some shortages in comparison with their conventional counterparts in terms of availability and variety of instruments in managing liquidity. In the conventional banking system, there is a well-developed interbank money market with a variety of instruments. Access to interbank money markets for short-term borrowings gives considerable flexibility to banks to adjust their short-term cash flows. Existence of secondary markets for financial instruments is also an important source of liquidity. However, these conventional mechanisms of liquidity management, including interbank market, secondary market financial instruments, and facilities from the central bank as the lender of last resort, are all based on interest and, therefore, not acceptable for Islamic financial institutions. This requires the development of similar instruments and mechanisms. However, before addressing these alternatives, let me point out the causes of liquidity risk in Islamic finance.

CAUSES OF LIQUIDITY RISK

Liquidity risk is one of the most critical risks facing Islamic banks for the following reasons:

- The limited availability of Shari'ah-compatible money market and interbank market instruments has restricted Islamic banks' options to manage their liquidity positions efficiently. Thus, most of the instruments used for liquidity management in Islamic finance, such as murbahah, wakalah, and salam sukuk, are not tradable in most Islamic financial centers. This is generally based on the restriction of the sale of debt in Islamic law because these instruments are, by nature, debt obligation instruments.
- The shallow secondary market is another source of liquidity risk. There are financial instruments that can be traded in the secondary market, such as sukuk, but despite the rapid growth of these instruments in the past few years, there is a problem of short supply, especially for investment-grade paper, and therefore, the market is characterized by a buy-and-hold culture. Yet, from a Shari'ah perspective, it is not permissible to trade financial claims unless such claims are linked to a real asset. Thus, the introduction of *sukuk* (Islamic bonds) is a good development that can provide the foundation for the development of secondary markets.[13]
- Even where instruments are available, the number of market participants is limited.

- Absence of a lender of last resort (central bank) is a problem,[14] as there is no basis for placement of short-term assets with central banks for reserve and other requirements because there are very often no Shari'ah-compliant papers or instruments to invest in. Yet, the system in most countries where Islamic banking operates is based on conventional banking systems.

- Generally, Islamic banks offer profit- and loss-sharing instruments to their customers. Thus, Islamic financial institutions are in general more liquid than conventional banks, as they are aware that their reliance on these instruments could trigger liquidity stress. The average liquid-to-total assets ratio for Gulf Cooperation Council (GCC)-based Islamic financial institutions rated by Standard & Poor's, for instance, was 30 percent at midyear 2007, compared with 18.1 percent for GCC-based conventional peers. This extra liquidity has a negative impact on profitability.[15]

- Most of the hedging risk techniques used by conventional institutions, such as derivatives, are not in compliance with Shari'ah and therefore are generally excluded in the industry's liquidity management system.

- A weak systemic liquidity infrastructure is another source of liquidity risk in Islamic financial institutions.[16] The lack of a cross-border liquid market infrastructure and instruments for the management of liquidity risk has been a long-standing challenge for the Islamic finance sector. The need and urgency for establishing a global Islamic liquidity management scheme is further underlined by the fact that the global commodity murabahah market is estimated at a staggering $1.2 trillion and constitutes the main underlying transactions of an Islamic liquidity management system.[17] Yet, the mechanism is criticized by some from within the industry, including Shari'ah scholars, due to deficient implementation by some institutions.

These factors have raised Islamic banks' exposure to liquidity risk and limited their ability to invest long-term, but this does not mean the window of creativity and innovation is closed. Many instruments have been introduced to address the issue, but a lot needs to be done.

CURRENT SOLUTION

Several developments have been taking place with a view to meeting the liquidity challenge facing Islamic financial institutions. A number of central banks are leading the quest for solutions to address the liquidity problem. Despite the limits of these initiatives and the fact that they are not immune from criticism, they pave the way for future development.

To resolve the differences in regulations regarding appropriate Shari'ah-compliant instruments, working on globally accepted liquidity management regulations and infrastructure could be a viable option. Establishment of a carefully designed and structured Global Shari'ah Supervisory Board could also be a step in the right direction.[18] Thus, it has been stressed that regulators and standard setters for Islamic financial institutions should ensure that the supervisory and legal infrastructure remains relevant to the rapidly changing Islamic financial landscape and global developments. Greater convergence and harmonization of regulations and products will facilitate efficient and sustainable growth. Addressing these challenges will require that Islamic banks and supervisors work together to develop the needed human capital.[19]

Several support institutions have been established to help solve the liquidity problem facing the industry.

- The **Islamic Financial Services Board (IFSB)** is addressing the issue of liquidity through its standards and has issued one of its early standards on risk management, with good sections on liquidity. Earlier this year, it issued a specific standard on liquidity management.
- The **International Islamic Financial Markets (IIFM),** which is very active in terms of harmonization and documentation, has already issued a standard agreement on murabahah and tahawut (netting) agreements and recently a standard agreement on profit rate swap. Moreover, the standard setter issued its standard on liquidity management in 2012.
- The **Liquidity Management Center in Bahrain** was established to manage liquidity more effectively. The institution issued a number of sukuk, but its activities have been curtailed in the last three years, perhaps due to the financial crisis.
- The recent institution mandated to resolve the issue of liquidity is the **International Islamic Management Corporation (IILM)**. Although it has not yet issued any tradable instrument, given the fact that IILM is being established by a number of central bank members of the IFSB, there is the suggestion that one way of addressing the issue of liquidity by the new institution will be through the issuance of highly rated instruments. This is an important factor for the capital rules under Basel 2. The high-quality, liquid, tradable, low-risk, Shari'ah-compliant financial instruments to be issued by the IILM at both the national level and across borders will enhance the soundness and stability of the Islamic financial markets. The instruments of the IILM are expected to be utilized in liquidity management as eligible collateral for interbank transactions and central bank financing, or through the trading of these instruments in the secondary market. As the IILM is intended to facilitate cross-border liquidity management, its instruments will be denominated in major reserve currencies. This is to ensure access to a large pool of global investors and broaden the range of its holders.[20] The challenge for the IILM is that there is a serious lack of Shari'ah-compliant AAA-rated paper. At the moment, the Islamic Development Bank's Islamic trust certificate program is the only institutional AAA-rated paper, apart from one or two other smaller issuers such as the International Finance Corporation, which has prompted some market players to question the availability of a large enough pool of AAA-rated assets suitable for securitization.[21]

Thus, the real challenge is developing suitable short-term financial instruments that are Shari'ah compatible and can be used for Islamic interbank money market transactions. Several experiences in the past decade in different regions of the Muslim world have addressed the situation.

MAIN EXISTING LIQUIDITY MANAGEMENT INSTRUMENT: COMMODITY MURABAHAH

The main liquidity management mechanism used by most Islamic financial institutions is commodity murabahah. It is generally implemented through the London Metals Exchange and, more recently, through trades based on palm oil contracts on the Bursa Suq Al Sila' Platform launched by Bursa Malaysia. The Bahrain Financial Exchange has recently also launched the Bait al-Bursa commodity murabahah trading platform.

Commodity murabahah is defined as an internationally acceptable form of short-term interbank deposit or placement.[22] It is one of the popular avenues of investment of short-term liquidity. It is widely based on commodities traded on a spot basis with 100 percent payment of the purchase price, then selling the purchased commodities to a third party on a murabahah basis for a deferred payment, with a maturity from one week to six months, and with spot delivery of the sold commodities. Most of these commodity murabahah deals are conducted in U.S. dollars.[23]

The global commodity murabahah market was estimated a few years back to be in excess of $1.2 trillion.[24] The mechanism needs fast execution and involves different time and geographical zones. Hence, the operational requirements are governed through a master agency murabahah agreement.

In practice, commodity murabahah may take several forms, based on the parties involved and their role in each transaction, depending on the responsibilities of the different parties. A simplified form is outlined in the following structure of commodity murabahah:

- An Islamic Bank (A) is having an excess of liquidity while another Islamic Bank (B) is short and is looking for immediate short-term liquidity.
- Islamic Bank (B) approaches Islamic Bank (A) to secure the short-term liquidity through commodity murabahah.
- Islamic bank (A) transfers to the account of Islamic Bank (B) $10 million and instructs the bank as its agent to invest the $10 million for one month by purchasing metal from the London Metal Exchange.
- Acting as an agent, Islamic Bank (B) buys a commodity from a broker A, value spot on behalf of the Islamic bank (A). The commodity is then credited to the Islamic Bank (B) account with broker A. Islamic Bank (B) will credit broker A's dollar account with $10 million.
- Value spot, Islamic Bank (B), acting as an agent on behalf of Islamic Bank (A), sells the commodity at cost plus markup on a deferred payment basis (one month) to Islamic Bank (B).
- Islamic Bank (B) sells on the commodity to a broker (B).
- On maturity (in one month), Islamic Bank (B) pays to the Islamic bank (A) profit (markup) plus the original investment of $10 million.
- Commission will be payable to Islamic Bank (as agency) and to the commodity brokers on buying and selling the commodities. These commissions will be built generally into the price quoted to the Islamic bank and not accounted for separately.[25]

During the early days of implementation of the international commodity murabahah, a number of international banks were appointed as agents to assist with the development of the wholesale asset flow. These appointments brought instant market experience and provided access to diversified global relationships that were targeted to accelerate low-risk asset generation.[26] Today, the practice is commonplace, and most Islamic banks are using it on a regular basis.

Benefits of International Commodity Murabahah

International commodity murabahah achieved some benefits. Thus, through murabahah allocation:

- Treasuries are able to match the maturities profiles of wholesale investments against projected deposit redemption.
- Islamic banks are enabled to manage and drive profit from short-term cash balances.
- The investment asset base of the Islamic banking sector has expanded.
- The burden of unallocated funds that, left idle, would both detract from investment performance and infringe on Shari'ah stipulations has been eased.
- High-yielding, relatively liquid, investment has been delivered to institutional and private investors seeking portfolio diversification.[27]

The mechanism has also its shortcomings.

Shortcomings of Commodity Murabahah

Murabahah has long been unpopular with ordinary Muslims, as well as some Islamic scholars and finance experts, due to the presumed similarity with the conventional mechanism of lending on interest. However, the vast majority of contemporary Shari'ah scholars approve it, provided it is implemented properly. Yet, although commodity murabahah has partially solved some of the problems of liquidity facing Islamic banks, it suffers at the same time from major weaknesses. These weaknesses include, among others:

- Flight of capital from the local economies to the international commodity market, depriving local economies of needed capital and investment opportunities.
- Commodity murabahah imposes severe limitations on local economic development and on the objective of promoting an active secondary market.
- The method is based on murabahah; therefore, it is only suitable for the investment of a surplus cash position and cannot be used for funding a shortage of cash position.
- More important, there is a possibility that some of these operations could be manipulated or misapplied and, therefore, transformed into fictitious trading on paper without satisfying Shari'ah requirements.[28]

- Cost of commodity brokerage: The use of an intermediary results in broker-age payout and transforms the mechanism into a less competitive product than its conventional counterpart.
- Doubt about the existence of sufficient metal to cover the transaction volume.
- The product was approved by scholars as an interim solution until the setup of a comprehensive Islamic money market.[29]

These problems are very serious and might hamper or slow the progress of developing a viable Islamic money market. Until recently, commodity muraba-hah as an instrument of treasury product was dominantly used by Middle Eastern financial institutions. The Malaysian market is dominated by other treasury products, structured mainly on the concept of sale of debt, criticized by the vast majority of contemporary Shari'ah scholars. However, commodity murabahah has been introduced recently in the Malaysian market as a treasury product, in a sign of the rapprochement between the two active markets in Islamic finance. The product was introduced with new positive additional features, as it utilizes crude palm oil contracts as its underlying asset rather than relying totally on the London Metal Exchange.

SALAM SECURITIES AS MONEY MARKET INSTRUMENT

Salam is defined as "a sale or purchase of a deferred commodity for a present price (bay'ajilin biajil)"[30] and "a transaction where two parties agree to carry out a sale/purchase of an underlying asset at a predetermined future date but at a price determined and fully paid for today."[31] In addition to the general conditions of an ordinary sale in Islamic law, salam has its own conditions. Thus, a salam contract must fulfill the conditions:

- It is necessary to precisely fix a period for the delivery of goods.
- Quality, quantity, and place of delivery must be clearly enumerated.
- A salam contract cannot be based on uniquely identified underlying assets. This means the underlying commodity cannot be based on a commodity from a particular farm or field.
- Full payment should be made at the time of making the contract.[32]

Salam is possible only for fungible goods or *mithli*. They are goods standard-ized into identical units. For instance, wheat, rice, barley, and other grains are of this type. Oil, iron, and copper are also mithli. Similarly, electricity measured in kilowatts could be considered a mithli. A seat on an airplane flight can also be mithli.[33]

Let us consider the following assumption of a corporation that needs funds:

- It requires for instance, USD50 million. It can use salam certificates equaling that amount in small denominations of USD10,000 each.
- Each certificate represents a salam contract. The seller is the corporation, and the buyer is the holder of that certificate that paid its nominal value.

- Each certificate promises on maturity (one year, for example) that the corporation will deliver to the holder a specified quantity of the underlying commodity, which is described fully on the back of the certificate or in the prospectus.
- Once the corporation receives the cash, it can use it for any purpose.
- On maturity, the seller will be delivering the sold goods in kind. For this purpose, the corporation will certainly buy on the open market and deliver to the certificate holder.
- The corporation floats these salam certificates, and it will receive immediately the face value of each certificate in cash, according to the majority of Muslim jurists, or three or more days later, according to the Malikis and some contemporary Muslim jurists.

Salam Sukuk and the Bahraini Experience

The Bahrain Monetary Agency issued a series of new Islamic financial instruments designed to broaden the depth and liquidity of the market. These instruments include short-term government bills structured under salam sukuk and introduced for the first time on June 13, 2001.

The initiative started on a monthly basis as a short-term government bills program of USD25 million. These Islamic short-term securities marked the beginning of a program that rolls forward the issuance of three-month securities that are designed to be a permanent feature of the Islamic financial system in Bahrain. The securities will provide a short-term investment opportunity for Islamic financial institutions. They are tendered for each month, and in the case of oversubscription, the securities are issued on a pro rata basis. So far, the demand has been exceptionally strong.[34]

Salam Sukuk Structure

Aluminum has been designed as the underlying asset of the salam contract. The government of Bahrain will sell aluminum to the buyer. In exchange for the advance payment that will be paid by the Islamic bank(s), the government of Bahrain will undertake to supply a specified amount of aluminum at a future date. At the same time, the Islamic bank(s) will appoint the government of Bahrain as an agent to market the quantity of aluminum at the time of delivery through its channels of distribution. The government of Bahrain will also undertake to market the aluminum at a price that will provide a return to the salam security holders.[35]

The investors will bear counterparty as well as market risks. The counterparty risk would arise with regard to the possibility of the government being unable to deliver the goods. The market risk would result from the government being unable to market the aluminum at the time of the delivery. However, these risks are mitigated by the structure of the deal. The risk translates into a sovereign risk, which is the government of Bahrain. Additionally, the CBB will secure that another Islamic financial institution will issue a guarantee to buy the aluminum from the new company in case the government fails to market the commodity. This guarantee will act as a credit enhancement that will provide additional security to salam sukuk holders against counterparty and market risks.[36]

Although the salam certificates have so far played a useful role in providing short-term investment opportunities for Islamic banks, the certificates would be much more useful if they could be traded in a secondary market. The issue is the point of difference of opinion among Shari'ah scholars. The majority[37] of Muslim jurists are of the opinion that it is not permissible to sell the purchased goods in a salam contract before taking possession. This means it is not possible to sell the salam certificate to a third party. They relied on the hadith of the Prophet to the effect that whoever makes salam shall not exchange it before taking possession.[38] It is based on such an argument that the Accounting and Auditing Organization of Islamic Financial Institutions (AAOIFI) standard on salam submitted that "it is not permissible to issue tradable bonds based on the debt from a salam contract."[39] However, this hadith is considered a weak hadith by some scholars. Therefore, it could not be the basis of any ruling.[40] A minority group, on the other hand, did not see any Shari'ah objection in reselling salam before taking possession, if it is sold to a third party and it is not a foodstuff. More important, it could be sold at the same price, a higher price, or a lower price.

Given the fact the salam certificates, in their present structure, are not tradable and aware of the need for medium- and long-term instruments, the CBB later introduced ijarah sukuk, which are more flexible and can be traded in secondary markets.

SHORT-TERM IJARAH SUKUK AS MONEY MARKET INSTRUMENT

The CBB has successfully launched the debut issue of a short-term, tradable ijarah sukuk in a yet another pioneering move by the CCB to develop Islamic banking, enhance investment opportunities for commercial banks, and address the issue of liquidity. The short-term ijarah sukuk is asset based and issued on a monthly basis by the CBB on the last Thursday of each month. Each issue is worth BD10 million (USD27 million) and carries a fixed rental return, based on the prevailing six-month LIBOR rate, with the return to be paid on maturity. The sukuk certificates are available to all Islamic and conventional full commercial banks licensed by the CBB, as well as pension funds in Bahrain. Other interested investors, who are allowed to subscribe through the eligible full commercial banks, include locally incorporated insurance firms, Islamic investment banks, and individual investors in Bahrain and elsewhere. It was the first short-term, tradable ijarah sukuk for the global Islamic banking industry. The sukuk can be traded to facilitate short-term Bahraini dinar liquidity management by Islamic financial institutions. It is held that the CBB might allow the subscribing institutions to use the short-term ijarah sukuk as collateral against short-term credit facilities from the CBB. This will add further depth to the primary Islamic debt market in Bahrain. The initiative will make available to Islamic financial institutions a greater diversity of investment choices, as enjoyed by their conventional counterparts.[41] The CBB now has a full complement of ijarah sukuk of short, medium, and long tenors. The ijarah sukuk are issued by the CBB on behalf of the government of Bahrain.[42]

The short- and medium-term ijarah sukuk as instruments of liquidity management have also been followed by the Central Bank of Malaysia. The Central Bank of Malaysia (Bank Negara) issued its inaugural Bank Negara Malaysia (BNM) Sukuk Ijarah with an issue size of RM400 million and a one-year tenor. The new Islamic monetary instrument was issued on a regular basis, with subsequent issues rang-ing from RM100 million to RM200 million. It is expected that there will be more issuance, depending on the pool of Bank Negara's underlying fixed assets available under the program. Foreigners could also invest in Bank Negara Malaysia sukuk ijarah, which will be issued via a special-purpose vehicle, BNM Sukuk Bhd. It is expected that most participants will come from banking institutions and that some corporations might also be interested in the instrument.[43]

The sukuk are based on the "sale and lease back" concept. The proceeds from the issuance are used to purchase the central bank's assets. The assets are then leased to Bank Negara for rental payment consideration, which is distributed to investors as a return on a semiannual basis. Upon maturity, which coincides with the end of the lease tenor, the sukuk are sold back to Bank Negara at a predetermined price. The new instrument is expected to add to the diversity of monetary instruments used by Bank Negara in managing liquidity in the Islamic money market. Due to its regular issuance, the sukuk ijarah is also expected to serve as a benchmark for other short- to medium-term Islamic bonds. The introduction of sukuk ijarah reflects also BNM's continuous efforts to spur product innovation and development to meet the diversified requirements of domestic and international investors.[44]

The use of ijarah sukuk as instrument of liquidity management has also been followed by the kingdom of Brunei. The government of Brunei has no external debt; therefore, the fundamental reason for the sale of these short-term sukuk is to develop Brunei as an Islamic market. Thus, the government launched an open-ended program called the Short Term Government Sukuk Al-Ijarah program that will allow issuance of Islamic commercial paper with maturities of three months and up to one year. The sale of certificates is assigned to five primary dealers: two local banks, Baiduri Bank Group and the Islamic Bank Brunei, and foreign banks Citibank Inc., HSBC, and Standard Chartered Bank. The government will lease back the assets, and the rental payments will be used to pay dividends to the debt investors. Though initially the sales will go through five primary dealers using a book-building process, the government may adopt an auction process later. Brunei short-term Islamic bonds are issued as a contribution to the Islamic capital market development and to be a reference for other Islamic countries. It is also intended to encourage other parties, including main corporate bodies in the country, to issue their individual Islamic bonds. These issuances are also aimed at reducing dependency on banks to get funds. Moreover, such issuances give the public the opportunity to invest in internal projects based on the principles of Islamic law. Finally, it is also hoped that it will reduce the amount of funds flowing out of the country. The Brunei government has thus issued, up to the middle of 2012, more than B$4.151 billion worth of short-term Sukuk Al-Ijarah securities since the maiden offering on April 6, 2006.[45]

INVESTMENT AGENCY AND LIQUIDITY MANAGEMENT

Wakalah is a contract whereby one party (the principal) places funds with the other party (the agent) to use it to finance any viable business activity for the benefit of the principal in return for a predetermined agency fee.

It is widely held that wakalah emulates the characteristics of a conventional money market placement and allows a much more efficient recycling of short-term liquidity in the Islamic banking system.[46]

Advantages of Wakalah

- No physical commodity is required, as is the case with murabahah or tawarruq.
- No intermediate party is involved and, therefore, no brokerage cost.
- It allows Islamic banks to accept liquidity from Islamic and non-Islamic financial institutions.
- It provides competitive pricing, as the wakalah's expected return is generally linked to market benchmarks.

For the bank to maintain its credibility and its depositor confidence, it invests the funds received from depositors under an Investment Agency Agreement only in existing projects or investment avenues having fixed return. These existing projects or investment avenues could be leased property generating a fixed return or leasing any equipment such as aircraft, ships, or sukuk instruments, in which the return is already known, or istisna projects with a predetermined markup.

The range of available products for liquidity management is not only diversified in terms of product characteristics but also based on country of origin. This is clearly evident in the musharakah, which are widely used in Sudan.

MUSHARAKAH CERTIFICATES AS MONEY MARKET INSTRUMENT: THE SUDANESE EXPERIENCE

The Sudanese experience in designing Islamic financial instruments for liquidity management is based on musharakah. The Central Bank of Sudan launched in 1998 the Central Bank Musharakah Certificates (CMCs). This is an equity-based instrument that is used against Bank of Sudan ownership in commercial banks. It is used by Bank of Sudan as an indirect instrument to regulate and manage liquidity within the banking system.

In 1999, the Ministry of Finance launched another instrument, called Government Musharakah Certificates (GMCs). They are also musharakah-based instruments that are used against the Ministry of Finance's ownership in some profitable public and joint venture enterprises in collaboration with some IMF staff. The certificates are meant to regulate and manage liquidity within the economy as a whole.[47]

The instruments enable the government to raise funds through the issuance of securities that promise the investors a negotiable return that is linked to the development in government revenue (a share in government revenue, for example) in return for their investment in the provision of general government services.[48]

The fund user is the government, which builds the infrastructure, and the fund suppliers are people who have savings to invest. The intermediaries are Islamic banks and other financial institutions. Once the government issues a particular sharing certificate, the Islamic banks and other financial institutions buy it out of the funds accumulated in their investment accounts or as insurance, as the case may be. The government's obligation to pay yearly dividends could be met through the bank, to which it may transfer its share of the declared profits. If the certificates have a maturity date when the government is offering to pay back the capital (with the final year's profit or minus the losses), this obligation, too, can be met through the banks. The government does not deal with the public directly. It transacts only with the Islamic banks and other financial institutions, which transact with the public. Those who do not wish to keep the certificate till maturity can sell, and those who missed the issue when it launched can buy. Thus, it will function like any other market.[49]

The successes of these two instruments and their wide market acceptability have encouraged the Bank of Sudan to introduce other types of instruments, such as ijarah sukuk, Islamic development sukuk, and government finance certificates.

MALAYSIAN ISLAMIC INTERBANK MONEY MARKET

The Malaysian experience is the most developed, and it adopted a wide variety of products to satisfy the market demand. Thus, besides the introduction of well-known products such as murabahah or short ijarah sukuk, the market has its own specific products, especially those based on the sale of debt. Bank Negara introduced the Islamic money market on January 3, 1994. The scope of activities of the Islamic Interbank Money Market (IIMM) included the purchase and sale of Islamic financial instruments among market participants (including the Bank) and interbank investment activities through the Mudaraba Interbank Investment (MII).

The Islamic financial instruments that are currently being traded in the IIMM on the basis of bai al-dayn and bay al-inah used a number of instruments. The following are the major instruments:

- Mudharabah Interbank Investment
- Bank Negara Negotiable Notes
- Islamic accepted bills (IAB)
- Government Investment Issue (GII)
- Wadiah and Daman
- Islamic Private Debt Securities (IPDS)
- Negotiable Islamic Debt Certificates (NIDC)
- Green Bankers
- Khazanah bonds
- Sell and Buy Back Agreement (SBBA)
- Ar Rahnu Agreement-I (RA-i)
- Sukuk BNM Ijarah (SBNMI)

Commenting on some of these products, observers have noted:

Even though some of these instruments are Shariah compatible, others seem to be controversial. The controversies surrounding these instruments are mainly due to the overemphasising on the use of bay al-inah contract in devising most IIMM instruments. For example, Government Investment Issue (GII) which was initially issued by the Government of Malaysia based on qard al-hasan (benevolent loan) principle, now replaced by bay al-inah, allowing it to be traded in the secondary market via the concept bay al-dayn (debt trading).[50]

The UAE Central Bank in 2010 started issuing the country's first Islamic certificates of deposits (ICDs) as part of a plan to create a new investment tool for Shari'ah-compliant banks in the country. The new ICDs would be issued in dirhams, U.S. dollars, and euros, and their maturity date would range between one week and five years and based on murabahah. The new ICDs are intended to absorb excess liquidity in Islamic banks in the country and allow them to invest such liquidity in dirhams in the local market "instead of turning abroad to invest in foreign currency."[51]

The Central Bank of Turkey, to address the liquidity problem of Islamic financial institutions (or participation banks, as they are called in Turkey), became a founding member of the IILM, mandated to resolve the issue of liquidity facing the industry worldwide, and contributed USD10 million to its equity. In another initiative to facilitate participation banks' liquidity management, the Undersecretariat of Treasury has started to issue revenue-indexed bonds, which are purchased by the participation banks. However, the "bonds" were not well received by the industry, and on February 19, 2012, some Shari'ah advisors stated that the revenue-indexed bonds (GES) are no different than government bonds in terms of interest charged. This has created a difficult situation for participation banks in Turkey, which hold $1 billion in GES. Participation banks quickly returned their Treasury-issued GES and exchanged them for the Islamic equivalent of bonds, called sukuk. Moreover, the Association of Turkish Participation Banks (TKBB) noted that the Shari'ah advisors' comments are a binding declaration for the TKBB and that there is a need for a new road map. According to the TKBB, three participation banks have $984 million worth of GES in their portfolios. Another $459 million held by individuals and institutions are the rest of the GES in Turkey. These GES, which were largely bought by conservative investors and participation banks, were issued by the government to increase the number of investors in debt bonds within the state and to diversify the available financial instruments.[52] Coupon payments for the instruments are linked to revenue from state-owned enterprises: the Turkish Petroleum Corporation, the State Supply Office, the State Airport Authority, and the Coastal Safety Administration.

ISLAMIC INTERBANK MARKET AND RECIPROCAL LOANS

To address the possibility of an Islamic interbank market to provide short-term liquidity to Islamic banks, three alternatives may be considered.

1. First, banks could have an agreement with other banks for mutual financing facilities, as is the usual practice of conventional banks, but within the framework of profit and loss sharing. Banks that are in need of more resources from others may enter into mutual agreements of profit- and loss-sharing arrangements. This would allow them place surplus funds, arrange liquidity when they need it, and balance their short-term assets and liabilities.
2. Second, there could be an interbank on the basis of a cooperative arrangement to extend reciprocal accommodation to each other on the condition

that the net use of this facility is zero over a given period. This could be on the basis of mutual borrowings canceling out mutual lending.

3. Third, the banks could create a common pool at the central bank to provide mutual accommodation. This method is multilateral in nature; therefore, it could avoid the disadvantage of the two previous methods of being bilateral. All banks may be required to contribute a certain percent of their deposits to this common pool, just as they do in the case of statutory reserve requirements. They would then have the right to borrow from this pool, with the condition that the net use of the facility is zero.[53]

However, the second and third propositions of interbank loans are based on the idea of mutual or reciprocal lending that is a point of disagreement among Muslim scholars. The majority of classical scholars, as well as many contemporary scholars, prohibit such a kind of transaction. The proposed structures rest essentially on the exchange of loans or the conditioning of a loan upon a counterloan. The simple form of the idea can be formulated as follows: I lend to you, provided that you lend to me (aslifini uslifuka).

Among the legal arguments advanced against the idea of reciprocal loans are the following:

• A loan is a gift, whereas if it is made contingent to another loan, it turns into a sale and thus deviates from its original nature and objective.
• Such a transaction will be a kind of qardan jarra nafan or "a loan that brings benefit to the lender," which is prohibited in Islam based on the ijma' of the Companions that a lender should not acquire any increment of the loan that was extended. A famous hadith is also reported in this connection, that "any loan that brings benefit (to the creditor) is riba."
• The reciprocal loan is based on two equal benefits or interests and their mutual setoff.

A minority of Muslim scholars did not see any Shari'ah objection to the idea of the reciprocal loan and argue that it is comparable to the idea of cooperative society or Jama and has the same spirit. These are mostly informal societies, wherein a group of employees or individuals may agree that each of them contributes a part of their income for the members of the society to benefit from the pooled amount, according to varying arrangements.[54]

However, the Shari'ah boards of several Islamic financial institutions have broadly approved the idea of the reciprocal loan.

Another product that deserves attention and is still under scrutiny and development is the Islamic alternative to repo.

ISLAMIC REPO

A repurchase agreement is a sale of securities coupled with an agreement to repurchase the same securities at a higher price on a later date. A repo is thus broadly similar to a collateralized loan. For example, dealer A can borrow $10 million overnight at an interest rate of 3 percent per annum by selling Treasury securities to a mutual fund and simultaneously agreeing to repurchase the securities the following day for $10,000,833 ($10 million + 1/360 of 3 percent of $10 million). The payment from the initial sale is the principal amount of the loan; the excess of the repurchase price over the sale price is the interest paid on the loan. As with a collateralized loan, the lender has possession of the borrower's securities during the term of the loan and can sell them if the borrower defaults on its repurchase obligation.[55]

To shed more light on the concept, let us consider the following transaction between a primary securities dealer and one of its clients, say, a municipality. The primary securities dealer in need of money calls the municipality and, in exchange for an MBS worth, say, $100, borrows $100 for a week. The understanding is that a week later, the primary securities dealer will return with $105 to get the MBS back. The extra $5 is the interest on the $100 principal, whereas the MBS is the collateral securing the loan. From the municipality's perspective, the municipality lends $100 to the primary securities dealer at $5 interest by borrowing the MBS for a week. If the primary securities dealer fails to come back with $105 at the end of the week, the MBS becomes the property of the municipality. If the municipality sells the borrowed MBS before the end of the week, then the municipality will need to buy the MBS back to return it to the primary securities dealer. If it is acceptable to the dealer, the municipality may instead buy a substitute (and most likely a cheaper) MBS. If the municipality fails to return the MBS or an acceptable substitute to the primary securities dealer, then the dealer keeps the $100 without paying any interest.[56]

In this transaction, the primary securities dealer enters into a sale and repurchase agreement or, in short, a repo. The municipality enters into a purchase and resale agreement, or a reverse repo. Thus, every repo is also a reverse repo and vice versa; the perspective depends on who is the seller and who is the purchaser.

There are a number of benefits in using repo that concurrently have been behind its rapid growth. These include greater liquidity and the ability to finance long bond and equity positions at a lower interest cost if they repo out the assets. The International Islamic Financial Market, in its paper on repo, listed the following benefits:

- An active repo market can lead to increase in turnover in the underlying bond, thereby improving liquidity and the depth of the market.
- For institutions and corporate entities, repos provide a source of inexpensive finance and offer investment opportunities to lend money at market rates, thus earning a good return. It is a cash management tool allowing the seller to maximize funding of its bonds inventory.
- Triparty repos offer opportunities for suitable financial institutions or clearing houses to act as an agent between the lender and the borrower.
- To cover a shortfall by borrowing the bonds on repo.[57]

Malaysia was among the first countries to introduce Islamic repo. The product is structured under bai al-inah, which is perceived as a suitable contract to be introduced in the Islamic Interbank Money Market. In this transaction, the Shari'ah-compliant asset (for example, Government Investment Issue) will be sold by a financier such as a central bank to the recipient bank at X price on deferred terms. Then, the recipient bank will sell back the asset to the financier on a cash basis at Y price. The deferred price of X is higher than the cash price of Y; hence the difference is regarded as profit to the financier. Both sale contracts are executed separately. The question is whether the application of bai al-inah, as explained previously, is acceptable in Shari'ah.[58] The Shari'ah advisory council of the Central Bank of Malaysia, in its eighth meeting held on December 12, 1998/23rd Syaaban 1419, resolved that bai al-inah transactions in the Islamic Interbank Money Market are permissible if they follow the mechanism that is accepted by the Shafii school of law and if the transacted asset is not a ribawi item.

However, most Shari'ah scholars view repos as explained here as inherently non-Shari'ah-compliant transactions and consider the repo rate, which is the price difference between the transactions, to contravene the ban on borrowing and lending on interest.

The guidelines on Islamic negotiable instruments (INI) issued by the Central Bank of Malaysia outline the repo mechanism in the following seven points, under the broader concept of the sell and buy back agreement (Islamic repo).

1. Under the sell and buy back agreement (SBBA), the transacting parties shall enter into two separate agreements as follows:
   - First agreement: The seller (owner) of INI sells and the buyer (investor) buys the instrument at a specified price agreed by both parties.
   - Second agreement: A forward purchase agreement whereby the buyer (investor) promises to sell back the INI to the original owner, who shall buy it back at a specified price on a specified future date.
2. Ownership of the INI shall be transferred to the buyer (investor) upon conclusion of the first agreement of the SBBA.
3. An INI may be sold under SBBA, subject to the following conditions:
   - An issuer shall not buy its own INI under SBBA.
   - The tenor of the SBBA must be within the tenor of the INI used for the transaction.
4. The INI used for the SBBA is not required to be delivered, unless otherwise agreed by the two transacting parties.
5. Where the SBBA transaction involves an INI that does not pay interim dividends or coupon profits (as in the case of NIDC), the amount of proceeds receivable by the seller under the first agreement of the SBBA shall not exceed the nominal value of the INI.
6. A licensed financial institution may provide on a regular basis a two-way quotation either by quoting rates or profit-sharing ratio to indicate its willingness to enter into SBBA.
7. Upon its release, the Guidelines on Sell and Buy Back Agreement shall govern SBBA transactions involving INI.[59]

Malaysia's repos are two-party agreements like those in conventional finance, but the Bahrain's repo transactions would involve three parties. In Bahrain's system, a bank seeking funds sells a sukuk to a broker, who then sells it on to the BMA in separate spot transactions. The bank that sought the funds promises to buy the bond from the BMA at a specified date and price. The BMA, as the legal owner of the asset, has no obligation to sell. But if the bank fails to keep its promise and the central bank takes a loss on a sale in the open market, it can claim compensation.[60]

Bahrain's central bank has also come up with an initiative in developing an Islamic repo to manage liquidity. The Bahraini version is not a two-party agreement but involves three parties. Thus, a bank seeking funds sells a sukuk to a broker, who then sells it on to the CBB in separate spot transactions. The bank that sought the funds promises to buy the bond from the CBB at a specified date and price. The CBB, as the legal owner of the asset, has no obligation to sell. But if the bank fails to keep its promise and the central bank takes a loss on a sale in the open market, it can claim compensation.[61]

However, according the IIFM, for this structure to serve in international or cross-border transactions, certain issues would need to be addressed, such as lack of margin maintenance, lack of an obligation on the CBB to sell at maturity to party A, and effectiveness in an insolvency of party A. Moreover, the product is based on CBB sukuk specifically, and therefore, there is an issue risk appetite outside the jurisdiction for this structure. The IIFM added that the structure is workable at a country level, where the central bank is the liquidity provider.

The report covers four concepts that were described and alludes to a fifth that is currently under discussion. The four concepts are the bilateral repo (I'aadat Al-Shira'a or IS), which is also the closest to a conventional repo whereby two parties agree to a sale by one party in the spot market with a repurchase of an identical security at a later date at a set price. Yet, it is recognized that if the set price does not depend on the market price at the time of repurchase, this raises issues of riba with the Shari'ah considerations. Moreover, it is suggested to use an identical security rather than the original security as a way of avoiding the problem of debt trading (bai al-inah). The second concept changed the purchase undertaking to a wa'd (unilateral undertaking to purchase or sell) but raised Shari'ah issues. The third concept is based a three-party structure. The three-party structure inserted a third party between the two parties, with a sale to the third party by the borrower and a purchase from the third party by the lender. There was also a purchase undertaking for a specified price between the borrower and the lender to return the securities for a prespecified sale price at maturity of the repo agreement. The issues in the three-party repo were covered more extensively than in bilateral repo. Yet from a Shari'ah perspective, there are issues with this concept as well, such as with the purchase undertaking, specifically whether it can be exercised by the lender (to force repurchase by the borrower) or whether it is a unilateral promise (wa'd) by the borrower to the lender.[62] The fourth concept is the collateralized structure.

The key difference between the new concept and a normal commodity muraba-hah is that the new concept is backed by another commodity using sukuk. The transaction is designed to facilitate short-term lending and borrowing at low risk, besides the existing interbank unsecured commodity murabahah. The transaction can be described now as secured commodity murabahah that is secured by an asset, and it is other than just another receivable on a counterparty.

This is important systemically because the failure of one institution would force the liquidation of a chain of interbank loans and could more easily spread across the Islamic banking system. As the troubled institution heads toward insolvency, the interbank markets would become harder and harder to access (because of concern by other banks of becoming unsecured creditors of a potentially failed bank). The difference with a commodity murabahah secured by a sukuk is that the cost of a counterparty failing is reduced (particularly if the collateral is high quality). All other things being equal, this would keep the lending channels open as long as the collateral is viewed as high quality.

The high-quality collateral can serve as a backstop to keep interbank money markets open even in a crisis because the failure of an institution would not have as much of a spillover effect onto its counterparties. They could keep lending so long as they were provided with good enough unencumbered sukuk as collateral, knowing that if the counterparty failed, they could recoup the principal amount lent by liquidating the collateral.

National Bank of Abu Dhabi (NBAD) and Abu Dhabi Islamic Bank (ADIB) jointly embarked on this initiative to formalize the Master Collateralized Muraba-hah agreement (MCMA) as the first such experience in the GCC.

THE WAY FORWARD AND REGULATORS' CONCERNS

Despite the efforts to address the liquidity risk in Islamic financial institutions, there are still a number of challenges that need to be addressed for an effective solution to the problem. Among others are the following:

- The unavailability of enough short-term instruments in which these banks could invest may hamper the development of an Islamic interbank market.
- Generally, there are only a few Islamic banks in one single country, which may make the functioning of such a market a bit difficult. Moreover, these banks are generally small in terms of their resources and may not be able to provide sufficient accommodation to other Islamic banks. Thus, there is a need for an institutional structure to facilitate such a market, especially when an Islamic interbank market can be internationally designed.
- Despite the success of the locally structured instruments, their volume, if they are confined to their local market, may not be suitable for the development of an Islamic secondary market that will solve the problem of liquidity. Therefore, the Islamic secondary market needs to be international in nature.
- The proposals advanced as the Islamic alternative to interbank, whether based on mudarabah, murbaha, or wakalah, have their shortcomings, and the design and use of sukuk for liquidity management requires detailed research if the Islamic secondary market is to succeed and the liquidity problem is to be resolved.
- The strong involvement of sovereign banks in sukuk issuance can make a real difference and, therefore, needs to be encouraged.
- If the active secondary market should be international in nature, there is a need for harmonization of products through the endorsement of different instruments by well-known scholars representing different regions. This will allow, for instance, products issued in Bahrain to be accepted in Malaysia, UAE, or any other country.
- Another key factor in the success of the Islamic sukuk market is the need for standardization of dealing and settlement practices of the different types of sukuk issued by Islamic financial institutions. This requires, in turn, the

issuance of guidelines that strengthen market practices at the international level.

- The international character of the market will allow addressing the problem of lack of awareness of attractive investment opportunities in other markets and facilitate raising funds and investments beyond national borders.

Most of the experiences described are confined to the local markets and do not carry any broader international acceptance. To support cross-border transactions by Islamic financial institutions in a globalized world and to ensure adequate market liquidity, international acceptance of at least some of these instruments is needed. It is necessary that Islamic finance practitioners and scholars look at the legal and technical hurdles that limit the international acceptability of these instruments and at the ways and means of addressing it. The role of infrastructure institutions such as AAOIFI, IFSB, IIFM, the Liquidity Management Center (LMC), and the International Islamic Rating Agency (IIRA) is important in this development.

Finally, for an effective liquidity management mechanism, there is a need beyond the capital market, money market, and the interbank market. It should be an effective and Shari'ah-compliant mechanism of lender of last resort. Few experiences are recorded in this area. Among others, we have the experience of Bank Indonesia in tackling the problem.

Under this mechanism, if an Islamic bank faces liquidity risk in the form of short-term funding difficulties and it fails to raise funds on the money market based on Shari'ah principles, Bank Indonesia will act as lender of last resort.

Another challenging concern facing Islamic financial institutions is how to manage liquidity in light of Basel 3. Obviously, Islamic financial institutions cannot invest in interest-based products. This makes the specific liquidity requirements of Basel 3 difficult to apply to them. There is also the complication that the outstanding stock of sukuk is not sufficiently large to enable all Islamic financial institutions to meet a liquidity ratio comparable to that mandated under Basel 3. Finally, the markets for sukuk are not always as liquid as those for conventional government bonds; therefore, even if an Islamic financial institution invests in them, it might not always be able to find a ready buyer when the need occurs.

These are genuine practical difficulties in applying Basel 3 to Islamic financial institutions. Even so, they should not get in the way of recognizing the important principle that Islamic financial institutions need to take liquidity risk just as seriously as conventional firms need to do. They need to make sure that they keep maturity mismatching to prudent limits. There needs to be a debate about what sort of limits would be prudent, but there is no doubt that limits are needed.[63]

Following the recent crisis, the role of liquidity in aggravating the situation and the proposed Basel requirement to maintain a sufficient cushion of high-quality liquid assets need to be carefully considered, as the infrastructure and tools for liquidity risk management by Islamic banks is still in its infancy in many jurisdictions. However, it has been pointed out that the very narrow definition of liquid assets that is currently proposed may exacerbate liquidity risks in many Islamic financial markets in which Islamic banks compete with conventional counterparts for the limited stock of Shari'ah-compliant government securities. This will certainly increase compliance cost and render the market illiquid when the demand exceeds supply, placing Islamic financial institutions at a disadvantage.

An adjustment that has been very helpful in interbank operations has been the reciprocal placement of funds on an interest-free basis, based on a relaxed interpretation of the legal maxim "Every loan which begets an advantage is riba." In this context, a loan is advanced for a certain period of time on an interest-free basis, and the other bank advances a similar amount in a different currency for a similar period of time as compensation. A reciprocal loan compensates the other bank for the cost of advancing the interest-free loan in the first place. Funds placed in nostro accounts with correspondent banks are in a similar category. The Islamic bank and the correspondent bank recover the cost of the interest-free deposit with each other in two ways: (1) by reciprocal exchange of funds and by mutually agreeing not to charge interest on either the vostro or nostro account, even if the accounts go into the red, and (2) the banking services are provided free by the correspondent bank for the Islamic bank, and by the latter for the former. It is true that in such a case, there is no explicit charging or paying of interest, but the benefits from keeping funds have been achieved in kind.[64]

It is reported that this product is implemented in Saudi Arabia, Kuwait, and Jordan, but further investigation is needed. Thus, Islamic financial institutions (IFI) use interbank compensating mutual financing facilities within the profit-sharing framework. This involves the exchange of interest-free deposits with arrangements to ensure that net balances average to zero in a defined period.[65]

CONCLUSION

Although a lot of effort has been recently made to address the issue of liquidity management in Islamic finance, the issue still requires more innovations. Infrastructure institutions in particular need to do more. The IFSB, besides issuing standards, needs to convince its members for better cooperation to resolve the issue, particularly the legal and regulatory dimensions. The AAOIFI needs to do more Shari'ah-related research on the issue, and the IIFM needs to double its efforts in terms of harmonization. The IILM has a leading role to play, and the institution needs to have close contact with the industry players and explain its future projects. Relations with Shari'ah scholars should not be limited to scholars on its board; it needs to forge relations with a wide range of scholars, especially those ready to conduct research. On the other hand, liquidity management in the industry is not just a business issue. It has also legal, political, and cross-border issues. Therefore, the IILM should not limit itself to its existing founding members but needs to get acceptance in the key markets and, therefore, leverage its relations with the IFSB and the central banks that make up its membership.

NOTES

1. J. L. Hanson, *A Dictionary of Economics and Commerce*, 6th ed. (London: Pitman, 1986).
2. Deric G. Hanson, *Dictionary of Banking and Finance* (London: Pitman, 1985).
3. William H. Baughin, Thomas I. Storrs, and Charles E. Walker, *The Bankers' Handbook*, 3rd ed. (Homewood, IL: Dow Jones-Irwin, 1988); *The Concise McGraw Hill Dictionary of Modern Economics* (New York: McGraw Hill, 1983).
4. See Chapra M. Umer, *Corporate Governance in Islamic Financial Institutions* (Jeddah, Saudi Arabia: Islamic Development Bank, Jeddah, 2002), 57.

5. Zeti Akhtar Aziz, "The Changing Landscape of Financial Regulation—Implications for Islamic Finance" (speech by the Governor of the Central Bank of Malaysia at the seventh Independence Federal Savings Bank summit on Global Financial Architecture, Manama, Bahrain, May 4, 2010).

6. Opening remarks by H. E. Rasheed M. Al-Maraj, Governor, Central Bank of Bahrain (first annual World Islamic Banking Conference Asia Summit, Singapore, June14, 2010).

7. Ibid.

8. Durmuş Yilmaz, Governor of the Central Bank of the Republic of Turkey, "Managing Liquidity in the Islamic Financial Services Industry" (speech at a conference organized by the Islamic Financial Services Board, Istanbul, April 6, 2011).

9. Mohamed Damak and Emmanuel Volland, *Risk Management for Islamic Financial Institutions: A Rating Perspective* (New York: Standard & Poor's, 2008).

10. Habhajan Singh, "Islamic Banks Grapple with Liquidity Risk Profile Issues," *The Malaysian Reserve*, Kuala Lumpur, March 30, 2009.

11. Maher Hasan and Jemma Dridi, "The Effects of the Global Crisis on Islamic and Conventional Banks: A Comparative Study" (IMF Working paper, September 2010).

12. Zeti Akhtar Aziz, "Global Financial Architecture: Challenges for Islamic Finance" (Governor's speech at the seventh Islamic Financial Services Board Summit, Manama, Bahrain, May 4, 2010).

13. For more details, see Muhammad Al Bashir and Muhammad Al-Amine, *Global Sukuk and Islamic Securitization Market Financial Engineering and Product Innovation* (Leiden, Netherlands: Brill, 2012).

14. Hennie Van Greuning and Zamir Iqbal, *Risk Analysis for Islamic Banks* (Washington, DC: World Bank, 2008).

15. Damak and Volland, *Risk Management for Islamic Financial Institutions*.

16. Singh, "Islamic Banks Grapple with Liquidity Risk Profile Issues."

17. Mushtak Parker, "Issues in Regulating Islamic Finance," *Central Banking Journal*, February 18, 2011. www.centralbanking.com

18. Yilmaz, "Managing Liquidity in the Islamic Financial Services Industry."

19. Hasan and Dridi, "The Effects of the Global Crisis on Islamic and Conventional Banks."

20. Yilmaz, "Managing Liquidity in the Islamic Financial Services Industry."

21. Parker, "Issues in Regulating Islamic Finance."

22. Ibid., 27.

23. Youssef Shaheed Maroum, "Liquidity Management and Trade Financing," in *Islamic Finance Innovation and Growth* (London: Euromoney Books, 2002), 165–166.

24. Parker, "Commodity Murabahah Attracting Investors," *Arab News, Saudi Arabia,* June 18, 2007. www.arabnews.com.

25. Bahrain Monetary Agency, *Islamic Banking and Finance in the Kingdom of Bahrain* (Manama: Bahrain Monetary Agency, 2002), 30.

26. Stella Cox, "Islamic Asset Management: An Expanding Sector," *Review of Islamic Economics*, No. 11, 2002, International Association for Islamic Economics, pp. 27–50.

27. Ibid.

28. Maroum, "Liquidity Management and Trade Financing," 165–166.

29. See Iqbal Khan, "Liquidity Management of Islamic Financial Institutions in the UAE" (seminar hosted by the Central Bank of UAE, Abu Dhabi, December 10, 2005).

30. Ibn 'Abidin, *Hashiyat Rad al-Muhtar,* Matba'ah Mustafa al-Babi al-Halabi (Cairo, 1966), 209.

31. Fahim Khan, "Islamic Futures and Their Market" (research paper no. 32, Islamic Research and Training Institute), 14; also see Obiyathulla Ismath Bacha, "Derivative Instruments and Islamic Finance: Some Thoughts for a Reconsideration" (unpublished paper, International Islamic University Malaysia, November 1997), 18.

32. êidd¥q al-ëar¥r, "al-Salam wa Tatb¥qŒtuhu al-Muasirah" (*Majallat Majma' al-Fiqh al-Islami* ninth session, 1996), 379–383; Nazih Hammad, "al-Salam wa tatabiqatuhu al Muasira" (*Majallat Majma' al-Fiqh al-Islami* ninth session, 1996), 553–555.

33. See Mohammad Ali El-Gari, "Developing Medium- and Long-Term Corporate Bonds" (paper presented at the international seminar The Economic and Financial Imperative of Globalization: An Islamic Response, Institute of Islamic Understanding, Malaysia, April 8–9, 1999), 11–12.

34. Khalid al-Bassam, "Recent Innovations in the Creation of the Islamic Financial Instruments in Bahrain," *Bahrain Dinar Digest,* Issue 1, Volume 1, January 2002: 8.

35. Ibid., 8–9.

36. Ibid., 4.

37. See Ibn Abidin, *Rad al-Muhtar* Matba'ah Mustafa al-Babi al-Halabi (Cairo, 1966), vol. 4, 209; al-Buhuti, Mansur Ibn Yunus. Kashaf al-Qina 'an Matn al-Iqna'. Beirut Lebanon. Dar al-Fikr. 1982–. Vol. 3, 293; Ibn Qudama, Muwaffaq al-Din 'Abd Allah Ibn Aḥmad. al-Mughni. Beirut. Dar al- Fikr. (n.d), vol. 4, 334.

38. Abu Dawud (n.d.), *Sunan AbuDawud,* vol. 2 (Cairo: Mustapha al-Halabi Cairo), 247.

39. Accounting and Auditing Organization for Islamic Financial Institutions, *Sharia'a Standards* 1423H-2002 (Manama, Bahrain: AAOIF), 167.

40. See Ibn Hajar *Talkhis al-Ḥabir fi Takhrij Aḥadith al Rafii al Kabir*, Sharikat al-Tbaah al-Fatimiyyah, Egypt (n.d.).

41. Bahrain Monetary Agency, "BMA Pioneers 6-Month Sukuk," *Capital Market Review,* September 6, 2005.

42. Ibid.

43. Bank Negara Malaysia, "Issuance of Sukuk Bank Negara Malaysia Based on Ijarah Concept," February 9, 2006: www.bnm.gov.my.

44. Ibid.

45. "Successful Issuances of Brunei Darussalam Government Short-Term Sukuk Al-Ijarah Securities 73rd Series," *Zawya,* June 4, 2012.

46. "European Islamic Bank Begun Accepting Wakalah Fund," *Gulf Daily News* 29, February 3, 2007.

47. See Sabir Mohammad Hassan, "Towards Fostering Financial Stability of the Islamic Financial Industry" (paper presented at the inauguration of the Islamic Financial Services Board, Kuala Lumpur, Malaysia, November 2002), 5.

48. See V. Sundrarajan, David Marston, and Ghiath Shabshigh, "Monetary Operation and Government Debt Management under Islamic Banking" (IFM working paper 144, 1998), 13.

49. Muhammad Najatullah Siddiqi, "Financing Infrastructure Building: Role of Islamic Financial Institutions" (paper presented in a seminar, Cooperation between Government and the Private Sector Financing Economic Projects, Center for Research in Islamic Economics, King Abdulaziz University, Jeddah, Saudi Arabia, 1999), 4–5.

50. Asyraf Wajdi Dusuki, "Commodity Murabahah Programme (CMP): An Innovative Approach to Liquidity Management," *Journal of Islamic Economics, Banking and Finance* 3, no. 1 (2007): 9.

51. Himendra Mohan Kumar, "Central Bank Islamic CDs Climb to Dh12b," *Gulf News,* June 3, 2011.

52. "Top Advisor to Participation Banks Says GES Equal to Gov't Bonds," *Today's Zaman* (Istanbul), March 29, 2012.

53. For more elaboration on this issue, see Umer Chapra, "Mechanics and Operations of an Islamic Financial Market," *Journal of Islamic Banking and Finance* 5, no. 3 (1988): 31–36.

54. For more details on the issue, see Rafiq Yunes al-Masri, "Reciprocal Loans," *Journal of King Abdul Aziz University: Islamic Economic* 14 (2002): 33–38; Saad Bin Hamdan

al-Lihyani, "Reciprocal Loans," *Journal of King Abdul Aziz University: Islamic Economic* 14 (2002): 39–46.

55. Michael J. Fleming and Kenneth D. Garbade, "The Repurchase Agreement Refined: GCF Repo," *Current Issues in Economics and Finance* 9, no. 6 (2003).

56. Viral V. Acharya and T. Sabri Oncu, "The Repurchase Agreement (Repo) Market," in *Regulating Wall Street—The Dodd-Frank Act and the New Architecture of Global Finance*, ed. Viral V. Acharya, Thomas F. Cooley, Matthew P. Richardson, and Ingo Walter (Hoboken, NJ: John Wiley & Sons, 2010), 319–351.

57. International Islamic Financial Market (IIFM) IIFM Reference Paper on I'aadat Al Shira'a (Repo Alternative) and Collateralization (Structuring Possibility). 28th July 2010, www.iifm.net

58. See Resolutions 45–52 of Shariah Advisory Council, Bank Negara Malaysia, www.bnm.gov.my.

59. Bank Negara Guidelines on Islamic Negotiable Instruments (INI). http://iimm .bnm.gov.my.

60. "Bahrain Gears Up for First Islamic Repo," *Gulf Times* (Doha, Qatar), March 8, 2006.

61. Ibid.

62. Backe Goud, "IIFM Islamic Repo Report" *Zawya*, August 4, 2010; Scottt Weber, "Retooling Liquidity Management," *Islamic Finance Asia*, November 2010.

63. Rashid Al Miraj, "Opening Address" (thirteenth AAOIFI–World Bank Annual Conference on Islamic Banking and Finance, Manama, Bahrain, October 23, 2011).

64. Abdullah Saeed, "Idealism and Pragmatism in Islamic Banking: The Application of Shari'iah Principles and Adjustments," *Journal of Arabic, Islamic and Middle Eastern Studies* 4, no. 2 (1998): 89–111.

65. Mustak Parker, "Shariah Compliant Repo: A Key Development," *Arab News*, August 11, 2010.

REFERENCES

Abu Dawud. n.d. *Sunan AbuDawud*, vol. 2. Cairo: Mustapha al-Halabi.

Acharya, Viral V., and T. Sabri. 2010. "The Repurchase Agreement (Repo) Market." In Viral V. Acharya, Thomas F. Cooley, Matthew P. Richardson, and Ingo Walter, eds. *Regulating Wall Street—The Dodd-Frank Act and the New Architecture of Global Finance*, 319–351. Hoboken, NJ: John Wiley & Sons.

Al-Maraj, Rasheed M. 2010. "Opening Remarks by the Governor, Central Bank of Bahrain." First Annual World Islamic Banking Conference Asia Summit, Singapore, June 14.

al-Masri, Rafiq Yunes. 2002. "Reciprocal Loans." *Journal of King Abdul Aziz University: Islamic Economic* 14, 33–38.

Al Miraj, Rashid. 2011. "Opening Address." Thirteenth AAOIFI–World Bank Annual Conference on Islamic Banking and Finance, Manama, Bahrain, October 23.

Aziz, Zeti Akhtar. 2010. "The Changing Landscape of Financial Regulation—Implications for Islamic Finance Speech." Seventh Islamic Financial Services Board (IFSB) Summit on Global Financial Architecture, Manama, Bahrain, May 4.

Aziz, Zeti Akhtar. 2010. "Governor's Speech." Seventh Islamic Financial Services Board Summit–Global Financial Architecture: Challenges for Islamic Finance, Manama, Bahrain, May 4.

Bacha, Obiyathulla Ismath. 1999. "Derivative Instruments and Islamic Finance: Some Thoughts for a Reconsideration." *International Journal of Islamic Financial Services* 1:1, 9–25.

Bahrain Monetary Agency. 2002. *Islamic Banking and Finance in the Kingdom of Bahrain.* Manama: Bahrain Monetary Agency.

Bahrain Monetary Agency. 2005. "BMA Pioneers 6-Month Sukuk." *Capital Market Review* 6.

Bank Negara Malaysia. 2000. *Guidelines on Islamic Negotiable Instruments (INI)*. www.bnm .gov.my.

Bank Negara Malaysia. 2006. "Issuance of Sukuk Bank Negara Malaysia Based on Ijarah Concept." www.bnm.gov.my.

Bank Negara Malaysia. Resolutions 45–52 of Shariah Advisory Council, Bank Negara Malaysia. www.bnm.gov.my.

Bashir, Muhammad Al, and Muhammad Al-Amine. 2012. *Global Sukuk and Islamic Securitization Market Financial Engineering and Product Innovation*. Leiden, Netherlands: Brill.

Baughin, William H., Thomas I. Storrs, and Charles E. Walker. 1988. *The Bankers' Handbook*, 3rd ed. Homewood, IL: Dow Jones-Irwin.

Chapra, M. Umer. 2002. *Corporate Governance in Islamic Financial Institutions*. Jeddah, Saudi Arabia: Islamic Development Bank.

Chapra, Umer. 1988. "Mechanics and Operations of an Islamic Financial Market." *Journal of Islamic Banking and Finance* 5:3, 31–36.

Cox, Stella. 2002. "Developing the Islamic Capital Market and Creating Liquidity." *Review of Islamic Economics* 11, 29.

Damak, Mohamed, and Emmanuel Volland. 2008. *Risk Management for Islamic Financial Institutions: A Rating Perspective*. New York: Standard & Poor's.

Dusuki, Asyraf Wajdi. 2007. "Commodity Murabahah Programme (CMP): An Innovative Approach to Liquidity Management." *Journal of Islamic Economics, Banking and Finance* 3:1, 1–23.

El-Gari, Mohammad Ali. 1999. "Developing Medium and Long-Term Corporate Bonds." The Economic and Financial Imperative of Globalization: An Islamic Response. Institute of Islamic Understanding, Kuala Lumpur, Malaysia, April 8–9.

Fleming, Michael J., and Kenneth D. Garbade. 2003. "The Repurchase Agreement Refined: GCF Repo." *Current Issues in Economics and Finance* 9:6, 9.

Gulf Daily News. 2007. "European Islamic Bank Begun Accepting Wakalah Fund" 29:320 (February 3).

Gulf Times. 2006. "Bahrain Gears Up for First Islamic Repo." March 8.

Hanson, Deric G. 1985. *Dictionary of Banking and Finance*. London: Pitman.

Hanson, J. L. 1986. *A Dictionary of Economics and Commerce*, 6th ed. London: Pitman.

Hasan, Maher, and Jemma Dridi. 2010. "The Effects of the Global Crisis on Islamic and Conventional Banks: A Comparative Study." IMF Working Paper.

Hassan, Sabir Mohammad. 2002. "Towards Fostering Financial Stability of the Islamic Financial Industry." Inauguration of the Islamic Financial Services Board, Kuala Lumpur, Malaysia, November.

Ibn 'Abidin. 1966. *îHashiyat Rad al-Muhtar*. Cairo: al- Al Babi al halabi.

Ibn Abidin. 1966. *Rad al-Muhtar*, vol. 4. Cairo: Al Babi Al-Halabi.

International Islamic Financial Markets. n.d. "Reference Paper on I'aadat Al Shira'a (Repo Alternative) and Collateralization (Structuring Possibility)." 28th July 2010, www.iifm.net.

Khan, Fahim. 1997. "Islamic Futures and Their Market," Research Paper no. 32, Islamic Research and Training Institute, Islamic Development Bank.

Khan, Iqbal. 2005. "Liquidity Management of Islamic Financial Institutions in the UAE." Seminar hosted by the Central Bank of UAE, Abu Dhabi, December 10.

Kumar, Himendra Mohan. 2011. "Central Bank Islamic CDs Climb to Dh12b." *Gulf News*, June 3.

Maroum, Youssef Shaheed. 2002. "Liquidity Management and Trade Financing." In *Islamic Finance Innovation and Growth*. London: Euromoney Books.

Parker, Mushtak. 2007. "Commodity Murabahah Attracting Investors." *Arab News*, June 18.

Parker, Mushtak. 2010. "Shariah Compliant Repo a Key Development." *Arab News*, August 11.

Parker, Mushtak. 2011. "Issues in Regulating Islamic Finance." *Central Banking Journal*, February 18.

Saeed, Abdullah. 1998. "Idealism and Pragmatism in Islamic Banking: The Application of Shari'iah Principles and Adjustments." *Journal of Arabic, Islamic and Middle Eastern Studies*, 4:2, 89–111

Siddiqi, Muhammad Najatullah. 1999. "Financing Infrastructure Building: Role of Islamic Financial Institutions." Seminar on Cooperation between Government and the Private Sector Financing Economic Projects, Center for Research in Islamic Economics, King Abdulaziz University, Jeddah, Saudi Arabia.

Singh, Habhajan. 2009. "Islamic Banks Grapple with Liquidity Risk Profile Issues." March 30.

Sundrarajan, V., David Marston, and Ghiath Shabshigh. 1998. "Monetary Operation and Government Debt Management under Islamic Banking." IMF Working Paper 144.

Today's Zaman. 2012. "Top Advisor to Participation Banks Says GES Equal to Gov't Bonds." *Today's Zaman*, March 29.

Van Greuning, Hennie, and Zamir Iqbal. 2008. *Risk Analysis for Islamic Banks*. Washington, DC: World Bank.

Weber, Scott. 2010. "Retooling Liquidity Management." *Islamic Finance Asia*. November.

Yilmaz, Durmuş. 2011. "Managing Liquidity in the Islamic Financial Services Industry." Conference on Managing Liquidity in the Islamic Financial Services Industry organized by the Islamic Financial Services Board, Istanbul, April 6.

Zawya. 2012. "Successful Issuances of Brunei Darussalam Government Short-Term Sukuk Al-Ijarah Securities 73rd Series." *Zawya*, June 4.

CHAPTER 8

Elements of Islamic Wealth Management

PAUL WOUTERS
Senior Foreign Lawyer AZMI & Associates—Advocates and Solicitors
(Malaysia–Singapore) CEO PT Senturiyon Global (Indonesia)

T he devout Muslim will be acquainted with the principles briefly explained here. This chapter therefore addresses some of the issues related to Islamic wealth management to a not yet introduced audience, in a language and point of view that they understand, without a priori assuming a conversion to Islam. It tackles some of the issues and explains differences from their conventional concepts and expectations.

RECOGNITION OF A DIFFERENT PARADIGM

Knowing that most readers will be novices to the concepts of Islamic wealth management, we briefly explore the Western eighteenth-century creed of the individual that created the present Western Weltanschauung, at least as far as money and finance are concerned: the survival of the fittest combined with the reassuring presence of the imaginary market equilibrium. *"My bank account and my financial assets are my concern only. I can dispose of them as and when I desire. I can use them or not use them at will."*

Conventional wealth management is in essence gaining maximum (dollarwise) short-term profitability on the individual bank account, assuming thereby the development of overall mid-term or even long-term prosperity of the community as an implicit result. How this happens remains unclear, but we have been taught that the community derives benefit from our egocentric activities in some way. Those of the readers who are educated in Western concepts will recognize this pattern.

As if the sum of all individual greed would make one good instead of just more greed! The assumption stems from a collusion of outdated (but popular and easily absorbed by the self-gratifying mind) nineteenth-century theories.

Talking economics, it is not a secret that Islam tends to favor a free market organization, private property, and limited government intrusion. One might therefore think that Islamic wealth management is the same as conventional wealth management, maybe with some perceived synthetic tweaks.

To savor this chapter properly, the reader therefore has to be aware that the offered alternative is much more than only a different way of doing things, just for the sake of being different.

It pays off to be aware of the existing paradigm of present-day Western-style culture. Most, indeed, think that all is the way it should be, the way it has been and always will be, although actually the average 1750 A.D. Western-educated person would be very astonished about the conceptual framework of wealth and the way modern individuals manage it.

Very briefly, Western thinking revolves around four circles. These concepts are always interlinked when—from a Western point of view—talking about *progress*. Indeed, when the West starts talking with the rest of the world, these notions are always mentioned together as a combined conditio sine qua non for development and wealth:

1. **Free market:** In Western thinking expanded to an absolute free market, all can be and should be and for everyone, and the government should only regulate (read: patch) the problems—reinforced by the myth of the market equilibrium that is supposed to end up in a middle road for the benefit of all.
2. **Democracy:** In the contemporary Western interpretation, the free striving for egocentric and short-term maneuvering of the individual actually will end up in the long-term benefit of society, again in the assumption that one striving in one direction will be balanced out with another striving in the opposite direction.
3. **Private ownership:** Again, in the absolute Western interpretation: *"absolutely MY money."* Limitations are only accepted as far as other individual rights are touched (thus confirming and reinforcing the individualism).
4. **Capitalism:** From an origin as a simple business model (sometimes confused with or equated with the free market) of optimizing the use of the assets in a business enterprise, but now focusing on the bottom line (money in the bank) only and again taken to absolute individual rights, assuming that market mechanisms will balance out.

The absolutism is, in turn, linked to an unshakable belief in the ever so popular survival of the fittest[1] ideology and the assumption that those on top will stay on top, which proves that the individual is the fittest (since he survived). And this persists, although the visual evidence shows that following unbalances, there is no tendency to equilibrium, but an even absolute gravitation toward crashes.

All these factors enhance the greed factor in every individual (my greed is good for me and by consequence for the community, and if not so, it will be balanced out) and have no boundaries but the conflicting rights of the other individuals. Rights of the community as such are basically declared void and are uttered for form only and again to confirm the individual. The community is there to guarantee the individual rights.[2] Human nature, of course, is happy with the ideology of the ego.

And all the time, everybody knows that the free market and individual rights should have boundaries other than just the rights of the others and sees the consequences of not respecting the natural limitations every day.

Even the 1948 Universal Declaration of Human Rights (UDHR) from the United Nations[3] is one such example of concordance with the ideology of the individual. After reading this introductory chapter, the reader will understand that it is not a coincidence that the 1981 Islamic Universal Declaration of Human Rights (IUDHR) from the Organization of Islamic Countries (OIC) appears to be in eternal conflict with and even juxtaposed to it.[4]

The four elements listed earlier tend to interact with each other (all referring to the ego) and are turned toward the greed zone by the Western interpretation of capitalism (in origin, a simple business model) that probably in turn is influenced by the four factors and the historical eighteenth-century striving for secularism (basically unloading ethics out of daily life), focused on the financial bottom line only: money.

All this is to show that the perception of the world around us is shaped by a coincidental string of (quasi) rational and scientific theories that appealed to the secular *homo rationae* who no longer accepts law or God, except for the self-invented laws that served his personal needs. It is a paradigm that is constantly on the move and that may balance from one side to the other.

But then here is the corrective offered by Islam: With full respect of the free market and the individual rights, al Qur'an gives the boundaries and shows the means to respect them. It offers a contemporary, competitive alternative, based on a free market, democracy, private ownership, and—why not?—capitalism,[5] that strives for optimal use of the available assets and profitability (in a broader meaning than money only) for the community within the framework of the needs and progress of the community and the acceptance of and submission to God. The *here-and-now-and-me* paradigm is translated to the *later-and-us* paradigm.

WHAT IS WEALTH IN ISLAM?

Talking about wealth, there are a few parameters that have to be accepted to develop a sustainable framework, such as:

1. Ultimately, all belongs to God.[6] Placing the ultimate ownership of things outside human reach changes the perspective of liability away from the ego and the immediate need to an accountability and long-term goal.
2. Man is only a temporary guardian receiving the wealth in trust.
   a. He has full ownership—the right to acquire, to use, and to dispose of— but not absolute ownership.
   b. He has no right to squander, hoard, or harm the rights of others or society.
   c. He is subject to a duty to use for the good of himself, his family, and the community—to spend it wisely and moderately for God's cause and society's prosperity in accordance with God's commandments.
   d. There is recognition and protection of individual ownership (within boundaries to protect the community).
   e. There is enhancement of the community through mutual responsibility and justice through redistribution and ethical behavior.
3. Working, trade, or investment and earning is an act of worship, and attached to that is a prohibition on unlawful earning sources and income.

    a. Acceptance of the free market (within boundaries) and government intervention (within boundaries) and respect of public interest.
    b. Exclusion of *Riba* (interest), *Gharar* (uncertainty), *Maysir* (gambling), cheating, and *Haram* (forbidden goods, actions, and industries).
    c. Through planning attain a proper use of the available assets.
    d. Real economy prevails on financial (synthetic) economy.
4. Wealth in itself is not good or bad; it depends on how it is used.
    a. It helps protect life and family.
    b. It helps development of the community, among other ways through *Zakat*, charity, investment, and redistribution.

It is a means and not an end, and the management thereof should be for the benefit of the community, directed to please God, and aimed to the life hereafter.

In Islam, mankind is the trustee of the Creator and everything belongs to ultimately Him. Social responsibility and accountability are essential to this concept.

As wealth is considered to belong to God, with mankind nothing other than its temporary guardian,[7] appropriate provisions related to the distribution and transmission thereof are important. With this in view, the testament and hereditary transmission become the key to wealth management,[8] which—and this is obvious now—involves lifelong responsibility.

Death is the key pivotal point in one's life, where one has to give account (present the final balance sheet) how wealth was acquired and managed, how wealth is handed down to the heirs, and more in general what one has done to gain access to heaven.[9] It is the moment of accountability toward God, the community, and the family.

Indeed, when one realizes that the wealth that one holds is not entirely one's own, the way it needs to be handled changes dramatically.

Wealth consists of *Mal*: those things that have permissible value (excluding carcasses and blood), create economic benefit, and are able to be possessed.[10]

Wealth management, *sensu lato*, has four aspects:

1. The proper acquisition of wealth.
2. The preservation and growth of wealth.
3. The correct expenditure (no hoarding and no spendthrift ways,[11] usage in favor of the community).
4. The (re)distribution of wealth (almsgiving) as detox, community builder, and justice provider.

Lots of so-called Islamic asset managers limit their services to the second item. Their focus rests on maximizing (from a conventional perspective) the short-term profitability (cash in the bank) of financial assets, using so-called Islamic-compliant assets (for instance, stock listed in one of the Islamic indexes), and trying to outperform conventional investment portfolios without any respect to the underlying Islamic values. Even when it would be the responsibility of the clients to take care of their overall end responsibilities, choosing Islamic-acceptable stock purely on short-term profitability and without respect to the requirements of the community is not at all Islamic, but conventional greed, hidden in an Islamic-looking jacket.

PIVOTAL ELEMENTS IN ISLAMIC WEALTH MANAGEMENT

As we have seen, the sum of all individual greed creates only more greed and does not balance out in favor of the long-term needs of the community. To develop a sustainable society, bonding between the individuals has to be encouraged (community building), and to fight envy, every individual needs to share in the prosperity of the community, thus helping him prosper and reach for a better future (redistribution).

Contrary to the contemporary Western approach, tangible, real wealth has to be created through the use of sustainable mechanisms instead of artificial financial bank money only (wealth creation).

Subsequently, wealth has to be handed down in such way that the needs of all those surrounding the individual are taken care of, without, however, dispersing it in an egalitarian, communist-style approach (wealth transfer and estate planning).

Redistribution and Community Building

The conventional Western world starts from *my money = my money* and a personal responsibility of the individual to pay dues (taxes) to the government and authorities that further are supposed to allocate these to the places where they should be used. The responsibility of the individual ending there, the individual can further concentrate on what he does best: making money and consequently paying taxes. The asset manager maximizes the cash profitability of the investments; the wealth manager has a broader approach, including financial estate planning.

Islamic wealth management acknowledges responsibility toward the community and redistribution as key concepts at the very start of the chain and not as an end result. And as we will see, *wealthy* is every individual eligible for paying *Zakat.*

Islamic wealth management therefore covers a much broader terrain than conventional wealth management. It also addresses the lower and middle classes of society and not only the upper-middle-class segment, the high-net-worth individuals (HNWI), and the extravagantly wealthy. The creation of wealth is treated at par with the subsequent protection and growth thereof.

The basic responsibility for the poor and the community needs rests on the shoulders of every individual (and not on the government) as soon as he has reached a basic level of wealth.

The major leveraging tools here are the *Zakat* ("wealth purification"), the *Sadaqah* ("voluntary charity"), and the *Qard Hasan* ("benevolent loan"). A more permanent purification can be attained by the dedication of a self-sustaining amount of wealth to God through establishment a *Waqf* ("charitable endowment").

Zakat (Wealth Purification)
Zakat—usually wrongfully translated to "wealth tax"—is paid at a level of 2.5 percent calculated on the wealth of the individual.[12] After prayer, *Zakat*, the third of the five pillars of Islam, is the second social-economic *Ibadah.*

Tazkiyah Al-Mal or purification of wealth indeed is not a cleansing process (of unlawful proceeds) but an act of purification of greed and selfishness. It purifies oneself and increases the remainder of the wealth. By doing so, the individual also becomes God-conscious in all financial dealings. The same goes for other forms of alms (*Sadaqah*) given to purify wrongdoings and as a pure, voluntary act of sharing.

Zakat is obligatory to all Muslims capable of paying it. Capability is referred to as *Nisab,* the minimum Zakatable amount.

It is meant to be used for eight *Asnaf* or categories of needy:

> Alms shall be only for the poor and the destitute, for those that are engaged in the management of the alms and those whose hearts are sympathetic to the Faith, for the freeing of slaves and debtors, for the advancement of God's cause and for the travelers in need. That is a duty enjoined by God. God is all-knowing and wise.[13]

Many Muslims do not mention *Zakat* when asked about their practice in alms-giving, since it is required for all, and giving in the amount of *Zakat* is just a duty. The real giving lies in giving beyond the required amount of *Zakat.*[14]

Many Muslims perceive that what they give does not really belong to them in the first place. To them, it belongs to God, and what they contribute is actually from God's property. Giving therefore increases their benefit from that property, and a significant number argue that if they do not give, they lose the money one way or another.

> We do not see money and our belongings as our real property. We see them as God's deposit on us. We can fulfill our responsibility to that deposit if we use it properly. Giving for the sake of God is one way of fulfilling that responsibility. . . When we give to others, we actually invest in ourselves. At first sight, it looks like we did something for someone else. But in reality, we discharge from a big responsibility to transferring God's property to those in need.[15]

Since *Zakat* is not a tax, it holds no revenue for the government. In most circumstances I've witnessed, the *Zakat* is contributed on a community level, where each participant often openly declares the amount of his contribution and strives to give more the next year, as it would testify to the benevolence of God the Almighty.

Besides the regular *Zakat* contributions, there is also the *Zakat Fitra*: This holds the purification of prohibited activities during Ramadan. It addresses all Muslims, wealthy or poor, the children and the dependents. Usually collected in cash, the distribution thereof is also spread over the eight *Asnaf* or categories of the needy.

Sadaqah (Voluntary Charity)

Islamic charity (and subsequent community building) is a well-known fact of life and a duty for every Muslim.[16]

Charity addresses poverty alleviation in general but also education, (scientific) research, and improvement of the community. I have witnessed occasional to regular contributions to local organizations helping the needy (in the broad sense of the word), upkeep of orphanages, support of schools, and so forth.

In principle, charity is not handed out to beggars, as begging is disapproved.[17]

Qard Hasan (Benevolent Loan)

The word *Qard* is derived from Arabic *Qirad,* which means "to cut," as it cuts a certain part of the lender's property by giving a loan to the borrower. *Hasan* is also an Arabic word and originates from *Ihsan* or "kindness to others." Therefore, the *Qard Hasan* is a gratuitous or benevolent loan given to needy people without requiring the payment of interest or profit. The receiver is required only to repay the original amount of the loan.[18]

Although it is not charity in itself (that would entail giving the money away), it is a charitable act and not a business transaction. The borrower can decide to reward the lender for his timely assistance and, at his sole discretion and without such being a stipulation of the original loan, decide on the amount of any reward as well.[19] Third-party guarantees, collateral, and mortgages are allowed.

Waqf (Charitable Endowment)

Waqf are charitable endowments, according to Islamic law. In this institution, a privately owned property, corpus, is endowed for a charitable purpose in perpetuity dedicated to God. The revenue generated thereof is spent for that charitable purpose. It stands out as one of the major achievements of Islamic civilization.[20]

From an origin restricted to real estate, they really came to full deployment in the sixteenth-century Ottoman Empire, when cash *Waqfs* were introduced and accepted.[21] Family *Waqfs*, humanitarian or charitable *Waqfs* providing education, health services, water, travelers' lodges, clinics and hospitals, centers for people with special needs, environmental protection, mosques, madressah, universities, and several other public utilities—they are available for a wide range of purposes.

The perpetual nature of the *Waqf* and its orientation to the welfare of the needy in the community make this dedication of a part of the wealth to God an ultimate vehicle, to be established during the lifetime or at death by will.

Wealth Creation

Man has to work to earn a living and to prosper.[22] The usual ways to acquire wealth are through inheritance, gift, labor, business, and partnerships (as a working partner, capital partner, or both),[23] according to Islamic standards.

Contrary to conventional wealth management, where the wealth or asset manager[24] only walks in when the client (or better: asks one to stay out till he or she) has acquired substantial wealth, the Islamic wealth manager will give comprehensive, holistic assistance covering all aspects of wealth generation, growth and protection, estate planning, and redistribution. How one makes and spends the money is as important as how one manages the money.

Wealth should not be squandered[25] or hoarded,[26] but rightfully spent. A part of that spending is the redistribution; another part is the rightful use of wealth for the benefit of the individual, the kinfolk, and the community at large. In addition, wealth and risk may be protected in a Shariah-compliant manner, as discussed in Chapters 7 and 12 of this volume.

Indeed, whereas conventional thinking focuses on the concept of *my money* and the maximization of individual, short-term profits, Islam focuses on the use of wealth for the benefit of the community and mid- to long-term optimization of profits and growth with same goal. This does not mean that the individual aspect disappears. It means that the most profitable way for the Islamic investor is not necessarily direct money in the bank but in synergy with the other goals.

And well-invested and spent money will be rewarded in both this life and the life hereafter.[27]

Investment

The need for the preservation of wealth is embedded in the religious principles. The investments themselves, therefore, cannot contravene those principles but, on the contrary, need to be in line with them.

Money cannot rest idle. Investment is needed for the preservation and enhancement of the wealth, in order (1) to pay [more] *Zakat* and (2) to take care of your life and the life of your family and the community, (3) with a reward in the life hereafter.

For starters, it may be stressed that investment in gold and silver in the Islamic world is not to be underestimated.

Equity   Investment in equities listed on the global stock exchanges really took off after the 1988 OIC Fiqh Academy Fatwa[28] (after five years of debate), allowing the establishment of the Dow Jones Islamic Market (DJIM) index, soon followed by several other index providers. Chapter 9 provides a full explanation of Shariah-compliant equity investment.

The 1988 Fatwa of the OIC Fiqh Academy and the derived index practice allowed massive activation of Islamic savings in the huge sphere of the conventional capital markets, up to then, for various reasons, problematic.[29]

At this point, it pays to recognize that the equities listed in these Islamic indexes are there simply because they meet (for whatever reason, if not purely coincidental) the Islamic financial criteria. Lots of the listed companies are not established within the Islamic world, so allocation of funds does not necessarily support the development of the economies within OIC spheres. They do not commit to the financial criteria themselves, which means that from time to time some company apparently haphazardly pops in or out of the Islamic indexes.

Another question that remains unresolved is adherence to Islamic business ethics, where some of the bigger companies have a tendency or reputation to adhere to questionable business practices. So far, the ethical vocation of Islamic investment tends to get lost in this area.

It may also be debated whether buying a participation from another investor[30] with an explicit intention to sell the same for a fast profit[31] really is an investment at all. And this is, moreover, in contemporary capital markets, where the market price of the shares no longer attaches to the underlying net asset value with a reasonable profit expectation but more often exceeds that value (future expectations only, so a fully speculative valuation). All this puts extra constraint on the conscious wealth advisor.

The positive side of the equation is that, according to Islamic standards, one can only sell what already exists and what one already possesses. Short selling, an enhancer of the 2008 financial crisis, bumps into Islamic hindrances. Since hedging often entails short selling, this part of the investment universe—which may lead to risk control or even risk mitigation—rests undeveloped, notwithstanding various Fatwa in favor of hedging, subject to conditions. Mid- to long-term developments will show the way.

If stocks are organized in investment funds, such funds will have a Shariah board to supervise the activities. Mutual funds, multiasset funds, unit trusts, and exchange-traded funds (ETFs) form part of the contemporary Islamic fund spheres.

Private Equity (Growth Capital) and Venture (or Seed) Capital   It has long been reasoned—and it still is in some circles—that private equity investment would be the natural habitat for Islamic finance.[32] The investor is exposed to risk for his part in the capital and is rewarded with a profit or loss (as opposed to a loan). Private equity also places the investor usually directly or at least close to the decision making of the target company, which gives extra leverage to clean the financial and business practices thereof, as opposed to mostly anonymous equity participations.

Experience teaches that—just as in conventional finance—portfolio diversification is essential and that real entrepreneurial spirit at this moment still is not abundant within OIC spheres, with their nascent economic development.

Conventional private equity lately is being heavily leverage (debt) oriented,[33] and alternative business models need to be enhanced.

The market is, however, already now in full development, and experiments (though still with relatively low financial input) with financial structuring and Islamic acceptable leverage hold bright prospects.

A basic Islamic private equity fund (IPEF) structure can be seen in Exhibit 8.1. Do note that variations are possible.

Sukuk   The benevolent loan (*Qard Hasan*) is commendable in Islam, but lending money against a profit (interest, *Riba*) is *Haram*. Whereas the global investor pool of so-called fixed-income instruments (lending and borrowing) is much bigger and more risk averse than the equity markets, the liquidities abundant on these markets have stayed out of reach for the Islamic investor.

A solution to this obstacle was developed in the form of Islamic Sukuk. These instruments offer the conventional or Islamic investor (1) access to the mostly stable but not fixed income of an underlying asset (real estate that is leased out, for example), (2) while giving title to that underlying asset (risk exposure), thereby completing the Islamic *Damanah* criteria: risk exposure brings profit sharing. Chapter 9 fully explains Sukuk structures.

At the birth of the Sukuk markets, conventional tax hindrances, obstacles to foreign ownership of real estate in Islamic countries, perceived lack of a legal framework (meaning that the existing framework did not match the expectations and desires of the common law–schooled legal advisors), ratings criteria, and so forth gave rise to the use of common law trusts and a catapulting of Islamic finance out of its legal habitat of the Shariah to foreign jurisdictions and legal systems with concepts that were not receptive or were even corruptive to the Islamic framework. The introduction of conditional and revocable trusts accompanied the naissance of purely asset-based Sukuk that granted only beneficial ownership to the Sukuk holders, with the underlying asset flow back to the originator in case of default,[34] thereby leaving the investor without claim on that asset. Hardly anybody cared for that aspect until, of course, the community got shaken up by the 2008 subprime crisis.

The crisis had, however, this positive effect, that the market tended to grow out of the asset-based phase to a real asset-backed Sukuk structuring that—to meet

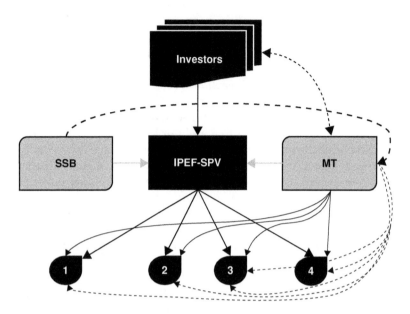

1. Shariah adviser (SA) or Shariah Supervisory Board (SSB) sets the Shariah statement of policy.
2. Investors finance the IPEF.
3. Management team (MT) identifies and acquires equity in the target companies (TC) on behalf of the IPEF.
4. SA monitors the follow-up of statement of policy and overall compliancy.
5. MT and Shariah compliance officer (SCO) monitor the TC for the IPEF—Shariah irregularities discovered in that reporting from the TC will be reported by the SCO to the SA.
6. MT keeps the investors updated on the development of the TC.
7. On decision of the IPEF, the MT ultimately executes the exit out of the TC through IPO/sale.
8. The profits/losses of that exit flow back to the IPEF that distributes them to the Investors.

Exhibit 8.1   Basic IPEF Fund Structure
Source: Paul Wouters. Islamic Private Equity Fund IPEF—basic notions, special edition to *Islamic Finance News* (Malaysia), 2008. For the Malaysian Guidelines and Best Practices on Islamic Venture Capital (the first ones available to the global Islamic finance community), one may consult www.sc.com .my/main.asp?pageid=936&menuid=&newsid=&linkid=&type= and www.sc.com.my/eng/html/ resources/guidelines/VC/0805_islamicVC.pdf.

investor requirements of stable income and lower risk exposure—most probably will develop into a mixture of underlying assets pertaining to various asset classes and hopefully also to a different risk profiling and pricing altogether. It would give the Sukuk a specific niche and leadership role.[35]

The downside, then, again is that also the conventional market wants to penetrate the resources of the relative unshaken Islamic community. A real mushroom of issuance is developing, draining liquidity out of the Islamic spheres. And then the typical conventional issuer, of course, chooses—when allowed to do so— the *minimum minimorum*: nontradable[36] asset-based *Murabaha* Sukuk. The pool of conventional money exceeding the Islamic sphere, the number and volume of those issuances might exceed the Islamic ones with the same number. It will be interesting to see whether Islamic finance can withstand the pressure thereof and build its own niche. The prospects do not appear to be too bright.

Failing sufficient offerings, the present secondary Sukuk market is rather restrained, which reinforces the reluctance of investors to sell any of their Sukuk holdings on these markets.[37] In that sense, the critical point of abundance still needs to be reached, after which the market will be set to grow exponentially.

Real Estate Investments   Chapter 18 of this volume discusses home mortgage financing, but wealth management also includes institutionalized real estate investments.

The financial paper derived from the real estate investment trusts (REITs) most often can be traded, thus giving them a far better liquidity position than any direct investment in the underlying real estate. It allows fast, major mobilization of money in a lawful way, with (compared to equity) relative low servicing needs. The overexposure to real estate investments in the Gulf Cooperation Council (GCC) became a direct consequence. The results were felt as a result of the fallout of the 2008 global financial crisis and its impact on the underlying real economy.

Since Malaysia has been the frontrunner in the regulatory development of the Islamic REITS, it may be interesting to make a short resume of their guidelines that are a yardstick for the industry:[38] Any Islamic real estate investment fund will have (depending on local regulations) a Shariah board or Shariah advisor who ensures full compliance with Islamic rules during the setup, functioning, and liquidation of the fund.

- Rental income from nonpermissible activities may not exceed 20 percent of the total turnover of the Islamic REIT (1.1.c).
- Maximum 20 percent of the floor area of a property can be utilized for nonpermissible activities (1.3).
- Cannot own properties in which all tenants conduct nonpermissible activities, even when the rental income thereof would be less than 20 percent of the total turnover (1.1.e).
- Cannot accept new tenants whose activities are fully nonpermissible (1.2).
- All forms of investment, including deposit and financing instruments, must be Shariah compliant (2).
- Property insurance must be based on *Takaful* except where *Takaful* schemes do not operate (3).

Rental activities that are classified as nonpermissible (appendix to the guidelines) are:

- Financial services based on *Riba* (interest).
- Gambling or gaming.
- Manufacture or sale of nonhalal products or related products.
- Conventional insurance.
- Entertainment activities that are nonpermissible according to the Shariah.
- Manufacture or sale of tobacco-based products or related products.

- Stockbrokering or share trading in Shariah-noncompliant securities.
- Hotels and resorts.

Liquidity Management   Not all the cash is invested all the time. Sometimes it is in transition from one investment to another; sometimes there simply is no suitable investment or other performing alternative available. Or the investor simply desires to keep an amount of cash in reserve for when and where needed.

Conventional finance is able to place the excess in liquidity *overnight* on the money markets against interest. But because interest-based lending is excluded to the Islamic investor, there is a problem.

Liquidity caused a growing problem in the financial management of Islamic financial institutions (IFI) and their institutional clients. In 2010, this led to the establishment of the International Islamic Liquidity Management (IILM) Corporation.[39] Based in Malaysia, it really is an international effort to boost and coordinate progress in this field. Although also active in product development, its direct influence will probably be limited to cross-border liquidity management.

Wealth Transfer and Estate Planning

Law of Inheritance (Faraid)   Conventional Western inheritance regulations tend to give a complete freedom of disposal in drafting a will[40] or make sure that the inheritance largely falls down to the legally protected children. In a slow movement over time, also the rights of the surviving spouse have been protected in the latest 50 years or so (often by a large portion in full of the estate and an important portion in usufruct on the rest, leaving the children only a notional and unreachable inheritance).

The Islamic law of inheritance (*Faraid*)—close to 1,400 years before our contemporary common and civil law framework—knows the following differentiators from most Western-style regulations:

- Parents, who actually have raised their children and most probably are at the low end of their revenue-generating powers, also inherit from their children.
- The surviving spouse inherits a reserved part, and the husband is actually committed to try to guarantee her a whole cycle[41] of life support after his death.[42]
- The somewhat broader family takes part in the inheritance.
- The disposable part of the inheritance is a maximum of a third, and the distribution among the heirs is fixed.
- There is no right of primogeniture (firstborn son).

First, all the costs of the funeral expenses have to be settled[43] and then the outstanding debts and legacies. Only then can an estate be distributed to the heirs. Any person dying and leaving an unsettled debt will have his soul dangling.[44]

Estate planning in the sense of optimizing tax and regulatory influences on transfer is acceptable.

Last Will and Testament (Wasiyah)   The redaction of the will is an essential item for the peace of mind of any Muslim[45]—at all times and especially before the commencement of the Hajj: Are all my debts and obligations properly settled? Have my wife and next of kin been taken care of? Did anyone find himself unluckily excluded, given the specific circumstances of the family composition, and has that been rectified? Was there any room left for charity?

The disposable part[46] of the inheritance is a maximum of a third. This is meant to allow for correction if the regular inheritance distribution omits somebody or leads to injustice and to donate for charity. Nonreceiving legal or nonlegal heirs— excluded because the Qur'anic heirs have depleted the inheritance in full—can be awarded parts of the estate.

It is prohibited to disown someone by will from his or her rightful part in the inheritance, just as it is void for the presumptive heir to waive or transfer a future chance of inheritance.

Within the framework of the disposable part of the inheritance, it is encouraged to donate to third parties not in line to inherit or to charities and to respect the Islamic parity between the lawful heirs. It is not encouraged to entrust one of the heirs with more than his or her just due (that is, favoritism of one of the children). It is advised to compensate for any effects of the unbalance that is created by some contemporary Western frameworks (such as loading women with same financial responsibilities as men) with gifts during the lifetime.

CONCLUSION

Islamic wealth management accompanies the individual throughout his or her life.

The unlucky person in need knows that there are explicit mechanisms weighing personally on the better-off individuals around him that will guide the community to alleviate the sorrow, contrary to the contemporary Western-style society, where an impersonal and invisible government is supposed to take care.

For the others, it focuses around two continuous pivoting points: the alms-giving (sharing and slow redistribution of wealth) and the rule of inheritance and last will.

The Islamic wealth manager will guide you by focusing on:

- Compliant wealth creation: using compliant financial and business tools for acquiring, sustaining, and expanding wealth, combined with well-designed family- and community-reinforcing spending mechanisms.
- Responsible job and business organization in all aspects.
- All this with the understanding that *wealth* does not start after six zeros on the bank account, but directly addresses all that pass the low Zakat threshold.

A conventional wealth manager uniquely targets the well-to-do part of society and preferably the HNWI, using mostly the *bottom-line-cash-in-the-bank* criteria, truncated down to asset management and estate planning.

Lots of Islamic wealth managers are looking to do exactly the same as conventional asset management services, using so-called Shariah-compliant investment products, instead of focusing on the overall holistic Islamic approach: commitment in personal, community, and business life to Islamic standards and living up to the redistribution mechanisms. Money and financial wealth are core elements, but they are not the bottom line, and profitability lies in the mid- and long-term improvement of the community, rather than short-term individual financial gain. And as we have seen, the mid- and long-term development of the community does not at all conflict with personal ambitions and needs—to the contrary. Giving is receiving, both in this life and the life hereafter.

There often remains frustration that not all conventional (synthetic) products are available yet, combined with a feeling that competition requires offering same type of products, structured in a compliant way.

The critic points out: If the only thing that changes is that I only invest in products because they happen to meet certain industry or financial screenings, then nothing really changed at all, and I could find myself in a Shariah-compliant greed paradigm. True Islamic wealth management focuses on the whole aspect of wealth, as set forth in Islam.

NOTES

1. Joseph Heath, *Economics without Illusions: Debunking the Myths of Modern Capitalism* (New York: Broadway Books, 2010); or Dan Ariely, *Predictably Irrational: The Hidden Forces That Shape Our Decisions* (New York: Harper Collins, 2008). But the literature is abundant for those interested enough to question economic ideology (law of supply and demand, pareto optimal, and the like are most of them theoretical dreams only, not attached to underlying reality) that apparently fails to help to avoid crisis (the number of bank and stock exchange crashes since 1850 is difficult to count) and even helps to generate them. The number of research articles by the Worldbank and the IMF on the subject is huge. They do see the problems, but in a baffling way, they refuse to take the consequences—blinded by the Western paradigms—and patch up rather than address the problems at the root and go for the Islamic alternative: free market with preset boundaries, conditional private property, and guided democracy. There are things one can do and things one cannot do, and one respects that. The larger debate on the economic alternative escapes the goal of this chapter.

2. See, for instance, article 29 (of 30) of the Universal Declaration of Human Rights: "(1) Everyone has duties to the community in which alone the free and full development of his personality is possible. (2) In the exercise of his rights and freedoms, everyone shall be subject only to such limitations as are determined by law solely for the purpose of securing due recognition and respect for the rights and freedoms of others and of meeting the just requirements of morality, public order and the general welfare in a democratic society. (3) These rights and freedoms may in no case be exercised contrary to the purposes and principles of the United Nations." It is immediately followed by the closing article 30: "Nothing in this Declaration may be interpreted as implying for any State, group or person any right to engage in any activity or to perform any act aimed at the destruction of any of the rights and freedoms set forth herein."

3. Available at www.un.org/en/documents/udhr/.

4. Available at www.alhewar.com/ISLAMDECL.html. The IUDHR was drafted in a more community-minded (rights and responsibilities) and contextual framework as opposed to the individualistic, literal Western (rights) UDHR approach. When two groups talk the same language (English), they assume that they are communicating. But when they live in a different paradigm and have a different use of language, they actually talk next to each other and keep repeating over and over the same arguments. They see that the other side grasps the words but *refuses to understand*, while resting blissfully unaware that they live in different realities and are producing nothing but thin air.

5. As long as this is reduced to a business model: optimal (according to Islamic standards) use of the assets available in an enterprise and in the community.

6. "It is He who has made the earth subservient to you. Walk about its regions and eat of His provisions. To Him shall all return at the Resurrection" (Al-Qur'an: Al-Mulk 67: 15).

7. "Narrated Ibn `Umar: I heard Allah's Apostle saying, 'All of you are guardians and responsible for your charges'" (Sahih Al-Bukhari, vol. 4, book 51:14).

8. "Narrated `Abdullah bin `Umar: Allah's Apostle said, 'It is not permissible for any Muslim who has something to will to stay for two nights without having his last will and testament written and kept ready with him'" (Sahih Al-Bukhari, vol. 4, book 51:1).

9. "Such are the bounds set by God. He that obeys God and His apostle shall dwell forever in gardens watered by running streams" (Al-Qur'an: An-Nisa' 4:13).

10. This could trigger a debate on the 1988 Fatwa of the OIC Fiqh Academy accepting the existence and economic value of intangible assets such as intellectual property (IP). Although this is used to cause lasting wealth transfer to the more developed world, it was one of the triggers of the dot-com crisis and the subsequent explosion of share values (fully decoupled now from underlying net asset value), without any Islamic reservation to the use thereof "inside the system." For the (Arabic only) web site of the OIC Fiqh Academy, see www.fiqhacademy.org.sa/. For most Fatwa translated to English, see among others www.isra.my/fatwas/organisation/oic-fiqh-academy.html.

11. "Stay in your homes and do not display your finery as women used to do in the days of ignorance" (Al-Qur'an: Al-'Azhab 33:33).

12. The exact calculation may differ from place to place and is—certainly for the first time—a task that may require some special attention.

13. Al-Qur'an: At-Tawbah 9:60.

14. Carolyn M. Warner, Ramazan Kilinc, Christopher Hale, and Adam Cohen, "Religion and Public Goods Provision: Evidence from Catholicism and Islam." Paper for American Political Science Association annual meeting, Seattle, 2011, p. 20.

15. Ibid., p. 24.

16. "Whoever does an atom's weight of good shall see it, and whoever does an atom's weight of evil shall see it also" (Al-Qur'an: Az-Zalzalah 99:7 and 8).

17. "Narrated Hakim bin Hizam: The Prophet said, 'The upper hand is better than the lower hand (i.e. he who gives in charity is better than him who takes it). One should start giving first to his dependents. And the best object of charity is that which is given by a wealthy person (from the money which is left after his expenses). And whoever abstains from asking others for some financial help, Allah will give him and save him from asking others, Allah will make him self-sufficient'" (Sahih Al-Bukhari, vol. 2:508).

18. "Those that preserve themselves from their own greed will surely prosper. If you give a generous loan to God, He will pay you back twofold and will forgive you. Gracious is God and benignant" (Al-Qur'an: At-Taghabun 64:17).

19. Ghazana Binti Said Atan, *The Concept of Al-Qard Ul-Hasan*: www.scribd.com/doc/22013726/Qard-Hassan.

20. Murat Cizakca, "Awqaf in History and Its Implications for Modern Islamic Economies," *Islamic Economic Studies* 6, no. 1 (1998); www.isdb.org/irj/go/km/docs/documents/IDBDevelopments/Internet/English/IRTI/CM/downloads/IES_Articles/Vol%206-1..Murat%20Cizakca..AWQAF%20IN%20HISTORY%20AND%20ITS%20IMPLICATIONS.pdf.

21. Murat Cizakca, "Incorporated Cash Waqfs and Mudaraba: Islamic Non-Bank Financial Instruments from the Past to the Future," MPRA Paper 25336, 2010 (original paper 2004); http://mpra.ub.uni-muenchen.de/25336/1/MPRA_paper_25336.pdf.

22. "Believers, when you are summoned to Friday prayers hasten to the remembrance of God and cease your trading. That would be best for you, if you but knew it. Then, when the prayers are ended, disperse and go your ways in quest for God's bounty. Remember God always, so that you may prosper" (Al-Qur'an: al-Jumu'ah 62:10).

23. Mudarib (working partner) and Rab al'Mal (financier, silent partner) in the Mudaraba partnership.
24. The main difference between the two is that the asset manager usually manages some of the assets or money of the client in specific asset classes (such as equity or bonds), whereas the wealth manager offers an overall service, including all the relevant asset classes and estate planning, all within the conventional, individualistic maximum of financial return against preferred risk profile.
25. "Lo! the squanderers were ever brothers of the devils, and the devil was ever an ingrate to his Lord" (Al-Qur'an: Al-Isra 17:27—Pickthall version).
26. "Never let those who hoard the wealth which God has bestowed on them out of His bounty think it is good for them: indeed it is an evil thing for them. The riches they have hoarded shall become their fetters on the Day of Resurrection. It is God who will inherit the heavens and the earth. God is cognizant of all your actions" (Al-Qur'an: Ali-Imran 3:181).
27. "Fear the day when you shall all return to God; when every soul shall be paid back for what it did. None shall be wronged" (Al-Qur'an: Al-Baqarah 2:281).
28. For the (Arabic only) web site of the OIC Fiqh Academy, see www.fiqhacademy.org.sa/; for the most relevant Fatwa translated to English, see, among others, www.isra.my/fatwas/organisation/oic-fiqh-academy.html.
29. Most obvious hindrances for the readers will be speculation and gambling arguments and the fact that the use of the limited liability company—as opposed to business partnerships—no longer has one or more managing partners with unlimited liabilities (the pure investors are also protected in the Islamic partnerships). The absence of such personal liability is an accidental by-product of conventional business structuring that, for instance, tries to patch up rather than solve the source of the problem known as nonliability and gives rise to the overdevelopment of corporate governance regulations, piercing the corporate veil notions and other fancy legal structures that again try to give some flesh to corporations. The 2008 global banking crisis made clear that lots of misfortune may have been prevented if the responsible people would not have had the protection shield of the limited liability between themselves and the other stakeholders (depositors, investors, regulators, and so forth).
30. Without direct benefit to the underlying company that usually does not even notice the change in the shareholdership and where zero of the proceeds of the so-called investment accrue to her.
31. Every day the newspapers are full of "market corrections due to profit taking"—did the investor become a profiteer only? Does investment entail commitment to sit out a business cycle or just participate or leave at will?
32. See, for instance, P. Wouters, "Islamic Private Equity Fund IPEF—Basic Notions," *Islamic Finance News* (Malaysia), 2008; for the Malaysian Guidelines and Best Practices on Islamic Venture Capital (the first ones available to the global Islamic finance community), see www.sc.com.my/main.asp?pageid=936&menuid=&newsid=&linkid=&type= and www.sc.com.my/eng/html/resources/guidelines/VC/0805_islamicVC.pdf.
33. And such meeting the interest-Riba and the debt ceiling constraints—both these aspects appear to warrant the development of an alternative private equity market and business culture that stays more to the real economy and better business ethics.
34. Could, for instance, be a sovereign that legally was not allowed to alienate the goods to foreign parties.
35. Some of these ideas, together with a basic introduction into Sukuk structuring, have been developed in P. Wouters, "Sukuk! Sukuk! My Kingdom for a Sukuk! A Brief Introduction in Sukuk Concepts," *Law Gazette* (Singapore), May 2011: www.lawgazette.com.sg/2011-05/101.htm, but Sukuk literature is abundantly available in the market.

36. Not important for them since they do not follow Islamic standards and will trade the instruments anyway.
37. Since there is not sufficient Sukuk for reinvestment available, what leaves the liquidity idle and nonproductive is what needs to be avoided, hoarding being unlawful in Islam.
38. *Guidelines for Islamic Real Estate Investment Trusts*, issued November 21, 2005; www.mifc .com/index.php?ch=134&pg=666&ac=61&bb=693.
39. See www.iilm.com/.
40. Giving rise to rather absurd donations to animals or exclusion of beloved ones that today are in an unfavorable position, but tomorrow might make up again.
41. Usually translated to her lifetime.
42. "You shall bequeath your widows a year's maintenance without causing them to leave their homes" (Al-Qur'an: Al Baqarah 2:240), usually interpreted as one life cycle instead of literally one year.
43. "God commands you to hand back your trusts to their rightful owners" (Al-Qur'an: An-Nisa' 4: 58). ". . . (the distribution in all cases is) after payment of any legacy they may have bequeathed or any debt they many have owed" (Al-Qur'an: An-Nisa' 4:11 and 12).
44. "It has been reported on the authority of 'Amr b. al-'As that the Messenger of Allah (may peace be upon him) said: All the sins of a Shahid (martyr) are forgiven except debt" (Sahih Muslim, vol. 6, book 20, number 4649).
45. "Narrated Abdullah bin Umar: Allah's Apostle said, 'It is not permissible for any Muslim who has something to will to stay for two nights without having his last will and testament written and kept ready with him'" (Sahih Bukhari, vol. 4, book 51:1).
46. "Narrated Ibn `Abbas: I recommend that people reduce the proportion of what they bequeath by will to the fourth (of the whole legacy), for Allah's Apostle said, 'One-third, yet even one third is too much'" (Sahih Al-Bukhari, vol. 4, book 51:6).

REFERENCES

Al-Qaradawi, Yusuf. 1997. *Wealth and Economy in Islam.* (Samir Al Tagi, trans.) Cairo: Islamic Inc.

Bank Sarasin. *Islamic Wealth Management Report 2010*, www.sarasin.ch/internet/iech/en/ index_iech/about_us_iech/media_iech/news_iech.htm?reference=103792&checkSum =66DA1EED4F66F891879BDB37881C9F09.

Bank Sarasin. *Islamic Wealth Management Report 2011*, www.iefpedia.com/english/wp-content/uploads/2012/02/islamic_wealth_management_report_2012-2.pdf.

Cox, Stella. 2002. "Islamic Asset Management: An Expanding Sector," *Review of Islamic Economics* 11:27–50.

Ghoul, Wafica Ali. *The Islamic Wealth Management Industry (IWMI): Is the Current Financial Crisis a Blessing in Disguise?* Beirut: Lebanese International University. Presented in Milan, November 18–19, 2009, "Moral Values and Financial Markets: Assessing the Resilience of Islamic Finance Against Financial Crisis." http://www.assaif.org/ita/Eventi/2009/18-19-novembre-2009-Milano-%22Moral-Values-and-Financial-Markets-Assessing-The-Resilience-of-Islamic-Finance-Against-Financial-Crisis%22/Wafica-Ali-Ghoul,-%22The-Islamic-Wealth-Management-Industry-IWMI-Is-the-Current-Financial-Crisis-A-Blessing -In-Disguise-%22,-Lebanese-International-University,-Beirut

Hoepnerab, Andreas G. F., Hussain G. Rammalc, and Michael Rezeca. 2010. *Islamic Mutual Funds' Financial Performance and International Investment Style: Evidence from 20 Countries.* Published 2011 in the *European Journal of Finance* 17 (9–10): 829–850. http://papers.ssrn.com/sol3/papers.cfm?abstract_id=1475037

Ibn Ashur (Muhammad Al-Tahir Ibn Ashour). 2006. *Treatise on Maqasid al-Shari'ah*. Lahore, Pakistan: The International Institute of Islamic Thought.

Khan, Muhammad Mustafa. 2005. *Islamic Law of Inheritance: A New Approach*, 3rd ed. Delhi, India: Kitab Bhavan.

Maulana, Justice Muhammad Taqi Usmani. 2000. *The Text of the Historic Judgment on Interest Given by the Supreme Court of Pakistan*. http://www.albalagh.net/Islamic_economics/riba_judgement.pdf Accessed August 10, 2012.

Mourad, Fares. 2011. "Managing Wealth—Islamically." Interview in *Islamic Finance Asia* (Malaysia), June.

Mubarak, Muath. 2010. "Islamic Wealth Management—A Paradigm Shift in Islamic Finance." *Islamic Finance News* (Malaysia), June 23.

Nyazee, Imran Ahsan Khan. 1994. *Theories of Islamic Law: Methodology of Ijtihad*. Lahore, Pakistan: The Institute of Islamic Thought.

Nyazee, Imran Ahsan Khan. 2000. *Islamic Jurisprudence: Usul al-Fiqh*. Lahore, Pakistan: The Institute of Islamic Thought.

Nyazee, Imran Ahsan Khan. 2009. *The Prohibition of Riba Elaborated*. Islamabad, Pakistan: Institute of Advanced Legal Studies.

Rasban, Sadali. 2006. *Personal Wealth Management for Muslims*. Singapore: HTHT Advisory Services.

Raysuni, Ahmad. 2006. *Imam Shatibi's Theory of the Higher Objectives and Intents of Islamic Law*. Lahore, Pakistan: The International Institute of Islamic Thought.

Sandwick, John. 2008–2009. "Untapped Potential of Islamic Wealth Management." *Islamic Finance Asia*, December–January.

Seng, Yeoh Keat. 2005. "Wealth Management in Malaysia." Presentation at CIMB Private Banking, Kuala Lumpur, Malaysia.

Siddiqui, Shahzad, and Siddiq Mohamed. 2009. "Contemporary developments and growing options in Islamic wealth management within North America and beyond." In Sohail Jaffer, ed. *Islamic Wealth Management: A Catalyst for Global Change and Innovation*. London: Euromoney, pp. 92–101.

Sulaiman Ibn 'Awad Qaiman. 2010. *Secrets of Leadership and Influence*. Selangor, Malaysia: Dakwah Corner Bookstore.

Thomas, Abdelkader. 2006. *Interest in Islamic Economics: Understanding Riba*. London: Routledge Islamic Studies.

Tuyser, C. R., D. G. Demetriades, and Ismail Haqqi Effendi. 2007. *The Mejelle—Being an English Translation of Majallah el-Ahkam-I-Adlyia and a Complete Code on Islamic Civil Law*. Kuala Lumpur, Malaysia: The Other Press.

Walkshausl, Christian, and Sebastian Lobbe. 2011. *Islamic Index Investing—The International Evidence*.

Warner, Carolyn M., Ramazan Kilinc, Christopher Hale, and Adam Cohen. 2011. "Religion and Public Goods Provision: Evidence from Catholicism and Islam." Paper for American Political Science Association, Seattle.

Wouters, Paul. 2008. "Islamic Private Equity Fund IPEF: Basic Notions." *Islamic Finance News* (Malaysia).

Wouters, Paul. 2010. "The Use of the Contract of Sale in Islamic Finance: General Concepts." *Law Gazette* (Singapore), September.

Wouters, Paul. 2011. "Sukuk! Sukuk! My Kingdom for a Sukuk! A Brief Introduction in Sukuk Concepts." *Law Gazette* (Singapore), May.

Yasaar Media. 2009. *Islamic Wealth Management 2009*. Dubai, UAE: DIFC.

Yusoff, Nik Mohamed Affandi Bin Nik. 2002. *Islam and Business*. Sepang, Malaysia: Pelanduk.

CHAPTER 9

Sukūk and the Islamic Capital Markets

An Introduction

MICHAEL J. T. McMILLEN*
Partner at Curtis, Mallet-Prevost, Colt & Mosle LLP

INTRODUCTION

The history of the Islamic capital markets is a short story: complicated, but short. The conception and birth of the equity side of the Islamic capital markets is associated with the year 1998 and the issuance of a *fatwā* to the Dow Jones Islamic Market Indexes (the "*DJIMI Fatwā*") by its *Sharīʿah* board. The DJIMI *Fatwā* addressed the standards that are applicable in connection with making a *Sharīʿah*-compliant equity investment. Those standards apply well beyond equity investing, including in respect of the finance side of the Islamic capital markets. The conception and birth of the finance side of the Islamic capital markets are tethered to the years 2001 to 2003 and to *Sharīʿah* Standard No. 17, *Investment Sukūk* (the "*AAOIFI Sukūk Standard*"), issued by the Accounting and Auditing Organization for Islamic Financial Institutions (AAOIFI).[1]

That description raises a few questions. Are the Islamic capital markets somehow different from the conventional markets? If they are distinguishable, are they symmetrical and integrated in some manner?

Capital markets are markets for equity and debt securities where business enterprises and governments raise long-term funds. The stock markets (broadly defined) are where equity securities are bought and sold. Debt securities are bought and sold in the bond markets. Primary markets[2] and secondary markets[3] exist for both equity and debt securities.

The *Sharīʿah* prohibits the purchase and sale of interest-bearing debt in any circumstance. *Sukūk*, the primary instrument used in the finance side of the Islamic capital markets, are not interest-bearing debt obligations; they are securitizations.[4]

---

*Partner of Curtis, Mallet-Prevost, Colt & Mosle LLP and Lecturer in Law at the University of Pennsylvania Law School. Member of the bar of the State of New York. © 2012 Michael J. T. McMillen. Copyright and all intellectual property rights reserved to Michael J. T. McMillen. This chapter is an abridgment of sections of a forthcoming book on Islamic finance and investment by Michael J. T. McMillen.

And *Sharī'ah*-compliant debt, such as lease rental obligations, are not traded in any debt market (secondary markets are largely nonexistent for *Sharī'ah*-compliant instruments). Thus, the finance side of the Islamic capital markets does not seem to overlap with the debt side of the conventional capital markets. To make matters a little more convoluted, in considering entrée to the Islamic finance markets, one must first consider some of the equity investment rules.[5]

This chapter considers the Islamic capital markets, particularly the finance (or non-interest-bearing debt) side of those markets. Specifically, it explores the nature of *sukūk* and their roles in those markets. The chapter begins with a brief definitional section, moves to an overview of the markets, and ends with a discussion of some structural matters.

SUKŪK

Definitional Matters

The AAOIFI *Sukūk* Standard was issued in 2003.[6] It defines *sukūk* as certificates of equal value put to use as rights in tangible assets, usufructs, and services or as equity in a project or investment activity. It distinguishes *sukūk* from pure equity, notes, and bonds. It emphasizes that *sukūk* are not debts of the issuer; they are fractional or proportional interests in underlying assets, usufructs, services, projects, or investment activities. *Sukūk* may not be issued on a pool of receivables that are not themselves *Sharī'ah*-compliant. Further, the underlying business or activity and the underlying transactional structures (e.g., the underlying leases) must be *Sharī'ah* compliant (e.g., no prohibited business activities).

The AAOIFI *Sukūk* Standard provides for 14 eligible asset classes. In broad summary, they are securitizations (1) of an existing or to be acquired tangible asset (*'ijāra;* lease), (2) of an existing or to be acquired leasehold estate (*'ijāra*), (3) of presales of services (*'ijāra*), (4) of presales of the production of goods or commodities at a future date (*salam;* forward sale), (5) to fund construction (*'istisnā';* construction contract), (6) to fund the acquisition of goods for future sale (*murābaha;* sale at a markup), (7) to fund capital participation in a business of investment activity (*muḍāaraba* or *mushāraka;* types of joint ventures), and (8) to fund various asset acquisition and agency management (*wakāla;* agency), agricultural land cultivation, land management, and orchard management activities.

Market Matters Prior to November 2008

Sukūk issuances were the strongest single element of Islamic finance until the onset of the 2007 financial crisis. Issuances fell off sharply in 2008 and have only slowly increased since then. Initially, some observers attributed the issuance decrease to the March 2008 statement of the AAOIFI *Sharī'ah* board regarding certain *sukūk* structures (the "*AAOIFI Clarification*"), characterizing it as new rules that were crippling the markets. Subsequently, it became apparent that the global financial crisis was the more likely, and certainly the more significant, causative factor.

A 2008 study provides insight into the *sukūk* markets from their inception to early November 2008.[7] From January 1997 to November 2008, US\$87.955 billion of *sukūk* were issued pursuant to 596 offerings. Approximately 35 percent of those issuances were characterized as sovereign and 65 percent as corporate.[8] Two countries predominated in the number of issues, and two countries predominated in the volume of issuances. Malaysia had 267 issuances (44.80 percent) and Bahrain had 150 issuances (25.17 percent), totaling 69.97 percent. By volume, Malaysia (US\$37.697 billion; 42.86 percent) and the United Arab Emirates (US\$26.977 billion; 30.67 percent) were predominant, the two countries totaling 73.53 percent. Gambia was third by number (36; 6.04 percent), and Saudi Arabia was third in volume (US\$8.225 billion; 9.35 percent). Average issuance size in the UAE was US\$793.46 million, in Malaysia was US\$141.19 million, and in Bahrain was US\$41.56 million.

Industry

Exhibit 9.1 summarizes issuances by volume and number, categorized by industry or use for issuances until November 2008.

Government issuances were almost 33.1 percent of all issuances, but only 8.3 percent of total volume, with a small average issuance size (US\$37.26 million). Financial services issuances comprised a quarter of all issuances by volume and 11.6 percent by number, with a relatively large average issuance size (US\$314.68 million). More than half of total volume and 40 percent by number were in four industrial segments: financial services, real estate, transport, and power and

Exhibit 9.1 Issuances by Industry Classification

Industry	Volume (US\$ millions)	% Total Volume	Offerings	% Total Offerings	Average Issuance (US\$ millions)
Financial Services	21,712.92	24.7%	69	11.6%	314.68
Real Estate	19,368.73	22.0%	67	11.2%	289.09
Transport	12,004.63	13.6%	40	6.7%	300.12
Power & Utilities	9,054.77	10.3%	22	3.7%	411.58
Oil & Gas	6,338.12	7.2%	20	3.4%	316.91
Government	7,340.65	8.3%	197	33.1%	37.26
Construction	4,254.04	4.8%	34	5.7%	125.12
Services	2,088.67	2.4%	7	1.2%	298.38
Telecoms & IT	1,836.32	2.1%	28	4.7%	65.58
Industrial Manufacturing	1,090.30	1.2%	21	3.5%	51.92
Conglomerates	1,014.88	1.2%	7	1.2%	144.98
Agriculture & Food	767.55	0.9%	52	8.7%	14.76
Consumer Goods	347.64	0.4%	11	1.8%	31.60
Mining & Metals	306.65	0.3%	4	0.7%	76.66
Basic Materials	169.10	0.2%	7	1.2%	24.16
Healthcare	128.08	0.1%	3	0.5%	42.69
Automotive	127.51	0.1%	6	1.0%	21.25
Travel & Tourism	4.69	0.0%	1	0.2%	4.69
Total	87,955.25	100	596	100	

Exhibit 9.2   Issuances by Type of *Sharīʿah* Structure

Structural Type	Volume (US$ millions)	% of Total Volume	Number of Offerings	% of Total Offerings	Average Issuance (US$ millions)
ʾIjāra	29,567.07	33.7%	225	37.8%	131.41
Mushāraka	27,339.01	31.2%	78	13.1%	350.50
Muḍāraba	10,305.37	11.8%	33	5.5%	312.28
Murābaha	8,065.00	9.2%	112	18.8%	72.01
ʾIstisnāʿ	5,022.20	5.7%	16	2.7%	313.89
Al-Istithmar	4,332.87	4.9%	4	0.7%	1083.22
Al Salam	2,337.73	2.7%	126	21.2%	18.55
Other	650.00	0.7%	1	0.2%	650.00

utilities. As a rough approximation, infrastructure issuances were 60 to 68 percent by volume (depending on the classification of government issuances).

What is not determinable from the foregoing data is of considerable interest. The type and degree of governmental involvement (ownership or support) cannot be determined. It is likely understated, given the degree of government ownership of so-called private corporate issuers. Cross-ownership and sovereign support are likely significantly greater than indicated in Exhibit 9.1. And the degree of overlap between and among categories is not discernible. For example, it is likely that a significant number of issuances in the real estate, transport, and power and utilities categories (and others) are also construction issuances. Similarly, it is difficult to tease out detailed information regarding infrastructure development.

SHARĪʿAH STRUCTURE

Exhibit 9.2 summarizes the frequency of usage of the different types of *Sharīʿah*-compliant structures for issuances up to November 2008.

Sukūk al-ʾijāra comprised the largest portion, both by number (37.8 percent) and volume (33.7 percent). Attention should be paid to the triad of structures addressed in the AAOIFI Clarification: *mushāraka, muḍāraba,* and *murābaha* structures. This triad comprised 52.2 percent by volume and 37.4 percent by number of all issuances. Only one issuance qualified as a securitization.

TENOR AND STRUCTURES

Tenor is a critical issue in the development of Islamic capital markets and a primary concern of practitioners. Exhibits 9.3 and 9.4 focus on the tenors of the different structural types for issuances up to November 2008.

Only 3.8 percent of issuances had a tenor of 20 years or more. However, this category represented 20.3 percent of the total volume. Long-term issuances were clearly large issuances, probably associated with large infrastructure projects. Considering long-term to be 10 years or longer, the figures were 16.8 percent by number and 38.9 percent by volume. The *mushāraka-muḍāraba-murābaha* triad predominated in the long-term category (63.6 percent in 20+ years; 52.0 percent in 10+ years).

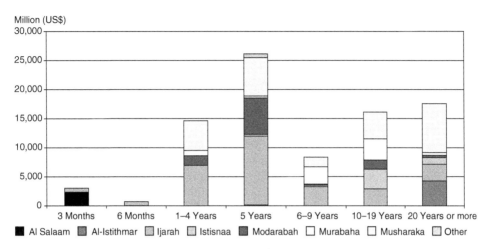

Exhibit 9.3 Tenor and *Sharī'ah* Structure by Dollar Volume

Malaysian issuances based on *mushāraka* and *murābaha* structures have been significant, although Middle Eastern *mushāraka* structures were also important in 2006 through 2008. *'Ijāra* structures were a distant second (13.6 percent in 20+ years; 31.6 percent in 10+ years), as was the *'istisnà'* (9.1 percent by number and 6.6 percent by volume in 20+ years; 13.3 percent by number and 13.6 percent by volume of 10+ years).

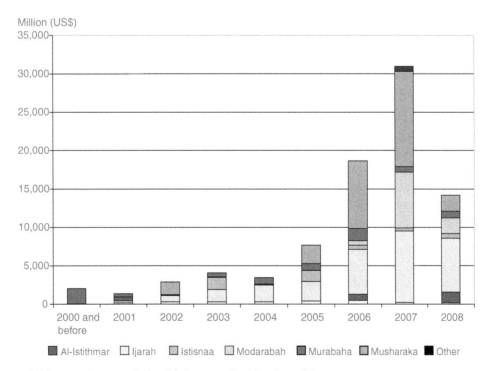

Exhibit 9.4 Tenor and *Sharī'ah* Structure by Number of Issuances

Medium-term financings were the most common, and the *'ijāra* structure predominated in this time frame. Five-year tenors comprised 19.2 percent by number and 30.2 percent by volume of all issuances. For six- to nine-year tenors, 26.9 percent of all issuances and 9.7 percent of the volume of all issuances were *'ijāra* structures. They comprised 53.42 percent by number and 58.48 percent by volume of financings of 1 to 9 years, 47.82 percent by number and 59.2 percent by volume of financings of 5 to 19 years, and 55.03 percent by number and 75.9 percent by volume in the 1- to 19-year grouping.

Medium-term *murābaha* structures are of particular interest. By number, they were 26.38 percent in one- to nine-year tenors, 33.07 percent in five- to nine-year tenors, and 50.96 percent in six- to nine-year tenors. Volumes show a different pattern: 8.70 percent in one- to nine-year tenors, 9.71 percent in five- to nine-year tenors, and 35.91 percent in six- to nine-year tenors. Significant medium-term *murābaha* issuance may be indicative of its use as revolving or working capital facilities. The suspicion is that many of these involve metals and may be unsalable in the secondary markets. By comparison, *'ijāra* structures were found in every tenor group and were strongest in the medium-term categories. Defining that term as from 1 to 10 years, the *'ijāra* constituted 45.19 percent by number and 44.99 percent by volume. If the definition is 1 to 19 years, the *'ijāra* was 43.81 percent by number and 33.82 percent by volume.

The *mushāraka-muḍāraba-murābaha* triad was a large segment of both the long-term and medium-term markets. It was 48.68 percent by number and 60.9 percent by volume of the 10- to 19-year class, and 51.52 percent by number and 56.6 percent by volume of the 10+ grouping. It comprised 70.88 percent by number and 54.5 percent by volume of the 1- to 19-year class, and 78.98 percent by number and 52.3 percent by volume in the 1- to 10-year category. One supposition is that the salutary goal of financing longer-term infrastructure projects may have been one of the pressures toward conversion of these structures (particularly the *mushāraka*) to more bond-type characteristics. Another supposition is that the conversion to bond-type structures facilitated the sale of these types of structures in the broader conventional markets.

Salam structures predominated in short-term issuances; overwhelmingly, they were issued from Bahrain and Gambia (as government funding issuances). They constituted 71.26 percent by number and 62.9 percent by volume of tenors less than one year, with the *'ijāra* constituting 38.71 percent by number and 37.1 percent by volume in that period. The predominance of *salam* structures in the three-month category is even more pronounced (91.18 percent by number, 77.20 percent by volume).

Exhibit 9.4 illustrates the increasing use of *sukūk al-mushāraka,* starting in 2005, and the consistent use of the *sukūk al-'ijāra*. The use of the *mushāraka*, particularly in the Middle East, diminished rapidly after issuance of the AAOIFI Clarification in 2008, although it remains a favored structure in Malaysia.

Exhibit 9.5 presents annual increases in tenor by number of issuances, and Exhibit 9.6 presents that information by dollar volume, in issuances up to November 2008. There was a notable drop-off of *sukūk* issuances in late 2008, as the financial crisis became more pronounced.

Clearly, there was a trend toward shorter-term issuances. In contrast, the medium-term categories were shrinking somewhat, and the long-term categories

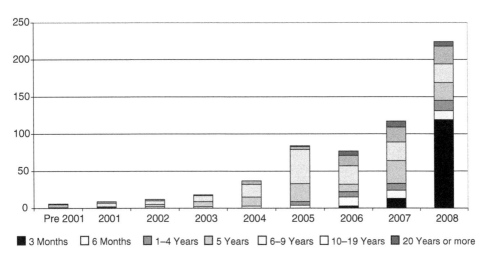

Exhibit 9.5 Annual Issuances in Tenor Categories by Number of Issuances

that developed in 2006 were stable in subsequent years, a trend that was welcomed by the infrastructure finance industry.

After a period of dormancy, *sukūk* markets are gaining strength. In the first nine months of 2011, US$63 billion of *sukūk* were issued globally, with Malaysia issuing 69 percent of all *sukūk* in the period (it was the only issuer in September).[9] Issuances from Gulf Cooperation Council (GCC) jurisdictions were US$7.6 billion in 2009 and US$6.1 billion in 2010. They jumped to US$17 billion in the first three quarters of 2011.[10] Qatar supplanted the United Arab Emirates as the top issuer, by volume, in the GCC.[11] Sovereign issuances constituted approximately 73 percent of all issuances globally.[12] Government-sector issuances were approximately 75 percent of all issuances, a percentage that is expected to increase. Banking and finance were

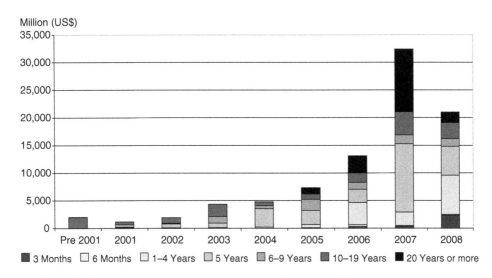

Exhibit 9.6 Annual Issuances in Tenor Categories by Dollar Volume

a distant second at 10 percent, and water and power were third at 8 percent.[13] As of the first half of 2011, approximately US$161.5 billion of *sukūk* were outstanding.[14]

Anecdotal evidence indicates that three structures are predominant at the present time, and the use of another structure is increasing. *Mushāraka* and *murābaha* structures are favored in Malaysia, and their use is increasing in those jurisdictions (in both number and volume). *'Ijāra* structures remain commonplace. Use of the *sukūk al-wakāla* seems to be increasing, with US$5.3 billion of new issuances in 2011 being wholly or partly structured using a *wakāla* (up from US$1.8 billion in the same period in 2010).[15] This structure is acceptable in both the GCC and Malaysia and allows incorporation of structures that cannot be traded on secondary markets (e.g., *murābaha* and *'istisnā'* obligations). These are trends worthy of attention and further study.

ISSUANCES SINCE NOVEMBER 2008

There was a pronounced downturn in *sukūk* issuance from the third quarter of 2007 until 2009. It is instructive to look at the *sukūk* markets as they existed at the end of the third quarter of 2011, as they existed at year-end 2011, and through the first quarter of 2012.[16]

In the first nine months of 2011, US$63 billion of *sukūk* were issued globally. Malaysia issued 69 percent of all *sukūk* issued globally in that period. Issuances from the GCC were US$22.4 billion (as compared with US$6.1 billion in 2010 and US$7.6 billion in 2009). A notable development in the third quarter of 2011 was the ascendancy of Qatar as the leading issuer by volume in the GCC, supplanting the United Arab Emirates. Sovereign issuances constituted approximately 73 percent of all issuances globally, and government-sector issuances were approximately 75 percent of all issuances. Banking and finance were a distant second at 10 percent of issuances, and water and power were third at 8 percent. Halfway through 2011, approximately US$161.5 billion of *sukūk* were outstanding. *'Ijāra* structures remained commonplace. *Mushāraka* and *murābaha* structures continue to be favored in Malaysia, and their use in *sukūk* was increasing in both number and volume. *Sukūk al-wakāla* began to increase during the second half of 2011, with US$5.3 billion of new issuances using the *wakāla* structure in whole or in part. That was an increase over the US$1.8 billion in the same period in 2010. The *wakāla* structure is acceptable in both the GCC and Malaysia and allows incorporation of structures that cannot be traded on the secondary markets (such as *murābaha* and *'istisnā'* obligations).

The year-end figures for 2011 show a total global *sukūk* issuance of US$84.4 billion, which is an increase of 62 percent over 2010, when US$52 billion were issued. See Exhibit 9.7. As of year-end, there were US$182 billion *sukūk* outstanding.

Of the US$84.4 billion of *sukūk* issued during 2011, US$58 billion, or 69 percent, were issued out of Malaysia, and US$19 billion, or 23 percent, were issued out of the GCC. See Exhibit 9.8, which shows issuances by country.

Government institutions issued 66 percent of all *sukūk*, or US$56 billion, in 2011. Financial services ranked second in volume of issuances with US$15 billion. Most issuances were domestic issuances (89 percent of the total, at US$75.8 billion). There were 14 international issuances equaling US$8.6 billion, up from 11 international issuances worth US$5 billion in 2010. Commensurate with domestic issuance and

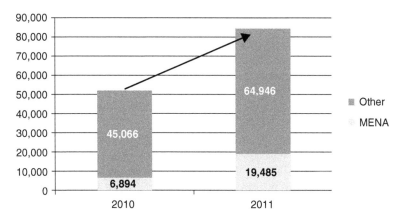

Exhibit 9.7 *Sukūk* Issuances in 2011 and 2010 (in Mn$)
Source: Zawya Sukuk Monitor.

the predominance of Malaysia as an issuer, 66 percent of all issuances were in the Malaysian ringgit, and 10 percent were in U.S. dollars. *Murābaha* and *'ijāra* structures predominated in 2011, although *mushāraka* issuances were significant, and *wakāla* issuances increased noticeably.

The first quarter of 2012 indicates strong *sukūk* markets. Global *sukūk* issues were US$43.5 billion, which is an increase of 55 percent from the first quarter of 2011. This is the best year on record. Malaysia continues to maintain the leading issuer position, with 71 percent of all *sukūk* issuances in the quarter, at US$31 billion. Saudi Arabia was second with 15 percent of all issues, at US$6.4 billion. Indonesia was the third-ranking issuer with US$3.4 billion, and the United Arab Emirates was the fourth-ranking issuer with US$1.9 billion. For the first time in history, *sukūk* issuances in the GCC exceeded bond issuances in the GCC.

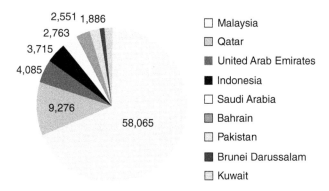

Exhibit 9.8 *Sukūk* Issuances in 2011 by Country (in Mn$)
Source: Zawya Sukuk Monitor.

STRUCTURAL MATTERS: *SUKŪK AL-'IJĀRA*

This section and the following sections provide an overview of generic forms of the more commonly encountered *sukūk* structures. Because of the frequency of its use and its importance in the global markets, the first structure to be discussed is the *sukūk al-'ijāra*. Each *sukūk* is built around a transactional form, and the transactional form that comprises the essence of the *sukūk al-'ijāra* is the *'ijāra*. It is therefore essential to begin with an overview of the *'ijāra*.[17]

An *'ijāra* is a *Sharī'ah*-compliant lease financing structure. It is a type of sale under the *Sharī'ah*. It is a lease of an object or services involving the transfer of the usufruct or *manfa'a* (the use of an object or the services of a person) for a rent (or hire) consideration. The nature of the *manfa'a* must be precisely defined; the rental consideration must be for a fixed value (a set fixed or variable rate), whether payable in a lump sum or installments; and the term of the *'ijāra* must be precisely determined. The rent may escalate or diminish during the term, so long as the amounts of such escalation or decrease are specified and known to both parties at inception. The lessor is responsible for structural maintenance of the assets and correlative obligations (e.g., property casualty insurance), and these obligations may not be passed to the lessee in the *'ijāra*. The lessor is entitled to rent as long as the lessee has the enjoyment of the leased assets as specified in the *'ijāra*.

Exhibit 9.9 depicts a generic *'ijāra* financing structure (without collateral security elements). A bank provides conventional interest-based financing in this

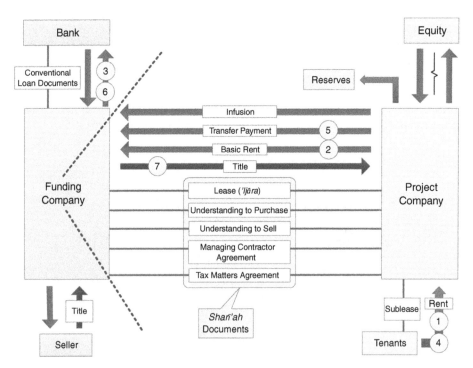

Exhibit 9.9 Generic *'ijāra* Transaction
Source: © 2009–2012, Michael J. T. McMillen.

bifurcated structure. The conventional loan documents and other noncompliant elements are shown to the left of the dotted line. All matters to the right of the dotted line are *Sharī'ah* compliant.[18]

The *Sharī'ah*-compliant investors ("Equity") infuse funds into the project company, usually by way of cash or in-kind capital contributions and loans. The precise infusion method depends on applicable tax strategies. The infused funds, together with funds made available by the bank pursuant to the conventional loan documents, are used by the funding company to pay for the acquisition or construction of the project.

The funding company is usually a bankruptcy-remote special-purpose entity established expressly for the financing transaction. Frequently, it is owned by a corporate service company; less frequently, by investors. It holds title to the assets comprising the project. And it is the borrower under a conventional interest-bearing loan with the bank. It also leases the assets to the project company pursuant to the lease (*'Ijāra*). The basic rent payable by the project company to the funding company under the lease (*'Ijāra*)[19] is structured to be exactly equivalent to the debt service payable by the funding company to the bank under the conventional loan documents[20] (steps ② and ③ in Exhibit 9.9). The income from the occupational tenant (step ①) is used to make the basic rent payment.

The other two *Sharī'ah* documents of relevance for payment purposes are the understanding to purchase and the understanding to sell (collectively, the "Understandings"). A payment under the understandings is referred to as a *transfer price* payment.

The understanding to purchase is a sale-and-purchase agreement that allows the funding company (at the direction of the bank) to cause the project company to purchase the assets comprising the project, in whole or in part, under certain defined circumstances. It is necessary because of, among other things, *Sharī'ah* principles prohibiting mandatory payment of future rents under an *'ijāra*, even in default scenarios. In a sale of the whole, the transfer price is equal to the aggregate amount outstanding under the conventional loan documents at the time of payment. In a partial sale, the transfer price bears a defined relationship to those outstanding amounts or is formulaically determined. Exercise is permitted for any lease event of default (functionally an acceleration) and for the equivalents of the conventional loan document mandatory prepayment provisions. For example, there may be payments to maintain different coverage ratios (e.g., loan-to-value or debt-to-equity) or because of sales of lots, homes, or condominiums or decreases in collateral values.

Using funds from the occupational tenant (step ④ in Exhibit 9.9), the project company makes payment of the transfer price to the funding company (step ⑤). The funding company uses those funds to make mandatory prepayments under the loan agreement (step ⑥). If the transfer price is paid in full, title is transferred to the project company or its designee (step ⑦).

The understanding to sell is a sale-and-purchase agreement that allows the project company to cause the funding company to sell the assets comprising the project, in whole or in part, under certain defined circumstances. Although the project company has the right to purchase all of the assets, that rarely occurs in practice because the rights are assigned to a third-party purchaser to avoid multiple asset transfer, recordation, and other taxes.

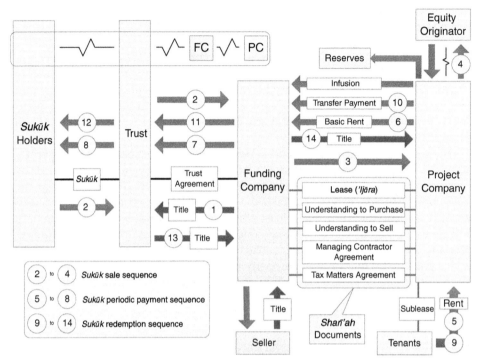

Exhibit 9.10   Generic *sukūk al-ʾijāra*
Source: © 2009–2012, Michael J. T. McMillen.

In the case of a purchase of the entirety of the assets, the transfer price is equal to the amounts outstanding under the conventional loan documents at the time of payment and is paid as set forth in steps ④ through ⑦. The transfer price in a partial payment will mirror the voluntary prepayment requirement of the conventional loan documents. Partial prepayments are commonplace, especially in condominium projects, single-family home projects, and other projects involving discrete groupings of separately functional assets and in circumstances where the project company desires to decrease the debt load.

The *sukūk al-ʾijāra* builds directly on the *ʾijāra* structure. A generic *sukūk al-ʾijāra* is graphically depicted in Exhibit 9.10 with the numerical key for the sequential progression.

Exhibit 9.10 illustrates a transaction in which preexisting *ʾijāra* transactions are used as the vehicle for a *sukūk*. The *Sharīʿah* documentation (including the lease (*ʾIjāra*)) is already in place at the inception of the *sukūk* transaction.

① The trust is formed. Title to the assets constituting the trust corpus are contributed by the funding company into the trust.
② The trust issues the *Sukūk* to the *Sukūk* holders, and the *Sukūk* holders make purchase payments.
③ The trust pays the entire amount of the issuance proceeds to the project company.

(4) The project company remits the issuance proceeds to the equity.

(5) The occupational tenants make periodic rent payments to the project company pursuant to the subleases.

(6) The project company makes periodic basic rent payments to the funding company pursuant to the lease (*'Ijāra*).

(7) The funding company transfers an amount equal to the basic rent payments to the trust.

(8) The trust distributes an amount equal to the basic rent to the *Sukūk* holders, pro rata.

(9) The occupational tenants make payments of rent to the project company under the subleases.

(10) The project company makes the transfer payment to the funding company under the understanding to purchase or the understanding to sell, as relevant, in respect of purchase and sale payments, in whole or in part.

(11) The funding company transfers an amount equal to the transfer payment to the trust.

(12) The trust distributes an amount equal to the transfer payment to the *Sukūk* holders, pro rata.

(13) The trust transfers title of the assets to the funding company upon payment in full of the transfer payment. (No such transfer is made in respect of transfer payments for partial payments.)

(14) The funding company transfers title to the property or assets to the project company or its designee upon a complete purchase and sale.

STRUCTURAL MATTERS: *MUSHĀRAKA* STRUCTURES

As indicated in Exhibit 9.2, the *mushāraka* is second only to the *'ijāra* in issuance volume. This is a purely *Sharī'ah*-compliant structure involving no conventional debt. It is based on joint venture concepts (*sharīkā, sharikāt mahassa,* or *mushāraka*). A generic transactional structure is illustrated in Exhibits 9.11 and 9.12, again focusing on the *sukūk* structure: the *sukūk al-mushāraka*.[21] Exhibit 9.11 focuses on the formation and funding of the *mushāraka,* and Exhibit 9.12 is directed to the repayment of the financing.

The members of the joint venture are (a) the *Sukūk* issuers and (b) the project company (often a developer and operator). The issuer is the finance partner and controls financial matters, and the project company is the technical partner and controls technical, construction, and operation matters, in each case as specified in the *Mushāraka* agreement. The allocation of management responsibilities between and among partners is quite flexible. Joint management is common.

Exhibit 9.11 illustrates that the issuer (a) is funded by the *Sukūk* issuance and (b) provides financing by making a series of capital contributions to the *Mushāraka* and acquiring interests (*hissas*) in respect of each capital contribution (steps (2), (3) and (X)). These contributions are made periodically (e.g., monthly) as financing is required and subject to satisfaction of conditions precedent that are quite similar to those in any conventional financing (e.g., milestone completion). The project company frequently contributes in-kind assets (as well as cash) (step (1)). This

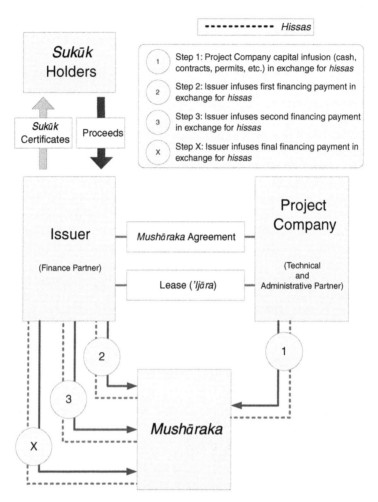

Exhibit 9.11 Generic *Sukūk al-'Ijāra*: Formation and Funding
Source: © 2009–2012, Michael J. T. McMillen.

may include land, rights under various project documents (construction contracts, supply and off-take agreements, etc.), and rights under permits. This is usually a one-time contribution made prior to any issuer contribution. Contributed capital is the property of the *mushāraka* and inures to the benefit of all partners.[22] The interests of the issuer are leased to the project company pursuant to the lease (*'Ijāra*) to allow the project company control of all relevant interests necessary for construction and operation of the project (and as a vehicle for cash flow equilibration).

Sukūk repayment is effected by periodic (say, quarterly) sales, by the issuer to the project company, of previously acquired *hissas*. As depicted in Exhibit 9.12, steps ① and ②, the *Mushāraka* makes a distribution of profits. The distribution ratio is weighted in favor of the project company, thereby providing the project company with funds to effect the *hissa* purchase. Payment of the *hissa* purchase price is shown as step ③, and by the dotted lines moving the *hissas* in the direction

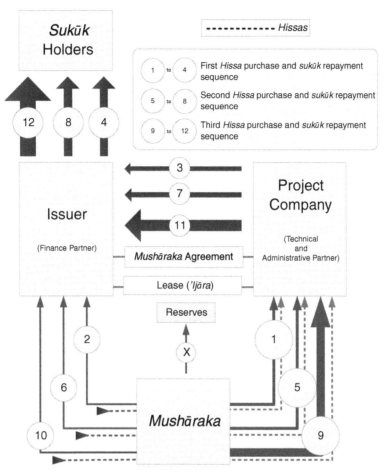

Exhibit 9.12 Generic *Sukūk al-Mushāraka: Hissa* Purchase; *Sukūk* Payment
Source: © 2009–2012, Michael J. T. McMillen.

of the project company (beneath the step ① designator). The issuer uses the funds obtained from the distribution by the *Mushāraka* (step ②) and from the payment of the *hissa* purchase price (step ③) to make a periodic payment to the *Sukūk* holders (step ④). The distribution-and-*hissa*-purchase sequence is repeated at the time of each payment to the *Sukūk* holders (i.e., steps ⑤ through ⑧ and steps ⑨ through ⑫). Upon payment in full of the *Sukūk*, all *hissas* will be owned by the project company (the *Mushāraka* will cease to exist).

A partner may not assume liability for the capital of another partner, including by way of guarantee (or assured, lump sum, or fixed-fee payment or profit from specific periods or activities). There may be guarantees to secure the partners against infringement, default, negligence, or breach by the managing partners. Absent agreement to the contrary, the liability of each partner is unlimited.

Profit and loss definitions are largely the same as with *muḍāraba*, but there are a few fundamental differences. Profit allocations may be in agreed ratios or in accordance with a points system where the points take cognizance of the amount of capital contributed and the period of participation. Generally, losses, up to the amount of a partner's capital contribution, are allocated in accordance with the relative capital contributions of the partners.

Careful structuring is required in the implementation of any *mushāraka* transaction.[23] That structuring must include precise discussions with the *Sharī'ah* scholars advising on the transaction with respect to each of the foregoing matters, among many others.

STRUCTURAL MATTERS: *SUKŪK AL-MUḌĀRABA*

The *muḍāraba* is, and has long been, a preferred method of financing, although it has not been frequently used in modern financings. A simple generic *sukūk al-muḍāraba* is illustrated in Exhibit 9.13.

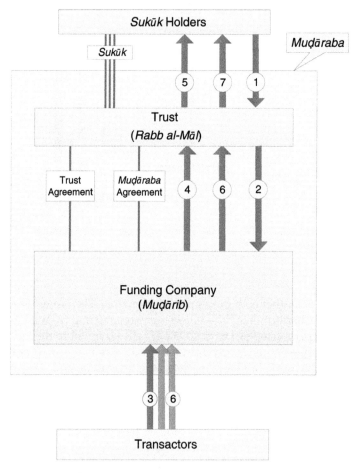

Exhibit 9.13   Generic *Sukūk al-Muḍāraba*
Source: © 2009–2012, Michael J. T. McMillen.

A *muḍāraba* is a profit-sharing partnership defined by the nature of the contributions of the *muḍārib* and the *rabb ul-māl* to the partnership.[24] One party acts as the *rabb ul-māl* (the capital provider). Steps ① and ② illustrate capital contributions by *Sukūk* holders to an issuer trust on behalf of the *Sukūk* holders and thence to the project company. The other party (the project company) acts as the *muḍārib* (the manager, developer, or operator) and contributes services (but, in the classical formulation, no capital). Steps ③ and ⑥ depict transactions between the project company *muḍārib* and different third-party transactors. A portion of the funds from those transactions is used to service the *sukūk* (steps ④ and ⑤ and steps ⑦ and ⑧).

The agreement of the parties governs the timing of, and conditions applicable to, the making of capital contributions. Thus, capital infusions may be structured to be periodic (resembling, for example, construction financing). The business of the *muḍāraba* may be specifically limited (e.g., as to scope, time, activities, and other factors) or unrestricted.

The *muḍāraba* does not necessarily, and need not, correspond to a secular legal category (such as a partnership). Thus, for example, it may be established with respect to a defined group of assets or activities.

A defining characteristic of the *muḍāraba* is that operational losses must be borne by the *rabb ul-māl,* absent infringement, default, negligence, or breach of contract by the *muḍārib*. The *muḍārib* suffers the loss of its services and therefore no loss of capital (unless the *muḍārib* also contributed capital).

The presumption, as a *Sharī'ah* matter, is that the *muḍārib* (not the *muḍuraba*) is responsible for operational expenses, including the purchase, transportation, storage, sale, and collection activities of a business. However, certain expenses are deductible from the *muḍāraba* funds prior to distribution of profits. Allocation of expenses is usually determined in consultation with the *Sharī'ah* board.

Profit allocations must be specified at the inception of the contract. It is permissible to provide for different percentages of profit distribution when the profit exceeds certain levels, thresholds, or amounts. There can be no predetermined or conclusive profit allocation to any of the parties, and arrangements allocating all profit or a lump sum to a single party are impermissible. Return of capital may not be assured or guaranteed. While the *rabb ul-māl* generally may not participate in the management or service component, some consent rights are permitted. Permissible rights are similar to those provided to limited partners in limited partnership structures (changes in business, sale of all or substantially all of the assets, bankruptcy declarations, and similar minority shareholder rights).

The following list illustrates a mixed structure *sukūk al-muḍāraba* for the construction and subsequent leasing of a project, such as a power, industrial, or real estate project, on land that has been purchased. In this example, there are six structural subsets (all references are to Exhibit 9.14):

1. The first is the *sukūk al-muḍāraba,* whose participants are a trust on behalf of the *Sukūk* holders, as *rabb al-māl*, and a funding company, as *muḍārib*. This is designated by the "*Muḍāraba*" call-out.
2. The second subset is an investment agency arrangement whereby funds are invested in *Sharī'ah*-compliant investments pending their expenditure from

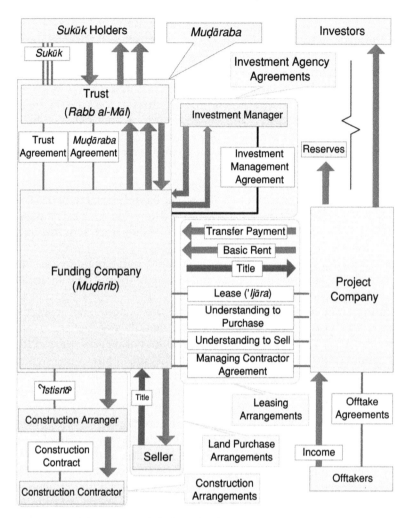

Exhibit 9.14 Mixed Structure *Sukūk al-Muḍāraba*
Source: © 2009–2012, Michael J. T. McMillen.

time to time. This is designated by the call-out titled "Investment Agency
Agreements."

3. The third subset is a land purchase arrangement with a third-party seller
   using funds obtained from the sale of the *Sukūk*. This is designated by the
   call-out "Land Purchase Arrangements."
4. The fourth subset is a construction arrangement for the project using the
   proceeds of the *Sukūk* issuance. This subset is designated as "Construction
   Arrangements."
5. The fifth structural subset is an *'ijāra* structure identical to that previously
   discussed. This structural subset is designated in a call-out as "Leasing
   Arrangements."
6. The final subset involves the sale of output from the project to third-party
   offtakers.

MATTERS OF CLARIFICATION

Sukūk are often referred to as "Islamic bonds." Although inaccurate, that characterization does express the desires of many market participants to trade them as bonds in the global markets. Those participants, including some banks and law firms, have structured *sukūk* issuances as tradable fixed-income bonds (rather than securitizations that pass through profits and losses of the underlying asset pool or business). Structuring in this manner makes the *sukūk* much easier to rate and allows law firms to render necessary opinions.[25]

In March 2008, after a year-long series of meetings and the circulation of a position paper, the AAOIFI *Sharī'ah* board issued the AAOIFI Clarification.[26] The AAOIFI Clarification applies to all *sukūk*, although it addresses specific issues pertaining to distinct types of *sukūk* (particularly *mushāraka* structures). The AAOIFI Clarification was thought to be necessary because of a series of post-2003 structural developments that rendered many *sukūk* to be, essentially, conventional bonds because (a) they did not represent ownership in the commercial or industrial enterprises that issued them; (b) they generated regular payments determined as a percentage of capital, rather than as a percentage of profit; and (c) through various mechanisms, they guaranteed a return of the principal at maturity.

Many *sukūk* were structured as entitlements to *returns from entities that were unrelated to profits* rather than profits from entities. Others included *murābaha* debt without ownership of tangible assets. The AAOIFI Clarification notes that tradable *sukūk* instruments must represent ownership (fractional undivided ownership) by the holders in actual assets that may be possessed and disposed of in accordance with the *Sharī'ah*. This reemphasizes that *Sharī'ah* principles applicable to asset possession and disposition must be at the forefront in structuring any *sukūk* instrument.

Concerns relating to regularized periodic payment structures focused on (a) payments to the fund manager to the extent that returns exceeded amounts due on the *sukūk* and (b) loans by fund managers to the *sukūk* holders or their proxies where returns were insufficient to pay fixed amounts on the *sukūk*. The issues pertaining to principal guarantees derived from the use of promises, by the issuer or fund manager, to purchase the subject assets at an amount equal to the original sale price of assets into the *sukūk* structure (i.e., at the principal amount of the *sukūk*).

Practitioners should be cautioned as to the limited precedential value, if any, of pre-2008 *sukūk* issuance documentation, to the extent impacted by the AAOIFI Clarification. It is clear that the AAOIFI *Sharī'ah* board intends to take a broader standard-setting role and to scrutinize *sukūk* structures and other Islamic finance products to ensure greater rigor in *Sharī'ah* compliance. Mimicry of conventional bond structures will not be acceptable. The industry has yet to learn where other oversight functions will be applicable.

OBSERVATIONS IN CONCLUSION

Sukūk have become the defining instrument of the finance side of the Islamic capital markets and will remain so for the foreseeable future. As presaged by the 2011 and first-quarter 2012 numbers, issuance volumes will increase markedly in the coming years. An emerging trend is an increase in corporate issuances. The trend was first discernible with government-owned corporates but will become increasingly apparent with privately held corporates.

The lease is a flexible financing device that is widely known and accepted throughout the world. Thus, it is likely that *sukūk al-'ijāra* will remain the predominant form of *sukūk*. Given the vibrancy of the Malaysian *sukūk* markets and the preferences of those markets for *mushāraka* structures, the *sukūk al-mushāraka* will also hold a prominent role. Issuances of *sukūk al-mushāraka* in the GCC and Middle East and North Africa (MENA) regions have decreased markedly since the promulgation of the AAOIFI Clarification and are not expected to rebound in the near future. However, the hallmark of the Islamic finance and investment industry is creativity, and there is every reason to believe that creative structures will emerge in the very near future. The move to *sukūk al-wakāla* may be an indication of an emerging structural trend.

The *sukūk* experience allows the observations that the Islamic capital markets have achieved broad recognition and acceptance and *sukūk* have achieved broad recognition and acceptance as the primary capital markets instrument. The direction in which creativity will take the markets is unpredictable. What can be confidently predicted is that the Islamic capital markets will emerge from the current financial downturn as a central feature of the Islamic finance and investment industry and will increasingly be integrated with the larger conventional capital markets. *Sukūk* will likely be the vehicle of choice in achieving that integration.

NOTES

1. In my opinion, these are two of five critical factors in the development of the modern Islamic finance and investment industry. The other three are the efforts of some *Sharī'ah* scholars to obtain *ijmā'* (consensus) as to certain critical matters; reconceptualization of the nominate contracts as building blocks, rather than rigid silos, in transactions and the ability to use more than one nominate contract in a transaction; and bifurcated transactional structures that allow both conventional Western institutions and *Sharī'ah*-compliant investors to participate in the transactions in accordance with their respective practices, constraints, and beliefs.

2. Markets where new public or private securities issuances are purchased directly from the issuer of those securities through the underwriting process in which some distribution risk is taken by financial services firms.

3. Markets in which previously issued securities are bought and sold. They include stock exchanges, other exchanges, bulletin boards, proprietary trading systems, and off-market systems.

4. *Sukūk* are securitizations of either assets (and their cash flows) or entire businesses (and their cash flows). They are not bonds. Each asset originator has a definable cost of obtaining funds from direct funding sources (i.e., the interest rate it must pay). The principle and purpose of asset securitization is to isolate certain of the originator's assets to allow an investor in those assets to provide lower-cost funding than the originator's direct funding cost absent such an isolation (taking into account transaction costs). One working definition of *securitization* is "the sale of equity or debt instruments, representing ownership interests in, or secured by, a segregated, income producing asset or pool of assets, in a transaction structured to reduce or reallocate certain risks inherent in owning

or lending against the underlying assets and to ensure that such interests are more readily marketable and, thus, more liquid than ownership interests in and loans against the underlying assets." Joseph C. Shenker & Anthony J. Colletta, *Asset Securitization: Evolution, Current Issues and New Frontiers*, 69 Texas Law Review 1369 (1990–1991), at 1374–1375. The segregated assets are instruments or obligations that involve some right to payment, such as lease payments, real estate mortgage loan receivables, credit card receivables, and royalties, among others. Benefits and criticisms of securitization are summarized at Michael J. T. McMillen, "Asset Securitization Sukuk and Islamic Capital Markets: Structural Issues in These Formative Years," *Wisconsin International Law Journal* 703, no. 25 (2008) (*"McMillen: Sukūk"*), pp. 731–737, and sources cited therein.

5. This chapter does not discuss the relevant equity-side rules set forth in the DJIMI *Fatwā* and progeny. Those rules have been applied in other areas, some being of relevance to *sukūk*. For example, the financial ratio tests may be of relevance for *sukūk* involving an underlying joint venture (e.g., *sukūk al-mushāraka* or *sukūk al-muḍāraba*). The core business tests are of relevance to any lease (*'ijāra*) arrangement, including a *sukūk al-'ijāra*. The tenants in the underlying *'ijāra* transactions must be in permissible businesses (not the manufacture, distribution, or sale of pork or alcohol for human consumption, pornography, prostitution, weapons of mass destruction, involvement in interest-based finance, or involvement in gambling, as examples). For a more complete discussion of these principles and their evolution and application, see Michael J. T. McMillen, "Islamic Project Finance: An Introduction to Principles and Structures," *Global Infrastructure* 1, no. III (2009), pp. 1–17, and McMillen: *Sukūk*, note 4, at 726–731.

6. The plural is *sukūk*; *sakk* is the singular.

7. Michael J. T. McMillen and John A. Crawford, "Sukuk in the First Decade: By the Numbers," *Dow Jones Islamic Market Indexes Quarterly Newsletter*, December 2008, p. 3, which is the source for all data in Exhibits 9.1 through 9.6.

8. The sovereign figure is likely greater because, for example, governmentally owned or controlled entities are not distinguished from privately owned or controlled entities, and government ownership is significant.

9. "USD 63 bn Sukuk Issued in First 9 Months of 2011," *Zawya Global Sukuk Review* September 2011, October 3, 2011, available at www.zawya.com/story.cfm/sidZAWYA20111003090112?zawyaemailmarketing (*"Zawya 3Q"*). See also Global Sukuk Report: H1–2011, Islamic Finance Information Service by ISI Emerging Markets (*"IFIS Report"*), p. 1 (copy on file with the author).

10. *GCC Sukuk Issuance Surges in 2011*, Emirates 24|7, October 8, 2011, available at www.zawya.com/story.cfm/sidZAWYA20111009030016/lok030000111008/GCC_sukuk_issuance_surges_in_2011?&zawyaemailmarketing.

11. IFIS Report, note 9, at 4. This was due, primarily, to a large (US$9 billion) issuance by the Qatar Central Bank.

12. IFIS Report, note 9, at 6. Again, government-owned corporates have been largely excluded.

13. IFIS Report, note 9, at 8.

14. Global Sukuk Report 1H2011, KFH Research Ltd and Kuwait Finance House, July 28, 2011, copy on file with the author (available with registration at http://kfhresearch.com/reports?id=1828).

15. Information on 2011 and 2012 issuances in the section "Issuances since November of 2008" is contained in "USD 85 Billion Sukuk Issued in 2011," *Zawya*, available at www.zawya.com/story.cfm/sidZAWYA20120110175320/Sukuk_record_year?zawyaemailmarketing; "2011 a Year in Review," *Zawya Sukuk Monitor*, "USD43bn Sukuk in 1Q12 Could Translate into USD120bnk in 2012," *Zawya*, available at www.zawya.com/story/1Q12_smashes_records-ZAWYA20120403111144/?goback=%2Egde_2600359_member_105513305.

16. See "The Rise of Wakala: Global Sukuk Review: August 2011," *Zawya Sukuk Monitor*, September 5, 2011, available at http://ae.zawya.com/sukuk/Story.cfm/ sidZAWYA20110905081630.

17. The discussion of *'ijāra* principles is based on, in particular, the *Majalat Al-Ahkam Al-Adliyah*, the translations of Judge C. A. Hooper, *Majalat Al-Ahkam Al-Adliyah* (an English-language translation prepared as *The Civil Law of Palestine and Trans-Jordan, Volumes I and II* (1933), and reprinted in various issues of *Arab Law Quarterly* 4 (1968), and C. R. Tyser, D. G. Demetriades, and Ismail Haqqi Effendi, "The Majelle: Being an English Translation of *Majallah El-AhkamI-Adliya and a Complete Code on Islamic Civil Law*" (2001) (the "*Majelle*"; article numbering is identical in each translation), at articles 404–611; Wahbah Al-Zuhayli (Mahmoud El-Gamal, translator, and Muhammad S. Eisaa, revisor), *Al-Fiqh Al-Islami wa-Adillatuh (Islamic Jurisprudence and Its Proofs), Wahbah al-Zuhayli, Financial Transactions in Islamic Jurisprudence* (2003), a translation of Volume 5 of *Al-Fiqh Al-'Islami wa 'Adillatuh*, 4th ed. (1997) ("*Al-Zuhayli*"), and "Shari'a Standard No. (9), Ijarah and Ijarah Muntahia Bittamleek," in *Shari'a Standards* 1425–6H/2004–2005 (2004) ("*AAOIFI Standards*"), at 135. More detailed discussions of the *'ijāra* structure are Michael J. T. McMillen, *Islamic Shari'ah-Compliant Project Finance: Collateral Security and Financing Structure Case Studies, Fordham International Law Journal* 24, no. 1184 (2000) ("*McMillen: Case Studies*"), and Michael J. T. McMillen, "Shari'a-Compliant Financing Structures and the Development of an Islamic Economy," *Proceedings of the Fifth Harvard University Forum on Islamic Finance: Islamic Finance: Dynamics and Development* (2002).

18. This chapter briefly summarizes payments of relevance to a *sukūk al-'ijāra* and related *Sharī'ah* documents. The managing contractor agreement has two functions: retaining the project company to perform various functions that the project company, as the lessee, cannot perform under the lease (*'Ijāra*) due to *Sharī'ah* restrictions; and removing the funding company from participating in making decisions and determinations. The tax matters agreement is a road map for the relevant taxing authority and is customized to each transaction, jurisdiction, and structure. The collateral security package is not discussed, despite its critical importance.

19. Most financings use complex account structures and lockbox structures. All payments are made into these accounts, and an escrow agreement directs the application of amounts.

20. All examples in this chapter assume the funding company to be a disregarded entity; that is not true in European jurisdictions, and the basic rent will have to be grossed up in those transactions, with the excess over debt service passed back to the equity in a tax-free jurisdiction.

21. An early use of this structure (1997–1998) in a Saudi Arabian electric sector financing is discussed in McMillen: Case Studies, note 16, at 1232–1236. *Sharī'ah* principles pertaining to a *sharikat* are set forth in the *Majelle*, note 17, at articles 1045–1403; Al-Zuhayli, note 17, at 447–481; and *Shari'a Standard No. (12), Sharika (Musharaka) and Modern Corporations* in AAOIFI Standards, note 17, at 197. The *mushāraka* is one of two structures (the *'ijāra* is the other) used for home ownership financings. More recently, it was used in bond *sukūk* that gave rise to the AAOIFI Clarification.

22. Contrast the *muḍāraba* in which the property is deemed owned by the *rabb ul-māl*.

23. In addition to a broad range of applicable *Sharī'ah* rules, there are various ongoing debates among the scholars with respect to structural issues, including the pricing of the *hissas*. These are not discussed. In addition, some structural elements in the *sukūk* context were the subject of the AAOIFI *Sukūk* Clarification.

24. The *Sharī'ah* principles applicable to the *muḍāraba* are discussed in *Majelle*, note 16, at articles 1404–1430; Al-Zuhayli, note 17, at 497–521; Muhammad Taqi Usmani, "The Concept of Musharaka and Its Application as an Islamic Method of Financing," *Arab*

Law Quarterly 203, no. 14 (1999); and "Shari'a Standard No. (13), Mudaraba," in *AAOIFI Standards*, note 17, at 227.

25. Necessary opinions in securitization *sukuk* are particularly difficult to render, particularly as regards "true sale" and similar fundamental concepts. See Michael J. T. McMillen, "Contractual Enforceability Issues: Sukuk and Capital Markets Development," *Chicago Journal of International Law* 427, no. 7 (2007).

26. This self-styled resolution or advisory is available at www.aaoifi.com (copy on file with the author). See also a previous, insightful, paper by Justice Mohammed Taqi Usmani, the chairman of the AAOIFI *Sharī'ah* Board: *Sukuk and Their Contemporary Applications* (undated; prepared in 2007).

CHAPTER 10

Shari'a-Compliant Mutual Funds

MONEM SALAM
President, Saturna Sdn. Bhd.
Former Director of Islamic Investing of Saturna Capital and
Deputy Portfolio Manager of the Amana Mutual Funds Trust

A mutual fund is an investment by a group of shareholders that is run by a professional fund manager. A mutual fund can be a corporation or trust that issues shares. The money is pooled for investment purposes, and the gains or losses are shared proportionally among holders. In addition, the mutual fund appoints a manager to run the fund. Investing in a mutual fund raises many concerns to Muslims about the Islamic legality of the investment itself. Yet, what many overlook is that a mutual fund is similar to Islamic investments: musharaka and mudaraba.

MUSHARAKA VERSUS MUDARABA

In a musharaka (equity partnership) transaction, two or more partners contribute capital to a project, though not necessarily in equal amounts. In this shared equity arrangement, a partner with a larger investment has proportionally more control over the decisions that are made and would absorb a larger percentage of any potential losses, again on a proportional basis. To make the terms of the agreement clear from the start, a musharaka contract must specify each partner's profit as a predetermined portion of whatever the total profit turns out to be. However, unlike the way loss is apportioned, profit isn't necessarily proportional to the investment amount.

Musharaka contracts may be either permanent or diminishing, also called *declining balance musharaka,* in which one partner eventually buys out the other with regularly scheduled investments in the partnership. Applied in simple partnerships, musharaka also sets a precedent for modern stock investing, as they are similar to joint-stock companies or corporations

To simplify, in musharaka, two or more partners supply capital to a joint venture, based on simple partnerships; it is the basis for equity investing, and it is commonly used for real estate financing.

In a mudaraba transaction, one or more partners supply the capital, and the other provides expertise and management to complete a joint venture. Any profit, which isn't predetermined, is divided using a ratio that is spelled out in the contract. While all potential financial losses are the sole responsibility of the partner or partners who invest the capital, the managing partner risks losing the time and effort spent on the project if it does not turn a profit. A mudaraba contract must specify how potential profits will be shared.

To simplify, mudaraba is an investment with a group of shareholders that is run by a professional fund manager. It is the basis for mutual funds, deposit accounts are required, and some arrangements require management fees.

"GENERAL NEED"

In a conventional world, can Muslims invest in a company if it is not 100 percent pure? The quick answer is yes. The longer answer comes down to a consensus among scholars about investing: that it is a general need or hajjah. What does it mean to have a "general need"? Investments one makes in the stock market are not black and white. If they were black and white between halal (permissible) and haram (forbidden), then one would know which company to purchase. Some people say that because interest is haram (forbidden) and all companies deal with interest, it makes investing in companies, and thus the stock market, haram. However, some things that are haram can be made halal if there is a necessity. This is called darurah (necessity), a concept within the bounds of Islamic understanding. In darurah, there is the underlying principle of hajjah, which is a legal maxim that states that when an activity in and of itself is halal, some haram elements may be permissible if prohibiting them would work against the general good. The principle of hajjah justifies participation in the stock market, even though modern companies inevitably operate with some level of interest.

Scholars have agreed that investments in stocks are a general need. If one were to examine all the types of investments from bank accounts, real estate, and commercial purchases, stocks (typically through mutual funds) are the only ones in which a small amount can be invested and outpace inflation. There are three factors scholars use to gauge if an investment falls into the general need category: minimal investment, outpacing inflation, and liquidity.

Inflation describes the persistent tendency of prices for goods and services to increase over time. Or if you look at it another way, inflation describes a gradual loss in the value of money. In either case, inflation means you can buy less and less with the same amount of money. But there are ways to avoid that risk and beat the toll that inflation takes on your financial security. The key is to invest in assets that, over time, have the potential to gain value more rapidly than the rate at which inflation eats away at the value of your money.

Liquidity is a measure of the percentage of a company's assets held in cash, cash equivalents, or accounts receivable. The acceptable level is typically set at 45 percent, because if it's more than 50 percent cash, it can be traded only at book value and would work against the general good. In this case, because the stock market is halal, stocks in principle are halal, too, and need not be forbidden to Muslim investors even if the corporations that issue them carry debt and pay or receive interest.

Stock market investments meet these three requirements, and based on that, scholars have said there is a general need. That also is the general consensus among scholars around the world. However, with all things, certain restrictions must remain, because though a company or investment may meet these requirements, there are halal and haram aspects a Muslim investor has to consider. For example, a company that can be avoided is one that sells pork or alcohol, but a company that cannot be avoided is one that has a bank account collecting interest. Interest is an evitable reality of our economic system.

STAKEHOLDER VERSUS SHAREHOLDER

If you own stock, you may be called a shareholder or a stakeholder. In fact, the words *stock* and *share* are often used interchangeably. To be precise, though, a share is a unit of ownership in a corporation, and stock is an investment that represents ownership, or equity, in a corporation. A stakeholder means you have control over the decisions being made in the company, and shareholders, although they are owners, don't make decisions. Shareholders just benefit from the company's growth and financial status. Though there is a difference between stakeholders and shareholders, guidelines for investment are specifically for those who are shareholders because the most likely scenario is that when buying stocks the investor will be a shareholder. Investors sometimes find themselves to be stakeholders when investing in a start-up, and those parameters allow that investor to decide the Islamic legality of the type of business they are investing in.

Regardless of the definition of mutual funds and stakeholders, most investors have some basic questions about investing as a Muslim

Does the company engage in haram business activities? Is the company's leverage, or debt ratio, too high? Is too large a percentage of the company's assets liquid, or in cash?

If the answer to any of the questions is yes, the company may fail the screening process. That makes its stock an unacceptable investment.

To simplify the task of identifying investments that meet specific criteria, financial institutions and analysts put companies through a series of screens, or questions. Islamic screens assess whether the business activities of the company are halal or haram.

When searching and choosing a company to invest your money, there is a halal screening test that can be implemented to help with the decision. The first guideline to use is the primary screen, which constitutes staying away from companies and investments that have revenues that are forbidden. An example of forbidden revenues would be an alcohol or pork manufacturer or a financial services company dealing in interest. If the primary revenues are halal, then the company is halal to invest in, provided a second set of criteria are verified, with nuances.

Let's compare the revenues of Target versus an airline, such as American Airlines. A portion of both companies' revenues is derived from alcohol sales. However, Target would be forbidden, and American Airlines would be acceptable. The reason is that Target is in the business of selling merchandise, and one kind of merchandise is alcohol. No matter how small, they have revenue from haram sources. In the case of American Airlines, however, the alcohol sales are an ancillary part of the business.

The second set of guidelines is to break down the financial statements into ratios to see if a company's debt/market capitalization adds up to be 33 percent.

The rule of 33 percent comes from an analogy cited in a hadith. The hadith tells the story of one of the Prophet's companions who was dealing with how to distribute his wealth after his death. He asked the Prophet, "O Prophet, I'm on my death bed, I am a wealthy man and I am survived only by one daughter." He proceeded to ask if he can give all his wealth to poverty, to which the Prophet responded "No." He then asked if he can give half his wealth to poverty, to which the Prophet responded, "No." The Prophet then said give a third, or 33 percent, of your wealth to poverty.

This hadith has led many scholars to implement the 33 percent rule on financial investments.

A company's size is determined by its market capitalization (market cap), which is computed by multiplying the number of existing shares by the current price per share. For example, a company with 100 million outstanding or floating shares worth $25 a share would have a market cap of $2.5 billion. Large-cap companies are those valued at more than $5 billion, mid-caps are valued between $2.5 billion and $5 billion, and small-caps are valued at less than $2.5 billion, although some sources use lower numbers.

The market cap is then divided by a company's total debt (short- and long-term) to get the debt/market ratio. If a company's debt/market ratio is less than a third, or 33 percent, then a company is deemed acceptable for investment.

To account for market volatility, returns are smoothed out by taking a 12-month trailing average. This requires investors to take an average of the entire year instead of only taking a snapshot of a company's immediate returns.

The third set of guidelines is called the 45 percent rule, which is a measure of the percentage of a company's assets held in cash, cash equivalents, or accounts receivable. The acceptable level is determined by dividing accounts receivable by total assets and is typically set at 45 percent because if it's more than 50 percent cash, the company can only be traded at book value, which would work against the general good.

The fourth guideline is the 5 percent rule, which simply outlines that a company's core business accounts for more than 5 percent of a company's revenue or gross income. For example if the sale of alcohol accounts for less than 5 percent of an airline company's revenue, alcohol is not a core business, and investing in that company's stock is generally acceptable.

The 5 percent rule is not restricted to perceived haram entities. It also examines the interest a company accrues. Because a company does not have to report its accrued interest, financial investors take current market values and rates and derive what the interest would be on that company's account.

This, in turn, allows financial investors to determine if the company fits the 5 percent rule.

A somewhat less stringent rule sets the standards for a core business at 10 percent, and different Islamic scholars may set different limits.

All of the aforementioned guidelines have been outlined and compiled to assist Muslims who are facing the tough decision of investment and finding the right company to fit their needs. In the complicated world of Shari'a law, haram and halal rules, and fatwahs, scholars have thoroughly researched the Quran and hadiths to compose these guidelines. Nothing has been presented without careful consideration.

Note that there are alternative screening methods. The Account and Auditing Organization for Islamic Financial Institutions (AAOIFI) and the Securities Commission of Malaysia (SEC), two standard-setting bodies for the Islamic financial industry, differ on which guidelines they consider. For example, the SEC implements a debt/market cap analysis, but it does not consider the 45 percent accounts receivable or 5 percent guidelines.

There is room for adjustment and growth, and room for incorporation of the guidelines that best work for your financial practices.

PURIFICATION

Shari'a prohibits Muslims from profiting, even indirectly, from unacceptable practices, so investors are expected to account for and give away any income derived from riba or other haram sources.

One reason Islamic mutual funds appeal to Muslim investors is that the vast majority of these funds calculate the tainted income that makes up part of the fund's income distributions. Some funds also calculate tainted total return figures, which take into account purification ratios for both dividends and capital gains.

The fund reports these figures to their shareholders so that the investors can calculate the amount of their fund income to give to charity. In some countries, though not in the United States, the fund itself handles the purification and distributes only acceptable income to its shareholders. In either case, this vastly simplifies the complexity of purifying investment income for individual investors.

Many Islamic scholars believe that purification of unacceptable income also requires Muslim stockholders and the managers of Islamic mutual funds to express public disapproval of a corporation's decision to earn unacceptable income. The corporation's annual meeting may be the ideal forum, but a letter to management will suffice.

Although individuals may not make a significant impression unless they own large blocks of shares, recent corporate history has made clear that institutional investors—such as mutual funds—or organized groups of investors who share a perspective often carry significant weight. For example, there's general agreement that several major corporations have revised their environment and workplace policies in response to shareholder pressure, especially pressure from mutual funds.

As shareholders, individuals and institutions have the right to submit shareholder resolutions on issues that concern them. They also have the right to vote against corporate acquisitions of or mergers with companies whose core businesses are haram. That action would apply even if the income from the proposed acquisition is small enough to enable the acquiring company to continue to qualify as an acceptable investment.

Dividend income also must be purified from haram or unknown sources of income. This is a requirement for dividend income, which is the revenue earned on stocks if the issuing company pays out a portion of its profits to its shareholders, but not for capital gains. This is because dividend income can increase your total return, which combines growth and income. Most U.S. stock dividends are taxed as long-term capital gains income. This income is a variable, is not guaranteed, and can be cut or even eliminated in a downturn.

In comparison, capital gains are a steady gain or growth of your entire investment or the value of your stocks in general. So if you buy a stock that gradually increases in value and hold it for 10 to 20 years, it's likely to provide some capital gains, or profit, when you sell. However, there are no guarantees about either the timing or the amount of any gains. You and other investors could end up with a capital loss if you sold a stock for less than you paid to buy it.

Scholars have agreed that dividend income cannot be purified by giving it away as zakah or for sadaqa. Remember, it is a purification of doing something wrong, so no personal benefit can be derived from it.

The Shari'a supervisory board is an entity unique to Islamic finance. It is made up of a team of Islamic legal scholars who establish the ground rules that govern the investments that a fund makes. That means not only avoiding stocks in those companies whose business activities are haram, or unacceptable, but also those that might be questionable. In short, the board's role is to ensure that the fund is in compliance with the letter and the spirit of Islamic investing. In addition to monitoring a fund's portfolio, the Shari'a supervisory board oversees its purification; advises on zakat, or charitable spending; and assists fund management in dealing with issues of concern to the Muslim community through shareholder resolutions and other tools of corporate democracy. A fund's board, usually three to five people, may either be a quorum of independent scholars or a council that is affiliated with the fund's promoter.

The Shari'a supervisory board approves initial screens to be used on choosing investments, and it monitors compliance at regular intervals. In Islamic banks, different from Islamic mutual funds, the board is given the complicated role of agreeing to complex contracts each time.

CONCLUSION

Investing in Shari'a-compliant mutual funds is compatible with and encouraged by Islamic principles. As long as the fund operates under the supervision of a qualified Shari'a supervisory board that both screens and monitors its portfolio, the investor can be assured that the fund complies with Islamic financial standards. Compliant funds are available internationally for investors at all levels of investment. These funds are performance rated (see Chapter 11 for more information) and adhere to international mutual funds' investment standards.

The Evolution of Shari'ah-Compliant Indexes and Why They Outperform Conventional Indexes over the Long Term

TARIQ AL-RIFAI
Director Islamic Market Indexes, Dow Jones Indexes

INTRODUCTION

The global market for Islamic financial services, as measured by Shari'ah-compliant assets, was estimated to be $1 trillion at the end of 2010, up 32 percent from 2007's $758 billion. Meanwhile, the Islamic fund market was reported to be $58 billion in 2010, up 7.6 percent from 2009. Clearly, the growth of Islamic banking has been one of the most important developments in global finance over the past decade.

Key centers of Islamic finance are concentrated in Malaysia and the Middle East, including Bahrain, Kuwait, Saudi Arabia, and the United Arab Emirates. Islamic finance is also expanding rapidly in Asian countries such as Bangladesh and Pakistan. Western nations looking to attract Islamic finance are attempting to make it easy for practitioners to establish operations. Countries such as Australia, France, and the United Kingdom are among the countries looking to develop opportunities for Shari'ah-compliant investors.

Interestingly, the rise in demand for Shari'ah-compliant products is coming from both Muslims and non-Muslims. Though Islamic banking institutions were bruised during the financial crisis, they were affected far less than those in the conventional banking system, which saw high-profile institutions collapse and suffer massive outflows of assets. Because Islam prohibits the use of interest-bearing debt, Islamic banks were buffered from the financial crisis. In addition, since the 1999 launch of the Dow Jones Islamic Market Indexes, there is now evidence that Shari'ah-compliant indexes outperform their conventional counterparts over the long term. This has led conventional investors to look closely at the Shari'ah-compliant investment philosophy.

THE EVOLUTION OF SHARI'AH-COMPLIANT INDEXING

Although the first Islamic banks were established in the Middle East in the 1970s, it would take another 10 years until Islamic equity funds were brought to market. Surprisingly, the first Islamic financial products were launched in the United States, followed by Singapore, South Africa, and Malaysia, before finally appearing in the Middle East.

Islamic funds were created as a result of strong demand by Muslim investors, who asked fund managers to create financial products that comply with Islamic investing principles—and they did. Swiss private banks were among the first to realize the potential of Islamic finance and did not want to miss the opportunity. These banks created tools for Muslim investors to gain exposure to the global equity market through their Islamic global equity instruments. However, without any alternatives, funds were benchmarked against conventional indexes such as the S&P 500, the FTSE All-World Index, and the MSCI Emerging Markets Index. For obvious reasons, none of these indexes provided a fair or satisfactory comparison. (Embedded within some of these indexes, for example, were industries and companies with high-leverage ratios—a financial situation that is inconsistent with Shari'ah principles.) By the mid-1990s, Islamic financial institutions, including DMI Group and Faisal Islamic Bank, started to build their own internal measurement gauges against which Islamic equity instruments could be benchmarked.

Finally, by 1999, a suitable alternative was provided as Dow Jones Indexes, seeing that Islamic finance was a growing market lacking proper benchmarks, created the Dow Jones Islamic Market Index—the very first Islamic financial index. Dow Jones Indexes' timing could not have been better. According to Morningstar, the number of Shari'ah-compliant funds reached 700 by year-end 2010—up more than threefold from 2003. Ernst & Young, meanwhile, estimates the value of these funds has grown to $58 billion in 2010 from $20 billion in 2003. Equity funds make up 40 percent of total investments, with fixed income 16 percent, real estate and private equity 13 percent, and cash, commodities, and other asset classes accounting for the balance.

With Dow Jones Indexes' new benchmark serving as the catalyst, other providers followed suit, providing healthy competition as well as unprecedented access to the Islamic fund market for investors.

Islamic indexes have changed the way the industry does business, offering transparency, low-cost solutions, standardization, and, most important, investability. They have also helped with product development, best practices, rules-based methodology and risk management.

INDEX DESIGN AND DEVELOPMENT

Shari'ah-compliant indexes differ from their conventional counterparts in at least three ways: Shari'ah supervisory boards establish investability guidelines and monitor the process, the guidelines are then applied to the universe of securities, and finally, purification rules are set to cleanse any impure profits from securities paying dividends.

1. Shari'ah Supervisory Boards

One crucial aspect of index construction is Shari'ah law, with decision making about compliance provided by well-respected and financially savvy Shari'ah scholars. To be included in an index, companies must meet Shari'ah guidelines for acceptable products, business activities, debt levels, and interest incomes and expenses. It is up to each index provider to develop its own screening methodology; however, Dow Jones Indexes took the critical extra step of establishing an internal Shari'ah supervisory board to provide qualified advice on compliance. This decision has been crucial with respect to consistency issues: A revolving-door policy, in which scholars jump on and off various boards of directors, is unhelpful, particularly when the board is expected to opine on important new developments.

2. Screening

One area in which there is little room for debate is screening. Shari'ah-compliant instruments and Shari'ah indexes generally prohibit investment in alcohol, pork, tobacco, weapons, gambling, pornography, certain leisure and entertainment businesses, and conventional financial systems.

Each index provider, however, approaches screening in its own way:

- The Dow Jones Islamic Market Indexes do not include companies involved in alcohol, conventional financial services (banking and insurance), pork-related products, entertainment, tobacco, weapons, and defense.
- The FTSE Shari'ah Global Equity Index Series also prohibits alcohol, tobacco, conventional finance, pork-related products, and nonhalal food production, packaging, or processing.
- The MSCI Islamic Index Series prohibits distillers and vintners, banks and insurance companies, aerospace and defense companies, casinos and gaming, hotels, resorts, cruise lines, and restaurants, as well as broadcasting and satellite movies and tobacco.
- The S&P Shariah Indexes prohibit alcohol, advertising and media (with the exception of newspapers), financials, gambling, pork, pornography, tobacco, and companies involved in the trading of gold and silver as cash on a deferred basis.
- The Russell-Jadwa index goes one step further, prohibiting the inclusion of companies involved in stem cells, human embryos, and genetic cloning.

(*Source:* iShares, Shari'ah Indexes, 2009)

However, this is only part of the picture. The Dow Jones Islamic Market Indexes prohibit *any* involvement in the activities mentioned, whereas the FTSE Shari'ah Global Equity Index Series allows companies to be included if the income on their total interest and noncompliant activities does not exceed 5 percent of the company's total revenue. Similarly, the MSCI Islamic Index Series prohibits only companies that derive more than 5 percent of their revenues (cumulatively) from any prohibited activities, as does S&P. Like Dow Jones Indexes, the Russell-Jadwa Shari'ah Index prohibits noncompliant companies from inclusion.

For Dow Jones Indexes, the exclusion of companies that are noncompliant is important. It is the only way, we believe, to ensure that an index is truly Islamic and that the index remains pure.

Screening is also not always a straightforward process. What happens when an index provider prohibits breweries from being represented in an index but then approves a supermarket that sells alcohol, or prohibits nonhalal meat producers but then includes McDonald's? It is not enough to have quantitative screening of stocks. We believe it is necessary to include a qualitative function that goes deeper. For Dow Jones Indexes, this involves an in-house research team that looks qualitatively at company information on an ongoing basis. The team examines many sources and considers how each company's revenues are broken down. The real work is in looking closely at the so-called gray areas.

Rather than exclude all supermarkets and hotels, for example, Dow Jones Indexes includes certain Gulf Cooperation Council region supermarkets and hotels that do not serve or sell alcohol. Companies in the gray area undergo an internal review, and they are also considered by the Quarterly Review Group. The information is then forwarded to Dow Jones Indexes' Shari'ah board for an opinion. Once a year, the group goes through each of the 65,000 securities that the indexes consider. On top of this, there are watch lists, on which are companies that have the potential to be of concern. Dow Jones Islamic Indexes also set up news filters to monitor company information on a daily basis to ensure that a company is prohibited that might be compliant one day but not compliant another.

Regular, qualitative scrutiny is particularly relevant when it comes to company debt. A stock may have a portion of Shari'ah-compliant debt, for example, which would not be apparent from information downloaded from a data vendor. This is often the case for companies in the Middle East.

Screening also applies for debt ratios. Dow Jones Indexes excludes companies with:

- More than 33 percent total debt divided by a 24-month average market capitalization.
- Companies with more than 33 percent cash and interest-bearing securities divided by a trailing 24-month average market capitalization.

Accounts receivable must also be less than 33 percent.

A debt-to-market capitalization ratio better captures the new economy, service-oriented companies, and companies that rely on larger amounts of goodwill. Debt-to-market capitalization is also more dynamic: It captures market-sector rotations. As it is market-value based, it is subject less to manipulations, as debt-to-market assets is an accounting treatment.

The methodology also provides faster accuracy about the health of a company. For example, companies like Enron, WorldCom, Tyco, and Global Crossing were all in the Dow Jones Islamic Market Index, but as their accounting issues came into the public domain, their market capitalizations were negatively impacted. Since they violated the debt-to-market-cap screen, they were removed from the indexes at the next quarterly review.

3. Dividend Purification

Index providers also have different approaches to dividend purification, a ratio that has developed over time in which a certain proportion of the profits earned through dividends (which corresponds to the proportion of interest earned by the company) must be given to charity. Shari'ah scholars have different opinions about purification. For the Dow Jones Islamic Market Indexes, dividend purification is not an issue because the indexes do not allow noncompliant companies to be included. For FTSE, appropriate ratios stand at 5 percent; MSCI Barra applies a dividend adjustment factor to all reinvested dividends.

PERFORMANCE: SHARI'AH-COMPLIANT INDEXES VERSUS CONVENTIONAL INDEXES

When Dow Jones Indexes launched the Islamic index family in 1999, it was difficult to assess its performance. It was clearly a niche market with growing demand, but no one would have guessed that Islamic indexes would outperform conventional indexes over the long run.

As you can see from Exhibit 11.1, the Dow Jones Islamic Market World Index has outperformed the Dow Jones Global Index by a significant margin.

When compared with other markets and regions, the Islamic indexes still outperform conventional indexes (see Exhibit 11.2). Across nearly every region, Islamic indexes perform better over the long run. This can be attributed to two main factors: First, Shari'ah-compliant screens remove all highly leveraged companies, which tend to be more volatile; they rise faster in bull markets and fall faster in bear markets. Thus, the extra volatility is removed. Second, Shari'ah-compliant screens tend to result in indexes that are overweight in certain industries—such as health care, technology, and oil and gas—yet are underweight in such sectors as financial services, insurance, entertainment, media, and hospitality.

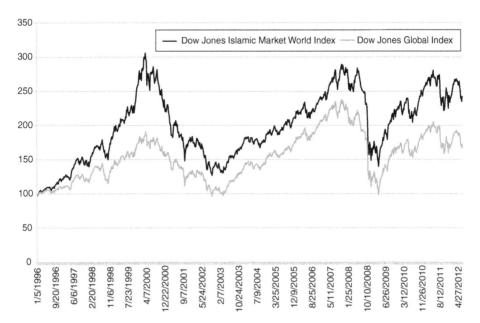

Exhibit 11.1 Performance of DJIM World Index versus DJ Global Index (January 1996 to October 2011)

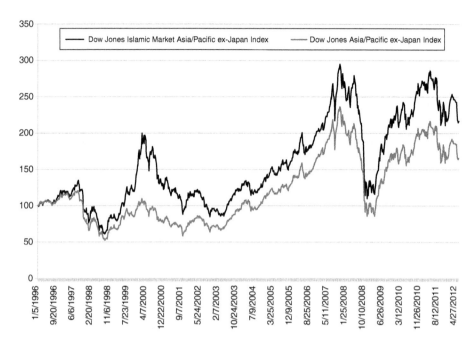

Exhibit 11.2 Performance of DJIM Asia Pacific ex-Japan Index versus DJ Asia Pacific ex-Japan Index (January 1996 to October 2011)

On the fixed-income side, Islamic finance still has not developed deep enough capital markets to sustain the demand for Shari'ah-compliant fixed-income securities. Nevertheless, the sukuk market (Islamic bond equivalents) has developed into a rapidly growing market and a key segment in the burgeoning Islamic finance industry. In 2006, Dow Jones Indexes partnered with Citigroup to launch the first sukuk index, the Dow Jones Citigroup Sukuk Index, which measures U.S. dollar-denominated sukuk issued globally and rated investment grade or above. To date, the index has proven to perform better than its conventional counterpart; however, due to its small size and some liquidity issues, it has been more volatile than the conventional bond index (see Exhibit 11.3).

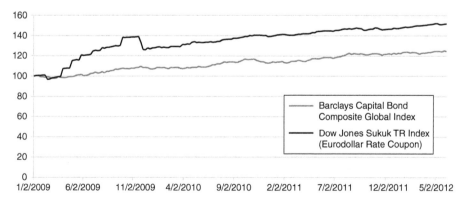

Exhibit 11.3 Performance of DJ Citigroup Sukuk Index versus Barclays Capital Global Aggregate Corporate Bond Index (October 2005 to October 2011)

FUTURE OUTLOOK AND TRENDS

Islamic indexes have always been at the forefront of developments in Islamic finance. They have helped shape the industry in many ways. For one thing, indexes have provided much needed transparency. In a post-financial-crisis world, this is crucial. Retail investors, particularly, put their trust in index providers and expect them to have completed due diligence on their behalf.

There are also investors who seek investability. Every index provider claims to be the most investable, but it is not about the total number of securities; rather, it's the Shari'ah compliance of those securities that really matters.

One important development over the last three years has been that of Shari'ah-compliant exchange-traded funds (ETFs). Though Islamic ETFs are a relatively nascent market (globally, there are fewer than 15 Islamic ETFs), these products are poised for growth, attracting retail and institutional investors alike with their accessibility. The first Shari'ah-compliant ETF was launched in Turkey in 2006, off the Dow Jones Islamic Market Turkey Index. Since then, there have been launches in many parts of the world, most recently in Saudi Arabia, where the Capital Markets Authority approved the kingdom's first ETF in May 2012. The Falcom Saudi Equity ETF is listed on the Tadawul Stock Exchange.

Another important development has been the listing of Islamic funds in key fund domiciles. A number of Shari'ah-compliant funds have been created as under-takings for collective investments in transferable securities (UCITS) products, for instance. Funds are being launched on a country-by-country basis, developing infrastructure to support Shari'ah needs. Luxembourg and Ireland started Islamic fund listings in 2007 and 2008, respectively. Asset managers continue to flock to the market, with some estimates suggesting there are now as many as 500 Islamic product providers worldwide.

Now that Islamic finance has developed a solid track record, it will continue to be a dynamic and evolving industry. Index providers, both the larger and the regional, will continue to evolve and stay on top of these developments. Today is an exciting time for the industry, as conventional finance begins to take a closer look at Islamic finance and see how it can learn from it. Time will tell if conventional finance develops some of the core principles of Islamic finance.

CHAPTER 12

Takaful

FARRUKH SIDDIQUI
President and Chief Operating Officer, Zayan Takaful

Perhaps no one would inherently associate concepts such as mutual protection, joint cooperation, risk sharing, and social responsibility with insurance. To most, insurance is a necessary evil that must be swallowed like a bitter pill to offset financial losses from the threat of risk inherent in every facet of life. How could this type of service have anything to do with the aforementioned ethical ideals? But this is exactly what Takaful, insurance designed to be in conformance with Islamic law, is based upon.

TAKAFUL EXPLAINED[1]

Insurance is "a contract (policy) in which an individual or entity receives financial protection or reimbursement against losses from an insurance company."[2] In Islam, this core principle of insurance is not forbidden; rather it is encouraged based on an essential aspect of Islamic belief, *tawakkul*, which means "complete 'reliance' on *Allah* (God) and 'trust' that He alone is sufficient for all of one's needs."[3] However, this "reliance" and "trust" does not mean that Muslims should abandon their own faculties by never studying for an exam and only praying that *Allah* will earn them an A+. Muslims are obligated to make a best-faith effort to achieve their aims and then rely on and trust *Allah* with sincerity of faith. One of the most famous traditions (*hadith*) on the subject states that when Prophet Muhammad (pbuh)[4] saw that a Bedouin had left his camel untied, the Prophet (pbuh) asked him, "Why don't you tie down your camel?" The Bedouin answered, "I placed my trust in *Allah*." The Prophet (pbuh) replied, "Tie your camel and place your trust in Allah."[5] Making a best effort to protect one's family and assets through the means of insurance, for example, is akin to the proverbial tying of the camel.

The Qur'anic injunction applied to Takaful underscores its underlying tenet as follows:

$$ \text{وَتَعَاوَنُوا عَلَى ٱلْبِرِّ وَٱلتَّقْوَىٰ وَلَا تَعَاوَنُوا عَلَى ٱلْإِثْمِ وَٱلْعُدْوَانِ} $$

And cooperate in righteousness and piety, but do not cooperate in sin and aggression.[6]

As enunciated by this verse, Takaful becomes an alternative to conventional insurance based on the concept of cooperation (*ta'awun*). In Takaful, members or participants make voluntarily contributions (premiums) to support a common goal of mutual protection.

Conventional insurance is structured as a contractual agreement (policy) between an insurance company and a consumer where in exchange for a fee (premium) the insurance company agrees to compensate a policy holder in the event of loss. The concept of paying another party a fee in order to "transfer risk" is prohibited under Islam because it introduces *gharar* (extreme uncertainty as to essential elements of an agreement) and *maisir* (gambling) to the transaction.

Takaful, however, involves sharing risk wherein participants voluntarily agree to subsidize each other's risk through a pool of voluntarily contributed funds. In a Takaful structure, the insurance company does not assume the risk of the participants, but simply plays the role of an operator (*wakeel*) who oversees the management and administration of the pooled funds. In the event one of the participants experiences a loss (claim), funds from the pool are used to help offset the financial burden of that loss. Since the insurance company is not being contracted to assume losses (which may or may not happen) and participants are making a voluntary contribution to a pool, rather than paying another party to transfer risk, Takaful structures do not involve *gharar* or *maisir*.

Along with this, conventional insurance structures violate Islamic principles by deriving income from impermissible activities such as investment in interest (*riba*)-bearing instruments and prohibited industries such as alcohol, pork, pornography, and gambling.[7] For example, conventional insurance companies invest premium funds based on a diversified investment strategy that calls for, among other things, investments in interest-bearing fixed income products and equities that could provide returns from prohibited industries. Under a Takaful structure, the operator will invest the pooled funds only in diversified investment vehicles that are compliant with Islam based on screens developed and approved by scholars proficient in Islamic jurisprudence.

Takaful implementation can be accomplished using various approaches acceptable to Islam. "Takaful models can be distinguished by the way contributions are managed, surpluses are distributed, funds are allocated, and fees are deducted."[8] The four common models known today are:

1. *Mudarabah.* This risk-sharing approach allows participants and an insurance company to share the risk and reward of the Takaful operation based on an equity partnership.
2. *Wakala.* This agency-based approach pays the insurance company a fee for administering the Takaful operation.
3. *Wakala/Mudarabah.* This hybrid approach pays the insurance company a fee for administering the Takaful operation, and investment returns are shared based on an equity partnership.[9]
4. *Waqf.* This is a trust- or endowment-based approach where the Takaful operation is self-reliant and all decisions are made by the participants.[10]

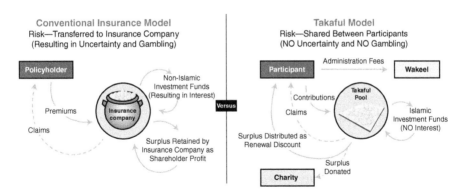

Exhibit 12.1 Conventional Insurance versus Takaful
Simplified rendering of a wakala-based Takaful model courtesy of Salaam Halal Insurance (defunct) and modified by Zayan Takaful, LLC.

As illustrated in Exhibit 12.1, conventional insurance companies are driven by maximizing returns and keeping the surplus from insurance proceeds and investment returns as shareholder profit. A Takaful company cannot do this. Therefore, the most beneficial feature of Takaful for consumers and society at large is that the surplus must be returned to the participants or donated to charity. A hybrid approach can also be adopted where the surplus is split between a portion returned to the participants and a portion donated to charity. Finally, in the event that the Takaful company has to shut down for whatever reason, the remaining pooled funds must be returned to the participants or donated to charity as agreed at the outset. This is different from conventional insurance, where the remaining funds are given to the shareholders only.

To summarize, the following ethical principles are at the heart of Takaful and must be incorporated as the foundational principles of any Takaful operation:

- Participants cooperate among themselves, making voluntary contributions to a pooled fund for the purposes of mutual assistance.
- Uncertainty is eliminated in respect of subscription and compensation.
- Losses are divided and liabilities spread according to the community pooling system.
- Surplus is returned to participants or donated to charity, including in the event of liquidation.
- Funds are invested based on Islamic guidelines that avoid interest and prohibited industries

It is the adoption of these core principles that makes Takaful acceptable under Islamic law and its conventional equivalent forbidden. Takaful might appear to be a new phenomenon, but its history dates back to the time of the Prophet Muhammad (pbuh) when various risk mitigation and mutual protection schemes were utilized to protect against the loss of life, property, and injury.[11] The emergence of Takaful in the modern context started with the formation of the first Takaful company in

Sudan in 1979.[12] Since then, the global Takaful industry has grown rapidly to an estimated premium volume in excess of $12 billion.[13]

Let's examine the state of the insurance industry today in order to ascertain why most people now cannot imagine insurance having anything to do with ethics or morality.

INSURANCE INDUSTRY TODAY

For many people, insurance is a service that you pay for and actually hope or pray never to benefit from because it means fear has become reality; that threat of risk has manifested into injury or damage, perhaps even of a catastrophic nature. Plus today the insurance industry is a black box full of actuarial analysis, rate calculations, and legalized language that frankly no one can be blamed for shunning. Therefore it is not difficult to see why insurance has become a commoditized product. It is needed but not necessarily wanted, so the impact that it has on the wallet should be minimized at all costs. Who actually even tries to understand the insurance they are buying by reading an insurance policy, anyway? Insurance policies are usually found buried at the bottom of the pile of stuff that people hope never to look at again. Although this is a prevailing sentiment for many, sophisticated consumers along with midsize to large businesses understand the value of insurance as a mechanism for protecting against and mitigating risk. If instituted properly, insurance can practically eliminate financial risk for a relatively nominal price.

Truth be told, this inauspicious reputation has been well earned by the insurance industry. Typically, compensation of insurance salespeople is heavily tilted toward commissions, which tend to be extremely volatile compared to the stability that a salary provides. This naturally leads salespeople to focus on their wallets instead of making an effort to understand the needs of their clients as they rush through the sale.[14]

> There are worse things in life than death. Have you ever spent an evening with an insurance salesman?
>
> Woody Allen

This justified yet shortsighted strategy typically leads to customer dissatisfaction and fuels the negative stereotype of the insurance industry. Moreover, insurance companies, focused on providing the maximum return to shareholders, go too far in cutting costs, including missing out on the key distinguishing feature of their offering, claims handling. Scan the Internet and you will find myriad consumer testimonials bemoaning their experience with insurance companies ranging from pricing to customer service to nightmarish claims experiences.

I don't mean to paint a gloomy picture, because there are a lot of great practitioners in the insurance industry who care about the customer. Plus ever since the dawn of the Internet and the more recent explosion of social networking and media, the dynamic is changing in favor of the consumer. But still, the insurance industry does not do a good job of educating the market with the aim of dispelling the negative perceptions that seem to always be mounting. Instead of distinguishing their products and services, most insurance commercials continue to highlight price, seemingly having embraced the prevailing sentiment that insurance is a commodity.

Admittedly still in the nascent stage of development, Takaful comes with great promise of changing the paradigm based on distinguishable product advantages through a fundamental shift toward ethical and moral considerations.

CAN TAKAFUL MAKE A DIFFERENCE?

Takaful has all the ingredients to live up to the ethical ideal it is based on, but, as with anything in life, preaching is one thing and practice is quite another. The financial crisis that started in 2007 and the resulting global mega recession and slow economic recovery present a model opportunity for Takaful to make an impact and grab significant market share. The stage is set, but will the industry produce the actors who are trained and willing to step up to the challenge? Let's examine the following five issues faced by conventional insurance and see how Takaful can resolve them to truly make a difference.

1. Product differentiation
2. Conflicting motivations
3. Insurance industry stereotype
4. The moral hazard predicament
5. "Surfing the green wave"[15]

One of the causes of the commoditization of insurance is that rarely is there a true *product differentiator*, so the industry is pushed into using price as a differentiator. The danger with this approach is fostering cutthroat competition driven by customers conditioned to make decisions based on price as the predominant factor. But in this environment rife with general discontent and ignorance, astute consumers are increasingly utilizing creative and nontraditional approaches to minimize their risk exposure and cost. Takaful companies can do well to position the unique benefits of their products to convince consumers that price is an important factor, just not the most important factor. Product compatibility with consumer needs and superior service prove to be more important in the long run. And Takaful consumers as participants have a say in the types of products and features that interest them, and they can also help develop a pricing advantage with good loss experience, so it is possible to have your cake and eat it, too.

The standard insurance contract creates *conflicting motivations* because the insurance company is a third party without any affiliation to the consumer or the risk being insured. It is only natural based on this contractual relationship that each party is looking out for its own interest. The insurance company wants to maximize profit by cutting costs and no area is off limits, including claims handling. Takaful companies, however, having been freed from the profit motive, are optimally situated to focus on what really matter in insurance: service and protection. Starting with the initial sales conversation and continuing through the manufacture and servicing of the insurance policy, Takaful companies have the unfettered opportunity to fully adopt industry best practices such as customized distribution channels, efficient distribution, performance-based compensation, centralized support functions, information technology (IT) and Internet proficiency, and decentralized organization.[16]

Takaful companies have to answer to only their participants, so instead of conflicting motivations, they can work to achieve uniform motivations. Their sales professionals can be compensated with a salary and bonuses tied to production and customer satisfaction so that they can become trusted advisors instead of pushy closers. Their service staff can be empowered to make real-time decisions and be measured against service benchmarks so they actually resolve customer issues instead of becoming robotic script readers who are incapable of problem solving, preferring to bounce customer calls from one department to another in a never-ending game of hot potato. Their management can create a culture encouraging and rewarding responsibility, benchmarking, and efficiency by supporting all segments of the organization through training, technology, and innovation.

Earlier in the chapter we discussed the *insurance industry stereotype*, explaining how it had developed with time due to key factors such as industry-wide sales practices and lack of education. As shown in the previous paragraphs, industry-wide practices can be corrected by Takaful companies as they look to achieve uniform motivations. The same opportunity exists on the market education front. The marketing, public relations, and business development units of Takaful companies have to work harmoniously to establish Takaful as a brand representative of an ethical alternative to conventional insurance. They have a fantastic story to tell that is rooted in reality and full of promise. Leveraging the Internet and social media effectively, they can focus on connecting with their target markets in ways unimaginable to their conventional counterparts. The opportunistic aspect of launching new and innovative products is that you can be proactive and dictate how your brand is to be positioned even in an industry that comes with historical baggage and preconceived notions.

Takaful companies have a wonderful opportunity to educate the market, and if they think through their story and present it with optimism and foresight, they should be able to attract attention from the public and media alike. They can leverage grassroots campaigns using traditional marketing strategies and engaging social media campaigns to drive interest, promote advocacy, and generate buzz. As part of this process, they should also show how Takaful is changing the insurance stereotype for the better by eliminating many of the practices that have fueled it and introducing new concepts that actually appeal to everyone's ethical sensibilities.

One of the chief benefits of realigning motivations in a meaningful way with Takaful is that it allows all stakeholders to strive toward the same goal of creating a stable and growing Takaful pool that is well positioned to serve its participants for the long haul. This approach goes to the heart of addressing the *moral hazard predicament* inherent in the polarity that is the conventional insurance system. The moral hazard of insurance has two dimensions: the passive and the active. The term is defined as "carelessness or indifference to a loss because of the existence of insurance." This is the passive aspect. The more insidious active aspect can be defined as "dishonesty or character defects in an individual that increase the chance of loss."[17]

One of the tangible benefits of Takaful is how surplus is treated. As opposed to conventional insurance companies, which treat surplus as shareholder profit, Takaful companies must return the surplus to the participants or donate it to charity. We will look at charity shortly, but let's talk about the impact of participants receiving their portion of the surplus. If Takaful companies successfully educate their consumers and carefully manage their operations to make surplus a reality, they greatly lower the probability of moral hazard becoming a significant factor in their enterprises. If consumers can clearly visualize the benefits of mitigating their risk through proper strategies designed for their particular exposures, they have an incentive to behave ethically and sensibly. To fully combat the active moral hazard, Takaful companies need to institute well-thought-out risk mitigation and prospect-filtering methodologies designed to identify problematic situations at the outset of a policy rather than discovering the problem at the time of a claim when often it is too late.

Zayan Takaful, working with a large specialized insurer, has piloted the first of its kind consumer Takaful program providing homeowners insurance in the United States. The company employs a property inspection process for its homeowners business, hiring trained property inspectors to file a report about every property that is initially insured by the program. The inspection is repeated every fourth year. During the inspection, pictures are taken and crucial house systems such as the roof, heating, wiring, and plumbing are evaluated based on age, current condition, and conformance with local building codes. This ensures that problems are identified and a process initiated to rectify them, and that active moral hazard identifiers such as concealment, misrepresentation, and fraud are discovered. On a few occasions the inspection process has led to Zayan Takaful refusing to insure a property after inspection. This has potentially led to significant savings and improved loss performance of its Takaful pool.[18]

Over the past few years, the chorus singing the virtues of ethics, morality, social responsibility, and protecting the environment has become louder and louder. The color green has become representative of this movement, and religious and nonreligious people alike have found a common platform to speak from. Certainly the financial meltdown of recent times and the hot air generated from the personal and corporate greed inflating the financial bubbles of the past couple of decades have given the green movement much to sing about. It is no longer possible to label green proponents as a fringe element, but some people are wondering and debating if this movement will last and when the right time is to begin "surfing the green wave." By implication, it is being suggested by some that all this "green" talk is just a wave, a trend, or a fad that will fade away on its own.

When you consider that children in this great country are living out of their parents' cars and washing up before school in local gas station and convenience store bathrooms,[19] you realize that the green wave must be allowed to endure in perpetuity. When you consider that even people who have jobs and savings are walking away from their homes just because they are underwater on their mortgages, to the point where cities such as Cleveland are spending hundreds of millions of dollars tearing down abandoned homes just to stabilize home prices in affected neighborhoods,[20] you realize the consequences of greed and overall apathy toward morality. Recent history is showing us that more and more people need to be made aware of the green wave so they can find the stroke to rise from under the water and ride the wave.

The reality is that our very modern problems are bringing very traditional virtues to the forefront. From average consumers who are embracing a green way of life in an ever-increasing capacity to pretty much every major corporation in some way or another positioning itself to be green, the signs are clear that the green wave is building momentum and is here to stay. Takaful companies should embrace this by setting aside surplus funds for charitable donations to stimulate further awareness of green initiatives, fund green entrepreneurial start-ups, and begin philanthropic initiatives focused on ethical and socially responsible projects, such as assisting financially struggling participants and non-Takaful policy holders who may have been denied claims due to no fault of their own and may be struggling with the resulting financial and societal ramifications. Additionally, by diverting investment funds away from socially irresponsible industries such as pornography and gambling, Takaful companies and participants alike should begin not only to make a difference for themselves but also, by integrating the principles of Takaful, to make an impact benefiting the greater good and well-being of local communities and the society at large.

IS TAKAFUL A GAME CHANGER?

The innate mutual nature of Takaful and its socially responsible investment mandate are what make it unique and truly set it apart as the ethical alternative to conventional insurance. Utilizing the principle of risk sharing, Takaful changes the motivation from conventional insurance companies seeking to maximize profits for their shareholders to participants sharing risk with the express aim of protecting each other and benefiting the society around them.

In this way, the unique and ethical foundation of Takaful opens up its appeal to a much larger audience than only Muslims. "The distinctive features of the Takaful product—such as transparency over product profitability, an element of profit share, and the limitations on acceptable investments (e.g., no alcohol, no gambling)—may be attractive to the growing 'ethical investment' segment."[21] Besides the natural affinity with consumers seeking ethical or socially responsible products, especially in the aftermath of the current financial meltdown, there is further practical evidence that other ethnic communities will also gravitate toward Takaful. The experience of the only provider of consumer Takaful products in the country has shown that even without a marketing strategy catering to the non-Muslim populace, members of niche ethnic communities that share cultural and linguistic affinity with different Muslim constituencies around the world are likely to see Takaful as a viable and natural alternative to conventional insurance. Zayan Takaful's customer base includes Hindus and Christian Arabs, along with non-Muslim African Americans. Once exposed to Takaful, people outside the Muslim faith have appreciated its ethical principles and have valued working with an organization that understands their culture and language requirements.[22] This is even more evident in regions where Takaful has a longer and more distinguished track record than here in the United States. For example, more than one-quarter of the policyholders of one of the Takaful operators in Malaysia are non-Muslim.[23]

For Takaful to become a game changer, its appeal must reach a large enough audience to actually make a difference and it must stand out from the crowd as a viable alternative. Therefore, correctly profiling their target markets and crafting a disciplined marketing and distribution strategy are two of the most important considerations that Takaful companies need to undertake at the outset. Here in North

America, Takaful companies should first naturally prioritize their core target market of Muslims. Because the census does not track religious affiliation, pinpointing the exact size of the North American Muslim market is a matter of wide disparity, with estimates ranging as low as 4 million between United States[24] and Canada.[25] Taking a balanced stance on the Muslim population in North America, we can safely assume a market size of 7 million in the United States[26] and 1 million in Canada,[27] representing a combined household count of 2 million.[28] Over the next 20 years, the Muslim American population is predicted to more than double, growing at least four times faster than the overall population.[29] This bodes very well for Takaful growth and forecasting in the future.

Looking beyond the core Muslim markets in North America and cautiously considering the appeal of Takaful within other affiliated ethnicities and the greater ethical consumer market, we can judiciously peg the market potential of Takaful in North America between 40 and 50 million,[30] including the 8 million North American Muslims. Other research has provided strong indications that the United States alone will make a significant contribution to the global Takaful premium potential, ranging from 10[31] to 20[32] percent. This is astonishing considering that the U.S. Muslim population cannot be rounded up to even 1 percent of its global counterpart, and clearly suggests a much larger cross-market appeal.[33]

The final point to consider when analyzing the game-changing potential of Takaful is legal and regulatory factors. In the United States, insurance regulation is controlled on a state-by-state basis, which does create a greater administrative and compliance burden for Takaful companies. But because state insurance departments have embraced technology and generally work together by setting up automated and uniform licensing and filing systems,[34] this hurdle is not as significant as it used to be. Plus the insurance regulations and laws allow great flexibility to set up Takaful operations either in partnership with existing regional and multinational insurers[35] or as stand-alone Takaful companies. Canadian law is more stringent, but there are realistic opportunities for collaboration with existing insurers for product development.

CONCLUSION

Takaful brings to the fore a realistic opportunity to fulfill the ethical promise imbued within the concepts of mutual protection, joint cooperation, risk sharing, and social responsibility. Besides the proof of concept that Zayan Takaful has been able to successfully navigate, there are not any other significant offerings in the market to date, but committed industry practitioners are working to bring better and more varied products designed to cater to the pent-up demand for Takaful in North America.

When planning and developing sincere Takaful offerings, practitioners must be diligent in abiding by the foundational principles that Takaful is based on, namely, solidarity, brotherhood, and ethics. The modern consumer tends to be sophisticated, astute, and able to recognize and reward innovative initiatives. Takaful practitioners must make their offerings transparent in accounting for surplus and investment guidelines; they must create product structures that are simple to understand, and implement them with sound actuarial, underwriting, and administrative analysis. These aims can be achieved by utilizing best-of-breed partners and service providers and an independent board of scholars specializing in Islamic jurisprudence who certify products based on adherence to Takaful principles and conduct regular operational audits to ensure that the overall enterprise is functioning within Takaful and ethical parameters. Finally, Muslim and ethical investors, businesspeople, and entrepreneurs need to carefully evaluate the Takaful market opportunity, and, if they agree with its immense latent potential, they should accept the challenge by funding and launching Takaful operations with vision, foresight, and patience that will be rewarded in the long term.

Takaful is here to stay based on what the global experience is demonstrating day by day, so it is time for Takaful to penetrate mature insurance markets such as North America. For those jaded by modern culture and experience and still not willing to accept the ethical principles and broad application of Takaful, our message should be that all good suggestions and ideas are welcome to develop an alternative system of insurance that can more holistically address the issues at hand than Takaful. All that is left to say is: "Aloha! It's never too late to learn to 'surf the green wave'!"

NOTES

1. This description of Takaful is generally accepted by Islamic scholars. As reference, see the Takaful presentation by Dr. Muhammad Imran Usmani at the Securities Exchange Commission of Pakistan (SECP) Takaful Conference on March 14, 2007.
2. *Insurance* as defined by www.investopedia.com.
3. *Tawakkul* as defined by www.dictionaryofspiritualterms.com.
4. Stands for "Peace be upon him," used by Muslims to show love and respect.
5. At-Tirmidhi; see also Saheeh al-Jaami' 1068.
6. Qur'an 5:2.
7. This is just an example of some clearly forbidden activities in Islam and should not be confused with the Islamic investment guidelines of any particular Takaful company.
8. "Takaful—Meeting the Growing Need for Islamic Insurance," Oracle White Paper, May 2008.
9. This model is the basis for the Zayan Takaful homeowners program in the United States.
10. This model is regarded as the purest form of Takaful by leading scholars such as Dr. Muhammad Imran Usmani.
11. See the "Takaful—Islamic Insurance" section of www.financialislam.com, where mutual protection schemes practiced in what is modern-day Saudi Arabia at the advent of the Prophet (pbuh) are described. These include Al Aaqilah, diya, and kafalah.
12. "Rating Takaful (Shari'a Compliant) Insurance Companies," A.M. Best, January 10, 2012.
13. *The World Takaful Report*, Ernst & Young, 2011.
14. Stephan Schiffman, *The 25 Most Common Sales Mistakes and How to Avoid Them*, 3rd ed. (Avon, MA: Adams Media, 2009), 57–60.
15. "Surfing the green wave" is used to describe a bicycle path in Copenhagen that lets commuters ride to the city center hitting only green lights (www.copenhagenize.com/2008/10/surfing-green-wave-in-copenhagen.html). It is also used at the Duke University Marine Lab by students denoting the practice of being green (www.nicholas.duke.edu/marinelab/experience/vid-greenwave). And it is used in the surfing world to describe environmentally friendly manufacturing practices (http://surfinjaco.com/2011/06/surfing-the-green-wave). In this chapter, "surfing the green wave" is being used generally for the green or ethical consumer movement.

16. "Six Habits of Highly Efficient Insurers," Arthur D. Little Publication, December 2008, www.adlittle.com/viewpoints.html?&no_cache = 1&view = 338.

17. George E. Rejda, *Principles of Risk Management and Insurance*, 5th ed. (Boston: Addison-Wesley, 1995).

18. Courtesy of Zayan Takaful, LLC.

19. Profiled during the 2011–2012 television season on *60 Minutes*, a weekly investigative journalism program broadcast on the CBS television network in the United States.

20. Ibid.

21. "Takaful: A New Global Insurance Growth Opportunity," Oliver Wyman Publication, October 2006, www.takaful.coop/doc_store/takaful/OliverWyman-TakafulOct06.pdf.

22. Courtesy of Zayan Takaful, LLC.

23. Ibid.

24. "Muslim Americans Survey," Pew Research Center, August 2011.

25. "Muslims and Multiculturalism in Canada" survey, Environics, March 2007.

26. "US Mosque Study—Report Number 1," Ihsan Bagby, 2011.

27. Canadian population growth from 2007 to 2011 extrapolated from "Muslims and Multiculturalism in Canada" survey, Environics, March 2007.

28. Based on the Zayan Takaful, LLC estimation for Muslim household size is of 3.92 rounded up to 4.

29. "The Future of the Global Muslim Population," Pew Research Center, January 2011.

30. Statistics cited in "Green and Ethical Investment Comes of Age," *Financial Times*, October 16, 2011, and "Ethical Consumption Makes Mark on Branding," *Financial Times*, February 20, 2007. These articles point to 33 percent to 50 percent of consumers willing to seriously consider ethical products and perhaps even pay more for them. For the extremely conservative market potential of Takaful in North America, I have considered what the market size would be even if only about 10 percent of the overall North American population gave serious consideration to ethical products and services. Additionally, the niche and related ethnic communities discussed are a buffer further showing the extremely conservative nature of this estimate.

31. "Takaful—Meeting the Growing Need for Islamic Insurance," Oracle White Paper, May 2008.

32. "Takaful: A New Global Insurance Growth Opportunity," Oliver Wyman Publication, October 2006, www.takaful.coop/doc_store/takaful/OliverWyman-TakafulOct06.pdf.

33. Ibid.

34. The National Association of Insurance Commissioners (NAIC) has set up an online platform greatly simplifying the compliance process for insurance brokers and insurers alike.

35. This is the approach taken by Zayan Takaful, LLC, in setting up its Takaful homeowners program.

CHAPTER 13

Islamic Human Resources Practices

WILLIAM MARTY MARTIN
Associate Professor of Management, DePaul University

S trategic human resources management (SHRM) aligns the human resources policies, practices, and procedures with the vision and strategy of the organization. The formulation of organization strategy involves a three-step process: analysis, synthesis, and creation. Strategic analysis deploys tools such as a SWOT analysis (strengths, weaknesses, opportunities, and threats), environmental scanning, and scenario planning, to name a few. After these strategic tools have been deployed, the data has to be translated and synthesized into knowledge that can then be transformed into the creation of strategies. Michael Porter outlined three generic corporate strategies: low cost, differentiation, and niche. Researchers (Boxall 2003) have posited that specific human resources strategies are aligned with each of Porter's three generic corporate strategies. For instance, a company with a low-cost corporate strategy may decide to offshore jobs to less expensive areas of production throughout the world. As an illustration, assume that a manufacturing plant moves production facilities from the United States to Indonesia: The human resources department must adjust scheduling to accommodate times of prayer for Muslim employees and assure that the meals provided in the cafeteria are prepared in accordance with Islamic traditions. This particular discussion is beyond the focus of this chapter but an understanding of how corporate and human resources strategies are aligned is critical to understanding the religious context of strategically managing human resources.

This brief introduction into the formulation of corporate strategy and SHRM sets the stage for the focus of this chapter, which seeks to address this question: What is the role of Islamic human resources management practices in organizations employing Muslim employees, located in predominantly Muslim countries, and/or governed by Shari'a principles?

This chapter will first explore the role of religion within the context of SHRM. Then, this chapter will briefly discuss a model of SHRM. After describing this model, each of the following functions of human resources management will be described from the perspective of Islamic human resources management practices (IHRMP) and finally specific recommendations will be presented. The human resources management functions of significance in this chapter are the following: recruitment/selection, onboarding, training/development, performance management, and compensation. These five functions are adapted from a description of human resources practices posited by Junaidah (2009). The exploration of Islam with regard to SHRM occurs within the context of the increasing globalization of business and its impact on SHRM (Owoyemi et al. 2011).

> The globalization of business is having a significant impact on human resources management practices and it has now become more imperative than ever for business organizations to engage in human resources management practices on an international standard. (p. 57)

This chapter looks at the SHRM-globalization linkage through the lens of religion in general and Islam in particular.

ROLE OF RELIGION IN SHRM

Religious diversity is becoming more of a reality in the United States (Eck 2001) and other countries (Smith, 2002). According to Kobeisy (2004), Islam is the second-largest and fastest-growing religion in the world. It has been estimated that more than 80 percent of Muslims live outside the Arab world and represent nearly one in five individuals in the world (Hoffman, Krahnke, & Dalpour 2004). In spite of these demographic trends, Muslims are often more visible in many cases than members of other religions because of their attire, with perhaps the exception of Orthodox Jews. Simply because demographics are changing does not mean that organizations are responding to these new demographic realities with regard to how they manage their human resources. Ahmad (2008) remarks, ". . . ignoring cultural and religious issues in management is committing corporate suicide" (p. 34). Bloomberg Finance (2011) outlines some of the legal considerations of managing human resources in Islamic countries and concludes the following in the Bloomberg Law Report:

> Multi-national businesses doing business in the Muslim World face numerous challenges in the human resources and employment law arena. Great care must be taken to understand what is specifically prohibited by local law and how local customs and traditions affect the workplace. (p. 10)

This chapter will focus upon unique IHRMP, realizing that there are common themes across all religions such as treating employees with justice (Hashim 2008).

Religion is a worldview (Ahmad, 2008). Islam as a religion is practiced differently in different countries based upon the distinctive cultures of those countries. As such, human resources management practices differ not only based upon religion but on how religion is interpreted in each particular culture of a given country. This holds true for many religions, including Islam. For instance, in Saudi Arabia, a company dress code may require that women wear an abaya, unlike in Morocco or Indonesia. Ahmad describes the difference between religion and culture as follows.

> . . . there is no distinct style of resources management that can be clearly identified as Muslims' management practices due to their world-wide presence facing different social and practical realities. (p. 36)

In short, the Muslim population is not homogeneous but heterogeneous (Asian 2006). This heterogeneity by national origin, culture, and even sect (e.g., Shia, Sunni) are all joined together by the common bond of Islam.

Rice (1999) asserts that human resources managers must maintain a dual focus on both religion and culture, not to the mention the intersection between the two. Some examples of how religion is expressed in organizations include but are not limited to the following:

- An employee of the Islamic faith requests breaks to pray on a daily basis.
- An employee of the Jewish faith requests not to be scheduled for work on Saturday.
- An employee of the Catholic faith requests not to be scheduled on All Saints Day.
- An employee of the Evangelical Christian faith requests to be allowed to say "Bless you" when greeting and saying goodbye to fellow employees and customers.

Religion is challenging for SHRM practitioners, yet if these practitioners rise to the occasion then there are benefits (Parboteeah, Paik, & Cullen 2009). According to Syed and Pio (2010), some of the benefits of managing diversity include the following: greater creativity, deepening relationships with diverse markets, enhanced flexibility, and improved problem solving.

ROLE OF RELIGION IN A POST-9/11 ENVIRONMENT

In the United States, reports of discrimination filed at the United States Equal Employment Opportunity Commission (EEOC) have increased 153 percent since 2002 (Al-Waqfi & Forstenlechner 2010) which is one year after September 11, 2001. Given the increase in discrimination toward Muslims in the workplace in the United States and other countries such as France, it is critical that employers be familiar and comply with the employment and labor laws in their respective employment settings. This view was first introduced by Ball and Haque (2003) with respect to public workplaces but holds equally true for private workplaces. A global review of the application laws prohibiting religious discrimination is beyond the scope of this chapter but is substantively addressed in the Bloomberg Law Report (2011).

Role of Shariah Law in SHRM

One of the core values in Islam is Shariah law—as is canon law in Catholicism, although to a lesser degree in the twenty-first century than during previous centuries. It has been observed that Islamic Financial Institutions (IFIs) follow the principles of Shariah law with regard to their operations and as such ". . . it is certainly logical to expect these organizations to inculcate Islamic principles in their HRM practices and policies" (Rhaman & Shahid 2010, 6). As an example, Islamic law forbids interest or *riba*. This has implications for the governance of employer-sponsored credit unions in which employees access credit union funds to make purchases for cars or houses or college tuition.

Model of SHRM

The nagging question among multinational companies, companies doing business in Islamic countries, and companies with Muslim employees is to what degree do these companies adapt their human resources management practices to reflect or align with the tenets of Islam. Pudelko (2004) advises that companies take the middle of the road approach, which means to engage in both universal human resources management practices and particular human resources management practices. Some have argued that there is currently no Middle Eastern HRM model (Mellahi & Budhwar 2006), yet others have argued that it is critical to develop an HRM model based upon the sociocultural context of a particular country (Khan 2011). Hoffman et al. (2004) recommend a two-prong approach: proactive stance and reactive stance. The proactive stance is to design and deliver education and training to prevent anticipated religious conflicts involving Muslim employees. The reactive stance is to formulate, communicate, and consistently enforce written policies to address religious conflicts involving Muslim employees when such situations arise. For example, a dress code that accommodates religious dress will distinguish forbidding specific attire for safety reasons versus other reasons.

In this chapter, we propose the blending of global best practices with tailored sociocultural and religious beliefs and practices at the local level as a way of balancing universalism and particularism. An analysis of the European Social Survey revealed that Catholic cultures lean toward particularism, in contrast with Protestant cultures, which gravitate more toward universalism (Nawojczyk 2006). This is important because it is the interaction between two or more cultures and religions, which define how accommodating each of the following human resources management functions will be undertaken in different companies.

Recruitment/Selection

Organizations of all types should recruit and select the most qualified talent. This is the case with respect to IHRMP, particularly as it relates to avoiding favoritism and nepotism, which is a tenet of Islam (Ali et al. 2000). Hashim (2008) further emphasizes the role of piousness and justice in the recruitment and selection process. In essence, hiring managers must focus on the merit and competence of the candidate from a Qur'anic standard (Ahmad 1995) and tell candidates the truth about the position and the organization (Hashim 2008). One of the hallmark Islamic principles to characterize the recruitment and selection process is that it be designed and implemented as just and free of any discrimination or bias (Azmi 2010). As such, companies should design recruitment and selection processes that place fairness and justice at the center with an emphasis of avoiding discrimination, favoritism, and nepotism.

Onboarding

Onboarding is the new term for employee orientation. Some refer to onboarding or orientation as organizational socialization. The goal of onboarding is to prepare the employee, his or her colleagues, and his or her manager for them to perform at the highest level possible in the shortest amount of time. As such, onboarding focuses on knowledge and skill acquisition as well as "learning the ropes" of the organization from cultural and political perspectives. As part of onboarding, employees need to know what is appropriate and inappropriate with respect to the expression of religious beliefs and religious speech. Rollins (2007) discusses how religious speech is often a source of conflict among employees. An effective onboarding program can eliminate some of this conflict if addressed up front. For instance, develop a clear policy about wearing a hijab or being given scheduled breaks to pray during working hours, not to mention a designated area for prayer. Accordingly, it is critical that intentional policies, programs, and processes be developed to orient new employees to the organization. This must also include a focus on religion and how religious diversity is accommodated within socio-cultural, legal, and organizational contexts.

Training/Development

Training emphasizes the continuing acquisition of new and existing skills in contrast to development that focuses upon education and training for a future role or for duties, which are not currently being used. Both are important but for different reasons. Training and development should be taken seriously by organizations, especially those organizations that are seeking to implement IHRMP. Another reason why training and development is essential is to counter some of the more commonly held biases and stereotypes, which even highly educated professionals hold for those who practice Islam (Ali et al. 2004). To this point, Hashim (2008) describes the dual role of the employee and the employer regarding training/development:

> It is obligatory for Muslim employees to seek knowledge and to serve [the] employer well. The employer, on the other hand, is responsible to provide opportunities to enable the employees to improve their competencies. (p. 150)

These dual duties between employees and the employer are characterized by some as a psychological contract. In this chapter, the emphasis is on the compliance with tenets of Islam rather than a psychological contract.

Managers also need to be trained to manage religious diversity (Cash & Gray 2000). This training should focus on the legal, cultural, and religious aspects of leading and managing a religiously diverse workforce (Cash & Gray 2000). Even if your workforce is all Muslim, they are not the same even if all of the employees are from the GCC. There are religious differences between Yemen and Oman as an example. And managers and employees need to know how to accommodate differences in ways that fit with a particularistic perspective.

As part of performance management, both managers and employees have a responsibility for career development. Azmi (2010) asserts that employers and managers should offer career development programs while at the same time Muslim employees should focus on the future with respect to their careers (Nasri & Ahmad 2006). According to Azmi (2010), the focus of Islamic training and development goes beyond the acquisition of knowledge and skills and includes an emphasis on the following tenets of Islam:

> ... on purifying one's soul (tazkiyah- al nafs), instilling Islamic values (al-ta'dib), understanding the philosophies of Allah's Oneness and Greatness (al-tawhid al-uluhiyyah and al-rububiyayah) and the concepts of working as a vicegerent (khal-ifah), a team (jama'ah), full submission to Allah ('ibadat) and a way to succeed (al-falah). (p. 2)

Hence, when developing training and development initiatives and programs, SHRM practitioners must incorporate religion in general and Islam in particular in any program which is offered and to also be sure to evaluate the effectiveness of such training and development on key performance indicators including differences in satisfaction, engagement, and loyalty among Muslim employees and other employees.

Performance Management

Performance management is more than a performance evaluation. Hashim (2008) argues that managers must demonstrate fairness when managing the performance of employees, including evaluating employees. Ali (2005) and Azmi (2010) acknowledge the challenges in assuring fairness in performance management due to a variety of factors. Azmi (2010) suggests that to maintain fairness, managers should be trained. Similar to other human resource management practices, performance management should be free of discrimination and bias (Junaidah 2007). Regard for fairness is so important that Azmi (2010) recommends that an appeals process be part of the performance management review for those employees who are not satisfied with their initial review.

Several researchers have found a positive relationship between loyalty and the Islamic work ethic (Ali & Al-Kazemi 2007; Yousef 2001) in diverse countries including Kuwait and the United Arab Emirates. In summary, managing performance is similar to recruitment and selection due to the focus upon fairness and eliminating any discrimination.

Compensation

Compensation consists of two major elements: monetary and nonmonetary. *Total reward management* is the new term used to describe compensation in organizations today. According to Hashim (2008), Islam forbids forced labor, while Ahmad (1995) emphasizes that compensation should be just and fair according to Islamic principles. Furthermore, Hashim (2008) addresses the adequacy of compensation, which is very relevant given the recent focus on income inequality throughout the globe:

> ... Islam emphasizes that workers should be given adequate and reasonable wages for their work, keeping in view the quality and quantity of work, their needs and requirement, and the overall economic condition of the society. (p. 151)

An interesting observation by Azmi (2010) is that married employees should earn more than unmarried employees based upon the assertion that married employees have children and unmarried employees do not have children. This begs the question as to what the human resource management practice ought to be in the case of married employees without children and unmarried employees with children.

With regard to gender, compensation should be managed without regard to gender (Azmi 2010). In designing pay structures, Junaidah (2007) suggests that attention be paid to pay structure so as not to promote dissatisfaction among employees. As such, compensation, both monetary and nonmonetary, ought to be aligned with the work that employees engage in rather than based upon nonwork matters such as gender, age, and religion.

CONCLUSION

It appears that one of the central themes regarding Islamic human resources management practices is the bond between employers and employees. Rousseau and Greller (1994) found that this relationship is not accidental but part of the intentional design process of human resource management processes and practices.

The key difference between IHRMP and other human resources management practices is the requirement that Islamic practices be based upon the Holy Koran and the teachings of the Prophet Muhammad (Rokhman 2010). Returning to the original question in this chapter, What is the role of Islamic human resources management practices in organizations employing Muslim employees, located in predominantly Muslim countries, and/or governed by Shari' a principles? The role is first to identify global best practices in SHRM and then to tailor those global best practices to align with the tenets of Islam and the particular sociocultural context of the country or countries in which you are operating facilities. This approach will enable executives and managers to begin with what is regarded to be "best in class" by SHRM practitioners and then make adjustments as necessary and appropriate to ensure a good "cultural fit" with the organization and the employees. This approach is similar to the construction of religious investment vehicles.

REFERENCES

Ahmad, K. 2008. "Challenges and Practices in Human Resources Management of the Muslim World." *The Journal of Human Resources and Adult Learning* 4:2, 34–42.

Ahmad, M. 1995. *Business Ethics in Islam*. The International Institute of Islamic Thought. Islamabad.

Ali, A. 2005. *Islamic Perspectives on Management and Organization*. Cheltenham, UK/ Northampton, MA: Edward Elgar.

Ali, A., and A. Al-Kazemi. 2007. "Islamic Work Ethic in Kuwait." *Cross Cultural Management: An International Journal* 12:2, 93–104.

Ali, A., M. Gibbs, and R. Camp. 2000. "Human Resources Strategy: The Ten Commandments Perspective." *International Journal of Sociology and Social Policy* 20:(5/6), 114–132.

Ali, S. R., W. Liu, and M. Humedian. (2004). "Islam 101: Understanding the Religion and Therapy Implications." *Professional Psychology: Research and Practice* 35, 635–642.

Al-Waqfi, M., and Forstenlechner, I. 2010. "Stereotyping of Citizens in an Expatriate Dominated Labour Market: Implications for Workforce Localization." *Employee Relations*, 32:4, 364–381.

Asian, R. 2006. *No god but God: The Origins, Evolution, and Future of Islam*. New York: Random House.

Azmi, I. A. G. 2010. "Islamic Human Resource Practices and Organizational Performance: A Preliminary Finding of Islamic Organizations in Malaysia." *Journal of Global Business and Economics* 1:1, 1–16.

Ball, C., and A. Haque. (2003). "Diversity in Religious Practice: Implications of Islamic Values in the Public Workplace." *Public Personnel Management* 32:3, 315–330.

Bloomberg Finance. (2011). "Doing Business in the Muslim World—Practical Issues for Employers and Employees." *Bloomberg Law Reports* 4:4, 1–10.

Boxall, P. 2003. "HR Strategy and Competitive Advantage in the Service Sector." *Human Resource Management Journal* 13:3, 5–20.

Cash, K. C., and Gray, G. R. 2000. "A Framework for Accommodating Religion and Spirituality in the Workplace." *Academy of Management Executive*, 14:3, 124–134.

Eck, D. 2001. *A New Religious America*. San Francisco: Harper.

Hashim, J. 2008. "The Quran-Based Human Resource Management and Its Effects on Organizational Justice, Job Satisfaction and Turnover Intention." *Journal of International Management Studies*, 3:2, 148–159.

Hoffman, L., K. Krahnke, and S. Dalpour. 2004. "Discrimination against Muslim Employees." *The Journal of Behavioral and Applied Management* 5:2, 137–152.

Junaidah, H. 2007. *Human Resource Management: Islamic Approach*. Saddle River, NJ: Prentice-Hall.

Khan, S. A. 2011. "Convergence, Divergence, or Middle of the Path: HRM Model of Oman." *Journal of Management Policy and Practice* 12:1, 76–87.

Kobeisy, A. 2004. *Counseling American Muslims: Understanding the Faith and Helping the People*. Santa Barbara, CA: Praeger Press.

Mellahi, K., and P. Budhwar. 2006. "Human resources management in the Middle East: Emerging HRM models and future challenges for research and policy." In P. Budhwar and K. Mellahi (Eds.), *Managing Human Resources in the Middle East*, 291–301. London: Routledge.

Nasri, M., and M. Ahmad. 2006. *Etika Perniagaan: Pendekatan Perspektif Islam* (2nd ed.). Saddle River, NJ: Prentice-Hall.

Nawojczyk, M. 2006. "Universalism versus Particularism through the European Social Survey Lenses." *Acta Physica Polonica B* 37:11, 3059–3069.

Owoyemi, O., T. Elgbede, and M. Gbajumo-Sheriff. 2011. "Human Resources Management Practices in Nigeria." *Journal of Management Strategy* 2:2, 57–62.

Parboteeah, K. P., Y. Paik, and J. B. Cullen. 2009. "Religious Groups and Work Values: A Focus on Buddhism, Christianity, Hinduism, and Islam." *International Journal of Cross Cultural Management* 9:1, 51–67.

Pudelko, M. 2004. "HRM in Japan and the West: What Are the Lessons to Be Learnt from Each Other?" *Asian Business and Management* 3:3, 337–361.

Rice, G. 1999. "Islamic Ethics and the Implications for Business." *Journal of Business Ethics* 18:4, 345–358.

Rokhman, W. 2010. "The Effect of Islamic Work Ethics on Work Outcomes." *Electronic Journal of Business Ethics and Organization Studies* 15:1, 21–27.

Rollins, G. 2007. "Religious Expression in the Growing Multicultural Workplace." *Journal of Diversity Management* 2:3, 2–12.

Rousseau, D., and Greller, M. 1994. Guest Editors; "Overview: Psychological Contracts and Human Resource Practices." *Human Resource Management Journal*, 33, 383–384.

Smith, T. W. 2002. "Religious Diversity in America: The Emergence of Muslims, Buddhists, Hindus, and Others." *Journal of the Scientific Study of Religion* 41:3, 577–585.

Syed, J., and E. Pio. 2010. "Veiled Diversity? Workplace Experiences of Muslim Women in Australia." *Asia Pacific Journal of Management* 27:1, 115–137.

Yousef, D. 2000. "The Islamic Work Ethic as a Mediator of the Relationship between Locus of Control, Role Conflict and Role Ambiguity." *Journal of Managerial Psychology* 15:4, 6–28.

Yousef, D. 2001. "Islamic Work Ethic: A Moderator between Organizational Commitment and Job Satisfaction in a Cross-Cultural Context." *Personnel Review* 30:2, 152–169.

CHAPTER 14

An Integrated Islamic Poverty Alleviation Model

ALI ASHRAF
University of New Orleans

M. KABIR HASSAN
University of New Orleans

POVERTY: CONCEPTS AND VIEWS

Poverty is a multidimensional economic phenomenon that has both political and social ramifications. It exists throughout generations and societies irrespective of cultural affiliation and geographical boundaries. Although the nature of poverty may vary from community to community, from culture to culture, and from time to time, poverty persists in both rural and urban areas alike; and also in both developed and developing economies.[1]

Definition of Poverty

Schubert (1994) identifies and establishes different poverty features. Poverty is less extensive in urban than in rural areas, as chances of employment and income growth in urban areas are higher. As agricultural activities are associated with the uncertainty of natural disasters and cyclical properties of crop and climatic cycle, the rural poor who are dependent on agriculture suffer from poverty of a seasonal nature.

The urban poor generally engage in low-skilled and low-paying jobs such as day laborer, mason, cleaner, and so forth. There is a cause-and-effect relationship between family size and poverty. Larger families are more likely to suffer from severe poverty than smaller ones. Lack of education and poverty also has a cause-and-effect relationship as lack of education leads to low levels of human capital and capacity. In general, poverty density is relatively higher in localities that lack infrastructure and facilities.[2]

Different Approaches to Antipoverty Programs

Antipoverty programs can be broadly classified into two strategies: (1) *indirect strategies* that formulate a macro-economic policy framework to ensure sustainable growth, higher employment, higher per capita income, and eventually reduction in poverty; and (2) *direct strategies* that target the underprivileged population and provide them necessary assistance to ensure credit access, improved health conditions, increased literacy rate, and ultimately eradication of poverty (Pramanik 1994).[3]

Indonesia, Malaysia, and Thailand are good examples of countries that have alleviated poverty through indirect strategies. These countries pursued consistent macroeconomic policies that ensured growth of 6 percent or greater and increased public spending on education, health, and family planning among others for decades. In contrast, Bangladesh is an example of direct policy application where government and nongovernmental organizations provide access to credit, health care, and educational services to targeted poor and underprivileged individuals (Centre for Policy Dialogue 1996).

ISLAM AND POVERTY ERADICATION

Islamic principles of poverty alleviation are based on the Islamic views of social justice and the belief in Allah Almighty. Islam defines poverty as a failure by individuals to fulfill any of the five basic human requirements of life: (1) religion, (2) physical self, (3) intellect or knowledge, (4) offspring, and (5) wealth.

The Islamic economy identifies individual differences among people as each person is endowed with different types and levels of human abilities. Thus, even though individuals are provided with equal opportunities, the economic status of two individuals may not be equal.[4] Therefore, poverty cannot be alleviated simply through income redistribution or by ensuring equitable opportunities for all. An Islamic approach to poverty alleviation would ideally involve a holistic approach including a set of antipoverty measures, such as (a) increasing income level with pro-poor programs, (b) achieving an equitable distribution of income, and (c) providing equal opportunities to all social segments.[5]

Poverty Eradication Strategies in Islam

The Islamic approach involves three distinct sets of measures: (1) positive measures, (2) preventive measures, and (3) corrective measures, as presented in Exhibit 14.1.

Positive Measures
Islam engages different positive measures in alleviating poverty: They include (a) income growth, (b) functional distribution of income, and (c) equal opportunity.[6]

a. **Income Growth:** Islam emphasizes moderate consumption behavior at an individual level that produces necessary savings for both the individual and the overall economy and also stresses the need for halal earnings. The Quran teaches that: (a) "A person gets what he or she strives for" (53:39), (b) "Earning a halal living is farz (obligatory) after obligatory rituals" (Al Baihaqui, Tabarani), and (c) "Do not make your hand tied to your neck, nor stretch it forth to its utmost reach, so that you become blameworthy and destitute" (17:29) (Sadeq 1995).

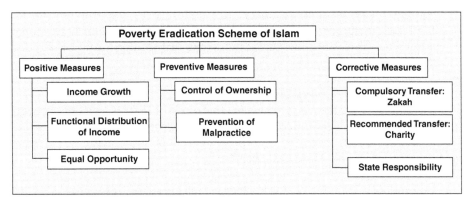

Exhibit 14.1   Poverty Eradication Scheme of Islam
Source: A. M. Sadeq, 1995, *Poverty Alleviation: An Islamic Perspective.*

b. **Functional Distribution of Income:** Functional distribution of income refers to equitable distribution of income among all the factors of production in absence of which high income growth alone may not be able to alleviate poverty. Islamic norms ensure that the principle for factor pricing is based on justice and fairness. The Quran teaches us that (a) "Allah commands justice and benevolence" (16:90); and (b) "Woe to those that deal in fraud; those when they receive from man take full measure, but when they give by measure or weight to others give less than due" (83:1–3).

Islamic approach recommends measures for an equitable distribution of income among factors of production such as profit sharing. Islam prohibits Riba (usury) and emphasizes the distribution of profits on the basic definition of ratio, rather than a nominal fixed interest among the stakeholders (Sadeq 1995).

Preventive Measures

Islamic economy also ensures preventive measures be taken so that wealth is not concentrated in a specific section of a population. These measures include: (a) control over ownership, and (b) prevention of malpractice.[7]

a. **Control of Ownership:** In Islam, ownership of everything belongs to Allah Almighty. Man has the secondary ownership, as trustee, for utilizing resources per the terms and conditions of the trust. In an Islamic economy, resources identified for public use, such as natural resources, cannot be privately owned. The state should own such resources so that they are accessible to all sections of the population when necessary. However, Islam allows private ownership in business and industry as long as they are performed based on Islamic ethics and norms.

b. **Prevention of Malpractice:** Islam identifies and prohibits malpractices that lead to economic disparity such as gambling, hoarding, cheating, bribery, and interest, called Riba. The Quran teaches us: "O ye believe! Squander not your wealth among yourselves wrongfully, except it be a trade by mutual consent" (4:29). In modern times, such malpractices take different forms. If all such malpractices, including corporate frauds and other white-collar crimes, are prevented, inequality in income distribution could be avoided (Sadeq 1995).

Corrective Measures of Poverty Eradication

This is the third set of antipoverty measures that attempt to foster wealth transfers so that wealth is not concentrated among the elite. Corrective measures include (a) compulsory transfers (Sikh), (b) recommended transfers (charity), and (c) state responsibility (enforcement and basic needs).

a. **Compulsory Transfer (Zakat):** Islam establishes Zakat as compulsory for all well-off Muslims. Zakat is a unique instrument for poverty alleviation as wealth is transferred from well-off people to worse-off people. Islam identifies Zakat as one of the five pillars. Anybody denying obligation of Zakat ceases to be a Muslim. According to the Quran: "The Zakat is meant only for the poor and needy, those who collect the tax, those whose hearts are to be won over, for the freeing of human beings from bondage, for the relief of those overwhelmed by debts, for the cause of God, and for the wayfarer: [this is] an ordinance from God—and God is All-Knowing, Wise" (9:60).

b. **Recommended Transfers (Charity):** Islam encourages charity and acts of benevolence rather than mandatory transfers like Zakat and Sadaqat al-Fitr. The Quran teaches us that (a) "And in your wealth, are obligations beyond Zakat"; and (b) "In their wealth, there is a known right for those who ask for it and for the deprived" (70:24–25). Thus, charity and other acts of benevolence are highly recommended. In the case of strong economic disparity or poverty, such transfers would become obligatory (Sadeq 1995).

c. **State Responsibility:** In the Islamic system, the state should be held responsible for maintaining a favorable environment for legal business and economic activities. The state should also protect its citizens from malpractice of any form. Finally, the state should enhance the institution of Zakat and provide equal opportunities for all.[8]

Comparison of Islamic Tools for Poverty Alleviation

In Islam, two charities—compulsory (such as Zakat) and optional (Sadaqa)—engage in initiatives of poverty alleviation through the redistributive approach. On the other hand, the third type of charity, Perpetual (Awqaf), is used to improve nonincome aspects of the poor, such as health and education as well as increasing their access to physical facilities, resources, and employment.[9] Exhibit 14.2 summarizes the key features of three basic tools of poverty alleviation and briefly compares them.

Zakat as a Tool for Poverty Alleviation

Islam establishes zakat as a compulsory charity tool that can be used on eight purposes. Five of these purposes are meant for poverty eradication among the poor,

Exhibit 14.2 Comparison of Poverty Eradication Tools in Islam

	Zakat	Lillah	Awqaf
Compulsory/ Voluntary	Compulsory	Voluntary	Voluntary
Rate	Fixed rate	Any amount	Any amount
Expense categories	Eight fixed expense categories	Flexible expense categories. Donor can decide.	Flexible expense categories. Donor can decide
Spend	Generally spent in one year	Generally spent in one year	Generally capitalized
Investments	Generally not invested—needs to be discharged as soon as possible	Generally not invested—may be discharged according to need and mandate	Invested in social or economic asset
Shariah governance: Liability	Liability for payment is governed by Shariah	Any person can give	Donor must be sane, of age, male or female
Mutawallee	Mutawallee not necessary	Mutawallee not necessary	Must appoint Mutawallee (trustee)
Document	No document necessary	No document necessary	May be done through an Awqafiyyah (donation deed)
Sadaqah Jariyyah	Generally not continuous	Generally not continuous	Always a continuous charity and continuous reward
Capital base	Not a capital base	Not a capital base	Forms a capital base for sustainable community development
Beneficiaries	Applied only to Muslims.	May be applied to all irrespective of creed.	May be applied to all irrespective of creed.
Time for payment	Generally paid in Ramadan	Can be paid at any time	Can be paid at any time
How payment is effected	Generally paid in cash or stocks	Can take the form of any asset	Can take the form of any asset—cash, land, coins, jewelry

Source: National Awqaf Foundation of South Africa. "Questions and Answers," 1993.

the needy, the debtors, the slaves (to free them from captivity), and the travelers in need. Other possible uses are the administrative cost of Zakat, "those whose hearts are made inclined" (to Islam), and in the way of Allah. Although eight possible uses for spending Zakat revenue have been mentioned in the Qur'an, there is general agreement that the first priority in the use of Zakat funds has to be accorded to the alleviation of poverty through assistance to the poor and the needy.[10]

- **The Nisab of Zakat:** There are several opinions regarding which articles would be considered for Zakat. One opinion considers that Zakat is imposed on only four types of agricultural products (wheat, barley, dates, and resin), gold and silver, and freely pastured camels, cows, and sheep. However, such items constitute only a part of the wealth of rich people of modern societies, as wealth and income have taken other forms. Another view of Nisab considers that Zakat must be imposed on the wealth and income of the rich that exceeds the normal and customary personal and family expenditures, such as business assets, bank accounts, financial assets, and rentable buildings (Hassan & Khan, 2007).[11]
- **Scope of Zakat:** Zakat can be used as part of a long-term strategy for poverty alleviation. The views expressed by the founder of three scholars of jurisprudence—namely, Shafi, Malik, and Ahmed bin Hanbal—are noteworthy. "According to Malik and Ahmed bin Hanbal, the amount paid in Zakat must be enough for one year's requirement. Imam Shafi treats this in a life-term perspective and maintains that the poor should be given Zakat enough for their lifelong requirements of a normal life span."[12] A Fatwa issued by the International Shari'ah Board on Zakat (ISBOZ) explains that Zakat funds might be used in undertaking development projects, educational services, and health care services as long as the beneficiaries of such projects fulfill the criteria to be recipients of Zakat.[13]
- **Zakat as an Alternative Source of Funding:** Zakat funds, if collected and managed properly, could be used to create a *pool of funds* that can be used in financing development activities and can replace government expenditures. In Bangladesh, Zakat funds could have contributed up to 21 percent of the Annual Development Plan (ADP) in 1983/1984 and up to 43 percent of ADP in 2004/2005; this amounts to Tk. 30,683 million in 1983/1984 and Tk. 220,000 million in 2004/2005.[14] In developing countries such as Bangladesh, foreign aid from donors contributes a significant portion of the development budget. If Zakat funds are properly managed, these funds could replace foreign aid and therefore significantly reduce the debt burden (Hassan & Khan 2007).

Awqaf

In the Arabic language, the word "Awqaf" literally means hold, confinement, or prohibition. In the Islamic system, Awqaf is a perpetual charity that means holding certain property and preserving it for the confined benefit of certain philanthropic purposes. Although Awqaf applies to nonperishable properties such as fixed property (land or buildings), it can be applied to cash money, books, shares, stocks, and other assets. The concept of Awqaf is a well-practiced phenomenon in recent times in both the Muslim and non-Muslim world. In North America, such Awqaf institutions are rendering a wide range of services by providing religious education, community services, and maintenance of mosques (Kahf).[15]

Kinds of Awqaf

Awqaf can be classified into different kinds based on its purpose or uses. The following are the most common Awqaf:

- **Religious Awqaf** focuses on maintenance of religious institutions, such as mosques and madrasas and their adjacent premises and properties.
- **Philanthropic Awqaf** aims at providing support for the poor, such as health services and education. In the early days of Islam, Prophet Muhammad (S.A.W.) initiated this type of Awqaf with the objective of reducing disparity and inequality among the social strata.
- **Family Awqaf** is a unique kind of Awqaf that ensures Awqaf proceeds are given to the family and descendents in the first place and then the excess be given to the poor. This is in contrast to traditional trusts in Western society that allow for no benefits toward the families and only to religious or philanthropic purposes (Kahf).

Legal Conditions of Awqaf

The creation of an Awqaf involves some legal obligations touching on the property, founder, purpose, and beneficiaries. Specifically, (a) the property must be a real asset that has some meaning of perpetuity such as land, buildings, camels, cows, sheep, books, jewelry, and so forth; (b) the property should be given on a permanent basis; (c) the Awqaf founder should be legally fit and able to take such an action (this means that a child, an insane person, or a person who does not own the property cannot make Awqaf); (d) the purpose of the Awqaf must be an act of charity from both points of view of Shariah and of the founder; and, finally, (e) beneficiaries, person(s), or purpose(s), must be alive and legitimate.

However, Awqaf can be made in cash as well. In the first century of Hijrah, a cash Awqaf was in practice in one of two forms: (1) cash for free lending to the beneficiaries, and (2) cash for investment and its net return as assigned to the beneficiaries.[16] Such cash Awqaf became very common in the later stage of the Ottoman Empire as well.

Scope of Awqaf as a Tool for Poverty Alleviation

As the primary focus of Awqaf is philanthropy, on principle, its objectives are in line with poverty alleviation objectives. In modern times, Awqaf can be rejuvenated through innovative approaches and at the same time comply with Islamic principles. Abdulhasan M. Sadeq (1995) presents an integrated approach on how traditional institutions of Awqafs may be revitalized through innovations.[17] Exhibit 14.3 delineates the basic mechanism of Awqaf certificate issuance suggested by Sadeq (1995). Awqaf certificates of different denominations can be issued to raise the cash Awqaf, so that a number of individuals or institutions may buy them and finance the development projects. Besides, cash Awqafs can be encouraged among people through building confidence on management.

Awqaf funds raised from issuing certificates and cash Awqafs can be used in creating a pool of funds (similar to the aforementioned pool of Zakat funds) for financing development projects. As Awqafs are generally applied on fixed assets, such assets are often underutilized. On the other hand, if cash Awqafs are raised

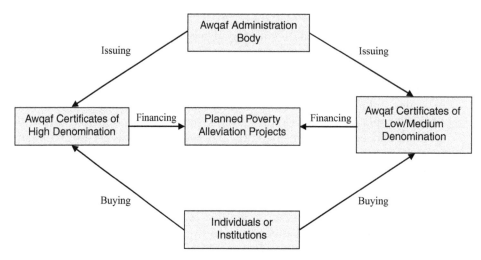

Exhibit 14.3 Issuing of Awqaf Certificates to Finance Development Project
Source: Abdulhasan M. Sadeq, 1995.

by issuing Awqaf certificates, they could be used more efficiently in a wide range of development projects.

Weakness of Traditional Zakat Management

In early Islamic states, Zakat funds were collected and managed by the state. However, Zakat management has gone through historical challenges after the extinction of early Islamic states. After the colonial era, a few Muslim countries such as Yemen, Saudi Arabia, Libya, Sudan, Pakistan, and Malaysia have opted for mandatory Zakat management through government. Other countries such as Egypt, Jordan, Kuwait, Iran, Bangladesh, Bahrain and Iraq, have formed specialized state institutions but participation by the public is voluntary.

However, in most Muslim countries, the contribution of Zakat from Zakat donors to such managed Zakat funds has been less significant for a variety of reasons: (a) individual Zakat donors prefer to choose to whom they should pay Zakat, which in some cases may be their close relatives and neighbors; (b) the low level of trust in the management of Zakat because of government involvement; and (c) more important, lack of trust in the national Zakat management fund, which has little knowledge regarding the eligibility of recipients.

Weakness of Traditional Awqaf Management

From the legal point of view, the ownership of Awqaf property lies outside the person who created the Awqaf. The Awqaf manager, also known as Mutawalli, is held responsible for the overall management of the Awqaf property to ensure the best interest of the beneficiaries. Usually, the Awqaf documentations mention how the Mutawalli should be compensated for this effort. If the document does not mention such compensation for the Mutawalli, the Mutawalli either volunteers the work or seeks assignment of compensation from the court.[18]

Historically, Awqaf played an important role in the socioeconomic development in Islamic societies during the early days of the Islamic era. In the early nineteenth century, a special ministry was established for Awqaf in the Ottoman Empire and different laws of Awqaf were enacted. The most important of these laws was the Law of Awqaf of November 29, 1863 (19/6/1280 of the Hijrah calendar) that remained in effect in several countries (Turkey, Syria, Iraq, Lebanon, Palestine, and Saudi Arabia) for many years after the break-up of the Ottoman Empire in 1918.

Over many centuries, the institution of Awqaf has been systematically destroyed by both the colonial rule, and later on, by postcolonial nationalization of Awqaf management. One reason behind the vengeance against the Awqaf institution was that religious education enjoyed major contributions, which was a cause of rebellion during colonial and postcolonial eras. This systematic destruction of Awqaf management has led to its present problems, including (a) low credibility of management because of government involvement, (b) lack of research about the modernization of Awqaf as an Islamic institution, and (c) lack of consensus among different schools of thought of Islam about Awqaf laws and their implications.

CONVENTIONAL MICROFINANCE AND ISLAMIC MICROFINANCE

Conventional Microfinance

Over the past three decades, microfinance has evolved as a major financial innovation in providing collateral-free credit access to the poor. Microfinance assumes that, to the microentrepreneurs, lack of collateral is the most important obstacle in availing formal credit and hinders the overall investment and profitability of the business. To this end, microfinance aims at providing collateral-free financial services to the poor to assist them in developing microbusinesses, increase their income level, and eventually get out of the poverty trap (Dichter 2007).[19]

However, the definition of microbusiness in microfinance is not well defined and it may vary from country to country depending on the country's stage of development, policy objectives, and administration, among other factors (World Bank 1998). Microbusinesses and medium enterprises are generally identified by the amount of fixed capital and the number of workers. They usually involve economic activities in three broad categories: production, trading, and providing transport services.[20]

Weaknesses of Conventional Microfinance

Although the key objective of microfinance is to provide access to credit to the poor, there has been much debate among development specialists regarding what activities actually constitute a microbusiness and whether or not microfinance is being used merely for consumption-smoothing purpose only. Microfinancers have been promoting nonfirm activities among the rural poor to counter the inherent seasonal trend of agroeconomic activity that generates irregular cash flows. However, in many cases the borrowers who take loans for microbusiness end up fulfilling immediate consumption needs, thus turning microfinance into a mere consumption-smoothing act.

Another problem with microcredit is the basic assumption that the poor can prove to be good entrepreneurs given access to credit. However, in developed countries, people usually prefer holding jobs to entrepreneurship, as entrepreneurship is more risky. There is no reason to assume that the poor can develop entrepreneurial skills after their experiences with basic economic activities that serve subsistence purposes only, such as going to a nearby commodity market to buy and sell basic consumption and agricultural products (Dichter 2007).[21] Apart from these crucial debates, there are some other impediments that endanger the desired effects of microfinance on poverty alleviation. We explain such problems in the following list (Ahmed 2002).

- **Asymmetric Information Problems:** Although conventional microfinancing institutions (MFIs) focus on participation of women in entrepreneurial development, eventually such loans may end up in the hands of male family members and used for other purposes, as the society itself is male dominated (Rahman 1999). Such diversion of credit can easily lead to higher loan defaults and lead to adverse selection problems for the microfinancing institutions.[22]

- **Economic Viability of MFIs:** One of the major financial challenges of the traditional microcredit institutions (hMFIs) is their high operating and administrative cost for monitoring loan operations closely as they engage in small collateral free credits to a large number of borrowers. Bennett (1998) reports that the administrative cost of five MFIs in South Asia is in the range of 24 to 400 percent per dollar lent. Besides this, another concern for conventional MFIs is their dependency on foreign aid. Ensuring constant and predictable foreign aid may become increasingly difficult in future in the changing business environment.

- **Charging Fixed Interest Rates:** Usually, MFIs pursue a standard and generalized policy of lending rates in different loan categories. However, profitability of a similar project may be different because of differences in geographic or demographic conditions. For example: a project located in a community better equipped with infrastructure may become more profitable than a similar project in a community that lacks good infrastructure. In such cases, charging a fixed specific interest rate irrespective of project features may be counterproductive from a poverty alleviation objective.

- **Higher Interest Rates and Focus on Short-Term Loans:** One of the reasons behind the most common allegation against conventional MFIs of higher interest rate is the imbalance in their investment portfolio and capital structure. Although the major portion of the capital and liability structure is long term, their investments are generally short-term-focused, which creates additional pressure on liquidity. As a result, MFIs charge higher interest on their clients to ensure short-term investable funds and to cover the high administrative costs.[23]

- **Low Rate of Return on Investment:** Conventional MFIs engage in financing microbusiness activities that usually substitute the agricultural or farm activities and require fewer skills. Often, such microbusiness activities are related to the production of basic commodities, transportation, and trading at smaller-scale ventures. However, as more and more households become involved in such ventures, return on such loans decreases as the supply side of such activities increases (Osmani 1989).

- **High Dropout Rate and Nongraduation from Poverty:** The objective of microfinance is to enhance microbusinesses and eventually alleviate poverty by ensuring a sustainable growth in the income level of the recipients. Unfortunately, as microbusinesses often involve very basic activities that possess low returns, the borrowers fail to attain desired income growth and fail to upgrade from poverty. Such nongraduation from poverty and other factors such as access to other competing MFIs for credits could lead to higher dropout rates. Karim and Osada (1998) report that there is a steady increase in the dropout rate from Grameen Bank (15 percent in 1994).[24]

- **Debt Trap:** Increased dropout and nongraduation from poverty among the borrowers may result in a vicious cycle of poverty. As conventional MFIs engage in strict recovery measures such as peer group pressures and social segregation, unsuccessful borrowers are to some extent forced to repay loans at any costs. Rahman (1996) discovered that the Grameen Bank borrowers often take loans from other sources to pay installments and are trapped in a spiraling debt cycle.[25]

- **Nonconforming to Popular Religious Beliefs:** A major challenge that conventional MFIs face while operating in Muslim communities is the nonconformance of the credit system to the popular religious beliefs. As usury (Riba) is prohibited in Islam, the clergy in the rural areas and conservative Muslim societies exhibit resistance to conventional microfinancing. Another issue is the focus of credit to women. In some cases, this focus has created social conflict in conservative populations. In extreme cases, although women are the recipients of credit, the credit ends up with the male member of the family, leading to misappropriations and credit diversion.

- **Credit Rationing:** Imperfect information on behalf of the loan officers and higher interest rates may lead to the problem of credit rationing where only projects with higher profit probability may be selected. That way, the true spirit of poverty alleviation through microcredit may be hampered and overall economic welfare may be endangered (Dhumale).[26]

Islamic Microfinance

Over the past three decades, Islamic banking has grown at annual rate of over 15 percent with an overall capitalization of US$1.3 trillion at present. (UN-HABITAT 1995).[27] Compared to Islamic banking, Islamic microcredit is an evolving concept with an outreach in mostly the Arab world and has grown considerably to more than 700,000 borrowers in 2003.[28] As an effective alternative to conventional microfinancing, Islamic microfinancing institutions (IMFIs) are evolving in different countries as well. Ahmed (2002) points out some elementary comparisons between IMFIs and conventional MFIs, as discussed in the following sections.[29]

Sources of Funds
Apart from the basic differences in principle between profit-based and interest-based systems, IMFIs differ from conventional MFIs in their liability and capital structure. Unlike conventional MFIs that depend on interest-free or low-interest

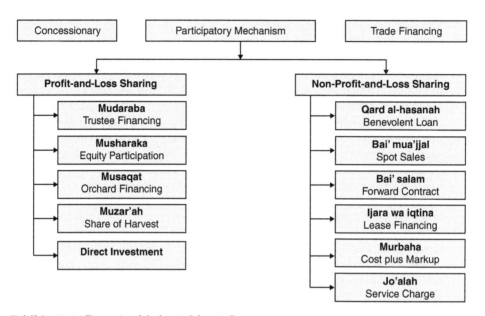

Exhibit 14.4 Financing Modes in Islamic System
Source: Kazarian 1993; Iqbal and Mirakhor 1987. Dhumale, Rahul, and Amela Sapcanin (2002), "An Application of Islamic Banking Principles to Microfinance," 7.

foreign aid, IMFIs may collect funds from religious contributions through the institutions of Awqaf, Zakat, and other charities.

Modes of Financing

While the conventional MFIs, asset portfolio is of fixed interest nature, IMFI-asset portfolios should feature diversity in terms of mode of financing and areas of financing. Exhibit 14.4 describes the basic categories of diversified financial products that the Islamic financing system offers.

Apart from interest-free loans (Qard-Hasan), the principles of Islamic financing can be broadly classified as partnerships (Shirakat) and exchange contracts (Mu'awadat). As depicted in Exhibit 14.4, the Islamic system engages in three categories of financing modes, among which participatory mechanisms can be relevant for Islamic microfinancing institutions (IMFIs).

a. **Non-Profit-and-Loss Sharing Modes:** Non-profit-and-loss sharing modes can include different transaction modes such as:
   - *Bay'-mu'ajjal:* This is a mode of deferred sale in which the object of the sale is delivered at the time of the contract but the price is paid later. The price can also be paid in future installments.
   - *Murabaha:* This is a special type of financial transaction, in which the IMFI buys a good or asset and sells it to the client at a mark-up. The client pays for the good or asset at a future date or in installments.
   - *Ijarah:* This is similar to a conventional leasing contract in which the client uses an asset by paying rent.

- *Ijarah wa iqtina':* This is similar to a hire-purchase scheme or a lease purchase scheme in which the installment includes rent as part of the price. When the installments are fully paid, the ownership of the asset is transferred to the client.

b. **Profit-and-Loss-Sharing Modes:** Among different profit-and-loss sharing modes, the following are most commonly practiced:

- *Musharakah:* This is an equity participation mode of contract in which the financer provides both equity and entrepreneurial skills on a project and shares in profit or loss on a fixed proportion. The *Musharakah* principle can be used in production (agricultural and nonagricultural). The IMFI can provide part of the financial capital to produce an output and in return receive a share of the profit.
- *Mudarabah:* Production undertaken under the *Mudarabah* principle implies that the IMFI provides financing and the client manages the project.
- *Muzara'ah:* This is an output-sharing contract specifically for agricultural production in which IMFI may provide the funding for the purchase of irrigation equipment, fertilizers, and other inputs that the landowner uses on his land to cultivate a certain crop.

AN INTEGRATED MODEL OF ISLAMIC MICROFINANCE, ZAKAT, AND AWQAF

Diversion of microcredit for consumption purpose by the borrowers is one of the important causes of credit default in conventional microfinance. Besides this, charging a generalized higher interest rate has also hindered poverty alleviation through credit rationing and adverse selection problems. These basic challenges of conventional microfinance can be resolved if IMFIs are designed in an integrated manner by incorporating the two basic and traditional institutions of Islam, the Awqaf and the Zakah, with Islamic microfinance into a single framework.

Although creating such a singular institution may be premature, in this paper we attempt to outline the novel idea of such an integrated institution. Such an integrated model may effectively resolve fund inadequacy of IMFIs by using funds from the Zakah and the Awqaf. The IMFIs may use the Zakah fund in disbursing funds to fulfill basic consumption needs for the hard-core poor target group in the first place, as on principle, no return can be realized from Zakah fund and the fund should be disbursed within one financial year. The Zakah fund may also be used to provide capital investment or provide the business initiation fund, and for that no return should be charged. However, the Awqaf funds may be used as investable funds to provide capital investment and working capital financing for the microbusinesses.

Such an integrated model may reduce the chances of loan default because the inherent tendency of the poor to use the loan fund for consumption purpose will be met. As their basic consumption needs are covered, the poor microentrepreneurs may be in a better position to focus on their business. Moreover, the IMFIs may initiate financing through different Islamic Shariah-compliant modes. Since Islamic financing modes are based on principle of social justice and equity and Riba is prohibited, IMFIs are likely to yield higher benefits if they are properly designed. Borrowers will have lower refundable loans, as a result of utilization of Zakah funds, it will result in less financial burden on the poor. The visible benefits of such a financing organization, in contrast to funding a conventional microcredit organization, will be greater.

Organizational Framework and Operational Procedure of Our Integrated Model

This section delineates a schematic arrangement for organizational framework and operational procedure of a plausible integrated model. It discusses the basic organizational framework, mission, and vision of organization, key functions, and possible credit delivery model.

    a. **Organization:** In modern times, management inefficiency and increased government involvement are two important factors leading to decrease in public participation in Zakat and Awqaf management funds. As a result, government and donor agencies are increasingly focusing on more private participation or NGO (nongovernment organizations) participation in different development initiatives. Considering these factors, we propose that an NGO abiding by Islamic ethics and norms with the poverty alleviation objective would be the ideal form of organization.

    b. **Mission and Vision:** The vision of the NGO should be to create a poverty-free society based on the Islamic principles of equality, social justice, and balanced growth. The mission of the NGO should be collecting Zakat and Awqaf contributions from a specified locality and providing a credit facility to the poorest segment of society.

    c. **Objective:** The main objective of the NGO should be to reduce poverty through the balanced growth and development of different segments of society. The NGO should focus primarily on developing microbusiness among the poor to enable them to attain a sustainable income growth and eventually get out of the poverty trap. In addition to its core service of providing collateral-free microfinance to the hardcore poor, the NGO may also provide financing for other items such as education, health services, and house building.

    d. **Key Functions:** Using an integrated approach, a single concern would be responsible for the management of Zakat, Awqaf, and Islamic financing. This organization would perform three key responsibilities:

        1. Collecting and managing Zakat funds from prospective Zakat donors and other Zakat fund management institutions.

        2. Collecting and managing Awqaf funds from prospective Awqaf donors, and other Awqaf fund management institutions.

        3. Providing microcredit to the poor on the basis of Islamic Sharia.

            In the initial phase, the NGO may concentrate on providing microfinance and collecting funds from other Zakat and Awqaf management organizations. However, as the organization becomes mature, it may engage in the management of Zakat and Awqaf funds and use them as a stable source of funds.

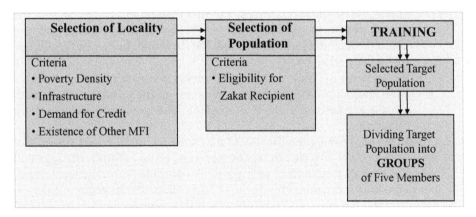

Exhibit 14.5 Operational Model

e. **Credit Delivery Model:** The proposed single-model NGO may adapt the success model of Amanah Ikhtiar Malaysia (AIM),[30] a successful microfinance institution in Malaysia. The success story of AIM provides empirical evidence that microfinance facilities may be delivered based on the adaptation of Islamic principles, group recovery, and a credit disbursement model similar to the Grameen Model.

In contrast to AIM, where the Malaysian government actively participates in lending interest-free capital and covers operational expenses, the proposed NGO may strive to be self-sufficient (meaning no government participation). In its initial stage, the NGO may undertake a few pilot projects to analyze the response of customers in different localities. Selection of such pilot projects may involve the following four-step process:

1. **Selection of Locality:** The NGO would focus on a location with a high poverty density. The selection of a locality would also depend on other factors such as: (a) a demographic study of the locality, (b) identification of probable microcredit project options, and (c) understanding of the prevailing infrastructure, which has important marketing and distribution impacts.
2. **Selection of Population:** After selecting a particular area, the NGO would select a target population. It may conduct a household survey, or use references from the existing survey data. Such populations can be selected on the basis of eligibility of Zakat funds or per capita income. In selecting individual members of the target population, persons eligible to receive Zakat contributions would be chosen first.
3. **Training:** This target population would be given vocational training in relevant areas. After successful completion of the training program, participants would be eligible for membership. Exhibit 14.5 summarizes the basic operational setup.
4. **The Group:** The basic units of the operational model are the groups. The mode of operation within groups would be based on the following principles:
   - The groups are made up of five individuals. Among the five persons of a group, the neediest person would be given credit first. After one

month, he or she would make the first installment payment, and the second person would be given credit. After another month, a second person would start repayment, and the third member would be eligible for credit, and so on.

- Repayments of credit would be in weekly installments.
- After they start receiving credit, members of the group would deposit a fixed amount each week as mandatory deposit and insurance for calamities.

f. **Organizational Structure:** The NGO may take its initial initiatives as *pilot projects*. Such *pilot projects* can be described as "units." A unit manager will lead the overall functioning of a particular locality and manage a number of credit officers who will disburse and collect the microcredit loans to and from the borrowers. Credit officers will be responsible for the overall credit appraisals, credit delivery, monitoring, and recovery process. One credit officer will be in charge of a number of group operations. In addition to regular credit officers, a team of two or three credit officers will be in charge of credit monitoring to determine whether credits are used properly. Such a team will also provide additional information, which will be used by unit managers and general management to analyze the model performance.

Financial Management Framework

This section discusses the financial management framework of the integrated model that is motivated to comply with Shariah principles and to ensure better utilization of Zakat and Awqaf funds with a developmental perspective.

Fund Management Principles

In the proposed model, the NGO will use Zakat and Awqaf funds as the two major sources of financing. On principle, Zakat funds do not need any return or repayment. Zakat funds would be used for two purposes: to fulfill basic needs and to provide capital investment so that a member can start a microbusiness.

Awqaf funds could be used as source of funding as well. From Awqaf funds, both capital and working capital investments could be made. In case of capital investment with Awqaf funds, the NGO would engage Mudaraba mode. However, in the initial phases, the NGO may engage Awqaf funding only for working capital investment. For operational simplicity, the NGO would prefer the Murabaha mode of financing for working capital, as this will also ensure that short-term credit is utilized in a proper way. Since the fee is fixed, the NGO will be assured of stable and predictable revenue during the initial years. As Zakat funds' investment in capital investment will not generate any revenue, the NGO will be better off investing in Murabaha mode for working capital financing.

In addition to these two major sources, the NGO would also collect funds from borrowings from Islamic banks and financial institutions, deposits from members, deposits from its employees, and deposit schemes for nonmembers. If needed, the NGO can also go to the capital market and raise funds through issues of share capital. In its overall financial operations, the NGO will comply with Islamic

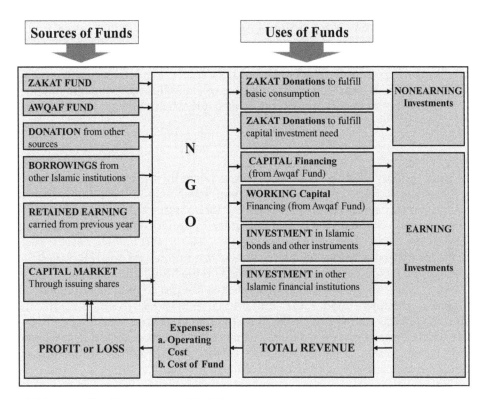

Exhibit 14.6   Fund Management Model

banking principles and Islamic Shariah benchmarks. Exhibit 14.6 illustrates a graphic presentation of the financial model of the NGO.

Sources of Funds

As previously mentioned, the NGO will raise funds from different sources with different contractual modes. In principle, the NGO will not engage in fund-raising activities that do not conform to the Islamic norms of banking. The NGO will collect funds from the following sources.

- Zakat contributions will be collected from prospective members, Zakat donors, or other Zakat-fund-management organizations. In the initial phase, the NGO might focus on its core function of microfinance instead of collecting and managing Zakat funds. In countries where the government, by law, does not enforce Zakat, collecting sizeable amounts of Zakat at the initial stage might be a challenge. However, considering the way that Zakat funds are collected, for any investment made on Zakat funds, no repayment or return can be charged.
- In the initial phase, the NGO might opt for a similar strategy in collecting Awqaf contributions. However, on investments made from Awqaf contributions, return and repayment can be charged on Mudaraba mode. All of them should, however, be used for benevolent purposes.

- Donations from other institutional and noninstitutional sources might require repayment of principle, and in some cases profits, in addition on Mudaraba mode.
- Borrowings from Islamic Banks and nonbanking financial institutes will be collected based on Shariah principles, especially through Mudaraba mode.
- The NGO can also generate funds from equity shares or from capital market participation.

Uses of Funds

The basic activity of the NGO is to provide credit for microbusinesses. As microbusiness requires credit for both capital investment and the fulfillment of working capital needs, the NGO can arrange for both in a balanced way. Its capital investments can create the base upon which to provide working capital credit or short-term credit. As mentioned earlier, the NGO would involve Zakat contributions for nonredeemable capital investment with no return only. However, the working capital credit will be delivered based on the Murabaha model.

Apart from these two basic investments, the NGO will also engage in Mudaraba investment modes after building its own capacity and its clients are well versed in accounting principles. In addition to investment in microcredit, the NGO will undertake diversified investment activities such as investing in Islamic bonds. Earnings from such nonoperational activities will provide a cushion during profit fluctuations resulting from uncertainties.

SUMMARY

Microfinance involves providing credit without collateral to the marginally poor. The traditional microfinance suffers from high default risk, high operational costs, and low returns. Successful NGOs like Grameen Bank, ASA, and BRAC have shown that even though there are such risks, microfinance can also be used to create and sustain successful businesses.

Weaknesses of conventional microfinance, such as charging high fixed interest rates, credit diversion, credit rationing, and nonconformity with the Islamic faith of majority population necessitates the creation of an Islamic microfinance. There is an opportunity for Islamic microfinance to grow by catering to the needs of the underprivileged Muslim population.

In our proposed model, we combine Islamic microfinance with two traditional Islamic tools of poverty alleviation such as Zakat and Awqaf in an institutional set-up. The inherent nature of the proposed model may ensure equitable distribution and welfare among the poor. As the model is based on profit-sharing and concessional contract modes, distribution of earnings should be allocated among different stakeholders such as depositors, shareholders, and investors in the NGO. The proposed model will be financially viable and sustainable in the long run, resulting from lower default rates, reduced by the proper use of Zakat funds, which do not require any return. This will create a win-win situation for all stakeholders.

If implemented, this model will contribute to poverty alleviation by combining all three approaches: positive measures (like increasing income growth through development of microbusiness for the poor), preventive measures (through ensuring functional redistribution among factors of productions), and corrective measures (engaging Zakat and Awqaf).

Unlike conventional MFIs, the proposed model will ensure that poor borrowers have less debt burden, as their capital investments will be partly met by funds from Zakat, which does not require any repayment. Since Islamic financing modes are based on profit-and-loss sharing principle, there will not be any fixed interest payment burden for the borrowers. All these factors will lead to lower default rates and higher graduation from poverty.

To sum up, the proposed Islamic microfinancing model will yield more benefit toward the overall social welfare. If such an IMFI is undertaken on a pilot project basis, and further operational adjustments are made accordingly, there may be a visible impact on poverty reduction among the targeted poor population. Finally, if a number of NGOs apply this model, the aggregate benefit will be greater.

NOTES

1. Datuk Dr. Syed Othman Alhabshi, "Poverty Eradication from Islamic Perspectives," p. 1.
2. M. K. Hassan and Md. Juanyed Masrur Khan, "Zakat as a Tool for Poverty Alleviation in Bangladesh" (2006), pp. 7–8.
3. M. K. Hassan, "The Role of Zakat in Poverty Alleviation in Bangladesh" (2006), pp. 6–7.
4. Alhabshi, pp. 3–4.
5. Hassan, M. K. (2006), "The Role of Zakat in Poverty Alleviation in Bangladesh," p. 13.
6. Ibid.
7. Ibid.
8. Ibid., p. 14.
9. Abdulhasan M. Sadeq, "Awqaf, Perpetual Charity and Poverty Alleviation" (1995), p. 137.
10. Hassan, "The Role of Zakat in Poverty Alleviation in Bangladesh," p. 16. Ashraf, Ali, and M. Kabir Hassan. 2007. "An Integrated Poverty Alleviation Model Combining Zakat, Awqaf and Microfinance." Paper presented at a UITS conference in Chittagong.
11. Hassan and Khan, "Zakat as a Tool for Poverty Alleviation in Bangladesh," pp. 10–11.
12. Hassan, "The Role of Zakat in Poverty Alleviation in Bangladesh," p. 16.
13. Monzer Kahf, "Role of Zakat and Awqaf in Reducing Poverty: A Case for Zakat-Awqaf-Based Institutional Setting of Microfinance" (2006), p. 10.
14. Hassan and Khan, p. 18.
15. Kahf, "Awqaf and Its Sociopolitical Aspects," p. 4.
16. Kahf, "Role of Zakat and Awqaf in Reducing Poverty: A Case for Zakat-Awqaf-Based Institutional Setting of Micro-Finance," p. 10.
17. Sadeq,"Awqaf, Perpetual Charity and Poverty Alleviation," p. 143.
18. Kahf, "Awqaf And Its Sociopolitical Aspects," p. 4.
19. Thomas Dichter, "A Second Look at Microfinance: The Sequence of Growth and Credit in Economic History," p. 1.
20. Habib Ahmed, "Financing Microenterprises: An Analytical Study of Islamic Microfinance Institutions" (2002), p. 3.
21. Dichter, "A Second Look at Micro-Finance: The Sequence of Growth and Credit in Economic history," p. 1.
22. Ahmed, "Financing Microenterprises," p. 7.
23. Islam, Land, and Property Research Series—Paper 8: "Islamic Credit and Microfinance," UN-HABITAT (2005), p. 12.

24. Ahmed, "Financing Microenterprises," p. 8.
25. Ibid.
26. Rahul Dhumale and Amela Sapcanin, "An Application of Islamic Banking Principles to Microfinance" (2002), p. 5.
27. Islam, Land, and Property Research Series, p. 5.
28. Dhumale and Sapcanin, "An Application of Islamic Banking Principles to Microfinance," p. 4.
29. Ahmed, "Financing Microenterprises," pp. 9–15.
30. Alhabshi, "Poverty Eradication from Islamic Perspectives," p. 1.

REFERENCES

Ahmed, Habib. 2002. "Financing Microenterprises: An Analytical Study of Islamic Microfinance Institutions," *Islamic Economic Studies* 9:2, 27–64.

Alhabshi, Datuk Dr. Syed Othman. "Poverty Eradication from Islamic Perspectives." http://elib.unitar.edu.my/staff-publications/datuk/JOURNAL.pdf. Last accessed on April 20, 2006.

Ashraf, Ali, and M. Kabir Hassan. 2007. "An Integrated Poverty Alleviation Model Combining Zakat, Awqaf and Microfinance." Paper presented at a UITS conference in Chittagong.

Bennett, Lynn. 1998. "Combining Social and Financial Intermediation to Reach the Poor: The Necessity and the Dangers." In Mwangi S. Kimenyi, Robert C. Wieland, and J.D.V. Pischke, editors, *Strategic Issues in Microfinance*. Hants, England: Ahsgate Publishing Ltd.

Centre for Policy Dialogue. 1996. "Experiences with Economic Reforms: A Review of Bangladesh's Development, 1995."

Dhumale, Rahul, and Amela Sapcanin. 2002. "Islamic Banking Principles Applied to Microfinance: Case Study: Hodeidah Microfinance Programme." Yemen, January 2002. www.uncdf.org/english/microfinance/uploads/thematic/Islamic%20Banking%20Principles%20Applied%20to%20Microfinance.pdf.

Dichter, Thomas. 2007. "A Second Look at Microfinance: The Sequence of Growth and Credit in Economic History." February 15. www.cato.org/pub_display.php?pub_id=7517.

Hassan, M. Kabir. 2003. "Financing the Poor: Towards an Islamic Microfinance." Mimeo, University of New Orleans, November.

Hassan, M. Kabir. 2006. "The Role of Zakat in Poverty Alleviation in Bangladesh," Paper presented at a conference in Dhaka, November 24–26.

Hassan, M. Kabir, and Junayed Masrur Khan. 2007. "Zakat, External Debt and Poverty Reduction Strategy in Bangladesh," *Journal of Economic Cooperation* 28:4, 1–38.

Kahf, Monzer. "Awqaf and Its Sociopolitical Aspects." http://www.awqafsa.org.za/.../Waqf%20&%20its%20Socio%20Political%20Aspects%20-%20Monzer%20Kahf.

Kahf, Monzer. 2006. "Role of Zakat and Awqaf in Reducing Poverty: A Case for Zakat-Awqaf-Based Institutional Setting of Microfinance." Paper for the Conference on Poverty Reduction in the Muslim Countries (Dhaka, November 24–26).

Kazarian, Elias. 1993. *Islamic versus Traditional Banking: Financial Innovations in Egypt* (Boulder: Westview Press).

National Awqaf Foundation of South Africa. 1993. "Questions and Answers." Accessed December 2007: http://awqafsa.org.za/.

Osmani, S. R. 1989. "Limits to the Alleviation of Poverty Through Non-Farm Credit," *Bangladesh Development Studies* 117:4, 1–18.

Sadeq, Abdulhasan M. "Awqaf, Perpetual Charity and Poverty Alleviation." Paper presented at a conference in Dhaka, 1995.

UN-HABITAT. 2005. Islam, Land, and Property Research Series—Paper 8: "Islamic Credit and Microfinance." http://www.unhabitat.org/downloads/docs/3546_13443_ILP%208.doc.

UN-HABITAT. 2005. Islam, Land, and Property Research Series—Paper 7: "Awqaf (Endowment) and Islamic Philanthropy." http://www.unhabitat.org/downloads/docs/3546_80031_ILP%207.doc.

World Bank. 1998. World Bank Operational Manual OP 8.30—Financial Intermediary Lending.

CHAPTER 15

How Does an Islamic Microfinance Model Play the Key Role in Poverty Alleviation?

The European Perspective*

SABUR MOLLAH
Associate Professor of Finance, School of Business, Stockholm University

M. HAMID UDDIN
Associate Professor of Finance, College of Business Administration, University of Sharjah

INTRODUCTION

The Secretary General of the United Nations declared 2005 as microcredit year for microfinance institutions (MFIs), for being so successful in alleviating poverty. Murdoch (1999), in this regard, has pointed out that lending to poor households is doomed to failure as the costs are too high, risks are great, saving propensities are too low, and few households have much to put up for collateral. But MFIs have overcome these criticisms by adopting group lending, which can mitigate these problems (Stiglitz 1990). Under group lending methodology, group members agree to shoulder a monetary penalty in the case of default. The group members have incentives to monitor each other, and can potentially threaten to impose "social sanctions" when risky projects are chosen. Neighbors can monitor each other more effectively than a bank. Thus, the potential for effective delegation evolves for monitoring microlending to borrowers.

Haqq (2011) has found that major microfinance institutions like the Grameen Bank and others operate with an "ignorance zone," as 98 percent of the participants

*An earlier version of the paper was presented at the Morality and Finance conference at Markfield Institute of Higher Education, Leicester, UK, October 3–5, 2011. We are grateful to Omar Sikder for assistance in collecting the literature.

are uneducated about the terms of credit and interest rates. Therefore, conventional MFIs have failed to ensure equal opportunities for the poor. Haqq's (2011) study has revealed that borrowers of the Grameen Bank pay an interest rate of around 40 percent, whereas the regular banks charge around 10 percent. This discrimination violates the social rights of the poor borrowers, since they pay higher interests than the wealthy borrowers in the regular banking system. This discrimination can only be possible from a business point of view and by ignoring social justice. As the poor borrowers cannot provide collateral, then an extra compensation may be needed to cover the additional default risk. However, this may frustrate the purpose of poverty alleviation that underlies any microcredit program. We argue that the Islamic Microfinance program can play a better role in delivering social justice to poor borrowers while alleviating their poverty at an accelerating rate. Moreover, the Islamic Microfinance model serves the societal needs for corporate social responsibility that is lacking in the neoclassical thought patterns of existing MFIs, which are driven by mere profit goals (see Ferro 2005).

Poor people seldom need any novel advice with financial support; instead, an integrated financial support plan is more important for them to come out of the poverty level. Conventional microfinance has successfully reached to the poorest groups of society but it lagged behind in providing favorable financial support in conditions that are relevant to the poor. The conventional microfinance institutions (MFIs) have different financial products aimed at reaching the poorest zones of society with small loans and strong monitoring systems for timely recovery. Such microfinancial products offered by the conventional MFIs perhaps become successful in making them very successful financial institutions in term of loan disbursement, recovery, profit earning, and so forth, but their contribution in poverty alleviation is yet to be determined. This is because the cost of borrowing from conventional MFIs is significantly higher than the cost in the regular banking system.

Academically, it can be argued that the higher cost of borrowing may prevent poor borrowers from rising above the poverty level. Since these borrowers are denied low-cost loans from regular banking systems, they are usually enticed by the easy loans offered by MFIs, which do not require collateral. Therefore, we have made efforts to understand how a low-cost microfinance program can be offered to the poor groups of society. It is believed that designing an integrated microfinance model based on Islamic principles can be useful to offer low-cost microloans while accelerating the process of poverty alleviation, which is the prime goal of any microfinance model.

Though at a very limited scale, the Islamic Microfinance Institutions (IMFIs) are in operation since 1983. The existing Islamic Microfinance (IMF) models operate based on single or combined applications of Mudaraba, Musharaka, and Murabaha (see Dhumale & Sapcanin 1999). These models have insufficient procedural guidelines on how the complex environment would be incorporated. In particular, the poorest of the poor groups need extra support, and thus the models should be complied with more flexibility and extra attention to this group. Wilson (2007) has projected the view that the Wakalah model could potentially be implemented in serving the poorest, and zakath and other donated funds could be used for appropriate situations. This argument is quite consistent with Obaidullah (2008) and Hassan and Ashraf (2010). Therefore, a model is urgently needed for optimum solutions to fill the gap in the existing IMF models where the poorest group "that deserves zakat" should be given special attention and the model should be easily understood by both bankers and the clients.[1]

The rest of the paper is designed as follows: section II contains a literature review, a brief review of the existing IMF models is incorporated in section III, section IV focuses on the European aspects and a proposed model, and concluding remarks are included in section V.

LITERATURE REVIEW

Dhumale and Sapcanin (1999) have introduced a technical note to include microfinance concept into Islamic Banking. Shariah-compliant financial products are in use only in Muslim countries, but a large majority (72 percent) of people living in Muslim countries do not use any formal financial services. Islamic Microfinance sells products mainly to microentrepreneurs, who normally borrow from friends, relatives, and quasifinancial institutions. However, Islamic Microfinance is mainly centered in a few countries,[2] such as Indonesia, Bangladesh, and Afghanistan. Islamic Microfinance is also found in other countries such as Jordan, Algeria, Syria, and Yemen. The most popular types of Islamic Microfinance products follow Murabaha,[3] Ijarah, Musharaka, and Mudaraba contracts. There is no evidence of Islamic microfinance in Europe or in the United States; therefore, the industry has yet to demonstrate that it can provide financial services that meet the needs of poor people on a larger scale.

The Islamic Banks do not engage in microfinance because of their belief that poor people are lacking skills and are not creditworthy (Murdoch, 1999). Lending to poor households is doomed to failure as the costs are too high, risks are great, saving propensities are too low, and few households have much to put up for collateral. The problems arise from the fact that financial institutions find it difficult to monitor poor borrowers and cannot perform with optimal confidence that enforces prudent behavior.

The Islamic Microfinance business model has two particular areas of importance: (1) operational efficiency and (2) risk management (Karim, Tarazi, & Reille, 2008). The Islamic Microfinance Institutions (IMFIs) should develop more novel techniques and practices to minimize costs and offer more attractive pricing to their clients. The conventional MFIs secure loans not by collateral but by strict discipline in collection processes and through group pressure. Authentication of schemes can be generated from financial specialists and Shariah experts.

While Takaful (Islamic insurance; please see Chapter 12 of this volume) on its own is not the solution to the poverty problem, it has to be recognized as an important component of any poverty alleviation strategy.[4] Without protection against losses and natural perils many individuals find themselves regularly falling back into poverty, which is not only disheartening but also renders ineffective development assistance in the long term. Takaful can provide the safety net for communities to achieve sustainable development of their standard of living, providing a basis for families to look to the future with a sense of security and optimism. As the Takaful and cooperative insurance concepts are so similar, there is no real obstacle for the more established cooperative to assist the Takaful movement to provide insurance products to low-income communities. The linkage between the two movements is such that where there are no Takaful schemes in place, Muslims are obliged to purchase their compulsory insurance needs from cooperative and mutual insurers. Takaful products in Muslim countries will protect the middle and working classes from falling into poverty in the event of a large or sustained loss, and micro-Takaful schemes based on cooperative and mutual principles will provide the poor with the protection they need to achieve sustainable poverty alleviation.

EXISTING ISLAMIC MICROFINANCE PRACTICES AROUND THE GLOBE

The Islamic Micro Finance (IMF) models consist of three main instruments[5] of Islamic finance (Mudaraba,[6] Musharka,[7] and Murabaha[8]). The Consultative Group to Assist the Poor (CGAP) reviews IMF programs of 125 institutions operating in 19 Muslim countries,[9] including Bangladesh, which has the largest Islamic Microfinance outreach with over 100,000 clients. The IMF is also concentrated in countries like Indonesia and Afghanistan. But it is still at its infancy in the rest of the Muslim countries, and as of now, no Islamic Microfinance exists in Europe and the United States. Most IMF programs operating in different countries apply the Murabaha model (cost plus markup sale) of financing and target female clients, as the conventional MFIs do (e.g., CGAP survey report has found that 59 percent of average IMFs clients in Bangladesh are females). It is also found that over 70 percent of IMFs concentrate on asset financing. The Musharka microfinance method is popularly adopted in Yemen.[10] In Malaysia, Islamic Microfinance is provided under BBA (*Bai Bithaman Ajil*[11]) and Murabaha concepts.[12] In a lecture at Harvard School of Law, Shyakh Yaquby stressed that most scholars prefer the Mudaraba concept.[13] Murabaha is preferred because the Qur'an and the Sunna have more references to deferred sales than to PLS partnerships (e.g., Goud, 2007).

Islamic Microfinance projects began in Sudan in the 1980s, and these IMFIs have only *mudarabah* and *qard al-hasan* products. However, the Islamic Microfinance program launched in Syria in 1998 used only the murabaha method. Indonesia presents probably the largest diversity of both conventional lending and Islamic Microfinance lending. Despite the fact that 97 percent of Indonesia's population is Muslims, only 11 percent of them understand the Islamic Microfinance products; therefore, a gap between public needs and Shariah product clearly evolves.[14]

The Qard-e-Hasana fund is widely used in Iran. These loans are free but there is an administrative expense. Depending on the size of the loan and the borrowers' ability to pay, borrowers have from one to two years to repay the *qard-e-hasana* loans. To become eligible for a *qard-e-hasana* loan, a borrower must be in urgent need, have at least one referee or guarantor, and demonstrate sufficient ability to repay the loan.

Hassan and Ashraf (2010) have developed the model Zakat and Awaqf funds for poverty alleviation with evolving concepts of Islamic Microfinance. Their model has the potential to rescue the poorest groups by supporting the loans from Zakat and microloans. In addition, a few other international organizations, such as the United Nations Development Program (UNDP), KfW (Kreditanstalt für Wiederaufbau), and FINCA,[15] have been instrumental in initiating Islamic Microfinance programs in Syria, Palestine, Northern Mali, and Afghanistan.

Shabrawy (2011) discusses the microentrepreneurs' activities in Bahrain in relation to IMFIs. The Family Bank is established as the first Islamic Microfinance bank in Bahrain with the prime objective to contribute to poverty alleviation and socioeconomic empowerment of the communities. An agreement for implementing the Grameen program has been signed between the Family Bank and the Grameen Trust.

A model for this is provided in the Deprived Families Economic Empowerment Program (DEEP) of IDB in Palestine. The project envisages three distinct types of intervention while ensuring a linkage between them. However, a recent Policy Paper on Poverty Reduction (Islamic Development Bank 2007) argues for an innovative approach for integration of the institutions of *zakah*[16] and *awqaf*[17] with poverty alleviation.

The Islamic Microfinance Services Providers (IMSPs) in Australia are fulfilling the microfinance needs of the Muslim community (Ahmed & Ahmed 2010). It concludes that IMSPs in Australia can proliferate in microfinance if they gradually advance toward undertaking more creative microfinance techniques to suit the financial needs of their clientele to facilitate their desired contributions in microfinance. There are currently three key IMSPs in Australia that offer these services—typically *Murabaha*, *'Ijara*, and *Musharaka* financing—which are generally used to purchase cars, homes, consumer durables, and small businesses.

Innovative methods are needed to serve the various financial needs of the poor. Since microfinance has high risk, microfinance programs are based on group sharing of risk and personal guarantee while maintenance of trust and honesty is tied to the availability of future funds. The existing IMF models are not effective enough in integrating the basic needs of the poor, such as education, training, and credit. However, the existing practices are lagging behind the pragmatic solutions to the real problems in a targeted and effective manner. An integrated model, therefore, has not yet been designed, which can address all the necessary aspects of the poor.

IMFIs: THE EUROPEAN PRACTICES AND POTENTIALS IN EUROPE

It is reported that the government of Luxemburg has been encouraging innovation in financial regulations in order to establish a hub for microfinance excellence in the European Union.[18] The report claims that the existing regulations in Luxemburg are compatible to the Islamic Microfinance environment, as it could be possible to combine religious economic principles with the Western governance framework to meet the needs of the poorest, who have been excluded from conventional interest-based microfinance solutions.

IMF schemes are organized around Zakat (obligatory charity), Sadaqah (voluntary charity), Quard Hasan (free loan), and Waqf (pure charity).

Although Islamic Microfinance has yet to be adopted in Europe, the Deutsche Bank and the Islamic Bank of Thailand are venturing to improve and increase interactions with Shariah-compliant microfinance. Luxemburg's MFIs are exploring new methods to stimulate microfinance investments. For example, the Luxemburg Microbanking Intermediary Scheme (LUXMINT) and Luxemburg Fund

Labeling Agency (LUXFLAG) have been established to improve performances and ensure transparent financial investments. They are working to improve confidence and recognition of MFIs in Europe. In consideration of these overall developments, it appears that conventional financial systems have failed to alleviate poverty by increasing the gap between rich and poor. Luxemburg wants to embrace the Islamic Microfinance models to mitigate financial injustice.

HOW SHOULD THE IMFIs OPERATE IN EUROPE?

Refugees from the war-affected Muslim countries such as Bosnia, Iraq, Afghanistan, and Libya are relocating to European countries. They are competing for resources and food and the local governments have not shouldered the responsibilities of caring for refugees. IMFIs can initiate the programs targeting

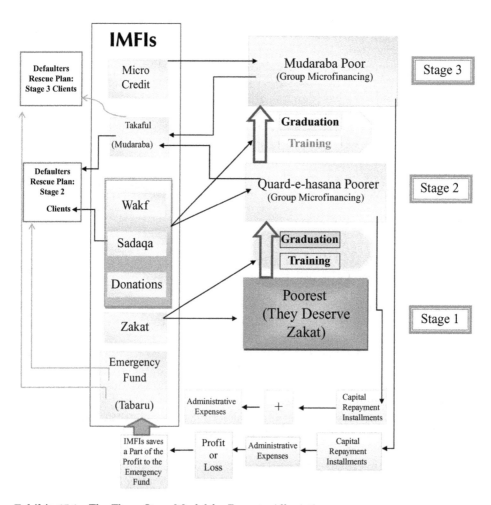

Exhibit 15.1 The Three-Stage Model for Poverty Alleviation

refugees to alleviate poverty. A three-stage integrated model could help to alleviate poverty in an effective manner.

> *Stage 1:* This group belongs to the poorest, who deserve Zakat. The group should be the primary target for the IMFIs. Zakat should be provided to fight poverty in the first instance. However, training should be organized on morality and ethics for this group. A part of this group could be promoted/appear as self-motivated—for example, those who can presumably take on the challenges for a better life—but they still need training.
>
> *Stage 2:* A group promoted from stage 1 will be given special training in their specific needs. This group does not deserve Zakat but a technical training should be organized. However, a Quard-e-hasana loan should be provided under group-financing framework with the condition of microsaving/takaful. They will be charged with administrative expenses.
>
> *Stage 3:* Upon successful promotion from stage 2, selected groups deserve expanded credit to set up microenterprises. IMFIs will sign up for Mudaraba (PLS) contracts.

CONCLUSION

Islamic Microfinance can adopt microfinance best practices without compromising Shariah compliance. Islamic Microfinance needs patronage, especially by the Islamic financial institutions that have developed over time, and it will bear fruit and contribute significantly toward poverty reduction.

The Grameen Bank, the most successful and established MFI based in Bangladesh, has adopted a group-based microfinancing model, which is a very popular method indeed. The key feature of their model is that group-based financing substitutes as collateral to mitigate default and delinquency risk. Therefore, group financing should be the key criterion for Islamic Microfinance.

Hassan and Ashraf (2010) have stressed that a fatwa has been issued by the International Shariah Board on Zakat (ISBOZ), which explains that Zakat funds might be used in undertaking development projects, educational services, and health-care programs as long as the beneficiaries of such projects fulfill the criteria to be recipients of Zakat.[19]

The Islamic Microfinance Institutions (IMFIs) should create Zakat funds and distribute them among the poorest groups. Waqf (plural: Awaqf) funds could be used to provide training to microentrepreneurs prior to providing them with any loans, since these destitute groups fulfill their basic needs of food and clothing through receiving Zakat. These clients could be disbursed Qurar-e-hasana[20] loans with the permission of a guarantor for payback. However, the guarantee of group defaulters of such microentrepreneurs can be paid off by Zakat/Takaful funds.[21] Group members should be encouraged to insure against future calamities or extreme needs by engaging in savings schemes. This is also integrated in the Takaful fund model (Islamic Insurance). IMFIs are also encouraged to generate rescue funds by contributing a part of their profit, which can be used in need to rescue the default credits from stage 3. I believe that the three-stage IMF model will be able to address the underlying problem in the conventional MFIs and alleviate poverty in a substantially better way.

NOTES

1. Eleven percent of Indonesian IMF participants understand the terms and conditions of loans (see Seibel, 2007).
2. These three countries capture 80 percent of global IMF.
3. Over 70 percent of the products.
4. See Sabbir Patel, 2011.
5. See Dhumale and Sapcanin (1999).
6. It is a profit-and-loss sharing (PLS) model.
7. Joint venture. Both bank and entrepreneur participate in capital and share profit and loss.
8. Cost plus markup sale. Banks buy some products and sell them to microentrepreneurs by adding a markup.
9. Afganistan, Bangladesh, Bahrain, Indonesia, Iran, Jordan, Lebanon, Malaysia, Mali, Pakistan, Palestine, Saudi Arabia, Somalia, Sudan, Syria, UAE, and Yemen.
10. See Chiara Segrado (2005).
11. Deferred payment sale.
12. Under the BBA concepts, financing is given directly to the client and a bank has nothing to do with what the borrower does after that. The amount given to a client is based on a "sale and deferred payment" method. Under the Murabahah concept, a bank buys what a client wants to buy directly from the supplier and sells it back to the client on the "cost-plus-profit" basis.
13. This is one of the popular financing principles of Islamic banking, in which the bank provides money and the entrepreneur acts as the manager. The bank bears the loss in case of default.
14. There are several reasons for the poor performance of Islamic Microbanks in Indonesia: (a) governance and management problems: many have been established by absentee owners for moral reasons, with an emphasis on social banking, and are managed by retired conventional bankers who lack dynamism and Islamic banking expertise, with dire consequences on performance; (b) inadequate internal control, mostly by absentee commissioners, and a lack of external auditing due to their small size, which is below the limit where auditing is required; (c) lack of popular demand for Islamic banking products; (d) emphasis on the informal sector and neglect of more profitable market segments; and (e) lack of mastery of overly complex Islamic banking practices.
15. A charitable microfinance organization.
16. It advocates creation of a *Zakah* Fund to (a) cover losses arising from the default of very small microenterprises; (b) cover part of expenses incurred by commercial banks in evaluating and financing microenterprises by the very poor; (c) provide *qard hasan* loans to reduce vulnerability of the nonpoor who are in danger of becoming poor due to external shocks through a system of microinsurance; and (d) build capacities to make households productive instead of focusing on income support.
17. Creation of mutual guarantee funds to pay for accidents, losses of property, and so forth.
18. Islamic Microfinance in Luxemburg, April 2009, by Vincent Linari-Pierron (Erniquin & Linari) and Elie Flatter (Ernst &Young).
19. Monzer Kahf (2006), "Role of Zakat and Awqaf in Reducing Poverty: A Case for Zakat-Awqaf-Based Institutional Setting of Microfinance," p. 10.
20. This mode allows for recovering actual costs through levy of service charge.
21. For a justification and elaboration of this idea, see M. A. Zarka, *Leveraging Philanthropy: Monetary Waqf for Micro Finance*, paper presented to a Symposium on Islamic Micro-Finance at Harvard Law School, Harvard University, April 2007.

REFERENCES

Ahmed, A.U.F., and A.B.R. Ahmed. (2010). Islamic Microfinance: A case study of Australia. *Journal of Islamic Economics*, 6 (1), pp. 59–80. Retrieved from www.ukm.my/hadhari/sites/default/files/prosiding/p14.pdf.

Dhumale, R., and A. Sapcanin. 1999. "An Application of Islamic Banking Principles to Microfinace: Technical Note." UNDP and World Bank.

Ferro, N. 2005. *Value through Diversity: Microfinance and Islamic Finance and Global Banking.* Milan, Italy: Fondazione Enrico Mattei.

Goud, B. 2007. "Overview of Islamic Finance." Presented at a seminar at Harvard Business School, April 13.

Haqq, Z. 2011. "Micro Credit under Grameen Bank." Paper presented at the 6th Annual London Business Research Conference, July 11–12.

Hassan, Kabir, and Ali Ashraf. 2010. An Integrated Poverty-Alleviation Model Combining Zakat, A-Waqaf and Micro-Finance. Paper presented at Seventh International Conference on the Tawhidi Epistemology: Zakat and Waqf Economy, Bangi.

Kahf, Monzer. 2006. Role of Zakat and Awqaf in Reducing Poverty: A Case for Zakat-Awqaf-Based Institutional Setting of Micro-Finance. Paper presented at the Conference on Poverty Reduction in the Muslim Countries, Nov. 24–26, 2006.

Karim, N., M. Tarazi, and X. Reille. 2008. "Islamic Microfinance: An Emerging Market Niche." *CGAP*, 49 (August).

Murdoch, J. 1999. "The Microfinance Promise." *Journal of Economic Literature*, 37, 1569–1614.

Obaidullah, M. 2008. "Introduction to Islamic Microfinance." *The Islamic Business and Finance Network (IBF NET).* Retrieved from www.microfinancegateway.org/p/site/m/template.rc/1.9.30212/.

Patel, S. 2011. "Takaful and Poverty Alleviation." The International Cooperative and Mutual Insurance Federation (ICMIF), UK.

Segrado, C. 2005. "Islamic Microfinance and Socially Responsible Investments." Paper presented at MEDA Project: University of Torino, August.

Seibel, H. D. 2007. "Islamic Microfinance: The Challenge of Institutional Diversity." University of Cologne, paper presented during a Symposium on Islamic Micro-Finance at Harvard Law School, April 14.

Shabrawy, A. 2011. "Innovation in Microentrepreneurship & Islamic Microfinance: The Model of Family Bank." Paper presented at 10th International Entrepreneurship Forum, Tamkeen, Bahrain, 9–11 January 2011.

Stiglitz, J. E. 1990. "Peer Monitoring and Credit Markets." *World Bank Economic Review* 4:3, 351–366.

Wilson, R. 2007. "Making Development Assistance Sustainable through Islamic Microfinance." Paper presented at IIUM International Conference on Islamic Banking and Finance, Kuala Lumpur, Malaysia, April.

PART II

Case Studies

CHAPTER 16

Islamic Finance in an Almost Postcrisis and Postrevolutionary World

As in Politics, All Islamic Finance Is Local

MARK SMYTH
Managing Director of Amanie Advisors S.Á.R.L.

To speak of the modern practice of Islamic Finance is to speak of an industry that is subtly complex and widely stratified. It is a movement, which carries with it a political connotation that can and often does frustrate its development. But as in politics, all Islamic finance undertakings are local, or at least possess a strong local flavor. Islamic Finance is both a wholesale and retail approach to banking and is practiced to varying degrees with varying success in all four corners of the globe. It is a way of structuring financial transactions that represent, in theory, a better and more sustainable approach to finance, but which struggles to reach the necessary scale that would allow its benefits to be felt in the larger world. Transactions can be subtly different from the conventional approach or represent a striking departure from tradition. Many key attributes are widely accepted; others remain contentious, which is not to mention the existence of, admittedly slight, regional differences of interpretation. Hopefully with that brief bit of wordplay one can begin to get a sense of the difficulty in making sweeping statements about the global Islamic Finance industry.

HISTORY

In broad terms, the modern Islamic Finance industry began to take shape in the early 1990s. While many individual initiatives, both in Malaysia and Arabia, can trace their roots back to the 1960s, and indeed Dubai Islamic Bank (1975) and Kuwait Finance House (1977) were firmly established in the 1970s, it was the 1990s that saw the industry take on a global dimension.

Bankers who were active in the Gulf in the 1980s will remember requests for "interest-free" accounts, which were gladly accepted, as they represented "free-money accounts," requiring no payment to the account holder. Also in the early 1980s, Malaysia began in earnest its push, by both the governmental and the private sector, to develop the industry. Malaysian efforts in those days were concerted and farsighted, though primarily focused on their domestic market. As a result of Malaysia's sustained development over the past 30 years, the country now has the most developed market for Islamic finance, is at the forefront of international efforts, and often drives cross-border innovation in the field.

In Arabia, the development was not primarily driven at the government level, but by the private sector in response to demand from high-net-worth investors. In time, however, regional Arab governments did adopt regulatory regimes to manage this market development. This push in the GCC represents a bottoms-up approach, which contrasts with Malaysia's PPP (Public-Private Partnership) or "top-down, bottom-up," or "government-directed" approach.

From the early 1990s, in various ways and in many countries, Islamic Finance products began to proliferate across the globe. Investment funds, initially equity-based funds that incorporated screens to prohibit investment in industries that run counter to Islamic teaching (interest-based banking, pork production, alcohol, gambling, and so forth) were among the early products that emerged during the 1990s. Later came the structuring of private equity and real estate portfolios that were designed to adhere to Islamic principles, which managed debt within Islamic structures and limits, and took a closer look at the activities of the end investment, mindful of established prohibitions. Over time, what was primarily a quiet way to structure club investments for a small percentage of Gulf Arabs and a self-contained project within Malaysia began to grow. Interest grew quickly among members of the press, academics, Muslim conventional bankers, and students in both the West and Muslim worlds. Links were established in many countries across the globe and businessmen formed more and more Islamic Financial institutions. At present Islamic banks and Takaful providers are a common site all around the globe and are growing in numbers, as is the case with Islamic funds, which have begun to rebound following the recent global crisis.

As the industry grew and took on an international character, it is not surprising that initiatives were established in Europe.

EUROPE

England, home to millions of Muslims and a well-established global hub for international finance, was a natural place for the industry to make inroads. London presently is home to four wholesale Islamic banks (Gatehouse, Bank of London Middle-East, Qatar Islamic Bank London, and EIIB) as well as one retail operation, Islamic Bank of Britain (IBB), which now has its headquarters in Birmingham. While retail penetration has been slow for IBB, it is hoped that two-way investment flows between regions will increase with activity from the four banks.

In Luxembourg, which is a major international domicile for investment funds, the push to attract more and more of this growing type of fund is widely supported. Though the number of Shariah-compliant funds is small, the hope is to attract the lion's share of new international funds and sukuk. The registration of new funds in Luxembourg fuels the countries vital fund services industry, which includes tax advisory, accountancy, fund servicing, administration, custody, and legal advice. The country also vies for the listing of Islamic sukuk, which in crude terms are often referred to as Islamic bonds.

In France, itself home to a large Muslim population, we see a complex approach to the industry with the major banks active overseas in investment banking and asset management, but with a rather opaque position with respect to their local retail market. In fact the retail market for Islamic finance in France illuminates clearly the key issues that present themselves to a country looking for a strategic approach to the industry. Among the issues confronting France and many other countries are the following:

- Facilitating FDI (Foreign Direct Investment): This is the easiest choice for a government to make. If making modest changes to the tax code for the purpose of putting Islamic-compliant structures on an even footing with conventional structures will allow for more overseas investment, then the answer for most countries is, yes. If it can be done with a minimum of political infighting, all the better.
- A Source of Profits for Big Banks: If a country is home to a number of large internationally minded investment banks, especially if they are active in emerging and frontier markets, then the potential exists for them to reap profits by arranging Islamic finance transactions. During good times in the economic cycle, this can be a helpful source of revenue for a nation's banking sector; however, like conventional investment banking, the business is highly cyclical. There is currently a global debate among the "big banks" about how to position Islamic finance. Is the sector large and robust enough to warrant an in-house team to concentrate solely on "Islamic deals" and support the related overhead (big salaries, big bonuses, expensive rents, and expensive airplane tickets)? At present, the answer is no. The preferred model is to have one expert within the group, a Global Head of Islamic Finance, who in the event of a transaction would lean upon the many skilled lawyers and advisory practices to structure the deal on the buy-side, and then sell the product as any other to their clients.
- Facilitating Market Activity: Another level of interaction with Islamic finance would be to take the free-market view that all legal economic activity is basically good (within limits) and that if Islamic finance is something in demand, then let us amend the regulatory hurdles and see what happens. It could be argued that the UK has taken this approach, which has resulted in a slow, slightly tepid market response, but one that has been accomplished with a minimum of political capital. The message from France seems to be more nuanced, or perhaps slightly conflicted: Active promotion of Islamic Finance in terms of capital market activity and inbound investment, coupled with silence on the retail side.
- Open up Retail Markets: This is the most difficult decision for governments, though the calculation is naturally different for Muslim-majority countries than it is for European or North American governments. In the West the issues at stake are many and involve a certain amount of political will. In Muslim-majority countries there are other issues as well as different political calculations.
  - For Western governments there exist a number of purely regulatory and tax issues. How to account for "participation banking" where the bank actually takes on risk for its deposit products? On the financing side,

making sure that duplication of transfer taxes is avoided for leasing structures is often an issue. Politically, the case must be made that Islamic
banking is something that is demanded from their Muslim populations
and something beneficial in its application, as very often action by an
elected parliament is required to affect the necessary legal changes. Also,
if the retail sector is to be opened up to Islamic banks, what will be the
effect on the existing high-street banks? Will they compete or let the Islamic
banks chip away at their market share? There also exists the more philosophical question, especially pertinent in France, which is: Do we want to
mix religion and banking? Should they not as a matter of principle be separate? An increasingly popular hybrid approach is to adopt a more neutral
"brand" to Islamic Finance, such as "Ethical Finance" or "Participation
Banking" and other variations that may help diffuse sensitivities.

- For governments of Muslim-majority countries, adopting Islamic finance
presents slightly different challenges. First, if Islamic finance legislation is
not currently in place, there is an issue of positioning. If the new banks
are Islamic, are the existing banks un-Islamic? Very often the existing
banks in nearly any country are government-owned and/or owned by
prominent business figures. Naturally proclaiming, by default, that the
old-line banks are somehow inferior morally in a country with strong
religious sentiments has potentially negative effects for all involved. In
all successful cases, the approach is to have a dual-system that includes
both "conventional" and "Islamic" banks; and which allows for Islamic
products to be offered through Islamic windows of conventional banks.
Such a parallel system allows both conventional and Islamic banks to
compete, ideally on an equal footing.

GOVERNMENT MOTIVATIONS AND APPROACHES

Why would a government, with only a slight minority of Muslim citizens, get
involved in Islamic Finance?

Inward Investment

On the wholesale level, it is primarily the opportunity to attract direct foreign
investment, and to reap a modest amount of bilateral goodwill with GCC countries by nurturing closer financial links. This is true of all countries. For all nations
appreciate, need, or desperately need foreign direct investment (FDI). The accumulation of capital that occurs in the Arabian Gulf as a result of energy resources is
a well-known economic phenomenon. In less politically correct days, the reinvestment of these capital surpluses (often to U.S. banks) was called "repatronization."
In the current more globalized world, Gulf investors have literally a world of
options available to them in terms of where to invest. It would follow then that
countries interested in being the recipient of Gulf capital would make a strategic
choice to find ways to accommodate Islamic finance structures.

Additionally, it should be noted that the Islamic Finance claim of being an
ethical alternative to the current system has an intellectual appeal to many, and not
just to Muslims (see Chapter 4, this volume). With a multitude of structural changes
now being applied to the existing financial marketplace, policymakers the world

over are looking for fresh ideas. Indeed, many of the current proposals—like the banning of short-selling and limiting the amount of debt governments and banks are allowed to carry—have direct parallels with the principles of Islamic Finance.

There is also a renewed interest among governments in the principals of "risk-sharing" seen in Islamic Banking. As we have recently witnessed in the conventional system, whereby banks take on all of the risk and all of the gains—that is, until the losses deplete all of their reserves (and in some cases all of their historical profits going backs hundreds of years) and nearly bankrupt the governments of their home countries—the appeal of a different model is clear. It should be stated, however, that fears of any "takeover" or significant "conversion" to the Islamic model are far-fetched at best, for in reality Islamic Finance is a very small percentage, likely less than 1 percent of global financial transactions. With the exception of Pakistan, a nation that has made various attempts at converting their banking system to an Islamic system, most Muslim-majority countries adapt a dual-system, which remains heavily tilted toward the conventional system. In the West, many countries allow for Shariah-compliant finance to varying degrees, and regulate them as they would any other conventional structure. Thus far, the business has been incremental and minute in relation to overall financial activity.

The idea of increasing the amount of "risk-sharing" is, however, problematic from a regulatory point of view. In the conventional model, safety schemes are devised to protect the bank account holder from loss and indeed, the bank from collapse; however, in the context of Islamic profit-sharing accounts, the formula is altered as both the bank and the client have, in a sense, a partnership agreement to share in the gains *and losses*; thus in theory banks have an increased incentive to more diligently analyze their lending and borrowers have greater incentive to make the undertaking (investment or loan) succeed. There exists a beauty in the simplicity of such a model, especially in light of the credit crisis, which saw the issuance of obscenely risky credits that were then quickly bundled and sold to others. Risky lending was permitted and encouraged precisely because the corresponding default risk would not be kept with the lender; in short there was a separation of any partnership relationship between lender and borrower. In the Islamic system the sale of debt is prohibited.

So what do senior government ministers and regulators think about Islamic Finance? Of course views vary widely. In Malaysia and some GCC countries, the highest levels of government actively promote its value and work to position themselves as Islamic Finance "hubs." Most of these leaders are keen to position their vision of Islamic Finance as an "alternative" and/or "parallel" approach, not wanting to upset the gains of the wider economy; for nothing frightens capital more than economic radicalism, especially within emerging or frontier markets where most Islamic finance is conducted. On the other end of the spectrum are alarmist voices, often in America, who see Islamic Finance as a generic threat, somehow related to "terrorist financing," or at best, a cynical and dangerous way to pander to "Middle East Dictators." It is, however, perhaps safe to assume that a consensus of informed elite opinion would characterize Islamic Finance as worthy of more study; potentially a helpful counterbalance to an increasingly mono-polar financial world; potentially a more equitable financial model for those with an interest; a helpful tool for attracting incrementally more FDI from GCC countries; and a challenge that has some potential to enfranchise Muslim communities in non-Muslim majority countries.

In the short term, however, the key issue remains the potential for increased FDI. With apologies to any remaining communists, increasing capital flows is a vital element to prosperity. Setting aside the contentious issue of so-called "hot money" into financial markets, FDI into infrastructure, industry, and development projects is an essential element to stability, growth, and prosperity; and indeed, they are the focus of the Islamic finance industry, which emphasizes "real," "tangible," or "hard investment" over speculation. Especially in the current climate where citizens of many nations are taking to the streets to protest economic conditions, the basic formula—more capital = more job creation = a greater degree of peace and prosperity—would dictate that governments are well advised to accommodate Islamic finance structures.

It should be noted, however, that the vast majority of investment from the GCC (and everywhere else Islamic Finance is practiced) is of a conventional nature. While estimates vary, Islamic finance is universally found to be only a small fraction of the total investment from countries active in the field. It is, however, growing; and one always hopes to be ahead of the curve.

If a government is comfortable making the necessary changes in hopes of attracting incremental investment (without expecting a petro-dollar windfall), it is hoped that long-term benefits will materialize. The required changes involve putting certain types of revenue on par with their conventional counterparts in terms of taxation, that is, interest payments and lease revenues, and waiving certain stamp duties on real estate transactions. Naturally these changes can either be easily tackled or lead a finance ministry into a legal/technical/political quagmire. The results are decidedly mixed and much depends on the political capital available for such changes and the efficiency of the legislative process. Not surprisingly, most countries get low marks on these counts, though not all. Many countries have passed laws and/or tax guidelines to facilitate Islamic Finance. These include all of the GCC countries, the United Kingdom, Luxembourg, Indonesia, Kazakhstan, and Japan, among others. A few, like South Korea, have measures pending. Additionally, it is often noted that countries whose legal systems take a "substance over form" approach, like the United States, are best equipped to facilitate transactions.

In keeping with the theme of Islamic finance being a local market, it should be stated that none of the macro trends or government-level motivations matter much to the individual promoter or project manager. If one has a limited partner or strategic investor, most often from the GCC or Malaysia, willing to contribute capital but only in a Shariah-compliant manner, all necessary steps will be taken to accommodate the investment. This will entail choosing competent lawyers who are well versed in Islamic finance structures, obtaining an endorsement of the project from expert Shariah scholars, choosing a custodian bank that is knowledgeable in the ways of Islamic transactions; and ultimately listing, when appropriate, the investment in a market that works on all of the standard basis (tax, ease of use, cost, and stability, among others).

Domestic Markets

The matter of allowing Islamic Finance alternatives to be sold to domestic retail clients is an entirely different matter. Whereas facilitating much needed inbound investment may justify amendment to the regulatory and tax regimes; upsetting the balance of play within a country's retail market can be a road riddled with obstacles.

Again, we can see how local politics can play a role in the development of Islamic Finance. In certain parts of the United States, the term "Shariah" itself has become a hot-button and highly politicized word, equated in the minds of those who seek to use it for political gain, with all manner of bad things.

In France, there exists a cherished brand of secularism, whose roots are indeed ethical and meant to provide for an equal playing field within the culture. Here we find a deep ideological struggle to undue elements of this approach and make special rules and exceptions that have a religious foundation. Added to this is the ever-simmering social unrest among segments of their Muslim immigrant populations, whose calls for greater economic opportunity pose a significant challenge for successive governments. Whether the practice of Islamic Finance would exasperate the divide within the country or prove helpful remains an unanswered question.

When proposing Islamic finance in Muslim-minority countries, there exists sociological questions related to the following basic question: We have X number of Muslims in our country, but will they go for Islamic banking? Here, whether speaking of the Arabs of France, the Turks of Germany, or the Uighur of China, there comes into the debate questions about the degree of religiosity. Does the given community understand the principles of Islamic banking to an appreciable degree? If so, are there significant pools of "money beneath the mattress" waiting for a Shariah-compliant alternative? What percentage would likely switch their banking to the Islamic model? In the current economic environment, especially among immigrant populations, are there more pressing economic concerns dealing with employment and wages that take precedence over the form of banking?

Retail Islamic Finance in Muslim-Majority Countries

One of the greatest acceptance rates for Islamic Finance can be found in Malaysia. The Muslims or Malays, aside from having a naturally higher comfort level with the idea of an Islamic bank, also benefit from over three decades of exposure to the industry. Malaysians have seen consistent high-level government support of the industry within the country and internationally, are exposed to large marketing campaigns, and have seen Islamic banks on the main street for a generation. In such an environment the level of wholesale suspicion of something new has largely been erased, though increased customer education about the products remains a challenge. From the Islamic financial institution prospective, this base comfort level among the population means that they can now actively expand their range of services from the traditional savings products, consumer loans, and equity funds to more sophisticated products.

Additionally, it is interesting to note that within Malaysia many institutions find significant buyers of their service among non-Muslim, particularly Chinese, communities, whether for takaful, lending facilities, or investment accounts. These consumers find either better value or greater comfort with Shariah-compliant alternatives.

THE ARAB SPRING

As of late 2011, it has become very clear that all of the above issues are very much in play in the aftermath of initial stages of the Arab Spring. As new democracies form across Arabia, all governments, both new democracies and remaining monarchies, have been quickly adopting Islamic Finance. While official attitudes and approaches on Islamic Finance were mixed across the Arab region in 2010, they are now unanimously behind the industry's further development. In the aftermath of the regime changes in Tunisia, Egypt, Libya, and beyond, there is now a shared interest among governments, their new political parties, prominent Muslim political voices, and businessmen to expand the role of Islamic Finance.

Tunisia

In the nation that sparked the current regional change, Islamic bank legislation was quickly adapted under the first interim government and the only existing Islamic Bank was taken under government control and away from the previous "old-regime" shareholders. Planned is the eventual sale of the Islamic Bank to private investors, a much more robust and regulated market for both conventional and Islamic Finance, and a larger role for Islamic Finance in particular. With the Islamic party, Ennahda, winning the first free elections in the current era, an expanded role for Islamic banking seems assured.

Egypt

In Egypt, the largest Arab country with a Muslim majority and in many ways the center of the Arab world, interim leaders took a Shariah-compliant funding program from the Islamic Development Bank in favor of the conventional program on offer from the International Monetary Fund to plug its budgetary gap. This was done in the early days of the new government, and with Islamic parties the clear winner of the early elections, nearly all stakeholders now see Islamic Finance as an integral part of the future financial landscape, for high-minded and political reasons alike. While the existing playing field for Islamic banks and windows is sparse, a medium-term learning curve will need to be scaled by the country's bankers and a smooth political transition achieved before significant growth will occur in this sector.

Libya

In Libya, following a bloody quest for independence from the long-time leader, among the very first proclamations from the National Transitional Council were measures to incorporate a greater role for Islam, which included reference to Islamic banking and the waiver of certain consumer debts. For a nation blessed with natural resources and large reserves, intermediation through Shariah-compliant methods would represent a great boost in size for global Shariah-compliant assets.

Oman

In the only GCC nation to forgo Islamic Finance, the ruler, in response to popular demand for Islamic Finance, has reversed course, adapted an Islamic banking law, and now actively promotes the industries development within its borders. In response, a number of high-level initiatives are currently underway to develop the sector in Oman.

Turkey

While not an Arab country, Turkey's economic success in recent years and its high-profile political leadership within the wider region has made it an inspiration to new governments in the Arab World. In Tunisia for instance, Ennahda party leaders are often found expressing their fondness for the Turkish model, as opposed to the Iranian model, of political and economic Islam. In Turkey, Islamic Finance is marketed as "participation banking" and is in its infancy, but growing quickly. In the fourth quarter of 2011, three of the four participation banks were raising capital internationally using Islamic sukuk instruments, and deal-making is active as business groups vie for stakes in what is anticipated to be a booming retail and corporate market for Islamic Finance in the years to come.

CONCLUSION

While the conditions and positioning vary throughout the world, the key elements of Islamic Finance—the avoidance of interest, asset-backed transactions, risk-sharing, and the avoidance of highly speculative and prohibited industries—continue to attract supporters. The development of the sector has been gradual over the past 30 years, but now seems to be finding potential areas of rapid growth opening up to its application. What used to be a GCC and Malaysian phenomenon has spread, albeit thinly, to parts of Europe, Sub-Saharan Africa, Central Asia, SE Asia, and most recently across North Africa. As regulatory regimes get put in place and new Islamic Financial Institutions are formed, the sector will move from a small-scale curiosity to a more robust and productive force for economic development. It is without doubt a sector to watch.

CHAPTER 17

Stepping Forward, Backward, or Just Standing Still?

A Case Study in Shifting Islamic Financial Structures Offshore

UMAR F. MOGHUL
Partner, Stephenson Harwood LLP

Public discourse surrounding the fundamental challenges facing the fast-growing Islamic finance industry are a welcome development and a sign of the industry's growing confidence and security. Among these challenges are the "adaptive strategies" being utilized to help enable establishment of the contemporary Islamic finance industry.[1] These strategies are understood, particularly within inner circles, to constitute a temporary means until such time as more authentic means become available and viable.

This chapter introduces an offshore leasing structure utilized as a key component of an Islamic acquisition structure in United States. Its development is important for a number of reasons. First, previous acquisition structures of global consequence, employing *murabahah* or *ijarah* as their basis, were developed as the result of significant efforts. In many respects, the subject structure may allow these accomplishments to be set aside, as will be explained below, but at a potentially significant cost with regard to the values and principles underlying Islamic finance. Second, this structure stands as evidence of the ability of Islamic law and the industry to respond to changing markets as well as social and political conditions. Third, the structure is a useful lens through which to discuss certain of the various theoretical and practical obstacles facing Islamic finance.

These challenges will be dealt with in some detail in this chapter. In particular, we will suggest an approach for the industry, to begin to turn toward notions of authenticity. By no means are these suggestions comprehensive. To do so, this chapter suggests a modified approach to the drafting and evaluation of contracts that better speaks to classical Islamic legal theory and contemporary factors and accounts for liability and risk assessment on a transactional level within a framework that is concerned with the characteristics of the desired Islamic financial marketplace. Last, the merits and limits of critiques of Islamic finance that rely primarily on the notion of legal purposes (*maqasid*) and economic theories will be presented.

THE SUBJECT TRANSACTION

The Dilemma—A Circular Triangle?[2]

A GCC-based Islamic investment company (the "Sponsor") sponsored a series of real estate acquisitions first in Europe and then in the United States. The dilemma presented at the center of this chapter began with adverse transfer tax consequences under applicable local law triggered by a typical Islamic acquisition structure (e.g., an *ijarah*- or *murabaha*-based one).[3] In this case, it was primarily Dutch transfer and income taxes that were most relevant.

These acquisitions also took place amid the prevailing global financial crisis (in which obtaining credit is arduous) and within an Islamophobic environment that persists in many, though not all, quarters of both Europe and the United States.[4] As much as Islamic finance has gained press attention and become more and more known, there remains in our experience a vast number of bankers and business types not yet acquainted with Islamic finance and many others who are simply unwilling, for whatever reasons, to engage therein. In our experience, when these realities are present they often slow and make inefficient the closing of Islamic transactions.

Adverse tax consequences were not expected in the United States due to the Islamic nature of the structure per se. It was the latter concern—the challenge in obtaining Islamic financing in the United States—coupled with the efficiency and cost savings gained by avoiding the challenge that pushed the use of a corollary of the European offshore structure for the Sponsor's U.S. investments.[5] So instead of the milestone Islamic financing structures developed with a tremendous degree of effort and now commonly employed in the United States, this circular lease structure was utilized.[6]

The Sponsor's aim then was to determine whether a structure could be designed, under Islamic and other applicable laws, so as to mitigate the effects of these adversities in both Europe and the United States. As the obstacles presented onshore, the thought was to somehow create a permissible offshore structure that would utilize conventional leverage onshore at the property level and yet allow Islamic investors to participate. As experienced practitioners are well aware, utilizing an Islamically permissible debt-based arrangement is the appropriate beginning point in such transaction structuring. It must also be noted that the parties were fortunate to be able to use as their basis a structure previously employed by another Islamic sponsor:[7] a closed loop of three leases modified by the parties, as shown in Exhibit 17.1.

The Lease Participants

Ownership of each of the three circular lease participants (Entity A, Entity B, and Entity C) was structured so as to be independent of one another to alleviate certain Islamic legal concerns (relating to the imposition of impermissible contractual conditions) and to perhaps thereby give the transactions a certain substance. Accordingly, the Sponsor appointed (and paid) two (already existing[8]) service providers to hold in trust all of the issued and outstanding shares in Entity A and Entity C, respectively, pursuant to nominee agreements under Cayman Islands law. Entity B

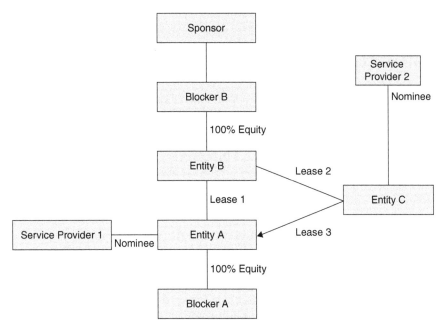

Exhibit 17.1 Circular Lease Structure

was indirectly owned by the Sponsor. The service provider-nominees also agreed (a) to pay over to the Sponsor all profits and dividends relating to such shares, and (b) to vote such shares as directed by the Sponsor. These service provider-nominees were not related to one another nor was there any common ownership among either of them and the Sponsor and/or its affiliates.

The Leases[9]

Lease One, between Entity A to Entity B, is a forward lease (*ijarah al-mawsuf bi-dhimma*) in which the full sum of the rent is paid in advance.[10] A forward lease "combines characteristics of two other contracts recognized by Islamic jurisprudence, i.e., a *salam* contract and an *ijarah* contract."[11] According to Nassar, the majority of jurists permit forward leases because "leasing an object is like selling it . . . and the sale of an object is valid whether the payment is immediate or delayed, so likewise is the lease [of an object]."[12] Hanafi jurists only permit forward leases with respect to a particular identified object (i.e., they do not permit unilateral substitution of the leased asset by the lessor). But the balance of jurists permit a forward lease (a) of described objects (i.e., not a particular object but any object meeting the stated description) and (b) of an object for which the lessor assumes responsibility to provide (i.e., allowing the lessor to charge another to provide such object).[13] Ibn Rushd said, "One of the conditions of forward *ijarah*, according to Malik, is that payment be immediate, in order to avoid the sale of a debt for a debt."[14] Expressing a similar concern, Shafi'i and Hanbali jurists, however, distinguished contracts formulated using the term *salam* or the like (e.g., *salaf*) in which case the payment must be received on the spot, but if such a term is not used (and so, for instance, the term ijarah were employed instead), then it is not necessary to make immediate payment.[15] The position of the Accounting and Auditing Organization for Islamic Financial Institutions (AAOIFI), as set forth in its Shari'a Standards, must be mentioned as well:

> An Ijarah contract may be executed for an asset undertaken by the lessor to be delivered to the lessee according to accurate specifications, even if the asset so described is not owned by the lessor. In this case, an agreement is reached to make the described asset available during the duration of the contract, giving the lessor the opportunity to acquire or to produce it. It is not a requirement of this lease that the rental should be paid in advance as long as the lease is not executed according to the contract of Salam (or Salaf). Should a lessee receive an asset that does not conform to the description, then he is entitled to reject it.[16]

AAOIFI thus appears to find greater merit in the Hanbali and Shafi'i positions. Lease One did not employ the terminology in question, but rather employed terminology of lease (in English). Immediate payment in full was integrated to address the cash flow needs of the transaction—and not to fulfill a requirement of law.

Neither Lease Two nor Lease Three is a forward lease; rather, rent is payable thereunder periodically. The Lease One agreement does not make mention of either Lease Two (between Entity B and Entity C) or Lease Three (between Entity C and Entity A), such as by conditioning the execution of Lease One on the execution of Lease Two or Lease Three. And neither Lease Two nor Lease Three makes mention of one another or of Lease One. Under the circular lease structure, what is leased to Entity B by Entity A is then leased by Entity B to Entity C, and finally from Entity C back to Entity A. Such subleasing is permitted by the majority of Muslim jurists, and according to the Majallat al-Ahkam it is even permitted prior to taking possession in the case of real property.[17]

The Leased Asset

The critical question in designing this circular lease structure was the nature of the leased asset itself.[18] Each relevant body of law brought to bear its own requirements and methods on this question.

For Dutch corporate and transfer tax purposes, the leased asset could not be construed (by Dutch authorities) as real property lest the aforementioned adverse tax consequences be triggered. The same may be said for U.S. tax purposes: if the leased asset is stated to be, or viewed by the IRS as, a real property interest, it would be subject to U.S. income tax. However, unlike the Dutch tax regime, the U.S. one may be said in many instances, including this one, to take a substance-over-form approach.[19] By that I mean the IRS will look to the economics of a transaction and characterize (or recharacterize) it accordingly, over and above the form or words of description used by the parties. It was therefore suggested that to satisfy these tax purposes, (a) the lease be one of shares in Blocker A placed between the circular lease arrangement and the property level entities, and (b) the initial lessor (i.e., Entity A) not have any direct enforceable legal relationship at the property level or with respect to the rental income and capital gains realized by the property. This raised the question, under Dutch, U.S., and Islamic laws, as to whether it is possible to lease shares and, if not, whether a lease agreement purporting to do so would be enforceable under the aforementioned laws and particularly those of the Cayman Islands, which expressly govern the circular lease arrangement.[20]

For Shari'ah purposes, a lease of real property is recognized and established both in theory and in practice, whereas the notion of leasing shares is novel (in our limited knowledge and experience). Consider for example AAOIFI Standard 9, Section 5/1/1, which reads:

The leased asset must be capable of being used while preserving the asset, and the benefit from an Ijarah must be lawful in Shari'a. For example, a house or a chattel may not be leased for the purpose of an impermissible act by the lessee, such as leasing premises to a institution dealing in interest or to a shopkeeper for selling or storing prohibited goods, or leasing a vehicle to transport prohibited merchandise.

And AAOIFI Standard 5/1/4, which reads:

The lessee must use the leased asset in a suitable manner or in conformity with common practice, and comply with conditions which are acceptable in sharia. You must also avoid causing damage to the leased asset by misuse through misconduct or negligence.[21]

In light of this standard, the parties considered what it would mean to lease shares or equity in a business entity. What use of the shares (e.g., the right to vote granted to its holder) would be sold to the lessor in a lease? Is there a common practice regarding leasing of equity on which to rely or from which to learn?

Having begun drafting the leases with the notion of leasing shares, the parties shifted, primarily in light of potential Shari'ah concerns, to a leased asset defined more vaguely so as to create space for each legal system to "succeed." Ultimately, the leased asset was contractually described as "an indirect interest arising solely from its ownership of the Company" (i.e., Blocker A). The phrase "in real property" describing the "indirect interest" could not be employed because of the probable resulting tax consequences under U.S. and Dutch laws. Moreover, the lease agreements expressly stated that the "Lessor shall not directly own or control, nor hold legal title to, or have direct beneficial interest in, any Real Property." A "direct beneficial interest," as defined by Dutch law, refers to a direct economic ownership interest of, in this case, the initial lessor (i.e., Entity A). Essentially, one has an economic ownership if one directly carries the risk of decrease and increase in the value of the subject asset (in this case, the real property) and would be directly entitled to the proceeds thereof. Given the stated rent amounts under, and other relevant terms of, the leases, this was held not to be the case. Hence, Dutch counsel informed that the nature of the leased asset, as it was described in the lease agreements, is that of an economic interest in the shares of the Cayman blocker company, and not in the underlying real property. In order to establish economic ownership in the underlying real estate under Dutch law, the lessor must have entered into an agreement with the owner of legal title of such real estate, pursuant to which the economic interest in the real estate transfers to the lessor. There was no such agreement and, to avoid a misinterpretation of the lease structure by Dutch tax authorities, it was made expressly clear in the lease agreements that each lessor will never directly enter into such an agreement.

From a Dutch and U.S. perspective, it was preferable to further strip away many common lease clauses from the three lease agreements, so as to prevent the characterization of the leases as real property, even if indirectly so. No lessor or lessee had actual access or use of the real property. Thus, typical lease provisions, such as the right to sell, convey, or transfer the asset, or permit certain uses thereof, or to make additions or alterations or inspections thereof, were deleted.

For Shari'ah purposes, the leases were deemed to be of a real property interest, albeit one that is removed from the real property asset itself by several inter-mediaries. As entry, use, or possession of the real property by any of the lease participants was not possible, the leased asset is thus quite different from that of a "typical" operating or finance lease—Islamic or otherwise. Under Cayman Islands law, which is perhaps most important since the leases were expressly governed thereby, the Sponsor was informed that such leases, given the leased asset descrip-tion, was an unknown and probably constituted an assignment or license of sorts, rather than a lease.[22] It would seem then that a resolution of what the leased asset is depends on the body of law from which the question is analyzed.

REFLECTIONS

The subject transaction, as noted previously, involves the use of successive leases to address adverse contextual factors, including tax treatment. This section will discuss in greater detail the key features of the circular lease structure, highlighting arguments from an Islamic legal perspective in favor thereof as well as opposed thereto. Finally, an outline of distinguishing criteria is suggested for application to future transactions.

Legal Structure and Strategem

The nominee arrangements used with regard to Entity A and Entity C were found from a Shari'ah perspective to constitute (sufficient) independence of the lease participants. Independence, in turn, gives the circular lease structure "substance" and, as such, they cannot constitute an impermissible legal stratagem (*hilah*). Prac-tically speaking, this arrangement also benefits the Sponsor by granting it a certain degree of control over its acquisitions for business purposes and in the unlikely event a nominee misbehaves. For example, if a nominee were to commit fraud and a court were to find the leases unenforceable, such fraud could create a number of challenges for the Sponsor. But is the value of such a benefit desirable precisely because of the circular lease structure? Is the problem it solves, in other words, a result of the use of the third party nominees?

Given (a) the Sponsor's direction to form each of the lease participants, (b) the *creation* of the nominee arrangement and thus any consequent indepen-dence, (c) the extent of the Sponsor's retained control over the shares, and (d) that the shares were held in trust by (and not per se sold, transferred, or conveyed to) the nominees under Cayman Islands law,[23] one might, on the other hand, contend that the independence of the nominees from the Sponsor is compromised so as to preclude a finding of independence of the three lease participants under Islamic laws.[24] If the lease participants are in fact one and the same legal person, is there a legal strategem (*hilah*) present?

Legal strategems (pl. *hiyal*) may be permissible or impermissible under Islamic law. Abdul Khir explains:

> The wide application of permissible *hiyal* in economic activities illustrates that *hiyal* play an important role in Islamic finance, as they alleviate financial predicaments and hardship . . . Impermissible *hiyal* are legal strategies that are exercised with the clear intention of an illegal end such as the negation of a Shariah ruling (*ibtal al-hukm*), the alteration of a Shariah ruling (*tahwil al-hukm*), the legitimization of the illegitimate (*tahlil al-haram*), and the transgression of basic Shariah principles (*kharm qawa'id al-Shariah*). Such *hiyal* are strictly prohibited for they are attempts to defeat the noble objectives of the Shariah.[25]

Abdul Khir continues to list factors that may help decide whether the hilah in question is permissible. These include: the actors' motivations, the objective of the Lawgiver (i.e., God), the means employed, public interest, and the law in both its original (*'azimah*) and concessionary forms (i.e., a *rukhsah*).[26]

Combining Contracts

The notion of combining contracts (*ijtima al-uqud*) is relevant to the circular lease structure insofar as the leases have been combined to create a closed loop.[27] However, typically the term *ijtima al-uqud* refers to "an agreement between two or more parties to conclude a deal involving two or more *different* forms of contracts of distinct features and legal characteristics to form a viable investment product."[28] The primary issue is the nature and combination of contracts, and not the validity of combination itself. According to Arbouna, "It may be suitable to state that the main impediments for disapproving tying arrangements or *ishtirat aqd fi aqd/bay'tayn fi bay'ah* are one of the following: (a) *riba*, (b) *gharar*, and (c) injustice, exploitation, and taking advantage of people's need."[29] This concern is highlighted by AAOIFI Standard 9, Section 3/4, which reads:

> The lessee may lease the asset back to its owner in the first lease period for a rental that is lower, same [sic] or higher than what he is paying if the two rentals are paid on a spot basis. However, this is not permissible if it should lead to contract of 'inah, by varying the rent or the duration. For example, it is not permissible if the first rental is one hundred *dinars* payable on a spot basis, for the lessee to sublet it to the lessor for one hundred and ten *dinars* payable on a deferred basis, or if the first rental is one hundred and ten *dinars* payable on a deferred basis, for the second to be for one hundred *dinars* payable instantly, or if the two rentals are of the same amount, but the payment of the first rental is deferred for one month and the second rental is deferred by two months."

While the synthesis at hand here is not of different contracts—such as (a) a loan and a lease or (b) a sale and a lease[30]—the aforementioned purposes (of avoiding *riba, gharar*, and so on) are at least worthy of further consideration because the very same asset is leased by a party and ultimately leased back to it by combining similar contracts.

From a Shari'ah perspective, the absence of any explicit statement in the leases tying them to one another or conditioning them on one another might be considered dispositive. On the other hand, regardless of the absence of an explicit statement to the contrary, the three leases would not have been entered into but for the others, so such a condition did exist *contractually* though not in the *written evidence of* such a contract.

Despite the complexity and sophistication of many Islamic transactions, there remains in my mind a fundamental point that may help resolve the persistent debate over form and substance.[31] Transaction parties engage one another in discussions and negotiations in a *majlis* (contractual session) whether conducted through a single, physical meeting of the parties or through a series of physical and/or telephonic and electronic interactions with one another spanning days, weeks, or months. In the course of this *majlis* (contractual session), the parties and their various professional representatives (such as lawyers and accountants) seek to reach an agreement regarding their business together. This agreement will likely comprise several components, all of which the parties each typically understand and discuss as, and agree to be, interrelated and interdependent, set forth in one or more definitive written instruments. The parties do not hold their agreement to be final unless and until the closing—whether physical or virtual—takes place, in which remaining details are finalized, definitive documentation representing the contract is completed and then signed, and signature pages are delivered to one another along with any exchange of countervalues. Separate written instruments, whether contracts or promises, are not understood, either by the parties and often the chosen applicable local laws as well, to mean that there are separate, independent agreements.

In light of this custom and its congruence with Islamic contract law theory, Islamic legal analyses should move toward an approach that assesses single transactions as a whole, integrating the myriad of written instruments together as written evidence of a single (greater) contractual agreement. This will help mitigate against instances in which strategies are employed to produce unacceptable legal and moral outcomes.[32] Furthermore, in light of the difficulties presented by the selection and enforcement of governing law clauses in Islamic transactions, an approach that analyzes a single transaction as the outcome of a single contractual agreement evidenced by multiple, related (whether expressly or otherwise) written instruments would align it with results that are likely under governing local laws using the same approach.[33] Shari'ah compliance could thus be furthered, not only by bringing form and substance together, but also by accounting for likelier outcomes upon litigation under local law where it seems the Shari'ah may otherwise be excluded.

While on the subject of motivations, it is important to note that the parties' motivations are best understood by them and those present in the *majlis* (as defined above). Often, in our experience, participation by Shari'ah advisors does not take place in the same manner or to the same extent as that of other professional advisors. Proper knowledge of Shari'ah by these participants, particularly lawyers, would be of significant benefit insofar as they may be able to guide parties' motivations toward improved mechanisms.[34]

Pricing

Pricing of the rent under each lease was done to enable cash to flow successfully between the offshore structure and offshore property investment. The forward lease rent amount, for example, was calculated to provide the amount of cash required to acquire real property. The payments under Lease Two and Lease Three were set high enough so as to enable periodic distribution of rent and other income such as that derived from property sales or any refinancings (of the conventional mortgage financing at the property level). Thus, one might successfully contend that the rent pricing was independent of the value of the leased asset and "when something is included unnecessarily in a contract as a countervalue or subject matter . . . [it] is indicative of the actual motive of the contracting parties."[35] Nevertheless, since these leases were not loans (or designed as financings), it would seem difficult to argue that the circular lease structure *itself* was *ribawi*.

But if the Sponsor's motivation was to overcome obstacles to Islamic finance in the United States and to enable a conventional secured credit facility at the property level, then we must ask: Is it permissible under Islamic law to avoid the adverse tax consequences and unfortunate social realities by arranging a ribawi transaction even if the Islamic Sponsor's investment financially therein is to some extent divorced legally through the previously described nominee arrangements? If this structure is more efficient than the Islamic financing structures developed in the United States, such as the *ijarah*,[36] is the former's use rightfully preferable over the latter? Will conventional markets (onshore) receive less education regarding Islamic finance if the Islamic structure is kept offshore? What other consequences, beneficial or harmful, might result? Are these questions better answered by an institution comprised of Muslim jurists, thinkers, and other policymakers rather than by way of a fatwa designed to speak at the micro or particular level?[37]

Maqasid al-Shari'ah

A number of commentators criticize the formalism of contemporary Islamic finance law, bringing up the notion of the purposes of the Shari'ah (*maqasid al-Shari'ah*) as not properly integrated into the legal analytical process. That the universals have in fact not been fulfilled appears to be an assertion that is generally not evidenced and stated in conclusory form.

The purposes of the Shari'ah are typically stated by Muslim jurists with quite a bit of breadth and abstraction; by definition, such breadth and abstraction brings with it a degree of ambiguity and indeterminacy, particularly considering if they are to be used as the basis of law making.[38]

While each law, when legislated and enforced, must be considered in light of the broader purposes, this begs, as Shakil insightfully notes, the question of whether our understanding of universals should trump the particulars?[39] Legislating on the basis of such purposes, or universals, would likely be a challenging undertaking creating greater legal ambiguity and variation than is found in the existing legal processes of Islamic finance.[40] A common criticism by those Muslim jurists who argue for rulings founded upon their '*ilal* (singular, '*illah*), or effective causes, against those who argue for rulings to be based upon their *hikam* (singular, *hikmah*), or rationale, is that the latter method may become too distant from the texts of the Shari'ah and thus proceed down a slippery slope.[41] Increased legislation may also upset those uncomfortable with the legal pluralism of Islamic law and those calling for increased standardization as well.[42] But this belies the very important point in Islamic jurisprudence that application of the particulars probabilistically[43] results in fulfillment of the universals.[44] If the universals are in fact not being achieved, is it possible something additionally is done to affect realization of the universals or are the particulars improperly understood and applied?

In the case of the subject transaction, which universal, if any, has been violated and how would that be proven? Or, was there in fact, first, a violation of a particular relating to (a) the meaning of ownership by finding (sufficient) independence in the nominee arrangement, (b) the nature of the leased asset, and/or (c) the distinction and separation of what were in fact a series of lease contracts contractually conditioned on one another?

If we contend that a particular has been violated, it becomes that much easier to argue that a universal has been violated; it might even be a valid (albeit rebuttable) presumption to make. If we hold that this structure is deemed "Shari'ah compliant" because of a technicality, would not that be the case with the commonly utilized *ijarah* acquisition financing structure as well?[45] And, as such, with the circular lease mechanism has Islamic finance moved forward, backward, or simply remained standing still?

It would be worthwhile to conduct a study of the various Islamic finance transactions and their impact on society to determine whether, and to what extent, the objectives of Islamic law are being realized. Such a study would be complicated by the fact that Islamic finance is a rather small piece of any given financial or economic market and that it exists within the dominant conventional regulatory paradigm and economic market. In assessing whether the substance of Islamic financial law is being met, Balz does, however, make an interesting point worthy of further consideration and analysis—namely, would contemporary Islamic finance, as a practice or industry, have prevented the current financial crisis and, if so, to what extent?[46] Such a study would call upon expertise across various disciplines from law and economics to a number of other social sciences.[47]

Economics

As others, Islamic economists often begin their analyses with an appeal to the objectives of Islamic Law. With regard to these, Dr. Nyazee reminds us of these two goals:

1. That the pursuit of human goals and the principle of utility based on human reason is not what is meant by maslaha . . .
2. That the goals determined for the Sharia by the Lawgiver may or may not coincide with the values determined by human reason. Thus, reasoning based upon the principles of utility or an economic analysis may sometimes be acceptable to the Sharia, but it may be rejected at other times when there is a clash of values.[48]

A key limitation to some Islamic economic analyses has been an attempt to subject *fiqh* to its principles and arguments, whereas theories of Islamic economics should be subject to, and drawn out from, *fiqh*. However the critique of *tawarruq* transactions presented by Siddiqui is excellent because it may be used to link economic consequences with legal particulars.[49] As such, his analysis helps inform whether and why implementation of particulars may fail to realize universals.

Siddiqui demonstrates that the regular usage of *tawarruq* generates the creation of a debt market.[50] It should be noted here that by debt market he does not refer to the simple creation of obligations. Citing numerous Muslim economists, he affirms:

> [A]s a method of creating additional or new wealth, debt creation (or debt-finance) is inefficient as well as inequitable. It is inefficient as the finance so provided goes not for the most promising projects for wealth production but to the most credit-worthy borrower. It is inequitable as it redistributes wealth in favor of suppliers of finance, irrespective of actual productivity of the finance applied.[51]

Tawarruq leads to a debt-based market, which, in turn, leads to the proliferation of debt as well as an increased scope for speculation. The point Siddiqui makes which I wish to emphasize and have considered with respect to financing transactions generally is that "financing facilitated by *tawarruq*, like its counterpart, lending in the conventional system, is free and unhinged from the real sector of the economy."[52]

Habil effectively connects such economics-based arguments to the legal underpinnings of risk and liability.[53] He designs a test to assess the object of financing and of contract in order to evaluate the merit of the transaction. He concludes, "whenever the object of the financing facility is actually the object of the contract, the requirement of *daman* is somehow fulfilled. . . If the true object of the financing transaction is not the actual object of the contract, then only unlawful *hila* is at work, as the underlying purpose of the transaction is to circumvent *daman*."[54]

Notwithstanding that the circular lease structure is not a financing mechanism, one can certainly raise the question of whether the leased asset was truly the subject of each of the leases and linked to a real asset, namely the properties. Finding the circular lease structure to be but a conduit to enable cash flow and conventional mortgage financing at the property level, one might conclude that its widespread use might generate the sort of debt market to which Siddiqui refers.

Siddiqui's analysis may also inform a discussion of the framework in which fatwa are issued. It is probably not within the purview of individual fatwa issuance (a legal particular) to develop broader economic policy and or to assess successful societal implementation of legal universals. But it would appear helpful if fatwa issuance fell within and under an institutionalization of the construction and assessment of universals by a body of Muslim jurists, economists, local law lawyers, and thinkers of other relevant disciplines.

CONCLUSIONS

This chapter presents a leasing transaction as a case study in order to assess the trajectory of contemporary Islamic finance and to explore questions of legal theory, law, and economics. In order to evaluate a transaction for compliance with Islamic law and ethics, we have proposed an approach of integrating written instruments relating to a single transaction together with Habil's proposal to assess whether the object of contract is the same as the object of financing. Such an approach, it is hoped, will help close the gap between form and substance, uphold the parties' motivations, and mitigate against the use of impermissible legal stratagems. Such an approach, moreover, will increase the likelihood of an adjudicated decision that is more consistent with the Shari'ah through application of governing local laws and authorities. Finally, the implementation of particulars more properly will more likely result in the realization of the purposes of the Shari'ah including, among other things, the likely intended economic consequences of the law of Islamic finance and investment.

NOTES

1. Aamir Rehman. 2010. *Gulf Capital and Islamic Finance: The Rise of the New Global Players.* New York: McGraw Hill, p. 115.
2. I am reminded of certain types of religious and theological questions regarding the possible and impossible for God. See Nuh Ha Mim Keller, *Sea Without Shore: A Manual of the Sufi Path*, pp. 333–34 (2011), commenting, "The possible or impossible for Allah Most High involves the divine attribute of *qudra* or omnipotence, 'what He can do.' This attribute in turn relates exclusively to the intrinsically possible not to what is intrinsically impossible, as Allah says 'Verily Allah has power over all things' (Koran 2:20), *thing* meaning only what in principle can exist. For example, if one asks, 'Can Allah create a square circle?' The answer is that His omnipotence does not relate to it for a 'square circle' does not refer to anything that in principle could exist: the speaker does not have a distinct idea of what he means, but is merely using a jumble of words."
3. Such consequences are not typically present in conventionally structured transactions. See also Kevin Conway, "Taxing Issues," *Islamic Business & Finance* 20 (September 2010).
4. Such an assertion hardly requires a citation. On the United States, see Sahar Aziz, "Terror(izing) the Muslim Veil," in *The Rule of Law and the Rule of God*, ed. Simeon Elsanmi (forthcoming, University of Virginia Press, Spring 2012), available at http://ssrn .com/abstract=1962313; Sahar Aziz, "Caught in a Preventive Dragnet Ten Years Later: Selective Counterterrorism Against Muslims, Arabs, and South Asians" (forthcoming, *Gonzaga Law Review*, Spring 2012), available at http://ssm. com/abstract=1825662. With regard to Europe, see Abdul Hakim Murad, "Can Liberalism Tolerate Islam?," *Osro Litteraturbuset* 20 (March 2011).
5. As practitioners will appreciate, the circular lease structure (described in greater detail below) is simpler and easier to effectuate in comparison with the now common *ijarah*-based acquisition financing structure. Moreover, because the circular lease structure can be established in a master lease format, it probably need only be set up once for a number and variety of transactions.
6. Islamic acquisition financing structures in the United States typically employ an ijarah-based structure, and less so a *murabahah*-based one in our experience. See, for example, Umar F. Moghul, "Separating the Good from the Bad: Developments in Islamic Acquisition Financing," *American University Intramural Law Review*, 23:4 (2008).
7. It is not known to the author whether in this prior structure the same, or similar, objectives were sought.
8. That is to say, these service providers were not created for this transaction nor are they akin to special purpose entities.
9. Although not discussed herein in any detail, it is worth noting that the circular lease structure is arranged as a master lease between the various lease participants. See, for example, Accounting and Auditing Organization for Islamic Finance Institution [AAOIFI] Standard 9, Section 2/2 (2008) [hereinafter AAOIFI Standards], which reads: "A master agreement may be drawn up covering a number of Ijarah transactions between the institution and the customer, setting out the general terms and conditions of agreement between the two parties. In this case, there may either be a separate lease contract for each transaction, in a specific written document signed by the two

parties, or alternatively the two parties may exchange notices of offer and acceptance by referring to the terms and conditions contained in the master agreement."

10. The AAOIFI Standards do not appear to discuss immediate or advance payments of rent in full. But see AAOIFI Standard 9, Section 4/1/4, which reads: "Urboun (i.e., earnest money) may be taken in respect of lease at the execution of the contract of lease and this is treated as an advance payment of the rental. If the ijarah contract is not executed for a reason attributable to the lessee, the lessor may retain the urboun. However, it is preferable for the institution to waive any amount in excess of the actual damage it has suffered, which is the difference between the rental specified in the contract of lease and the actual rental obtainable in an Ijarah contract with another lessee."

11. Ahmad Muhammad Mahmud Nassar, "The Parameters of Forward Ijarah and its Application in Financing Services in Islamic Financial Institutions" (2009) (on file with the author). This article is neither dated nor does my copy use page numbers.

12. Ibid.

13. Ibid.

14. Ibid. (quoting Ibn Rushd, *Bidayat al-Mujtahid*, vol. 2, p. 182). Nassar further informs: "It is permitted to securitize the benefits that are the subject matter of the forward ijarah contract, and which have become a debt obligation upon the lessor. It is then permissible to buy and sell them. That is because a stipulated benefit is by its nature amenable to transactions by means of an ijarah contract; so, likewise, it can be traded by the original renter; who gains the right to it by the ijarah contract. He can rent it to a third party, who can rent it to a fourth party, who can rent it to a fifth. The price can be the same as the original rental or higher or lower. It doesn't matter, in this regard, if the original ijarah contract was for a particular object or a specified description. . . That is because, from a fiqh standpoint, it doesn't matter if the benefit that the ijarah contract bestows right to is connected to a particular object or a generic object that the lessor undertakes responsibility to provide, as long as it is sufficiently described with specifications that make it determinate and, thus, valid for purposes of transaction." See ibid.

15. Ibid. (quoting Sharh Muntahah al-Iradat, 2, p. 36).

16. AAOIFI Standard 9, Section 3/5.

17. See Mohamed Ali Elgari, "Special Features of the Right of Usage and the Consequences of Its Transfer," presented to The Sixth Conference of the Shariah Boards of Financial Islamic Institutions and The Accounting and Auditing Organization of Islamic Financial Institutions, p. 8 (n.d.). See also p. 8 (quoting Mawahib al-Jalil: "The lessee can take the usufruct in full, either personally or through others; and he can lease out what he has leased for the same fee, or for more than it or for less . . . because he owns the usufruct of the contract, which gives him the right to transfer it to whomever he chooses, like anything else he owns. Therefore he can lease out what he has himself rented").

18. Other basic rules of the ijarah may be found in Muhammad *Ayub, Understanding Islamic Finance*, pp. 279–305 (2007); and Wahbah al-Zuhayli, *Financial Transactions in Islamic Jurisprudence*, vol. 1, p. 381 (trans. Mahmoud El-Galal 2003). Regarding forward leases, see also Abdul Satter Abu Ghuddah, "Practical Application of al-Ijarah al-Mawsufah Fi al-Dhimmah" (Forward Ijarah) (n.d.; on file with the author).

19. While Islamic finance is often criticized for its legal formalism, consider that to satisfy Dutch legal concerns, among other things, the term "rent" was amended to "lease payment" in each lease agreement.

20. In light of recent court decisions, the question of governing law has received increased attention within contemporary Islamic financial discourse. See, for example, Julio C. Colon, "Choice of Law and Islamic Finance" (2011), available at http://ssrn.com/abstract=1856351; Zulkifli Hasan and Mehmet Asutay, "An Analysis of the Courts' Decisions on Islamic Finance Disputes," *ISRA International Journal of Islamic Law*, 3:2,

67 (2011) (referring to the defense as unethical). Both of the foregoing articles address the recently arisen defense that an Islamic transaction was not Islamic despite Shari'ah advisory approval. Some have insensitively termed this Shari'ah risk, but the risk is not of or relating to the Shari'ah.

21. See also Elgari, supra note 17, p. 3 (informing that "Jurists have explicitly stated that a lease can only be for a benefit that can be taken without consuming the object [that provides it."]).

22. A Cayman Islands legal opinion, which might have provided some comfort, would therefore have been a significant undertaking (and was not undertaken).

23. The Sponsor declined a more expensive option of utilizing a special trust under the Special Trusts (Alternative Regime), 1997 under the laws of the Cayman Islands. Such a trust, often termed a *STAR trust,* may be a pure purpose trust for noncharitable purposes and for the benefit of individual beneficiaries. For purposes of this discussion, the use of such a vehicle would have made a more definitive separation of ownership of the shares from the Sponsor by having the trust actually legally own the shares. See Cayman Islands Trusts Law (2011 Revision), Section VIII.

24. This is an interesting example of how local and Islamic laws intersect, where the former informs an understanding of the facts to which the latter is applied to create legal determinations.

25. See Mohamed Fairooz Abdul Khir, "Shariah Parameters of Hiyal in Islamic Finance," *ISRA International Journal of Islamic Finance,* 2:2, 159 (2010).

26. Ibid., p. 161. Abdul Khir's more exact list is as follows: "1. The usage of the hiyal must confirm to the objectives of the Lawgiver (qasd al-Shari') based on the Shariah hierarchy of priorities . . . 2. The motive of the individual (qasd al-mukallaf) must comply with the objective of the Lawgiver (qasd al-Shari) without any contradiction . . . 3. The wasilah (means) employed in hiyal must not lead to negation of qasd al-Shari' . . . 4. The maslahah intended from the exercise of hiyal must be actual, prevalent and accredited by the Shariah . . . 5. A hilah that has a time limit must not be exercised continuously, while a hilah without a time limit can be prolonged." Ibid., pp. 161–64.

27. Ijarah contracts may be executed in respect of the same asset for different periods for several lessees, provided that two contracts are not executed in respect of the same asset for the same period. Such an arrangement is called "successive leases," because each Ijarah is considered as being successive to the previous one and not concurrent with it on the basis of its being a future Ijarah . . ." See AAOIFI, Standard 9, Section 4/2/1. The present case may be distinguished by the fact that a single lessor is not leasing to several lessees concurrently. Thus, the present case of a "closed loop" of leases does not appear to be explicitly addressed by AAOIFI standards.

28. Mohammed Burhan Arbouna, "The Combination of Contracts in Shariah: A Possible Mechanism for Product Development in Islamic Banking and Finance," *Thunderbird International Business Review,* 49:3, 341, 344 (May–June 2007).

29. Ibid., p. 346.

30. "An asset may be acquired from a party and then leased to that party. In this case, the Ijarah transaction should not be stipulated as a condition of the purchase contract by which the institution acquires the asset." AAOIFI Standard 3/2.

31. We will show below the importance of form and its relationship to substance in Islamic jurisprudence—often overlooked probably because it is not understood.

32. Habib Ahmed, "Maqasid al-Shari'ah and Islamic Financial Products: A Framework for Assessment," *ISRA Intil. J. of Islamic Finance,* 3:1, 149, 150 (2011) (stating "Products that combine different *legal* Islamic contracts and produce *illegal* outcomes in substance or violate the legal maxims will be contrary to the spirit of Shari'ah principles" [emphasis supplied]).

33. In our experience, many Islamic transactions commonly select UK law as the governing law and some others use the laws of the State of New York. On the question of governing law, see infra note 20.

34. Hasan and Asutay, supra note 20, p. 69 (stating, "[A] sound legal framework is dependent on the instrumental function of its legal fraternity. Lawyers, judges, legal advisors, Shari'ah scholars, and other professionals in Islamic finance should acquire sufficient knowledge on the traditional Islamic legal concepts and be able to apply them in the context of modern finance and the law of international finance").

35. Abdul Khir, supra note 25, p. 60. If the leased asset (as described above) is unintended by the parties as either the true subject matter or motivation of the leases, then it is unnecessary. This is a factor in assessing whether the mechanism is an impermissible legal stratagem (*hilah*).

36. See supra note 5. It should be noted that the circular lease structure is simpler from the point of view of documentation and once established it can be used for multiple transactions. It is thus less costly. It also avoids the need to have possibly lengthy discussions with financiers regarding Islamic finance since conventional financing is used at the onshore level.

37. See also Arbouna, supra note 28, p. 366 (stating, "Last but not least, the fact that Islamic banking needs viable products to compete in a global finance should not be a ground for defeating the purpose and principles of Islamic law for prohibiting certain transactions"). Does the circular lease defeat such purpose and principles?

38. See generally Mohammed Hashim Kamali, *Principles of Islamic Jurisprudence* (2003), pp. 264–305.

39. Mansoor Shakil, "Theory of Higher Objectives of Islamic Law vis-à-vis Islamic Finance: A Study of Imam Shatibi's Theory of the Higher Objectives and Intents of Islamic Law and Its Relevance to Islamic Finance," *Islamic Finance: Innovation and Authenticity* 65:83 (S. Nazim Ali, ed., 2011).

40. For instance, the Shari'ah grants a concession to the traveler with respect to *salat* and fasting. The *'illah* of the legal dispensation is travel (*safr*), and the *hikmah* is the prevention of hardship. So should this dispensation be extended to all other cases of hardship, however slight, or confined to the hardship specific to travel? Where do we draw the line in extending the applicability of this concession? Is hardship and its corollary, benefit, too ambiguous, uncertain, and variable to legislate upon? The majority of Muslim legal scholars, comprised mostly of Hanafis and Shafi'is, contend that rules of the Shari'ah are founded upon their *'ilal* and not upon their *hikmah*. See Umar F. Moghul, "Approximating Certainty in Ratiocination How to Ascertain the *'illah* (Effective Cause) in the Islamic Legal System and How to Determine the Ratio Decidendi in the Anglo American Common Law," *Journal of Islamic Law* 4:125 (147, Fall/Winter 1999).

41. Moghul, supra note 40, p. 28 (citing Bernard Weiss, The Search for God's Law: Islamic Jurisprudence in *The Writings of Sayf al-Din al-Amidi*, p. 581 [1992]).

42. Consider Moghul, supra note 40, p. 196 (quoting Joseph Schacht, "Problems of Modern Islamic Legislation," *Studia Islamica* 12, p. 108 (1960), stating, "This solution of codifying Islamic law, states Professor Joseph Schacht, ignores the fact that "Islamic law being a doctrine and a method rather than a code . . . is by its nature incompatible with being codified, and every codification must subtly distort it"). Ibid., p. 197 (stating "Another important consideration pointed out by [Sherman] Jackson is that in codifying Islamic law, the Muslim jurists' authority is, for the most, replaced by the state, and Islamic law, it must be mentioned, is a jurist's law.") See Sherman Jackson, *Islamic Law and the State: The Constitutional Jurisprudence of Shihab al-din-al-Qaral*, p. xvii (1996). Also consider the following remark by Harlan Fiske Stone regarding the common law tradition: "By the very process of codification we would destroy those elements in the common law system

which have given it its vitality and its great practical utility; viz., the power of the judge to create law as it arises and the consequent capacity of the law itself to adapt itself to actual situations by the elaboration of minute and precise rules of action." Ibid., p. 196 (quoting Richard B. Cappalli, *The American Common Law Method* 62 [1997], quoting Harlan Fiske Stone, "Some Aspects of the Problems of Law Simplification" *Columbia Law Review* 23, 313 [1923], reported in *Essays in Jurisprudence and the Common Law*, p. 139 [Arthur Goodhart, ed., 1931]).

43. By this it is meant that the law's purposes are more likely than not (i.e., p > .5) to be achieved.

44. Ibid., p. 160 (stating, "The Hanafi and Shafi'i schools of law maintain that the illah must be both evident and constant. In their view, the *'illah* secures the *hikmah* in most cases, for the *'illah* is the probable indicator of the fulfillment of the *hikmah*. Their objection to the Maliki and Hanbali reasoning is that the *hikmah* of a particular ruling is often latent, obscure, and thus extremely difficult to ascertain with precision and clarity. However, the possibility that a *hikmah* could be *zahir* [evident] and *mundabit* [of inherent determinacy], in which case it could be properly regarded as the *'illah*, is not ruled out").

45. See supra note 5 and accompanying discussion.

46. Kilian Balz, *Breaking the Formalist Deadlock? Islamic Investment and Corporate Social Responsibility in Islamic Finance: Innovation and Authenticity*, pp. 251–252 (S. Nazim Ali, ed., 2011); Aamir Rehman, "The Relevance of Islamic Principles to the Global Financial Crisis, Panel Discussion on the Evolution of Global Financial Crisis from the Current Crisis," Harvard Law School Islamic Finance Project (March 16, 2009).

47. This point raises the questions of whether and how academic institutions or other organizations could be utilized to conduct such research and make policy recommendations.

48. See Shakil, supra note 39, p. 83 (quoting Imran Ahsan Khan Nyazee, *Islamic Jurisprudence*, pp. 196–97 [2000]).

49. Muhammad Nejatullah Siddiqui, Economics of Tawarruq: How Its Mafasid Overwhelm Its Masalih 2 (February 2007) (on file with the author).

50. Ibid., pp. 2–3.

51. Ibid., p.fa 3.

52. Ibid.

53. See Abdurrahman Habil, *Authenticity of Islamic Finance in Light of the Principle of Daman, in Islamic Finance: Innovation and Authenticity* (S. Nazim Ali, ed., 2011), 89.

54. Ibid., p. 108.

CHAPTER 18

Islamic Mortgages

BY DAVID LOUNDY
Chairman of the Board of Directors and Chief Executive Officer, and
Head of Religion-Based Financing for Devon Bank in Chicago

I n Islamic finance circles, it is the big mega-transaction high-value corporate
financing deals that make the news. However, at a retail level, it is home
buying that makes up the higher individual transaction volume. To purchase
a home, the demand for financing is high, the transaction sizes are reasonably
high in relation to customer resources, and thus the need for financial assistance in
making such a purchase is also high. On the investor side, home finance is often seen
as attractive because people will let a lot of other needs go unmet before they are
willing to risk their families being thrown out in the street for nonpayment on their
home financing. Home financing is also asset-backed financing with collateral that
has a readily accessible market should liquidation be necessary. Home financing is
seen as more stable than a lot of other potential financing transactions.

The number of homeowners versus home renters varies depending on country.
This is due to definitions of "ownership," differences in financing options, state
subsidies, ability to own and track property titles, cultural value of ownership,
and so forth. In many countries, elaborate homeownership infrastructures are
developed to support the long-term financing of home purchases. Such support
may be in the form of standardized products, purchase or payment subsidies, tax
benefits, or secondary-marketing funding mechanisms and the like.

Buying a home is often the most expensive purchase an individual or family
will ever make, and a cash-purchase is usually beyond most people's means. Prices
are often much higher than annual incomes.[1] Even where a family saves to buy a
home, prices often escalate faster than savings.

MAJOR FINANCING MODES

In the world of *Shariah*-compliant financing, there are a number of structures that
are used to finance home purchases. The most common are *murabaha* (sometimes
referred to as *bai bithaman ajil*), *ijara wa iqtina*, and diminishing *musharaka*.[2]

These modes are often confused by customers who pick up a little knowledge
but not enough to fully differentiate the forms. Thus it is not uncommon for
customers to ask about profit sharing upon the sale of a property when the financing
mode does not involve a profit or loss share.

Before discussing the various modes, it is worth discussing the intent of Islamic finance in general, and the criticism that attaches to these financing models. Islam prohibits *riba*. As a shorthand, *riba* is often defined as "interest" but more broadly the prohibition on *riba* covers exchanges based on the time-value of money. The prohibition prohibits investment returns without commensurate risk. It prohibits certain kinds of exchanges of like commodities with a differential in value built into the equation.

It is commonplace that an Islamic "financing" transaction is designed to mimic, as closely as possible, a conventional loan that Islam would otherwise prohibit. For some people, this in itself is sufficient to invalidate all of Islamic banking—the "intent" is the same. While many would agree that this state of affairs is not ideal, that does not mean that the entire industry lacks legitimacy. The products may be designed to be economically similar to conventional financing but, properly implemented, the products do involve distinct legal structures that differ from conventional loans in more or less subtle ways, some of which will be discussed later in this chapter. (In fact, some see the similarity to conventional financing as a means of showing the products' fairness—by allowing for comparison shopping, customers can see how costs for a religiously compliant product differ, and where differentials may be warranted and where they may be unfair.) While the products' similarities to conventional loans may help them fit into existing financial systems, the means by which the products reach their ends are intended to be wholly Islamic. As customer and investor risk tolerances evolve, there will be opportunities for Islamic finance products to distinguish themselves further in their economic performance from conventional loans and not just in their structures.

One of the most-used transaction forms for home financing is the *murabaha* transaction (sometimes referred to as *bai bithaman ajil*). This can be summarized as a "cost-plus sale" trade transaction. In such a transaction, the customer identifies the property it wishes to acquire. Generally the customer then arranges the details of the purchase transaction. However, instead of borrowing the money and purchasing the property with the loan proceeds, the customer then enters into an arrangement with the financier. The financier steps in and purchases the property instead of the customer. Properly done, and unlike with a conventional loan, the financier must take ownership of the property and have the risk of loss should something happen to the property. The more remote the financier's ownership of the property becomes, say, by using the customer as the financier's agent, the more doubt cast on the legitimacy of the transaction. Once the financier owns the property, the financier then sells the property to the customer, generally at a higher price, paid over time, but at no interest. The amount at which the property is sold to the customer may be calculated to be the approximate equivalent to how much the financier might expect to make over the term if the property acquisition was financed with an interest-bearing loan.

The *murabaha* transaction, however, is not a "loan." The customer was never given any money. It is a trade transaction. More specifically, it is a "credit sale" in which a piece of property is sold in installments by the financier to the customer. The customer is paying the financier its purchase price (essentially, all principal), rather than "returning" the financier's principle plus interest. This also means that the contract has no interest rate. Although an interest rate may have been used in calculating the financier's mark-up at which the financier sells the property to the customer, once the amount of the *murabaha* debt is calculated, as between the customer and the financier, the interest rate ceases to exist. If the customer does not pay on time, there is no interest rate "clock" ticking and increasing the amount of the debt owed. The financier takes on this additional risk over that present in a conventional loan. Similarly, if the customer wishes to pay early, say, in six months instead of 25 years, there is no interest rate that can be invoked to demand that the total of the *murabaha* debt be discounted in exchange for early payment—this becomes the customer's additional risk over that of a conventional loan. Realistically, the financier may discount the *murabaha* debt in exchange for early payment, either out of an internal desire for fairness or because an external legal system requires discounting independent of the terms of the transaction contracts, but the transaction structure itself does not require discounting. Ironically, in some places, insisting on full payment of the *murabaha* debt upon early payment may make a non-interest-bearing transaction a usurious one under local laws due to the imputation of an interest rate, which could potentially be very high.

An *ijara wa iqtina* transaction can be summarized as a "rent to own" transaction. It is also a form of trade transaction. Again, the customer identifies the property and agrees with the seller on basic terms. Again, the financier steps in and buys the property in the financier's name, with no money being lent to the customer. The customer then purchases the property from the financier, at the financier's cost, paid over time. At the end of the payment stream, the purchase price has been paid in full, and the customer takes title to the property. However, because the financier retains title to the property until it is paid off, the customer also pays the financier rent for the customer's use of the property. While it is not necessary to do so, it is often structured so that the combination of "on account" payments toward the purchase of the property along with lease payments resemble the same payments that would be made on a conventional amortizing loan.

Unlike a *murabaha* transaction, which is necessarily fixed at the beginning and does not change, while the purchase obligation in an *ijara* transaction may be fixed, the lease does allow for quite a bit of flexibility. The method by which the rent is calculated must be established up front, and any adjustments made must be outside of the control of the parties to the transaction, but the rent can be either fixed or tied to an index and adjusted at any agreed-upon interval. Some jurisdictions, however, may have legislation that limits how often the rent may change or how much the rent may change either during a defined period (say, per year) or over the life of the transaction.

Tying the rental rate to an index creates questions of legitimacy in some peoples' minds. Some people object that the index by which the rent is calculated may be an interest-based index, such as the U.S. Wall Street Journal Prime lending rate, or the London Inter-Bank Offering Rate (LIBOR). It is important to understand, however, that the transaction involves a lease payment. It is a payment made for use of a property owned by another. Although the setting of the lease payment may be tied to an interest-based index, it is not interest being paid—it is rent being paid. Because of the desire to distance Islamic financing transactions from the use of indices that create such questions of appearance, a number of Islamic banks and other policy and governance institutions recently launched the Thomson Reuters Islamic Interbank Benchmark Rate[3] as an alternative to using an interest-based index. Again, however, the index is only a benchmark by which returns are calculated, and the selection of index does not change the source of the returns being paid.

An *ijara* transaction does not suffer from concerns over discounting of debt as does a *murabaha* transaction. Because the property is being purchased from the financier at the financier's cost, there is no issue of discounting in exchange for early payment. To pay early, the customer simply pays off the balance of the purchase price and any fractional month's rent owed.

Because the financier owns the property for the duration of the transaction, the financier is required to bear certain risks associated with the property. Some of these expenses may be recouped as part of the rent paid by the customer. Again, the more of these responsibilities that are pushed off on the customer, the more the transaction's legitimacy is subject to being questioned.

A diminishing *musharaka* transaction is a form of partnership transaction. Unlike with a *murabaha* or *ijara* transaction, there is an investment aspect to a *musharaka* transaction based on a coinvestment by the financier and the customer, and the venture's performance over time.

As is the case with the other transactions, the customer identifies the property it would like to acquire and comes to an agreement with the seller on the basic terms of the purchase. The financier, in partnership with the customer, then steps in and they jointly purchase the property from the seller. In the case of a home acquisition, the financier generally puts in the bulk of the investment. The partnership agreement between the customer and the financier lays out each party's respective rights and obligations, such as which will provide maintainance and ensure that any taxes or other expenses are paid. As an investment, the agreement will provide how any profits from the venture are to be divided between the parties. Particular to an Islamic partnership, however, is a requirement that any losses be borne based on each party's level of equity investment in the venture. If one party has invested 75 percent of the money, that party generally bears 75 percent of any economic loss that may result. Again, the more that is done to skew this result, the more such attempts will call into question the legitimacy of the transaction.

While this may describe the arrangement at a static point in time, the transaction does not stay static. Specifically, because one party is using the property as its home, and the other is not using it at all, the customer will rent the financier's interest in the property. This lease will be essentially identical to the rental use of a property described in the *ijara* transaction above. As a "diminishing" *musharaka*, over time, the customer will buy out the financier's interest in the property according to the terms set in the partnership agreement. As a result, the percentage of the property on which rent is owed will diminish along with the financier's ownership percentage, and the transaction may end up looking very much like an amortizing loan in its "normal course" payment stream, though there may be a profit or loss share upon the sale of the property during the transaction that would not exist with a conventional loan.

Like an *ijara* transaction, there is no issue of discounting debt as there is with a *murabaha* transaction—the customer purchases the financier's remaining partnership interest as provided in the partnership agreement along with any fractional month's rent, and the transaction is complete. Also as is the case with an *ijara* transaction, a *musharaka* transaction allows the rent to be either fixed or tied to an independent index, which may vary over the life of the transaction.

Unlike the other financing models mentioned, a *musharaka* transaction is an equity transaction rather than a debt transaction. Both parties to a *musharaka* transaction have an ownership interest in the property, not just contractual rights to use or contractual rights to pay. As a result, some people consider this the only acceptable form of Islamic financing transaction to use; however, the Quran specifically endorses trade transactions and has no exclusive blessing reserved for equity transactions. Also, in some regulatory environments, *musharaka* transactions are either not allowed, or are restricted in their usage by some financiers, precisely because of the transaction's profit and loss share nature. Many banking regulators do not approve of supervised banks, for instance, agreeing in advance to share prospective losses with their customers.

CHOOSING ONE MODE OVER ANOTHER

So how does one choose which mode to use for financing a home purchase? To some extent, there may be no choice to make—you may be limited based on what providers are available in the area to finance a home purchase and which models those providers offer. If you do have a choice available, one issue worth considering is the degree of religious acceptability. While it would be great if this was a simple "yes" or "no" decision, in practice, the quality of products may vary along a continuum, and it is always best to examine options that are available to ensure that a particular option lives up to your personal standards of religious acceptability.

A common method of examining a product is to compare its performance and cost structure to that of a conventional loan. Often conventional loans have a very well-established infrastructure, both for costs and pricing, and thus disparities between them and Islamic financing transactions will be readily apparent. The difficulty with this view is that the volume of Islamic financing transactions is often much smaller, and the providers are often smaller, and thus there may not be the economies of scale necessary to get the best pricing that may be available for conventional loans. Additionally, the structure of an Islamic financing transaction often dictates some higher transaction costs that may not apply to conventional loans. For instance, with a *murabaha* or an *ijara* transaction, the property is purchased not once, but twice (once by the financier and once by the end customer), and thus any costs associated with a property transfer, such as deeds being recorded or transfer taxes may be (at least) double what they would be for a conventional loan. It is important to look at how these costs may differ over the expected life of the transaction, not just at a single point in time. Some structures may have some initial additional costs, while other structures may have ongoing additional costs.

One distinguishing characteristic between the different modes is timing of ownership. Customers often have strong cultural or personal preferences as to the actual ownership of their homes that may encourage the use of a particular model. Generally speaking, with a *murabaha* transaction, title is transferred to the customer at the beginning of the transaction, with a mortgage retained by the financier as security for the payment of the debt owed. With an *ijara* transaction, title is transferred only at the end of the transaction, with the financier retaining ownership to the property as a security interest during the duration of the transaction. For a diminishing *musharaka* transaction, ownership is transferred, in part, with each payment made over the duration of the transaction.

FINANCIAL PERFORMANCE

As to the financial performance of one structure over another, there is a fundamental difference between a *murabaha* transaction and either an *ijara* or a *musharaka* transaction with an adjustable rent. This is because the *murabaha* is necessarily fixed in its terms over the life of the transaction, whereas the rental-based transactions may fluctuate if the rent is tied to an index. Whether this is a good thing or a bad thing depends on whether you are the homebuyer or the investor, and based on whether the index is adjusting up or down. This distinction disappears when the rental transactions use a fixed rent that does not adjust over the life of the transaction.

However, there are other cases where there may be economic differences between the transaction types. In the case of a *murabaha* transaction, if payments are missed, the total of the *murabaha* debt owed does not change, even though such inconsistent payments would result in more interest being owed in the case of a conventional loan. In the case of one of the rent-based transactions, if a payment is missed, the purchase commitment has not changed and is still owed, but there may be back rent that is owed due to the missed payment. Of course, as a profit-and-loss-based transaction, a diminishing musharaka transaction may produce an economic difference if the property is sold prior to the transaction running full term, depending on the property's valuation on sale and how the profit-and-loss aspect is incorporated into the transaction.

It is worth pointing out that just as is the case with conventional loans, there exists opportunities to arbitrage between types of Islamic financing transactions. Such arbitrage also reduces the value of creation of more novel transaction forms that are tied, for instance, to non-interest-based indices. For instance, a customer may purchase a property with an *ijara* transaction in which the rent is tied to a national index of rents. However, if that index moves out of sync with conventional interest rates, the customer may be in a position to refinance the *ijara* with another Islamic financing transaction based on a cheaper interest rate rather than the independent rental index. As long as such refinances, and customers' proclivities toward them, are available, it will be hard to establish a pricing mechanism truly independent of conventional interest rates.[4]

On the homebuyer side, there may be other issues to recommend one transaction structure over another for use in purchasing a home, depending on the local laws where the structure is being used. These issues are most often related to concerns over ownership, or more often taxes that may have to be paid on the transactions. Some countries, such as the United Kingdom, have worked to amend local laws to put the tax status of Islamic financing transactions on equal footing with conventional loans used to finance home purchases by eliminating the otherwise applicable double "stamp duty" (transfer tax). Other jurisdictions have not been so generous, however. For instance, in New York state in the United States, there is a mortgage tax that applies to any mortgage recorded against a property based on the principle amount of the mortgage. While this is straightforward with a conventional mortgage, with a *murabaha* transaction, for instance, the entire debt to be paid over the term of the transaction becomes principle and thus taxable, resulting in far higher mortgage taxes owed than would be the case with conventional mortgages—or even with an *ijara* transaction. A financier is left to decide whether it will risk being only partially secured, whether it will not use *murabaha* as a financing model in the state, or whether it will risk pricing itself out of the market due to the taxes that apply to the transaction form.

INVESTOR RISK

On the investor side, the transaction forms provide three different types of risks to manage—credit risk, pricing risk, and liquidity risk. Credit risk is the smallest of the increase in risks to manage. The reason why is that the risk in an Islamic financing transaction is very similar between modes and as compared to conventional lending. When an investor decides to put its money at risk with a specific customer, whether in the form of a conventional loan, a debt-based Islamic financing transaction, or an equity-based Islamic financing transaction, the investor still wants to minimize risk. In any of these forms, the investor's capital is at risk. Whatever the form, the investor is hoping and expecting to be paid. Whatever the transaction form, the investor wants to know that the customer has the character and capacity to perform its obligations. As a result, the underwriting standards applied in evaluating the customer are not likely to differ based on the transaction form.

In the case of a *murabaha* transaction, the inability to "run the clock" does provide a potential additional risk to an investor, but this is not likely to present a profound difference. If a customer pays, there is no problem. If a customer stops paying and is unable to regain his or her footing, then whatever the transaction form, the investor and the customer are facing a workout in which the investor is trying to best preserve the value of its investment, regardless of whether there is an interest rate resulting in a yet larger amount owed that the investor will never recover. In the case of a customer who pays, stops paying, but then recovers, had there been a running interest rate, or had rent been accruing, the customer would owe more as a result of the gap that will not be owed with a *murabaha* transaction. In such a case, the gap is not likely to be very large, or the transaction would have ended up as a workout, and the investor is probably likely to be grateful to have made a recovery on its investment. In the case of a diminishing *musharaka*, there is additional credit risk due to the profit and loss sharing aspects of the transaction. Depending on how the contracts are arranged, there is also an arbitrage concern because a customer may be tempted to refinance out of a profit-sharing position and thus avoid any need to share gains with the financier. If there is a loss to be realized, the customer is in the same place they would be with a short sale on a conventional loan—in all likelihood, the financier will bear the largest share of the loss upon sale of the property. The same loss will be assumed with a *murabaha* or an *ijara* transaction if the customer does not have the resources to make the financier whole, and, in the case of an Islamic financing transaction, may have no obligation to make the financier whole outside of the surrender of the property.

PRICING RISK

Pricing risk relates to an investor tying up its money long-term. The longer the term of an investment, the greater the chance that what started out as a good deal winds up out of sync with current market conditions. While a customer may have an opportunity to refinance if market rates move away from the customer's favor, the investor may not have the ability to recast a transaction to match market conditions. The only chance that an investor may have to account for these pricing risks is upon the commencement of the transaction. This can be done by either restricting the term of the transaction, or by using a transaction, such as a rent-based transaction, that allows the tying of the pricing to an external index.

In the case of a *murabaha* transaction, the pricing is necessarily fixed at the commencement of the transaction. While a financier can always voluntarily make it easier for a customer to pay, the financier cannot make it harder. In some areas, where long-term fixed-rate home financing is the norm, this forces an Islamic financier to either fall out of step with the rest of the home financing market, or to accept long-term pricing risk. A *murabaha* "balloon," where payments are small and level until the last large one, may not be a reasonable means to reduce this risk because of the difficulties of refinancing a *murabaha* transaction should the customer be unable to make the balloon payment. For religious reasons, it may not be easy to refinance a *murabaha* balloon with another *murabaha* transaction. It is not the equivalent to a conventional loan where there may be a constantly renewing series of, say, five-year balloons.

A *musharaka* or *ijara* transaction eliminates some of this pricing risk by allowing the parties to tie the rent to an external index, which, if well chosen, will allow the removal of much of the market risk. It is worth pointing out, however, that for a long-term Islamic financing transaction, even though the rental rate may reset based on an index, that does not mean that the rental rate can be reset due to changes in the customer's credit quality.

Perhaps one of the most important investor risks is liquidity risk. Home financing transactions are generally relatively large, may be high volume, and are often long term. An investor is going to have limited capacity to finance home purchases using its own funds. While a large investor may have a large portfolio capacity with which to finance these transactions, certainly smaller investors, such as individuals or housing cooperatives, will not be able to finance many of these transactions without running out of available funds. In some cases, investors may issue bonds or otherwise raise funds to increase their "on balance sheet" portfolio capacity. However, another "off balance sheet" solution to this capacity limitation is to package home-financing transactions and sell them into the secondary market, generally as an Islamic bond, or *sukuk* offering. Such bonds focused on home financing are commonplace offerings from entities such as Cagamas in Malaysia, and Islamic financing transactions may be included with conventional mortgages in bonds issued in the United States by entities such as Fannie Mae or Freddie Mac.

The packaging of these home-financing transactions into securities is also affected by the transaction structure. Specifically problematic are *murabaha* transactions, as these are considered debt transactions of a fixed value. If a house costs 100, and it is sold to the customer for 150 paid over 25 years, the *murabaha* debt is 150. The equivalent loan principal, however, is 100. For a conventional loan, the financier may sell the loan into the secondary market for 102. Under most interpretations of Islamic law, however, the sale of a 150 debt for 102 would be a *ribawi* transaction and thus prohibited. This is the reason that some of the Cagamas bonds are not well regarded outside of Malaysia—while some Malaysian *Shariah* scholars have permitted such transactions, not all scholars accept such a securitization as permissible. A similar case exists in the United States where some scholars have permitted the discounted secondary market sales as being the only way available to avoid killing the bulk of the U.S. Islamic home finance industry due to its lack of capacity and better alternatives for producing needed liquidity.

The securitization of *musharaka* and *ijara* transactions, again, does not suffer from the same shortcoming that plagues *murabaha* transactions. Because these transaction forms involve a customer buying a property from the financier at cost, there is no issue of discounting debt. Because the income paid to the investor is in the form of rent, the transactions are considered, for investment purposes, to be transactions in real estate, not transactions in debt.

SUMMARY

As has been discussed, by design, there is often little performance difference between conventional mortgages and Islamic home financing transactions. There are small differences dictated by the necessities of the transaction structures and how they may fit with local laws. The industry, however, is still fairly immature. Most countries have not built up the infrastructure to support Islamic financing transactions, letting them stand on the same footing as conventional loans. There may be additional taxes and transaction costs, there may not be a robust secondary market, and the economies of scale may not exist, producing even pricing. Islamic financing is still, in many countries, a case of fitting a square peg into a round hole. There is generally interest and motivation to expand availability and encourage home ownership, but the level of accommodation differs widely. Some countries will establish laws making it easy to use Islamic structures to finance homes, but other countries will simply stand by their existing legal framework and invite providers to figure out how to make their products fit within that framework.

While the products do differ in structure from conventional loans, and in some cases may perform similarly to conventional loans, in most cases only customers that care about the religious aspects are willing to use these products because of their additional transaction costs—we do not see the "cross-over" use of these products by non-Muslims. The reason for this lack of cross-over is because of the products' "copy-cat" nature. The products offer nothing particularly unique in terms of performance—only religious accommodation. This is not a necessary state of affairs. However, for the products to offer unique traits that would appeal to a broader audience, there must be both investor acceptance of this difference, and customer acceptance. If investors are not willing to put their money into financing home purchases that may produce a different risk/reward balance than a conventional loan, there will be no creative products. Similarly, if customers are not willing to purchase homes using a financing model that may perform differently from their neighbors' financing transaction, or if they refinance whenever there is a divergence in performance, there will never be more creative products that may appeal to a broader audience.

As a result of the global credit crisis, the phrase "creative financing" is currently out of fashion. However, there is a determined search to define responsible "lending" that allows consumers long-term stability, such as that offered by home ownership. People are looking at Islamic financing models to see what they may have to offer. It is likely that Islamic financing models will be used with increasing frequency, and in places where they are not labeled as "Islamic" but are simply used as an expanded tool set in places where they can be made to perform differently from conventional loans.

NOTES

1. See "Global House Prices/Price to rent ratio/Price to income ratio," http://canadabubble .com/bubble-watch/73-global-house-pricesprice-to-rent-ratio-price-to-income-ratio .html, accessed October 30, 2011.
2. Istisna, or "build to suit," financing is considered outside the scope of this chapter, as it is more specialized in its use for construction financing, and is less of a commodity product than the other models discussed here.
3. See "Thomson Reuters Launches World's First Islamic Interbank Rate," http:// marketwire.com/press-release/thomson-reuters-launches-worlds-first-islamic-interbank -rate-nyse-try-1589778.htm, accessed November 29, 2011.
4. Please note that under *Shariah*, there are some limitations as to when a transaction may be refinanced, the details of which are beyond the scope of this chapter.

CHAPTER 19

Shari'a Quality Rating

NASIR ALI MERCHANT
Islamic International Rating Agency

INTRODUCTION

The "Shari'a" (the Islamic Law) Quality Rating aims to provide information and independent assessment regarding the Shari'a compliance of Islamic financial institutions or conventional institutions providing Islamic banking or financial services, as well as of Islamic financial products such as Sukuk.

Difference between a Credit Rating and Shari'a Quality Rating

The Shari'a Quality Rating differs from a Credit Rating in that the latter is an evaluation of the solvency of financial institutions and their capability and willingness to repay their obligations. A Shari'a Quality Rating, on the other hand, is rather concerned with issuing an independent opinion primarily about compliance mechanism for financial institutions, securities, or financial products.

Rationale for Shari'a Quality Rating

The differential factors between a Shari'a compliant institution from others is that it is required to be engaged in activities that are compliant with the Islamic Law (i.e., Shari'a) in accordance with the directives from the Shari'a Supervisory Board (SSB) of its own institution. Therefore it is very important for all the stakeholders, such as the investor, regulator, employees, and general public, to be confident that there is an independent, complete, and robust process to meet this requirement. Shari'a Quality Rating seeks to fulfill this very need of the stakeholders.

Benefits of Shari'a Quality Rating

The benefit for the investors would come from the comfort that the institution in which they are investing the funds has a proper mechanism to implement the Shari'a laws.

The benefit for the regulator comes from the fact that if most of the institutions are rated on a comfortable level in the Shari'a Quality rating mechanism, then the reputation of the regulator is enhanced.

The benefit for the institution obtaining Shari'a Quality Rating is that it can demonstrate the robustness of the mechanism of following the Shari'a fatwas as directed by its Shari'a Supervisory Board. This in turn can bring more confidence and investment in the institution.

One of the major benefits of the availability of ratings as a tool is to make sure that competition will lead to the improvement of Shari'a Quality of Islamic finance. And this will not happen unless a mechanism for such assessment of legitimacy and its disclosure to the public is in place.

Subjects discussed in this chapter will be more directed toward the Shari'a Quality rating of an entity rather than the product, as the later tends to be more specific to the particular needs of the product. The reader will be introduced to the Metholodogy, Training, and Standards used to rate individual companies according to the quality of its Shari'a oversight.

METHODOLOGY: THE MAIN INGREDIENTS

Shari'a Quality Rating tries to assess a large number of factors in an Islamic financial institution. The following sections describe the main constituents of this rating methodology.

Shari'a Supervisory Board (SSB)

Accounting and Auditing Organization for Islamic Financial Institution (AAOIFI)'s definition of SSB states that

> A Shari'a supervisory board is an independent body of specialized jurists in *fiqh almua'malat* (Islamic commercial jurisprudence). However, the Shari'a supervisory board may include a member other than those specialized in *fiqh alrnua'malat*, but who should be an expert in the field of Islamic financial institutions and with knowledge of *fiqh almua'malat*. The Shari'a supervisory board is entrusted with the duty of directing, reviewing and supervising the activities of the Islamic financial institution in order to ensure that they are in compliance with Islamic Shari'a Rules and Principles. The fatwas, and rulings of the Shari'a supervisory board shall be binding on the Islamic financial institution.

The purpose of SQR is not to make a judgment on how Shari'a scholars have reached an Islamic conclusion, that is, a fatwa on a certain process or product. This is the area of expertise of the scholars and it is assumed that they would issue a fatwa after complete understanding of the product or the process and understanding the consequences of their decisions.

During the rating exercise, one needs to take into account the local regulations, as an institution operating in a certain country will have to abide by those regulations, even if there is a perceived conflict.

What rating methodology seeks to understand is:

- The process of appointment of the Shari'a committee: Whether this is approved by the shareholders, by the board, or by the management. For a better-governed institution, it is also advisable that while the process starts at the management level, the final approval needs to be given by the shareholders of the organization.

- The remuneration of the Shari'a committee: The rating seeks to determine who is the authority to fix the remuneration, that is, either the management, the board, or the shareholders. Often shareholders vest this power through the board. The rating also tries to understand whether the remuneration is appropriate for the work done by the SSB, considering also the local context.
- Terms of agreement: Whether there is an explicit agreement between the SSB and IFI on the terms of engagement. Often while doing practical work, we have found that this document is sometimes not present or, if available, is quite vague. The rating also seeks to see whether the terms of engagement have actually been accepted by SSB.
- Composition of the SSB: While there is no fixed or optimal formula for composition of the SSB, the rating process inquires into how many members serve on the board and whether the number of members is sufficient to do justice to the work undertaken by IFI. In some jurisdictions, instead of a board, the regulators allow one person to be Shari'a Advisor, who is then assisted by a team of junior Shari'a scholars.
- Services of external consultants: The rating also seeks to understand whether the SSB has at its disposal the services of experts in the fields of business, economics, law, and others, and also whether such services have been obtained in the past.
- Engagement of SSB members: One of the concerns often expressed in the Islamic Finance arena is that there are a few Shari'a scholars who are present on a number of boards. Some scholars also offer their own consultancy services. While in principle there is nothing wrong with this, the concern expressed is that some of them may not be in a position to do justice to their work. The rating seeks to understand, to the best possible extent, the other engagements of the SSB member.
- Meeting of SSB: Again there is no fixed or optimal formula as to how many times an SSB shall meet. However, the rating expects that they will meet at least once a quarter. It was observed that although some SSBs meet only once a year, there are institutions where an SSB meets six or more times in a year. While the higher number of meetings is not a guarantee of better quality of work, nevertheless, a high frequency of meetings does suggest the commitment of SSB members and a possibility that the issues pertaining to Shari'a may be resolved quickly.
- Agenda and minutes of SSB: Moving from the number of meetings, the rating assesses the quality of the meetings through the agenda, minutes, and duration of the meetings. This gives an idea of the kind of discussions that have taken place, the issues presented in the meeting, and the process of giving decisions on those matters.
- Reports of SSB: The rating inquires into the kind of and quality of reports produced by the SSB. The SSB produces at least one report, which is included with the annual report of the company. The contents of the report are reviewed to see what assurances it is providing to the stakeholders. Other than that, the rating asks whether the SSB produces any other report. In a more ideal scenario, the SSB should produce a report on a quarterly basis based on the work that it has done during the quarter. While the number of reports is important, the quality of each report in terms of what it covers

and what kinds of suggestions it provides to the management for further improving the Shari'a governance process is equally if not more important.

- Standing of the SSB in the organization: The rating also seeks to understand the position of the SSB in the organizational hierarchy. Does it report to the shareholders or to the board or to the management? Also, are the SSB members also employees of the organization and, if so, is there a possibility that their organizational hierarchy may affect their work?
- Interaction of stakeholders with SSB: The rating considers what kind of interactions happen between the SSB and the other stakeholders of the organization. For example, is it mandatory for the SSB head to be available at the annual general meeting of the organization? Does the SSB or its head attend the board meetings regularly? Does the head of the organization attend all the SSB meetings to provide them with input from the management?
- Involvement of the SSB in employee selection: The rating seeks to understand whether there is a formal (and/or binding) role of the SSB in selection of employees for an IFI, particularly at the more senior level. Most of the time we have found that this is not present in the organization. An IFI, by its nature, is different from other organizations and therefore it may be better if the SSB is involved in the selection process of more senior employees.
- Participation of the SSB in training: The rating also tries to understand if the SSB members are involved in training; this suggests that the employees may be provided appropriate kinds of training as the SSB members tend to understand the organization better than outsiders.

Internal Shari'a Control (ISC)

The Internal Shari'a Control is the unit responsible for ensuring that the fatwas and decisions of the SSB are implemented in the organization. Therefore it is of prime importance to understand the composition, competence, and working mechanism of ISC. Below is a list of a few items that the rating seeks to understand.

- Process of appointment of the ISC: The ISC would be an integral part of the organization. Therefore it is important to understand who appoints the ISC and the reporting line of the ISC. Does the SSB have any control over appointments and the workings of the ISC?
- Mandate of the ISC: The rating seeks to establish the completeness of the document pertaining to the function and mandate of ISC and whether or not the SSB's approval has been taken in this regard.
- Independence of ISC: The rating seeks to understand if ISC is an independent unit in the organization or whether it is a part of the internal audit process. If it's a part of internal audit, does it have separate Shari'a auditors or do the same auditors who undertake the financial and compliance audit also do the Shari'a audit? Often in small or new organizations, the internal audit also does the Shari'a audit but for that they need to have the necessary competence. Also, there may be a need to have a clear policy of establishing a separate ISC unit over the next few years.
- Education and experience of ISC team: Continuing from the above, the rating seeks to establish whether the ISC team has the necessary education and

experience to carry out the Shari'a review work. It needs to be understood that a Shari'a review is a separate process from the general audit and even if the internal auditors are performing the Shari'a audit, they should have proper education, training, and experience to fulfill their duty.

- Continuous training: The rating also seeks to establish the mechanism through which continuous training is provided to the ISC team, including the head of the team. This is established through the courses that they attend and the additional qualifications that they obtain during their association with the organization. While most of the IFIs undertake this job seriously, at some organizations this process needs to be further strengthened.

- Documents for ISC work: The rating reviews the kind of policy documents and manuals available for the ISC team to carry out their duties. It establishes the completeness of those documents, approving authority, and the process of updating those documents, among other things.

- Planning of work: The due diligence done during SQR tries to understand the process of planning before the actual work. Planning includes obtaining background information about the activities to be reviewed, obtaining SSB fatwas in this regard, and communicating with all necessary people about the planning. This is normally done through an annual Shari'a audit plan. The rating seeks to establish the appropriateness of the plan and timing and approval of the plan. The plan should be approved at least two months before the beginning of the work and the approving authority should be both management and SSB. In some instances, this process was found to be incomplete or the plan was approved much later than the desired dates.

- Executing the plans of a Shari'a review: A review would determine whether the plan was implemented in the desired manner. What kind of documents were reviewed, what was the mode of collecting information from the management, what kind of documents were prepared to record the observations of the Shari'a reviewers, and were the observations discussed with the relevant management authorities?

- Shari'a review reports: The rating seeks to understand the frequency and detail of the reports that are prepared by ISC and the authority to whom these reports are sent. What is the process of discussing these reports with the management? If the observations are repetitive in nature, what is the process through which management seeks to eliminate these repetitive observations?

- Follow-up process: The whole process of planning, reviewing, and reporting would be of little relevance if a proper follow-up is not done on the reports produced by the ISC. The rating determines if there is a proper mechanism for the follow-up and what steps are taken if the observations made in the reports are not addressed.

ACCOUNTING STANDARDS

The rating seeks to determine which standards have been followed for the preparation of accounts of the company and, specifically, whether the company has followed Accounting and Auditing for Financial Institutions (AAOIFI) standards. In this regard, it should be noted that while a number of jurisdictions have adopted

AAOIFI standards for IFIs, there are some places where both AAOIFI and other standards are applicable and there are also a number of jurisdictions that have not adopted AAOIFI standards. The rating takes into account the local regulations and does not put any institution in an inferior position due to its compulsion of adopting local regulations.

TRAINING AND HUMAN RESOURCES

There is a general perception that the Islamic Finance professional does not have the optimal education and training to conduct his work. While this perception is not true, nevertheless the fact remains that the training and management of human resources needs to be strengthened in the IFIs. The rating seeks for the following:

- Training of the new employees: The rating tries to establish what kind of training is available for new employees. The new employees will be at various levels of management, that is, entry level, middle level, and senior level, and the rating review understands whether there are separate and complete programs available for the employees who have joined the organization, especially if they are coming with little or no knowledge about Islamic Finance.
- Continuous training: Apart from the training at the inception stage, the rating seeks to understand the mechanism through which the regular employees are provided training. This includes whether the employees are sent outside the organization or if there is an in-house mechanism available for training. It seeks to understand in quantitative terms how many hours the employee on average spends in training. This review of training is not restricted to the middle- or junior-level employees but, perhaps more important, the rating inquires into whether senior management and the board is also given training on the various developing aspects of Islamic finance.
- Quality of training: The rating tries to establish the quality of training imparted through the quality of trainers and training material and the relevance of training courses to the work of employees.
- Involvement of the SSB and ISC in training: The rating inquires into whether the SSB and ISC are involved in training the employees. It takes particular note if the SSB members are involved in designing and delivering the training course to employees. In a number of organizations, this process is still at a developing stage.
- Encouragement for additional qualifications: The rating determines whether the organization encourages the employees to obtain additional qualifications in Islamic Finance. This encouragement can come from allowing them to attend the training during work hours, reimbursing their fees, and developing a mechanism for the promotion of employees obtaining additional qualification.
- Impact of training on the employees: Training in itself will not yield results in the absence of a process that determines the impact of training on the work. The rating inquires whether such an evaluation system is available and whether there is a reward system established for those employees who can convert the training toward improvement in their work.

ZAKAT

Zakat is an important part of the Islamic Finance system. The rating seeks to establish what kinds of systems are in place for this purpose. The system for zakat is evaluated at three levels:

1. Shareholders: The rating inquires whether the organization has a mechanism to remind the shareholders about their duty for zakat and assist them for this purpose.
2. Board of directors, management, and employees: The rating also seeks to understand if the organization ensures that the board of direction as well as the employees are aware of their responsibilities.
3. Customers: The rating seeks to establish if the organization reminds the customers for the zakat and also if there a mechanism available to assist them in calculation of zakat. A number of organizations were visited that do not remind the customers about their zakat obligations, but do provide the facility to the customers for calculation of zakat.

CORPORATE SOCIAL RESPONSIBILITY

There are certain matters under CSR that by and large are considered mandatory for the IFIs. These include:

1. Policy for screening clients: While to some extent this policy will be similar to the Know-Your-Customer (KYC) policy prevalent in other conventional financial institutions, for IFIs this should also include a review of compliance of prospective clients' investments with Islamic law. Like for example, if the client is involved in industries that are forbidden by Islam. It is obvious to state that there must exist a written policy in this regard with the approval of SSB.
2. Policy for earnings and expenditure prohibited by Shari'a: Again, the rating seeks to establish if there is a written policy available, duly approved by the SSB. The policy should define a procedure where each of such material transactions is properly recorded, along with the reasons that such transactions were undertaken and how the IFI is going to dispose of such revenues (and assets and liabilities). The policy may also include the procedure of how to avoid such transactions in future in terms of finding alternatives for such kinds of transactions.
3. Policy for fair treatment with clients: The rating seeks to understand if there is a policy document available specifying what it will do to ensure fair treatment to the clients. One of the aspects in this regard is the disclosure policy, which is dealt with separately in this chapter. Other than disclosures, the policy will state how the IFI will develop and maintain its contracts; how it will seek approvals from the SSB; how it will help clients understand clearly the terms and conditions of the contract, the rights and responsibilities of each party, and the remedies available to each party in case of breach of terms of contracts. The policy may also state the SSB

policy on the issue of fees for late payments, in what circumstances the late payment charges will be taken, and how they will be allocated (e.g., to charity). It may also state the broad policy of allocating profits between the clients (as the fund owner) and the bank (as manager), and how deductions (like, for example, profit equalization reserve or investment risk reserve) would be made.

Apart from that, the CSR policy may also discuss the following:

1. Policy for Qard Hassan: The policy will state the decision about establishing a Qard Hassan, sources of these funds, and the purpose for which the funds would be utilized. The policy shall also state the appropriate decision-making body for the disbursement of these funds, how the IFI would ensure that those funds are returned on time, and the conditions for the write-off of such loans.
2. Policy for charitable activities: A large number of IFIs have established a fund for charitable activities. The rating seeks to understand the procedure in this regard. It looks for a policy that demonstrates how the fund was created and at what level the decision was taken. How is the mechanism ensured for allocating funds for charitable purposes? What is the guideline for selecting individuals or companies that will benefit from these funds? What is the decision-making body for approving allocation of such funds? Is there a process in the organization to evaluate the impact of charitable activities on the society? Many of the organizations visited have such a policy; however, in some cases, the policy did not cover all the aspects as mentioned above.

There may be certain other policy documents in this aspect, which may include policies for assisting some disadvantaged groups in the society, for promoting micro and small businesses, and for Waqf management.

Modes of Financing

The Shari'a Quality Rating seeks to understand what kinds of models of financing the IFI is engaged in and what it plans to do in future. While Islamic Finance allows for asset-based transactions like Murabaha and Ijarah, Shari'a scholars emphasize that along with that, the IFI must also ensure the inclusion of a decent proportion of equity-based transactions like Mudarabah and Musharakah. While it is easy to understand the limitations in this regard, in part due to the fact that the Islamic Finance Industry is a niche industry, nevertheless what the rating seeks to establish is the proportion between these two broad categories of transactions. Even if the percentage of equity-based transactions is very low, due to the limitations in the system, the rating seeks to determine whether the organization has the commitment to increase this proportion as and when circumstances permit. This is primarily done through a policy document that defines the commitment of the stakeholders in this regard and the process and time lines which through this objective would be achieved.

Identity and Corporate Image

All kinds of organizations have a certain appearance through which they are identified. This is not confined to banking and finance, but is present in all kinds of industries, such as manufacturing or service-related industries. Therefore, it is expected that an IFI would have a certain kind of identity and image by virtue of which it is defined as belonging to Islamic Finance. The list in this regard may be exhaustive, but certain things that are considered include:

1. Mission and Vision Statements: It is expected that an IFI would explain in its mission and vision statements about their identity as an institution offering Shari'a-compliant services and their commitment toward maintaining their business in this manner. A large number of organizations have shown their Islamic inclination in this regard.
2. Marketing Campaign: It is expected that the marketing campaigns and distributions of IFI reflect their Islamic identity. The marketing campaigns and documents should be ethically balanced, promoting business without an exclusive focus on profits that may induce inappropriate behavior/consumption and unsuitable products inconsistent with Islamic, social, and cultural norms.
3. Place for Prayers: It is expected that IFI would have a dedicated place for prayers and also a process through which it is made known to the employees that prayer times have arrived.
4. Dress Code: It is expected that IFI would persuade its employees to have a proper dress code as is prescribed by the religion.

Transparency and Disclosures

While all the conventional institutions have a policy for proper disclosures to stakeholders and to a large extent are driven by law, the responsibility for IFI in this regard increases as the religion puts special emphasis on complete transparency and disclosures. The list for disclosures may be very long but has been summarized for reference purposes. The organization should make arrangements for complete disclosures on the following:

- All financial aspects, such as assets, liabilities, equity, profit and loss, cash flow, and so forth.
- The profile of the shareholders, board of directors, and key management.
- The remuneration paid to the board of directors and key management.
- The views of the external parties like auditors, rating agencies, and regulators.
- The policy for screening clients.
- The policy for Zakah.
- The policy for Qard Hassan for charitable activities.
- The policy for distribution of profits to the clients.
- The policy for deductions in form of reserves like profit equalization reserves (PER) or investment risk reserve (IRR) or any other such reserves.
- The disclosures about the future direction of the company and the businesses that it plans to engage.

As mentioned earlier, the list can be exhaustive, but these items have been listed as examples.

It is equally important not only that the disclosures are made, but that they are made in a timely manner and through a medium that is readily accessible to a large number of stakeholders. For example, the website of the institution should have updated information. The disclosures regarding material financial and nonfinancial information and material changes should be published in leading newspapers, or sent to the customer's addresses. The bottom line is that the organization should try to ensure that all the stakeholders of the organization are informed with relevant and updated information.

CONCLUSION

Shari'a Quality Rating (SQR) was designed in order to give information to the external stakeholders about the robustness of the compliance mechanism of an Islamic Finance Institution. At the same time, SQR also attempts to encourage institutions to take steps to help improve the functioning of the organization and the development of Islamic Finance and the overall community. It is expected that over time, when the SQR service is accessed by a large number of institutions, it will promote a healthy competition among the institutions, which will lead to an improvement in the overall Islamic Finance system.

CHAPTER 20

Islamic Mutual Funds' Performance in Saudi Arabia

HESHAM MERDAD
Assistant Professor, Department of Finance and Economics, King Fahd University of Petroleum and Minerals

M. KABIR HASSAN
Associate Professor and Chair of Finance Department, University of New Orleans

Unfortunately, most empirical studies that discuss Islamic mutual funds still do not provide a definite answer to this most critical question: Is investing in Islamic mutual funds associated with any cost? Some researchers conclude that investing in Islamic mutual funds comes at no cost because their findings indicate no evidence of any performance differences between Islamic and conventional funds. On the other hand, some researchers conclude that there is a cost because Islamic mutual funds provide investors with lower returns than conventional mutual funds. Such inconsistent results exist because the Islamic finance and investment field is relatively new compared to its conventional counterpart, and thus the Islamic mutual fund literature is still in its infancy.

This chapter carries the critical investigation of Islamic mutual funds to Saudi Arabia. Saudi Arabia is considered an ideal experimental environment to conduct this empirical study for two important reasons: First, Saudi Arabia alone possesses the largest amount (52 percent) of Shariah-compliant fund assets worldwide.[1] Second, Saudi Arabia is considered one of the few countries that strictly adhere to the Shariah law. (In fact, Saudi Arabia's law is based on the Shariah law, the legislative framework that regulates all aspects of life, both private and public, in the Arab world.) Studying Islamic mutual funds located in Saudi Arabia is thus a good place to start investigating how Islamic mutual funds differ from their conventional counterparts.

In our study we assess the performance and risk factors of Saudi Islamic mutual funds relative to Saudi conventional mutual funds for the period from July 2004 to January 2010. (Although Merdad, Hassan, and Alhenawi (2010) address the same issue, their paper is only a case study that focuses on mutual funds managed by HSBC Saudi Arabia Limited.) To our knowledge, this is one of the first papers to examine the Islamic mutual fund issue in the context of Saudi Arabia. The uniqueness of this paper lies on the fact that it employs a unique sample set of Saudi funds in terms of size, diversity, investment goals, and geographical focuses.

Findings suggest that the risk-return profile of Saudi Islamic fund portfolios is sensitive to different geographical focuses: The locally focused Islamic fund portfolio underperforms its peer, the locally focused conventional fund portfolio, during the overall and bullish periods, but outperforms during the bearish and the financial crisis periods. In other words, locally focused Islamic funds punish investors less than conventional funds do during adverse economic conditions. This assessment is consistent with other studies, such as Abdullah, Hassan, and Mohamad (2007), and Kräussl and Hayat (2008). The results for the Arab- and internationally focused fund portfolios, however, indicate that the Islamic fund portfolio underperforms its peer the conventional fund portfolios during all four studies periods.

The body of this paper unfolds in five sections: (1) a discussion of the previous literature; (2) a presentation of the hypothesis and the data; (3) an explanation of the methodology; (4) an analysis of the empirical results; and (5) concluding statements.

PREVIOUS LITERATURE ON ISLAMIC MUTUAL FUNDS

Ahmed (2001) provides a primer on the performance of 13 Islamic equity funds in Saudi Arabia. Only two institutions manage these funds: the National Commercial Bank (NCB) and Al-Baraka Group. However, no statistical tests are reported in his study.

Elfakhani and Hassan (2005) use a sample of 46 Islamic mutual funds from January 1, 1997, to August 31, 2002, to examine the performance of Islamic mutual funds relative to Islamic and conventional market benchmarks. They employ different risk-adjusted performance measures such as Sharpe, Treynor, and Jensen alpha. Moreover, they employ an analysis of variances (ANOVA) statistical test. (The section in this paper titled "Methodology" explains how several of these and other measures mentioned throughout our article are calculated.) Overall, their findings suggest that no statistical evidence exists for any performance differences between Islamic funds and the employed market benchmarks. Their findings do suggest, however, that Islamic mutual funds offer a good hedging opportunity against market downturns.

Abdullah, Hassan, and Mohamad (2007) compare the performance of 14 Islamic funds relative to 51 conventional funds in Malaysia during the period from 1992 to 2001. They employ different measures such as the adjusted Sharpe, Treynor, adjusted Jensen alpha, Modigliani and Modigliani (MM) measure, and the information ratio. They find that conventional funds perform better than Islamic funds during bullish trends; but during bearish trends, Islamic funds perform better. They conclude that Islamic funds offer hedging opportunities against adverse market trends. They also find that conventional funds have diversification levels that are marginally better than Islamic funds, but both funds are unable to achieve at least 50 percent of the market diversification level.

Kräussl and Hayat (2008) use a sample of 59 Islamic equity funds (IEFs) to examine the performance of these funds relative to Islamic and conventional market benchmarks during the period from 2001 to 2006. They employ a set of measures such as the Jensen alpha, Sharpe, Treynor, Modigliani and Modigliani (MM), TT, and the information ratio. They find that, on average, there are no significant performance differences between IEFs and the employed market benchmarks (both Islamic and conventional). However, taking a closer look at the bear market of 2002, they document that IEFs significantly outperform the Islamic and conventional market indices using conditional CAPM. Analyzing the risk-return characteristics of IEFs, they find that IEFs possess superior systematic risk-to-return ratios. Therefore, they argue that these IEFs "seem most attractive as part of a larger fully diversified portfolio like a fund of funds."

Abderrezak (2008) examines the performance of 46 Islamic equity funds (IEFs) relative to conventional funds, ethical funds, and Islamic and conventional market indices during the period from January 1997 to August 2002. He employs several methodologies such as the Sharpe ratio, the single-factor model, and the Fama and French three-factor model. He finds that IEFs are 40 basis points more expensive than their conventional peers. Furthermore, he finds that IEFs consistently underperform their respective Islamic and conventional market benchmarks. Finally, he finds that there are no performance differences between IEFs and ethical funds.

Muhammad and Mokhtar (2008) use weekly net asset values (NAVs) of nine Islamic equity funds in Malaysia in order to examine their performance relative to the Islamic market index, Kuala Lumpur Syariah Index (KLSI), for the period from 2002 to 2006. To assess the performance of these funds, they employ the Sharpe and Treynor ratios. They find that eight of these funds underperform the KLSI. However, they find mixed results when they employ the standard deviation, coefficient of variation, and the systematic risk (beta) to assess the level of risk associated with these funds.

Hoepner, Rammal, and Rezec (2009) use a unique dataset of 262 Islamic equity funds from 20 countries and 4 regions in order to examine the performance of these funds relative to constructed portfolios that have exposure to national, regional, and global markets. Furthermore, they control for different investment styles by employing a conditional three-level Carhart model. The results show that Islamic funds from eight nations (mostly from the western regions) significantly underperform their respective equity market benchmarks, that funds from only three nations outperform their respective market benchmarks, and that Islamic funds are biased toward small stocks. Furthermore, they find that Islamic funds from the Gulf Cooperation Council (GCC) and Malaysia do not significantly underperform their respective market benchmarks nor are they biased toward small stocks. Finally, they argue that Islamic equity funds can offer hedging opportunities because their investment universe is limited to low debt-to-equity ratio stocks.

Merdad, Hassan, and Alhenawi (2010) use a sample of 28 Saudi mutual funds managed by HSBC in order to examine the performance of 12 Islamic funds relative to 16 conventional funds during the period from January 2003 to January 2010. They use several performance measures such as the Sharpe, Treynor, Modigliani and Modigliani (MM), TT, and Jensen alpha. Furthermore, they employ the Treynor and Mazuy model to examine the Saudi funds' selectivity and market-timing abilities. They find that Islamic funds underperform conventional funds during both full and bullish periods, but outperform during bearish and financial crisis periods. Furthermore, they find that HSBC managers are good at showing timing and selectivity skills for Islamic funds during the bearish period, and for conventional funds during the bullish period. They also assert that Islamic mutual funds do offer hedging opportunities during economic downturns.

THE HYPOTHESIS AND DATA

This section explains details and processes necessary to understand the development of our hypothesis and the sources of Saudi mutual find data we examine.

Hypothesis Development

An Islamic mutual fund is similar to a conventional mutual fund in many ways; however, unlike its conventional counterpart, an Islamic mutual fund must conform to the Shariah law mandates. Shariah law encourages the use of profit-loss sharing and partnership schemes, and forbids *riba* (interest), *maysir* (gambling and pure games of chance), and *gharar* (selling something that is not owned or that cannot be described in accurate detail, i.e., in terms of type, size, and amount) (El-Gamal, 2000).

Shariah law also governs several aspects of an Islamic mutual fund such as its asset allocation (portfolio screening) and many investment and trading practices. In terms of asset allocation, conventional mutual funds can freely choose between debt-bearing investments and profit-bearing investments, and invest across the spectrum of all available industries. On the other hand, an Islamic mutual fund must set up screens in order to select those companies that meet its qualitative and quantitative criteria set by the Shariah guidelines.

Qualitative screens are used to filter out companies based on the nature of their business or securities that contain one of the Shariah-prohibited elements (e.g., involving *riba*, *maysir*, or *gharar*) or companies that conduct unethical business practices per Shariah law, such as companies that are engaged in nonmedical alcohol, pork production, illegal and intoxicating drugs, gambling, adult entertainment, and tobacco. As a result, all fixed-income instruments such as corporate bonds, treasury bonds and bills, certificates of deposit (CDs), preferred stocks, warrants, derivatives (e.g., options and futures) are excluded from the Islamic funds' investment universe.

As for governing investment and trading practices, Islamic mutual funds cannot trade on margin (i.e., they cannot use interest-paying debt to finance investments). Also, they cannot engage in sale and repurchase agreements (i.e., repos or buy-backs), which are considered akin to indirect interest charges. Also, unlike conventional mutual fund managers, Islamic fund managers are not allowed to speculate. An Islamic economic unit is expected to assume risk after making a proper assessment of risk with the help of information. Only in the absence of information or under conditions of uncertainty is speculation akin to a game of chance and considered reprehensible (Elfakhani and Hassan, 2005).

Based on these conditions and exceptions, there are several restrictions and necessary adaptations to which Islamic mutual funds must commit before they can earn an Islamic title. Due to the nature of these restrictions and necessary adaptations, the following can be hypothesized: First, an Islamic mutual fund exposes investors to less risk than a conventional mutual fund. Second, an Islamic mutual fund rewards investors with less return than its conventional mutual fund counterpart.

Saudi Mutual Fund Data

The Saudi mutual fund sample is unique in terms of size, geographical focuses, diversity, and investment objectives. To our knowledge, no other study has used a Saudi mutual fund sample in such a way as the one employed in this study.

The selected sample data consist of daily net asset values (NAVs) of 143 out of 234 mutual funds available in Saudi Arabia during the period from July 2004 to January 2010. Information on these funds is obtained from three main sources: (1) the official site of the Saudi Stock Exchange (Tadawul),[2] (2) the official site of HSBC Saudi Arabia Limited,[3] and (3) the Zawya database.[4]

The Saudi mutual fund population has six regional focuses: local, international, Arab, Asian, U.S., and European. To enhance comparability, this empirical study gathers the five latter (i.e., all the nonlocal) mutual funds into one regional group called "internationally focused funds." As a result, Saudi mutual funds that make up the sample used in this empirical study will have only three main geographical focuses (local, Arab, and international). Locally focused funds are those that invest in assets located only in Saudi Arabia. Arab-focused funds are those that invest in assets located only in countries that are members in the League of Arab States, excluding Saudi Arabia. Finally, internationally focused funds are those that invest in assets located in all countries, excluding Saudi Arabia and members of the above-mentioned Arab league.

Exhibit 20.1 breaks down the sample based on the three geographical focuses (local, Arab, and international), investment goal classifications (growth, income, capital preservation, and income and growth), and Shariah compliancy subcategories (Islamic and conventional).

Results show that there are 67.13 percent (96 of 143) Islamic mutual funds and 32.87 percent (47 of 143) conventional mutual funds. These percentages are quite similar to those for the entire Saudi mutual fund population where there are 62.39 percent Islamic mutual funds and 37.61 percent conventional mutual funds. Also, results show that out of 143 funds in the sample, there are 82 (57.34 percent), 19 (13.29 percent), and 42 (29.37 percent) funds that are local, Arab, and internationally focused, respectively.

Furthermore, results show that locally focused Islamic funds that are growth orientated dominate the sample with 33 out of 143 funds (23.08 percent). However, Islamic and conventional funds that are internationally focused *and* have an income and growth investment objective are the least represented in the sample, where there are only 2 out of 143 funds (1.40 percent) of each type. Also, results show that among all 20 available Arab-focused funds in the Saudi mutual fund population (not tabled), there are 19 Arab-focused funds in the fund sample and they are all growth oriented and only invest in equity.

The end-month Saudi Interbank Offering Rate (SIBOR) with one-month maturity has been collected from Bloomberg for the period from July 2004 to January 2010. In this empirical study, SIBOR with one-month maturity serves as a proxy for the monthly risk-free rate.

Exhibit 20.1 Mutual Fund Sample Based on Geographical Focus, Investment Goal, and Shariah Compliancy

The following table presents the selected sample of 143 mutual funds in Saudi Arabia for the period from July 2004 to January 2010. Funds are categorized based on three main geographic focus categories (local, Arab, and international), Shariah-compliancy subcategories [Islamic (Is.) and conventional (Cn.)], and investment goal classifications [growth (G), income (I), capital preservation (CP), and income and growth (I&G)].

	Investment Goal Classifications and Shariah Compliancy Subcategories																
	G				I				CP				I&G				Total	
Category	Is.	%	Cn.	%	Is.	%	Cn.	%	Is.	%	Cn.	%	Is.	%	Cn.	%	Total	%
Local	33	23.08	20	13.99	8	5.59	4	2.8	7	4.9	3	2.10	4	2.80	3	2.10	82	57.34
Arab	14	9.79	5	3.50	0	0	0	0	0	0	0	0	0	0	0	0	19	13.29
International	14	9.79	3	2.10	8	5.59	4	2.80	6	4.20	3	2.10	2	1.40	2	1.40	42	29.37
Total	61		28		16		8		13		6		6		5		143	
%	42.66		19.58		11.19		5.59		9.09		4.2		4.2		3.5		100	
Total funds based on investment goal classification	89				24				19				11				143	
%	62.24				16.78				13.29				7.69					

There are six different market indices used to benchmark the performance of Saudi funds, and they fall under two main groups. The first group includes the Islamic indices: (1) Global Index of the GCC Islamic (to mainly benchmark locally focused Islamic funds),[5] (2) MSCI Arab Markets Domestic Islamic Index excluding Saudi Arabia (to mainly benchmark Arab-focused Islamic funds), and (3) MSCI World Islamic Index (to mainly benchmark internationally focused Islamic funds). The second group includes the conventional indices: (1) Tadawul All Share Index (TASI) (to mainly benchmark locally focused conventional funds), (2) MSCI Arabian Markets Domestic Index excluding Saudi Arabia (to mainly benchmark Arab-focused conventional funds), and (3) MSCI World Index IMI (to mainly benchmark internationally focused conventional funds).

The monthly historical prices of both Islamic and conventional indices from July 2004 to January 2010 are obtained from three main sources: 1) the official website of the Saudi Stock Exchange (Tadawul), (2) the official website of the Global Investment House,[6] and (3) the MSCI Barra.[7]

Finally, to enhance comparability, the sample timeframe is divided into four different periods depending on different stock market trends in Saudi Arabia. Such division will hold throughout the entire study. These periods are: the overall sample period (from July 2004 to January 2010), the bullish period (from July 2004 to February 2006), the bearish period (from March 2006 to January 2010), and the recent 2008 financial crisis period (from September 2008 to January 2010).

METHODOLOGY

This section of the chapter details the methodology used to calculate non-risk-adjusted returns and simple risk-adjusted performances measures.

Non-Risk-Adjusted Returns

From the daily net asset values (NAVs), the monthly NAVs for all funds are calculated as follows:

$$R_{it} = \left(\frac{NAV \text{ on Last Day of Month } (t)}{NAV \text{ on First Day of Month } (t)} - 1 \right) \qquad (20.1)$$

where R_{it} is the monthly return for fund (i) at month (t).[8]

Note that the methodology is based on using a portfolio approach in order to diversify away fund-specific risks and to facilitate comparison between the entire Islamic and conventional Saudi mutual funds industries. Thus, Saudi mutual funds in the selected sample are grouped into portfolios based on the following characteristics: the funds' three main geographical focuses (local, Arab, and international), the funds' Shariah compliancy (Islamic and conventional), and four different stock market trends in Saudi Arabia (overall, bull, bear, and the recent 2008 financial crisis periods). Also, note that all formed portfolios are equally weighted and formed on a monthly basis.[9]

Fund portfolios are calculated as follows:

$$R_{pt} = \frac{\sum_{i=1}^{n_t} R_{it}}{n_t} \tag{20.2}$$

where R_{pt} is the monthly return for portfolio (p) during month (t), n_t is the total number of individual funds during month (t), and R_{it} is defined as in equation (20.1).

Simple Risk-Adjusted Performance Measures

This section explains several calculation methods and ratios in the financial industry to measure and adjust risk.

Sharpe and Modified Sharpe Ratios

The Sharpe ratio is derived by Sharpe (1966) as an absolute risk-adjusted performance measure. Thus, no market benchmark is needed to calculate the Sharpe ratio. The idea of this ratio is to see how much additional return is received for additional volatility of holding the risky asset over the risk-free asset. Thus, this ratio measures how well a portfolio compensates investors for the additional risk taken. The risk in the Sharpe ratio is measured by the portfolio's standard deviation, which represents the total risk (diversified and undiversified risks). This ratio is useful in ranking portfolios because a higher ratio is only warranted if return is higher with the same level of risk or if the risk is lower with the same level of return. The Sharpe ratio is calculated as follows:

$$S_p = \frac{\overline{R_p} - \overline{RF}}{\sigma(R_p)} \tag{20.3}$$

where:

S_p: Sharpe ratio for portfolio (p)
$\overline{R_p}$: Average of monthly return for portfolio (p)
$\overline{RF}$: Average risk-free rate measured by SIBOR one-month maturity
$\sigma(R_p)$: Standard deviation of the portfolio (p)

The Sharpe ratio is very difficult to interpret, however, and could lead to spurious portfolio ranking when the excess return is negative. In other words, it is not always true that the portfolio with the higher ratio is the best portfolio. For example, if two portfolios, A and B, have excess average returns of –5 percent and standard deviation of 20 and 25 percent, respectively, then the Sharpe ratio is –0.25 and –0.20 for A and B, respectively. According to the Sharpe ratio, portfolio B has a superior risk-return profile when compared to portfolio A. However, that is not true because B is considered more volatile than A.

As a result, Israelsen (2005) proposes a modification to the Sharpe ratio to overcome the spurious portfolio ranking when excess return is negative. He introduces an exponent to the denominator of the Sharpe ratio that is equal to the portfolio excess return divided by its absolute value. It is worthy to note that the modified Sharpe ratio coincides with the original ratio when the excess return is positive, and is superior to the original ratio when the excess return is negative. Therefore, only the modified Sharpe ratio results are reported in this study and it is calculated as:

$$Modified\ S_p = \frac{\overline{R_p} - \overline{RF}}{\frac{\overline{R_p} - \overline{RF}}{\sigma(R_p)(|R_p| - \overline{(RF|)})}}$$ (20.4)

where *Modified S_p* is the modified Sharpe ratio for portfolio (*p*) and the reset is defined as in equation (20.3).

MM Measure

Modigliani and Modigliani (1997) propose this measure as a relative risk-adjusted performance measure. It is very intuitive and easy to interpret and it is also considered an extension to the Sharpe ratio. This measure shows the return the portfolio would have gained if it had the same risk as the market benchmark. The risk is measured using the total risk: the standard deviation. According to this measure, the most appealing portfolios are those with the highest MM values. MM is calculated as follows:

$$MM_p = (\overline{R_p} - \overline{RF})\frac{\sigma(RM)}{\sigma(R_p)} + \overline{RF}$$ (20.5)

where MM_p is the Modigliani and Modigliani measure for portfolio (*p*), $\sigma(RM)$ is the standard deviation of the market index, and the rest is defined as in equation (20.3).

Treynor Ratio

The Treynor ratio measures the excess returns over the riskless asset that could be earned per unit of market risk. Market risk or systematic risk is measured by the portfolio's beta, which measures the co-movement of the portfolio with the market. Since the Treynor ratio normalizes excess return by the portfolio's beta instead of the portfolio's standard deviation, then the Treynor ratio is superior to the Sharpe ratio in assessing the risk-return profile if the fund is a part of a larger fully diversified portfolio. This is because the relevant risk in such circumstance is the market risk (beta). It is calculated as follows:

$$TR_p = \frac{\overline{R_p} - \overline{RF}}{\beta_p}$$ (20.6)

where $\overline{R_p}$ and $\overline{RF}$ are defined as in equation (20.3) and

TR_p: Is the Treynor ratio for portfolio (*p*)
β_p: Portfolio's beta—estimated using a single-factor model (CAPM) as is shown in following equation:

$$R_{pt} - RF_t = \alpha_p + \beta_p(RM_t - RF_t) + \varepsilon_{pt}$$

where:

R_{pt}: Returns for portfolio (p) at months (t)

RF_t: Risk-free rate measured by SIBOR with one-month maturity at months (t)

α_p: The intercept for portfolio (p). In this model it is called the Jensen alpha index

β_p: Beta or the market risk for portfolio (p)

RM_t: Return on the market index at months (t)

ε_{pt}: The error term with zero mean

TT Index

The TT index is an extension to the Treynor ratio. The TT measure is proposed by Bodie, Kane, and Marcus (2005) and it measures the excess return of a portfolio per unit of systematic risk (beta) above the excess return on the market, which by definition has a beta of one. Thus, one can look at the TT measure as the difference between the portfolio and the market Treynor ratio. It is calculated as follows:

$$TT_p = TR_p - (\overline{RM} - \overline{RF}) \qquad (20.8)$$

where TT_p is the TT index for portfolio (p), $\overline{RM}$ is the average monthly return for the market index, TR_p is defined as in equation (20.6), and $\overline{RF}$ is defined as in equation (20.3).

EMPIRICAL RESULTS

This section includes the three exhibits, each in two parts, which present the empirical results for locally focused, Arab-focused, and internally focused portfolios.

Locally Focused Portfolios

Exhibit 20.2 reports the results for only the locally focused fund portfolios. The market indices used to benchmark the performance of these locally focused portfolios are also locally focused, and they are: (1) GCC Islamic: Global Index of the GCC Islamic, and (2) TASI: Tadawul All Share Index.

Exhibit 20.2—Panel A—reports the non-risk-adjusted return mean and variance results for the locally focused fund portfolios and market benchmarks. The results indicate that the locally focused Islamic portfolio during the entire studied period is 0.17 percent less risky than its peer, the locally focused conventional portfolio, and that difference in the total risk is considered statistically significant at 1 percent. Even though the locally focused Islamic portfolio has less total risk exposure than its peer, the results during the entire studied period indicate that there is no statistical evidence that shows any differences in the performance (non-risk-adjusted return) between the Islamic and the conventional locally focused fund portfolios.

Breaking the sample period into the bull, bear, and financial crisis periods, the results indicate that the locally focused Islamic portfolio is also considered

Exhibit 20.2 Results for the Locally Focused Portfolios

The total sample consists of 143 mutual funds (96 Islamic and 47 conventional) in Saudi Arabia for the period from July 2004 to January 2010. From these funds, equally weighted monthly return portfolios are formed based on the following characteristics of the funds: (1) geographical focus (local, Arab, and international), (2) Shariah compliancy (Islamic and conventional), and (3) different market trends (overall period: July 2004 to January 2010, bull period: July 2004 to February 2006, bear period: March 2006 to January 2010, and financial crisis period: September 2008 to January 2010). The SIBOR with one-month maturity serves as a proxy for the risk-free rate. All panels in this table report the results for only the locally focused portfolios. The market indices used to benchmark the performance of these locally focused portfolios are also locally focused, and they are: (1) GCC Islamic—Global Index of the GCC Islamic, and (2) TASI—Tadawul All Share Index. Panel A reports the non-risk-adjusted return mean and variance results. Panel B reports the results from the simple risk-adjusted performance measures (modified Sharpe, MM, Treynor, and TT). All standard errors from all regressions are corrected for heteroscedasticity problems using White's (1980) correction test.

Panel A: Non-Risk-Adjusted Returns (Locally Focused Portfolios)

	Overall Period		Bull		Bear		Financial Crisis	
	Mean	Variance	Mean	Variance	Mean	Variance	Mean	Variance
Islamic portfolio	0.31%	0.17%	2.27%	0.04%	-0.52%	0.21%	-0.77%	0.20%
Conventional portfolio	0.38%	0.34%	3.66%	0.08%	-1.02%	0.39%	-1.40%	0.48%
The difference	**-0.07%**	**-0.17%***	**-1.38%***	**-0.04%***	**0.49%**	**-0.18%****	**0.63%**	**-0.28%****
GCC Islamic	0.94%	0.96%	7.70%	0.29%	-1.94%	0.97%	-3.36%	0.98%
TASI	0.46%	0.91%	5.89%	0.24%	-1.85%	1.03%	-1.61%	1.00%

Panel B: Simple Risk-Adjusted Performance Measures (Locally Focused Portfolios)

	Index	Overall Period		Bull		Bear		Financial Crisis	
		Islamic	Conv.	Islamic	Conv.	Islamic	Conv.	Islamic	Conv.
Modified Sharpe Ratio		0.96%	1.82%	96.23%	116.06%	-0.04%	-0.08%	-0.04%	-0.10%
MM	GCC Islamic	0.37%	0.45%	5.48%	6.55%	-1.44%	-1.75%	-1.84%	-2.05%
	TASI	0.36%	0.45%	5.00%	5.97%	-1.49%	-1.82%	-1.86%	-2.07%
Treynor	GCC Islamic	0.11%	0.21%	8.71%	9.85%	-1.95%	-2.34%	-2.13%	-2.43%
	TASI	0.09%	0.18%	5.11%	6.03%	-1.81%	-2.14%	-1.99%	-2.20%
TT	GCC Islamic	-0.55%	-0.46%	1.29%	2.43%	0.26%	-0.13%	1.33%	1.03%
	TASI	-0.09%	-0.01%	-0.49%	0.43%	0.31%	-0.02%	-0.28%	-0.50%

*, **, *** significant at 10%, 5%, 1%, respectively.

313

significantly less risky than its peer, the locally focused conventional portfolio. That is, the locally focused Islamic portfolio is considered 0.04, 0.18, and 0.28 percent less risky than its peer during the bull, bear, and financial crisis periods and that difference in the total risk is statistically significant at 10, 5, and 5 percent, respectively.

The performance results of these portfolios from each of these three market trends (bull, bear, and financial crisis) also reveal the following: During the bull period the locally focused Islamic portfolio significantly (at 10 percent) underperforms the locally focused conventional portfolio, and that underperformance averages about 1.38 percent per month. However, during the bear and financial crisis periods, the non-risk-adjusted return results reveal no statistical evidence that shows any differences in the performance between the Islamic and the conventional locally focused portfolios.

Exhibit 20.2—Panel B—reports the simple risk-adjusted performance measures for the locally focused fund portfolios. The results indicate that the locally focused Islamic portfolio underperforms its peer, the locally focused conventional portfolio, during both the overall and bull periods, but performs less badly than its peer during the bear and financial crisis periods. This is true regardless of the simple risk-adjusted performance measure used and regardless of the locally focused market benchmark employed to adjust for risk.

Arab-Focused Portfolios

Exhibit 20.3 reports the results for only the Arab-focused fund portfolios. The market indices (i.e., the Morgan Stanley Capital Index, MSCI) used to benchmark the performance of these Arab-focused portfolios are also Arab-focused and they are: **(1) MSCI Arab Mrk Islamic**, MSCI Arab Markets Domestic Islamic Index excluding Saudi Arabia and **(2) MSCI Arab Mrk Index**, MSCI Arabian Markets Domestic Index excluding Saudi Arabia.

Exhibit 20.3—Panel A—reports the non-risk-adjusted return mean and variance results for the Arab-focused fund portfolios and market benchmarks. The results indicate that the Arab-focused Islamic portfolio during the entire studied period is 0.14 percent more risky than its peer, the Arab-focused conventional portfolio, and that difference in the total risk is considered statistically significant at 10 percent. Even though the Arab-focused Islamic portfolio is more risky than its peer, the results during the entire studied period indicate that no statistical evidence exists to indicate any differences in the performance between the Islamic and the conventional Arab-focused fund portfolios.

Breaking the sample period into the bull, bear, and financial crisis periods, the results show that during the bull and financial crisis periods there is no statistical evidence that any risk differences between the Islamic and conventional Arab-focused fund portfolios exist. However, the results during the bear period indicate that the Arab-focused Islamic fund portfolio is considered 0.19 percent more risky than its peer, the Arab-focused conventional fund portfolio, and that total risk difference is statistically significant at 10 percent.

Looking at the performance of these Arab-focused portfolios during these three periods (bull, bear, and financial crisis periods), the non-risk-adjusted return results

Exhibit 20.3 Results for the Arab-Focused Portfolios

The total sample consists of 143 mutual funds (96 Islamic and 47 conventional) in Saudi Arabia for the period from July 2004 to January 2010. From these funds, equally weighted monthly return portfolios are formed based on the following characteristics of the funds: (1) geographical focus (local, Arab, and international), (2) Shariah compliancy (Islamic and conventional), and (3) different market trends (overall period: July 2004 to January 2010, bull period: July 2004 to February 2006, bear period: March 2006 to January 2010, and financial crisis period: September 2008 to January 2010). The SIBOR with one-month maturity serves as a proxy for the risk-free rate. All panels in this table report the results for only the Arab-focused portfolios. The market indices used to benchmark the performance of these Arab-focused portfolios are also Arab-focused and they are: (1) MSCI Arab Mrk Islamic—MSCI Arab Markets Domestic Islamic Index excluding Saudi Arabia and (2) MSCI Arab Mrk Index—MSCI Arabian Markets Domestic Index excluding Saudi Arabia. Panel A reports the non-risk-adjusted return mean and variance results. Panel B reports the results from the simple risk-adjusted performance measures (modified Sharpe, MM, Treynor, and TT). All standard errors from all regressions are corrected for heteroscedasticity problems using White's (1980) correction test.

Panel A: Non-Risk-Adjusted Returns (Arab-Focused Portfolios)

	Overall Period		Bull		Bear		Financial Crisis	
	Mean	Variance	Mean	Variance	Mean	Variance	Mean	Variance
Islamic portfolio	-0.03%	0.45%	2.54%	0.26%	-1.12%	0.49%	-2.43%	0.67%
Conventional portfolio	0.70%	0.31%	3.67%	0.19%	-0.56%	0.31%	-1.69%	0.50%
The difference	*-0.73%*	*0.14%**	*-1.13%*	*0.06%*	*-0.56%*	*0.19%**	*-0.74%*	*0.17%*
MSCI Arab Mrk Islamic	0.98%	0.95%	6.33%	1.23%	-1.29%	0.67%	-3.64%	1.14%
MSCI Arab Mrk Index	0.77%	0.61%	4.63%	0.58%	-0.87%	0.55%	-3.05%	0.99%

Panel B: Simple Risk-Adjusted Performance Measures (Arab-Focused Portfolios)

	Index	Overall Period		Bull		Bear		Financial Crisis	
		Islamic	Conv.	Islamic	Conv.	Islamic	Conv.	Islamic	Conv.
Modified Sharpe Ratio		-0.02%	7.79%	44.48%	77.24%	-0.10%	-0.05%	-0.21%	-0.13%
MM	MSCI Arab Mrk Islamic	-0.16%	1.03%	5.21%	8.84%	-1.35%	-0.95%	-3.18%	-2.58%
	MSCI Arab Mrk Index	-0.08%	0.88%	3.68%	6.18%	-1.19%	-0.84%	-2.97%	-2.41%
Treynor	MSCI Arab Mrk Islamic	-0.61%	0.94%	12.34%	12.54%	-1.92%	-1.43%	-3.57%	-3.04%
	MSCI Arab Mrk Index	-0.47%	0.74%	6.83%	8.86%	-1.79%	-1.30%	-3.45%	-2.90%
TT	MSCI Arab Mrk Islamic	-1.33%	0.23%	6.30%	6.49%	-0.37%	0.12%	0.17%	0.69%
	MSCI Arab Mrk Index	-0.97%	0.24%	2.48%	4.51%	-0.65%	-0.16%	-0.30%	0.25%

*, **, *** significant at 10%, 5%, 1%, respectively.

indicate that no statistical evidence exists for any differences in the performance between the Islamic and the conventional Arab-focused fund portfolios.

Exhibit 20.3—Panel B—reports the results from the simple risk-adjusted performance measures for the Arab-focused fund portfolios. The results indicate that the Arab-focused Islamic portfolio underperforms its peer, the Arab-focused conventional portfolio, during both the overall and bull periods. However, contrary to what is observed when analyzing locally focused portfolios (Exhibit 20.2—Panel B) the results from this panel reveal that the Arab-focused Islamic portfolio performs worse than the Arab-focused conventional portfolio during both the bear and financial crisis periods. These results hold regardless of the simple risk-adjusted performance measure used and regardless of the Arab-focused market benchmark employed to adjust for risk.

Internationally Focused Portfolios

Exhibit 20.4 reports the results for only the internationally focused fund portfolios. The market indices used to benchmark the performance of these internationally focused portfolios are also internationally focused (per Morgan Stanley Capital Index, MSCI) and they are: **(1) MSCI World Islamic**—MSCI World Islamic Index and **(2) MSCI World Index**—MSCI World Index IMI.

Exhibit 20.4—Panel A—reports the non-risk-adjusted return mean and variance results for the internationally focused fund portfolios and market benchmarks. The results indicate that the internationally focused Islamic portfolio during all studied periods is considered slightly more risky than its peer, the internationally focused conventional portfolio. That is, the Islamic portfolio is 0.01, 0.003, 0.01, and 0.04 percent more risky than its peer during the overall, bull, bear, and financial crisis periods and that difference in the total risk is statistically significant at 1, 1, 5, and 10 percent, respectively. Even though the internationally focused Islamic portfolio has more total risk exposure than its peer, the results during all studied periods indicate that no statistical evidence exists to show any differences in the performance between the Islamic and the conventional internationally focused fund portfolios.

Exhibit 20.4—Panel B—reports the results from the simple risk-adjusted performance measures for the internationally focused fund portfolios. The results from this panel are very similar to the results reported in Exhibit 20.3—Panel B, where the Arab-focused portfolios are discussed. The results indicate that the internationally focused Islamic fund portfolio underperforms its peer, the internationally focused conventional fund portfolio. This is true using all measures, regardless of the sample period under examination and regardless of the internationally focused market benchmark employed to adjust for risk.

CONCLUSION

This paper investigates one of the most important issues raised in the Islamic mutual fund literature: Does investing in Islamic mutual funds come at any cost? Findings from this paper suggest that the risk-return profile of Saudi mutual fund portfolios depends on the geographical focuses of these fund portfolios. That is,

Exhibit 20.4 Results for the Internationally Focused Portfolios

The total sample consists of 143 mutual funds (96 Islamic and 47 conventional) in Saudi Arabia for the period from July 2004 to January 2010. From these funds, equally weighted monthly return portfolios are formed based on the following characteristics of the funds: (1) geographical focus (local, Arab, and international), (2) Shariah compliancy (Islamic and conventional), and (3) different market trends (overall period: July 2004 to January 2010, bull period: July 2004 to February 2006, bear period: March 2006 to January 2010, and financial crisis period: September 2008 to January 2010). The SIBOR with one-month maturity serves as a proxy for the risk-free rate. All panels in this table report the results for only the internationally focused portfolios. The market indices used to benchmark the performance of these internationally focused portfolios are also internationally focused and they are: (1) MSCI World Islamic—MSCI World Islamic Index and (2) MSCI World Index— MSCI World Index IMI. Panel A reports the non-risk-adjusted return mean and variance results. Panel B reports the results from the simple risk-adjusted performance measures (modified Sharpe, MM, Treynor, and TT). All standard errors from all regressions are corrected for heteroscedasticity problems using White's (1980) correction test.

Panel A: Non-Risk-Adjusted Returns (Internationally Focused Portfolios)

	Overall Period		Bull		Bear		Financial Crisis	
	Mean	Variance	Mean	Variance	Mean	Variance	Mean	Variance
Islamic portfolio	0.21%	0.02%	0.62%	0.004%	0.04%	0.03%	−0.13%	0.06%
Conventional portfolio	0.29%	0.01%	0.45%	0.001%	0.21%	0.02%	0.06%	0.03%
The difference	*−0.08%*	*0.01%****	*0.17%*	*0.003%****	*−0.18%*	*0.01%***	*−0.19%*	*0.04%**
MSCI World Islamic	0.41%	0.21%	1.04%	0.08%	0.14%	0.26%	−0.62%	0.57%
MSCI World Index	0.24%	0.25%	1.15%	0.07%	−0.15%	0.32%	−0.66%	0.73%

Panel B: Simple Risk-Adjusted Performance Measures (Internationally Focused Portfolios)

	Index	Overall period		Bull		Bear		Financial Crisis	
		Islamic	Conv.	Islamic	Conv.	Islamic	Conv.	Islamic	Conv.
Modified Sharpe Ratio		−0.001%	1.17%	51.97%	53.19%	−0.004%	−0.001%	−0.01%	−0.001%
MM	MSCI World Islamic	0.08%	0.33%	1.73%	1.77%	−0.43%	0.04%	−0.58%	−0.05%
	MSCI World Index	0.06%	0.33%	1.65%	1.68%	−0.50%	0.02%	−0.67%	−0.07%
Treynor	MSCI World Islamic	−0.22%	0.07%	2.12%	3.73%	−0.79%	−0.26%	−0.71%	−0.15%
	MSCI World Index	−0.25%	0.07%	2.06%	3.79%	−0.89%	−0.29%	−0.81%	−0.17%
TT	MSCI World Islamic	−0.36%	−0.07%	1.36%	2.98%	−0.66%	−0.13%	0.01%	0.57%
	MSCI World Index	−0.21%	0.11%	1.19%	2.92%	−0.47%	0.13%	−0.05%	0.58%

*, **, *** significant at 10%, 5%, 1%, respectively.

assessing the locally focused fund portfolios, the total risk results indicate, as hypothesized, that statistical evidence exists to show that the Islamic fund portfolio is, indeed, less risky than the conventional fund portfolio. This is true regardless of the period under examination. Even though the Islamic fund portfolio is less risky, there is no statistical evidence that the performance (using non-risk-adjusted returns) of such portfolio is different from that of the conventional fund portfolio. This is also true during all periods except the bull period.

However, when risk is adjusted, results provide a different story. As hypothesized, all simple risk-adjusted performance measures show that the locally focused Islamic fund portfolio underperforms its peer, the locally focused conventional fund portfolio, during both the overall and bull periods. That underperformance could mainly be attributed to the lower level of risk assumed. Furthermore, all risk-adjusted performance measures show that the locally focused Islamic fund portfolio performs less badly than its peer, the locally focused conventional fund portfolio, during both the bear and financial crisis periods. Such finding is not surprising given that the Islamic fund portfolio has less risk exposure, and therefore is not going to perform worse than the conventional fund portfolio in adverse market trends. Note that all these results are observed regardless of the market benchmark used to adjust for risk.

As a result, it would be beneficial for investors to include Saudi Islamic mutual funds that are locally focused in their portfolios during a bear and/or a crisis period in order to help hedge the downside risk in such adverse economic conditions. Finally, it is worthy to note that such results are very much consistent with other studies, such as Abdullah, Hassan, and Mohamad (2007), and Kräussl and Hayat (2008).

On the other hand, results from analyzing both Arab- and internationally focused fund portfolios are very similar to each other and at the same time contrary to both the hypothesis and the results from analyzing the locally focused fund portfolio.

That is, the variance results indicate that during the overall period, both Arab- and internationally focused portfolios are considered more risky than their respective conventional counterparts. However, the non-risk-adjusted return results during the same period indicate that there is no statistical evidence that any differences exist in performance between the Islamic and the conventional fund portfolios that are both Arab- and internationally focused. Similar results are observed during all other three periods (bull, bear, and financial crisis periods) for the internationally focused fund portfolios. However, for the Arab-focused fund portfolio, these results are only observed during the bear period.

When risk is adjusted, however, the results indicate that the Islamic fund portfolio, regardless if it was Arab- or internationally focused, performs worse than its peer, the conventional fund portfolio. This is true regardless of: the simple risk-adjusted measure used, the sample periods under examination, and the market index used to adjust for risk.

In sum, investors might benefit by considering investments that adhere to the precepts of the Shariah law (i.e., locally focused funds that invest in assets located only in Saudi Arabia). On the other hand, it seems that investors might incur a cost by considering investments that adhere to the Shariah law (i.e., Arab- and/or internationally focused funds that invest in assets located in countries other than Saudi Arabia).

NOTES

1. See "GCC Mutual Fund Industry Survey 2010." Dr. Gıyas Gökkent, the editor and author of this study, which was released on February 9, 2011, is the Group Chief Economist in the National Bank of Abu Dhabi. (GCC refers to the Gulf Cooperation Council; see note 5.) The study can be found in the following link: www.nbad.com/economic/countries/gcc_mf_industry_survey2010.php. Note that *Shariah* is an Arabic word that refers to the legislative framework that regulates all aspects of life, both private and public.
2. Source: www.tadawul.com.sa.
3. Source: www.hsbcsaudi.com.
4. Zawya is one of the leading Middle Eastern business information firms. Their main website is www.zawya.com. We would like to express deep appreciation to Mr. James Randall, the international business manager, for providing access to the database.
5. Gulf Cooperation Council (GCC) members include Saudi Arabia, United Arab Emirates, Kuwait, Qatar, Bahrain, and Oman. This index is used to benchmark locally focused Islamic funds instead of the Saudi Arabia Islamic index because the later is relatively new and lacks data that goes back to July 2004.
6. Source: www.globalinv.net.
7. Source: www.msci.com. The MSCI data contained herein is the property of MSCI Inc. (MSCI). MSCI, its affiliates (and any other party involved in, or related to, making or compiling any MSCI data) make no warranties with respect to any such data. The MSCI data contained herein is used under license and may not be further used, distributed or disseminated without the express written consent of MSCI.
8. Conventionally, mutual fund returns are calculated as capital gains plus income (dividends). However, because obtaining data on dividends was very difficult, dividends are not accounted for in this study.
9. According to Hoepner, Rammal, and Rezec (2009), "It is common practice to analyze portfolios of assets with religious of ethical characteristics based on equal weighted rather than value weighted portfolios. This practice ensures a focus on the assets religious or ethical characteristics and substantially reduces the risk of bias due to idiosyncratic return characteristics of a specific asset." This is why in this empirical study all formed portfolios are equally weighted portfolios.

REFERENCES

Abderrezak, Farid. 2008. "The Performance of Islamic Equity Funds: A Comparison to Conventional, Islamic and Ethical Benchmarks." Retrieved July 27, 2012, from Failaka: http://s3.amazonaws.com/zanran_storage/www.failaka.com/ContentPages/42957265.pdf.

Abdullah, Fikriyah, Taufiq Hassan, and Shamsher Mohamad. 2007. "Investgation of Performance of Malaysian Islamic Unit Trust Funds." *Managerial Finance*, 33:2, 142–153.

Ahmed, Osman Babikir. 2001. *Islamic Equity Funds: The Mode of Resource Mobilization and Placement*. Jeddah, Saudi Arabia: Islamic Research and Training Institute, Islamic Development Bank.

Annuar, M., Mohamad Shamsher, and M. Ngu. 1997. "Selectivity and Timing Evidence from the Performance of Malaysian Unit Trusts." *Pertanika Journal of Social Science and Humanities* 5:1, 45–57.

Bodie, Zvi, Alex Kane, and Alan Marcus. 2005. *Investments*, 6th edition. New York: McGraw-Hill.

Carhart, Mark M. 1997. "On Persistance in Mutual Fund Performance." *Journal of Finance* 52:1, 57–82.

Chen, C., F. Cheng, S. Rahman, and A. Chan. 1992. "A Cross Sectional Analysis of Mutual Fund's Market Timing and Security Selection Skill." *Journal of Business Finance and Accounting* 19, 659–674.

Elfakhani, S., and M. Kabir Hassan. 2005. "Performance of Islamic Mutual Funds." *Economic Research Forum*, 12th Annual Conference, Cairo, Egypt, 1–33.

El-Gamal, Mahmoud Amin. 2000. "A Basic Guide to Contemporary Islamic Banking and Finance." Unpublished paper, Rice University: Retrieved July 27, 2012, www.lariba.com/knowledge-center/islamic-banking-guide.pdf.

Fama, Eugene F., and Kenneth R. French. 1993. "Common Risk Factors in the Returns on Stocks and Bonds." *Journal of Financial Economics* 33, 3–56.

Grinblatt, Mark, and Sheridan Titman. 1992. "The Persistence of Mutual Fund Performance." *Journal of Finance* 47:5, 1977–1984.

Hoepner, Andreas G. F., Hussein Guizar Rammal, and Michael Rezec. 2009. "Islamic Mutual Funds' Financial Performance and Investment Style: Evidence from 20 Countries." Retrieved July 27, 2012, from Social Science Research Network (SSRN): http://ssrn.com/abstract=1475037.

Israelsen, Craig L. 2005. "A Refinement to the Sharpe Ratio and Information Ratio." *Journal of Asset Management* 5:6, 423–427.

Jegadeesh, Narasimhan, and Sheridan Titman. 1993. "Returns to Buying Winners and Selling Losers: Implications for Stock Market Efficiency." *Journal of Finance* 48:1, 65–91.

Jensen, Michael C. 1967. "The Performance of Mutual Funds in the Period 1945–1964." *Journal of Finance* 23:2, 389–416.

Kon, S. 1983. "The Market Timing Performance of Mutual Fund Managers." *Journal of Business* 56, 321–347.

Kon, S., and F. Jen. 1979. "The Investment Performance of Mutual Funds: An Empirical Investigation of Timing, Selectivity and Market Efficiency." *Journal of Business* 63, 261–278.

Kräussl, Roman, and Raphie Hayat. 2008. "Risk and Return Characteristics of Islamic Equity Funds." Retrieved July 27, 2012, from Social Science Research Network (SSRN): http://ssrn.com/abstract=1320712.

Lintner, J. 1965. "The Valuation of Risk Assets and the Selection of Risky Investments in Stock Portfolios and Capital Budgets." *Review of Economics and Statistics* 47:1, 13–37.

McDonald, John G. 1974. "Objectives and Performance of Mutual Funds." *Journal of Finance and Quantitative Analysis* 13, 311–333.

Merdad, Hesham, M. Kabir Hassan, and Y. Alhenawi. 2010. "Islamic versus Conventional Mutual Funds Performance in Saudi Arabia: A Case Study." *Journal of King Abdulaziz University: Islamic Economics* 23:2, 161–198.

Modigliani, Franco, and Leah Modigliani. 1997. "Risk Adjusted Performance." *Journal of Portfolio Managemen* 23, 45–54.

Muhammad, N. M., and M. Mokhtar. 2008, June. "Islamic Equity Mutual Fund Merformance in Malaysia: Risk and Return Analysis." Paper presented in the Malaysian Finance Association (MFA), 11th International Conference at Kuching, Malaysia.

Obaidullah, Mohammed. 2005. *Islamic Financial Services*. Jeddah, Saudi Arabia: Islamic Economics Research Center.

Rao, Dabbeeru N. 2006a, August 1. "Performance Analysis of Mutual Funds in Saudi Arabia." Retrieved March 14, 2010, from Social Science Research Network (SSRN): http://ssrn.com/abstract=921523.

Rao, Dabbeeru N. 2006b, November. "A Four-Step Model to Evaluate Mutual Funds: A Case-Study for Equity Mutual Funds in Saudi Arabia." Retrieved April 13, 2010, from Social Science Research Network (SSRN): http://ssrn.com/abstract=946937.

Rao, Dabbeeru N. 2006c, December 21. "Analyzing Balanced, Debt and Liquid Funds: A Case-study of Mutual Funds in Saudi Arabia." Retrieved April 20, 2010, from Social Science Research Network (SSRN): http://ssrn.com/abstract=952975.

Shamsher, Mohamad, M. Annuar, and Hassan Taufiq. 2000. "Investment in Unit Trusts: Performance of Active and Passive Funds." Proceedings of FEP Seminar 2000: Issues in Accounting and Finance 2, Universiti Putra Malaysia Press, Serdang, 129–141.

Sharpe, William F. 1964. "Capital Asset Prices: A Theory of Market Equilibrium under Conditions of Risk." *Journal of Finance* 19:3, 425–442.

Sharpe, William F. 1966. "Mutual Fund Performance." *Journal of Business* 39:1, 119–138.

Treynor, Jack, and Kay Mazuy. 1966. "Can Mutual Funds Outguess the Market?" *Harvard Business Review* 44, 131–136.

White, Halbert. 1980. "A Heteroscedasticity Consistent Covariance Matrix Estimator and a Direct Test of Heteroscedasticity." *Econometrica* 48, 817–838.

CHAPTER 21

Shari'ah-Compliant Real Estate Investment in the United States

JOHN L. OPAR

Partner, Shearman & Sterling LLP

The *Shari'ah* countenances an asset-based system of investment that promotes ethical activities and prohibits the use of conventional leverage. Given these basic tenets, it is no surprise then that real estate has been at the core of the brief history of compliant investment in the United States. The reasons are understandable. First, real estate offers an obvious target for an asset-based investment system. Second, concerns about noncompliant (or unethical) use of the asset can be readily evaluated by review of leases and visual inspection. Finally, the very nature of real estate as a tangible asset eases the concerns with participating in an investment with noncompliant leverage. While one must consider the effects of project-level debt, there is no need to be concerned about internal or imbedded company-level leverage, as has plagued compliant private equity and capital markets investors. The possibilities for noncompliance are lessened relative to investments in operating businesses.

In the earliest days, compliant investors targeted the least complex of real estate holdings—parking garages. They afforded investors a steady revenue stream and a nonmanagement-intensive asset, with essentially no concern for noncompliant use. As compliant investment has evolved in the United States, multifamily has become the asset class of choice, again offering a steady revenue stream with limited issues of noncompliant use. Verging further afield, some investors have targeted industrial properties, which typically house only one or two tenants, often in the logistics business, thus keeping relatively simple the diligence for noncompliant uses. Investments in office properties have also been undertaken, with single tenant properties the easier targets.

THE PROPERTY UNDER CONSIDERATION

For purposes of our discussion, let's posit a compliant investor considering an investment in a multifamily rental property in New York City, with some additional but limited commercial space for rent. Let's further assume that fee title to the property (perhaps through a condominium structure) will be acquired and that the investor is not adverse to third-party leverage on the property if the same can be structured in compliance with the *Shari'ah*.

Perhaps the first decision for the investor will be whether to undertake the investment outright (and likely hire third-party property management and leasing agents) or to pursue the investment in a joint venture with a local operator/investor, most likely a noncompliant person. The choice between the approaches—wholly owned versus joint venture—raises obvious tradeoffs. Does the investor consider itself sufficiently well versed in local market conditions to underwrite and close on a remote investment, and does it have in place in the United States a sufficient infrastructure to manage the asset? While the investor could engage third-party agents to assist with property management and residential and commercial leasing, none of those agents will have invested anything more than its time and thus will not have aligned its interest with the investor by putting its own capital at risk.

On the other hand, while a third-party co-investor/operator solves the interest alignment problem, the question remains whether the co-investor will recognize and appreciate the matters of concern to the compliant investor. Today, many if not most significant real estate operators understand at least the basic principles underlying the *Shari'ah* and are prepared to entertain compliant structures. Non-compliant investors will, however, view the structures as less than ideal—limiting the universe of financing sources to those willing to accommodate Islamic structures; raising additional operating issues, such as treatment of interest on security deposits; and perhaps restricting uses of any commercial space at the property. (For instance, can ancillary retail be leased to banks or to restaurants serving alcohol?)

Let us assume that the investor has elected to acquire the property in joint venture with a local operator.

DILIGENCE

One of the basic principles of Islam is the prohibition against investment in activities that are *haram* (forbidden). This proscription extends to investing in real estate that is used for impermissible purposes. Classic examples of forbidden uses include tobacco and alcohol, pork, interest-based banking, insurance, gambling, pornography, and weaponry. Thus it is important that the advisers to a compliant investor review any current or contracted-for uses of the property to confirm the absence of any impermissible activities.

As noted above, the analysis with respect to multifamily property is quite straightforward and, while attention must be paid to common areas and amenities, one would be surprised to discover any impermissible activities in the basic use of the residential portion of the property.

Complications arise, however, when, as in our example, use of the property extends to commercial activities. Thus, even a small amount of commercial space to be used for nonliving purposes requires careful examination. If the space is leased to service providers such as dry cleaners, there should be no issue; and one can catalog any number of activities that would similarly be permitted. But warning signs should appear if current uses include food establishments or groceries that would likely serve or sell any number of products considered *haram*.

The legal documentation relating to the entire investment should be reviewed. The presence of conventional debt secured by the property should not present a problem so long as the debt is satisfied upon the compliant investor's acquisition of the property or a structure is put into place isolating the compliant investor from any project-level debt. Leases should also be reviewed. Many states require that residential tenants receive interest on security deposits; in other cases, interest is provided for by contract as a minor tenant benefit. Where interest payments are optional, the offending provisions can be removed from the lease form, thus reducing the level of noncompliance as leases roll. Where interest payments on security deposits are mandated by law, the investor and its property manager should then consider how to isolate any deposit accounts and to avoid any noncompliant payments flowing from or to the investor.

The existing residential leases will almost certainly be in the name of the current property owner. Who will assume these leases upon our client's investment? Will they be assumed by the compliant investor (the master tenant in the typical *ijara*, or lease, structure), or will they be assumed by the master landlord? If the former, will tenants question entering into leases with a party not obviously the owner of the property? If the proposed landlord is XYZ Tenant LLC, have we complicated leasing operations?

COMPLIANCE DETERMINATION

First, a brief note on the compliant investor's advisory team. As U.S. legal advisers, we expect to work closely with the client's *Shari'ah* adviser or board of advisers on issues of possible noncompliance. Typically, the adviser will review the rent roll for the investment property and a narrative of the uses of any commercial space to identify possible noncompliance. The adviser may also consider uses of common amenities for the residential tenants. Is there a clubhouse (or the equivalent) where alcohol is served? For some investors even joint male/female uses of common facilities will be examined.

At present, there does not exist any single public or private governing authority in Islamic jurisprudence to offer uniform prescriptions on issues of impermissible activities or interpretation of other principles of compliant investment. While there is some movement toward a consistent cross-jurisdiction approach, for now, in each transaction, one must rely on the client's adviser to determine the acceptability of an investment in light of this client's sensibilities. While there is a great deal of uniformity on basic principles, there can be, as one would expect, divergence on some of the particulars. While recognition of some "impurity" in a compliant investment has been with us for at least the last decade—largely traceable to the Dow Jones fatwa in 1998—there may still be differing views on the permissible levels of such impurity.

- Will the presence of a single automated teller machine (ATM) amount to noncompliance of the entire asset? Advisers may agree that immaterial noncompliance will not render an entire investment impermissible—perhaps the stand-alone ATM would fall into this category. If so, must the income associated with that ATM still be segregated and donated to charity?
- May a compliant investor acquire a residential property subject to a lease to a restaurant that serves alcohol if the space occupied by the restaurant or the rental income from the restaurant, or both, are not material to the overall investment? If so, is all revenue from the restaurant deemed tainted or can a portion of the rent be isolated on the basis of the square footage of the

beverage operation or the percentage of revenue derived by the restaurant from sales of alcohol? Should the monies be segregated at the revenue or income level?

- Some advisers have agreed that immaterial, but impermissible, operations at a potential investment property can be segregated. In this approach, space occupied by a noncompliant tenant is effectively "walled off" from the investor by literally excluding the leased space, for so long as the space is occupied for impermissible purposes, from the premises leased to the compliant investor. This pseudo-condominium structure would trap any noncompliant revenue of the master landlord. Query then whether that revenue must be donated to charity or whether it can be used to pay expenses relating to obligations, such as maintaining property or casualty insurance, retained by the master landlord, recognizing that there may remain some indirect benefit to the tenant, albeit remote.

The practice is not uniform, but many compliant investors would expect that the investment target, the structure of the investment, and the relevant documentation would be expressly approved by the *Shari'ah* adviser(s) and be the subject of a formal fatwa. With programmatic investments, investors may be comfortable with a program or fund-level review by the adviser(s) with attention to specific transactions as the need arises.

THIRD-PARTY FINANCING

Virtually all commercial properties these days bear some level of secured debt, as the use of leverage can enhance returns. For the compliant investor, directly acquiring a property with conventional leverage is not an option. Similarly, it would be difficult for a compliant investor to invest in an existing ownership vehicle where conventional leverage is involved.

All cash or all equity investments are not uncommon among compliant investors. Those comfortable with the property being subject to conventional debt have customarily used the project *ijara* structure to isolate the investor from any responsibility for the conventional debt. However, as Umar Moghul describes in Chapter 17, *Stepping Forward, Backward, or Just Standing Still?* a few alternatives to the project-level *ijara* structure are being developed.

THE *IJARA* STRUCTURE

A simplified version of the project-level *ijara* structure is shown in Exhibit 21.1. The structure is designed to isolate the investor from any obligation with respect to any conventional debt encumbering the property. Title to the asset is taken in the name of a corporate or similar vehicle. From time to time these vehicles have been owned by corporate service providers. But, more recently, lenders such as Fannie Mae and Freddie Mac have preferred that the ownership entity/borrower be owned by more substantial, though necessarily noncompliant, deal participants. The project is then leased through the *ijara* to an entity owned by the compliant investor and any joint venture partner. Thus the only obligation of the compliant investor and

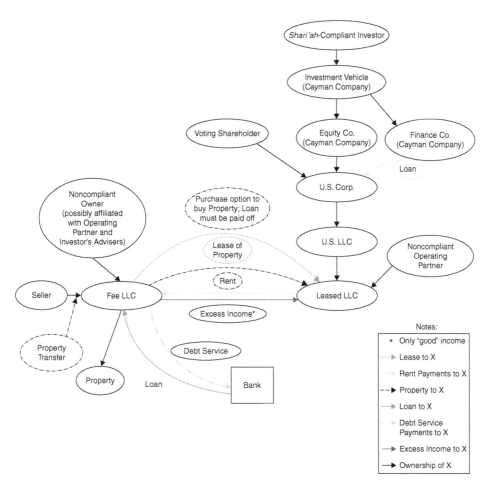

Exhibit 21.1 Project-Level *Ijara* Structure

its partners is to pay rent under the master lease. While not uniformly agreed, most advisers opine that the rental rate may be calculated taking into account the master landlord's obligation to pay debt service and other transaction costs, so long as the master tenant has no obligation to the lender. The *ijara* has been variously termed a "master lease" or a "net lease." I believe the latter characterization misleading in that a net lease would typically require that the tenant assume all property-related obligations. Here, the only obligations delegated to the tenant are those that can be performed by the tenant in accordance with the *Shari'ah*. Thus, for example, the obligation to maintain casualty or property insurance remains with the landlord, as only compliant forms of insurance, that is, *takaful*, could be maintained by the tenant/compliant investor.

The *ijara* has also been likened to financing leases common to a variety of sophisticated investment structures. That analogy is also problematic, in that various features common to financing leases would run afoul of the *Shari'ah*. Financing leases often attempt to shift all risks of ownership to the tenant. Islamic principles would not permit the tenant (*musta'jir*) to assume responsibility for all such risks. As noted earlier, certain obligations inherent to ownership and not typically transferred with the usufruct (i.e., the rights or enjoy the property) must be retained by the master landlord (*mu'jir*). Similarly, other provisions, such as the right of the landlord to accelerate all rent upon a default, may be inconsistent with a compliant lease. These limitations may be addressed, however, by the parties entering into separate contractual arrangements independent of, but parallel to, the *ijara*. The limitation on acceleration of rent may be addressable, for instance, by the master landlord and master tenant entering into separate put and call arrangements whereby transfer of ownership of the property can be compelled for separate consideration, and which may in turn be used to satisfy the secured debt.

The intent of the *ijara* is to isolate the compliant investor from any obligations arising out of any conventional leverage secured by the property. Today, most lenders require some form of guaranty, though often limited to responsibility for "recourse carve-out" events—that is, events such as theft or waste where the value of the lender's collateral is impaired. In the case of properties wholly owned by a compliant investor, prospective lenders should be advised at the earliest time that no form of guaranty or credit support can be made available. In the case of properties owned by the compliant investor in a joint venture, the joint venture partner is often asked to provide any necessary guaranties. This also has the advantage of allocating the risk of so-called recourse events, such as misappropriation of funds, to the party likely responsible in fact for administering property operations. A point of negotiation in the joint venture documentation will be whether claims under these guaranties can, at least in some cases, be shared with the investor through capital credit or indemnity. A related query involves whether this creates an impermissible link between the investor and the conventional debt.

Continuing with the joint venture scenario, the operating partner should be advised early on that its economic stake in the property will be held through an ownership interest in the master tenant. This can appear counterintuitive to third parties, especially if the partner currently owns the property and is introducing the compliant investor to an existing arrangement. Tax treatment is one important reason to maintain the preferred approach in which all investors hold their interests through the master tenant. United States income tax law generally follows a "substance over form" approach. Where, as here, the economic benefits and risks associated with the ownership lie with the master tenant, most tax advisers will conclude that the master tenant is the owner of the property for tax purposes and thus the party entitled to depreciate the property. If ownership is split between the operating partner and the compliant investor, with one holding through the master landlord and the other through the master tenant, determining the owner of the property for tax purposes may be more difficult. While the focus here is on United States investments, note that the *ijara* structure may in fact be easier to implement here than in Europe. We do need to take care that the master lease does not trigger transfer taxes (and it would not in New York so long as the term of the master lease is sufficiently short). In most states and localities in the United States, leases of relatively short duration—not deemed to be equivalent to fee ownership—are not subject to transfer tax. However, in Europe, the master landlord may be treated as a separate taxpayer and the master lease may be subject to additional stamp duty.

JOINT VENTURE MATTERS

If the compliant investor elects to proceed in joint venture, its joint venture partners must become well versed in the principles of the *Shari'ah* as they relate to the operation of the asset. Routine approaches, such as charging and collecting default interest, can create compliance issues. Similarly, the operating partner must be attuned to the limitations on use of the property. These matters are generally not burdensome in multifamily properties as one ordinarily finds only limited amounts of commercial space. However, imagine co-investors in properties with large blocks of space that would otherwise be leasable for financially attractive, but impermissible, uses (e.g., retail banking or insurance). These co-investors should be advised in advance that certain financial opportunities must be foregone and should agree that the overall transaction represents a fair consideration for this limitation. Otherwise one can imagine the co-investor demanding some financial adjustment for adhering to these limitations.

The joint venture documents must also be considered in their own right for potential areas of noncompliance. It would not be unusual, for instance, for a partnership or limited liability company operating agreement to provide for so-called default loans as a remedy for failure of a partner or member to contribute its required share of additional capital. For the compliant investor, such interest-bearing loans would be anathema, and adjustments to equity-sharing ratios would provide a more appropriate remedy. That said, preferential equity returns can themselves raise questions of compliance. While preferred stock has long been recognized as possibly contrary to Islamic principles promoting an even and fair sharing of risk and reward, analogous issues can arise in partnership or operating agreements. Equity investors, as passive capital investors are sometimes characterized, often bargain for a preferred return (i.e., one senior in payment to other distributions), in exchange for granting the operating partner a greater share of profits over a specified hurdle return. Some scholars have questioned whether this arrangement—even though seemingly negotiated at arm's length and agreed to be a fair result to the noncompliant investor—are consistent with the *Shari'ah*. Some prior return to the other investors may be necessary to alleviate this concern.

FINANCING MATTERS

As noted above, most sophisticated lending institutions in the United States today have some familiarity with Islamic structures and are comfortable financing within these structures. In fact, not an insignificant amount of debt subsequently placed in the securitized markets over the last decade reflects ownership through compliant structures. For many lenders, the principal (and sometimes only) concern is whether the master lease is subordinate to the secured debt. Confirmation of such subordination may be sufficient comfort as the lender is assured that its lien can be foreclosed free of the master lease structure. Other lenders have, however, required additional assurances, as, for instance, that the rental flow from the actual space users cannot be interrupted, as perhaps by a bankruptcy of the master tenant. This has in turn led to the use of "bankruptcy remote" vehicles throughout the structure. Lenders may also be concerned that the actual occupancy leases, if held by the master tenant, may be "trapped" and the rental income thus unavailable to the master landlord and its lender if the *ijara* is terminated without concurrent repayment of the debt secured by the property. Thus, some lenders will insist that the occupancy leases be collaterally assigned to the master landlord (and then to its lender) as further security for repayment of the loan to the master landlord.

TAX STRUCTURING

Any review of real estate investment in the United States by Islamic investors should at least touch upon tax considerations. Since 1980 and the enactment of the Foreign Investment in Real Property Tax Act, non-U.S. investors in real estate have generally been treated on a par with U.S. taxpayers. Foreign investors resident in countries with tax treaties with the United States may still be able to take advantage of some reduced rates. However, none of the GCC countries has a tax treaty with the United States at the moment and, as tax authorities have become more focused on eliminating "treaty shopping" and restricting tax treaty benefits to true residents of the applicable jurisdiction, investors from nontreaty countries have generally borne a fairly high tax burden on their equity investments in U.S. real estate. While mezzanine debt investments can be structured in a tax-advantageous manner, the use of mezzanine debt by a compliant party would not be acceptable absent a restructuring that would entirely change the character of the income received from that of interest to a compliant payment. Islamic investors do, however, have some opportunity to use internal debt arrangements to facilitate a more tax-efficient structure. While it may seem counterintuitive, so long as there is commonality of ownership between the borrowing and lending vehicles and thus no imposition of a financial burden on a third party, those arrangements should not run afoul of Islamic precepts.

CONCLUSION

In sum, U.S. real estate remains an attractive target for compliant investors. Product is readily available in the favored asset classes. Lenders are generally receptive to the use of the *ijara* structure in transactions involving investors comfortable with the use of leverage in a compliant manner. And U.S. tax law imposes few obstacles to implementing compliant structures with minimal additional tax burdens.

CHAPTER 22

Risk and Derivatives in Islamic Finance

A Shariah Analysis

DR. MUHAMMAD AL-BASHIR MUHAMMAD AL-AMINE
Group Head, Shari'ah Assurance Department, Bank Al Khair

Risk management is at the heart of any financial intermediation process, in particular at a time when volatility in financial markets is affecting Eastern and Western markets and when economic crises are heating different parts of the world. Islamic financial institutions are no exception. Similar to their conventional counterparts, they face many challenges in adequately managing these risks.[1] Yet the issue of risk management was at the center of the Islamic finance industry even before the crisis. This could explain the fact that among the first standards to be issued by the Islamic Financial Services Board (IFSB) is the standard on risk management, a vivid sign of the importance of the issue for Islamic financial institutions.

More importantly, while addressing the risk issues, the IFSB pointed to an important regulatory factor that needs to be taken into consideration by industry players. It noted that regulating risk issues for Islamic financial institutions would not be achieved while working in isolation of the wider international financial system. Thus it has been clearly noted that, "While the Basel Committee on Banking Supervision (BCBS) has published documents setting out sound practices and principles pertaining to credit, market, liquidity and operational risks of financial institutions, the present Guiding Principles serves to complement the BCBS's guidelines in order to cater for the specificities of IIFS."[2]

Thus, while the different risk issues affecting conventional financial institutions are also present in Islamic finance, some of these instruments require careful analysis before being adopted into Islamic finance, not only because of the controversy surrounding them even in the conventional financial discussions but also because of the differences of opinion among Shariah scholars in accommodating them in Islamic finance. This is evident in the case of derivatives instruments more than in any other financial product. This chapter analyzes how to develop Shariah-compliant derivatives instruments that would serve in managing risks in Islamic transactions while avoiding, as much as is possible, the negative implications of modern derivatives instruments.

The derivatives market has recently attracted more attention against the backdrop of its role in the financial crisis, fraud cases, and the near failure of some institutions. Although the financial crisis has primarily been caused by structured credit-linked (such as sub-prime) securities, which are not derivatives, policy makers and regulators have started to think about strengthening regulation to increase transparency and safety, both for derivatives and other financial instruments, given the widely acknowledged assumption that the use of unregulated derivatives have aggravated the situation.[3]

ISLAMIC DERIVATIVES AND RISK MANAGEMENT

The importance of derivative instruments as tools of risk management is a key part of the modern financial system. However, due to their early development as part of a conventional financial system or their association with financial and economic crisis, as noted above, these instruments may not be easily accepted in Islamic finance due to Shariah-compliance issues. This does not mean that the use of the existing derivatives instruments, even after being adapted to Islamic rules, or the development of new instruments having similar economic purposes is not feasible. The cornerstone for the development of such instruments will rely on their Shariah basis and whether they contravene Shariah principles or not. The importance of these instruments was stressed by many scholars and practitioners, as well as by credit ratings agencies such Moody's. In recent research Moody's maintains that the Islamic finance industry faces the need to develop its own derivative products that don't just duplicate conventional derivative instruments; the industry is under obligation to maintain its special status as a Shariah-compliant financial system, which makes them very attractive to a large population of Muslims, and at the same time is obliged to reduce the risk exposures of Islamic financial institutions (IFIs) and to improve their overall creditworthiness.[4]

Thus, it has been maintained that:

> If employed with care, derivatives can enhance efficiency in IFIs through risk mitigation, thereby making them more competitive as well as appealing to customers. However, their application in Islamic finance is highly controversial for reasons of speculation and uncertainty, two practices forbidden under Shari'ah.[5]

Besides the issues of speculation and uncertainty covered by the principles of *gharar* (excessive risk), we have also the fundamental issue of interest, another investment aspect that affects the nonpermissibility of derivatives. Moreover, the varying scholarly opinions on the legitimacy of derivatives have so far translated into a total prohibition of these instruments in some countries and limited implementation in others. This has resulted in a cautious approach by the Islamic finance industry practitioners toward derivatives.

Nobody in the industry, however, is denying the crucial role of derivatives as risk management tools in the conventional financial system and the need to develop similar tools in Islamic finance. Thus, Standard & Poor's for instance notes that:

The management of market risks is made more difficult for Islamic banks due to the limited number of risk management tools/instruments available to them. For example, it is difficult for an IFI to use hedging instruments such as derivatives as they are generally forbidden.[6]

BASIC FEATURES OF SHARIAH-COMPLIANT DERIVATIVES

This chapter briefly analyzes basic derivatives instruments from an Islamic point of view, their economic benefits, and their reason d'être. The main scope of this analysis is limited to derivative transactions based on commodities and shares, and it excludes the use of these instruments in their present forms in interest rate, currency, and stock indices due to the involvement of *riba* (interest) and excessive risk (*gharar*). It does outline the Islamic alternatives based on Islamic profit-rate swaps or currency exchange, however, and discusses a reference to the recent efforts by the International Islamic Financial Market (IIFM) and the International Swap and Derivatives Associations (ISDA) to standardize the present practices of these new hedging instruments.

Insisting on derivatives based on commodities and shares' trading first is justified by the fact that Islamic finance is an industry based on a close link between finance and the real economy; therefore, starting with commodities is natural. Moreover, the economy of many Muslim countries where Islamic finance is flourishing is based on commodities and, therefore, hedging risk related to the trading of these commodities will arise. Unfortunately, Muslims have ignored the obvious logic of establishing a Shariah-compliant derivatives market in these commodities in particular, and in the most fundamental commodity in the modern world, namely oil and its derivatives. Thus, one observer, after addressing some of the economic benefits of derivatives in oil trading noted:

> However, it is clear that these advantages are not being exploited in the market of all the countries that produce or consume this important commodity. Indeed the benefits that flow from the derivatives trading are concentrated in a very few countries. The principal exchanges for trading energy are in New York, London and Singapore. Other off-exchange markets flourish in London, the US and various countries in Europe and have following in countries of the Far East. However, many of the producing countries, particularly in the Middle East and Latin America, seem to be excluded from the benefits that the derivatives trading in oil can bring. This situation cannot remain indefinitely. It must be becoming increasingly clear to those in economic decision making positions in producing countries that there are substantial benefits, in terms of both increased revenue and control over pricing and distribution which derivatives trading produce. It can only be a matter of time before they seek to obtain these benefits for their own economies.[7]

Based on the above, it is clear that the establishment of an Islamic derivative exchange for oil trading is a necessity given the fact that the majority of the members of the organization of oil producing countries (OPEC) with the exception of Venezuela are Muslim countries.[8] Recently, Saudi Arabia, through its national oil company, has broken new ground. As the world's largest oil exporter, Saudi Arabia is seeking to capitalize on its refining strength and run its own oil-trading book—buying and selling gasoline, gas oil, and other fuel to balance the needs of its expanding system and to turn a profit. Aramco Trading is venturing into derivatives, such as futures and paper trading, in a significant cultural change. It is reported that the company has already lined up an 80-person team that includes risk management specialists lured from top Western trading houses for that purpose.[9] The move is long overdue but a step in the right direction. It should be noted that Malaysia has long established its derivatives market with regard to palm oil. The pressing question now is, to what extent will such markets be Shariah compliant? And to what extent could a derivative market enhance Islamic finance?

Research on derivatives from a Shariah perspective is still in its early stages. The general response of Muslim jurists is so far negative. Although the issue has been addressed by a number of institutions, such as Makkah-based Fiqh Academy,[10] the Islamic Fiqh Academy based in Jeddah in different seminars and workshops,[11] the Permanent Research Committee of the Board of Great Scholars in Saudi Arabia,[12] and the Accounting and Auditing Organization of Islamic Financial Institutions (AAOIFI),[13] the outcome of these discussions has been to urge the prohibition of derivatives. These judgments should not be considered the final Shariah ruling on the issue because certain shortcomings have been associated with these resolutions.[14] Therefore fresh discussion on the issue is a must. Reaching a solution is possible given the flexibility of Islamic law on one hand and the broader sphere of the concept of freedom of contract on the other, in particular as it has been pointed out by a recent International Money Fund (IMF) working paper:

> There are indeed a number of Islamic financial instruments with derivative-like features which could help agents reduce risks and that could form the basis for designing Shari'ah-compatible derivatives.[15]

At the same time it is pertinent to note that a derivatives market from an Islamic perspective will have its own scope, and therefore, many of the bad effects of the conventional derivative market may not be expected to be part of a Shariah-compliant derivatives structure. For instance, the following four restrictions need to be highlighted.

1. An Islamic derivative market will not include underlying asset instruments, such as a collateralized debt obligation (CDO) or credit default swap (CDS) given the fact that such instruments are not Shariah compliant by nature due to the fundamental Shariah principles of banning the sale of "debt for debt" as long as it leads to *riba* (interest). However, looking at the events leading to the crisis it has been observed that the financial system grew increasingly complex and nontransparent as the CDOs in turn were bought up by structured investment vehicles (SIVs) that, for their part, issued bonds (CDO-squared) that were in turn bought up by other SIVs that issued bonds (CDO-cubed) to finance their purchase, and so on and so forth.[16] As Umer Chapra noted:

   > When there is excessive and imprudent lending and the lenders are not confident of repayment, there is an excessive resort to derivatives like the credit default swap (CDS) to seek protection against debt default. The

buyer of the swap pays a premium to the seller (a hedge fund) for the compensation he will receive in case of debtor default. This may not have created any problem if the protection was provided to the actual creditor. However, in a typical swap deal, a hedge fund will sell the swap not to just one bank but also to several other wagers who are willing to bet on the default of that specific debtor, even though they may not have themselves lent to that debtor. These wagers may again resell the swaps to others, thereby unduly accentuating the risk. Accordingly the notional amount of outstanding derivatives rose to the high of $692 trillion (including CDRs or cash deposit ratio of $62.2 trillion) in the first quarter of 2008, but declined thereafter to $600 trillion (including CDRs of $54.6 trillion) in the second quarter. However, even after the decline, it is more than ten times the size of the total world output of $57 trillion.[17]

2. Any foreign exchange market from an Islamic perspective will be limited to serve genuine real economic business and not just exist for speculative purposes; this is based on the Islamic law principle that money is just a medium of exchange and not a commodity by itself.

3. An Islamic derivatives market would be well regulated so that it can serve the genuine need of the economy and not the greed of rogue and unscrupulous traders as it is incumbent upon such a market to uphold its principles of avoiding *gharar* (excessive speculation) and *maysir* (gambling).

4. An Islamic derivatives market should be designed more on an equity-based financial system that prefers profit-loss sharing instruments, therefore limiting the need to resort to derivatives as they exist in the conventional financial system.

SHARIAH ANALYSIS OF DERIVATIVES INSTRUMENTS

The four main derivatives instruments are called *forward, futures, options*, and *swaps*. This paper analyzes the main objections against these instruments from a Shariah perspective. The discussion on the forward contract draws an analogy between the conventional forward contract and similar contracts in Islamic law such as *bay al-salam, bay al-istisna*, and *bay al-sifah* and how each one of these contracts could be the basis for the adoption of the forward contract. It also rebuts the claim that there is no benefit in the conventional forward contract or that it contradicts the principle enshrined in the *hadith* (i.e., a category of religious literature that communicates actions and sayings in the tradition of Islam): "Do not sell what is not with you."

The Forward Contract: A Shariah Evaluation

A forward contract is an agreement to exchange values in the future at a predetermined price. It plays a vital role in international financial markets and serves as the building block for more advanced and sophisticated financial instruments. The primary function of the forward market is to hedge against unexpected and undesirable price fluctuations.[18] Without forward contracts, business trade and

planning would be greatly hindered.[19] Some Muslim scholars acknowledged the
benefits of these instruments[20] and many[21] have rejected the claim that there is
no benefit in such a contract.[22] However, the forward contract in its actual form
has no exact counterpart in Islamic law. Some scholars have drawn a similarity
between the forward contract and *bay al-salam* on the one hand and *bay al-istisna*
on the other. Furthermore, some have tried to establish the legality of this contract
under *bay al-siffah* (sale by description).

Salam is defined as "a sale or purchase of a deferred commodity for a present
price."[23] It is the closest contract to the conventional forward contract. Some have
considered it as the Islamic alternative to the forward contract[24] and they are
insisting that for the forward contract to be accepted in Islamic finance it shall fulfil
the conditions of *salam*. Although there are similarities between the two contracts,
in *bay al-salam* full payment at the time of agreement is a requirement according to
the majority of scholars. They argue that in fact a *salam* contract is a kind of sale of
debt for debt, which is prohibited in the Shariah, and because *salam* is allowed as an
exception it would therefore not be permissible to adjust the contract.[25] The Malikis
on the other hand allowed delay payment for three days without any condition,
and with different conditions in other different cases.[26] (Maliki is one of the four
schools of religious law or jurisprudence [Fikh] in Sunni Islam, along with Hanifi,
Shaf'i, and Hanabali.) It is observed that based on the Maliki opinion why not
allowing deferment of both countervalues as it is the case in a forward contract.
It is clear that the Maliki opinion is based on the conclusion that the deferment
of the price in *salam* for three days neither involves *riba* nor *gharar*, otherwise *riba*
or *gharar* could not be allowed either for three days or more or less time. This is
also confirmed by the Maliki insistence that the above rule could not be applied
to currency exchange because it will lead to clear *riba*. Even a delay of one hour or
just the disappearance of one of the contracting parties from the session of contract
is not permissible.[27]

Extending the Maliki opinion to the modern type of forward contract will
establish an analogy (or *qiyas*) between the two contracts. However, such *qiyas*
would be impossible if we consider the permissibility of *salam* as an exception, as
the majority of scholars maintain it to be. This claim was refuted, however, by some
classical and some contemporary scholars.[28] Thus, one may conclude that requiring
the condition for the price of *salam* to be delivered at the time of the conclusion
of the contract is not based on the fear of *riba* or *gharar* but on the assumption
that the permissibility of *salam* is against the norm of *qiyas*. However, as it has
been maintained above, such a claim cannot be justified in Islamic jurisprudence.
Therefore, one can conclude that the modern forward contract is a valid contract
by way of analogy to *salam*.

Besides *salam*, the forward contract has similarities with the contract of *istisna*
accepted by some early scholars and unanimously by contemporary ones. *Istisna*
is a contract of selling a manufacturable entity with an undertaking by the seller
to present it manufactured from his own material, with specified descriptions and
at a determined price. Unlike *salam*, in *istisna* it is not a condition to advance
the payment, though it is permissible to do so; it could be deferred or made in
installments.[29] Thus, from the contractual specifications, *istisna* is more in line with
the conventional forward contract, where the price is not paid in advance. Deferring
price in *istisna*, according to the classical scholars, is allowed on the basis of *istihsan*

(preference) and need. Therefore, one may argue that the need for the modern forward contract is similar to that of *istisna*, if not much greater, and therefore it should be allowed on the same grounds. (The difference that *istisna* is a production contract while the forward contract is a trading contract seems to be irrelevant.)

Another contract having similarities with the forward contract is *bay al-siffah*, the sale of something that is not present at the time of contract but very well described and to be delivered in the future. Although *bay al-siffah* is accepted by the Hanafis[30] and Hanbalis,[31] the Maliki's approach[32] is much broader and more in line with the analogy to the forward contract. It is maintained that firstly, in *bay al-siffah* as well as in the forward contract, the contract is based on a detailed description of the subject matter, relying on previous observation or the presence of a sample. Secondly, in both contracts the subject matter of the contract is not present and the parties have a real intention to execute the contract according to the time and place specified. Thirdly, both contracts fulfill the characteristics of *bay al-siffah* and not *bay al-aayan*, which is the sale of an asset present at the time of contract. Lastly, in both contracts both countervalues are deferred although the price could be paid by installments as well.[33]

Some scholars argue that there is an extra *gharar* in deferring both counter-values (as opposed to the deferment of only one), as it is the case in *salam*, and therefore the forward contract is nonpermissible due to the extra risk involved. There seems to exist in both situations a possibility for the price of the commodity to fluctuate during the period of maturity of the contract. Therefore, one of the parties will bear the consequences of this fluctuation (this is what always occurs in the case of *salam*). Thus the level of risk in both situations is the same.[34] The contracting parties will clearly specify the price and the subject matter when the agreement is written. Therefore, the possibility of dispute is minimal; the history of forward transactions is a good example.[35]

Another issue closely related to the permissibility of the forward contract is that of *gharar* and the possibility of the seller being unable to make delivery due to difficulties in procuring the subject matter of the contract. However, this seems to be very remote and the ability of the seller to acquire the subject matter of the transaction could not be compared to cases of selling "birds in the sky" or "fish in the deep sea," which represent the standard concept of *gharar*. Similarly, there is no risk regarding the subject matter of the contract since it is well defined and not similar to cases such as "I am selling to you what is in my hand" or "what is in my box" without showing it.[36]

Some scholars have also rejected the forward because it contradicts the *hadith*: "Do not sell what is not with you."[37] However, for Ibn al-Qayyim the issue in this *hadith* is not about the existence or nonexistence of the subject matter but about risk, or *gharar*, and whether it is impossible to deliver the subject matter whether it exists or not.[38]

As such, the conventional forward contract has great benefits, and it could be accommodated in Islamic law whether under the general theory of contract and conditions or by analogy to *salam*, *istisna*, or *bay al-siffah* since it does not involve *riba* or *gharar*. Moreover, it is not included in the prohibited forms of selling debt and does not oppose the principle "do not sell what is not with you."

The forward contract has overcome some of the problems associated with risk, but it is still associated with other problems, such as double coincidence, and, more importantly, counterparty risk, by defaulting to honor one's obligation. Thus, the need for the futures contract arises. However, from a Shariah perspective, the admission of the forward contract will be the cornerstone in admitting the futures contracts given the fact that the futures contracts are forward contract trading in an organized market with the presence of a clearinghouse and brokers. Although there are Shariah issues that need to be addressed, most of these issues are administrative issues that could be easily accommodated under the basis of *maslahah* ("public interest"). Therefore, the next logical step will be the Shariah position regarding options.

Concept and Scope of Options

> An option contract conveys the right to buy or sell an underlying commodity at a specified price within a specified period of time.[39] The important feature is that the buyer of the option is not obliged to complete the deal and will do so only if changes in price make it profitable to do so. He is protected from unfavourable market movements but is still able to profit from movement in the buyer's favour. The risk of loss is carried by the seller, who charges the buyer a fee for taking on this risk.[40]

Despite the widely held position against options, some scholars have stressed the need for a cautious adoption of options in Islamic finance due to the need associated with these instruments.[41] Among these benefits we may mention an increase in the liquidity of the market, a reduction in the effect of fluctuations in the prices of securities, and an opportunity for investors to rearrange their investment portfolio by choosing the most appropriate position for their preferences based on the risk-return trade off.[42] Thus, there are many legitimate and Islam-sanctioned desirable uses of options, in particular, the hedging aspect of options which is not contradictory to the Shariah.[43] Thus follows the need to better understand the real implications of these contracts and the purpose they serve and then modify them to achieve our objectives while avoiding legal and Shariah problems and complications.[44]

There are many option types in finance, such as exotic options and compound options. The focus in Islamic finance, however, is the basic types, namely, call and put options. A call option gives the holder the right to buy an asset by a certain date for a certain price. A put option, on the other hand, gives the holder the right to sell an asset by a certain date for a certain price. Similarly, the discussion in this chapter is limited to options in commodities and the possibility of shares trading, since other forms of options are irrelevant due to *riba* (interest) or *gharar* (excessive risk).

It has been proposed that *khiyar al-shart* and *bay al-arbun* can be used as tools in risk management and as possible alternatives to options. However, for a real paradigm shift to occur in the discussion of options, it is necessary to discuss the permissibility of selling such rights from a Shariah perspective. This is prompted by the fact that the Fiqh Academy issued a resolution stressing that the subject matter in options, as they are traded, are not *mal, manfaah,* or *haqq mali*, which could be legally exchanged, but are illegal types of contract. The AAOIFI standard followed, as did additional research papers. Thus, the issue of rights of sale, as they exist in the context of options, is one of the hotly debated issues raised against the permissibility of options. This chapter argues in favor of the sale of such rights relying on the general principles of Islamic commercial law and by referring to specific cases where a right is sold or exchanged for money. Included among the cases highlighted (and explained in the following paragraphs) are the sales of the rights in *khiyar al-shart*, the rights of *shuf'ah* (preemption), the rights of easements (*huquq al-irtifaq*), and other similar cases. Finally, the present study raises the issue of involvement or otherwise of gambling in options and provides a suitable response.

Some scholars have argued that conventional options could be accommodated in Islamic law through *khiyar al-shart*,[45] while others did not see any grounds for legalizing options by making an analogy to *khiyar al-shart* (option of stipulation).[46] *Khiyar al-shart* refers to an option in which a condition stipulated in the contract, whether to confirm the contract or to cancel it in a specific period. It provides a right to either of the parties, or both, or even to a third party, to confirm or to cancel the contract within a stipulated time period.[47]

Despite the differences in using *khiyar al-shart* as a replica of an option, no one objects that *khiyar al-shart* could be used as a tool of risk management in its own right. However, for *khiyar al-shart* to serve a real mechanism of risk management with real practical outcome, we should consider *khiyar al-shart* as a contract in line with *qiyas* and not against it. Thus, when individuals buy stock using *khiyar al-shart*, they look at the up or down trend of the stock they have bought or sold; they are not just looking to avoid possible cheating by their counterpart in terms of the price or a possible defect in the commodity or stock they bought or sold. At the same time, they are not asking for an option because they have no sufficient knowledge of the subject matter they have agreed to buy. They are buying these stocks with a view of seeing if the later price is in their favor, in which case, they will exercise the option in order to benefit from the price differential, and if the opposite situation occurs they will leave the option to expire without exercising it.

Thus, in the above scenario *khiyar al-shart* could be used to manage risk. However, if the right to exercise an option could be exchanged it would make *khiyar al-shart* almost similar to conventional options. Some scholars have discussed the possibility of charging a fee or premium for the option in *khiyar al-shart* so as to match the conventional option.[48]

In contrast, some argue that *khiyar al-shart* is merely tolerated by way of exception; it is not permitted in order to allow a benefit from price movement, and therefore, the period of *khiyar al-shart* should not exceed three days as it is stated in the *hadith*.[49] However, it is worth noting that Ibn Taymiyyah and Ibn al-Qayyim vigorously refuted the claim that *khiyar al-shart* is allowed against the norms or *qiyas*. Moreover, if it is established that the permissibility of *khiyar al-shart* is in line with *qiyas*, there is a need to establish whether the right provided in the *khiyar* is a right that could be the subject of a sale transaction or not.

Some researchers compared the right in conventional options with that of *khiyar al-shart* and concluded that the right in *khiyar al-shart* is not a property right (*haqq mali* and, therefore, it could not be inherited or exchanged).[50] To address the issue, several points and questions need to be clarified. First is whether this right is related to property (*haqq mali*) or not, because according to the generally held view, if a right is related to property then it could be exchanged. Muslim jurists usually tackle this question when it is connected to the possibility of inheriting such a right. The Malikis and Shafis consider that such a right is related to the benefit of a property and, therefore, it can be inherited.[51] The Hanafis, on the other hand, maintained that it could not be inherited because it is a kind of desire, opinion, and willingness, and such willingness will no longer exist after the death of the beneficiary of the option, as is the case with his other attributes.[52] The Hanbalis have, on the other hand, considered such a right as inheritable only if the beneficiary has requested its inheritance before his death.[53]

Regarding the inheritance of the right to *shuf'ah*, the different schools of Islamic law[54] have taken a similar stand to that on *khiyar al-shart* and adopted almost the same line of argument. Therefore, it could be argued that if these rights could be inherited because they are rights related to property, then they could be exchanged as well based on the argument that every right related to property could be exchanged. Therefore, the right to an option of stipulation, or *khiyar al-shart*, and the right to *shuf'ah* could be exchanged. And if these rights could be exchanged despite the fact that they are pure rights, then the right to option (as in conventional options types) could also be exchanged. Moreover, the Malikis did not see any objection in selling the right in *khiyar al-shart* and *shuf'ah* after receiving it because it is an established right, and as such it could be exchanged like any other right.[55] This opinion has also been reported from Abu Ishaq Ibrahim Ibn Ahmad al-Mirwazi, one of the leading Shafi scholars.[56]

Moreover, it is reported in a Hanafi fatwa that "if a person sells a house to another with an option of stipulation or *khiyar al-shart* for three days, then the buyer requests the seller to drop his right for option in exchange for a specific amount of money or a specific commodity, such a transaction is legal and the amount added would be considered as an increase in the price of the house. Similarly, if the option is in favour of the buyer and the seller requests him to drop his right for option and confirms the contract, the transaction is legal and it will be a deduction from the initial price."[57]

A similar analysis was made by Abd al-Rahman al-Sa'di while addressing the issue of *sulh* (reconciliation), maintaining that to drop one's right in preemption (*shuf'ah*) or his right in option of stipulation (*khiyar al-shart*) in exchange for some money is a kind of *sulh*. The argument of the early Hanbalis that these rights are not legalized for financial benefit is correct, but individuals may accept to drop or relinquish their right in *shuf'ah* or *khiyar al-shart* in exchange for money, and they may not agree to relinquish their right without it; such an exchange is in line with the general principles, and there is no explicit evidence that prohibits it.[58] Similarly, 'Ali al-Khafif, while touching on the different opinions about the sale of right in pre-emption (*shuf'ah*), questions the Hanafi's opinion that such a right could not be sold.[59]

Thus, to claim that a pure right, such as the right of *shuf'ah* or *khiyar al-shart*, cannot be exchanged is just the opinion of some scholars. Some submit following the argument as unfounded: that the right in an option is similar to that of *shuf'ah*, and since the right to *shuf'ah* could not be exchanged, then the right to option likewise cannot be exchanged. Moreover there is no text from the Qur'an or the *sunnah* to prohibit the sale of such right. Therefore, it is incumbent upon those who prohibit the sale of such a right to provide the evidence.[60]

The term *arbun* refers to another classical instrument that has similarities to an option. Arbun can be defined as "a transaction whereby the buyer pays only a small part of the price of a commodity, on the understanding that the seller will retain this amount if the sale is not finally concluded due to withdrawal of the buyer."[61] Although there is some disagreement among the classical schools of Islamic law about the legality of arbun, the majority of contemporary Muslim jurists have opted for the permissibility of the contract.

To give an example of how arbun works in commodities, we may choose the following example given in literature[62] to show its similarity to an option. Let us assume you have decided that you want to buy a new car. You select the type of car you want and go to your local dealer. At the dealer's showroom, you decide on the exact specifications of your car's color, engine, size, wheel trim, and so forth. The car is on offer at £20,000, but to guarantee that price you must buy the car today. You do not have that amount of cash available and it will take a week to organize a loan. You offer the dealer £100 as arbun if he will just keep the car for a week. At the end of the week, if you buy the car, the £100 will be credited toward the price, but if you do not turn up, the £100 remains with the seller (i.e., the £100 is his whether or not you buy the car). Thus, you have entered into an arbun in the present example, while it is also a call option contract in conventional finance, as in this example. If, during the week, you discover a second dealer offering an identical model for £19,500, you will not take up your option with the first dealer. The total cost of buying the car is £19,500 + £100 = £19,600, which is cheaper than the first price you were offered. However, if you find that the first dealer's price is lower than the second dealer's and buy the car from the first dealer, the car will cost a total of £20,100. If you decide not to buy the car at all, you will lose your £100 to the car dealer. Thus, you are hedging against a price rise in the car.

Questions may be asked about whether *arbun* is a kind of clause for liquidated damages or a kind of penalty that will be imposed upon the one who fails to honor his obligation as a compensation of imminent harm, or is it something else? If we consider *arbun* as a kind of clause for liquidated damages, this would mean the damage should be assessed by a court of law even if the parties have agreed at the beginning to a certain amount of compensation. Similarly, questions arise if the *arbun* is intended to compensate for the harm suffered by the owner of the commodity because the commodity has been reserved for the buyer and the owner has waited for the seller to ratify the contract, or if the opportunity to sell that item at a good price has been lost, and court intervention is necessary. More importantly, if the terms agreed upon are more than the real damage, the court would reduce it to the appropriate amount, and if it is less, then the one who fails to honor the obligation should be mandated by the court to pay more. This is totally different from the nature of *arbun*, which cannot be subject to the court's intervention in the normal circumstances. Moreover, in the case of liquidated damages, the occurrence of the damage is a condition for receiving the compensation. If no damage has happened, then there are no grounds for compensation; this is not the case with *arbun* where the beneficiary is entitled to it whether there is damage or not. Therefore, it seems that what is paid as *arbun* is in exchange for the right to cancel the contract and not as compensation for the damage. As such, *arbun* could vary according to the underlying asset's price and the period of *arbun* guaranteed, and remove the need for court intervention.

Arbun and Call Option

Achieving a balance between *arbun* and a call option is not difficult[63] given the fact that the basic rationale of an option resembles that of *arbun*, especially in the sense that both can be used as risk-reduction strategies.[64] More importantly, the *arbun* contract can be analogized to the pure call option and the contract could be devised with results and pricing identical (or nearly identical) to the call option.[65] Moreover, the previous examples make it obvious that *arbun* could serve the basic role of a call option without major differences. Thus, it could be concluded that *arbun* could be the Islamic alternative to a call option without contravening Shariah principles. However, the question remains as to what would be the Islamic alternative to a put option.[2]

The possible alternative to a put option in connection with *arbun* is to make it a condition in the contract that if the seller fails to fulfil his contractual obligations, he should pay the buyer a certain amount in the form of reverse *arbun*. Thus, if the seller, who has already received the *arbun*, fails to fulfil his obligation, he should return the first *arbun* twice as compensation to the buyer.[66] Practically it seems that there is a difference between the original *arbun* and the reverse *arbun*. In both cases, the payment is in exchange for the right to cancel the contract or an option with a price. It is also argued that by giving this right to both parties, the transaction will be much fairer and just than giving it to just one party.[67] It also seems that such a stipulation does not contradict the objective of the contract or any explicit text. Moreover, it is to the benefit of the contract and agreed upon by both parties. Thus, it is upheld that the reverse *arbun* is legally permissible and could serve as an alternative to a put option.

It is worth looking now into the five points of difference between option and *arbun* as postulated by some contemporary Muslim jurists. These objections could be summarized as follows:

1. An option requires payment for something that is a mere intangible "right." The right of the option is given to the buyer as well as to the seller, while *arbun* is given only to the buyer.
2. The objective of options trading is not for the benefit of the contract but rather the parties are looking for price differentials.
3. The underlying assets in an option are not restricted to a commodity, as in the case in *arbun*, but they could also be stock indices, which are a kind of gambling.
4. The price of an option is determined by the movement of interest rates, which is not Islamic in practice.
5. If the option is in currency, not even forward sales are allowed since currencies can be exchanged only on the spot.[68]

It is clear that objection #1 is the most important one, targeting the essence of the contract by invalidating its subject matter. However, based on the analysis of the right in *khiyar al-shart* and the right of *shuf'ah*, as well as other similar rights, it can be concluded the right of option is a property right and can be the subject matter of a contract.

Concerning the second point in #1—namely the right of both parties to rescind the contract in an option, while in *arbun* it is only granted to the buyer—it could be argued that even if this right is guaranteed to the seller, there is no *riba* or *gharar* involved in such a transaction. Moreover, such a transaction does not contradict any specific Shariah text. Similarly, the right to option in *khiyar al-shart* was originally guaranteed to the seller but it was later extended by way of *ijtihad*, or reasoning, to the buyer or to both. Therefore, extending the right in an *arbun* to the seller could be handled similarly.

Regarding objection #2, whereby the parties are just looking for price differentials and are not willing to fulfil the objectives of the contract, it could be said that not every issue of price differential requires excessive speculation. Moreover, the price-differential issue could also be raised against other transactions, such as share trading (*khiyar al-shart*).

Objection #3 concerns the subject of the underlying asset in options, which is not limited only to the commodity as is the case with *arbun*, but could also be currency and even stock indices. (Note that this chapter's discussion is limited to the use of options in commodity and share trading but not in stock indices or interest rate.)

As for objection #4, that the movement of interest rates determines the price of options, it could be said that in an ordinary *arbun* market there is no possibility of directly determining the price through interest. Moreover, the determination of the rate of return (Islamic financial institutions use LIBOR, the London Inter-Bank Rate) as a benchmark, and some leading Muslim scholars and economists respond that given the lack of an Islamic representative rate of profit (and as long as conventional financial system dominates the world financial markets), Muslims may have to bear with the use of LIBOR as an approximate benchmark, at least in the initial phase of development of Islamic finance.[69] Thus, to rely on LIBOR in order to determine the rate of return does not question the Islamic-compliance issue of a transaction because it is not part of the contract itself."[70] Lastly, it should be noted that among the five factors affecting options pricing, namely strike price, underlying price, time to expiry, volatility, and interest rate, interest rates have the least influence on options.[71]

Thus, it is clear that none of these objections against *arbun* as an alternative to options are well founded, and we could conclude that it is possible to use *arbun* as an alternative to a call option while "the reverse *arbun*" could be used as alternative to a put option. Although *arbun* could achieve many aspects of options as a tool of risk management, this role will be restricted if we uphold the view that a right (as it is in an option) could not be exchanged.

It seems from the above that the sale of pure rights is at the heart of the legality of options contracts, because if the subject matter of a contract is invalid, the whole contract is invalid. The argument that option trading involves the sale of a pure right is correct; however, to claim that such a right could not be considered as subject matter of a contract in Islamic law is unwarranted. As it has been shown above with the right in *khiyar al-shart* and that of *shuf'ah*, such rights could be the subject matter of a contract by reference to the views of early Muslim scholars on the subject of *huquq mujarradah* (abstract rights).[72]

The discussion on derivatives from Shariah perspective would not be complete without an investigation into the issue of speculation and gambling as basis to declare derivatives non-Shariah compliant.

HEDGING, SPECULATION, GAMBLING, AND DERIVATIVES

Hedging is a process used to minimize losses in commodity marketing and processing that stem from adverse price fluctuations. Hedging plays an important role as a tool of risk management.

Generally Muslim scholars consider hedging as valid from the Shariah point of view if the issue of contract is permissible, but speculation is rejected.[73] The dilemma rises because it is somehow difficult to make the distinction between hedging, a needed factor to manage risk, and speculation, which is generally connected with crises and market crashes. A similar confusion is apparent between speculation and investment. The situation is aggregated by the fact that a limited level of speculation is not only needed but is necessary, for the smooth functioning of any exchange.[74] As such, it has been pointed out that eliminating speculation altogether, whether in ordinary sales or in derivatives, is impossible. However, if a limited level of speculation is necessary, the question then becomes how to draw the line between this limited scale of speculation and that which is excessive.[75] Some have maintained that speculation would be acceptable when it is part of some real activity and helps to shift risks from the vulnerable producers, who cannot afford bearing all the risk, to those who can afford to bear it.[76]

A well-regulated market may reduce speculation to an acceptable level. Thus, it is upheld that in its strictly literal sense, there is "nothing" objectionable about speculation in the Islamic framework. In fact, no law can be enforced against such a prima facie speculation, as it involves lawful activities of buying and selling.[77]

However, a well-regulated market may reduce speculation to an acceptable level. Thus, there is a need for a well-organized derivatives market. Moreover, such regulations are administrative requirements for the protection of investors and could be easily adopted in Islamic law under the basis of *maslahah*.[78]

Another issue raised with regard to the prohibition of options is gambling, generally defined as the voluntary risking of a sum of money (called a stake, wager, or bet) in the outcome of a game or other event.[79] The underlying object of a contract of gambling is risk and nothing else. It does not relate to the exchange or production of real goods or services.[80] The characteristic of being a genuine commercial transaction marks the difference between betting, wagering, gaming, or gambling and entering into a future contract. The transaction is genuine because it was an open type commercial transaction, conducted in a publicly controlled exchange where what is being purchased is known to all persons, with no hint of it being disguised as something else.[81]

Although some scholars cited gambling as one of their arguments against options,[82] the issue is well summarized by the late Sami Hammud in this response to debate on the issue: "To say that this contract is similar to gambling is not true. It is not a gambling contract in the eyes of one who is expert in the field."[83] Thus, to claim that options in commodities and stocks in particular are a form of gambling is not supported by any legal or economic evidence.

SHARIAH-COMPLIANT SWAPS

The recent development on derivatives from a Shariah perspective is the profit-rate swap and the foreign-exchange swap mechanism. Although these products have been in the market for several years now and selectively applied by several Islamic financial institutions, the products witnessed a further step forward when the International Islamic Financial Market (IIFM) and the International Swaps and Derivatives Association (ISDA) came up with a master agreement for a profit rate swap (*mubadalatul arbaah*) as a mechanism for Islamic financial participants to hedge against fluctuations in the profit rates that are used to determine the cost of Islamic financial products.

The master agreement is expected to facilitate this process by lowering the costs compared to having the participants custom build a profit-rate swap. Without the master agreement, there would be fewer transactions, which would make an impact on the "real economy" because fewer companies would have the opportunity to fix their financing, and effectively shift the management of interest-rate fluctuations to institutions that have a focus on managing those changes.[84]

Islamic banks' retail product offerings tend to be generally fixed-rate *murabaha*-based products for regular customers, while the corporate customers are offered facilities based on floating benchmarks. Thus from the banks' point of view there is a liquidity mismatch with Islamic deposits being of much shorter tenor (three to six months) compared with Islamic investments of longer maturity, and also fixed versus floating rate exposure. Corporate clients also require a more sophisticated product set to manage their own risk positions through the banks. Therefore, Islamic banks require Islamic tools to manage interest rate risk and foreign exchange (FX) risk.

The objective behind an Islamic profit-rate swap is effectively the same as that underlying a conventional interest-rate swap, namely to manage exposure to interest-rate movements. Thus it is designed to protect financial institutions from fluctuations in borrowing rates and to provide a risk-control mechanism. The widespread availability of hedging instruments acceptable in Islamic finance will ensure that investors and customers with different banking requirements, as well as Islamic financial institutions that require balance-sheet management, can enjoy benefits that conventional banks have been experiencing for many years.

A profit-rate swap is best analogized to a conventional interest-rate swap. Under a conventional interest-rate swap the parties agree to exchange periodic fixed and floating payments by reference to a preagreed notional amount.[85]

An Islamic profit-rate swap is basically an agreement to exchange profit rates between a fixed-rate party and a floating-rate party, or vice versa, implemented through the execution of a series of underlying Shariah contracts. In the current market a further contract called the *wa'ad* contract is being used to ensure the swap reaches maturity. A *wa'ad* is a binding unilateral promise and is binding one-way only. Before each commodity *murabaha* stage and reverse *murabaha* stage in the following structure, a *wa'ad* is given by each counterparty, respectively. The *wa'ad* ensures that the promisee undertakes to enter into that relevant commodity *murabaha* or reverse-commodity *murabaha* trade. This will continue until the swap expires.

Under this profit-rate swap, the parties enter into *murabaha* contracts to sell Shariah-compliant assets (often London Metal Exchange–traded metals) to each other for immediate delivery but on deferred payment terms. A term *murabaha* is used to generate fixed payments and a series of corresponding reverse *murabaha* contracts are used to generate the floating-leg payments.[86]

The structure is, to some extent, similar with the "parallel loans" structure that was used by institutions in the earliest examples of conventional swap transactions.

As in a conventional swap transaction, the parties, namely the "bank" and the "counterparty," agree on the terms of the transaction (i.e., the trade dates, the fixed rate, the floating rate, the assets to be traded, and the notional cost price). On each trade date, the bank and counterparty will enter into two *murabaha* agreements (each having three requirements); the first example has a floating rate while the second is based on a fixed rate.

First Murabaha Agreement ("floating leg")

1. The counterparty will sell to the bank an amount of commodities the value of which will be the notional cost price.
2. The sale price for these commodities will be cost price + profit.
3. The profit element will represent the floating rate (calculated against the notional cost price).

Second Murabaha Agreement ("fixed leg")

1. The bank will sell to the counterparty an amount of commodities the value of which will be the notional cost price.
2. The sale price for these commodities will be cost price + profit.
3. The profit element will represent the fixed rate (calculated against the notional cost price).[87]

The net result of these trades is that on each trade date the amount of commodities sold under each *murabaha* will be the same and the cost price will be the same, and these will effectively be netted off by way of sales to a third-party broker; only the profit element will differ, and, as in a conventional interest-rate swap, the net beneficiary (of the difference between the fixed and floating rate) is dependent on whether the fixed or floating rate was higher.[88]

The following is an example of a basic profit-rate swap using a *murabaha* structure:

- Bank A has a fixed-rate investment profile from its purchase of Islamic assets maturing in five years and paying semiannually.

- Bank A wishes to swap its fixed-rate payment profile with a floating-payment profile. Bank A may decide to enter into an Islamic profit-rate swap with counterparty Bank B.
- Bank A receives a cash flow from its investment every six months on a fixed-rate profit margin.
- Bank A gives a *wa'ad* thereby promising to enter into commodity purchase.
- Bank B (counterparty) sells an asset (base metals) to Bank A on a *murabaha* basis at a selling price that comprises both principal and profit margin to be paid upon completion of subsequent transaction (floating-rate portion). Thus the commodity *murabaha* transaction is executed.

Murabahah Floating Rate

- Prior to six months, Bank B gives a *wa'ad* so that it promises to purchase commodities from Bank A. Bank A will sell an asset to Bank B at a selling price of notional principal, plus a markup based on the prevailing profit rate (agreed spread plus current benchmark). Thus the reverse commodity *murabaha* is executed by the two parties (reverse commodity *murabaha* as seen from Bank B's point of view).
- Payment of selling price by both Bank A and Bank B is netted-off.
- The net difference is profit, and is paid to the swap counterparty as initially agreed between both counterparties in the Master Agreement.
- Floating profit rate is repeated every six months until maturity.
- During commodity trades Bank B can also act as agent for Bank A in the commodity trades between the brokers and facilitate the individual legs involved in the process.
- The costs of the actual commodity trades vary from broker to broker; generally over the last few years broker fees will run between US$20 and US$30 for every million traded.[89]

In the swap no actual payment is made, as the principal amount upon which total payments are based are merely notional; this is in line with what happens in a conventional IRS. From Shariah the principle of *muqasah* (set-off) has been utilized.

Also, profit rate swap may be structured as a series of *wa'ads* (unilateral promises) whereby each party undertakes to the other to swap relevant fixed- and floating-rate payments at some particular point of time in the future.

The foreign-exchange swap is also one of the new hedging mechanisms in Islamic finance. It should be clear at the outset that one of the important conditions for currency exchange in Islamic law is that such an exchange must only be an on-the-spot transaction and therefore no deferment is permissible. To address the issue, the industry developed two mechanisms that provide Muslim investors with a means that can allow them to hedge against exchange fluctuation. The first is based on *murabaha/tawarruq* while the second is structured under the concept of *wa'ad*.

The Islamic foreign-exchange mechanism based on the *wa'ad* structure involves on-the-spot exchange of currencies at the beginning and the promise or undertaking to execute another currency exchange at the future date based on the rate determined today. The concept is widely practiced in the industry and the basic concept is approved by AAOIFI.

An investor that has $14.5 million can sell these U.S. dollars to the bank on spot basis to obtain its equivalent in euros. This is a common transaction that does not contravene any Shariah principle. Thereafter the investor will get a *wa'ad* or undertakes to enter into a contract of currency. The future exchange of currencies will be based on an exchange rate that is referred to today's rate. So at the future time, the investor will get back the U.S. dollars without being exposed to the risks of currency fluctuation.[90]

CONCLUSION

This chapter on derivatives instruments shows that the admission of derivatives contracts in Islamic finance depends fundamentally on the type of contract used, the subject matter of the contract, and the way the commodities are traded. Therefore, totally rejecting or accepting these novel strategies of risk management without genuine investigation will be premature and unwarranted. Despite the fact that almost all derivatives instruments are totally new to Islamic financial law, the possibility of admitting some of these instruments, or finding the suitable alternative for others, is very high and requires further collective research and investigations on the Shariah foundations.

NOTES

1. Anouar Hassoune, "Risk Issues in Islamic Financial Institutions," *Moody's* (January 2008), 1.
2. IFSB, "Guiding Principles of Risk Management for Institutions (other than Insurance Institutions) Offering Only Islamic Financial Services" (2005), http://www.ifsb.org/standard/ifsb1.pdf (accessed July 31, 2012).
3. Deutsche Börse Group, "The Global Derivatives Market," White Paper (April 2008).
4. Anouar Hassoune, "Derivatives in Islamic Finance: Examining the Role of Innovation in the Industry," *Moody's* (April 2010).
5. Ibid.
6. Mohamed Damak and Emmanuel Volland, "Risk Management For Islamic Financial Institutions: A Rating Perspective," Standard & Poor's (January 15, 2008).
7. Edward J. Swam, *Derivatives Instruments Law* (Cavendish Publishing Limited, 1995), p. 87.
8. For more details on the issue see Muhammad Al-Bashir Muhammad Al Amine, *Risk Management in Islamic Finance: An Analysis of Derivatives Instruments in Commodity Markets* (Brill's Arab and Islamic Law, 2008).
9. *Gulf Times*, "Aramco Breaks New Ground with Oil Trading," Reuters, May 14, 2012.
10. For the complete text of the resolution see Al-Majma' al-Fiqhi al-Islami li-Rabitat al-'Alam al-Islami, *Qararat Majlis al-Majma' al-Fiqhi al-Islami*, seventh session, from 11–16 Rabi' al-'Akhir, 1404 "Suq al-'Awraq al-Maliyyah wa al-Badai'i (al-Bursah)" pp. 120–124.
11. The first time the issue was raised in the sixth session in Rabat, Morocco, in 1989.
12. General Secretariat of the Great Ulama's Board, *Islamic Research Magazine* [several issue nos.] (1996); no. 46: 26–140; no. 47: 23–120; no. 48: 27–90.
13. AAOIFI Shariah Standard no. 20.
14. For more details see Muhammad Al-Bashir Muhammad Al-Amine, *Risk Management in Islamic Finance: An Analysis of Derivatives Instruments in Commodity Markets* (Leiden, The Netherlands: Brill, 2008).

15. Andreas A. Jobst and Juan Solé, *Operative Principles of Islamic Derivatives—Towards a Coherent Theory*, IMF Working Paper (March 2012).

16. Reinout M. Wibier and Omar Salah, "The Credit Crunch and Islamic Finance: Shari'ah-Compliant Finance against the Backdrop of the Credit Crisis," TISCO Working Paper Series on Banking, Finance and Services No. 01 (2011).

17. Umer Chapra, "The Global Financial Crisis: Can Islamic Finance Help Minimize the Severity and Frequency of Such Crisis in the Future." Paper presented at the Forum on the Global Financial Crisis at the Islamic Development Bank (October 25, 2008); Bank for International Settlements (BIS) (September 2008), *BIS Quarterly Review: International Banking and Financial Market Developments* (Basel:B15).

18. Philippe Jorion and Marcos De Silva, *The Importance of Derivatives Securities Markets to Modern Finance* (Chicago: Catalyst Institute, 1995), 222.

19. Anthony F. Herbst, *Commodity Futures Markets, Methods, of Analysis, and Management of Risk* (New York: John Wiley & Sons, 1986), 3.

20. See Abd al-Wahhab and Abu Suaiman "[aqd al-Tawrid Dirash Fiqhiyyah Tahliliyyah," paper presented to the twelfth session of the Islamic Fiqh Academy (2007), 7; Hasan al-Jawhiri, "Uqud al-tawrid wa al-Munaqasat," paper presented at the twelfth session of the Islamic Fiqh Academy, Rabat, Morocco, p. 3; Mukhtar al-Salami, "Ta'jil al-Badalain fi al-'Uqud," paper presented in Nadwat al-Barakah al-Tasia' 'asharah lil iqtisad al-Islami, Makkah al-Mukarramah (December 2–3, 2000), 5.

21. See al-Darir, *al-Gharar wa Atharuhu fi al Uqud*, p. 316; Isawi Ahmad, "Bay ['al-Dayn wa Naqlihi," pp. 169–170; Mukhtar al-Salami, "Ta'jil al-Badalain fi al-'Uqud," paper presented in Nadwat al-Barakah al-Tasia' 'asharah lil iqtisad al-Islami, Makkah al-Mukarramah (December 2–3, 2000), 3; Ahmad Ali Abd Allah, "al-Bay [ala al-Siffah," paper presented in Nadwat Bank al-Shamal lita'sil al-[amal al-Masrifi (June 20–21, 1997), 4; Hasan al-Jawhiri, "Uqud al-tawrid wa al-Munaqasat," paper presented at the twelfth session of the Islamic Fiqh Academy, Rabat, Morocco (2007), 5.

22. Ibn Taymiyyah, *Nazariyyat al-'[aqd*, p. 235; Ibn al-Qayyim *I'lam al-Muwaqq'in an Rab al-'Alamin*, vol. 3, p. 9.

23. Ibn Abidin, *Hashiyat Rad al-Muhtar* (Cairo: al-Babi al-Halabi, 1966), 209.

24. Sudin Haron and Bala Shanmugan, *Islamic Banking System Concept and Application*, Kuala Lumpur: Pelanduk Publications (1997): 180; Muhammad Akram Kan, "Commodity Exchange and Stock Exchange in Islamic Economy," *American Journal of Islamic Social Sciences* 5:1 (1988), 92–114.

25. See, for instance, Ibn al-Humam, *Sharh Fath al-Qadir*, vol. 5, Bulaq, Egypt: al-Matba'ah al-Amiriyyah (1937): 337; Al-Nawawi, *al-Majmu*, vol. 9, p. 208; in Qudama, *al-Muqhni*, vol. 4, p. 324; Ibn Hazm, *al-Muhalla*, vol. 9, p. 109.

26. For more details about the Malikis opinion, see al-Hattab, *Mawahib al-Jalil li-Sharh Mukhtasar Khalil* Mustapha al-al-Halabi, vol. 4, p. 514–517; al- Khirshi, *Sharh al-Khirshi ala Mukhtasar Khalil*, Beirut: Dar Sadir, vol. 5 p. 202–203; and Ibn Rushd, *Bidayat al- Mujtahid*, vol. 2, p. 202; Al-Darir, *Al-Gharar wa Athruhu fi al-Uqud*, pp. 461–462; Ibn Abidin, *Rad al-Muhtar'ala al-Dur al-Muqhtar*, Cairo: al-Babial-Halabi, vol. 4, p. 288.

27. Ibn Abd al-Bar, *al-Kafi*, vol. 2, p. 4.

28. See, for instance, Siddiq al-Darir, "al-Salam wa Tatbiqatuhu al-Mu'asirah," *Majallat Majama al-Fiqh al_Islami*, vol. 9, ninth session (1996): 379–383; Ibn al-Qayyim, *'Ilam al-Muwaqq'in an Rab al-'lamin*, vol. 1 p. 350; Ibn Hajar, *Fath al-Bari*, Maktabat al-Kulliyat al-Azhariyyah, vol. 9, p. 305; Izz Al-Din Ibn Abd al-Salam, *Qawa'id al-Ahkam fi Masalih al-Anam*, Cairo: Maktabat al-Kulliyat al-Azhariyyah (1968): (2), 111–112; Nazih Hammad, "al-Salam wa tatbiqatuhu al-Muasirah," *Majallat Majma' al-Fiqh al_Islami*, vol. 9, ninth session (1996): 553–555; Majama' al-Fiqh al_Islami, *Majallat Majama' al-Fiqh al_Islami* (discussions about *salam*) ninth session, 1996, no. 9, pp. 643.

29. For more details see Muhammad al-Bashir Muhammad al-Amine, *Istisna [Manufacturing Contract in Islamic Banking and Finance: The Law and Practice]* (Kuala Lumpur, Malaysia: A. S. Nordin, 2001).

30. Ibn Abidin, *Rad al-Muhtar ala al-Dur al-Mukhtar*, Dar al-Kutub al-Ilmiyyah, Beirut, vol. 4, p. 21.

31. al-Buuti, Kashshaf al-Qina' vol. 3, p. 164.

32. al-Zuqani, *Sharh al-Zuqani ala Muqtasar Khalil*, Beirut: Dar al-Fikr 1978, vol. 5, p. 38. Ibn Qudamah, al-Mughni, Dar al-Fikr, Beirut, vol. 4, p. 56.

33. See Abd al- Wahhab Abu Suaiman, "Aqd al-Tawrid Dirasah Fiqhiyyah Tahliliyyah" (paper presented to the twelfth session of the Islamic Fiqh Academy, Morocco, Egypt, 2000), 2–3.

34. Ibid., 346–347.

35. Mukhtar al-Salami, "Ta'jil al-Badalain fi al-'Uqud" (paper presented in Nadwat al-Barakah al-Tasia' 'asharah lil iqtisad al-Islami, Makkah al-Mukarramah, December 2–3, 2000), 3.

36. Ibid., 44–47.

37. Abu Dawud, *Sunan, hadith* no. 2187.

38. Ibn al-Qayyim, *I'lam al-Muwaqqi'in*, vol. 1, p. 219.

39. Hans R. Stoll and Robert E. Whaley, *Futures and Options Theory and Applications* (Mason, Ohio: South-Western Publishing Co., 1993), 6.

40. Securities Commission and Securities Institutes Education, *Malaysian Futures and Options Registered Representatives* (MFORR) (course presented in Kuala Lumpur, Malaysia, 1997), 2.

41. See Fuad al-Omar and Mohammed Abdl-Haq, *Islamic Banking Theory Practices and Challenges* (New York: Oxford University Press, 1996), 92–93; Obiyathulla Ismath Bacha, "Derivatives Instrument and Islamic Finance: Some Thoughts for Reconsideration," pp. 1–2; Mohammad Obaidullah, "Islamic Options—Engineering Risk Management Solutions," *New Horizon* (May, 1998), 6; Islamic Finance Net, "Islamic Financial Derivatives" (discussion forum), *International Journal of Islamic Finance and Services* 1:1 (April–June 1999), 9. Available online at http://islamic-finance.net/journals/journal.

42. See Mohammad Ali El-Garie, "Towards an Islamic Stock Market," *Islamic Economic Studies* 1:1 (December 1993), 12.

43. Mohammad Ali El-Garie, "Stock Exchange Transactions: Shari'ah Viewpoint," *Encyclopaedia of Islamic Banking*, London: Institute of Islamic Banking and Insurance, London, 1995, p. 170.

44. See Mohammad Ali El-Garie, note 42, p. 13; Robert W. Kolb, *Option The Investor's Complete Toolkit* (New York: New York Institute of Finance, 1991), 7; Securities Commission and Securities Institutes Education, *Malaysian Futures and Options Registered Representatives* (MFORR) course (15).

45. Mohammad Hashim Kamali. *Islamic Commercial Law: An Analysis of Futures and Options*, Selangor, Malaysia: Ilmiah Publishers (2002); Yousuf Sulaiman, "Rai' al-Tashri al-Islami fi Masa'il al-Bursah," *al- Mawsua' al-' Ilmiyyah wa al-' Amaliyyah lil bunuk al-Islamiyyah*, Cairo: al-Ittihad al-Dawli lil- Bunuk al-Islamiyyah, 1982, vol. 5, pp. 428–445; Ali Abdul Qadir "Ta'qib 'ala Rai' al-Tashri al-Islami fi Masa'il al-Bursah," *al- Mawsua al- Ilmiyyah wa al-'Amaliyyah lil bunuk al-Islamiyyah*, Cairo, al- Ittihad al-Dawli lil- Bunuk al-Islamiyyah, 1982, vol. 5, pp. 438–443; Shahat al-Jundi, *Mu' amalat al-Bursah fi al- shari[ah al-Islamiyyah*, Cairo, Dar al-Nahdah, 1988; "Financial Engineering with Islamic Options," *Islamic Economic Studies* 6:1, November 1998, pp. 73–103.

46. See Ahmad Muhyi al-Din Hassan, *'[amal Sharikat al-Istismar*, pp. 268–271; Samir Ridwan, *Suq al-'Awraq al-Maliyyah*, p. 361.

47. Abd al-Rahman al-Jizari, *al-Fiqh ala al-Madhahib al-Arbaa*, Dar al-Rayyan li al-Turath, Cairo, n.d., vol. 3, p. 155.

48. See Kamali, *Islamic Commercial Law*, pp. 356–357. Ali Abd al-Qadir, "Ta'qib 'ala Rai' al-Tashri al-Islami fi Masa'il al-Bursah", *al-Mawsuah al-Ilmiyyah wa al-'Amaliyyah lil bunuk al-Islamiyyah*, vol. 5, p. 441; Shahhat al-Jundi, *Mu'amalat al-Bursah*, p. 151.

49. Ahmad Muhyi al-Din Hassan, *'[amal Sharikat al-Istismar*, pp. 268–271; Samir Ridwan, *Suq al-'Awraq al-Maliyyah*, p. 361.

50. Abdal-Wahhab abu Sulaiman, "al-Ikhtiyarat" *Majallat Majama al-Fiqh al-Islami*, 6:1, pp. 307–308; Abu Qhuddah, "al-Ikhtiyarat", *Majallat Majama al-Fiqh al-Islami*, 6:1, p. 334.

51. See for instance, al-Nawawi, *al-Majmu*, vol. 9, p. 222; al-Dasuqi, *Sharh al-Dasuqi ala Muqtasar Khalil*, vol. 3, p. 102.

52. al-Kasani, *al-Bada'i'*, vol. 5, p. 264.

53. See for instance, Ibn Qudamah, *al-Mughni*, vol. 3, p. 518; Ibn Muflih, *al- Furu with Tashih al-Furu*, vol. 4, p. 91.

54. See for instance, Ibn Qudamah, *al-Mughni*, Maktabat al-Jumhiriyyah, Cairo, vol. 5, p. 375; Ibn al-Humam, *Sharh Fath al-Qadir*, vol. 7, p. 446; al-Mirdawi, *al-Insaf*, vol. 6, p. 298; al-Shirazi, *al-Muhazzab*, Dar al-Fikr, Beirut, vol. 2, p. 283; Ibn Rushd, *Bidayat al-Mujtahid*, Dar al-Fikr, vol. 2, p. 198.

55. Imam Malik, *al-Mudawwah al-Kubra*, Dar al-Fikr Beirut, vol. 4, p. 216; *Hashiyat al-Ruhuni ala al-Zurqani*, Dar al-Fikr, Beirut, vol. 6, p. 264; al-Mawwaq, *al-Taj wa al-Iklil*, with *Mawahib al-Jalil*, vol. 5, p. 318.

56. See Al-Nawawi, *Rawdat al-Talibin wa Uddat al-Muttaqin*, al-Maktab al-Islami Beirut, vol. 5, p. 111.

57. al-Fatawa al-Hindiyyah, Dar 'Ihya al-Turath al-Arabi, Beirut, 1986, vol. 3, p. 45; *Fatawa Qadi Khan*, Mawlawi Niyaz Muhammmad Kuwanti, Bulishistan, 1985, vol. 2, p. 371.

58. See Abdal-Rahman bin Nasir al-Sa'di, *al-Mukhtarat al-Jaliyyah min al-Masa'il al-Fiqhiyyah*, al-Riasah al-Ammah li Idarat al-Buhuth al-'Ilmiyyah wa al-Dawah wa al-Irshad, Saudi Arabia, 1985.

59. See Ali al-Khafif *Ahkam al-Mu[amalat al-Shar'iyyah*, Dar al-Fikr al-Arabi, Cairo, 1996, vol. 3, pp. 171–172.

60. For more details, see Muhammad Al-Bashir and Muhammad Al-Amine (note 14).

61. Mohammad Ali El-Garie (note 43, p. 14).

62. Reuters Limited, *The Reuters Financial Training Series, An Introduction to Derivatives* (New York: John Wiley & Sons, 1999), 79.

63. See Mohammad Ali El-Garie (note 14).

64. Mohammad Hashim Kamali, *Islamic Commercial Law* (Malaysia: Research Centre International Islamic University, 2000), 357.

65. Frank E. Vogel and Samuel Hayes III, *Islamic Law and Finance, Religion, Risk, and Return* (Leiden, The Netherlands: Brill, 2008), 162.

66. al-Sanhuri, *al-Wasit*, vol. 1, p. 261, and *Masadir al-Haqq*, Dar al-Maarif, Cairo, vol. 2, p. 96.

67. Rafiq al-Misri, "Bay[al-[arbun," p. 730.

68. Mukhtar al-Salami, "al-Ikhtiyarat," *Majallat Majma' al-Fiqh al-Islami*, p. 233; al-Zuhaili," al-Ikhtiyarat," *Majallat Majma' al-Fiqh al-Islami*, p. 256; Abu Ghuddah, "al-Ikhtiyarat," *Majallat Majma' al-Fiqh al-Islami*, p. 334.

69. Umer Chapra, "Islamic Banking and Finance: The Dream and Reality," *Hamdard Islamicus* 22:4, 1999, p. 74.

70. Sami Hasan Hamoud, "Progress of Islamic Banking: The Aspirations and the Realities," *Islamic Economic Studies* (June 1994): 125–126.

71. See note 62, p. 88.

72. For more details, see Muhammad Al-Bashir Muhammad Al-Amine, note 14.

73. See *al-Fatawah al-Iqtisadiyyah al-Sadirah an Nadwat al-Barakahli al-Iqtisad al-Islami*, edited by Abd al-Sattar Abu Ghuddah et al. (Jeddah, Saudi Arabia: Dallah al-Barakah, 1995), 42.

74. Ahmad al-Ashkar, "Toward an Islamic Exchange in Transitional Stage," *Islamic Economic Studies* 3:1 (1995), 82–83.

75. Mohammad Hashim Kamali, "The Permissibility and Potential of Developing Islamic Derivatives as Financial Instruments," *IIUM Journal of Economics & Management* 7:2 (1999), 77.

76. Fahim Khan, *Islamic Futures and Their Markets*, Research paper no. 32, Islamic Research and Training Institute, Jeddah, Saudi Arabia, IDB (1996), 46.

77. See Muhamad Akram Khan, "Commoditiy Exchange and Stock Exchange in Islamic Economy," *American Journal of Islamic Social Sciences* 5:1 (1988), 101.

78. For more details see Muhammad Al-Bashir Muhammad Al-Amine, note 14.

79. *The Encyclopedia Americana*, International Edition (University of Michigan: Grolier Incorporated, 2001).

80. Mohammad Al-Garie, see note 43, p. 5.

81. See Paul Latimer, "Futures Contracts and Gaming Laws," *The Company Lawyer International* 14:3 (December 1993), 67–71.

82. *Majallat Majama' al-Fiqh al-Islami*, 1990, vol. 1, p. 568.

83. Ibid., p. 593.

84. Blake Goud, "Profit Rate Swap Master Agreement," posted on Sharing Risk dot Org blog, March 27, 2012, http://investhalal.blogspot.com/2012/03/profit-rate-swap-master-agreement.html (accessed July 31, 2012).

85. Priya Ubero and Nick Evans, "Profit Rate Swap," www.docstoc.com/docs/71602854/PROFIT-RATE-SWAP-By-Priya-Uberoi-Senior-Associate-Derivatives# (accessed July 31, 2012).

86. Ibid.

87. Qudeer Latif and Susi Crawford, "Introduction to Islamic Financial Risk Management Products," www.qfinance.com/financial-risk-management-best-practice/introduction-to-islamic-financial-risk-management-products?full (accessed July 31, 2012).

88. Ibid.

89. Kazi Hussain, "Hedging Market Risk in Islamic Finance," *World Commerce Review* 2:3, pp. 22–24.

90. Asyraf Wajdi Dusuki, "Shariah Parameters on the Islamic Foreign Exchange Swap as Hedging Mechanism in Islamic Finance," *ISRA International Journal of Islamic Finance* 1:1 (2009).

CHAPTER 23

Islamic Microfinance

BLAKE GOUD
Principal, Sharing Risk, and Correspondent for the Americas, *The Islamic Globe*

W ith the growth in Islamic finance as well as microfinance, it is perhaps surprising that the Islamic microfinance industry has been very slow to develop. Microfinance is a concept, pioneered in Bangladesh by the Grameen Bank, in Bolivia by BancoSol, and in Indonesia by Bank Rakyat, where poor borrowers who are overlooked by the formal banking system receive small loans from microfinance institutions (MFIs) to start microbusinesses.[1] In most cases, the MFI makes loans to groups of people (in many cases, focused on women).

The reason the MFI focuses on groups of borrowers, rather than lending to one at a time independently of the group, is that the typical clients of MFIs are excluded from normal banking because they have no assets to post as collateral against the loan they are receiving and are therefore seen as poor lending risks by the banks. In a group lending system, each borrower in the group is responsible for the other members' loans. If one borrower defaults on her loan, the other group members will not usually be required to repay the defaulted loan. Instead, if one of the group members defaults on her loan, the other group members will lose further access to credit. This provides an incentive for group members to monitor the other members and generates social pressure on other members, making them more likely to repay. This social pressure, referred to as social collateral, has led many microfinance institutions to report high repayment rates, in some cases up to 99 percent.

Microfinance is not a new concept although it has only recently become part of the formal financial system. For years before microfinance was formalized, groups of individuals joined together to pool their resources to finance large purchases, through a Rotating Credit and Savings Association (RoSCA). In a RoSCA, all participants are required to contribute an equal amount each period, say $1, and they take turns getting the entire amount contributed in that period. If the RoSCA is made up of 20 people, then every month, there would be $20 available to distribute to one member. Over the course of 20 months, each group member receives a $20 lump sum that they can use as they choose.

The difficulty of formalizing the RoSCA model is that there is no way to force a group member to keep contributing after receiving the $20, except the possibility of social exclusion if one member receives the funds in one month and then stops contributing in following months. There is also a limitation that inhibits growth: If you are the final member of the group, you will have to wait 20 months (in our hypothetical example) to get the funds, which is worth much less than if you were chosen to receive the first $20 because individuals value $1 today more than $1 a year (or two) from now.

The microfinance model addresses the limitation of RoSCAs by raising a larger amount of capital from either investors or donors and, when added to the deposits it is able to accept from individuals, allows it to offer a much greater volume of loans than a RoSCA. However, like a RoSCA, the traditional group-based microfinance model continues to leverage social pressure on borrowers to repay their loans and not default like the RoSCA (and unlike a regular bank).

In the decades since the Grameen Bank, BancoSol, and Bank Rakyat Indonesia began offering microfinance, the product offering has grown with individual loans, consumer consumption financing, for-profit MFIs, and the development of much more sophisticated lending software to make the microfinance institutions more efficient. The microfinance industry has also had its share of problems, with overlending in Uttar Pradesh, India, leading to waves of borrowers strategically defaulting (i.e., defaulting on loans even if they have the economic ability to continue paying). There have also been questions about how much profit MFIs should be making, particularly after several nonprofit MFIs, such as Comparamos in Mexico and SKS Microfinance in India, converted into for-profit companies and launched initial public offerings (IPOs).

While the conventional (interest-based) microfinance industry has grown rapidly over the past 35 years since Professor Muhammad Yunus began offering small loans to the rural poor in Bangladesh, the Islamic microfinance industry has not grown as rapidly. In a broad survey of Islamic microfinance institutions, the Consultative Group to Assist the Poor, the microfinance arm of the World Bank, estimated that as of 2007, there were 380,000 clients from Islamic microfinance institutions compared with 77 million clients of conventional microfinance institutions.[2]

In the remainder of this chapter, I will describe the types of products used by microfinance institutions to compare and contrast conventional microfinance and Islamic microfinance, provide several case studies of Islamic microfinance institutions, and conclude with a look into the future of Islamic microfinance based on the experiences described in the case studies.

CONVENTIONAL MICROFINANCE PRODUCT OFFERINGS

Microfinance institutions began with only one product offering—small business loans—but have expanded into other areas of financial services: savings products, insurance, money transfer, leasing, and consumer finance. When describing the areas of finance that an Islamic microfinance institution should target, the longer history of conventional microfinance institutions can be instructive.

Microcredit

The mainstay of microfinance institutions is the provision of microcredit. These are small loans—the average size ranges from several hundred dollars to several thousand dollars depending on the location—provided to poor borrowers to start businesses or to finance consumer purchases. The loans typically carry interest rates that are higher than commercial bank loans, but far lower than informal lenders charge. A Consultative Group to Assist the Poor (CGAP) study that analyzed 555 MFIs across the world found that the average interest rate charged was 26 percent.[3]

The high level of interest rates charged on microcredit loans has drawn criticism towards MFIs.[4] In some cases the criticism is deserved, such as when borrowers are provided much more credit than they can afford (Uttar Pradesh) or where the degree of profits to private ownership is seen as excessively high. The latter criticism has been most common when for-profit MFIs like Comparamos in Mexico or SKS Microfinance in India have gone public and made their owners millionaires.

However, there are many reasons besides excess profits or relentless growth at all costs for explaining why microfinance interest rates are higher than commercial bank loans in the same country. The simple formula that banks, including MFIs, use to determine interest rates is:

$$R = \frac{AE + LL + CF + K - II}{1 - LL}$$

Interpreting this formula, administrative expenses (AE), loan losses (LL), the cost of funds (CF), and the MFIs-required capital (K) increase the interest rate it must charge to break even, while the income on its nonloan assets (II) lowers the interest rate. In most MFIs, the largest contributor to high interest rates is the administrative expense of lending. It is far more costly to administer 10,000 loans of $100 than it is to administer 10 loans of $100,000, so the administrative expense as a share of outstanding loans is much higher in MFIs.

An offsetting factor that explains why so many borrowers have repeatedly used microfinance loans, despite their high cost, is that businesses with little free capital can often generate high returns on whatever capital they are provided, benefiting the client who can generate income in excess of the interest paid on the microfinance loan.

Microsavings

In addition to providing loans, many microfinance institutions offer deposit products to help their clients build up assets, as well as to provide security for their loans. In the latter case, many MFIs require a certain amount of money be put into a savings account with the MFI each period as a condition for granting a loan. This provides a service to the client—a safe place to store money—while also providing some cushion for the MFI by reducing the loan losses it must realize if a client defaults (although it may raise some issues due to the compulsory nature).

In the absence of MFIs offering savings, the poor often find it difficult to save. For example, in the United States, an estimated 56 million people—20 percent of the population—do not have a bank account and are forced to use more costly companies like payday lenders, check-cashing services, or money transfer companies to perform services that they would receive for free from a bank.[5]

In developing countries, saving is accomplished through other means, often by storing assets in-kind, such as by owning livestock.[6] While this kind of saving can provide a store of value and even a return on the investment, it is inefficient because assets often have to be purchased or sold in relatively large amounts and can be vulnerable to death from drought, for example, a time when an owner would be more in need of the savings the assets represent.

Microinsurance

One of the newer areas of microfinance is microinsurance. There are many different types of microinsurance, but one of the most common is health insurance. Some forms of health insurance offer protection just against high-cost events, where the insured person would not be able to afford treatment or care out of his or her own resources (or would be forced to sell off productive assets to pay for this care). Other types of microinsurance that several studies have found are in the highest demand cover lower-cost care such as outpatient healthcare.[7]

Other forms of microinsurance available are crop and livestock insurance, weather insurance, life insurance, and insurance to cover minor property damage. In addition to these supplemental forms of insurance, many MFIs will embed a form of life insurance into their microcredit programs so that if the borrower dies, his or her family will not have to make repayment.

ISLAMIC MICROFINANCE PRODUCT OFFERINGS

Islamic microfinance has expanded beyond its initial focus on providing Shari'ah-compliant credit. In addition to the traditional microlending, Islamic microfinance institutions offer deposit products, as well as micro-*takaful*, a Shari'ah-compliant form of insurance.

Microcredit

The Islamic microfinance industry has far less of a track record than conventional microfinance, so the microcredit aspect represents a larger proportion of Islamic microfinance institutions' (IMFIs) activities. There are four methods for extending credit on a microlevel, which mirror the types of contracts used by Islamic banks with the exception being the fourth: *qard al-hasan*. The other three, in the order in which they are used: *murabaha*, *ijara*, and *mudaraba/musharaka*.[8]

In *murabaha*, instead of lending money to clients, the clients request that the bank purchase a good for them, which is then purchased by the bank and re-sold with a markup to the client. In order to make it a "credit" product, rather than just a sales product, the bank will allow the client to make equal installment payments over several weeks or months.

IMFIs offer both traditional leases and financial leases using *ijara*, although the financial lease is different than a conventional financial lease in how the transfer of ownership is made. In the *ijara* used to finance the purchase by the client of an asset, the IMFI purchases the asset and leases it for a fixed period, with fixed periodic payments. After the lease ends, ownership of the asset is transferred to the client, through either a sale for a nominal price or as a gift, and is not technically part of the *ijara* itself.[9] The main difference from a conventional lease is that the

IMFI is responsible for the costs associated with maintaining and insuring the asset (using *takaful*, the Islamic custom of pooling money to cover a cost).

One area where microfinance—and large-scale Islamic finance—has not explored, despite the contention by many Islamic financiers and academics that it represents a more "authentic" form of Islamic finance, is *mudarabah* and *musharaka*. These two products, respectively, are similar to venture capital and joint ventures. Under a *mudaraba*, the IMFI provides financing to clients and agrees to a profit-sharing split. Any financial losses are borne by the provider of capital. Over the course of the agreement, the clients make profit-sharing payments to the IMFI, as well as buying one share of the IMFIs investment in their microbusiness. This will reduce future profit-sharing payments, so unlike in conventional microfinance, the clients' payments will be decreasing during the term of the *mudaraba*.[10] A *musharaka*-based microfinance product works similarly to a *mudaraba*, except that both the client and IMFI contribute capital to the business, and therefore both are liable for losses, in proportion to the amount of capital they contribute. The periodic profit-sharing payments and share purchases by the client operate the same way.

The final product mentioned above for Islamic microfinance is *qard al-hasan* (a benevolent loan). There have been attempts to incorporate it into Islamic microfinance, but it is difficult to sustain because the lender is prohibited from accepting any amount in excess of the amount lent when it is repaid and is also expected to forgive the loan if the borrower cannot repay. As a financing product, *qard* loans will not be sustainable on their own, although there is probably a scope for *qard* loans to be used by IMFIs in their charitable activities.

Microsavings and Micro-*takaful*

Islamic microfinance has been relatively slow to develop microsavings and micro-*takaful* products relative to conventional microfinance institutions. The typical form of savings products with Islamic banks—which are carried over on the microfinancing level—are *mudaraba* and *wadiah*. A *mudaraba* deposit provides the depositor with the prospects of returns on the deposit from the profits generated with the funds. However, it also puts the funds at risk of loss, although typically the depositor will not be forced to bear a loss unless the total loss exceeds the total capital of the IMFI and it fails. In contrast, a *wadiah*-based deposit account gives the depositor assurance that the deposit will be safeguarded (*amanah*) and can be withdrawn on demand, but no profits are paid on the deposit amount.

Micro-*takaful* can also function in a way similar to a savings product because unlike conventional insurance, the premiums paid by the clients remain owned by the insured clients. Each period, the IMFI is paid a management fee (either flat or based on the return generated by investing and managing the *takaful* pool) and losses are covered out of the pool of funds, with gains on the investments made with the funds returned to the pool. The net amount remains owned by the policyholders, although typically it is not returned but is credited against the next period's premium to ensure that there will be sufficient funds to pay future claims. However, in some cases, the funds remaining are paid out on a specified date in the future.[11]

CASE STUDIES

In order to understand the gap between the promise of Islamic microfinance and its current state as the small niche of Islamic finance, much as Islamic finance remains a niche within conventional finance, we will survey a few illustrative examples of the Islamic microfinance industry as it is practiced.

Islami Bank Bangladesh Ltd. and the Rural Development Scheme

Islami Bank Bangladesh (IBBL) was one of the first Islamic banks in Bangladesh and was established in 1983. As of September 30, 2011, IBBL had total assets of 376 billion BDT ($5 billion) and revenues of 30 billion BDT ($397 million) for the full year 2010. In 1995, the bank launched the Rural Development Scheme (RDS) as a pilot project near one of the bank's branches in one district of the country. Since then, the RDS expanded to areas around 144 branches of the bank and serves 501,941 clients and has disbursed a cumulative 28.1 billion BDT ($370 million).[12] As of June 30, 2010, these clients are located in 61 of the country's 64 districts in 22,763 centers and work through 128,583 groups of mostly women (85 percent of clients are female).[13]

The RDS grew from its roots as a pilot project through the bank's branch network, which provides a lot of the human resources for administering the centers, although each center also has its own (self-elected) Centre Leader and Deputy Centre Leaders who are also clients of the RDS. Each branch that is involved with the RDS program surveys villages within 10 kilometers where communications between the village and branch are easy and, so long as it expects at least 400 potential clients in the 10 kilometer area, it begins with four to six villages of two to eight groups per center.

The financing is provided using a number of products, but the most commonly used is *bai-muajjal*, which is a form of credit sale where the bank buys a good on behalf of the client and resells it to the client with repayment in installments. One of the main differences between *bai-muajjal* and *murabaha* is that where the cost-plus-profit figures are disclosed to the client in a *murabaha*, they do not have to be disclosed in *bai-muajjal*. Other forms of financing used by the RDS are *ijara*, *bai-salam*, *murabaha*, *mudaraba*, and *musharaka*. Unfortunately, the RDS does not make available information about the relative uses of each form of financing.

The RDS program provides financing for both agricultural and nonagricultural industries including crop production, livestock, rural transportation, and rural housing. One of the criteria used to select villages for expansion of its RDS program, besides being close to an existing IBBL branch, is the presence of enough off-farm business opportunities. The duration for which the loans are extended varies depending on the business that is being financed, although most are for one year.

In 2005, the RDS was expanded to provide additional financing to group members who have reached the maximum amount through a Micro Enterprise Investment Scheme (MEIS). The MEIS provides financing of between 50,000 and 300,000 BDT ($659 to $3,955). As of June 2010, 1.5 BDT billion ($20 million) is outstanding, and 3.6 billion BDT ($48 million) has been disbursed in total since 2005.

The financing begins eight weeks after a group member joins the group, with a maximum of 10,000 BDT ($132) and is increased in successive loans up to a maximum, which varies between 20,000 and 50,000 BDT ($264 to $659) depending on the business. The financing cost for clients varies over time, but is currently 12.5 percent with 2.5 percent rebated with timely repayment. As is common in conventional microfinance, the RDS does not require any collateral from borrowers, but each group member is responsible for the repayment of loans provided to the other group members. Repayment is made in 45 equal weekly installments (for a 12-month duration).

Along with repayment each week, the group members are required to deposit 25 BDT ($0.33), 20 BDT of which is deposited into an account for the group member and the remaining deposited into an account controlled by the RDS center. The Centre Fund is used for *qard* loans to members of the center, decisions for which are made by the Centre Leader and Deputy Centre Leader. The *qard* loans are primarily made to fund the construction of tube wells to provide clean drinking water to the members. As of 2008, 11 million BDT ($141,000) had been spent constructing over 5,500 wells.[14]

There is, unfortunately, little research on the profitability of the RDS and the impact that the RDS has had on the communities in which it operates. The impact analysis has focused on using surveys with small samples. M. R. Kroessin, while focusing on the relationship between the RDS and its dual focus on financial services and on promoting Islamic ideals, describes the RDS as a "still marginally profitable product for the bank," which is not surprising given the relatively lower cost of the financing (12.5 percent) versus the 30 percent interest rate charged by Grameen Bank.[15] However, like the Grameen Bank, the RDS reports high repayment rates of 99 percent as of June 2010.[16]

Afghanistan

Afghanistan is one of the least developed countries in the world, following decades of war and for the last 10 years has faced an internal conflict between the government and the Taliban, making it a difficult environment for microfinance. Most of the microfinance in Afghanistan is supported by international organizations including the World Bank and USAID, the development aid agency of the U.S. government. The economy is highly focused in agriculture, with 32 percent of GDP generated from agriculture as of 2008 (excluding opium production), although in terms of employment, 79 percent of the labor force is employed in agriculture.[17]

The microfinance efforts began in 2003 with the formation of an apex organization, the Microfinance Investment Support Facility for Afghanistan (MISFA). The MISFA was funded by the World Bank's Afghanistan Reconstruction Trust Fund (other funding is provided by the Canadian, UK, and Swedish international development agencies) and since its inception, it has provided funding to 15 microfinance institutions in the country, including two that offer Shari'ah-compliant financing. The two organizations engaged in Islamic microfinance are the Foundation for International Community Assistance (FINCA), which focuses on village banking, and the World Council of Credit Unions (WOCCU), which provides funding and support to credit unions.

Some of the additional funding to these MFIs was provided by USAID through a series of funding programs beginning with the Rebuilding Agricultural Markets Program (RAMP) from 2003 to 2006. This was followed by funding under the Agriculture, Rural Investment, and Enterprise Strengthening (ARIES) from 2006 to 2009, and most recently the Rural Finance and Cooperative Development (RUFCOD) program, which began in 2009 and is scheduled to continue through the end of 2012.

The earliest Islamic microfinance program in Afghanistan was provided by FINCA-Afghanistan, developed beginning in 2003, and implemented in 2004. This product initially used a *murabaha* approved by scholars at Al Azhar University in Egypt, which was not widely accepted within Afghanistan and was mispriced so that it could not cover costs and discouraged smaller borrowers.[18] This forced FINCA to redevelop three *murabaha*-based products in consultation with religious scholars within Afghanistan, which were launched in July 2006.[19] The three products are Women's Murabaha Group, Market Murabaha Group, and Business Murabaha Agreement, two group and one individual lending program (see Exhibit 23.1). In addition to the financing provided through FINCA, clients are provided with "market-oriented skills training and business development support" from the International Rescue Committee.[20]

FINCA's client base grew rapidly from 2004 to 2008 but sharply contracted after 2008 due to deterioration of security conditions, business losses, and inflation, something that was widespread across the microfinance industry in Afghanistan, in addition to concerns about fraud on the part of clients. In addition, there was an increasing number of client dropouts across the MFIs in Afghanistan, although roughly half were from FINCA. Many of the client dropouts seen by FINCA were a result of FINCA's decision to stop disbursing funds to clients who were delinquent on previous loans.[21] From 2008 through 2010, FINCA wrote off a substantial portion of its microfinance portfolio, resulting in a significant drop off in the number of clients and in the outstanding loan portfolio, from a peak of $11.8 million in 2007 to $1.7 million in 2010. The total number of clients dropped with the decline in the loan portfolio from 63,571 in 2007 to 10,697 in 2010.

Exhibit 23.1 FINCA Afghanistan Product Details

Product	Group Size	Average Loan Size	Financing Cost (% per month)	Initial Loan Cycle	Subsequent Loan Cycle
Women's Murabaha Group	10+	$250	2–3%	6–9 months	12 months
Market Murabaha Group	3–40	$400	2–3%	5 months	6–10 months
Business Murabaha Agreement	Individual	$1,000	2%	6–9 months	6–12 months (2nd) up to 18 months

Source: Paul Robinson and Nimrah Karim. (2008). FINCA's Experience in Afghanistan. Presentation made at the International Islamic Finance Forum, Dubai, UAE, April 13–17, 2008; and FINCA Audited Financial Statements (2010).

While the portfolio has shrunk significantly since the peak in 2007, its quality is beginning to improve. In 2009, of the 33,289 clients, 20,609 (62 percent) were overdue amounting to $1.4 million (40 percent) of the $3.6 million loan portfolio. In 2010, 4,429 clients out of 10,697 (41 percent) were overdue amounting to $0.3 million (19 percent) of the $1.7 million portfolio. As of the most recent audit for 2010, FINCA was not receiving funds from USAID directly, although it still received support both from its parent organization FINCA International as well as MIFSA.

The other MFI offering Shari'ah-compliant financial services in Afghanistan is the World Council of Credit Unions (WOCCU), an apex organization of world credit unions that is involved in establishing credit unions in Afghanistan. The difference between a bank (or bank-like MFI) and a credit union is that the former is owned either by individuals or another company, while a credit union is owned by its members and limits the loans it provides to members of the credit union.

Unlike FINCA, which saw its growth spike prior to 2007 before shrinking dramatically, WOCCU started slowly with two credit unions in 2004, the Balkh Savings and Credit Union in Mazar-e-Shareef, and the Jawzjan Savings and Credit Union in Sheberghan. The two credit unions grew relatively slowly having only 4,915 depositors (members), of which 1,869 borrowed from the credit union by 2006. In the first few years the project was funded by MISFA, as well as by the First America Credit Union in Utah, before being subsequently funded by the USAID ARIES program.

Where the FINCA program ran into difficulties from the large scale and appears, as a result, to have lost momentum, the WOCCU program ran into problems early on, when a general manager of the Balkh Savings and Credit Union was discovered to have concealed the status of many loans and to have provided loans outside of the loan approval process. As a result, the WOCCU program recognized the hazards where one individual was able to conceal information under the current loan monitoring system.[22] Based on the limited loan losses since this discovery, it appears that WOCCU has implemented changes to limit the ability of one person to control loan approvals and monitoring.

In 2006, when the WOCCU Islamic Investment and Finance Cooperatives (IIFCs) began to receive funding from USAID through the ARIES program, the growth began to accelerate, with the number of depositors increasing to 41,324 in 2009 from 8,498 in 2007.[23] Despite the more rapid growth in depositors (members) than borrowers during these years, the total loans outstanding still far outnumber the value of deposits held. By 2009, the total loans outstanding across the 27 IIFCs was more than $4 million compared with just $870,000 in total deposits.

Like FINCA, the primary loan product is based on *murabaha*, although the WOCCU IIFCs are unique with their several savings products, based on *wadiah* and *mudaraba*. Comparing the terms of the loans (see Exhibit 23.2), it is clear that they are similar to the terms of FINCA's loans with markups under the murabaha of 2 percent per month (a flat fee that is not increased continues to accrue in excess of the initial amount).

After the ARIES program ended in 2009, the WOCCU IIFCs began receiving funding through the RUFCOD program from USAID and by 2011 saw growth to 40 IIFCs, including more locations through the South and East of the country, where the security situation continued to remain poor. Both depositor (member) numbers

Exhibit 23.2 WOCCU's IIFC Product Details

Product	Client Focus	Loan/Deposit Size	Return / Markup	Terms
Savings				
Current Account		No min/max	None	Term Deposit (varies)
Investment Account		No min/max	3–7.5% (varies by IIFC)	
Individual Savings		No min/max	3–5% (varies by IIFC)	
Individual Development Accounts	Women, students, and low-income earners	400–2,500 AFN ($8–50)	Initial deposit amount matched by IIFC grant	2-year Term Deposit
Business Development Accounts	Public or private sector employees	Max 10,000 AFN ($200) in year 1, 15,000 AFN ($300) in year 2	Initial deposit amount matched by IIFC grant	2-year Term Deposit
Loans				
Cooperative Group Loan	Home-based businesses (women); Farmers (men)	Max of 250,000 AFN ($5,000)	2% per month (flat markup)	6–9 months
Business Loan—LoC	Traders or public or private sector employees	Up to 50% of annual salary	2% per month (flat markup)	6–9 months

Source: WOCCU. 2010. WOCCU-IIFC Program Brief No. 1. Madison, WI: WOCCU.

and saving amounts and the total value of the loans outstanding continued to rise at a strong pace, reaching 70,047 members in March 2011 with savings of $2.08 million and loans outstanding of $14.47 million. Despite the rapid growth, WOCCU's IIFCs continue to report low rates of delinquency (2 percent of the portfolio is delinquent more than 30 days). During 2011, WOCCU began piloting a new product, funded in part by the United Kingdom's development agency to offer farmers with greater, longer funding through both existing *murabaha*-based lines of credit and new *ijara* financing.

The original IIFCs in Balkh and Jawzjan that were established before 2006 have reached operational self-sufficiency, and while WOCCU plans to open three more by the end of June 2012, it is focused on ensuring that when the RUFCOD program ends in December 2012, the existing IIFCs will be close to operational self-sufficiency.[24]

Sanduq in Syria

The preceding two case studies were focused in Asia but given the prominence of Islamic finance (on a macro level) in the Arab world it is reasonable to expect an example from the Middle East. It is notable that, even as the Islamic finance industry grew rapidly in the region, the development of Islamic microfinance was almost entirely absent. However, there is one prominent example of Islamic microfinance that has existed since 2000 in Jabal al-Hoss, one of the poorest areas of Syria, near the city of Aleppo.

The microfinance begun under the Rural Community Development Project from the UN Development Program (UNDP) in Jabal al-Hoss is similar to the FINCA financing in Afghanistan using a village lending model. However, in contrast to the FINCA model, the organization is member owned, even where it leverages external financing to expand its operations. The Rural Community Development Project leveraged already existent *sanduq* (sing. *sanadiq*) village groups where members contribute capital and members can borrow from the fund to finance income-generating activities or meet short-term needs.

In general, the income generating activities are financed using a *murabaha* with a fee of around 1 percent per month, included in the cost of the goods as a fixed markup, rather than accruing as interest. The short-term funding, which is often offered in smaller amounts than the *murabaha*, is extended as a *qard al-hasan*, with repayment having principal only and no profit margins.

The original project sponsored by the UNDP began in 2007 and ran out of funding on schedule in 2007. Subsequent to the end of the UNDP funding, the International Fund for Agricultural Developments' Near East, North Africa, and Europe (NEN) Division picked up the project to continue the expansion to new villages. By 2010, there were 76 *sanduq* with 13,500 clients, of whom 45 percent are women. Throughout the first 10 years of the *sanduq*, more than 22,000 loans were extended for $17 million, with an average of $772 per loan.[25]

In contrast to most microfinance institutions where loan sizes increase over time, the *sanadiq* saw loan sizes decline over the length of the project. In the first three years of the program, between 2000 and 2002, the loans began at 50,000 SYP ($1,014 at July 2012's exchange rate), increasing to 150,000 SYP over four 3-month loans.[26]

Unlike most microfinance institutions, the *murabaha* financing provided to clients of the *sanadiq* are repaid in one payment upon maturity, whereas in most other microfinance—Islamic or conventional—repayment is made weekly, biweekly, or monthly to make monitoring easier. Over time, the *sanadiq* financing was structured to encourage monthly repayment rather than repayment upon maturity by lowering the profit margin charged on installment loans. Unfortunately recent data on repayment rates are not available, although in the first few years, the *sanduq* were reported to have more than a 98 percent repayment rate and had the ability to generate dividends for members of between 30 percent and 40 percent of the capital contributed by the indigenous community members, despite reporting operational self-sustainability ratios of less than 100 percent (meaning the *sanduq* continued to rely on financing provided by the UNDP).[27]

CONCLUSION

The theory of Islamic microfinance has thus far gone further than the practice. There are many ideas for how a *mudaraba*- or *musharaka*-based product could be adapted for use by Islamic microfinance institutions. However, there are few instances of Islamic microfinance institutions moving beyond the *murabaha* model. There is also scant data on the effectiveness of Islamic microfinance models, either compared to the baseline conditions before the products are available or in comparison with conventional microfinance.

The primary differentiating factors in the Islamic microfinance structures detailed in this chapter are (1) whether the MFI is owned by its members/clients or by an outside group; (2) whether the products are offered on an individual basis or through a group or village lending model; and (3) whether the MFI is primarily focused on financial performance, whether that is generating profits for shareholders or just ensuring that the MFI is financially sustainable without external support.

Yet, even the simple factors that differentiate the Islamic MFIs profiled in this chapter have not been investigated in any formal way to determine which models provide superior outcomes for clients, MFIs, and the communities in which they operate. It is the view of the author that this type of analysis is necessary before discussions about how more complex products like *mudaraba* and *musharaka* can be adapted for the Islamic microfinance industry can be productive.

This will likely be a disappointment to the proponents of Islamic microfinance who generally want to avoid seeing it become—like the macro Islamic financial industry—a replication of conventional products. However, as discussed earlier in this chapter, the costs of microfinance are high and anything adding complexity to the product will add costs that either have to be borne by the microfinance clients or by the MFI, making it even more difficult for a financially sustainable Islamic MFI to emerge.

NOTES

1. Nial Hermes and Robert Lensink. 2007. "The Empirics of Microfinance: What Do We Know?" *Economic Journal* 117 (February), F1–F10.

2. Nimrah Karim, Michael Tarazi, and Xavier Reille. 2008. *Islamic Microfinance: An Emerging Market Niche*, CGAP Focus Note No. 49, August 2008.

3. Richard Rosenberg. 2009, February. "The New Moneylenders: Are the Poor Being Exploited by High Microcredit Interest Rates?" CGAP Occasional Paper No. 15.

4. Richard Rosenberg. 2002. *Microcredit Interest Rates.* CGAP Occasional Paper No. 1.

5. Brigit Helms and Xavier Reille. 2004. *Interest Rate Ceilings and Microfinance: The Story So Far.* CGAP Occasional Paper No. 9.

6. Renée Chao-Béroff. 2003, July. "Rural Savings Mobilization in West Africa: Guard Against Shocks or Build an Asset Base?" *MicroBanking Bulletin*, 16–17.

7. Microinsurance Learning & Knowledge (MILK). 2011. "What Do We Know About the Financial Value of Microinsurance for Poor Clients: A Snapshot." MILK Brief #4.

8. Nimrah Karim, Michael Tarazi, and Xavier Reille. See note 2.

9. Mohammed Obaidullah. 2008. "Introduction to Islamic Microfinance." IBF Net Ltd. Retrieved July 31, 2012, from http://ssrn.com/abstract=1506072.

10. Azhar Nadeem. December 3, 2010. "Islamic Business Contracts and Microfinance—A case of *mudaraba*." MPRA Paper No. 27194.

11. Box 2 in Karim, Tarazi, and Reille (2008), p. 3.

12. Islami Bank Bangladesh Ltd. (2012). Performance of RDS. Retrieved July 31, 2012, from www.islamibankbd.com/rds/performance.php.

13. Ibid.

14. Mohammad Main Uddin. 2008. "Credit for the Poor: The Experience of Rural Development Scheme for Islami Bank Bangladesh Ltd." *Journal of Nepalese Business Studies* 5:1, 71.

15. Mohammad Raif Kroessin. 2010, November. "Re-thinking Development: 'Islamist' Banking and the Case of the Islamic Bank's Rural Development Scheme in Bangladesh." Paper presented at the DSA conference, "Values, Ethics and Morality" (p. 8).

16. Islami Bank Bangladesh Ltd., see note 12.

17. CIA World Factbook. 2011. Afghanistan. Retrieved July 31, 2012, from https://www.cia.gov/library/publications/the-world-factbook/geos/af.html.

18. Academy for Educational Development. 2007. "An Overview of ARIES and Islamic Finance." Retrieved July 31, 2012, from http://mltraining.kdid.org/es/library/overview-agriculture-rural-investment-and-enterprise-strengthening-aries-aries-islamic-finan

19. Paul Robinson and Nimrah Karim. 2008, April. "FINCA's Experience in Afghanistan." Presentation made at the International Islamic Finance Forum, Dubai, UAE.

20. Maliha Hamid Hussein. 2009. "State of Microfinance in Afghanistan." Report prepared for the Institute of Microfinance as part of the Project on State of Microfinance in SAARC Countries (p. 16).

21. Ibid., p. 31.

22. World Council of Credit Unions. 2008. "Supporting Credit Union Developments in Afghanistan: An Overview of Issues Important to the Development of Shari'a-Compliant Cooperative Finance." Research Monograph. USAID Cooperative Development Program. Retrieved July 31, 2012, from www.ruralfinance.org/fileadmin/templates/rflc/documents/1209565120610_Credit_union_in_afganistan.pdf

23. WOCCU. 2010. *WOCCU-IIFC Program Brief No. 1.* Madison, WI: WOCCU.

24. Barry Lennon, senior vice president at WOCCU (personal communication, June 21, 2011).

25. IFAD. 2010, November. "Rural Finance in Selected IFAD-Financed Operations." Presentation from the IFAD NEN Division Tuscany Retreat.

26. Omar Imady and Hans Dieter Seibel. 2005. "Sanduq: A Microfinance Innovation in Syria Driven by Shareholder Value." NENARACA Newsletter, September 2003 (revised April 2005).

27. Ibid.

About the Editor

Karen Hunt-Ahmed is the president of Chicago Islamic Microfinance Project, a not-for-profit economic development organization that provides business education and Shari'a-compliant microcredit to entrepreneurs in Chicago. She left a position as visiting assistant professor of finance and management at DePaul University to devote time to the project and remains a lecturer in Islamic economics at DePaul. She received a BA and MBA from Washington University in St. Louis and a PhD from the University of Chicago. She has worked in the banking sector in Chicago and in private equity in Dubai, United Arab Emirates. Her research interests include culture and identity, financial empowerment, Islamic finance, microfinance, and the socialization of economic behavior. Dr. Hunt-Ahmed is a Faculty Fellow of DePaul's Egan Urban Center.

Dr. Hunt-Ahmed lives in Wilmette, Illinois, and enjoys karate. She lived in Dubai for many years and has traveled extensively in the Middle East, Pakistan, Africa, and Europe.

Index